GN00838402

Published by:
Yore Publications
12 The Furrows, Harefield,
Middx. UB9 6AT.

© Tony Brown 1996

....

All rights reserved. No part of this publication may be reproduced or copied in any manner without the prior permission in writing of the copyright holder.

British Library Cataloguing-in-Publication Data.
A catalogue record for this book
is available from the British Library.

ISBN 1 874427 61 5

YORE PUBLICATIONS specialise in football books, generally of an historical nature, including Club Histories, Who's Who Books, and general interest - both League and non-League. Three free newsletters per year are issued.

For your first newsletter please send a S.A.E. to the above address.

Paul Wain can be contacted via the publishers should the reader have, or know of, any rare/interesting photographs relating to Notts County, especially any of the missing 19th century team groups.

Printed and bound by The Bath Press

DIRECTORS, MANAGEMENT, AND PLAYERS: 1994/95 SEASON

Back: Johnson, Agana, Murphy, Cherry, Reece, Slawson, McSwegan, Legg,

Second Row: Jones (Asst.Man.), Gallagher, Short, Simpson, Cox, Sherlock, Walker, Lund, Yates, Mills, Matthews, Gaunt (Youth Coach) Pettitt (Physio.)

Third Row: Butler, Emanalo, Thomas, Mrs. Pavis (Director), Mounteney (Vice Chair.), Pavis (Chairman), Slade (Manager), Ward (Director), Hook (Chief Exec.), Turner, Devlin, Jemson

Front: Pearson, Needham, Ridgway, Ludlow, Galloway, Worboys

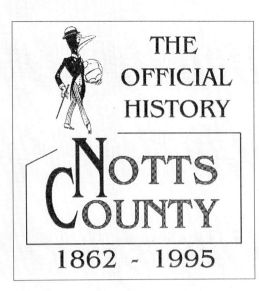

THE OFFICIAL HISTORY

NOTTS COUNTY

1862 - 1995

TONY BROWN
Assisted by
Paul Wain & Keith Warsop

INTRODUCTION

Notts are oldest club in the Football League. They have played more games in the League than any other club. Consequently, I have faced considerable difficulties in attempting to compile the "complete" record. The fact that the club was probably at its peak more than 100 years ago means that there needs to be as much emphasis on the Nineteenth Century as there is on the Twentieth!

I am indebted to many people for their help in writing the book. Thanks must go to Keith Warsop and Paul Wain above all. Keith is a long standing member of both the Association of Football Statisticians and the Association of Cricket Statisticians and Historians. He is the author of "The Magpies" (Sporting and Leisure Press, 1985), now well out of print, but still readily available for loan in Nottingham's libraries. Without Keith's statistics, carefully compiled whilst researching his own book, this one would not have been possible. I am also indebted to him for allowing me to base many items in the "A to Z" chapter on his notes. Paul is a real "Magpie", with a large collection of photographs and memorabilia of the club. It is thanks to him that we have been able to include probably the most comprehensive set of team groups ever seen in a book such as this. Paul had the job of writing all the captions to go with the photographs, a not inconsiderable task.

The statistical pages in the book are based around computer spreadsheets and databases. This has helped to eliminate many errors, but can also easily create new ones! Any mistakes are down to me, not the computer. Of course, the compilation of a book such as this causes many problems; as recently as August 1994, my sources disagreed as to who came on as substitute. Goal scoring details are also open to interpretation. For example, the first goal scored at Meadow Lane is sometimes credited to Emberton; his cross was touched into the goal by Matthews. Mick Vinter's goal against Fulham is sometimes credited as an "own goal" by Gale.

The players' section owes a large debt to Michael Joyce, Terry Woodhouse and Martin Green. Other help has been received from Brian Tabner (attendances), Brian Bent, Geoff Grain, John Lamb, Bill Wylie and Alan Feebery amongst others. Don Starr, Keith Warsop, Colin Slater and David Stapleton read my proofs and I am grateful for their comments.

Finally, thanks to the people at the club for their help and advice.

ACKNOWLEDGEMENTS

Thanks are extended to the numerous supporters, ex-players, and their relatives, for making available photographs and other memorabilia, which have been used for many of the illustrations used in the book.

Every effort has been made to trace the source of illustrations and to ensure that copyright has not been infringed. Permission to use a number of photographs, whose copyright is hereby acknowledged, has been received from the Nottingham Evening Post, J.M.S. Photography and EMPICS.

Tony Brown

DEDICATION

This book is dedicated to the "Fifty Year Club"; the good people who have been supporting Notts for all that time. You have had more downs than ups, but did see Tommy Lawton in his prime!

Contents

INDEX

(Applies to General text and 'A-Z sections only, i.e. pages 7-86 incl.)

Chapter 1
Gentlemen: 1862 - 1882

If you were transported back to 1862, you could be forgiven for assuming that the group of young men playing with a large muddy object in open fields near Nottingham were engaged in a game of rugby rather than football, or maybe just a general brawl! If a player caught the ball, he could run with it until tripped or hacked to the ground; "hacking" was a sharp kick to the shins. If the ball was on the ground, both sets of players would form a scrum round the ball and attempt to move it forwards. A participant admitted that, *"frequently, rough play was engaged in,"* and you can imagine that tempers were short in the general melee. Another account described the players as *"a set of harmless lunatics, who amused themselves by kicking one another's shins, but did no great harm to the public at large."*

The traditional forms of village football were curtailed by legislation and the increased industrial growth of mid 19th century Britain. The public schools had taken the lead in writing down the rules of the game for others to follow. However, each school had different ideas on the size of the pitch, the size and shape of the ball, how much handling was allowed, and whether or not hacking was permitted. The forerunners of the Notts club would have adopted whatever practices suited them best, and as all their early games were between the members themselves, the rules would not have been of the utmost importance.

A Sheffield club had been formed a few years before, in 1857. Sheffield adopted a set of eleven rules. These were based, we believe, on the laws in use in the public schools and at Cambridge. Pushing with the hands was allowed, but not hacking or tripping. Running with the ball in the hands (as practised at Rugby school) was not allowed. However, the ball could be caught, provided it had not touched the ground; a free kick then followed (similar to the "mark" in today's rugby football). The ball could also be pushed on with the hand. There were no off-side rules, so players known as "kick-throughs" were positioned permanently in the opponents' half. There was no limit on team size, and whatever size or shape of ball that happened to be handy was used. Referees were unnecessary, as the two captains would settle any dispute.

The Nottingham Guardian of November 28th 1862 carried the following report:
The opening of the Nottingham Football Club commenced on Tuesday last at Cremorne Gardens.

A side was chosen by W. Arkwright and Chas. Deakin. A very spirited game resulted in the latter scoring two goals and two rouges against one and one.

A rouge was a feature of the Sheffield rules from 1861. A ball passing though the inner posts, four yards apart, scored a goal. Four yards on either side of the posts were two rouge flags. A rouge was scored if the attacking team were the first to touch the ball down after it was over the goal line and between a rouge flag and an inner goal post. Cremorne Gardens was an open area in the Meadows, bordering onto the south end of Queen's Walk. The Cremorne public house now covers most of the site. We don't know if this game was organised by forerunners of the Notts club. An early account suggested that the founders of Notts first played in The Park, an area of Nottingham now filled with many interesting large Victorian houses. The Park was once the deer park of the Castle, and provides a natural amphitheatre under the sandstone rocks on which the Castle stands. Houses had been built in the area since the 1830s, but the central part, with its roads arranged as concentric ovals, had yet to be developed. Nottingham was in the process of rapid growth in 1862, but not quite the City we know today; only seven years had passed since a man sold his wife for a shilling and a pint of beer!

We have very little information on the first few years of the club's existence. Its members would perhaps be aware of the development of the game in Sheffield; 15 organised teams were active by 1862. A club in Lincoln started in 1861, playing a mixture of rules from Marlborough, Eton and Rugby. The London clubs met in October 1863 to try to agree a set of rules. The first draft of the new "Football Association" rules allowed running with the ball and players could be hacked. There were no height restrictions to the goals. Touch downs by the attacking team over the goal line resulted in a kick at goal from a "15 yard" line. In other words, rugby football! The secretary of the Sheffield club had not attended the meeting, but wrote in November with his comments. After many discussions, the FA's rules came more into line with those of Cambridge; hacking and running with the ball were banned. As with the Sheffield game, catching the ball was allowed, and a free kick followed if the player made a mark with his heel. Goals were set at 8 yards wide, but without a crossbar.

The tradition that Notts were formed in 1862 has had too long a life to be challenged in this book; anyway, it would mean repainting the grandstand! Headed notepaper used by the club in the 1880s gave 1860 as the year of foundation. Of course, young men who later formed the club may have been playing in the Meadows or the Park in 1862. Also playing, however, were the shinney (hockey) players on the Forest who were later to form the second oldest Football League club in 1865. No one suggests Forest were formed earlier than 1865! The true date of Notts' foundation has to be the meeting at the George Hotel on 7th December 1864. Mr. Frederick C. Smith of Bramcote was invited to be president; John Patterson was treasurer, and Messrs Hack, Wright, Crompton and Browne formed the committee. Patterson's first task was to collect the 5 shilling membership fee (25p), a not inconsiderable sum in those days, equivalent perhaps to membership of a modern day golf club. The report of the meeting mentions the presence of, *"the President, Thomas Wright"*, thus confirming that some sort of organisation existed before the inaugural meeting.

The committee was instructed to decide on the playing rules the club would follow, and obtain "caps and uniforms". We learn they were playing in blue caps a month later, but perhaps the "uniforms" came later. The club's first formal game was played the next day, a twenty-a-side knock about with another group of young men from a club known as Trent Valley. The committee no doubt considered where to play the game. The best places to look were the local cricket grounds or large open spaces such as the Forest.

Cricket grounds in those days did not have a well tended "square" in the middle of the ground; indeed, in the early days of the game the "away" captain was given the choice of where to pitch the wickets. Cricket grounds had the merit of being flat, with short cropped grass, and a pavilion for changing (if you were lucky). The committee decided to play on the Meadows cricket ground. This area, and Queen's Walk that runs alongside it, had been set aside as open spaces in the 1845 enclosure act for Nottingham. The open space is still there, now known as the Queen's Walk Recreation Ground. Bowling and putting greens have eaten into the corner, but there is still a football pitch marked out, for the primary school next door.

Of course, there were no pitch markings in 1864. Flags may have marked the corners of the pitch, and goal posts were required. If children's games today are anything to go by, play would have continued when the ball went off the pitch, but technically, the first player to touch down the ball was entitled to kick it back into play. Later, this became a one handed throw; the two handed overhead throw came in 1882. We don't know if any goals were scored in the game with Trent Valley. Play started at 2 p.m. and lasted until some time after sunset! *"The exhilaration produced and the kindly feeling engendered disposed many to wish that the contention might be continued by moonlight"*, said the reporter of the Nottingham Daily Guardian.

The players wore long flannel trousers (maybe their cricket flannels), everyday shirts without collars, and their working boots with nailed soles.

The first real test of the club's mettle followed on January 2nd 1865 with the first match against Sheffield, again played on the Meadows. This was Sheffield's first "out of town" match. This is how the Nottingham and Midland Counties Daily Express saw the game, played under "Nottingham rules":

> FOOTBALL - SHEFFIELD v. NOTTS. Yesterday, a game at football was played on the Meadows Cricket Ground between the Sheffield and Notts. clubs. The weather was extremely cold, still there was a large number of spectators present, who appeared to enjoy the excitement of the sport with a zest only exceeded by that of the players themselves. The Sheffield party were distinguished by scarlet shirts and caps, the Notts. men hoisting blue caps, the distinction between the two sides thus very apparent to the visitors. The game was kept up in a spirited manner, the Sheffielders scoring the only goal obtained. Richard Daft took a most prominent and active part for the Notts. club and "all but" managed a goal for them by a clever kick, which one of the Sheffield men succeeded in stopping at the last juncture. In obtaining their goal the Sheffield club appeared up to the game, as they kept their men well positioned on the field, whilst, in some instances, an overcrowding was visible in the ranks of the Notts. club, which rather mitigated against their chance. Towards the close of play, the Notts. party seemed to improve, and, for a club of such recent origin, they acquitted themselves remarkably well. Seventeen players contended on each side.

The reporter can be excused for not noticing that there were eighteen players on both sides! Supper at the George followed. The Notts team had its share of star players. Richard Daft was shortly to be acknowledged as the best batsman in English cricket, and retained that position until W.G. Grace's day. Charles Frederick Daft, Richard's brother, was a professional cricketer too, and also ran a sports outfitters shop in Lister Gate.

And who where the others? Many came from the lace trade; not surprising, given that a good proportion of Nottingham as a whole worked in the lace trade at that time. Edward Birkhead Steegman worked in the family lace business. So did Christopher Silvester Wardle and Alexis Blake Baillon. Frederick Chatwin Smith was one of Bramcote's chief landowners and built Chilwell Church. His money came from the family bank overlooking the Market Square in Nottingham, now Smith's Branch of the National Westminster. Frederick organised the rebuilding of the bank in 1878, causing the removal of several shops and the creation of Exchange Walk. There was certainly a good sprinkling of public school men in the team, each with his own interpretation of the rules no doubt!

A fifteen-a-side game followed at Lincoln in March. The return game with Sheffield took place on March 23rd 1865, Sheffield again having the best of things by one goal to nil.

Next season, competitive matches did not get underway until January 1866. *"We wuz robbed,"* appears to be the tone of the report of the first game against Sheffield on January 25th 1866. Though losing 1-2, Gilbert Packer can claim the first recorded goal for Notts.

The return game in March found Bramall Lane in bad condition, and incessant rain spoiled the game. Sheffield scored the only goal in the second half. Two weeks later, Sheffield travelled to Battersea Park in London to meet a representative team drawn largely from Barnes and the Wanderers. London had an easy win, 2 goals and 4 touchdowns to none.

Notts' first game with Forest took place on March 22nd 1866 when 13 of Notts were due to meet 15 of Forest. In the end, 11 of Notts played 17 of Forest! No goals were scored. The return game took place on April 19th, this time intended to be 11-a-side, though only 10 of Forest turned up on the day. *"A pleasant and well contested game"* with *"many splendid kicks made by both sides,"* again ended scoreless. The Notts line up included "Stranger", but the suspicion is that this was the reporter putting down "a stranger".

The Lincoln club resigned from the FA, but the FA president, Pember, wasn't too unhappy since Lincoln liked, *"hacking, throttling and other harsh practices."* The FA agreed to Sheffield's proposal to limit the height of the goal by means of a tape, 8 ft above the ground (though Sheffield then moved the tape to 9 ft in their rules in 1868!)

The 1866/67 season opened with a practice match at Frederick Smith's estate at Bramcote. A team chosen by Mr Smith played one chosen by E.B. Steegman. Two guest players, Mr. G. Pym (Civil Service) and H.W. Chambers (Sheffield), also joined in. Harry Waters Chambers was a solicitor and friend of Nathaniel Creswick, one of the founders of the Sheffield club. Chambers was later secretary of Sheffield for 22 years and the club's representative at meetings of the Football Association. Mr. Smith's side scored the only goal, and although Mr Steegman's team managed three touch downs, no goals followed. Next week, the home game with Forest took place at the Meadows. Notts were now attired in orange and black stripes. Forest scored an early goal; the rule then was the teams should change ends, so now Notts had the strong wind behind them. John Hack's, *"well directed kick"* brought the equaliser. Strong forward play by Notts was not enough to get the winner.

In February, Notts played what was essentially a practice game with the "old public school men"; those in the club who had had a private education. The list of players for the public schools illustrates both the background of many of the club members and also provides some important clues to the nature of the rules followed by the club at the time.

The "opposition" was:

F.C. Smith (Rugby)	A. Deedes (Winchester)
J. Patterson (Charterhouse)	T. Elliott (Repton)
C. Rothera (Rugby)	G. Fellows (Repton)
C. Elliott (Uppingham)	T. Crompton (Rugby)
J. Lambert (Rugby)	T.P. Keely (Repton)
J. Keely (Oundle)	

With so many Rugby men in the team, it would be surprising if the game was more akin to the sport you would see on the Nottingham Rugby Ground at Beeston, rather than at Meadow Lane! However, Notts are believed usually to have played the Sheffield rules, though at least some games are recorded as "Nottingham Rules". Small variations in rules could of course be used to strategic advantage!

Notts recorded their first win against Sheffield in the Bramall Lane encounter in February 1867. Charles Rothera scored the only goal, and Notts also managed a rouge. The return game on March 14th was notable for being the first occasion on which Notts hired the Trent Bridge cricket ground, later to become the home of both Forest and Notts. Forget about the shape and look of the present day ground. When William Clarke had laid out the ground in 1838 the first priority was a palisade fence right around the playing area so that admission could be charged to watch the game. There was precious little else inside the fence until a single-storey pavilion was built in front of the Trent Bridge Inn. The ground stretched to where Fox Road now is, but the Bridgford end of the ground ended in front of the site of the current pavilion. It is possible then that the first football pitch ran parallel with the Radcliffe Road, though later it became established at the Fox Road end, so as to avoid encroaching on the cricket "square".

Though a good crowd could be expected for football, this was by no means the main attraction at Trent Bridge in the winter months. Coursing attracted large crowds, to watch pairs of dogs chase live rabbits, accompanied by much betting of course! Pigeon shooting (with real birds naturally) was also a frequent event, and "Pedestrianism" (athletics meetings) were popular with the betting fraternity.

It would seem that most of the games played in 1867/68 can be regarded as club games or practice games. The first game was against the Robin Hood Rifles. Concern over French troop movements in 1859 led to the creation of a number of volunteer corps, rather like the modern Territorial Army. They wore uniforms of Lincoln Green, and met at the Castle for drills and training. Boys used to drills at their public school were eager to join the adult version, so it is not surprising to find Mr. Deedes (ex Winchester) was a Captain in the Robin Hoods. Some of the other Notts team represented were Ensign W. Elliott, Sergeant H. Browne and Privates Lambert and Hack.

With the wind in their favour, Notts could only show two shots over the tape in the first half. After half time, *"a splendid bit of play by the forward men of the club resulted in a most cleverly kicked goal by Mr. J.C. Hodges. The goal was acknowledged by both sides as the best bit of play they had ever seen."* Notts were due to play Sheffield on 28th November, but no report of the game has been found.

Eleven of the Town played 11 of the County at the Meadows on December 12th, and a practice match with Forest followed on the 26th. Forest had their first "out of town" match with Sheffield Norfolk arranged for the 28th, so this was perhaps a "warm up" for that match. A return game with the Robin Hoods and two games with the "old public school men" completed the season.

Elsewhere, the FA amended the offside law so that the forward pass was allowed. Sheffield's proposals for rouge flags and changes to the handling rules were presented to the FA but rejected. Lincoln rejoined, but whether or not they were still hacking and tripping we do not know!

The club organised an amateur athletics meeting at Trent Bridge on May 7th 1868. E.B. Steegman had attended a similar event organised annually by the Sheffield club, and Notts saw the meeting as a way to raise funds for the club. Some events were restricted to club members; Mr. C. Wilde won the longest kick at football with 139 yards 3 inches. J.C. Hodges should have won the 120 yards, but seems to have mistaken the winning post to let H.J. Pfungst into first place in 14½ seconds, with Charles Rothera second. The 440 yard race for scholars under 16 years of age was won by Arthur Ashwell, later to play an important role in the club's survival, and one of the first on the board of directors when it became a limited company. Dinner followed at the George, where the trophies were presented, all manufactured by Mr. Everington, silversmith of Pelham Street.

For reasons difficult to tell at this remove, the next season, 1868/69 was a quiet one. The first games were played with Newark, but fixtures with Sheffield and Forest were allowed to lapse. Maybe "off the field activities" in arranging athletics meetings were to blame. Profits expected from these events turned out to be substantial losses incurred and caused membership fees to double.

The summer of 1869 was perhaps the pinnacle of Richard Daft's cricket career. He scored 103 not out against the MCC and 93 not out against Surrey, finishing with an average of 49.40. Although pitches were much improved since Parr's day, remember they were still not the flat strips as used today. However, matters at the club improved rapidly, and 1869/70 was the most successful season to date. In eleven games just one was lost.

Trent Bridge was intended to be used to entertain Sheffield, but the game had to be moved to the Meadows to make way for rabbit coursing. Trent Bridge now sported a cinder running track.

Clifton colliery opened in 1870. Just down the road from the Meadows cricket ground, the colliery became a major employer for people living in the district, over a thousand by 1900, and stimulated the building of more of the terrace houses that helped transform the open "meadows" into densely packed housing.

Two new forces began to change soccer's direction about this time. County associations formed under the aegis of the FA, and international matches and representative games occurred. Both of these lifted players out of their home base at the clubs, and brought them into contact with other people's ideas about the game. The first England v. Scotland international took place in March 1870, but in reality was only "Scots players in London clubs" against "English players in London clubs". Sheffield had continued its games with London, and December 1870 saw the first North v South game at the Oval. Charles Rothera of Notts captained the North (despite not appearing for the club in season 1870/71) and E.H. Greenhalgh was also in the team. The South won 1-0. Football Association membership had risen to 39 clubs, a dozen or so of these from the provinces.

The summer of 1871 found W.G. Grace scoring a century at Trent Bridge, and the opening of the new bridge over the river nearby, to replace the old, many arched, structure. In London, the FA decided to introduce a Challenge Cup on knock-out principles. Although school matches at Harrow are often quoted as the model for a knock-out tournament, it is equally likely that the example of coursing (where dogs were matched in pairs until only two were left for the final) was equally influential. Anticipating trouble in the cup-ties, neutral umpires and a referee to arbitrate between the umpires if necessary were introduced for the games. Entries were predominantly from London; only Donnington School from Spalding and Queen's Park from Glasgow came from elsewhere. Quite why this was so is unclear. Maybe fixture lists had already been drawn up, maybe London was too far away to consider, or maybe the provincial clubs just were not interested in the activities of the "London" Association.

Or maybe it was still arguments over the rules. Sheffield made some revisions to their rules in 1871, retaining the 9 ft cross bar, and introducing a "one person" offside rule. That is, if the attacking player was nearer the goal than any defender, he was offside. The defending side was allowed to handle the ball within three yards of the goal, but the position of goalkeeper, as we know it, was still to be created; any of the defenders could handle the ball. Otherwise, handling was slowly being written out of the association game.

Indeed, folklore has it that members of the Hallam club in Sheffield would play with coins (florins) in their hands to ensure they were not tempted to touch the ball.

Notts' games with Sheffield were both lost by one goal to nil. In October 1871, Sheffield had played a representative London team at Bramall Lane. London had agreed to play Sheffield rules. *"The strategic management of players in regular positions"* helped Sheffield to win by 3-1. One of the goals was scored when a London defender was caught with the ball in his hands and was bundled over the line. For most of the Nineteenth century, a goalkeeper's lot was not a happy one. Banish from your mind the athletic, gymnastic 'keepers of today. The attributes required then were as much brawn as possible in order to stand firm against the onrushes of the opposition. The Royal Engineers in particular were noted for their forcible play. It was about this time that the designated goalkeeper became the only man able to handle the ball. He was allowed to do this anywhere in his own half of the field. He was not allowed to run with the ball, but could bounce it out from his goal.

Notts generally had a poor season in 1871/72. Four games were won in the early part of the season, but in the new year seven matches were played without a victory. The trip to Lincoln on February 8th proved an embarrassment as only five players made the trip, and local players were pressed into service to make up the numbers. Nottingham was in the grip of a small-pox epidemic in the early part of 1872, but Sheffield came in March for the annual fixture. Next season saw the first "real" international between England and Scotland, which took place in Partick in November 1872. E.H. Greenhalgh and J.C. Clegg (of Sheffield) were the only men of the north in the England team. No goals were scored. Greenhalgh also played in the return game in March 1873, with England this time running out easy winners by 4 goals to 2. Clegg said later of the first game, *"none of the Southern amateurs spoke to me."* March 17th 1873 saw Notts meet a representative London side at Trent Bridge. No goals resulted.

For the 1873/74 season, Trent Bridge became the home of the club, with just occasional matches played else-where. A new pavilion had been built on the south side of the ground, replacing the old, single storey building which stood behind the Trent Bridge Inn. The "Football Annual" for 1873 was impressed by the vast size of the ground. Notts played another home game with London at Trent Bridge in November, winning by two goals to nil. 1,500 people attended (though 10,000 had seen Grace get his century). There was a small amount of crowd trouble, for a well known bare knuckle fighter of former years, Bendigo, was charged with being drunk and disorderly - having been caught throwing turnips at passers-by. Bendigo was spending his retirement from the boxing ring working as a waiter in the new pavilion.

James Grundy died in November 1873, and many of the Notts players attended the funeral. The Nottingham Journal commented that, *"football is almost, if not quite, as popular as cricket"*. Grundy was an outstanding bowler for Notts CCC, taking all 10 wickets on four occasions.

The Forest club had an important fixture against the Royal Engineers on December 23rd, and the presence of Notts' men A.B. Baillon and C.J. Spencer must have strengthened the team. The players at this time were all amateurs playing for the love of the sport. There was no problem about being a member of more than one club, except in cup ties, where the FA had ruled that you could only play for one club each season. Samuel Weller Widdowson is usually thought of as a Forest player, but he played more than twenty games for Notts over seven seasons. Sam is credited with the invention of shin pads, when he cut down some cricket pads and strapped them to his legs. The Rev. J.R.B. Owen played for Derbyshire, Notts and Sheffield, where he was capped by England in 1874.

In March, Notts made the trip south to play two games against London at the Oval. Easy victors in the first game, London made nine changes for the second match two days later which was drawn.

Heading the ball became common in the Sheffield game around this time. Early balls had the panels held together by a button at each end of the ball, and heading was unwise, but as stitched balls became widely used, the only damage likely to the head was now from the lace, or the sheer weight of the ball if wet. Crossbars rather than tapes were introduced for the goals, though these were not made mandatory until 1882.

The club headed north in January 1875 for their first meeting with the famous Queen's Park club in Glasgow. Formed in 1867, Queen's Park remained undefeated until February 1876 when they lost to the Wanderers in London. Notts lost by six goals to nil, probably out-thought tactically by the Scots. The English game had settled on a 1-2-2-6 formation, whilst the Scots played 1-2-2-3-3. A return game was arranged for March 8th 1875. Although losing again, Notts at least had the distinction of being the first English club to score against them.

The reporter of the Sporting Life caught the train from St. Pancras in the summer of 1875:

> Alighting from the carriage (at Midland Station), the visitor is faced by a full length life sized painting of Richard Daft in batting attitude, with the address of his cricketing depot. Entering the street, Summers' Hotel is seen immediately opposite the station door. Hailing one of the commodious white-roofed cabs, whose horses have a sort of tin pail instead of a nose bag, the cricketer is soon on his way to the Trent Bridge, passing by the King's Meadows and noticing en route the prevalence of the moustache

movement and the external cleanliness of the houses, with their lace curtains. An approach, resembling on a smaller scale, that of Battersea Bridge, leads us to the handsome new bridge, built just above the old bridge, a good deal after the design of Westminster Bridge, and which was opened in July 1871. The piers of the old bridge are still left to the right of the new structure and must be dangerous to craft in the rapid stream. In point of picturesqueness the old bridge over the Trent was superior to its handsome successor. The house (the Trent Bridge Inn) is on the left-hand side immediately after crossing the bridge. Entering the enclosure, we see at a glance that it is rather small for county cricket, that the light is good, that the turf on the outskirts might be more level, and that the ground is inclined to be damp and spongy, and is at the same time rather bleak. Altogether, although the wickets are good, the Trent Bridge contrasts unfavourably with the Forest Ground. Calling to a friend to send down a ball or two for practice, the visitor is politely informed that none but members of the county club or the opposing eleven are allowed to practice here, so that he must get one of his own side, or a ground man to bowl him an over or two. The pavilion, built last season, will probably together with the result of the expenditure to be incurred on account of benches for the general public, now supply the necessary sitting accommodation, the absence of which was previously the chief exception the spectator could take to the arrangements. The sheds are to the right and left of the entrance and a small wooden house, the property of the Bank Club, faces the pavilion. There are also a scoring box and two telegraphs. As well as a cinder track, halfway round the ground, the accommodation usually boasts a tent for ladies, which is well patronised, many of the county families driving down to see play in the afternoon.

Notts FC's close ties with Notts CCC continued. Edwin Browne, who became the Notts FC secretary in 1883, was assistant secretary of the cricket club.

On 26th February 1877, the Sheffield and London rules finally came into alignment. The way was now open for the game to spread without having to argue about the rules. As a consequence perhaps, Notts entered for the F.A. Cup (then known as the London Association's Cup) in 1877/78. Provincial clubs were drawn in groups for the early rounds; there were six "northern clubs"; Sheffield, Darwen, Manchester, Druids (from Ruabon) and Shropshire Wanderers. Notts were drawn with Sheffield, having already included the traditional friendly games in their fixture list.

On the day of the cup-tie, the reporter was as perplexed as the Notts public to find that Arthur Cursham was turning out for Sheffield.

"Some little surprise was expressed that A.W. Cursham should have transferred his services to the Yorkshire town. He is one of the leading members of the Notts. club, with which he has been associated for some years, and it was somewhat surprising to find him in the ranks of the enemy on Saturday last."

The report continued:

> The Sheffield players arrived on the ground shortly before three o'clock, and they made up a remarkably strong team, which included the brothers Clegg, Matthews, the Sorbys, and others whose names are well known in connexion with

HARRY CURSHAM: A 'star' in the pre-League days. Pictured in his England kit.

football. The home club was fairly represented, though owing to an unfortunate accident to Pearson, they had to play one short during the latter part of the game. Shortly after three o'clock Notts., having won the toss, E.H. Greenhalgh kicked off towards the West Bridgford goal, and five minutes afterwards the ball was near to the Sheffield stronghold, that the services of the goal keeper were needed. The attack was successfully repelled, and the Sheffielders attempted a similar move, a few minutes later though without any issue, though the ball went dangerously near the Notts. posts. H. Greenhalgh was however equal to the occasions, and the contest was again waged in the centre of the inclosure with no material advantage to either side. Jessop, playing back, did very good service in the early part of the game, his action being prompt, and his kicking forcible, and H. Cursham and Widdowson, the latter always a favourite, did most of the hard work for Notts. At twenty minute to four o'clock, the game having been in progress for about half an hour, Keely, on behalf of Notts., effected a run up, and H. Cursham, taking the ball at the right moment, sent it through the posts. Thus the first blood was drawn by Notts., amid hearty applause from the bystanders. Without loss of time the "leather" was again set in motion and Notts. tried hard to make a second score, but it was now the visitor's turn, and taking advantage of a weak point in the arrangement of the field, one of the brothers Clegg got a famous run, nor was his career checked until the ball was safely in the keeping of A.W. Cursham, who succeeded in putting it through the posts. Both these goals were obtained before the call of "half time." With the change of ends came a more exciting state of things, and Notts. seemed to be getting the best of it. On more than one occasion they got the ball in dangerous proximity to the Sheffield goal, and but for the timely intervention of Ellison, the goal keeper, they would have advanced their position. The play of H. Cursham for Notts. was superb, and in a less degree that of Widdowson, Oliver and one or two others was noticeable. In the course of the afternoon a dispute arose which caused a short suspension. It seems the ball was put through the Notts. posts after it had touched the boundary, and as the umpires could not agree upon the point, the referee was appealed to, and a "no goal" was declared. Once during the latter half of the game the visitors very nearly gained a second goal - which would have decided the match in their favour - the ball striking the horizontal bar, but generally, Notts. had the best of it, a remark which applies more especially to the latter half of the game. At a quarter to five o'clock "time" was announced, the match being drawn.

The Sheffield team was M.J. Ellison (goal), J. Collins, T. Willey, W.H. Clegg, R.A. Sorby, J.C. Clegg, A.W. Cursham, T.H. Sorby, A. Denton, W.A. Matthews, and Rev. J.R.B. Owen. Owen was the second Sheffield man with Notts connections. The umpires were Mr. A. T. Ashwell (Notts.) and W. Chambers (Sheffield), who was probably the same man that had joined in Mr. F.C. Smith's practice match in 1866. The referee who saved Notts' blushes was not mentioned.

The accident to Pearson must have been serious, but other changes were forced on the team for the replay. Sheffield ran out easy winners, with Arthur Cursham scoring two! Quite what his clubmates made of this we don't know; he was back in the Notts team on December 20th when they lost by two goals to one at Bramall Lane. Perhaps things were finally settled by the return game in February when Notts ran up seven without reply, six of these by the Curshams; 3 for Charles, 2 for Arthur and one for Harry for good measure.

Nottingham football was now getting more competitive perhaps. Notts cancelled fixtures with Forest for two seasons because the garibaldi reds were "too artisan"; a sign, perhaps, that the public school background of the Notts players was still predominant. However, they were drawn together in the Cup in 1878/79, with Forest having the better of things, and no doubt feeling rather smug about it!

Getting to the games proved somewhat easier after 17th September 1878. The Nottingham and District Tramway's Company first route opened, from St. Peter's Church to Trent Bridge. The horse drawn tram would get you there in ten minutes for a penny. The service terminated at the Town Arms, on the north side of the bridge, but you could always get Mr. Mann's horse bus if the last few hundred yards were too much for you! The trams were probably busy on the evening of the 14th October 1878 when Notts enjoyed their first floodlight game with Derbyshire. 1878 also saw the first telephone call in Nottingham, between the police station in St. Johns Street and the Castle Museum, and the first use of electric arc lights for street lighting.

The referee's whistle supposedly came into use in 1878. This seems to be one of those long standing stories that should be taken with a pinch of salt. The game was supposed to be between Forest and Sheffield Norfolk, but Forest hadn't played Norfolk since 1874. Also, the game was still controlled by the two umpires, one in each half of the field, who only intervened "on appeal", just as in cricket. The referee stayed on the touchline. So what did he need a whistle for? To blow for full time perhaps. It is more likely that the whistle appeared in the 1880s, when the referee got onto the pitch and began applying the rules directly, rather than waiting for an appeal from the players.

We have a first hand account of Saturday nights in Nottingham in 1879; nothing much has changed perhaps!

Pleasure, sometimes rough and unrefined, but always harmless, now holds the sway. Pattern-girls in new frills, menders with retrimmed bonnets, machine girls wearing the "latest from Paris," laugh and joke with a good sprinkling of the opposite sex. The clocks have chimed seven, eight, nine, and the numbers increase. A band is playing selections from the latest opera here, and an organ is grinding away there. Bingham's and the Cafe are crowded to excess, while from the public houses issues forth a monotonous hubbub whenever the swinging doors are thrown open. Never was a livelier scene witnessed in the Boulevards of gay Paris than the Long Row now presents, but the inevitable "hour of Cross" arrives and cuts it off in its glory. It is eleven o'clock, and the promenade becomes more thronged than ever; reeling men, noisy women, musical youths and giggling girls jostle with one another. Fights, brawls and policemen without end mark the close of the day, for Bacchus is the reigning monarch.

Home games for season 1879/80 were played at the Beeston Cricket Club's ground. This had been laid out in 1866 on land immediately to the south of Beeston Station on the Midland Railway, a site now covered by car parks, concrete and a bowling green. Notts had played the Cup-tie with Forest at Beeston in November 1878, and Wright's Directory of 1879 reports that practice sessions on Thursday afternoons were held there. The ground was described in 1867 as, *"one of the finest in England,"* and it was later to find favour with W.G. Grace as he compiled yet another century there. The Author once asked the groundsman if the bowling greens were the original turf; *"not bloody likely"* he said *"I sweated buckets to lay the top soil."* Beeston is seemingly just part of Nottingham's urban sprawl, but it is important to remember that the Nottingham population in 1879 would have regarded this move with the same raised eyebrows as the people of Luton do when a move of the football club to Milton Keynes is discussed. It was a long walk to Beeston for those who could not afford the horse bus or the train!

The move to Beeston lasted for just one season, for the club moved back to a new ground in the Meadows in 1880, at the south end of Queen's Walk, just to the south of the Meadows Cricket Ground. The Castle Cricket Club had recently laid out a new ground in the Whey House Field, near the Trent. Notts played here for the next three seasons. The ground was later developed with a new pavilion (1886) and a track for bicycle races, but was in the way of the Grand Central Railway's new lines at the turn of the century. A settled team had a mixed season, the highlights being an 8-1 thrashing of Sheffield and a 15-1 demolition of Newark. The Cup brought the first meeting, and a defeat, against Aston Villa, who had beaten Forest in the previous round.

For the meeting with Sheffield in December 1880, Notts sported their new uniform of Cambridge blue and chocolate, *"one of the most unique and striking combinations I remember having seen"* said the local reporter.

Chapter 2
Players: 1880 - 1890

Gates of 5,000 were now common for games played in the North of England, though not in the South. There was talk of money being played to players. The game was beginning to attract people who were impressed by the commercial possibilities, not just the sporting. Indeed, Derby County was established in 1884 to help the flagging finance of the Derbyshire Cricket Club. Juggling a club's finances was no easier then than now; a decline in Notts' membership in 1881 led to a crisis of confidence and the first of many rescue plans. The meeting at the Lion Hotel led to a vote, with the motion to continue proposed by Arthur Ashwell, the winner of the under 16 race at the first athletic meeting in 1868.

Season 1881/82 brought more high scoring games, but this time it was the Notts' keepers' turn to watch the ball fly past him. Trips to Blackburn and Queen's Park resulted in 10 goal defeats. If an excuse was needed for the game, the players could point out that they had caught the train from Nottingham on Friday evening and travelled overnight to Glasgow. In the Cup, Wednesbury Strollers were defeated easily enough, but they protested about the referee and one of the Notts' players. The game was ordered to be replayed, allowing Notts to run up their (then) record win, 11-1, with Harry Cursham scoring six of them. A return game with Aston Villa was the reward. Two closely contested games ended 2-2 after extra time, but Villa again had the best of things in the second replay.

1882/83 saw the fixture list reach its longest yet. Two Harry Cursham goals saw Notts record their first win in a friendly game with Aston Villa, a result repeated when the clubs met in the Cup for the third year running. Notts had by now established a strong line up, with Macrae and the two Curshams in the England game with Scotland in March 1883. The settled team was rewarded by the results, including big wins over Sheffield and Blackburn Rovers. Cup form was good too, helped by some gamesmanship! There was no fixed day for a Cup round to be played at this time; the clubs just had to play the game before a specified date. Notts repeatedly put off their fourth round tie with Sheffield Wednesday because they, *"couldn't raise a team".* This didn't prevent them beating the Sheffield club 8-2 in the interim! Having beaten Wednesday and Aston Villa, Notts travelled to the Oval in London for the semi-final

where they lost 1-2 to the Old Etonians. *"The gentry turned out in their carriages in large numbers"* says the report. Many Notts supporters made the trip to London, carrying chocolate and blue cards with "Play up Notts" written on them. H.T. Moore had been taken ill before the game, which led to late changes to the line-up. Harry Cursham gave Notts the lead in the first half, but the Old Etonians equalised after 60 minutes, and scored the winner six minutes from time.

If you were looking for a "golden age" of Notts football, then the early 1880s would be a strong candidate. For three or four years, Notts ranked as one of the leading clubs in the land. It is also worth noting that this period coincided with an outstanding period for the Notts Cricket Club, with four successive county championships won. Blackburn Rovers would perhaps lay claim to being **the** best team of the period, with an outstanding record in the Cup, but Notts had some success against them in friendly matches. Later in the decade, the honorary title of leading club passed to Preston North End, who earned the title of "The Invincibles".

The club settled at Trent Bridge for the 1883/84 season. There were still no permanent structures for watching games, apart from a small stand at the Radcliffe Road end, and the (rather distant) pavilion of course. Harry Cursham scored 37 goals for Notts that season. It is often overlooked that the leading goalscorer in the F.A. Cup is not Ian Rush or Dennis Law (on 41), but Harry Cursham with 49. He scored two others in the "void" game with Wednesbury Strollers in 1881, but these are not included in the record. His goals in 1883/84 contributed to the local paper's report of the season as, *"the best yet".* Notts again reached the semi-final of the F.A. Cup, after they were perhaps a little lucky in the replayed game with Bolton Wanderers when the umpire disallowed a Bolton goal and awarded them a free kick instead. Unsportsmanlike behaviour from the neutral spectators in Birmingham was held to be a contributory factor to the semi-final defeat. However, Harry Cursham had been moved to the centre for the game, and perhaps the rhythm of the team was disrupted.

The forward line of Arthur and Harry Cursham, John Dixon and William Gunn boasted four England internationals, the latter player also representing England at cricket. Arthur Cursham played his last game for Notts in his benefit game against Queen's Park in April 1884, and immediately caught the boat to start a new life in Florida. The proceeds from the game of £284 were presented to his brother, the Rev. F.C. Cursham, at the club's annual dinner in May. By Christmas, Arthur was dead, of yellow fever. Black armbands were worn in his respect for the game against Blackburn Rovers in January 1885.

Notts made steady progress in the Cup of 1884/85, and a new record crowd of 17,000 squeezed into Trent Bridge to see the round six tie with Queen's Park. After a 2-2 draw, Notts tried to claim the match since Queen's Park refused to play extra time. The FA accepted the Scottish club's argument that encroachment by spectators onto the playing area made further play dangerous, and a replay took place the following Saturday at the Derby Cricket Ground.

Programme for the F.A.Cup match versus Sheffield F.C. Founded in 1857, they are the only surviving club older than Notts County. N.B. A printer's error states '1884', whereas the match was played in January 1885.

ately recognised professional players, a real break with tradition when you remember the public school beginnings of the club and the snobbish behaviour over the Forest fixtures. The six registered professionals were W. Gunn, M.Sherwin, E.Harker, H.W. Emmitt, H.T. Moore and A. Peters.

A new landmark appeared in May 1885, when the new Trent Bridge Inn opened. It had been built to the rear of the old inn, which would have stood where the dual carriageway road is now. The two inns stood side by side for a while until the old one was demolished. The new pavilion opened at the ground (the one still in use today) in June the following year.

The new season was enlivened by the club's record win, a 15-0 demolition of Rotherham Town in the Cup at Trent Bridge in October 1885. Notts can truly claim to have won "by a cricket score" as the Notts cricket team were bowled out for 13 at Trent Bridge by Yorkshire in 1901, with Wilfred Rhodes taking 6 wickets for 4 runs.

Strong fencing was erected to avoid a repeat of the trouble at Trent Bridge. Queen's Park were the better team on the day and won by two goals to one.

By this stage in the development of the game, professionalism was well established in the Northern clubs, but technically still outlawed by the Football Association. With things coming to a head, some clubs still considered it prudent to withdraw from the Cup for 1884/85. A meeting of the F.A. on 20th July 1885 finally accepted that professionals were part of the English game; the Scots were to remain amateur until 1893. On the 30th July 1885, the Scottish FA wrote to the 58 players in England who had been registered as professionals; 57 of these were with Lancashire clubs and the other with Aston Villa. Notts were one of the clubs who immedi-

The trip to Glasgow in October 1885 resulted in the customary defeat by Queen's Park, but as the club had also agreed a fixture with Walsall Swifts on the same day, two "first" teams had to be fielded. The Cup brought a surprise. After scoring 26 goals in their first three ties, little trouble was expected from a visit to Blackpool to play South Shore. Not for the last time in their history, Notts were beaten by unfancied opposition. Shortly afterwards, a reasonably strong first team travelled to Wellingborough to play a friendly game with the Grammar School. Harry Jackson scored 8 of the goals in an 11-3 victory.

Lack of a settled team may have contributed to some of the topsy-turvy results in 1886/87. William Gunn was away, touring Australia with Shaw and Shrewsbury's cricket team. 9-1 and 11-0 victories over the Sheffield club and Lockwood Brothers respectively were counterbalanced by two visits to Lancashire in November. Preston demolished them 0-14, and three weeks later Accrington ran up eight without reply. Another good Cup run took Notts to a quarter final tie with West Bromwich Albion at Trent Bridge, but a good crowd of 13,067 saw them lose 1-4.

The F.A.Cup semi-final between West Bromwich Albion and Preston North End was played at Trent Bridge later in 1887. A brick wall had been built along the Gamston Lane end of the ground (now the Radcliffe Road End) in 1884, but a free view of the ground could be gained by climbing the trees that lined the road. Regrettably, a labourer fell from one of the trees whilst watching the game, broke his spine and died. A covered stand had now been built at the Fox Road end of the ground; there was some hissing from this stand when the players were late starting the game with Mitchell's St. George's in October 1887.

In December, the club had a return fixture with Leek in their list, but the opportunity arose to play a more lucrative friendly at Preston. Two "first teams" therefore had to turn out again. As the reserve team were also in action at Kettering, a good idea is gained of the playing strength of the club at that time. When Halliwell turned up in February 1888, they were none too pleased to find the "first team proper" were in Glasgow, playing Queen's Park.

Fine tuning by the Football Association of the laws of the game continued. Once a ball had crossed the line it was agreed to be "out" of play under all circumstances. Formerly, the umpires had allowed play to continue if the ball curved back into play before touching the ground.

The fixture list was still expanding, and the need to pay the players was forcing the clubs to take a more business like approach to the game. Small Heath, later Birmingham City, became the first club to set itself up as a limited company, a move which the Athletic News later recommended all clubs to adopt. It was partly from these commercial pressures that the suggestion to form a "league" was debated and finally agreed on 23rd March 1888. Notts may consider themselves fortunate to be part of the original twelve clubs. Their playing record against the other eleven who formed the League was not brilliant in 1887/88, though there was a notable 8-2 victory over Aston Villa. However, the fact that the club had the use of Trent Bridge must have been an attrac-

tion, for it could hold larger gates than most other grounds at the time. The claims of the Forest club were somewhat negated by the fact that they remained amateur. Meanwhile, Notts Rangers laid claim to outperforming both senior clubs in 1888! However, the League decided that one club per town was enough. Twelve clubs was thought to be the maximum number, and therefore 22 Saturdays would be required for fixtures, with spare ones left for cup-ties and friendlies.

The Football Association was unsure how to handle this new organisation, potentially one that would be at odds with it. The Cup arrangements for 1888/89 were decided on the past season's performance, not whether clubs were in the League or not. Thus, Everton, Stoke and Notts were obliged to play in the qualifying rounds, despite having League fixtures arranged on dates that ties had to be played. On three occasions, the Notts reserve team played in the cup-ties, with two of the games taking place at Trent Bridge before the scheduled League match. Coincidentally, this was the first season that qualifying rounds had been used, in an attempt to avoid more embarrassments like the 26-0 thrashing of Hyde by Preston the previous season.

A press report of Notts' first ever home League match, 6th October 1888.

NOTTS. V. BLACKBURN ROVERS.

This League match was commenced on the Trent Bridge Ground immediately after the conclusion of the Cup tie, and at this time there were quite 4,000 people present. The Notts. team included Allin, of Burton. Jardine took the place of Hodder on the left wing, and that player assisted Albert Moore on the opposite side. The Rovers kicked off, and play had been started about two minutes, when the Rovers' goal was endangered. Daft put in a good shot, but the ball just passed over the bar. At the other end Southworth made a similar shot, and the ball being brought down a sharp struggle took place round the Blackburn goal, but although Daft stuck to the ball manfully he was eventually deprived of it. Two corners shortly afterwards fell to the home side in succession. Nothing was done with them. Uninteresting play followed, neither side showing their best form for some time. The ball, however, passed quickly from one end to the other, and each goalkeeper was called upon to repel weak attacks. One of the Rovers' men—Beverley—received a shaking from Allin. Immediately after the game was restarted Allin centred the ball splendidly, and Daft shot it through, scoring the first point for Notts. amidst applause, after 35 minutes' play. A minute later, however, a sharp struggle occurred round the Notts. goal, and Fecitt equalised by a beautiful overhead kick. There was some enthusiasm shown now as the game waxed warm, and each team strove hard to put in a leading point. C. Shelton shot grandly into the Blackburn goal, but Arthur was all there and relieved his side. Guttridge fouled the ball in front of his own goal, and from the free-kick Holland was called upon to save.

The first League fixture took Notts to Everton on 15th September 1888. Defeats at Stoke and Aston Villa would have left Notts at the bottom, but the League was still considering how to rank the clubs, and two points for a win and one for a draw was not agreed until 21st November 1888. Results improved a little, but Notts could not claim to have a had a successful first season in the League. The players were largely those who played in recent seasons and it became obvious that fresh blood was needed. First, the club had to survive the re-election process, which involved the last four clubs in the table. It turned out to be a narrow thing, the club gaining only seven votes, just two more than Birmingham St. George's.

The game is troubled in the 1990's by the activities of player's agents, and "bungs" or signing on fees. It is a mistake to consider this as just a current phenomenon. Agents were just as active in the 1890s, probably more so. Scotland was the main hunting ground, with big signing-on fees, attractive salaries, part time jobs, and accommodation offered to Scottish players to move south. Agents working for Notts secured the services of Macmillan, Ferguson and Calderhead for the 1889/90 season. The agents were helped by the lifting of some of the stringent restrictions on professionals in May 1889, and many other clubs signed their share of Scots. Notts were also after James Oswald, who had also received an offer from Preston.

Trent Bridge - photo' taken towards the pavilion end. The stand on the left was re-erected at the Meadow Lane of Notts' new ground in 1910.

Thomas Selby wrote to Edwin Browne in June 1889 saying it would be, *"the greatest capture Notts ever made if it comes off."* It did! Oswald scored 15 goals in 19 games, but the end result was a rise of just one place, in the second season of the League, to 10th. Oswald was missing for the fixture with Aston Villa in November 1889. Notts asked the famous amateur player Tinsley Lindley to play at centre forward. Lindley was one of the great centre forwards of the time, winning 13 England caps and playing for Cambridge University, Corinthians and Forest. With Forest playing in the Football Alliance, not the League, Notts anticipated no trouble with his registration as an amateur player. However, Villa raised the matter with the League, believing Notts had pulled a fast one. Notts were fined £5 and became the first club to have a point deducted from their playing record. Lindley, a barrister, led an appeal, complaining that the club had suffered two punishments for one offence. The point was reinstated but the fine increased to £25! Crowd trouble reared its head on 14th December 1889 when Wolves were the visitors. Also, Sheffield Wednesday complained to an FA Committee about the rough play of Clements in a cup-tie the previous season. The complaint was duly recorded in the minutes.

Notts took the step of becoming a limited company in 1890. The "Notts. Incorporated Football Club" is their company name, not Notts County! The F.A. were asked to agree on the change of name, from Notts FC to Notts Incorporated FC.

Chapter 3
Halcyon Days: 1890 - 1900

The increasing competitiveness and commercialisation of football meant it was necessary to sort out how the game was controlled on the pitch. The referee's powers had increased in 1888, for he was on the field (though the whistle was optional) and the umpires were becoming a hindrance, if only by getting in the way. So, in 1891, the umpires were banished to the touchline and given the job of linesmen. The white flags they had used on the pitch to wave at the players stayed with them so they could indicate when the ball was over the line. Goal nets were also introduced in 1891. After a trial game in Liverpool, they were used for the North v, South game, played on Forest's Town Ground in January 1891. Fred Geary of Everton can therefore claim to be the first player to "put the ball in the net" in a competitive game. Geary was born in Hyson Green, Nottingham and was on the books of Notts Rangers and Notts (making two appearances in 1887 and 1888) before joining Everton. The inventor of goal nets, Mr. Brodie, had taken out a patent on the idea, which led to some debate with the F.A. as to how he would be paid. Nevertheless, after interviewing him on 4th February 1891, the F.A. agreed on March 11th that nets would be used for the 1891 Cup Final.

Also new in 1891 was the penalty kick. Notts had a starring role in its creation, following a cup-tie with Stoke in February that year. Interestingly, there was no requirement to mark the penalty spot at first (12 yards from goal) but all the other players had to stand 6 yards behind the 12 yard line. Moreover, not only could the goalie choose to stand up to 6 yards out of his goal, he was also not required to stand still until the ball was kicked! Pitch markings now had a strange look to the modern eye. Around each goalpost was a 6 yard semi-circle, from within which goal kicks could be taken. There was a centre spot and a half way line, but no 10 yard circle. Reporters were still expected to sit at a trestle table, open to the elements. The Evening News reporter complained bitterly that his notes had turned to pulp during a wet second round cup-tie with Burnley.

Season 1890/91 saw a welcome resurgence of form in the League, and an outstanding Cup run took them to the final for the first time, to meet Blackburn Rovers at Kennington Oval. Notts were the strong favourites to win the cup, and could point to a 7-1 victory over Blackburn just a week before.

John Forbes, captain of Blackburn Rovers wrote of his side, *"The team is in strict training all week, and the men are confident that they can win the cup."* James Oswald wrote from the Ashover Hydropathic establishment where the Notts men spent the week, *"To tell the truth, I really cannot say in what condition our team will be in on Saturday, but I can assure you this much, that we shall give the Rovers as hard a game as ever they got in their lives."* The Star provided the following pen pictures of the Notts team:

James Oswald, the captain and centre forward, has the reputation of being about the best man in his position in the kingdom. Previous to joining Notts in 1889, Oswald was in the ranks of the Third Lanark (Glasgow) and played for Scotland against England at the Oval two years ago. The success of the Notts team is greatly the result of Oswald's tuition, knowledge of the game, and splendid generalship. He is 23 years of age, weighs 10st. 10lb., and stands 5ft. 6½in.

Andrew McGregor (outside right) is a canny Scot of 24 summers who joined Notts this season. He previously played for Wishaw Thistle, where he was soon marked as a player of exceptional ability. He is only 5ft. 5½, but with 11st. of flesh he can move at a great pace.

T. McInnes (inside right) is the littlest and lightest fellow in the team, standing 5ft. 5in., weighing 9½ stone. He came from Clyde (Glasgow) to Notts last season, and he straightway became a favourite with the Trent Bridge crowd. His trickiness is proverbial, and as an all round player he is a gem of the first water. He is 22 years of age and played for Scotland against Ireland two years ago.

Harry Daft (outside left) is one of the only two men in the team who belong to Nottingham. He is 25 years of age, 5ft 9½in., and weighs 11st. He has played in international matches three years in succession, and is one of the best left wingers in England. He is noted more for his great speed and clever centres than for passing or dodging. Daft has played for Notts and the Corinthians.

William Locker (inside left) is a Derbyshire man, and came from Long Eaton Rangers to Notts at the beginning of the season. He is a hard worker and backs up Daft most assiduously. Locker is seldom brilliant, but has a knack of scoring goals, and I fancy this is the most useful quality a player can possess. He is 24 years of age, 5ft. 6½in., and weighs 10st 4lb.

Alfred Shelton (left half back) is a Nottingham man, and has played football for the greater part of his 26 years. For three years in succession he has played in international matches, and at the present time he is about the best man in his position in England. He is 5ft 8in., and weighs 11½ stone.

David Calderhead (centre half-back) played for the Queen of the South Wanderers (Dumfries) before he came to Notts two years ago. His play is characterised by great coolness and judgement, while he places the ball beautifully to his forwards. He is 5ft. 10in., 24 years of age, and weighs 11st 8lb.

In all likelihood **Thomas McLean** will play at right back, but if not Ferguson will take his place. McLean is an old Vale of Leven player but has now assisted Notts for three seasons. Although only 5ft. 6in., and 10st. 5lb., he is a strong defender and a magnificent kicker.

John Hendry (full back) is the heaviest man in the Notts team. He weighs 13st., stands 5ft. 10½, and is 22 years of age. Hendry made a great name in the ranks of the Glasgow Rangers before he joined Notts this season. His play is of the robust type, and he never loses his head, nor has he yet seen the man he is afraid of.

J. Thraves (goal) is a native of Stapleford, and has only this season been identified with first class football. Since George Toone was hurt in January last Thraves has occupied his position with great success. He is 20 years of age, 5 ft. 6in., and weighs 11st 4lb.

THE NATIONAL FOOTBALL CUP.

NOTTS. V. BLACKBURN ROVERS.

PORTRAITS AND BIOGRAPHIES OF BOTH TEAMS.

To-day, for the first time since the establishment of the National Football Cup, Nottingham will be represented in the final tie. Both the Notts. and Forest teams have in years past done honour to the football merit of the town by entering the penultimate round, but each club had to succumb to the fortune of war. Notts. have contested two semi-finals, being beaten first of all by the Old Etonians and then by Blackburn Rovers, whose career in the Cup competition has been wonderfully brilliant. They have six times secured the honour of contesting the final tie, and after emulating the example of the Wanderers by winning the Cup three years in succession, went one better and won it for the fourth time, though with an interval of a season. Both Notts. and the Rovers have had some ill-luck with their players this season; but the cruel fate that has pursued Notts. has perhaps hardly been paralleled by any other club. To have both goalkeeper and full back disabled is such ill-luck as a club neither anticipates or is prepared for. However, the accident to Toone was the means of introducing to first-class football a remarkably smart youngster in Thraves, the second team goalkeeper, and up to the present McLean's injury has not materially prejudiced the chance of Notts. in the Cup.

A preview of Notts' appearance in the 1891 F.A.Cup.

Though Notts were the clear favourites, past form counted for nothing on the day. A rather unsettled side were soon behind when Dewer scored for Blackburn after just 8 minutes. After 30 minutes, John Southworth, the Rovers international centre forward scored the second, and Townley added a third eight minutes later.

Notts had a better second half, with Oswald scoring after 70 minutes, but the Cup went deservedly to Blackburn for the second year in succession. 23,000 spectators saw the game, and receipts were £1,454.

Notts had a friendly game arranged with Derby County the following Monday at the Derbyshire County Cricket Ground. After the game, the players caught the train to Nottingham's Midland Station where a large number of supporters had gathered. The players, *"preferred obscurity to publicity,"* and went their separate ways, though Messrs Shelton, Calderhead, Ferguson and Thraves later made their way to the Notts' club room, in Thurland Street. Secretary Edwin Browne thought they were beaten; *"by bad luck rather than fair play."* He also regretted to hear that *"on a certain ground in Nottingham, the result at half time was received by the supporters of a certain club, not with disappointment, but with absolute cheering"*!

Prospects for the next season, 1891/92, looked good. Only Andrew McGregor was not available from the previous year. The left wing had been strengthened by the arrival of Harry Walkerdine, who had been part of the Gainsborough Trinity team that had won the Midland League. However, injuries, loss of form, and the failure of the new man Abrahams to replace McGregor led to a disappointing finish of eighth.

In the Cup, Notts were drawn at Sunderland whom they had beaten in the semi-final the previous year. Training at the Tynedale Hydropathic Establishment at Hexham had not really prepared them for the ground conditions. Despite magnificent weather, the ground was covered two inches deep in sand, but with a liberal coating of ice along the centre line. Notts protested about the conditions before the game but it went ahead, with them losing 0-3. Their protest was upheld, but the replay a week later was of no help to them; with Osborne out through injury they lost 0-4. This result probably had nothing to do with the smoking concert held at the Mechanics Hall between the two games! A formidable programme of vocal and instrumental selections had been prepared, with a *"really almost impossible bill of fare"* having been arranged. Tom McLean was presented with a clock and a purse of gold to celebrate his marriage, and numerous toasts were drunk.

Defeat in the Cup did not help the finances. Not for the last time in the club's history, gates were down and the financial situation was not good. Players' salaries had been raised following the Cup run the previous season, and, *"a good deal of money had been spent on the reserve men, who had proved of little use to the club."* The Chairman declared his intention to reduce wages for the next season (though, *"they would still be paying as high wages as probably any other team in the league"*). The meeting decided not to call up the £3 per share on the 260 that had been issued, but agreed to hold a bazaar for club funds.

In the early 1890s, the first flush of commercial opportunism had passed in the game, and Notts were not the only club in financial difficulties. Though average earnings were 30/- (£1.50) a week, some players salaries had risen to the then astronomical heights of £6 per week, equivalent no doubt to today's £20,000 a week superstars. Many clubs found they could not compete, and in 1893 tried to restrict player's wages to £140 a year. The proposals were defeated, though a maximum wage was later to be forced on the players.

1892/93 brought the first taste of relegation. Form up until Christmas was all right, but a run of six consecutive defeats left them bottom, and facing a test match with Darwen, the champions of Division 2. The game was played on Ardwick's ground at Hyde Road, Manchester. A defeat consigned them to the Second Division. Form after Christmas had not been helped by the story of Harry Daft's toe. Daft had not reported for the New Year tour to Scotland, blaming an injury. The club doctor was insistent that Daft could travel. The directors were not amused that one of their professional players was not obeying orders, and Daft was dropped.

Daft demanded a transfer, the directors hesitated, especially when it was learned that Forest had offered to take him on. A public meeting was convened, with Harry's father, Richard, presenting his side of the story. Harry did eventually play a few games for Forest, but the breach was healed and he returned to Notts' colours the following season.

So, 1893/94 found them visiting many grounds for the first time, including a trip to London to meet the only Southern team in the League, Woolwich Arsenal. League form was good enough for third place, and a test match with Preston, which was lost. However, this was the Magpies' year in the Cup, overcoming Forest and Blackburn Rovers on the way to the Final.

The Final tie was to be played on Everton's new ground at Goodison Park. Notts spent the week before the final at West Kirby, which, according to the sports correspondent of the Nottingham Guardian *"at first sight recalls to mind the general surroundings of the popular Lincolnshire watering place, Skegness."* Mornings were devoted to a little running and sprinting and afternoons were spent on gentle walks. *"Only on one occasion have the players had a look at the ball, moderate exercises with the dumb bells being considered sufficient."* Abstemiousness was strictly enjoined, a glass of beer only being allowed with dinner and a bottle of stout each night.

- The 1894 F.A.Cup winning team -
(Back) Bramley, Harper, Calderhead, Toone, Hendry, Shelton, Joe Goode (Trainer).
(Front) Watson, Donnelly, Logan, Bruce, Daft.

Notts made a positive start to the game, with Bruce getting in the first shot on goal. A few minutes later, another Bruce effort hit the crossbar. Then Donnelly hit the post, but Watson was following up to score the first goal. Bolton now pressed, and strong appeals for a penalty were turned down when Hendry appeared to trip a Bolton forward. Notts again pressed strongly, and with many Bolton men trapped upfield, Logan ran through to score the second after half an hour. After half time, Bolton caused some early pressure, but soon play was concentrated back in the Bolton half. Logan scored an excellent solo goal in the 67th minute, and three minutes later volleyed home the fourth goal, and his hat-trick. He could have had four, and only a brilliant save by Bolton's goalkeeper saved further embarrassment as Notts continued to press. With just three minutes left, Toone in the Notts goal could only parry a shot to Cassidy who scored Bolton's consolation goal. 37,000 had been at Goodison Park to see the first Second Division side win the Cup. Gate receipts were £1189.

The team had arranged to return to Nottingham on the Saturday evening, and the streets from the town centre to the Midland station were packed with a *"dense mass of people"* awaiting their return, so much so that it was difficult for the reporter even to walk to the station. A brass band was playing popular songs of the day, including "The man who broke the bank at Monte Carlo". An open conveyance drawn by four horses was reserved for the players. Under the gas lights of Station Street it was difficult to get a good view, but the new electric lights used by many of the shops in Carrington Street gave the crowd a better sight of the players and the Cup. It took 35 minutes for the coach and four to reach the club's headquarters, which had now moved from Thurland Street to the Lion Hotel in Clumber Street. Latecomers had no chance of getting near to the hotel, and had to stand in Pelham Street or High Street to try to catch a glimpse of the players. There were the usual speeches and toasts, and the trophy was displayed on the balcony.

Jimmy Logan was only to play one more Cup game for Notts before moving on, and his end was tragic. After spells at Dundee and Newcastle he moved to Loughborough of the Second Division. Loughborough somehow mislaid their kit on the way to play Newton Heath in Manchester. For some reason they were unable to borrow any, and elected to play in their everyday shirts. It rained during the match, and they had no change of clothes, so had to keep them on for the train journey back to Loughborough. Logan caught a chill, but managed one last appearance in a League game the following week. The chill turned to pneumonia from which he died in 1896, aged 26. He was buried in Loughborough, in a pauper's grave.

Chadburn was the only new player for the 1894/95 season. Old rivals Sheffield Wednesday proved too strong in the Cup so Notts fell at the first hurdle. Logan and Daft played their last games for the club. Second place in the table at the end of the season meant another play off match, this time against Derby County at Filbert Street, Leicester. Again they were unsuccessful. Things got even worse next season, with a fall to tenth place.

Moves to strengthen the team gave grounds for optimism in 1896. In at full back came T.G. Prescott and W. Gibson. Calderhead was still playing at centre half. New signings John Murphy and T. Boucher provided the strike power that had been missing in the previous seasons. Murphy scored 22 goals in 28 starts, Boucher 22 in 30. The championship of Division Two was still not enough to ensure promotion, but the test matches had been rearranged as a "mini-league" rather than a one-off match. In the event, home and away games with Sunderland and Burnley produced two wins and two draws, and saw Notts back to Division One.

1896 rule changes saw the introduction of corner flags, and a measure of additional protection for goalkeepers. Now they could only be charged if they were playing the ball. This proved open to interpretation however, and goalkeepers were still getting flattened and asking for more protection. The law changed again in 1897 to allow charging only when holding the ball. In the modern game, the goalkeeper has more space then ever before, but as late as 1957 an F.A. Cup final result was influenced by the ability of a forward to charge a goalkeeper.

An international match was arranged for Trent Bridge on February 20th 1897, when England met Ireland. No player from Notts was selected, but the great Steve Bloomer of Derby County was playing. Also, a replayed semi-final was played there.

The new season, 1897/98, proved disappointing. Notts finished 13th place in the League, and Forest snatched the headlines in Nottingham with an F.A. Cup win. Goals were hard to come by, Boucher ending top of the list with just 7 goals. 1898/99 got off to a better start, with Notts unbeaten after the first 8 games. The secretary Mr. Harris reported to the October shareholders meeting at the Lion Hotel that the season to date had been a greater financial success than any of its predecessors, and promised that the hunt for experienced players would continue. Crowds of between 15,000 and 20,000 were now coming regularly to Trent Bridge. John Lewis, one of the leading referees of his day, was somewhat concerned about safety: *"Under no circumstances should a crowd be allowed to enter the playing* field. Trent Bridge is a place where they do it at the end of every match. Some of these days you'll hear of serious trouble on the Notts. ground. If the crowd suddenly took it into their heads to go for the referee, the latter would be surrounded in a few minutes without chance of escape. He would get hurt, the ground would be closed and a fine old club would be injured simply because the officials now do not anticipate such a possibility by making proper and convenient provision for the referee."

It was Loughborough's turn to suffer a financial crisis. Notts coffers were sufficiently healthy for Mr. Harris to send a cheque for £10. Tom Prescott was given a benefit. Notts had been impressed by his play in a friendly with Liverpool South End in 1896 and signed him on at once. He settled at once into the side as a reliable full back, with excellent tackling skills and clean and safe kicking. He was very quick to recover if beaten, his speed making him a match for the fastest forwards. It's not known if the Notts crowd ever sang, *"You'll never beat Tom Prescott,"* but it is doubtful! He was to play on with Notts until 1904, scoring just one goal.

The game away to Preston on November 4th 1899 was David Calderhead's last appearance for the club. He was still regarded as a great half back, though admittedly less speedy than when he played internationals for Scotland. The programme notes said: *"He retains that excellent judgement for which he is justly famed; feeding his forwards with a master hand (or should we say feet). A well preserved athlete, and an exemplary captain. A steady industrious, gentlemanly player commanding respect of opponents, spectators and committee; he has done as much as any one to reinstate Notts. County in its present highly satisfactory position."* He was dropped for the Forest game, and replaced with McDonald, recently signed from Port Vale. Caldershead was the last remaining player from the Cup winning side, and the local papers seemed genuinely sorry about the directors decision to drop him.

There was no shortage of opportunity to catch up with other results in 1899. The half time results board first appeared at Trent Bridge for the Everton game on December 3rd 1898. The Nottingham Evening Post ran editions at 4, 5, 6 and 7 o'clock with the special football edition following at 8 o'clock on Saturdays. The first cricket test match at Trent Bridge took place in 1899 when England met Australia; the football stands were pressed into use, including the new stand which stood roughly where the Taverners' stand is now. Like the modern stand, it was angled slightly towards the cricket square so could be used for both sports. The stand was later dismantled and moved across the river to Meadow Lane.

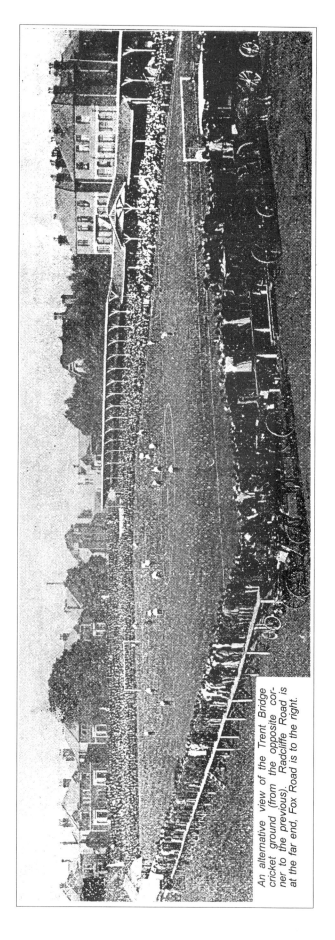

An alternative view of the Trent Bridge cricket ground (from the opposite corner to the previous). Radcliffe Road is at the far end, Fox Road is to the right.

Chapter 4
Edwardians: 1900 to 1919

Notts settled into a period of un-spectacular life in the First Division, lasting until 1913, and third in 1901 was the highest position reached. Apart from 9th position in 1910, the rest of the time was spent in the lower reaches of the division. Relegation could have happened in 1905 when they were bottom, but the decision to add two more clubs to the First Division gave them a reprieve. Cup progress was also unspectacular during this period, the club going out in the first round more often than not. Just two players won international caps, Percy Humpheys for England and Arthur Green for Wales, though Walter Bull, Harry Fletcher, Percy Humphreys, Ted McDonald and Tom Prescott all played for Football League representative teams.

The third place finish in 1901 might have been better but for a poor start to the season, just one win in six matches, and another spell of four consecutive defeats in November. Liverpool, on the way to their first championship, were easily beaten in October, and a large crowd assembled for the Boxing Day game with Forest. Forest were in first place, five points clear of Liverpool, and seemingly headed for their first championship, with Notts back in fifth. A big gate saw centre forward Ross score the only goal to give Notts a 1-0 win. By April, Notts were in second place, one point behind Sunderland but four ahead of Liverpool who had three games in hand. A win for Notts at Anfield on April 8th was crucial to their title hopes, but Liverpool were the better team on the day and won 1-0.

Hopes for better things in 1901/02 were soon quashed by two successive defeats at the start of the season. New signings were Innes from Gillingham and Humphreys from QPR. By the Boxing Day game at the City Ground, Notts were 15th of 18, with the clubs below them all having games in hand. This time Forest won by the only goal. Notts were still in desperate trouble when they travelled to Anfield on 15th February, but a goal from Ross gave them victory and only one more game was lost. Back into the team for three games in January was goalkeeper Toone.

1902/03 was little better, though this time it was the end of season games that left them down in 15th place. Making his debut was Arthur Green, who made an effective strike force with Humphreys. Next season, Green was top scorer with 20 League and Cup goals,

including seven penalties. 1904/05 was one of those seasons best forgotten, like some around 90 years later perhaps! Only one home game was won all season, attendances dropped, and just 36 goals were scored in 34 games.

NOTTS. PLAYERS FOR 1905-6.

REILLY, M.—Popularly known as "Gunner" Reilly; 5ft. 11½in.; 13st. 9lb. A native of Ireland, and an Irish international. A custodian who built up a reputation in the Army, and afterwards played for Portsmouth. Comes to Notts from Dundee. Has represented the Army, Hampshire, and Forfarshire. First season.

IREMONGER, A.—Aged 20; 6ft. 4in.; 12st. Reserve goalkeeper. Affects his more famous brother James in build and appearance. Hopes to emulate the Forester in gaining his international cap. Has something to learn, but shows great promise. Second season. Native of Wilford.

MONTGOMERY, J.—Born Chryston, Glasgow, June, 1876; 5ft. 8in.; 12st. 10lb. For eight seasons a loyal servant of the club. A vigorous left full back and a beautifully clean kick. Lacks only speed.

GRIFFITHS, A.—An Astonian; 5ft. 9in.; 11st. 8lb. Notts made a half-back of him for one season with fair success, but he prefers the second line, and has done good service there. Third season.

ROBERTSON, S.—Born Cowdenheath, Fifeshire; 23 years of age; 5ft. 8½in. Was on the league list for Dundee, with whom he played as a half-back three seasons ago. Has the reputation of being a sturdy full back, which Notts hope he will enhance.. First season.

WILKINSON, J. W.—Hucknall Torkard, born October, 1883; 5ft. 8in.; 12st 5lb. A "nippy," industrious full back for the Reserves last season. Very popular with the Thursday afternoon contingent; a good "header." Second season.

The 'Post Football Guide' first appeared in 1905. This extract includes Albert Iremonger - just another young hopeful!

Making his debut at Sheffield Wednesday on April 1st was a goalkeeper who no doubt caused some merriment amongst the Wednesday fans. Albert Iremonger stood 6ft 5in at a time when the average footballer was probably around 5ft 9in. In team group photographs you will invariably find Albert at the back, shoulders slightly hunched so that the photographer could get him in the frame. Albert retained his place for the next game, played 22 next season, and went on to set appearance records for Notts that still wait to be beaten. His run of 211 consecutive League games will probably stand for all time. He was never selected for a full international, but played in one representative game for the North v. South. Some blamed this lack of selection on his willingness to debate the state of the game with anyone, including the referee. Once, seeing a Notts man about to be sent off the field, he is reported to have asked the referee not to, *"as there will be nothing left in our pockets when we get back to the dressing room!"*

Trent Bridge around 1905. Arthur Green tussles with a Middlesbrough defender.

On another occasion, he raced to the centre of the field to argue a goal decision with referee J.T. Howcroft. The "Linford Christie" of the day was Hutchings, a sprinter from Australia; *"Iremonger,"* said Howcroft, *"I'll give you 10 seconds to get back into your goal." "Who do you think I am, Hutchings?"* asked Albert. His last game was in 1926, when he left for Lincoln. Another player making his debut in 1904/05 was Teddy Emberton, whose career at wing half was to last 365 games.

The decision to extend the First Division by two clubs, by promoting two from the Second Division and not relegating Bury and Notts, thus kept the club in the top flight in 1905. Season 1905/06 started a little brighter, and the crowds improved. Perhaps play was helped by the directors deciding that smoking would not be allowed in the dressing room! However, inconsistencies returned and the club stayed near the bottom for this season and the next. 1906/07 was enlivened by a good Cup run, with an attractive third round tie at home to Tottenham Hotspur from the Southern League. Such was the interest in the game that the directors considered hiring the City Ground, but they eventually decided to use Trent Bridge, with a one shilling gate instead of sixpence (5p instead of 2½p). A record crowd of 25,000 packed in, setting a new record for gate receipts. 'Spurs were despatched 4-0, but a visit to West Bromwich (then in Division 2) saw them lose 1-3. Financially, the Cup run had done the club a world of good, and the year saw record profits.

1907/08 found Notts in their by now customary position, 18th out of 20. Needing to win the last two away games, it took a penalty five minutes from the end of the final game to keep them up. Humphreys had gone, to Leicester, and coming in for the last seven games was a young centre forward called Jimmy Cantrell, signed from Aston Villa together with outside right Rowland Harper. Jimmy soon established himself as a sharp goalscorer, netting 64 times in 131 games for the club before his transfer to 'Spurs in 1913. Cantrell returned to work at the Ordnance Factory in Nottingham during the First World War, and played many games for Notts as a guest player, before returning to 'Spurs. He was a member of their Cup winning team in 1921, and after retirement, he ran Ye Olde Corner Pin on the corner of Clumber Street in Nottingham; what he would make of its current role as a Disney Store is anyone's guess! 18 goals from him helped Notts to 15th in 1909 and he scored 22 next season as Notts rose to ninth. It might have been a higher finish but for a run of eight games without a win at the end of the season. This included the last game played at Trent Bridge, on April 16th 1910.

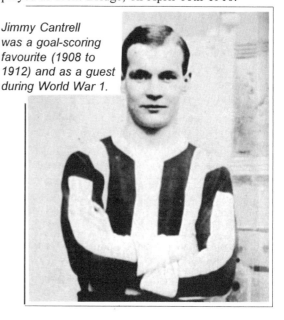

Jimmy Cantrell was a goal-scoring favourite (1908 to 1912) and as a guest during World War 1.

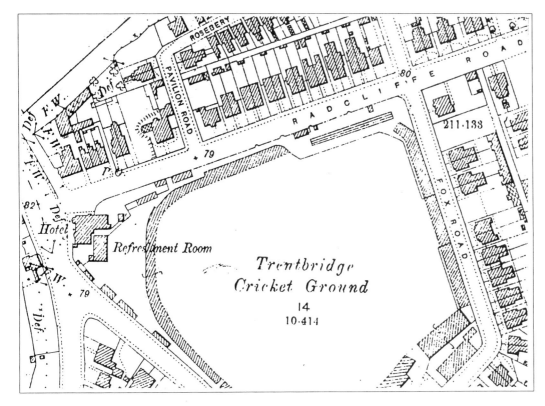

The Trent Bridge Ground in 1901.

The football ground ran parallel to Fox Road. The stand at the West Bridgford end was moved to Meadow Lane in 1910

The Football League was not pleased with Notts having to ground share with Forest at the start and end of the season when cricket took precedence at Trent Bridge; some clubs had claimed that this had been a disadvantage to them. The facilities at Trent Bridge were adequate, but only temporary terracing could be provided on the cricket ground side. Of course, by today's standards, spectator comforts at the games was minimal, and a look at the photograph of the final game makes you wonder just how much of the play the average spectator saw. There were 13,000 there for the Villa game, whereas somehow 25,000 had squeezed in to see the Cup-tie with Spurs.

The site chosen for the new ground was a flat piece of land off Meadow Lane, bounded on one side by a stream and on the other by terrace housing. As it was near the cattle market, the space had become rather a dump for rubbish of one sort or another. The rent was agreed with the council, and a hectic programme of work began in 1910 to have the ground ready for the new season. Mr. W. Shepherd was appointed as architect. One problem was what to do with the stream, which restricted building on what is now the County Road side, though there was no road there at the time. The solution was a small stand placed in front of the stream, stretching three quarters of the way along the pitch. The covered part was described as being similar to the old stand on the Fox Road side of Trent Bridge. The main stand was of similar design to that at the City Ground.

It was decided to re-use the stand from Trent Bridge at the Meadow Lane end of the ground. Earth had been dumped to form the "Spion Kop", and there was space left at the back of the bank for further extension. Soil had to be dumped to level the playing area, and four large drains were installed under the pitch. Stands, terracing and pitch were all completed in the close season.

Appropriately, it was Forest who provided the opposition in the first League game at the new ground, now called "The County Ground". The newspaper report opens:

> There were some rousing scenes on Saturday in connection with the County Ground in Meadow Lane, the admirably equipped and splendidly compact new home of the Notts. F.C. Spectators rolled up in numbers which had no parallel in the club's long history, and on all hands was to be found evidence of the interest and enthusiasm which the launching of the new undertaking had aroused. Moreover the good wishes of the powers that be in the football world, of the city fathers, who stand in position of landlords to the club, and of friends and rivals alike, found hearty expression at a function which the directors could not have had more convincing testimony of the wisdom of their decision to acquire headquarters of their own.

> In honour of the day, flags and bunting were freely employed around the ground. The old club flag floated proudly from a lofty mast at the Meadow Lane end, and in the opposite corner, a brand new emblem, mounted on a flagstaff of Ruddington oak, presented by Major Ashworth, offered its mute welcome to the thousands of spectators who came to witness the first match.

(Above) The Lord Mayor's party at the Meadow Lane ground opening (the stand transferred from Trent Bridge is in the background.... (Below) The original stand, on what became known as the County Road side (it was replaced in 1925 by the more familiar gabled stand.

The directors had invited the Mayor to lunch, with most of the City Council, the local Member of Parliament, and representatives of the Football League, including the president John McKenna. The Mayor said he would like to see more Notts born men in the team! After lunch, the dignitaries paraded to the centre of the ground for the Mayor to declare the ground open. The band played the National Anthem, and the crowd cheered vociferously. Forest spoiled the party by holding the Magpies to a 1-1 draw. An unexceptional season followed, with a respectable mid-table finish.

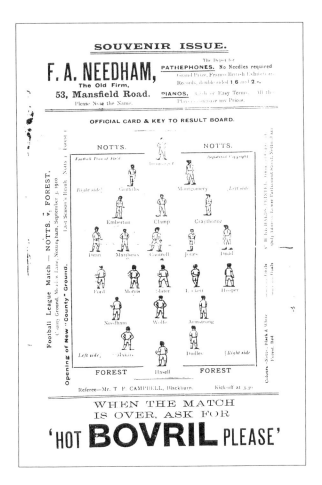

The cover of the programme
for the first match at Meadow Lane.

Albert Iremonger, a Magpies legend;
photographed with brother Jimmy, who played
for Forest and later became the Notts trainer.

Notts (in white shirts) in action at Newcastle, October 1910. Left to right: Sam Richards, Billy Flint, and Ike Waterall.

The club slipped to 16th in 1911/12. Cantrell was injured and played just 23 games, and goal scoring was proving difficult. The following season, goals dried up all together. Twenty of the games ended without a Notts goal, probably not helped by the sale of Cantrell to Tottenham Hotspur. Naturally, it was back to Division 2. The only bright spot was perhaps the form of Peart, who scored 7 goals in 11 games towards the end of the season.

There were not many grounds for optimism when season 1913/14 got underway, but the forward line began to find form, and results improved. A run of eight successive wins between January and March put them in a strong position, which was eventually crowned by the Second Division Championship itself. Peart finished with 28 goals from 30 games, and his strike partner Richards got 21 from 36. Recognition for Peart came when he was selected to play for the Football League. A celebratory tour to Barcelona followed, with three consecutive victories over the home club.

Season 1914/15 was overshadowed by the outbreak of war. The football authorities had no precedence to work with, and a feeling of "it will all be over by Christmas" encouraged them to press on with League and Cup competitions. However, the demands of the Western Front were beginning to be felt, and footballers were among the many to enlist. The season finished with Notts in 16th place in the First Division. It was clear that organised, professional football could not continue and the Football League was suspended (though, in Scotland, the First Division of the Scottish League continued throughout the War). However, Saturday half-holidays continued, and some entertainment was necessary for the many people contributing to the War effort in the United Kingdom. The English clubs were organised into regional leagues. Guest players were allowed, and a welcome returnee to the black and white was Jimmy Cantrell. Eventually, four complete seasons of wartime football were played, and clubs did not return to pick up where they'd left off in 1915 until August 1919.

Championship Certain—Promotion Secured.

LOOK OUT FOR NEXT SEASON

Standing on the verge of achievement so far as promotion is concerned, Notts. County to-day had the task of meeting Barnsley at Oakwell—a task much more difficult than the division status of the home side would imply. Away from home the Yorkshiremen have hardly been brilliant, but on their own territory they have not dropped a point since December 20th, and as a consequence eight successive wins have been placed to their credit. Notts. were highly desirous of breaking that sequence, and were out in their most serious and formidable mood. Leeds, Bradford, and Hull had all been victorious at Oakwell earlier in the season, and in this Notts. had cause for encouragement, for all three of them suffered disaster at the hands—or feet—of the Meadow-lane brigade.

The match was regarded as a big attraction in the ball. Emberton and Morley saved shots from the return.

Later the home outside right came down again with Allsebrook still hanging on him with bull-dog tenacity. Bartrop put over, and Iremonger effected a glorious save from Halliwell, grabbing the ball full length.

Henshall and Peart fought for an opening, but Barnsley packed their goal.

A second corner was awarded to Barnsley, and Allsebrook easily cleared Bartrop's return.

Peart broke away, and Henshall put behind. Downs miskicked, but Richards was too far behind the ball to benefit. Henshall brought Cooper to his knees.

Jennings also was injured in colliding with Barson, but resumed after attention.

Iremonger once more saved finely from a corner returned by Bartrop, and Wigmore sent over the bar.

Although relegated at the end of the 1912/13 season, Notts soon returned to Division One. The victory at Barnsley on 4th April 1913 secured the Second Division Championship. Promotion was celebrated with a banquet.

Notts. County Football Club.

Celebration Banquet

WELBECK HOTEL,

Tuesday, April 28th, 1914.

PRESIDENT:

J. T. FARR, ESQ., C.C.

E. H. LEE, PRINTER, NOTTS.

Chapter 5
Doldrums 1919-1947

Some familiar faces were on view for the 14,000 people who came to the first peacetime game with Burnley. Albert Iremonger was back in goal, whilst Richards and Peart still provided striking power. However, the old faces were perhaps too old, and a run of eight games without a win in the new year left Notts a task they could not recover. 21st place and relegation followed for the third time.

Many team changes from week to week left Notts in sixth place in 1920/21, and next season saw them even lower, 13th. However, 1921/22 saw an excellent F.A. Cup run, one indeed that we still wait to see repeated!

It wasn't easy getting to the semi-final; every tie needed a replay, and the meeting with Bradford City needed two. Old foes West Bromwich and Aston Villa were met and defeated, and a semi-final against a "middle of Division One" Huddersfield was looked forward to with confidence. Notts had won the Cup once already as a Second Division club, why not do it again! Luck ran out on the day, and Notts went down 1-3 at Turf Moor, Burnley.

For the next few seasons, the Notts full back pairing of Ashurst and Cope were to gain something of a reputation for their exploitation of the offside trap. Bill Ashurst was an outstanding full back, who went on to gain England caps with Notts. He was one of the Leeds City players "auctioned off" by the League following the suspension of the club for financial irregularities in World War One. Lincoln City snapped him up, and he moved to Notts from there in 1920. Until 1925/26, offside was determined by three players, not two, so only one of the full backs needed to be forward to catch the opponents out. This defensive tightness helped Notts to the Second Division championship in 1922/23. Only 46 goals were scored in the 42 games, but only 34 were conceded, and six of these were in one game. Notts were helped by the general competitiveness of the division, and their total of 53 points is equal to the record "low" for a championship club in Division Two under the old system of "two points for a win".

(Left) The toss-up at the 1920/21 season F.A.Cup match with Aston Villa, before a then record Meadow Lane crowd of 45,014. (Below) Next year, the tenth F.A.Cup match saw Notts lose to Huddersfield in the semi-final.

May 1922, the Notts party before a match in Barcelona.
(Players only) Standing: Dinsdale, Streets, McPherson,
Death, Gibson. Front: Kemp, Platts, Cope (kneeling),
Ashurst, Cook and Marriott.

The reward was three seasons of First Division football that were destined to be the last Meadow Lane saw for a very long time. 1923/24 was notable for three Cup-ties with Crystal Palace that all ended goalless. The League position was 10th, and ninth the next season, both of which could be considered satisfactory. 1924/25 had promised better things, for Notts had risen to the top of the table on November 1st with a home victory over Manchester City, and were still there three weeks later. Only one goal was conceded in home games, a record they maintained until Christmas Day. However, seven games without a win in December and January left them with no chance of the championship.

1925/26 proved a struggle and resulted in bottom place once more. The new offside rules led to a glut of goals in the League, and some said it was the new rules that had caused Notts' downfall. It is more likely that injuries and the consequent break up of a settled team were more to blame. Albert Iremonger was given a free transfer and played his last game for Notts on the final day of the season. Notts went out with a flourish, beating Huddersfield Town who had just won their third consecutive championship. Billy Flint was also given a free transfer. Billy had made his debut in 1908/09, and played 376 League games for Notts, many as captain.

Two seasons in the lower reaches of Division Two followed, with a welcome rise to fifth place in 1927/28.

Goal scoring was in the hands of B.R. "Paddy" Mills, signed from Hull City where he had also been a prolific scorer. His brother, 6 ft. tall Percy Mills, made his debut in 1927/28, and was to go on play more than 400 games for the club at full back. Percy became the club's penalty expert.

"THIS OUGHT TO HAVE BEEN A FOOTBALL GROUND."
"AYE, AND THAT THE GRAND STAND"

A new landmark opened in Nottingham on May 22nd 1929 - the new Council House. Underneath the foundation stone is a casket containing local newspapers and a set of coins from a farthing to a sovereign. It is one of two things in the City centre which strikes a newcomer as "odd". To most people, a council house is a small terrace dwelling for the working class, not a huge edifice made of Portland Stone. The other oddity is that lots of buses are called Arnold! (Arnold is one of the City's suburbs).

- The long, and fondly, remembered first choice defence and half-back line of the 1920's -

(Left to right, top to bottom)

Albert Iremonger - quite a character! Bill Ashurst - an England international

Horace Cope - later went to Arsenal. Billy Flint - a forward from 1909 (and later right-half) to 1926.

Norman Dinsdale - the regular centre-half, 1920-28. Hayden Kemp - skilful half-back, 1920-31.

Season 1929/30 proved to be a new low. Tom Keetley had been signed from Doncaster Rovers to replace Paddy Mills, but illness restricted his appearances. By the end of March, there was optimism about avoiding relegation, but six consecutive defeats sent them down to the Third Division as bottom club. Also making his first appearance that season was a young Alf Feebery, later to form a dependable full back partnership with Percy Mills.

Tom Keetley

Alf Feebery

Alf Feebery's brothers Albert and Jack played League football. Albert played for Coventry and Crystal Palace in the Southern League, and was captain of the Third Division championship winning team when Palace joined the Football League. Jack played for Bolton between 1908 and 1920, then moved to Exeter City and Brighton. He made a wartime appearance for Notts as a guest player. Other brothers Arthur, Ernest and Horace were professional footballers without

The Keetley's and the Feebery's are two of the largest sets of brothers to have played in the English game. Four of Tom's brothers played League football; Charlie with Leeds United, Frank with Derby County and Doncaster, Harold with Doncaster, and Joe with a number of clubs. Also, brother Albert was with Burton Albion, and Arthur at Tottenham (though he made no first team appearances).

out making a League appearance.

Tom Keetley found the Third Division defences suited him nicely. He scored 39 goals in just 34 games to set a single season scoring record for the club which still stands today. Notts got off to an excellent start with an 18 match unbeaten run, and had no difficulty winning their way back to Division Two.

A pause in training during the 1930/31 promotion season. Henshall (Sec./Manager), Jakeman, Feebury, Stimpson, Maw, (not known), Fenner, Wightman (Coach), (not known), Bisby.

George Stimpson, Percy Mills and goalkeeper Jimmy Maidment defend against Chesterfield - 1932/33 season.

GALLACHER'S ARTISTRY A DELIGHT

Famous Scot Captains Notts. in First Match

ATTENDANCE DOUBLED

Hopes of further improvement came to nought; four seasons in the lower half of the table found them relegated again in 1935. This time there was no easy way back, though they reached second place in 1937. Much of this was due to the inspired signing of Hughie Gallacher. Hughie was one of the immortal "Wembley Wizards", the Scottish team who had beaten England 5-1 in 1928. After a successful career with Newcastle, Hughie was nearing the end of his career, but his skill on the ball brought him 25 goals from 32 games. Nearly 10,000 people were added to the gate when he made his debut in September 1936. Notts had another famous forward on their books that season, but injury restricted James Smith to just three appearances. Smith was a Scottish International and holder of the all-time scoring record in a single season, scoring an amazing 66 League goals for Ayr United in 1927/28.

Gallacher moved on to Grimsby Town in 1937/38. His replacement was another famous player, Bill "Dixie" Dean of Everton. Dean holds the English scoring record of 60 goals for Everton in 1928, but was 31 years old and no longer wanted at Goodison Park now that a young Tommy Lawton was on the books. Dean played just three games for Notts before needing an ankle operation, and further injuries in 1938/39 restricted him to only 6 more games and just 3 goals. Notts allowed him to leave for a season with Sligo Rovers in Ireland.

This programme cover style lasted from 1920 to 1934, but with the club's attempt at a new image was dropped.

Peace in Europe was uncertain in the summer of 1939, but there was no reason not to plan for the 1939/40 season. Numbers on a player's shirt now became compulsory. Notts were active in the transfer market with no less than six new signings. Results from the games on August 28th and September 2nd were encouraging, and the prospects for promotion seemed excellent. Alas, all to no avail. War was declared on September 3rd, and League football was suspended immediately. The two matches were struck from the official record, so the six players never "officially" played for the club. For the record, they were Thomas Chester and Frank Rayner, transferred from Burnley, James Knox from St. Mirren, where he was the leading scorer, James Mackenzie from Cardiff, Albert Ringrose from Spurs, and Eric Weightman from Chesterfield.

Players' contracts were cancelled, and Notts' new signings dispersed to find a job. After some urgent planning sessions, a few friendly games were organised, and official football restarted in October 1939 with regional leagues. Player registration rules were relaxed, so that guest players could join the team. This led to Aldershot becoming the "team of talents" as many famous players passed through the army camp there during training!

Wartime football was not easy. Transport difficulties meant players were often not able to get to the ground, and young men from local clubs were drafted in to make up the numbers. Though a few senior players could appear regularly, the spectators were treated to an ever changing array of talent (or not, as the case may be!).

A young Billy Wright made a few appearances for Notts as a guest player, and showed enough talent for the local reporter to comment on his skills. Clubs had to decide whether or not to continue from season to season; there were no cash handouts to help, and crowds of 2000 or so were needed to break even. Enemy bombers over Nottingham caused considerable damage to the pitch and the north end of the main stand at Meadow Lane in May 1941, causing the club not to play at all in season 1941/42. They were back in action for 1942/43, with an even greater mix of experienced players, reserves, colts and guest players. One of the guests was a certain Tommy Lawton, playing centre forward against Forest on April 24th 1943.

1943/44 resulted in a total of 129 players appearing for the club during the season! New manager Major Buckley had something to do with that. Buckley was famous in the 1930s for his youth policy at Wolves, and he set to work with similar vigour at Notts, throwing likely recruits into action at the earliest opportunity. Buckley's appointment was a sign that the club was determined to achieve success when the war had ended; his wages were reported to be the highest in the country at £4000 per year.

A young "Bevin Boy" named Jackie Sewell joined the team in 1944. A coal shortage had forced the Minister of Labour, Ernest Bevin, to introduced a bill in December 1943 by which youths ready for call up would be diverted to the mines. Boys as young as 14 volunteered. Jackie had been spotted playing for Whitehaven and was asked to come to Nottingham. He made his debut as a 17 year old.

An enemy raid on the night of 8/9 May 1941 produced bomb craters at Meadow Lane.
With the subsequent closing of the ground, 1941/42 became the club's only season when there was no football played.

VE Day on May 8th left little time for planning the 1945/46 season. The F.A. decided to re-introduce the F.A. Cup, using the 539 entries received for the 1939/40 competition; in the event only 223 clubs were able to take part. League competitions remained temporary, and guest players were allowed in League games, though they were restricted to three after November 1945. Guests were not allowed in the Cup.

Notts were optimistic about the new season, and issued a souvenir brochure. George Cottee had taken over as President in January 1945, following the death of Mr. Shipstone. The brochure carried advertisements from many well known Nottingham companies; Marsdens (grocers for the "quality"), Henry Barker, the Dale, Rio and Grove Cinemas, Smart and Brown, Turner's Bread and Tobys, "the store of excellence and worth". One of the guest players featured in the brochure was Flying Officer Ian McPherson, awarded the DFC in 1944 and the bar seven months later. McPherson moved to Arsenal and Glasgow Rangers, but re-joined Notts in the 1951/52 season. Also featured in the brochure were Lance Corporal Cyril Hatton, who saw service in France, North Africa, Italy and Germany, Private Norman Rigby serving in India, and L/AC J.K. Marsh, was stationed in the Sudan.

Making his debut at the start of the season was Jesse Pye. His skilful play at inside forward made an immediate impact, and he was selected to play in the Victory International against Belgium in January 1946, scoring one of England's goals in a 2-0 victory. Jesse was transferred to Wolves and went on to win more England caps. In October 1945, the club took a team to Germany for a friendly game against an Army XI in Cologne.

26,000 people came to Meadow Lane to see normal service resumed in August 1946. Considerable activity in the transfer market had brought a number of new faces to Meadow Lane, and one welcome return; Billy Corkhill came back from Cardiff City. Corkhill and Bill Fallon were the only links to pre-war years, so nine of the team were making their Football League debut for Notts. Included in their number was Canadian centre forward Fred Whittaker, whose signing was the result of a transatlantic hop by manager Stollery. Jackie Sewell's contribution was 21 goals in 37 games, but generally goal scoring proved difficult and the final position in the table was a disappointing twelfth. A welcome signing in January was Eric Houghton, who had won many England caps whilst playing for Aston Villa. He had a reputation as one of the hardest kickers of a dead ball.

Jesse Pye and manager Frank Buckley during the 1945/46 season - when Notts played in black and white hoops.

## Chapter 6

The Lawton Era: 1947 - 1952

Even today, more than 40 years on, the words "The Lawton Era" raise fond memories for Nottingham people of a bygone age, even for those of us too young to experience it at first hand. An age of flat hats and raincoats with belts. Queues for Corporation buses in the town centre to take you to the game, or a trolley bus ride to Trent Bridge. Wooden rattles loud enough to wake the dead. Fog. Sweets for the kids if the ration books allowed it. Threepence for the programme so you know what the half time scores meant when the man hung the numbers next to the letters. And 40,000 or more to watch a Third Division match.

Seldom has one man endeared himself to a City like Tommy did. There was the very fact of him coming. Why should an established international player with a First Division club, still only 28, join one in the Third? It took a record fee to get him; £20,000, made up of £17,500 and a player valued at £2,500. Then there was the style of his play. Never one to shirk a challenge, it's surprising how often the local paper has to report, *"Lawton was carried from the field with concussion."* It would be reasonable think that this was due to the heavy footballs, but apparently Tommy hung in the air for so long and climbed so high that his jaw often made contact with the head of the defender on his way down! The local paper reports him playing in a daze for 84 minutes of a game in September 1949; two days later he's back in action, right as rain.

Then there were his goals. *"Back arched like an angry snake"* said one report. Our children will have the benefit of archive film of every goal scored today, we have only memories and press reports to

go on. Still, if we had to nominate a "goal of the century" it would be hard to beat Tommy's goal against Forest in December 1949. The photograph shows him 10 yards from goal, whilst the Forest keeper can do no more than wave his arms in the air. The ball is already in the net, the result of a perfect header from a Frank Broome corner kick.

The Lawton era is not just about Tommy of course. By one means or another, a Third Division team was graced by players of considerable merit. Jackie Sewell was now a key member of the team. Eddie Gannon (an Irish international) is rated by many as the best wing half to play for the club. Tommy Deans was signed from Clyde in October 1949 for £6,500. Another interesting signing was Frank Broome from Derby, no stranger to Meadow Lane after his wartime appearances. Tommy Johnston joined from Forest, and went on to score 88 goals in 267 games for the Magpies.

The surprise was that it took three seasons for the team to gain promotion. Lawton's arrival in November 1947 put 10,000 on the home gates, and the Boxing Day game with Swansea in 1947 caused the gates to be locked with 45,116 inside and an estimated 10,000 left outside! Sixth place in 1947/48 was perhaps the best that could be hoped for following a poor start to the season. In 1948/49, a home scoring record of 68 goals against 19 in 21 games was offset by a poor away record. There were many highlights in the Lawton era for those fortunate to be there. Ipswich Town were beaten 9-2 in September 1948, with four goals for Tommy. Alan Brown, a £10,000 signing from First Division Burnley, and Oscar Hold, from Norwich City, made their home debuts in that game. Newport County arrived on 15th

Tommy Lawton

RESULT:
NOTTS. COUNTY 11
NEWPORT CO. 1

SCORE SHEET:
14 min...Johnston for notts. .. 1—0
18 min. Sewell for Notts. .... 2—0
24 min. Sewell for Notts. .... 3—0
26 min. Lawton for Notts. .. 4—0
29 min. Sewell for Notts. .... 5—0
34 min. Johnston for Notts. .. 6—0
38 min. Houghton for Notts. .. 7—0
64 min. Sewell for Notts. .... 8—0
69 min. Lawton for Notts. .. 9—0
82 min. Carr for Newport .... 9—1
84 min. Lawton for Notts. ... 10—1
89 min. Lawton for Notts. .... 11—1

Little John's Notes

Notts. forwards again demonstrated their prowess in this match. In the first 38 minutes cracked into the Newport defence no fewer than seven goals—this against a team who had won their Cup-tie at Leeds the previous week, and had not lost a match in the last six.

They were beaten in every department, and the home attack was so virile that Newport scarcely knew the way they were going.

And so it was in the second half, though fewer goals were scored.

This was the third time this season that Notts. had scored nine goals in a match. The team spirit was magnificent and the defence was all that was to be desired.

—:o:—

*The famous 11-1 victory
over Newport County
in 1948/49.*

LEAGUE III SOUTH

	P	W	D	L	F	A	P
Swansea	24	16	4	4	51	17	36
Brighton & H.A.	24	12	9	3	34	24	33
Bristol Rovers	25	14	3	8	38	32	31
Bournemouth	26	13	5	8	39	31	31
Swindon	26	13	6	8	40	41	30
Millwall	26	10	8	8	44	40	28
Norwich City	24	11	5	8	46	30	27
NOTTS. CNTY.	25	12	3	10	76	42	27
Reading	23	12	2	9	42	16	26
Ipswich	23	10	4	9	45	43	24
Port Vale	24	10	0	10	33	28	24
Bristol City	23	8	6	9	26	33	22
Torquay Utd.	24	8	6	10	32	49	22
Walsall	23	9	3	11	34	38	21
Exeter City	24	8	5	11	32	50	21
*Leyton Orient	25	7	7	9	37	41	21
Northampton	24	7	6	11	32	37	20
Watford	25	7	5	9	37	35	20
Newport County	24	7	5	12	47	64	19
Aldershot	24	6	6	12	29	35	18
*Southend Utd.	22	4	9	9	21	26	17
Crystal Palace	24	3	6	15	14	46	12

* Denotes to-day's match not included.

Bournemouth 1 Reading .. 3
Half-time: 1—0.

Bristol City 1 Norwich C 6
Half-time: 0—1.

Exeter C . 2 Torquay U 0
Half-time: 1—0.

Ipswich ... 2 Swansea .. 0
Half-time: 1—0.

Millwall ... 1 Aldershot 1
Half-time: 0—0.

NOTTS. 11 Newport .. 1
Half-time: 7—0.

Port Vale . 3 Brighton .. 4
Half-time: 2—3.

Swindon .. 2 Northmptn 2
Half-time: 1—0.

Walsall ... 0 Bristol R . 1
Half-time: 0—0.

Watford . 2 Crystal P . 0
Half-time: 0—0.

Leyton O . 2 Southend . 0
Half-time: 1—0.

—:o:—

January 1949 unbeaten in 6 games and expected to give Notts a close game. Result? 11-1 to Notts, their biggest League win. Two Newport supporters planted two leeks on the centre spot at half time; perhaps a comment on their clubs' defence! Away from home it was a different story; it took until Christmas Day for Notts to record the first win.

*Mascots parade around the ground in front of enthusiastic
supporters before a cup-tie in the late 1940's.
This photograph captures perfectly the spirit of the era.*

A good cup run took them to Liverpool in the 4th round, and 61,003 were at Anfield, just 33 below the club record at the time. Chances fell to both sides in a goalless first half. Billy Liddell scored for Liverpool in the 58th minute as the result of a free kick in the penalty area, and chances which fell to Hold and Lawton were saved.

A surprise came in February 1949, when it was announced that Mr. Stollery had resigned as Manager through ill health. Secretary Wilf Fisher took over team responsibilities until Eric Houghton's appointment the following May. Shortly afterwards, Eddie Gannon left, for Sheffield Wednesday. The season ended with Notts a disappointing 11th in the table, and only one win in the last seven games.

The new season of 1949/50 opened in a heatwave. The police thoughtfully provided buckets of water to deal with cases of fainting in the 33,000 crowd, and at least 30 people needed treatment. A win was followed by an away defeat; the press were concerned that this was to be a repeat of the story from the previous season. However, this was the only defeat until December, and hopes rose that this was to be Notts' season. Lawton was still the crowd puller, scoring 31 goals that season from his 37 starts. Some of these were penalties, but unusual for Tommy, who admitted that taking one was the thing he liked doing least in football!

The highlight of the first part of the season was undoubtedly the visit to the City Ground in December to play Forest, the first League game against them since 1935. An all-ticket crowd of 37,903 saw Horace Gager lead out the Forest team of Walker; Thomas, Hutchinson; Anderson, Gager, Burkitt; Scott, Love, Ardron, Capel and Kaile. Chances had fallen at both ends when Sewell forced a corner for Notts. in the 28th minute. Broome pulled it well back to Lawton for the header of the century! *"I never hit a ball as hard before"* he said after the game, *"everything went exactly right. I just got clear and my jump was carrying me forward as I met the ball full on my forehead."* People still talk about it in Nottingham, even those of us that weren't there! Forest had the advantage of the wind in the second half, and should have scored when Love missed a straightforward chance. Lawton broke away on the right with nine minutes left, and centred for Broome to score. Capel replied, but only three minutes remained. Desperate attempts to score in the gathering gloom came to nothing, leaving Notts the victors and strengthening their lead at the top of the Division.

Lawton threatens the Brighton defence before a 34,000 crowd in the run-in to promotion. (11th March 1950).

Injuries at the turn of the year lead to a small crisis of confidence and three successive defeats, but they remained at the top of the table. The Lawton goal touch returned when his pulled muscle allowed him to rejoin the team, and Notts looked forward to Newport's visit in February. Only seven goals scored this season, three for Sewell! Notts eventually sealed promotion with a 2-0 win over Forest on 22nd April 1950.

Notts completed the double over their Forest neighbours. The attendance of 46,000 was an all-time record for a Meadow Lane League match. Players nearest to the camera (from left), Harry Adamson, Roy Smith (goalkeeper), and Norman Rigby (number 3).

An all-ticket crowd of 46,000 saw the game, when the kids were allowed over the boundary wall. Tension rose after a goalless first half. In the 58th minute, the defenders concentrated on Lawton as Johnston's corner headed for the far post where Jackie Sewell headed in. Two minutes later, a Deans' free kick found Tommy's head, and that was that.

The new season back in Division Two began inauspiciously; it was the seventh game when a win was finally recorded. The players decided that the Magpie on the new club badge was to blame, so they were unstitched for the game against Barnsley on 28th October. The first home win followed of course, and Lawton's first goal of the season. In September, Notts had paid a new club record fee of £25,000 to bring Leon Leuty from Bradford. Leuty had had a trial for Notts in 1941, injuring himself in one of the bomb craters! The season continued on a disappointing note, with the events of March 1951 causing considerable controversy at the time. Sheffield Wednesday wanted Jackie Sewell, and were prepared to break the transfer record to get him.

A typical programme cover of the 1949/50 season (this one was the title clincher versus Forest). This style first appeared in 1934 - in chocolate and blue (the club's new colours) - but changed back to black and white from 1935/36. The style was revised at the start of the 1951/52 season.

Notts were said to be reluctant to part, but Sewell eventually signed for £34,500. He was still only 23 years of age, and had overtaken Keetley as Notts' leading scorer with 97 League goals, a total only surpassed to this day by Les Bradd and Tony Hateley. He won a Second Division championship medal with the Wednesday and a Cup Winners medal with Aston Villa, but also had the dubious distinction of playing with four relegated clubs; Wednesday twice, Aston Villa and Hull City. He was also in the England teams that lost 3-6 and 1-7 to Hungary. The Notts' directors bore the brunt of the spectator's unrest about Jackie's departure; the Southwell branch of the Supporter's Club threatened a boycott.

The first game back in Division Two - 1950/51 season. Jackie Sewell challenges the Coventry goalkeeper, Billy Evans is on the left.

Chapter 7
Fall: 1952 - 1969

17th in Division Two in 1951 was followed by 15th a year later. 1951/52 had started well; four wins out of five took them to the top of the table. A new star was "boy prodigy" Ron Wylie, a cultured inside forward who immediately displayed a feeling for the game that belied his years. Ron was to play more than 200 games for the club until his transfer to Aston Villa in 1959. The Lawton era ended with his transfer to Brentford in March 1952 as player/manager.

The next two seasons found Notts still in the lower reaches of the division, but at last a settled team emerged which promised better things. The club finished seventh in 1954/55, and threatened to go to Wembley after good Cup wins against Middlesbrough, Sheffield Wednesday and Chelsea left them with a home tie against Third Division York City. A new ground record of 47,310 squeezed into Meadow Lane, but this was York's year, and Notts lost 0-1.

Chelsea (First Division Champions-elect) were beaten in this 5th round F.A.Cup match. Gordon Bradley and Leon Leuty defend against Roy Bentley.

Arthur Bottom scores for York City in the shock 6th round Cup defeat. The crowd of 47,310 is the all-time Meadow Lane record.

The club and the City were rocked in December 1955 by the death of Leon Leuty from leukaemia, only a few months after his last League appearance. He made five appearances for the England 'B' team, and was strongly tipped to win a full cap. He had won an F.A. Cup winner's medal with Derby County in 1946. A run of six consecutive defeats made relegation a possibility for Notts in 1955/56, but they finished three points clear of the drop. Next season they were also 20th, but in 1957/58 a late surge by Lincoln City consigned Notts back to the Third Division.

Tommy Deans leads out Aubrey Southwell, Gordon Bradley, and the rest of the team, at Fulham in September 1954.

Two years later, Forest were in Division One, heading for an F.A. Cup win, the League championship and Europe. County were heading for Division 4. So did fortunes and luck change that day? What if Forest had lost to Goole, and Notts had won 6-0? Well, probably nothing would be different, but I sometimes wonder!

The Rhyl defeat meant another change of manager. Frank Broome took on the job as caretaker, and this was followed by the popular decision to give the permanent position to Tommy Lawton. Tommy had found the player/manager's job at Brentford a bit of a struggle, but had joined Arsenal as a player to bow out of the Football League in fine style. He had then joined non-League Kettering as manager. He brought Jack Wheeler from Kettering, as trainer. Jack held this position for twenty six years, never missing a first team match. His final count of games was 1,398. At Notts, Tommy was unable to stem a run of poor results, and was relieved of his duties the following summer, with the club back in Division Three.

It would be an overstatement to pretend that a club's fortune turned on a single game, but from a perspective of nearly 40 years on it doesn't seem so far fetched to make such a claim.

In January 1957, Forest and Notts had been drawn at home to non-League opposition in the third round of the Cup. The Forest game was due to kick off at 2.45 and the Notts game at 3.15. My friends and I decided to pay our 6d. to watch the Forest game. By leaving a few minutes early, we could hop over Trent Bridge in

New manager Frank Hill meets some of the players (1958/59). From left, Frank Cruikshank, Peter Russell, Bert Loxley, Frank Hill and Ron Wylie.

time for Notts to open their exit gates for us to watch the last 20 minutes free! Forest duly despatched Goole Town 6-0, and we ran over the bridge expecting to see more goals at Meadow Lane. 1-1 when we arrived; 2-1 to Rhyl within minutes, 3-1 to Rhyl at the end!

1958/59 was the first year of a "combined" Third Division in the Football League. The top teams from the old Third Divisions North and South formed the new Third Division, with clubs in the lower half forming Division Four. As has happened so often in League history, a relegated team can continue to struggle in their new surroundings,

A 1958/59 forward line - Don Roby, Ron Wylie, Jack Lane, Stan Newsham and Tommy Asher.

and so it was with Notts. The club stayed down at the bottom all season, eventually finishing 23rd. Making his debut was a young man signed just as Tommy Lawton left the club, Tony Hateley. He marked his debut with a goal. Tony was to become an honoured member of the "great centre forwards" club at Notts; his headers brought back fond memories of the Lawton era.

A young player called Jeff Astle made a few appearances in 1961/62, but the next season was to see a "strike partnership" that would be worth a bob or two in today's game; Jeff and Tony Hateley playing up front together. In the last 25 games of the season they knocked in 30 goals between them as Notts rose to seventh position.

Notts. back in Div. III with well-earned point

By Lawrie Simpkin

ALDERSHOT 1   NOTTS. COUNTY 1

THIS well-earned point booked Notts. County a place in Division III next season—unless the Magpies suffer heavy defeats in their last two games and Northampton run up cricket scores in winning their remaining matches and then goal average would be the deciding factor. To celebrate there was after-dinner champagne on the long journey home.

Notts first taste of life in the League's basement was fortunately brief. Goals were plentiful, indeed Notts failed to score in only 3 games out of the 46. Though crowds were down at first, a winning team soon brought the spectators back. More than 25,000 came to see the Cup-tie with Bath City in December 1959, but again Notts were playing the role of the gentle giant, slain by the non-League team.

There were faint hopes of further promotion in 1961, but a run of defeats in March and April put them out of the running. Next season, 1961/62, Margate's visit for the Cup third round replay in November caused a wry smile at the time. It was the custom in those days for each club to keep the floodlights on half power during the pre-match warm up, and turn them up when play started. Notts' lights were a bit outdated by this time, and the Margate players claimed afterwards that they kept waiting for them to brighten, not realising that they were already on full!

NOTTS. COUNTY
FOOTBALL CLUB

1862   1962

VERSUS

AN ENGLAND XI

CENTENARY SOUVENIR PROGRAMME
WEDNESDAY, MAY 2nd, 1962 · PRICE 6d.

The main playing event of the Centenary year in 1962 was a game with an England X1 on May 2nd 1962. The two teams were as follows. Notts: Peter Butler, Richard Edwards, Tony Bircumshaw; John Sheridan, Alex Gibson, Gerry Carver; Keith Fry, Roy Horobin, Tony

Hateley, Bob Forrest, Peter Bircumshaw. England: Alan Hodgkinson (Sheffield United); Don Howe (WBA), Mick McNeil (Middlesbrough); Stan Anderson (Sunderland), Joe Shaw (Sheffield United), Alan Deakin (Aston Villa); Mike Hellawell and Jimmy Bloomfield (Birmingham City), Alan Peacock (Middlesbrough), Derek Kevan (WBA), Peter Thompson (Preston North End). The England XI won 3-1 before 11,022 spectators, Hateley scoring for Notts.

Tony Hateley was sold in the summer of 1963, to Aston Villa. His replacement for 1963/64 was Terry Bly, a prolific goal scorer for Peterborough. Alas, he could not reproduce this form at Notts. Five consecutive defeats at the start of the season was just a foretaste of what was to follow, and perhaps Notts' worst season of all time left them bottom of Division Three. Seven seasons followed in the Fourth Division. Not surprisingly, a financial crisis threatened the club's existence until a local businessman Bill Hopcroft joined the Board in 1965 and made a much-needed injection of cash.

Alex Gibson: He clocked up 347 League appearances between 1960 and 1969.

The club's record low point in the Football League came in 1966/67 when they were 20th, avoiding the need to apply for re-election by a fraction.

David Needham made his debut at centre half in 1966, the start of a long and successful career with Notts. After more than 400 games for the club, he had a brief spell at QPR before becoming a key member of the great Forest teams of the late 1970s. Another good player was Les Bradd, signed in October 1967 from Rotherham United. He scored 10 goals in 28 starts in his first season, en route to becoming the club's all-time top goal scorer with 125 League goals.

Brian Stubbs and Don Masson made their debuts in 1968/69. Stubbs went on to make 426 League appearances in the period up to 1979/80. Masson, regarded as perhaps the best passer of the ball in Notts' history, played 401 games in two spells, and won Scottish International honours with Queen's Park Rangers.

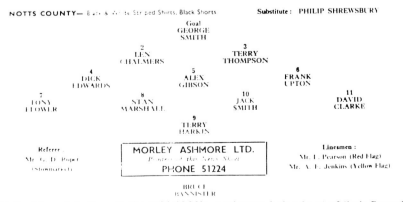

Notts hit rock bottom in the mid-1960's, and were helped out of their financial crisis by Bill Hopcroft

Chapter 8
Resurgence: 1969 - 1984

Looked at from today's perspective, the period from 1964 to 1984 was a good one to be a Notts supporter. Despite bouncing around in Division 4 at the start of the period, at least they were never relegated!

Plenty of room on the terraces! Meadow Lane in the late 1960's.

Still in the late 1960's. The old Meadow Lane stand and wooden boundary fence; they survived into the 1970's.

(Above) Don Masson leads out Notts for the last game in Division Four, versus Exeter City
(Below) Enthusiastic supporters salute the manager and players after the 1972/73 season Tranmere match

Much if not all of the credit for the club's resurgence was due to Jimmy Sirrel. Jimmy was appointed manager in November 1969 by new Chairman Jack Dunnett, a Labour MP with a Nottingham constituency. Jimmy set out to rebuild the team around the footballing skills of Don Masson. Some of his initial astute purchases included Arthur Mann, Kevin Randall, Ray O'Brien, Steve Carter, Willie Carlin, Bill Brindley, and the welcome return of Tony Hateley. Hateley's total of 22 goals in 29 games was a major contribution to the promotion campaign of 1970/71. The next season coincided with Aston Villa's visit to the Third Division, and a crowd of 37,462 was at Villa Park in November to see the Magpies lose by the only goal. Promotion to Division Two finally came in 1972/73.

Life back in the Second Division saw local derbies with Forest resume in 1974/75. A record transfer fee was received for someone who was going to prove difficult to replace - Don Masson. Though Don had almost joined Bournemouth some years before, he eventually signed for QPR for £100,000 where he was to gain international honours for Scotland. Pedro Richards made his debut at full back, the first of 399 League appearances for Notts. A notable feat occurred on 16th November 1974 in the game against Sheffield Wednesday. Ian Scanlon scored three goals, one a penalty, in less than three minutes! Not a League record, but certainly a club record.

Season 1975/76 opened in a promising manner, with six wins and two draws in the first eight games. The signing of Ray O'Brien from Manchester United had boosted the defence, and a League Cup visit to First Division Leeds United in October had resulted in a 1-0 win. Then two Les Bradd goals saw off Everton in round four after a 2-2 draw at Goodison Park. However, the first age of Sirrel came to an end when he was offered the manager's job at First Division Sheffield United. His successor was a man who had come from Brentford with Sirrel, Ronnie Fenton. Despite Fenton's best efforts, and those of his assistant Colin Addison, the promotion chase fell away and Notts finished fifth. Les Bradd scored his one hundredth goal for the club.

Next season saw the Magpies finish in eighth position. Dave Needham went to QPR after 430 games, only Albert Iremonger having played more. 10,500 spectators turned up for his testimonial game. Fenton's time as manager ended with the club back at the bottom of Division 2. Jimmy Sirrel's time at Sheffield United had not proved successful, and he was a popular choice with the supporters when he returned to the manager's seat again. More fresh blood arrived, in David Hunt, Iain McCulloch and Jeff Blockley. 1977/78 ended with the club just escaping relegation. A welcome return was given to Don Masson in 1978 when he rejoined from Derby County.

Ian Bolton and Brian Stubbs challenge in the Forest goalmouth - 1975/76 season.

1975/76: Ian Scanlon shoots past Paul Reaney in the Leeds goal. In the background, the old Meadow Lane stand.

Trevor Christie was signed from Leicester in 1979, and with the transfer of some of the old guard, 17th position was probably the best anyone would have hoped for. Christie went on to score 64 goals in 186 League games, a good strike rate in the modern game. Though little fancied as promotion candidates at the start of 1980/81, Howard Wilkinson's coaching perhaps suited the playing style of Don Masson and newcomer Eddie Kelly. The team got off to a good start with 23 points from the first 28 available. By mid-January, hopes had slipped with a run of eleven games without a win. A good away record, and mixed results from the other clubs at the top, meant that Easter arrived with the club back in a healthy position. Promotion was clinched in the penultimate game at Chelsea. A soggy night failed to dampen the enthusiasm of the crowd at the last home game with Cambridge, and a celebration banquet followed the match.

Notts win the 1975/76 pre-season Shipp Cup. Players in full view are: Ray O'Brien, Brian Stubbs (with trophy), David McVay, David Needham, Eric McManus and Ian Bolton.

The Magpies were to spend three consecutive seasons in the top flight. Expensive signings had to be made and the wage bill rose, but attendances were disappointing. There were some excellent results, starting with a 1-0 win at Aston Villa in the first game of 1981/82. 26,000 people were at the City Ground in January 1982 for the re-opening of the local derbies, and goals from Hooks and Christie gave the Magpies a 2-0 victory. The new signings included a trio of internationals from abroad; Rachid Harkouk (Algeria, via QPR), John Chiedozie (Nigeria, via Leyton Orient) and Aki Lahtinen (Finland). With Raddy Avramovic (Croatia) in goal, the team had quite a cosmopolitan feel! The good results were balanced by some unexpected defeats, which left them in 15th place in 1981/82. Iain McCulloch was Notts' player of the year and top scorer with 16 goals. He played (as an over-age player) for the Scottish Under-21 side and was listed in Scotland's 40 for the World Cup.

In 1979, Tommy Lawton opened the 'Wall of Fame' in the supporters room. Tony Hateley (above) was included amongst the stars

Jimmy Sirrel is applauded after the last match of the 1980/81 season, and the club is back in the First Division after 56 years.

Next season brought another 15th place finish. McCulloch was injured and missed the first six games. Brian Kilcline was the first Notts player to win an Under-21 cap for England. 23,065 watched an exciting derby with Forest at Meadow Lane in December 1982; 2-2 at half time, but Christie scored the Notts winner even though McCulloch was sent off. A few days later, the ex-Forest striker Justin Fashanu was signed, and went on to score 7 goals in 15 games that season, before injury cost him his place in the team. Jack Wheeler was forced to step down as trainer and received due reward for his many years of service; honorary membership and a seat in the directors' box.

Larry Lloyd took over as manager in the summer of 1983 after Howard Wilkinson moved on to Sheffield Wednesday. Another ex-Forest star came to the club when Lloyd signed Martin O'Neill. Though the team looked good on paper, results were disappointing. The club never recovered from a run of seven consecutive League defeats in September and October, though 5-2 and 6-1 home wins over Aston Villa and Sunderland respectively gave spectators some grounds for optimism. Also, a rare F.A. Cup run to the sixth round gave a brief vision of a trip to Wembley. One win in the last seven League games left them in 21st place, and relegated to Division Two.

(Left) Rachid Harkouk scores the goal at Chelsea on 2nd May, that finally c l i n c h e d promotion to Division One in the 1980/81 season.

(Below) First Division action, at home to Manchester United. Players from the left: Rachid Harkouk, Ray Wilkins, Brian Kilcline, Gary Birtles and T r i s t a n Benjamin.

Chapter 9

Change: 1984 - 1995

Relegation from the top flight produces many management difficulties. There isn't the money to pay top wages, and it is not unreasonable for good players to want to remain in the top flight.

Relegation season, 1983/84: Near ever-present John Chiedozie on target in a home match.

Trevor Christie joined Forest, John Chedozie went to Spurs after scoring his last goal in a pre-season friendly at Exeter City. Iain McCulloch's leg was so badly broken in a collision with the Manchester United goalkeeper in April 1984 that he was never to play League football again. The lack of a settled side makes winning runs difficult to string together, and Football League history is littered with examples of clubs who have suffered two relegations in successive seasons; such was Notts' fate in 1984/85, and not for the first time. Larry Lloyd and Richie Barker's spells as manager had come to an end, and Jimmy Sirrel took up the reins again.

Sirrel set out to build a new team based on youngsters, and nearly made the play-offs in 1986. The financial situation was bad again, and a crisis meeting drew 1,500 supporters to the Astoria night club on September 15th 1986, with many more locked outside. £2 million debts had forced the directors to consider putting the club into liquidation.

(Right) Steve Sims with the County Cup which was won against the odds when Forest were beaten 2-1 in the Final.

The start of a new era at Meadow Lane in 1987.
From left: New Chairman Derek Pavis and Directors Frank Allcock, Bill Hopcroft and John Mounteney.

In scenes probably reminiscent of the 1881 crisis meeting, the players and directors pledged to carry on with financial support from the fans. A friendly match with Forest brought 3,299 to Meadow Lane, and added £14,000 to the survival funds. 1986/87 ended with the club in 7th place in Division Three, though a win in the final game at York would have seen them into the play-offs.

A new chairman followed, local businessman Derek Pavis, and he appointed a new manager, John Barnwell. The re-building exercise began again, with new arrivals Geoff Pike (as captain), Paul Hart (as player-coach), Gary Mills and Gary Lund. Gary Birtles came from Forest, where he was in a second spell after an unhappy time with Manchester United. Andy Gray was loaned from Aston Villa, so another famous striker was seen at Meadow Lane. Fourth place in Division Three at the end of 1987/88 was disappointing, but it gave Notts a chance of promotion via the play-offs. The home game with Walsall was lost 1-3, and a draw was all that could be managed at Walsall.

A string of poor results at the start of 1988/89 saw the end of John Barnwell and the appointment of a young manager with a successful record at Scarborough, Neil Warnock. Warnock persevered with most of the players used by Barnwell, and brought in Steve Cherry and Phil Turner. 1989/90 saw the club finish in third place and qualify for the play-offs. Bolton were beaten in the qualifying game, to set up the club's first ever visit to Wembley Stadium, where they met Tranmere Rovers in the play-off final. Tommy Johnson and Craig Short goals saw Notts back to Division Two.

You would not have expected much from Notts during most of 1990/91. By early April they seemed out of contention for a play-off place, but a string of seven consecutive victories lifted them into fourth place. Middlesbrough were beaten by the only goal in the first round of the play-offs to set up the second Wembley visit in two seasons. Brighton and Notts drew almost 60,000 spectators to the game, with Notts the easy winners by 3-1. Tommy Johnson scored two of the goals, and was leading scorer in the League with 16. Most unexpectedly, the club were back in the top flight!

NOTTS COUNTY FOOTBALL CLUB

3rd Division Play-off Winners

WEMBLEY STADIUM
Sunday 27th May 1990

Another victorious visit to Wembley in 1991. (Above) Phil Turner holds up the Second Division play-off trophy, alongside Dean Yates, Tommy Johnson, and Paul Harding. (Below) Some of the jubilant Notts supporters.

The stay at the top proved to be for just a single year. 1991/92 was a season-long and unsuccessful struggle against relegation. Warnock kept faith largely with the players who had won promotion, but record signing, Tony Agana from Sheffield United, could manage only one goal in 13 appearances. Attendances were again disappointing. Big fees were received from Derby County for Tommy Johnson towards the end of the season, and for Craig Short a few months later.

The 1992/93 season opened in the "new" Football League Division One with Leicester City as the first visitors to the "new" Meadow Lane. A major building effort in the close season had transformed three sides of the ground with modern, "all seater" stands.

17th place was the result of the season which saw Warnock depart and Mick Walker promoted to the manager's seat. Dean Yates skills in defence were missed as he needed major surgery on a knee ligament.

(Left) When Wembley was visited again, in 1991, Notts County became the first team to secure promotion twice via the play-offs, and in two consecutive seasons.

(Below) The County Road stand and Meadow Lane end, taken during the match versus Crystal Palace in the 1991/92 season.

(Above) The same view a few months later, and ready for the forthcoming 1992/93 season.

THE RAPIDLY CHANGED FACE OF MEADOW LANE FROM SUMMER 1992

(Top left) The former rear view of the County Road stand (now the 'Jimmy Sirrel Stand'). (Bottom left) The Kop end at the last match of 1991/92 (v. Luton) - work had already started. (Top right) Summer 1992, work is already well underway. (Bottom right) all work was completed within 17 weeks, and ready for the first match of 1992/93 (v. Leicester)

Next season saw a resurgence of League form, only a few points short of the play-offs and with an interesting diversion in the Anglo-Italian Cup.

Though not attracting huge numbers of fans to the games, the final against Brescia was played at Wembley Stadium, making it visit number three (and the first defeat) for the faithful.

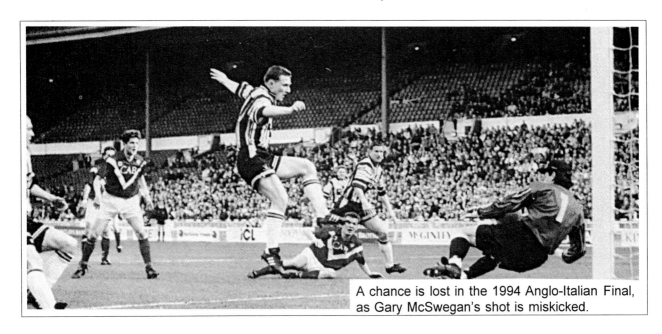

A chance is lost in the 1994 Anglo-Italian Final, as Gary McSwegan's shot is miskicked.

(Above) Proud manager, Mick Walker, leads out the team (and mascot), at Wembley.

(Left) Former YTS trainee Michael Johnson, was a near ever-present defender during the 1993/94 season.

Finally, 1994/95 brought a troubled year of managerial changes and an unsettled team. The club found itself back in a position it knows quite well; relegation for the 13th time, a League record.

If there was a bright spot, it was the win over Ascoli in the Anglo-Italian Cup at Wembley as Notts reached the final for the second year in succession. Relegation from Division One meant it was an honour they could not defend in 1995/96.

1995: The Anglo-Italian Cup. Phil Turner clutches the trophy, followed by Stevo Chorry and Paul Devlin - and about to receive the fans acclaim.

When you read these pages, time will have passed and given a new perspective to the recent seasons. Are they a springboard to twenty years of sustained growth? Are they a sign of further decline? The game itself is subject to increasing financial pressures from the players and their agents as well as from the world outside. Certainly, a club like Notts cannot survive without considerable investment by the directors and the supporters. Though we can hope to see exciting young players learning their craft at Meadow Lane, it is unlikely they can be kept through the days of their playing maturity. Should the club's role therefore be as a "feeder" to other clubs? Can Nottingham support two Premiership clubs (when it has failed to do so in the past)? Time will tell. Though it is unlikely to be me who writes the 150th anniversary booklets in 2012 (or 2014!) I believe my successor will have many new stirring deeds to recount, hopefully led by a strapping goal scoring centre forward.

NOTTS COUNTY

A - Z

ABANDONED GAMES

The club have been involved in the following instances of Football League matches having to be abandoned through weather conditions:

Nov. 23rd 1889   Div. 1   Stoke (a), fog, 90 mins. Result 2-2.
Jan. 12th 1901   Div. 1   Bolton Wanderers (a), fog, 25 mins. Score 0-0.
Mar. 30th 1903   Div. 1   Aston Villa (a), rain, half-time. Score 0-1.
Jan. 6th 1906   Div. 1   Bolton Wanderers (a), rain, half-time. Score 0-2.
Oct. 12th 1912   Div. 1   Tottenham Hotspur (a), fog, 82 mins. Score 3-1.
Mar. l0th 1934   Div. 2   Bradford Park Avenue (h), rain, 16 mins. Score 0-0.
Dec. 25th 1937   Div. 3S Gillingham (a), fog , 37 mins. Score 0-1.
Dec. 3rd 1960   Div. 3   Halifax (h), rain, half time. Score 0-2.
Mar. 25th 1965   Div. 4   Millwall (h), rain, half-time. Score 1-2.
Dec. 28th 1965   Div. 4   Tranmere Rovers (h), fog, 14 mins. Score 0-0.
Dec. 11th 1976   Div. 2   Burnley (h), frost, half-time. Score 0-0.

Though ninety minutes were played in the Stoke match of 1889, the match was declared void because of the fog. The re-arranged match was also drawn, 1-1. The First Division match against Birmingham on September 19th, 1925 was halted for a period of 50 minutes, due to torrential rain but play was resumed and the match completed. Notts won 1-0.

Notts lost 6-0 in a Football League game at Preston on December 12th, 1891. Heavy snow and extreme cold led to five Notts players walking off! The score at the time was 0-4, and Preston scored two more against the remaining five men (Osborne had gone off early in the game after a scuffle with Drummond and had not returned). Preston protested; the League ordered that the result should stand but that another game should be played on January 25th, with Preston receiving half the gate. The other half was to be split between the Football League and Notts. Preston won the game 6-2. Notts received the sum of £10 8s.

A wartime Midland Section league match was abandoned on February 9th, 1918. The game against Huddersfield was 0-0 at half time; the re-arranged game was won 2-1 by Huddersfield. Two other war time games were abandoned, but the results were allowed to stand. These were a Midland Section game with Bradford City on January 26th, 1918 (0-0, after 60 minutes) and a League Cup North game with Mansfield Town on January 15th, 1944 (0-1, after just 15 minutes).

In recent seasons, stricter rules for referees mean that games are often called off well before kick off if conditions are bad. On January 10th, 1987 the players did not agree with the referee when he postponed the scheduled game with Newport County, and held a practice match on the pitch!

ABSENTEES

The club were a man short for the Football League game at Preston on March 31st, 1893. The absentee was goalkeeper George Toone who missed the train. For economy reasons the directors had not sent a reserve player for the match so full-back Jack Hendry went into goal and the Magpies, playing with ten men, lost 0-4. On a number of occasions goalkeepers have been absentees from a League match and so another player went into goal with a reserve making up the team. The majority of cases occurred during the very bad winter of 1946/47 when goalkeeper Harry Brown, who had to travel up from London, failed to turn up on three occasions when selected, in each case because of train timetable disruptions. Canadian centre-forward Fred Whittaker went into goal twice and half-back Bill Corkhill once.

In the match v Sheffield United (a), Division 1, Dec. 26th, 1906, half-back Reuben Craythorne was in goal in place of Bob Suter who was delayed by the railways. The reverse procedure was the case v Newport County (a), Division 4, Feb. 28th, 1970. The club's nominated substitute missed the coach and reserve goalkeeper Barry Watling had to fill the role. During the match Don Masson came off injured and Watling went on to replace him.

In pre-Football League days, there were a number of occasions when the side took the field with only ten, and a few times, with nine players. The record for absentees though was the game with Lincoln (a), on Feb. 8th, 1872, when no fewer than seven selected players failed to turn up. The side was made up to 11 with spectators at the Lincoln ground and despite this the club lost by only 0-1!

AGE
The oldest player to appear in a Football League match is Albert Iremonger who was 41 years and 320 days old when he played in goal against Huddersfield Town on May 1st 1926. Next comes Bill Corkhill at 41 years 142 days in his final game at Barnsley on Sep. 12th 1951. The youngest player in the Football League was Tony Bircumshaw at 16 years 54 days. He made his debut against Brentford on April 3rd, 1961.

AMATEURS
All players were regarded as amateurs until the legalisation of professionalism by the Football Association on July 20th, 1885. Many amateur players were members of more than one club, and could play for which ever one they chose. However, F.A. Cup rules restricted a player to appearing for only one club in any season. As the professional game grew, the number of amateur players declined, especially since the Second World War. The F.A. abolished the distinction between professionals and amateurs in 1974.

The following players gained amateur international honours whilst with the club:

Barry, L.J. (1)	England v Ireland, 1923/24
Jones, B. (1)	Wales v Scotland, 1934/35 (one of three players named Jones signed from Swansea Town in 1934, Bryn Jones never appeared in the first team)
McCavana WT (1)	Ireland v. Scotland 1948/49

ANGLO-ITALIAN CUP
The present version of this was introduced in 1992/93 and competed for by clubs from the second divisions of English and Italian Football. The competition has excited little interest except amongst Notts supporters who were rewarded with two Wembley finals in 1994 and 1995. Earlier manifestations of the competition included tournaments for Third Division and non-League clubs.

ANGLO-SCOTTISH CUP
The tournament started life as the Texaco Cup and originally included clubs from Northern Ireland also. It became a pre-season tournament. The Scottish clubs withdrew in 1981 and the competition evolved into the Football League Group Cup. Notts reached the semi-finals in 1977/78 and the final in 1980/81, losing to Chesterfield over two legs. A play off game with Sheffield United was required in 1977/78 when the clubs finished with the same points in the "mini-league" preliminary round.

APPEARANCES
The player with most League appearances in total is goalkeeper Albert Iremonger (564) followed by Dave Needham on 429 (including appearances as a substitute).

The record for the number of consecutive appearances in the Football League is also held by Albert Iremonger. From February 9th, 1907 he did not miss a match until suspended in 1912. His run ended on October 19th, 1912, a total of 211 consecutive Division 1 appearances. Altogether, his consecutive appearances totalled 222 for he also played in 11 F.A.Cup games.

ASSOCIATE MEMBERS CUP
Associate members of the Football League are the members of the (new) Divisions Two and Three who do not have full voting rights. A knock-out tournament for these clubs has been played since 1983/84 under a variety of sponsors'

names. This doesn't help the fans get very enthusiastic about the competition and some spectacularly low attendances have followed. 200 turned up in 1985/86 to see Peterborough play Aldershot in a preliminary round game even though neither could qualify and the semi-finals had already been played! In the years that the Magpies entered, it was known as the Freight Rover Trophy, the Sherpa Van Trophy and the Leyland DAF Cup.

Notts' composite record in the Associate Members Cup is played 22; At home, won 3, drawn 4, lost 2, goals for 8, against 10. Away from home; won 5, drawn 2, lost 6, goals for 15, against 18.

ATTENDANCES

Early "gates" are unreliable. They were usually estimated by the newspaper reporter, who would sometimes add *"at the kick off, the attendance was ...."*, implying that more spectators would arrive later. The club would have been able to make a better guess by the money taken at the gate, and sometimes this information was given to the press. Since 1925, clubs have been required to report their attendances to the Football League.

The largest League attendance for a Notts match was at Goodison Park on 20th October 1951 when 49,604 saw the game with Everton. At Meadow Lane, an all-ticket crowd of 46,000 was said to have watched the game with Forest on 22nd April 1950. The best attendance in the modern stadium is 18,655 against Forest on February 12th, 1994. In the F.A. Cup, the Magpies visit to Anfield on January 29th, 1949 drew 61,003 to see the game with Liverpool. At home, 47,310 saw the 6th round tie with York City on March 12th, 1955. Notts' four visits to Wembley drew crowds ranging from 59,940 (the 1991 play off against Brighton) to 11,704 (for the 1995 Anglo-Italian Cup Final).

The early days of League football saw some very small gates. The crowd at Crewe Alexandra for the game with Notts in 1894/95 was reported as *"a few dozen"* at the kick off. 300 came to Trent Bridge the previous season to see Crewe, who were obviously not the greatest attraction of the time! In recent years, the "miscellaneous" tournaments have been notable if only for setting record lows at many clubs. Just 1,616 turned out to see Notts play Peterborough in the Leyland DAF Cup at Meadow Lane on December 12th, 1989.

The best season for attendances at Notts' games, home and away, was 1950/51. An average of 27,933 saw the 42 games. The worst season was 1895/96 when the average was 3,569. In recent times, the worst season was 1985/86, with 4,405. Notts' average home attendances are as follows:

Season	Av.	Seaon	Av.	Season	Av.	Season	Av.
1890	3620	1914	11579	1949	29976	1973	10701
1891	7140	1915	9684	1950	34659	1974	11911
1892	4692	1920	16050	1951	30047	1975	10927
1893	7367	1921	15789	1952	26260	1976	12414
1894	3164	1922	11738	1953	19285	1977	10943
1895	4464	1923	14476	1954	16277	1978	9268
1896	3400	1924	16048	1955	16891	1979	9281
1897	4667	1925	13476	1956	15414	1980	8805
1898	8573	1926	14908	1957	15627	1981	9551
1899	10911	1927	9825	1958	14441	1982	11628
1900	8276	1928	11065	1959	9523	1983	10790
1901	9706	1929	15090	1960	13821	1984	9463
1902	9294	1930	11333	1961	11908	1985	6211
1903	8726	1931	12257	1962	8352	1986	4404
1904	10411	1932	11998	1963	6867	1987	4729
1905	8294	1933	11015	1964	6322	1988	6336
1906	10083	1934	12037	1965	5609	1989	5675
1907	9947	1935	10984	1966	4957	1990	6151
1908	10158	1936	7320	1967	4354	1991	8164
1909	10395	1937	14129	1968	5640	1992	11135
1910	10105	1938	12567	1969	4778	1993	8151
1911	13184	1939	10410	1970	5779	1994	8314
1912	10447	1947	15405	1971	10757	1995	7195
1913	11895	1948	25157	1972	13941		

The season is the final year of the season; e.g. 1995 is season 1994/95.
Games where the attendance is not known have been excluded from the analysis.

AWAY RECORDS

Notts have avoided the ignominy of failing to win away from home during the course of a single season, but managed just one win on 6 occasions, most recently in 1977/78. The most wins during a season are 11 in season 1970/71 (23 matches), followed by 10 in 1965/66.

The best goals total away from home is 41 in 1959/60. The lowest is 7 (from 17 games) in 1901/02.
The number of times each result has occured in Notts' 1,941 away games is as follows (Notts' score first; i.e., 1-0 is an away win for the club):

0- 0	139	1- 0	119	2- 0	64	3- 0	20	4- 0	8	5- 0	1	6- 0	1		
0- 1	170	1- 1	205	2- 1	105	3- 1	57	4- 1	20	5- 1	5	7- 1	1		
0- 2	156	1- 2	169	2- 2	90	3- 2	26	4- 2	7	5- 2	4	8- 1	1		
0- 3	104	1- 3	124	2- 3	54	3- 3	25	4- 3	6	5- 3	1				
0- 4	51	1- 4	44	2- 4	30	3- 4	10	4- 4	2	5- 4	2				
0- 5	21	1- 5	37	2- 5	15	3- 5	5	4- 5	1						
0- 6	16	1- 6	7	2- 6	4	3- 6	2								
0- 7	2	1- 7	3	2- 7	1	3- 7	1								
0- 8	2	1- 9	3												

BASS CHARITY VASE

Organised by the Bass brewery in Burton upon Trent, dating back to the 1880s. Entries are by invitation, but the Notts' minute books show that sometimes they declined to play when asked. The Vase has been competed for by reserve teams in recent times, with Notts successful in three consecutive years from 1988. Results of first team matches can be found under "friendlies".

CLOSURE

German air raids on Nottingham in May 1941 caused heavy damage to Meadow Lane. The club did not play during season 1941/42 as a consequence.

CLUB NAMES

Some of the clubs met by Notts in League and Cup games later changed their names.
Woolwich Arsenal became Arsenal in 1914.
Burslem Port Vale became Port Vale in 1907.
Rotherham Town and Rotherham County merged to become Rotherham United in 1925.
Ardwick became Manchester City in 1894.
Newton Heath became Manchester United in 1902.
Stoke City played as Stoke until 1925.
Small Heath Alliance and Small Heath were names for Birmingham until 1905; "City" came in 1945.
Clapton Orient became Leyton Orient for the 1945/46 season. They played as "Orient" from 1966 to 1987.
Burton Swifts and Burton Wanderers merged to form Burton United in 1901.
Chester City played as Chester until 1983.
Gateshead (now defunct) played as South Shields until 1930.
Hartlepool United were Hartlepools United until 1968, and played as Hartlepool from 1968 to 1977.
Leicester Fosse became Leicester City in 1915.
Swansea City were Town until 1970.
Walsall played as Walsall Town Swifts until 1895.
The original Accrington club left the League in 1893; they were not the same club as Accrington Stanley.
Leeds City were closed for financial irregularities in 1919; they were not the same club as Leeds United.

COACH

The role of "coach" is a modern one, since his duties in former times would have been the responsibility of the manager and perhaps the trainer. Indeed, the post is sometimes called "assistant manager" rather than coach. Colin Addison was appointed assistant to Ron Fenton in 1975. Jimmy Sirrel had Colin Murphy with him as coach and assistant manager in 1977/78. Later, Howard Wilkinson and Larry Lloyd had responsibilities for first team coaching, with Sirrel as General Manager. Other men to hold the position of first team coach are Dick Bate, Alan Hill, John Newman, Mick Jones, Wayne Jones and Russell Slade.

COLOURS

The first recorded club colours were amber and black horizontal stripes and this was the case at least until 1872. The next reference to colours, in 1880, is to chocolate and Cambridge blue halves and these remained the club colours until the formation into a limited company in the summer of 1890. From this point the club colours have mainly been black and white but there have been changes in the style of shirt. Stripes were in favour until the club won promotion to Division 1 in 1922/23. From then until the end of season 1925/26 the colours were white shirts with a black "V" and a Magpie on the breast of the shirts. They then reverted to stripes.

The next change was for the season of 1934/35 when the club went back to chocolate and blue but these colours were used for only a few games before switching to black and white stripes again. During the later war years another design was used, broad horizontal stripes. When the Football League resumed operations in 1946/47 the design was white shirts with black collars and cuffs. Black and white stripes came back into favour at the start of 1952/53. For 1962/63, white shirts with a black circle around the neck were used, with the club's badge on the shirts. In 1963/64 they went back to black and white stripes and stayed that way throughout the 1970s.

Fashion and sponsor's requirements now dictate a change of detail every season! In general, the black and white stripes have remained. There were three thick stripes from 1977/78 to 1982/83, then the shirts went pinstripe. After reverting to "normal" stripes, a sponsors name appeared on an inelegant "bib" under the players chin, fortunately now replaced by a square "label" on the player's chest. Small splashes of yellow have appeared in recent seasons. The black shorts went white in 1994.

The report of the game at Blackburn Rovers on December 15th 1888 says that some Notts players were dressed in white shirts, and some in Blackburn Rovers' colours. The report also mentions that the game was played in a dense fog, which must have made the referee's job interesting! The referee in the game at Huddersfield on November 25th, 1989 must have been equally confused. The Notts' black and white stripes proved indistinguishable from the home team's blue and white stripes. Notts emerged for the second half wearing yellow and black check shirts borrowed from the home club.

On 19th November 1949, the club found themselves without a convenient change strip for the visit to Torquay. Eric Houghton called at his old club and Notts played the game in borrowed Aston Villa shirts.

CORINTHIANS

The most famous of all English amateur clubs was formed in 1882. Leading amateur players of the day were asked to play for the Corinthians but could also turn out for their home clubs of course. For example, Harry Cursham played for them from 1882 to 1886 and was a member of their committee.

Notts first played them in 1884/85, and matches continued until 1906/07. Notts' record was:
Played 20; won 9, drawn 3, lost 8. 48 goals for, 46 against. The Corinthians amalgamated with the Casuals in 1939.

CRICKETERS

The early history of Notts FC coincided with the reign of Notts County Cricket Club as the best county side in England. It is not surprising that many cricketers turned out for Notts during the winter. In season 1883/84, no less than six of them were in the team; Mordecai Sherwin, Herbert Emmitt, William Gunn, Arthur and Harry Cursham, and John Dixon. In addition, Harry Moore and Stuart Macrae made appearances for the Nottinghamshire Colts cricket team. William Gunn was capped for England at football in 1883/84 and played in eleven test matches against Australia from 1886 to 1899. John Dixon was another "double" international.

Overseas cricket tours started as early as 1859. Players not available for the club because of touring commitments included Richard Daft, William Gunn and Mordecai Sherwin.

Other Notts footballers who played for Notts CCC are Harry Daft (Richard's son), W.A. Flint, F.H. Guttridge, A. Iremonger, G.M. Lee, T. Lindley, T. Simpson and S.W. Widdowson. Notts men played for other counties of course. The last example was Dennis Oakes who played for Warwickshire in 1965 and made his final appearance for Notts in 1971.

FAMILIES

Brothers: There have been many instances of brothers appearing for the club. Included below are details of when brothers appeared together in Football League matches.

Edward and William May were twin brothers who made two appearances together in 1888/89. Ike and Albert Waterall appeared together between 1910/11 and 1912/13. A third brother, Tom, played during the 1906/07 season along with Ike but the two never appeared together in a match. Alf and Abe West played in one match together, in 1912. This was Abe's only appearance for the club and would most likely never have occurred if the original match against Tottenham had not been abandoned.   Percy and Bert "Paddy" Mills appeared together in two matches during the 1927/28 season and 15 matches in 1928/29. James and John Oswald appeared together in 19 matches during the 1889/90 season. Chris and Craig Short played many games together between 1990 and 1992.

In the 1961/62 season two sets of brothers appeared together! Peter and Tony Bircumshaw and Peter and John Butler played against Portsmouth on Feb. 24th, 1962 and against Barnsley on March 3rd. Two sets of brothers also appeared against Derby County on Dec. 22nd, 1888.   Alf and Charles Shelton appeared in fifteen matches together that season while Edward and William May played in two. The Sheltons also appeared together in four matches during the 1890/91 season.

Father and son: George Toone played between 1889/90 and 1901/02 while his son, George junior, played one match in 1913/14. Harry Daft played between 1884/85 and 1894/95 while his father, Richard, captained the club in the late 1860s.

General: For seven seasons the brothers Albert and James Iremonger were on the staff of the club. James was appointed trainer in 1919/20 after playing for Forest; Albert finished his long playing career with the club at the close of the 1925/26 season.

In pre-Football League days, three brothers from the Greenhalgh family played regularly in the same team. They were Harold, Ernest and Richard. Harold was the regular goalkeeper for seven seasons. Ernest won international caps at three quarter back. The three Curshams (Arthur, Charles and Harry) also appeared in the same side in the late 1870s.

Full back Bob Worthington played in all 46 League games in 1970/71. His brothers Frank and Dave were also "ever present" that season; Frank with 42 games for Huddersfield Town, Dave with 46 for Grimsby Town.

Percy Mills' grandson Nigel Pearson is the current Middlesbrough full back and captain.

FLOODLIGHTS

The first game by floodlights in England took place at Bramall Lane, Sheffield, on October 14th, 1878. The lighting was considered to be a great success and other such matches soon took place in various parts of the country. The first one involving Notts County was against Derbyshire at Trent Bridge on November 30th, 1878. The power was generated on the ground by two portable engines - one behind each goal driving Siemens dynamos. The report in the Nottingham Daily Express gives some details: the two machines were, *"capable of producing equal to 6,000 and 3,000 candles respectively. Each lamp was suspended on a pole about 15ft in altitude, about 20ft in front of each of the goal posts which were about 110 yds apart. Behind each lamp was a reflector so as to cast the light over the space occupied by the players. The current was conveyed to each lamp by cables of copper wire insulated by gutta percha, the positive wire being about 1/8 inch in diameter and the negative wire about 1/4 inch."* The occasion was not such a success as the one at Sheffield. The report continues: *"The night was somewhat foggy and it was a source of regret that more lights were not brought into requisition. One at least was required to give a satisfactory effect especially as the light affixed near the upper goal flickered at times considerably, added to which the light on several occasions went out entirely. But with regard to the low lamp or the one placed near the right wing of the new cricket pavilion, we should state that it worked admirably. At 8 o'clock the upper light suddenly went out and it transpired that the belt of the driving engine had flown off. The engine had accordingly to be stopped and as a consequence of the stoppage the other light went out and the vast crowd were left in utter darkness and some groans were raised. The inconvenience was however quickly remedied."* Notts won the match, which kicked off at 7.15, by one goal to nil, scored by T.A. Oliver after 47 minutes. The attendance was estimated at 4,000 and the report concludes: *"Financially the match was a marked success but regarded as an exhibition of the electric light it was scarcely so successful as could have been desired."*

Floodlit football under more modern conditions was prohibited by F.A. resolutions and progress was not made until a new resolution of January, 1951 reduced the ban to competitive matches only, dependent on the ruling of the authority concerned. Among the pioneers who installed floodlights at this period was Notts County and the first match under lights at Meadow Lane was against Derby County on March 23rd, 1953. The result was a 1-1 draw and a crowd of 20,193 saw the game.

Within three years floodlit football became permissible in both F.A.Cup and Football League but with the improved and higher standards of lighting it soon became necessary for new floodlights to be installed at Meadow Lane. These were officially opened at the match against Port Vale on October 11th, 1962. A new set of lights were installed in time for the start of the 1977/78 season, and these were replaced by the latest set when the ground was redeveloped in 1992.

F.A. CUP
The Challenge Cup competition was proposed in 1871 and got underway with an entry of 15 clubs for season 1871/72. Notts were one of the first of the present day League teams to enter the competition, in 1877/78. They have won the trophy once (1894), been beaten finalists once (1891) and semi-finalists on three other occasions. Harry Cursham of Notts is the leading goalscorer of all time in the competition, with 49 goals. He scored another two goals in a cup tie that was later declared void.

Notts were the first Second Division side to win the Cup. The trophy they received was won by Aston Villa the following season, but was stolen from a shop window in 1895 and never seen again. It is believed to have been melted down in order to make counterfeit coins. A replica was made, and used until 1910. It was then replaced by the Bradford-made trophy we are familiar with today. The first winners were Bradford City! As this third cup was getting a little battered, an exact duplicate has been made and was first presented in 1992.

Notts complete record in the F.A. Cup is: Played 276; at home, won 71, drawn 30, lost 35, goals for 315, against 160. Away from home, won 50, drawn 18, lost 72, goals for 210, goals against 254. 122 diferent clubs have been met. The most regular opponents are Aston Villa, with twelve meetings including replays. Bolton Wanderers have been played on nine occasions, Sunderland and Sheffield Wednesday on seven. Nottingham Forest have been played six times.

FOOTBALL LEAGUE
Notts County were founder members of the Football League, formed on April 17th 1888 at a meeting held at the Royal Hotel, Manchester, following preliminary meetings at Andertons Hotel, Fleet Street, London, during March. A Second Division was added in 1892, when members of the Football Alliance were admitted. "One off" games known as test matches were used for a few seasons to determine promoted and relegated clubs. The League ran with two divisions until 1920, when the Southern League was incorporated to form a third division. Next season, 20 Northern clubs formed the Third Division North, the earlier division being then renamed as the Third Division South. In 1958, the top clubs in the two third divisions formed the new Third Division, the others joining Division Four. In 1993, the First Division clubs became the constituents of the Premier League, and the three remaining Football League divisions were renamed as One, Two and Three.

Two points for a win was introduced part way through the first season in 1888/89, and was used until 1982, when it became three points. Goal average (goals for divided by goals against) was used to separate clubs level on points until 1976; then goal difference was used (goals for minus goals against). The "new" Football League prefers "goals for", but if two clubs have the same number, goal difference is then used.

The club's first match in the Football League was versus Everton at Anfield on Sept. 15th, 1888, resulting in a 2-1 defeat. The highlights of Notts' achievements are:

Most wins in a season:	30 in 1970/71 (Div. 4, 46 matches)
Fewest defeats in a season:	7 on six occasions, the latest in 1980/81 (42 games).
Fewest wins in a season:	5 in 1888/89 (Div. 1, 22 matches); 1904/05 (Div. 1, 34 matches)
Most defeats in a season:	28 in 1963/64 (Div. 3, 46 matches)
Most draws in a season:	18 in 1968/69 (Div. 4, 46 matches)
Most goals scored in a season:	107 in 1959/60 (Div. 4, 46 matches)
Most goals conceded in a season:	97 in 1934/35 (Div. 2, 42 matches)

Fewest goals scored in a season:	28 in 1912/13 (Div. 1, 38 matches);
Fewest goals conceded in a season:	31 in 1893/94 (Div. 2, 28 matches), 1924/25 (Div. 1, 42 matches)
Longest unbeaten run:	19 matches from April 26th, 1930 to Dec. 6th, 1930
Longest unbeaten run (home):	25 matches August 17th 1970 to August 14th 1971
Longest unbeaten run (away):	10 matches July 24th 1971 to October 30th 1971
Longest winning run:	8 matches from Jan. 17th to March 14th, 1914
Longest run of home wins:	14 matches Sep 17th, 1959 to Feb 13th, 1960
Longest run of away wins:	5 matches Sep 15th, 1896 to Oct 31th, 1896
Longest run of drawn matches:	5 matches Dec 2nd to Dec 21st, 1978
Longest run of defeats:	7 matches from Sept. 4th to Nov. 2nd, 1912; Apr. 8th to May 6th, 1933 (the last seven matches of the season) and Sep. 3rd 1983 to Oct. 16th 1983..
Longest run without a win:	18 matches from Nov. 26th, 1904 to Apr. 8th, 1905
Longest run without a home win:	13 matches (Dec. 3rd, 1904 to Sep. 23rd, 1905, and Nov. 24th, 1979 to April 26th, 1980.
Longest run without an away win:	24 matches Dec. 23rd, 1933 to Jan. 30th, 1935
Longest run without a drawn match:	22 matches from Feb. 14th, 1903 to Nov. 7th, 1903; and from Sept. 12th, 1959 to Jan. 9th, 1960.

Notts complete aggregate performance in the Football League (to the end of season 1994/95) is as follows.
Played 3882:   won 1443, drawn 944, lost 1495. Goals for 5670, against 5813.
Home: won 995, drawn 483, lost 463. Goals for 3533, against 2186.
Away: won 448, drawn 461, lost 1032. Goals for 2137, against 3627.

FOOTBALL LEAGUE CUP
At the annual meeting of the Football League in May, 1960 a proposal that they should introduce their own Cup competition was accepted and approved by 31 votes to 16. Whereas entry to the competition was originally optional it has been compulsory since 1971. Initially unpopular with the leading clubs, the competition grew in stature once the decision was made to play the final at Wembley. The competition has been known by sponsors names since 1981; Milk Cup (1981/2 to 1985/6), Littlewoods Challenge Cup (1986/7 to 1989/90), Rumbelows League Cup (1990/1 to 1991/2), Coca Cola Cup (1992/93 onwards).

Notts' best seasons in the competition were in 1963/64, 1972/73 and 1975/76, when they reached the fifth round. The best wins are 6-1 against Bolton Wanderers on Oct. 30th 1984, 5-0 v Swindon Town on Oct.17th, 1962 and 5-0 v. Mansfield Town on Aug. 30th 1988. The biggest defeat came at home to Newcastle United on Oct. 5th 1993 when they lost 1-7.

Notts' complete record is: Played 102;
Home: won 30, drawn 7, lost 14, goals for 107, against 67.
Away: won 13, drawn 10, lost 28, goals for 51, against 95.

FOOTBALL LEAGUE GROUP CUP
A competition for League clubs played in 1981/82, to replace the Anglo-Scottish Cup after Scottish clubs withdrew. Notts did not progress beyond the preliminary stage.

FULL MEMBERS CUP
Full Members of the Football League were those who played in the old Divisions One and Two. These clubs were full members and each had a vote; third and fourth division clubs (associate members) had four votes between them. The tournament ran from 1985/86 to 1991/92. Notts entered in 1990/91 and 1991/92 when it was known as the Zenith Data Systems Cup.

GATE RECEIPTS
As with transfer fees, this section is particularly vulnerable to inflation as will be seen from the following progressive table of the gate receipts record at Magpies' home matches:

£564 11s 4d.	v. Nottm Forest (Trent Bridge)	Oct. 8th, 1898, Division I
£1,335	v. Tottenham Hotspur (Trent Bridge)	Feb. 23rd, 1907, F.A.Cup
	(this was a shilling gate, i.e. double the normal admission)	
£2,103 1s 8d.	v. Sheffield Wednesday (Meadow Lane)	Dec. 27th, 1920, Division 2
£4,129	v. Aston Villa	Jan. 29th, 1921, F.A. Cup
£5,631 14s 6d.	v. Portsmouth	Feb. 2nd, 1952, F.A. Cup
£6,425 5s 6d.	v. York City	Mar. 12th, 1955, F.A. Cup
£9,611	v. Aston Villa	Mar. 4th, 1972, Division 3
£14,022	v. Nottingham Forest	Dec. 26th, 1973, Division 2
£23,215	v. Leeds Utd.	Jan. 3rd, 1976, F.A. Cup
£30,654	v. Aston Villa	Jan. 5th, 1982, F.A. Cup
£124,539	v. Manchester City	Feb. 16th, 1991, F.A. Cup

These details must be read in relation to the minimum admission charges which used to be laid down by the Football League. This is how prices rose until the 1970s. Prior to World War I: 6d.; 1919/20 1s.; 1942/43 1s.3d.; 1951/52 1s.6d.; 1955/56 2s.; 1960/61 2s.6d.; 1965/66 4s.; 1968/69 5s.; 1970/71 6s.; 1972/73 40p. (8s.); 1975/76 65p; 1976/77 80p; 1977/78 90p. Notts share of the F.A. Cup final receipts in 1894 was £199 6s 8d. The first game at Meadow Lane attracted 27,000 people who paid £755, the best for a League game at that time.

GOAL AVERAGE
The club have been saved from relegation by a superior goal average once and also avoided having to apply for re-election for the same reason. In 1897/98 the five bottom teams in Division 1 all had 24 points with Notts County finishing fourth from bottom. However the League was extended after that season so the two bottom teams, Blackburn Rovers and Stoke, were re-elected to Division 1. In 1966/67 the club finished fifth from bottom in Division 4, having a superior goal average to Rochdale who thus had to apply for re-election. A superior goal average kept the club off bottom place in Division 1 in 1888/89 above Stoke but they still had to apply for re-election.

GOAL KEEPING
The Notts goalkeepers with the best defensive records are as follows (minimum 50 games):

	Games	Goals	Av.
B.J. Watling	65	68	1.04
R.E. Brown	113	125	1.10
G. Blyth	99	120	1.21
C.E. McManus	229	298	1.30
A. Iremonger	564	740	1.31

In terms of clean sheets, the best performances have come from:

	Games	No.	Av.
G. Blyth	99	37	37.37%
R.E. Brown	113	41	36.28%
G.H. Streets	133	43	32.33%
A. Iremonger	564	183	32.44%
B.J. Watling	65	21	32.20%

Goalkeeper Gordon Bradley scored a goal against Leicester City in 1956/57. He had given up his position in goal after an injury but continued playing on the wing.

GOAL SCORING
Individual

The record individual goalscoring aggregate for a single season in Football League matches is held by centre-forward Tom Keetley who scored 39 goals from 34 games in Division Three South, 1930/31. The club's leading goalscorer in League matches is Les Bradd with 125. Next come Tony Hateley (109), Jackie Sewell (97), Tom Keetley (94), Don Masson (92) and Tommy Lawton (90). The most prolific scorers in non-League days were Harry Cursham and Harry Jackson. Cursham scored over 150 goals in friendly games, two in the Football League and 49 in the F.A. Cup. Centre forward Jackson scored 94 goals in 123 known appearances, including 40 goals in 32 games during season 1885/86.

To compare rates at which goals were scored in the League, dividing the number scored by the appearances made by each player (assuming a minimum of ten games) provides the following top five: Tom Keetley (0.91 goals per game), James Logan (0.76), Hughie Gallacher (0.71), John Murphy (from the 1890s, 0.65) and Jack Peart (0.62).

Leading F.A. Cup scorers are Harry Cursham (49), Harry Jackson and Richard Daft (both 19), William Gunn and Tommy Lawton (both 13). Leading Football League Cup scorers are Trevor Christie(10), Jeff Astle(9) and Les Bradd(7).

Dave Watson's two League goals were 17 years apart! He scored in October 1967, then moved to Rotherham, Sunderland, Manchester City, Werder Bremen, Southampton, Stoke City, Vancouver Whitecaps and Derby County before returning to Notts to score his second goal in April 1985. Bill Corkhill's two F.A. Cup goals were scored 15 years apart. He joined the club from Marine (Crosby) in 1931 and moved to Cardiff in 1938. After wartime appearances for Mansfield he rejoined Notts in 1945 and played on until 1951. Later, he became senior coach to the Notts FA.

The fastest goal scored for the club is by Barrie Jones against Torquay United on March 31st 1962. The goal was timed at 6 seconds after the kick off.

The individual scoring record in one game is held by Harry Jackson, who scored eight of the eleven goals against Wellingbrough Grammar School on February 4th, 1886. This was a friendly game. The leading scorer in a competitive game is Harry Cursham with six, against Wednesbury Strollers in the F.A. Cup, December 10th, 1881. In Football League games, four players have scored five goals; Daniel Bruce, Harry Daft, Robert Jardine and Bertie "Paddy" Mills.

The player with most hat tricks is Tom Keetley with ten. He scored hat tricks in three consecutive away games in 1930/31. Ian Scanlon's hat trick took just 2 minutes 45 seconds in a Second Division game with Sheffield Wednesday in November 1974.

Jimmy Cantrell scored 78 goals in First World War games to add to his 64 League goals for the club, a total of 142.

Team
Notts record wins in the Football League are 11-1 v. Newport County, Division 3 (South), Jan 15th, 1949, and 10-0 v. Burslem Port Vale, Division 2, February 26th, 1895. The heaviest defeats were 1-9 reverses at Aston Villa (Sep. 1888), Blackburn Rovers (Nov. 1889) and Portsmouth (April 1927). Having lost 0-8 to West Bromwich in October 1920, Notts won the return game 2-0 just one week later!

In F.A. Cup games, Rotherham Town were beaten 15-0 in the first round on October 24th 1885. Notts lost 1-8 to Newcastle United in the third round of Jan. 8th, 1927. Newcastle also inflicted Notts' heaviest defeat in the League Cup, 1-7 in 1993/94.

GROUNDS
The men who formed the club met originally in the Park Hollow. When they began to meet outside opposition in 1864/65, the ground of the Meadows Cricket Club was used. Occasionally Trent Bridge cricket ground was hired for a major match such as those against Sheffield, London or Queen's Park, Glasgow. For season 1877/78, the club moved to the ground of Beeston Cricket Club. In 1880/81 came another move, this time to the ground of the Castle Cricket Club, back in the Meadows. After three seasons there, the club became regular tenants of Trent Bridge Cricket Ground following Nottingham Forest's move from that venue to Parkside, Lenton. Because Trent Bridge was also needed for cricket, the club sometimes played matches early or late in the season at other grounds, utilising both the Meadows and the Castle grounds for this purpose. Later they also used Forest's Town Ground and City Ground.

Following representations from the Football League in 1902 about playing all their home matches at the same venue, the club began to look around for a new ground. What is now the Sir Julien Cahn Memorial Ground, Loughborough Road, West Bridgford, and a plot of land on Meadow Lane were both inspected but no action was taken and the City Ground continued to be used occasionally. In 1908, the Trustees of Trent Bridge Cricket Ground decided not to renew the club's lease when it expired in 1910. Forced now to look elsewhere, the club moved rapidly to rent ground from the City Council on Meadow Lane and the new "County Ground" was ready for the opening of the 1910/11 season. The stand at Trent Bridge (that stood where the Taverners Stand is now) was dismantled and taken to the new site at the Meadow Lane end. A main stand and a cover for the other "County Road" side of the ground were built during the close season, to the design of the architect Mr. Shepherd. Earth was dumped in order to form the kop. There was no County Road at this time; the Tinkers Leen flowed along behind the stand, and it is reported that a man was stationed on its banks with a net to fish the ball out when necessary. A new County Road stand was built in 1925.

The ground suffered bomb damage in 1941 which led to the club closing down temporarily for the 1941/42 season. 10 to 12 feet in height was added to the kop in 1949 to help accommodate the huge post war crowds. The old Meadow Lane stand was demolished in 1978, and squash courts and offices built on the site. The changing rooms were moved from the main stand to this new building. Terracing was rebuilt in 1980 to provide more crash barriers. The pitch had to be shortened by six feet in the summer of 1985 as spectators in the sponsors' boxes at the Meadow Lane end couldn't see the goalmouth directly below them.

Although there was much speculation over the years about a new stadium to be shared with Forest, first at Colwick, and then at the Wilford power station site, nothing was agreed. Meadow Lane was looking increasingly decrepit when the bold decision was made to rebuild; in any case, the Taylor Report had forced clubs to plan "all-seater" stadiums. Three new stands were erected in a frantic summer of work during 1992, leaving just the main stand in its original state. This was replaced in the summer of 1994. The new County Road stand is named after Jimmy Sirrel, and the new main stand after the chairman, Derek Pavis.

HEIGHT

Shortest

The shortest player to appear in a Football League match for the Magpies is probably Steve Holder who played once in 1969/70, coming on as a substitute against Northampton Town at Meadow Lane, April 24th, 1970. His height was given as 5ft. 3in. Next come Willie Carlin (1971/72 to 1973/74) and John Gissing (1957/58 to 1960/61). Both were 5ft. 4in. These were all forwards or midfield players. The shortest full-backs appear to have been Tom Prescott (1896/97 to 1904/05) and Andrew Mosley (1908/9 to 1909/10), both of whom were 5ft. 7in. Henry Sissons played in one test match, against Derby County in 1895. He was reported to be just 5ft. tall.

Tallest

Goalkeeper Albert Iremonger (1904/05 to 1925/26) was on record until recent years as the tallest player to appear in any Football League match. His height is given as 6ft.5in. or sometimes 6ft. 5½in. Next comes William Gunn, the cricketer and winger for Notts FC, who played in only three Football League games but was a regular member of the team earlier in the 1880s. He was 6ft 2½in. In 1906/07, in addition to first choice goalkeeper Iremonger, the reserve Bob Suter, who played in four matches, was 6ft 1in.

HOME RECORDS

Notts won only one home game in season 1904/05, a dubious distinction shared with Loughborough (1899/00), Arsenal (1912/13), Blackpool (1966/67) and Rochdale (1973/74). Notts were unbeaten at home in season 1970/71, winning 19 out of 23 games. 19 games were also won in season 1959/60.

1948/49 was the best season to see Notts score goals at home; 68. The poorest season was 1904/05, when just 16 goals were scored in 17 games.

The number of times each score has occcured in Notts' 1,941 home League games is as follows:

0- 0	159	1- 0	169	2- 0	173	3- 0	88	4- 0	50	5- 0	27	6- 0	8	8- 0	1
0- 1	102	1- 1	207	2- 1	164	3- 1	97	4- 1	50	5- 1	25	6- 1	11	8- 1	2
0- 2	55	1- 2	122	2- 2	92	3- 2	65	4- 2	20	5- 2	13	6- 2	4	9- 0	3
0- 3	35	1- 3	46	2- 3	32	3- 3	23	4- 3	9	5- 3	4	7- 0	1	9- 1	1
0- 4	10	1- 4	20	2- 4	11	3- 4	9	4- 4	2	5- 4	2	7- 1	3	9- 2	1
0- 5	2	1- 5	9	2- 5	1	3- 5	4	4- 5	1			7- 2	1	10- 0	1
0- 6	1	1- 6	1	2- 6	1							7- 4	1	11- 1	1
0- 7	1														

INTERNATIONALS

ENGLAND

After five unofficial "England v Scotland" matches played at The Oval cricket ground, with both sides selected by the Football Association, official internationals began with the match England v Scotland at Glasgow on Nov. 30th, 1872.

The club's first international player was Ernest Harwood Greenhalgh who played three-quarter back for England in this match. To date, the last Notts player to represent England was Tommy Lawton against Denmark at Copenhagen on Sept. 26th, 1948. The following is a complete list of the club's internationals:

Ashurst, W. (5 appearances): Sweden (2) 1922/23; Scotland,Wales, Belgium, 1924/25.

Only 5ft 9½in., but more than 12st. of solid muscle that could stop any winger in his tracks! Bill Ashurst started with Leeds City and was bought by Lincoln City at the "player auction" when Leeds were wound up for financial irregularities. He joined Notts in 1920. He had a good turn of speed and would probably have been at home in the modern game. He became renowned for his operation of the "offside trap" with his Notts colleague Horace Cope. Later moved to West Bromwich Albion.

Cursham, A.W.(6): Scotland, 1875/76; Scotland, 1876/77; Scotland, 1877/78; Wales,1878/79; Scotland, Wales, 1882/83. An outstanding forward, Arthur played for the Nottingham Law club and for Notts from 1871 onwards. Born in Wilford in 1853 and educated at Oakham School, he was also a cricketer of note, making his debut for Notts CCC in 1876, and later also playing for Derbyshire where he owned a colliery. He also played football for Sheffield FC, causing consternation when he chose to play for them rather than Notts when the clubs met in the F.A. Cup in 1877. Captained England in the games with Scotland (1877/78) and Wales (1878/79). In 1884, he played his last game for the club and emigrated to Florida to run a plantation. A testimonial game at the Castle Ground against Queen's Park raised £284. By Christmas he was dead, of yellow fever.

Cursham, H.A. (8): Wales,1879/80; Scotland, Wales, Ireland, 1881/82; Scotland, Wales, Ireland, 1882/83; Ireland, 1883/84 Born in 1859 and educated at Repton. Perhaps the first of the great goal scorers in the English game. Harry holds the record for the most goals scored in the F.A. Cup, with 49. Dennis Law and Ian Rush are next, on 41. He followed his brothers Arthur and Charles into the Notts' team, marking his debut in 1877 in true strikers fashion, with a goal! At home on either wing or in the centre, and had good dribbling skills. He played for long enough with Notts to see Football League action, making his last appearance (converted to full back!) in February 1891. Harry also played for the Corinthians, Thursday Wanderers (Sheffield) and Grantham. He played two first class cricket matches for Notts CCC. The first. a trial in 1880, was followed 24 years later when he was asked to captain the side against the South African tourists.

Daft, H.B. (5): Ireland,1888/89 ; Scotland, Wales, 1889/90; Ireland, 1890/91; Ireland, 1891/92. Son of Richard Daft. Described as a fast and tricky left winger, good at creating goal scoring chances for others. Harry was born in Radcliffe on Trent in 1866 and educated at Trent College. Also played for the Corinthians from 1887 to 1890 before he became a professional and served on the F.A. committee. He joined Forest for a brief spell after a disagreement with the Notts' directors, and later went to Newark. Though his batting skills did not match his father's, his cricketing career lasted 15 seasons, ten of those as a regular member of the Notts CCC side. He scored 4,421 runs at an average of 16.11. Had a trial for the English lacrosse team.

Dixon, J.A. (1): Wales, 1884/85 John Dixon was a stalwart of Notts cricket and the Dixon Gates at the main entrance were erected in his honour in 1933. He was captain of the cricket team for 11 years, scoring the then highest individual total of 268 (not out) in 1897, and a member of the test selection committee from 1910 onwards. He was a partner in Dixon and Parker, manufacturing clothiers, whose shop is still to be found in Friar Lane, Nottingham. Born in Grantham in 1861, Dixon was educated at Nottingham High School and Chigwell Grammar School. He made his debut for Notts FC in 1883 at inside forward, where he was a creator of goals rather than a scorer. Also played for the Corinthians. Ill health caused his retirement from football in 1888.

Dobson, A.T.C. (4): Ireland,1881/82; Scotland, Wales, Ireland, 1883/84 Born in Nottingham in 1859. A fine full back, with terrier-like tackles. Handicapped, it is said, by poor eyesight. Also played for the Corinthians, as did his brother Charles.

Dobson, C.F. (1): Ireland, 1885/86 Brother of Alfred, and a half back. Made his debut in 1879/80, and played long enough to record a single League appearance in the first season, 1888/89.

Greenhalgh, E.H. (2): Scotland (2), 1872/73 A three quarter back, whose special task was to protect the goalkeeper from the onrush of the opposing forwards. He was one of the two northern players in the first "official" English team. He was an influential figure in the development of the game in Nottingham, making his debut in 1869 and playing regularly until his final appearance in 1883. Became secretary of Greenhalgh's FC in Mansfield, where he was proprietor of Field Mill. Greenhalgh's played on ground at the back of the mill, now the home of Mansfield Town.

Gunn, W. (2): Scotland, Wales, 1883/84

William Gunn is perhaps best known as an outstanding cricketer, playing in nine tests, and joint founder of Gunn and Moores' sports shop in Nottingham. He used his height to great advantage on the wing and also played in the centre. Later became a club director.

Humphreys, P. (1): Scotland, 1902/03

Percy Humphreys joined Notts from Queen's Park Rangers. He made over 200 appearances for the club and scored 73 goals before moving to Leicester Fosse. Played at inside forward and centre forward for Notts, showing fine skills on the ball and a good shot. Later played for Chelsea and Tottenham Hotspur before becoming player-manager at Hartlepools United.

Lawton, T. (4): Scotland, Sweden, Italy, 1947/48; Denmark, 1948/49

Tommy had made 19 full England appearances with Everton and Chelsea and had played regularly in wartime internationals. There was much speculation when he joined Third Division Notts as to whether he would keep his England place. In the end, he played just four more times. Tommy was born in Bolton in 1919, and signed as a professional for Burnley in 1936, moving to Everton in 1937 where he won a League championship medal in 1939. After leaving Notts, he was player-manager at Brentford. He finished his League career with Arsenal, joining them in 1953. Tommy's everlasting fame is due to his heading ability, but he was equally brilliant with the ball on the ground.

Macrae, S. (6): Scotland , Wales, Ireland, 1882/83; Scotland ,Wales, Ireland, 1883/4

One of the first "foreigners" in the England team, Stuart was born in Scotland, at Port Bannatyne in Bute in 1857. A half back, he was noted for his dribbling skills and his rugged tackling. Also played for the Corinthians (1883-90) and Newark where he was a maltster.

Moore, H.T. (2): Ireland, 1882/83; Wales, 1884/85

Born in Nottingham in 1861. A full back, noted for his ability to send the ball vast distances upfield. A regular player for Notts from 1881 to 1888.

Morley, H. (1): Ireland, 1909/10

Herbert Morley joined Notts from Grimsby Town and retired during the First World War. He was a tall and hefty right back, and an acknowledged expert at playing the offside game.

Morse, H. (1): Scotland, 1878/79

A strong and fast running half back. Made his debut for Notts in 1878 and played until 1882. Moved to centre forward for the 1880/81 season, scoring an average of a goal a game in that position.

Shelton, A. (6): Ireland, 1888/89; Scotland, Wales, 1889/90; Scotland, Wales, 1890/91; Scotland, 1891/92

Played at half back, and noted for his hard work and composure. Later moved to Loughborough, then returned to work at the Cammell Laird works in Nottingham where he was unfortunately killed by a collapsing crane in 1923. His brother Charles made one appearance for England (against Ireland, in 1888) but was a Notts Rangers player at the time. He moved to Notts for the 1888/89 season.

Toone, G. (2): Scotland, Wales, 1891/92.

Notts' goalkeeper, the man who missed the fixture at Preston in 1893. Played for Nottingham Jardines (a works team) and Notts Rangers, making his Notts debut in 1889. Joined Bristol City for a season, returning to Notts for three games in 1901/02, before retiring to run a pub in Nottingham. He missed the 1891 final through injury, but was in the winning team of 1894.

Goals: Harry Cursham scored five goals for England, including a hat-trick against Ireland at Belfast, 1883/84. The other Notts players to score for England are H.B. Daft 3; T. Lawton 2; A.W. Cursham 2; and W. Gunn 1.

One full international has been held on a Notts ground. England versus Ireland was staged at Trent Bridge on Feb. 20th, 1897, England winning 6-0.

Near miss: H.T. Cope was selected for the England versus Ireland match in 1925/26 at Belfast but had to withdraw because of injury. He was not subsequently selected.

Though Sam Weller Widdowson is properly recognised as a "Forest cap" when he played his one international game in 1880, he had been a regular member of the Notts team also until 1879.

Unofficial internationals: F.H.Broome v Australia (2), 1951 Commonwealth tour (including hat-trick in match at Sydney); Jesse Pye v Belgium at Wembley, 1945/46 victory international (scoring one goal). Jackie Sewell toured Canada with an F.A. party in May-June, 1950, scoring seven goals. He won full England caps with Sheffield Wednesday.

SCOTLAND
Strangely enough, there have been no full Scottish internationals from Notts. When the club had its strongest collection of Scottish players in the 1890s the Scottish F.A. was ignoring Anglo-Scots in its international selections. James Oswald won one cap with Third Lanark before joining Notts, and two afterwards, when he played for St. Bernards and Rangers. David Calderhead won one cap in 1889. In recent years, Don Masson won 17 caps, but none during his two spells at Meadow Lane. If it is any consolation, Iain McCulloch won two Under 21 caps for Scotland whilst with Notts.

WALES
Davies, W. (6): England, Scotland, Ireland, 1928/29; .England, Scotland, Ireland, 1929/30
Willie Davies was an established international when signed from Cardiff City in March 1928. He had a fine turn of speed, was a clever dribbler, and could play on either wing. He played 73 games before leaving for Tottenham Hotspur. He won 17 caps in total, the rest with Swansea and Cardiff.

Green, A.W. (5): England, 1902/03; Scotland, Ireland, 1903/04; Ireland, England, 1905/06
Another in the line of Notts' goalscoring centre forwards, Arthur Green scored 56 goals in 134 games after signing from Walsall. He later moved to Nottingham Forest. He won one cap with Aston Villa and two more with Nottingham Forest.

Lawrence, E. (1): Scotland, 1931/32.
Signed from Clapton Orient where he won one cap, Eddie Lawrence was a skilful wing half with good distribution skills. He later moved to Bournemouth before returning to Orient. After his playing days ended, he returned to Nottingham to do some scouting for Notts.

Morgan, J.R. (2): England, Scotland, 1879/80
Morgan was on the staff of Derby School and played three games for Notts in 1879/80. He also played for Cambridge University and the original Swansea club.

Goals: Arthur Green scored a hat-trick versus Ireland at Wrexham, 1905/06. Willie Davies scored two goals versus Scotland at Glasgow, 1928/29.

NORTHERN IRELAND
O'Neill, M. (8) 1983/84 to 1984/85
A clever and industrious midfield player and an important member of Forest's winning team of the late 70's. Martin moved to Norwich and came to Notts at the age of 32. Won 64 caps in total, the rest with Distillery, Forest, Norwich City and Manchester City.

Wilson, K. (15) 1991/92 to 1993/94
Notts most capped player. Kevin Wilson gained 40 caps in all, with Ipswich and Chelsea as well as Notts.

EIRE
Fallon, W.J.(5) Hungary,1934/35; Hungary,1935/36; Hungary, Switzerland, France, 1936/37
A fine winger signed from the Dublin club Dolphin. Later joined Sheffield Wednesday where he won four more caps.
Gannon, E. (1): Switzerland, 1948/49
A "classic" wing half, rated by many who saw him as one of the best players ever to appear for Notts. Capped 13 more times with Sheffield Wednesday and Shelbourne.

Moulson, C. (2): Switzerland, France, 1936/37
 Capped twice with Lincoln City before joining Notts.

O'Brien, R. (4): Norway, Poland, 1975/76; Spain, Poland, 1976/77•
 A dependable full back with a goalscoring touch.

McDonagh, J. (12): 1984 to 1986.
 Goalkeeper, signed to replace Raddy Avramovic. Won 12 caps with Everton and Bolton before joining Notts in 1983.

OTHER
Harkouk (Algeria), **Chiedozie** (Nigeria), and **Lahtinen** (Finland) all made appearances for their country whilst with Notts.

INTER-LEAGUE GAMES

The first representative Football League side ,which drew 1-1 with the Football Alliance at Sheffield on April 20, 1891, included two Notts County players, H.B.Daft and T. McInnes. Both were also in the Football League side for its first match against the Scottish League, at Bolton on April 11th, 1892, when the result was 2-2. These Football League teams included Scots who were playing for English clubs and one of whom was McInnes who scored one of the goals against the Scottish League. The complete list of the club's Inter-League representatives is:

Ashurst, W. (1)	Irish League, 1923/24
Bull, W. (1)	Scottish League, 1900/01
Craythorne, R. (1)	Irish League, 1906/07
Daft, H.B. (2)	Football Alliance, 1890/91; Scottish League, 1891/92
Fletcher, H. (1)	Irish League, 1898/99
Humphreys, P. (1)	Scottish League, 1902/03
Iremonger, A. (2)	Irish League, Southern League, 1911/12
McDonald, E. (1)	Irish League, 1902/03
McInnes, T. (2)	Football Alliance, 1890/91; Scottish League 1891/92
Peart, J.G. (1)	Scottish League, 1913/14
Prescott, T.G.(1)	Scottish League, 1898/99

Scorers: Apart from McInnes's goal against the Scottish League in 1891/92, the only other Notts player to score in an Inter-League match is H. Fletcher, one goal against the Irish League in 1898/99

KICK OFFS

Under the early rules of the game, the teams would change ends whenever a goal was scored.. The team losing the goal was allowed the kick to restart the game. Later, when teams changed ends at half time only, it became the practice to toss for the choice of ends at the start of the game. Later, the winning captain was allowed the kick off instead, so allowing his opponent the choice of ends.

It is reported that Notts kicked off at the start of both halves in the game with Chesterfield in October 1969.

LIMITED COMPANY

The club became a limited liability company during the summer of 1890. Moves to bring about this change were initiated by Mr. Arthur Williams who proposed a resolution to that effect at the general spring meeting of the club, held at the Lecture Room of the Albert Hall, Apr. 28th, 1890. The resolution was as follows:

 That this meeting, believing it is necessary to place the Notts. Football Club on a sound financial basis, hereby directs the Committee to register the club under section 23 of the Companies Act, 1867, with limited liability. That subject to the approval of the Board of Trade the Share capital shall be 500 shares of £5 each, upon which £2 per Share shall be at once pair up, such Shares to be allotted to such persons as the Committee, and after their appointment, the Directors, may approve of. That each shareholder shall have the right of free admission to all matches in Nottingham, under the management of the club. The holder of one share shall be qualified to be a Director of the club. That each shareholder shall only have one vote, whatever the number of shares he holds that every transfer of a share shall be approved of by the Directors before registration of his transfer. That the profits, or other income of the Club shall be applied solely in promoting its objects, and that no portion thereof shall be paid by way of dividend or bonus to the shareholders. That the meeting also directs that after such registration of the Club Season Tickets at 10s. 6d. each, to admit the holder and one lady to all matches in Nottingham, under the management of the Club, shall be issued to persons not Shareholders.

The resolution was carried and further meetings were held during the summer to establish the new organisation. The club was registered under the title of "The Notts Incorporated Football Club" (still the official name). There were 12 directors as follows: A.T. Ashwell, A. Barlow, B.F. Blackburn, A. J. Chamberlain, T. Cooper, W. Gunn, R. Halford, A. Lofthouse, F. P. Norris, W.B. Scottorn, H.Vickers, and A. Williams. The first meeting of the Board was held at the Lion Hotel on Aug. 19th, 1890. Williams was elected Chairman.

In March 1928, the club's financial position was described by the then chairman of the Board, Alderman Henry Heath as *"the worst in the club's history."* After taking advice from financial experts it was decided to put The Notts Incorporated Football Club into liquidation and to float a new limited liability company, Notts County Football Club Ltd.

Steps were taken to float the new company during the summer of 1928, but the public made a poor response to the share offer and at the Board meeting of Oct. 10th, 1928 it was resolved *"that the Notts County Football Club Ltd. go into voluntary liquidation and that the Board of Directors revert to the Articles of Association originally published by The Notts Incorporated Football Club"*. The proposed new club was officially wound up at a meeting on Nov. 14th, 1928. A new share issue was made in 1966.

The following men have been Chairman of the Board:
A. Williams 1890-92; R. Deplidge 1892-95; Ald. H. Heath 1895-1930; Lord Belper 1930-1935; C.G. Barnes 1935-56; L. Machin 1956-64; C.F. Williamson 1964-66; W.A. Hopcroft 1966-69; J.J. Dunnett MP 1969-87, D.C. Pavis 1987 onwards.

Alderman Henry Heath was elected to the board on June 5th, 1893, was chairman from 1895/96 to 1930/31 and relinquished his seat in 1934/35. He was then elected an honorary director and so, at his death in 1943, had kept up a connection with the club for 50 years. William Gunn was elected to the club's first board when the limited company was formed in the summer of 1890, retaining his seat until his death in 1921, a spell of 31 years. His first appearance as a player for the club was in the 1881/82 season, thus giving 40 years service on and off the field. Gunn is the only director to turn out as a player while actually serving on the board. He made two Football League and one F.A. Cup appearances after his election.

MANAGERS
In the early days, men who performed the tasks of a manager were not given that title, so there is some confusion between men who would now be regarded simply as secretaries and those who had anything at all to do with team management. Before the formation of the limited company in 1890, the committee or one of its sub-committees were responsible for team selection and this practice continued during the time of the early boards of directors. For instance, at the inaugural board meeting on August 19th, 1890 it was resolved *"that Messrs A. Barlow, W. Gunn, A. Lofthouse, F.P. Norris and W.B. Scottorn be, and they are hereby appointed, a committee to be called "The Team Management Committee" with power on behalf of the Board of Directors to manage the League team during the next football season, subject to the Board of Directors - such committee in cases of emergency also to have power to select the players for such team."* This arrangement lasted for a few seasons but generally the team was selected at Board meetings.

It was on May 30th, 1913 that the Board decided to advertise in the Athletics News for a team manager following the resignation through illness of the secretary, Mr. T.E. Harris. In the event the post became one of secretary-manager and on July 16th, 1913 Mr. Albert Fisher was appointed the club's first secretary manager, his duties to commence on August 1st. However at this stage the team was still selected at Board meetings and although Mr. Fisher soon began to decide on the line-up himself, his choice had to be approved by the Board.

In 1923/24, Charles Bell was appointed team manager under Mr.Fisher but he was what would now be regarded as coach and had little or no say in team selection. In more recent times, the position of "coach" has sometimes clouded the question of who selects the team.

The complete list of managers from the appointment of Albert Fisher is as follows:

Albert Fisher	August 1st 1913 to May 31st 1927 (secretary-manager)
R.C. White	July 17th 1917 to Jan 29th 1919 (during Mr. Fisher's absence in the armed forces)
Horace Henshall	June 1st 1927 to May 5th 1934 (secretary-manager)
Charlie Jones	May 5th 1934 to Dec. 6th 1934
David Pratt	April 28th 1935 to June 28th 1935
Percy Smith	July 19th 1935 to Oct. 31st 1936
Jimmy McMullan	Nov. 10th 1936 to Dec. 29th 1937
Harry Parkes	Jan 11th 1938 to July 13th 1939
J.R. ' Tony ' Towers	July 13th 1939 to July 14th 1942
Frank Womack	July 14th 1942 to Nov. 4th 1943
Major Frank Buckley	March 1st 1944 to May 11th 1946
Arthur Stollery	June 12th 1946 to Feb. 15th 1949
Wilfred Fisher	Feb. 15th 1949 to end of season 48/49 (caretaker)
Eric Houghton	May 25th 1949 to Sep. 1st 1953
George Poyser	Oct 22nd 1953 to Jan 7th 1957
Frank Broome	Jan 7th 1957 to end of season 56/57 (caretaker)
Tommy Lawton	May 7th 1957 to July 1st 1958
Tim Coleman	July to October 1958 (caretaker)
Frank Hill	Oct. 17th 1958 to Oct 31st 1961
Tim Coleman	Oct 31st 1961 to June 31st 1963
Eddie Lowe	July 1st 1963 to April 12th 1965
Tim Coleman	April 12th 1965 to Dec 10th 1965, then as advisor to March 1966
Andy Beattie	Dec 10th 1965 to March 18th 1966 (as managerial advisor, with Coleman and Peter Doherty)
Jack Burkitt	March 18th 1966 to Dec 6th 1966; resigned Feb. 23rd 1967
Andy Beattie	Dec 6th 1966 (acting); Feb 23rd 1967, general manager
Billy Gray	March 13th 1967 (team manager)
Andy Beattie	Team selection from start of 67/68 to Sep 23rd 1968
Billy Gray	Sep 28th 1967 to Sep 23rd 1968
Jack Wheeler	Sep 23rd 1968 to Nov. 19th 1969 (acting manager)
Jimmy Sirrel	Nov 19th 1969 to Oct 16th 1975
Ron Fenton	Oct 16th 1975 to Oct 6th 1977
Jimmy Sirrel	Oct 6th 1977 to Aug. 1982, when he became General Manager
Howard Wilkinson	Aug. 28th 1982 to June 24th 1983
Larry Lloyd	July 7th 1983 to 21st October 1984
Ritchie Barker	Nov. 5th 1984 to April 19th 1985
Jimmy Sirrel	April 19th 1985 to June 1987
John Barnwell	June 3rd 1987 to Dec 2nd 1988
John Newman	Dec 2nd 1988 to Jan 5th 1989 (caretaker)
Neil Warnock	Jan 5th 1989 to Jan 14th 1993
Mick Walker	Jan 14th 1993 to Sep 14th 1994
Russell Slade	Sep 14th 1994 to Jan 12th 1995
Howard Kendall	Jan 12th 1995 to Apr 1st 1995
Wayne Jones, Steve Nicol	Apr 1st 1995 to Jun 5th 1995 (caretakers, with Dean Thomas)
Colin Murphy	June 5th 1995 (with Steve Thompson as team manager)

Albert Fisher had brief spells as a player with a number of Scottish and English clubs before joining Merthyr Town in the Southern League as secretary-manager. Impressed with his efforts in his only season at Merthyr, the directors brought him to Notts. He had a successful first season with the players already at the club, leading them to promotion from Division 2. His highlight as a manager was the Magpies trip to the F.A. Cup semi-final in 1922. He resigned after the disappointing 1926/27 season, with the club back down in 16th place in Division 2. *Horace Henshall* was a fast running forward who had made many appearances for Notts each side of WW1, joining from Aston Villa, and leaving to become reserve team coach at Sheffield Wednesday. He spent three years as manager of Lincoln City before returning to Notts as manager.

His new spell began inauspiciously, with Notts relegated to the Third Division for the first time, despite Henshall's signing of Tom Keetley from Doncaster. However, the team bounced back after one season, with Keetley scoring 39 goals in 34 games. Henshall resigned as manager in 1934, stayed on as secretary for a year, and then ran the Navigation Inn near the ground.

Charlie Jones' spell as manager was a brief one. He made 100 appearances at outside left for Forest before moving to Arsenal in 1928, where he played 214 games for the famous Herbert Chapman side, winning three championship medals. Arsenal were not pleased when Notts "poached" him to be their manager, but neither were Notts pleased with his results as the side sank to the bottom of the table. With only one win in 17 games he was sacked. *David Pratt* played for Bradford City and Liverpool, and had had a successful spell as manager of Clapton Orient when he joined Notts in April, already relegated to Division Three. Unable to work the way he wanted to, he resigned in June after eight weeks in charge and returned to his native Scotland to manage Hearts. *Percy Smith* played for Preston and Blackburn and then managed Nelson and Bury before taking over at Spurs in 1930. He introduced an attacking, short passing game which was later to become a Spurs trademark, but relegation in 1935 led to an acrimonious departure. He had just over a year as Notts manager, signing Hughie Gallacher just before leaving for Bristol Rovers. *Jimmy McMullan* had a long spell as a player with Manchester City, and captained the famous Scottish "Wembley Wizards" side that beat England 5-1 at Wembley in 1928. After spells as manager at Oldham Athletic and Aston Villa he joined Notts in November 1936 and was thus re-united with Hughie Gallacher, another of the Wembley Wizards.

Harry Parkes' period as manager was also a brief one. He made his playing debut for West Bromwich Albion against Notts in 1907, and later joined Coventry City in the Southern League. He had spells as manager with Newport County, Chesterfield and Lincoln City, where he won the Third Division North championship in 1932. He moved to Mansfield before joining Notts in 1938. He signed the famous Bill "Dixie" Dean in March 1938, but injuries restricted Dean to just 3 goals for the club. Parkes retired in the summer of 1939. *Tony Towers* took over, made some new signings, and then found himself swept up into the confusions of wartime football. *Frank Womack* had been in charge at Leicester City and encouraged young players into the team. After he left in 1943, the club turned to the legendary "Major" *Frank Buckley* to see them through the rest of the war period. Buckley had been in charge at Wolves for 17 years, and was renowned for his somewhat unconventional methods of supposed "monkey gland" injections for the players, and the use of psychologists. He resigned from Notts in 1946 to take on the challenge of getting Hull City to the First Division (Hull remains the largest English city never to have had a First Division club).

Arthur Stollery was Chelsea's trainer just before WW2. During the war, he served as a PE expert in the RAF. He made an immediate impact at Meadow Lane by flying to Canada to sign Fred Whittaker. This was nothing compared with what was to follow in October 1948 - the signing of Tommy Lawton for a record fee. Tommy had known Arthur at Chelsea, and that played a part in his decision to join the Third Division club. Ill health forced Stollery's resignation in February 1949. The club secretary, *Wilf Fisher* looked after playing matters until the end of the season, whilst the ambitious directors looked round for a successor. *Eric Houghton* had been playing for Notts since 1946, after a long and successful career at Aston Villa. He led the talented team to promotion in his first season in charge, but after selling Sewell and Lawton, fortunes declined. Houghton resigned and rejoined Aston Villa, where he was to manage the 1957 F.A. Cup winning side. *George Poyser* was a full back with Mansfield Town and Port Vale before having a long spell at Brentford. He was coach at Wolves when he took over at Notts. The highlight of his period at the club was the run to the sixth round of the cup in 1955, but he was sacked after the defeat by Rhyl in 1957.

Frank Broome had a distinguished playing career with Aston Villa and Derby County, winning seven caps for England and taking part in the "Nazi salute" game with Germany in 1938. He played in the Notts team from 1949, leaving to join Tommy Lawton at Brentford. He rejoined Notts as assistant trainer in 1955, and took over the reins as caretaker manager following Poyser's dismissal. His successor was *Tommy Lawton*. Lawton's spell as player-manager at Brentford had not ended successfully, and he joined Arsenal as a player in 1953 at the age of 33. He moved into management with Kettering Town, and was a popular choice to come to Notts as manager. However, the club's playing record in 1957/58 was poor, compounded by the fact that Forest had won promotion. Relieved of the manager's duties, he considered playing again, but settled for retirement in July 1958. *Frank Hill* had been another of Chapman's Arsenal team of the 1930s, and had managed Crewe, Burnley and Preston before joining Notts. Though his first season in charge saw the club relegated to Division Four, he did lead them back at the first attempt, and introduced a young Tony Hateley to the side. His contract was not renewed in November 1961 and he later worked at Charlton.

Tim Coleman was a Nottinghamshire man who started playing with Grimsby Town before his transfer to Arsenal for a record fee at the time. He won a championship medal in 1933 and then moved on to play for Middlesbrough and Norwich. He joined Notts as assistant to Frank Hill and introduced Jeff Astle to the side when he took over as manager. *Eddie Lowe* won three international caps with Aston Villa and played over 500 games for Fulham. He joined Notts as player-manager, making eight appearances the first season, and one next. His first decision was to sell Tony Hateley to Aston Villa for £20,000, but his successor Terry Bly did not reproduce the scoring form that he had shown with Peterborough. Notts dropped to the bottom of Division Three and found themselves back in the bottom drawer. Lowe was sacked when results did not pick up in 1965. Tim Coleman resumed control, and with *Andy Beattie* helped steer the club through a financial crisis. Andy Beattie won Scottish International caps with Preston, guested for many clubs during WW2, and managed or scouted for a dozen or so more, including a spell in charge of the Scottish team. He took over from Billy Walker as Forest's manager in 1960. Beattie joined Notts as a professional advisor and general manager, and later looked after team selection when Jack Burkitt was taken ill.

Jack Burkitt was a top class wing half who had captained the victorious Forest side in the 1959 Cup Final. He took over with the Magpies in mid-table in the Fourth Division and results were not going too well the next season when he was forced to take leave of absence before retiring as manager. He later worked as trainer at Derby County with Brian Clough and Peter Taylor, and ran the Post Office on Oakdale Road. *Billy Gray* was another Forest player who had played in the 1959 Cup Final. A classic winger, he had also played for Leyton Orient, Chelsea and Burnley. He was player-manager at Millwall and manager at Brentford before joining Notts. Gray was unable to shift the club from the lower reaches of the Fourth Division, and just one win in nine games forced his resignation. His signings included Les Bradd and Don Masson. The club turned to trainer *Jack Wheeler* as acting manager, which stretched to 14 months in charge, more than many another "permanent" manager has enjoyed!

A man with a chirpy grin and typically "dry" Scottish humour was appointed manager in November 1969, for what turned out to be the first of three separate spells in charge. *Jimmy Sirrel* played for Celtic after the war, and then joined Bradford, Brighton and Aldershot. He had had two years hard work as manager of Brentford before joining Notts. A rejuvenated team stormed to the Fourth Division championship in 1971, helped by the re-signing of Tony Hateley. He built a team around Masson, Needham and Bradd that was good enough to finish fourth and then second in Division Three, thus returning the Magpies to Division Two for the first time since 1958. Seeking a new challenge, Sirrel resigned to manage Sheffield United, but couldn't rediscover the magic he had created at Meadow Lane. He was sacked in September 1977 but was only out of work for two weeks before rejoining Notts. In the interim, *Ronnie Fenton* had kept the club in the top half of the division. Fenton played primarily at West Bromwich, and joined Notts as youth team coach. After taking over as manager he brought Colin Addison in as coach. Fenton was not the first nor the last manager to find a run of bad form costs you your job; ten games without a win at the start of season 1977/78 brought him the sack. He later worked as assistant manager to Brian Clough on the other bank of the Trent.

Sirrel's second spell in charge lasted until July 1982, when he became general manager and later, a director. If his earlier achievements were considerable, he capped this by leading Notts back to the First Division in 1981, when they finished second in Division Two. They also reached the final of the Anglo-Scottish cup that season. Sirrel handed over the ropes to a young coach whose playing career with Sheffield Wednesday and Brighton had not been particularly spectacular. *Howard Wilkinson* kept the club in 15th place in Division One before leaving to take Sheffield Wednesday to promotion and then the winning of the League championship with Leeds United. His successor was *Larry Lloyd*. As a player, he was at the heart of the defence of two clubs who enjoyed tremendous success, Liverpool and Nottingham Forest. He played in both of Forest's European successes and won four England caps. He joined Wigan Athletic as player-manager, took them to promotion, but was then sacked. With Notts, he signed O'Neill and Fashanu, but was sacked when the Magpies found themselves back at the bottom of Division Two. *Richie Barker* returned to the club he had played for in the late 1960s after managing Shrewsbury Town and Stoke, and being assistant manager at Wolves. He was unable to stop the decline in the club's fortunes and was sacked in April 1985.

Back came Jimmy Sirrel for the third time. There was no magic this time, but they maintained a respectable position in Division Three. He retired in May 1987 to do some scouting for Derby County. The new manager was *John Barnwell*, a midfield general with Arsenal, Forest and Sheffield United. He started in management with Peterborough and then joined Wolves. There he sold Steve Daley for more than a million pounds, and then signed Andy Gray for £1.4 million. However, results were mixed, and he resigned from Wolves. Spells in Saudi Arabia and Greece followed. Notts reached the play-offs under his management, but he was sacked the following December with the club struggling in Division Three.

John Newman had been assistant-manager and coach under Barnwell, and assumed the role of caretaker for a month. *Neil Warnock* had played in the lower divisions of the Football League, but established his reputation as a manager by taking Scarborough to the Conference championship and automatic promotion to the Football League. Warnock revitalised Notts' playing record, and Wembley victories in successive years in the play-offs took the club back to the top flight. Life in the First Division was always going to be difficult with limited resources, and Warnock found past achievements no security when he was fired in January 1993 with the club back in Division Two.

Mick Walker took over team affairs, and enjoyed moderate success in 1994, reaching the final of the Anglo-Italian Cup at Wembley and narrowly missing a play-off place. Walker had been with the Magpies since 1980, helping to develop the youth scheme. However, indifferent early season form found him replaced by *Russell Slade*. Slade had also been at the club for many seasons, working with the youth team and the reserves. Within weeks, *Howard Kendall* was appointed as manager, with Slade continuing as his assistant. Kendall had a distinguished playing career with Preston, Everton, Birmingham and Stoke. He was player-manager at Blackburn Rovers, then led Everton to League and Cup triumphs. Later he managed Athletico Bilbao and Manchester City before returning for a second spell at Everton. Kendall was unable to improve the teams' League performances, though was in charge at Wembley when the Magpies won the Anglo-Italian trophy. He was sacked in March 1995 and replaced by caretaker-managers Wayne Jones, Steve Nicol (signed by Kendall from Liverpool) and Dean Thomas. In June 1995, *Colin Murphy* was appointed as General Manager, with *Steve Thompson* in charge of team matters.

Magpies' players have gone on to manage elsewhere, notably David Calderhead and Herbert Chapman. Calderhead was in charge of Chelsea for 26 years, from 1907 to 1933, a feat never likely to be repeated! Chapman played seven games for the club in 1903/04 and went on to gain outstanding success as a manager with Huddersfield Town and Arsenal.

Jack Peart was manager of Fulham when he died in 1948. Tommy Johnston managed Rotherham United when they reached the League Cup Final in 1961, and also managed Grimsby Town and Huddersfield Town.

NAME
The club has never had the company name of "Notts County", though of course it trades under that name. In the early years, they were just known as "Notts.", with the full stop, indicating "the club from Nottingham". Some reports spell the name out in full; "Nottinghamshire". It was only with the growth of the game in the 1880s that it became necessary to distinguish Notts. from other Nottingham teams like Olympic, Mellors and Rangers. In match reports, you will still find them called Notts., but Notts County is used in fixture lists from the early 1880s. Also, when the Nottinghamshire F.A. was formed in 1882, it became necessary to distinguish the club side from the county representative side (even if the club side was called "County"!)

In 1890, the club applied to the Football Association for a change of name, from "Notts. FC" to "Notts. Incorporated FC", and it is by this name that they were registered as a limited company. An attempt was made in the 1920's to reform the club as "Notts County" but this came to nothing, and the official title of the club at Company House remains Notts Incorporated.

NICKNAMES
The club have been nicknamed "The Magpies" ever since they changed their colours from chocolate and blue to black and white at the time of the conversion to a limited company in 1890. Before this they were known as "The Lambs" and the two nicknames ran in harness for a number of years. Even in the early 1900s, newspaper writers switch between the two during the same match report. For instance, the Nottingham Daily Express of April 11th, 1893, reporting a friendly at Kettering, says: *"The first appearance of the "Magpies" in Northamptonshire had been sufficiently advertised, consequently a large number of spectators assembled to see the famous "Lambs."*

The origin of the name "Lambs" as applied to Notts County is more obscure. In the 18th Century, the mob of hooligans from the Narrow Marsh slums were known as the Lambs, particularly with regard to their activities at elections. When England played Nottingham on the Forest at cricket in 1817, the crowd, who invaded the pitch, were described as "the Lambs." In their early days, Notts County were notorious for rough tactics, especially in the Birmingham area, and it is likely that this is the reason for "The Lambs" being appropriated for the town's football club - namely, their very un-lamb like behaviour on the field of play!

NOTTS COUNTY CUP

This competition was instituted by the Nottinghamshire F.A. in 1936/37 and continued until the outbreak of war. It was restarted in 1960/61. Only the three Football League clubs who are members of the Notts F.A., Notts County, Nottingham Forest and Mansfield Town, compete for the trophy although in pre-war seasons Newark Town, now defunct but then in the Midland League, also took part.

The Magpies' first match in the competition was against Mansfield Town on Oct. 14th, 1936, resulting in a 5-1 win for the club. This remains their record win in the competition and Harry Mardon's hat-trick is still the club's only one in County Cup matches. This victory qualified Notts to meet Nottingham Forest in the final at Meadow Lane on Oct. 28th, 1936. The result was a 1-0 win for the Magpies after extra time, and they thus became the first holders of the County Cup. Since then the club have won the trophy in 1962/63, 1974/75, 1975/76, 1984/85 and 1993/94.

The attendance for the game with Forest on April 14th, 1964 was 14,442, the best at Meadow Lane. 22,851 saw the game with Forest at the City Ground on May 9th, 1967.

PENALTY KICKS

The penalty kick was introduced into the Football League for the 1891/92 season. Among the incidents which influenced its introduction was one during the F.A. Cup match between Notts County and Stoke at Trent Bridge on Feb. 14th, 1891. Stoke, losing 1-0, were in a scoring position with goalkeeper George Toone well beaten but left-back John Hendry fisted the ball away. Stoke were awarded a free-kick but the ball was cleared and Notts went on to win 1-0.

The first recorded scorer from a penalty for the club was Jimmy Logan in the F.A.Cup match against Burton Wanderers on Feb. 10th, 1894. In a Football League match the first recorded Notts. penalty scorer was Elijah Allsopp against Bury on Nov. 24th, 1894.

The first use of the penalty kick as a tie-breaker in a competitive match was in the County Cup semi-final against Mansfield Town on May 1st, 1975. After a 0-0 draw, Notts won 5-4 on penalties.

Most penalties converted in a season is seven, by Arthur Green (1903/04), Kevin Randall (1972/73) and Ray O'Brien (1979/80).

Messrs Randall, Masson and Stubbs all missed the same penalty against Portsmouth on September 22nd 1973. The kick was retaken twice because of encroachments and the third was missed!

PLAYER OF THE YEAR

First presented in 1965 by the Supporters' Club to the Notts County footballer voted Player of the Year. The winners are:

1964/65:	George Smith	1980/81:	Don Masson
1965/66:	Brian Bates	1981/82:	Iain McCulloch
1966/67:	Alex Gibson	1982/83	Raddy Avramovic
1967/68:	Keith Smith	1983/84	Chiedozie/Christie *
1968/69:	Don Masson	1984/85	Pedro Richards
1969/70:	David Needham	1985/86	Tristan Benjamin
1970/71:	Brian Stubbs	1986/87	Dean Yates
1971/72;	Les Bradd	1987/88	Geoff Pike
1972/73:	Roy Brown	1988/89	Chris Withe
1973/74:	Don Masson	1989/90	Phil Turner
1974/75:	John Brindley	1990/91	Craig Short
1975/76:	Ray O'Brien	1991/92	Steve Cherry
1976/77:	Arthur Mann	1992/93	Dave Smith
1977/78:	Mick Vinter	1993/94	Phil Turner
1978/79:	Eric McManus	1994/95	Shaun Murphy
1979/80:	David Hunt		

John Chiedozie and Trevor Christie shared the award in 1984.

PLAYERS

The first-ever season of the Football League in 1888/89 consisted of a programme of only 22 matches. In these matches 33 players represented the club and this remained the most players ever used by Notts until recent seasons. A new record was set in 1994/95 when 36 players made first team appearances.

The lowest number to represent the club in a Football League season is 17 during the Division Four championship winning campaign of 1970/71. This figure was equalled in 1908/09 in Division One but the programme then was of 38 matches.

PLAYER'S UNION

The first Player's Union was formed in 1897 and lasted until 1901. The Union won a significant victory against Notts in 1898; the club were forced to pay wages and expenses to a player who had to undergo treatment for an injury received during a game. David Calderhead served on the Management Committee, and Walter Bull played for an English XI against a Scottish XI at Ibrox Park on Mar. 26th 1900, one of three fund raising "internationals" organised by the Union.

The Union reformed in 1907. Harry Mainman was elected as the first chairman of the new organisation; he had played 130 games for Notts at his retirement in 1906/07. When tackling, he was said to be able to wrap his legs "like an octopus" around opposing forwards.

The Union reformed again after the First World War, with Harold Henshall serving on the Management Committee. It was renamed the Professional Footballer's Association in 1958.

PLAY-OFFS

Play offs were introduced in 1986/87 to settle League promotion and relegation issues. Four teams take part in each of the three competitions with two semi-finals (played over two legs) and a final. The finals were also played over two legs, but since 1990 have been a single game at Wembley Stadium. Notts have appeared in three play-offs, failing at the two legged semi-final stage in 1987/88 (Third Division), but successful in two successive seasons - 1989/90 (Third Division) and 1990/91 (Second Division)

POINTS

Two for a win:
The club's record season for point scoring was in winning the championship of the Fourth Division in 1970/71 when they totalled 69 points from the 46 games played. In a 42 match season, the record is the 59 points obtained in 1930/31 when the club were champions of the Third Division South. In a 38 match season the best is 53 points in 1913/14 when champions of the Second Division.

Three for a win:
The best season with three points for a win was season 1989/90, when 87 points were gained in Division Three.

PROGRAMMES

When the Author was a lad, programme vendors used to shout *"Programmes, card of the match, three pence."* Programmes were originally just that, a single sheet of card with a stylised picture of the players on one side, and advertisements on the back. Cards such as this date back to the 1880s.

By the 1890s, the number of pages had increased. The players' names still appeared on the front page, in 2-3-5 formation. Though the other pages were largely for advertising, some editorial comment appeared. Cards for Notts and Forest games were printed by Mr. C.H. Richards of Lower Parliament Street. A good reason for buying the Richards' card was the introduction of a results board in 1898. The card provided the key to the letters on the board, to show which game was which. Due to appear on 19th November, it was reported that the board could not be completed in time, and so the half time scores would be carried round the ground on a board attached to a post. The main board was ready for the game against Everton on December 3rd 1898. Programmes followed the same style until just before World War One.

The next three styles of programme were relatively long lasting, from 1920-34, 1934-51 and 1951-61. A black and white cover with a County logo and an advertisement meant that the general style remained unaltered throughout this time. Then as now, advertisements had a large part to play in the contents!

The years since 1961 have seen the programme contract and expand in physical dimensions and contents: centenary year programmes were a handy pocket size 11cm by 14cm, and a newspaper style format was adopted in the mid 1970s. The use of colour makes todays' programme attractive, but regrettably indistinguishable from the offerings of most other League clubs.

The price is not shown on early programmes, but was held at 2d. from 1919 to 1948/49. By 1970, the cost had risen to 1s., 1980 to 25p, and 1990 saw the first £1 programme.

PROMOTIONS
Notts have been promoted on 11 occasions, the same number as Birmingham City. The club with the best promotion record is Grimsby Town on 12, which gives Notts something to aim at in future seasons!

PROTESTS
During the early days of competitive football, protests were almost as much part of the game as bookings and sendings off are now. Notts were involved in a number of notorious protests.

1881/82: County beat Wednesbury Strollers 5-3 at the Castle Ground in the second round of the F.A.Cup on Nov. 24th, 1881. Strollers protested that the result should have been 3-3, claiming two of the goals had been allowed by the referee who was a Nottingham man, L.O. Lindley; also that Notts full-back H.T. Moore was not properly qualified and played under the name "Wheeler", plus the fact that the crowd had encroached on the pitch and threatened the visiting team and umpire. The F.A. upheld the protest and ordered a replay on a neutral ground with a neutral referee. This was duly played at Derbyshire County Cricket Ground on Dec. 10th, 1881, resulting in an 11-1 win for Notts.

1889/90: County lost to Sheffield Wednesday 5-0 at Olive Grove in the third round of the F.A.Cup on Feb.15, 1890. Notts protested about the state of the pitch and the weather conditions. The game would never have started under today's rules; rain and snow fell in sheets before and during the game. Wednesday also protested, just in case they lost. The protest was upheld and the match replayed at the same venue on February 22nd. This time County won 3-2, but Wednesday protested that Notts had included three ineligible players. This protest was also upheld, and the next replay was at the Derbyshire cricket ground. Wednesday won 2-1. Notts are reported to have considered another protest, but probably thought better of it!

1891/92: Notts lost to Sunderland 3-0 at the Newcastle Road ground in the first round of the F.A.Cup on Jan. 16th, 1892. They protested about the state of the pitch and the weather conditions. The protest was upheld and the match was replayed at the same venue on Jan. 23rd. This time Sunderland won 4-0.

RE-ELECTION
Although the club have never been forced to apply for re-election to Divisions Three (South) or Four, they did have to submit to this indignity in the days when the Football League consisted of just twelve clubs. The seasons involved were the very first two of the League, 1888/89 and 1889/90. At that time the four bottom clubs had to apply for re-election and in 1888/89, Notts finished 11th. All four clubs regained their places but Notts finished bottom of the four in the voting, just two votes ahead of Birmingham St. George's. The poll was: Stoke 10, Burnley 9, Derby County 8, Notts County 7, Birmingham St. George's 5, Sheffield Wednesday 4, Bootle 2, Sunderland 2, Newton Heath 1, and no votes for Grimsby, South Shore, Sunderland Albion and Nelson. The club finished 10th in 1889/90 but this time Aston Villa and Bolton Wanderers were voted in without going to the poll. After that Notts and Burnley were voted back in without any worries but Sunderland were elected in place of Stoke.

There was a struggle to avoid having to apply for re-election to Division 4 in 1966/67, 1967/68 and 1968/69. In the first of these seasons the club finished in 20th position out of 24, missing one of the bottom places on goal average ahead of Rochdale. Both teams had 37 points but Rochdale's goal average was 0.030 worse. For 1967/68, the final position was 17th, five points ahead of a re-election position after wins in the last two matches of the season. Early in 1968/69, the club were bottom of the Football League after taking only eight points from the first 16 matches but after a revival they finished 19th, three points ahead of York City who were forced to apply for re-election. York actually beat Notts 2-0 on April 23rd, but County then took three points from their two remaining matches.

RELEGATIONS

The Magpies have been relegated on 13 occasions (upto 1994/95), more than any other Football League club. Next come Birmingham City on 11, then Grimsby Town, Preston North End and Bolton Wanderers on 10.

RESERVE TEAM

Matches by a Notts' second team developed during the 1870s and by the 1880s a full reserve team programme was in operation. For a few years at the beginning of the 1890s the reserves played under the title of Notts Rovers and it was as the Rovers that they joined the Midland Alliance in 1890/91, winning the championship in their first season of league football.

Competitions played in:

Midland Alliance	1890/91 to 1892/93
Friendlies	1893/94
Notts League	1894/95 to 1903/04
Midland League	1904/05 to 1906/07
Notts League	1907/08
Midland League	1908/09 to 1912/13
Central Alliance	1913/14 to 1914/15
Midland League	1919/20 to 1923/24
Midland Combination	1924/25 to 1926/27
Midland League	1927/28 to 1938/39
	1945/46 to 1957/58
Football Combination	1958/59 to 1966/67
North Midland League	1967/68 to 1981/82
Central (Pontins) League	1982/83 onwards

In addition the following competitions:

Midland Midweek League	1933/34 to 1934/35
	1950/51 to 1959/60
Midlands Senior League	1944/45
Central Alliance	1956/57
North Midlands Combination	1957/58 to 1959/60
Midland Intermediate League	1960/61

The following championships have been won:

Midland Alliance	1890/91
Notts League	1903/04 and 1907/08
Central Alliance	1914/15
Midland League	1954/55
Midland Midweek League	1957/58
North Midland League	1973/74

RUGBY FOOTBALL

The Notts' directors gave permission for a Rugby League Test match to be staged at Meadow Lane during the 1911/12 season. Accordingly, England met the touring Australian team on December 6th, 1912, the result being a win for England by 5 points to 3.

During World War Two, Notts Lincs and Derby XV met an RAF XV at Meadow Lane under the Union code on March 3rd 1945. The RAF won 10-9 before 2,500 people. Rugby League returned in 1986 when the Mansfield Marksmen met Fulham before 950 spectators.

SEASONS

The length of the season was extremely short in the early days of the club, running from early November until the middle of March. With the expansion of the fixture list, the season began to grow, and from 1876/77, the club usually began their fixtures early in October and completed them by the end of March. The next major expansion of the season took place after the formation of the Football League and was directly due to the large number of Scottish professionals the club signed on. To enable the wage bill to be met, it was necessary to play an extensive range of away friendly matches with a guaranteed cash return. Almost the whole of April 1890 was taken up with such matches. At this stage the season settled down to run from September 1st until the last Saturday in April. This remained the norm until after the First World War when, for 1919/20, the season ran from August 30th until May 1st.

Throughout the inter-war years, the last Saturday in August until the first Saturday in May was the general rule, except for charity games which could be played later if permission was obtained.

The big freeze-up of 1946/47 saw that season extended until the end of May, the Magpies last match being on May 29th, the latest date on which they have played a League fixture. The following season saw the programme begin a week earlier, on August 23rd, and this became the practice until the late 1960s.

Nowadays, seasons are stretched by pre-season tournaments and friendlies, and the end of season play offs. Notts can claim to have played competitive football every month of the year! They met Brighton in the 1991 play-off on June 2nd, and played a Watney Cup tie and an Anglo-Scottish Cup game in late July.

SECRETARIES

In the early days of the club playing members also filled the various official posts. The first non "player-secretary" was Edwin Browne, the assistant secretary of the Nottinghamshire County Cricket Club, who took office for the 1882/83 season. Another type of secretary developed just before the First World War and continued to be popular until the start of the Second War. This was the "secretary-manager", whose duties included running the team as well as the secretarial work. The first secretary-manager appointed by the Magpies was Albert Fisher who took office on August 1, 1913. Following the resumption of the club's activities in 1942, Wilfred Fisher became the full-time secretary, to be succeeded by Charles "Chick" Heath and Dennis Marshall. Previous to this, Mr. Fisher had worked in the office and handled much secretarial work for the so-called secretary-managers. The complete list of secretaries is as follows:

J. Patterson 1864 to 1866; E.B. Steegman 1866 to 1868; C.L. Rothera 1868 to 1870; F.W. Rothera 1870 to 1872; E.H. Greenhalgh 1872 to 1879; T.A. Oliver 1879-80; H.T. Morse 1880-81; H.A. Cursham 1881-82; E.C. Browne 1882-83 to June 1893; T.R. Featherstone June 1893 to Dec. 1893; T.E. Harris Dec. 1893 to June 1913; G.E. Osborne Mar. 1913 (appointed during illness of Mr. Harris) to Aug. 1913; A. Fisher (secretary-manager) Aug. 1913 to May 1927; R.C. White July 1917 to Jan. 1919 (during .Mr. Fisher's absence in the armed forces); H.V. Henshall June 1927 to April 1935 (secretary-manager to May 5, 1934, then continued as secretary only); D. Pratt (secretary-manager) April 1935 to June 1935; F.J. Smith (secretary-manager) July 1935 to Oct. 1936; J. McMullan (secretary-manager) Nov. 1936 to Dec. 1937; H. Parkes (secretary-manager) Dec. 1938 to July 1939; J.R. Towers (secretary-manager) July 1939 to July 1942; W. Fisher July 1942 to Nov. 1956; C.H. Heath Nov. 1956; D. Marshall Feb. 1973, L.G. Hayward, June 1981; Ken Mott 1983; Neal Hook 1984 (also as Chief Executive), Ian Moat 1995.

SUBSTITUTES

From the 1965/66 season the Football League allowed one substitute per game in place of an injured player. The F.A. and Football League Cup competitions allowed one substitute from the following season. With the start of the 1967/68 season substitutes were allowed without the need for replacing injured players only. This recognition that substitutes could be used for tactical reasons led to an increase to two per game, and in 1994/95 two outfield players plus a goalkeeper.

Notts first substitute called on was Dennis Shiels who came on for injured outside-right Brian Bates after 75 minutes of the Division Four home game against Lincoln City on Feb. 5th, 1966. It is believed that Notts were the last League club to first use a substitute that season. The first substitute to score a goal for the club in a Football League match was Richie Barker. He netted against Southport on March 13th, 1971, after replacing Les Bradd.

Before the substitute rule was introduced for competitive matches, they had sometimes been allowed in friendlies by mutual consent. The earliest record of one being used was in the match against Leek on December 17th, 1887, when Brown was substituted, having hurt his shoulder. Another example was the game with Rangers on Jan. 2nd, 1902 when Walter Bull replaced Ellis Gee at outside-left after half-time.

961 substitutions have been made in 823 League games to the end of 1994/95. 151 different players have made an appearance as a substitute; the players with most are W. Fairclough (32), I.J. McParland and M. Vinter (both 31). 154 players have been substituted; the players who have taken an early bath most often are T. Johnson (37), L. Bradd (35) and G. Lund (32). 29 substitutes have scored goals; the leading three are M. Vinter (5), G. Lund and T. Christie (both with 4). The numbers of substitutes used in League games are as follows:

1965/66	3	1980/81	23
1966/67	11	1981/82	29
1967/68	24	1982/83	33
1968/69	15	1983/84	27
1969/70	17	1984/85	27
1970/71	19	1985/86	28
1971/72	32	1986/87	35
1972/73	23	1987/88	45 (13)
1974/75	22	1988/89	54 (15)
1975/76	31	1989/90	46 (16)
1976/77	32	1990/91	53 (17)
1977/78	30	1991/92	63 (27)
1978/79	22	1992/93	63 (21)
1980/81	28	1993/94	39 (8)
		1994/95	64 (21)

Numbers in brackets are the number of games in which two substitutes were used.

SUNDAY GAMES

Sunday games are now regular occurrences, but it was not always so. The Football League first sanctioned Sunday matches during the power crisis of 1974. The club's first was against Crystal Palace at Meadow Lane on Sunday, January 20th, 1974. The match against Nottingham Forest at the City Ground was also played on a Sunday, in this case March 3rd, 1974.

The Club's first Sunday game of all, dates back to the third match of the first continental tour to Denmark in 1910 when they beat a Danish XI 2-1 in Copenhagen on June 5th.

TEST MATCHES

When Division Two of the Football League was formed for the 1892/93 season it was decided that promotion and relegation should be decided by means of Test matches between the clubs involved. For three seasons the arrangement was that the top team in Division Two met the bottom in Division One on a neutral ground, the runners-up met the second from bottom and the third placed team met the third from bottom. The winners of the three matches, or replays where necessary, went into Division One for the following season.

From 1895/96, for three seasons, a different system was used. This time only the top two and bottom two teams were involved. They played in a mini-league, each team meeting the two from the rival division but not the one in their own division. This meant that they each played four matches and from the resulting mini-league the top two went into Division One the following season. The method was abandoned after 1897/98 when the League was extended and automatic promotion and relegation introduced.

Notts were involved in test matches in 1893, 1894, 1895 and 1897.

THIRD DIVISION CUP

At the 1933 annual meeting of the Football League the Southern and Northern sections of the Third Division were given permission to run their own knock-out cup competitions and these were continued until the outbreak of World War Two. Following Notts' relegation from Division Two in 1934/35, they took part in the Southern Section Cup from 1935/36 to 1938/39 inclusive. The club's best season was 1936/37 when they reached the semi-finals, playing a 1-1 draw with Watford. Because of fixture congestion the replay was held at the start of the 1937/38 season, the Magpies losing 8-3, their record defeat in the competition. Immediately afterwards they again met Watford in the second round of the 1937/38 competition (having a bye in the first round), losing again, this time 2-0.

THROW INS

Andy Legg won a place in the Guinness Book of Records with his ability to throw the ball. His official world record is 41.6 metres and he has a "personal best" of 46.5 metres.

TOURS

Notts' first visit overseas was to play three games in Denmark in June 1910, at the invitation of the Akadezuisk Boldklub. A guarantee of £200 was accepted. Three games against Danish XI's resulted in two wins and a draw.

Promotion to Division One in 1914 was celebrated with a trip to Spain for three games against Barcelona. Notts won all three, by 3-1, 4-2 and 10-3! The journey took 39 hours of non-stop travel, taking in the midnight boat to Calais, train to Paris, coaches to the Quay d'Orsai station, and a change at Toulouse. The Spanish frontier was reached at 3am, where the luggage was examined by the Spanish customs. The Barcelona team had three English professionals, one of whom was Greenway, formerly with Woolwich Arsenal. Admission to the ground for the games was two pesetas, the equivalent then of 1/7d. The ground was described as *"hard as flagstones"*, with not a blade of grass. In the final game, Notts reached half time 1-2 down, so nine of the goals came in the second half. A number of the party went to see a bullfight; director Alderman John Houston wrote subsequently that, *"the view of all was that it is a disgusting and cruel performance, and the sooner Spanish people exchange it for football, the better for the Spanish people."*

A second trip to Spain took place in 1922. A match was played with St. Mirren, also on tour, resulting in a 1-2 defeat. Two games with Barcelona then followed. Other trips were to Denmark in 1923, and Central Europe in 1925, with games in Vienna and Prague.

Notts visited Cologne in October 1945 to play one game against the British Army XI, winning 5-2. Other tours since the war have seen the club in East Africa, Holland, Italy, Spain and Gibraltar.

The first season of the Football League coincided with a tour of a party of footballers from Canada. Their trip included games with many of the League clubs. Notts met them on October 4th 1888 and won 2-0 at Trent Bridge.

TRIAL MATCHES
Up until the start of the Second World War, official trial matches were held by the England selectors. The club's representatives in these were:

Ashurst, W	England v Rest, 1924/25
Barry, L.J.	Amateurs v Professionals, 1923/24; England v Rest, 1925/26
Bull, W.	North v. South, 1899/00 & 1900/01
Chapman, H	North v South, 1882/83
Cursham, H.A.	North v South, 1882/83 & 1883/84
Dobson, A.T.C.	North v South, 1881/82, 1882/83 & 1883/84
Emberton, F.P.	Stripes v Whites, 1910/11
Greenhalgh, E.H.	North v South, 1870/71
Gunn, W.	North v South, 1883/84 & 1885/86
Iremonger, A.	Stripes v Whites, 1910/11
Macrae, S.	North v South, 1883/84
Moore, H.T.	North v South, 1882/83
Morley, H.	Whites v Stripes, 1909/10
Prescott, T.G.	North v South, 1898/99
Rothera, C.L.	North v South, 1870/71
Shelton, A.	Whites v Stripes, 1889/90, North v South, 1890/91
Toone, G.	North v South 1890/91, Whites v Stripes, 1891/92
Walkerdine, H.	Whites v Stripes, 1891/92

TRAINERS
The position of the trainer evolved during the 1880s along with the growth of professionalism. As with many other traditional football occupations it is difficult to define just who the first trainer was. However, by 1890 the position was being filled by Henry Kirk, although during the club's F.A.Cup run in 1890/91, former goalkeeper and Notts CCC wicket-keeper Mordecai Sherwin was called in to take charge. It is clear that the directors were not completely satisfied with Kirk for in 1891/92 former centre-half Herbert Emmitt was offered the job but he declined. The players themselves put in a petition to retain Kirk and he stayed until the club were relegated at the end of the 1892/93 season; perhaps the reason why the players were happy with him may have something to do with lax discipline!

Nowadays, trainers prefer the name of "physio" and spend more time in the dressing room with potions, sprays, and exercise machines, than they used to do in the old days, when a bucket of cold water and a sponge was enough! For instance, in October 1932, Alf Feebery went down injured in the game at Swansea. Trainer Banks applied the sponge and told Alf to carry on. Alf collapsed a few more times, and on each occasion the sponge worked its magic. At half time, Alf found he couldn't get his boot back on. He went to hospital where it was discovered that he had played for twelve minutes with a broken leg!

The Notts trainers have been:

1893-1903	Joe Goode	1945-1948	T. Radcliffe
1903-1905	G. Swift	1948	Bill Corkhill (acting)
1905-1917	Tom Prescott	1948-1956	Bill Moore
1919-1927	James Iremonger	1956-1957	Vic Potts
1927-1929	Tom Radcliffe	1957-1983	Jack Wheeler
1929-1934	Fred Banks	1983-1986	John Short
1934-1936	Bill Seddon	1986-1989	Wayne Jones
1936-1938	T. Radcliffe	1989-1992	David Wilson
1938-1940	Ernie England	1992-1994	David Lawson
		1994-	Dennis Pettit

Whilst holding the post of trainer, Joe Goode appeared in the first team for the United Counties League match against Sheffield Wednesday in 1894/95. Jack Wheeler's record as trainer lasted 26 years and included over 1,000 consecutive matches, including a spell as caretaker-manager when he said it felt as though he was running the club single handed! Wheeler was goalkeeper at Kettering with Tommy Lawton, and came to Notts with Tommy. He was renowned for George Formby impressions with his ukulele; more of a threat than a promise to the players perhaps! He had a well deserved testimonial game in 1971, against Nottingham Forest.

TRANSFER FEES
In 1922 the Football League passed a regulation that all transfer fees should be treated as private and confidential so that fees as stated in the national and local press are only estimates. Because of the League ruling, Notts are unable to confirm the figures given here which have been taken from newspapers and football annuals.

The first four-figure transfer in which the Magpies were involved appears to be the sale of centre-forward Jimmy Cantrell to Tottenham Hotspur in Oct. 1912. The fee was £1,500. The record between the wars was £3,000, paid to St. Mirren in 1933 for George Walker.

Tommy Lawton was signed from Chelsea in November, 1947 for a fee of £20,000. This was the British record at the time, not bad for a Third Division club! The British record was again broken when Jackie Sewell was transferred to Sheffield Wednesday in March, 1951; the fee was £34,500. Notts record signing became Leon Leuty, who cost £25,000 when he signed from Bradford in 1950.

Notts record signings are now Tony Agana, who cost £750,000 from Sheffield United in November 1991, and John Chiedozie, who cost £600,000 when signed from Leyton Orient in August 1981. The record fees received are £2,500,000 from Derby County for Craig Short in September 1992, and £1,300,000 from the same club for Tommy Johnson in March 1992. Mark Draper's transfer fee of £1,250,000 when he moved to Leicester City in 1994 had to be settled by a tribunal after the clubs could not agree.

TRAWLERS
Notts had a trawler named after them in the 1960's. It eventually sank in Reykjavik harbour.

UNDER-21 CAPS

England	Scotland
Mark Draper (3) 1991,1992	Iain McCulloch (2) 1982
Tommy Johnson (5) 1991,1992	
Brian Kilcline (3) 1983	
Dean Yates (5) 1989	

UNITED COUNTIES LEAGUE
The United Counties League was formed during the summer of 1893. There were two sections, based on the West Midlands and East Midlands. Its aim was to fill up some of the dates between cup-ties near the end of the season which until then had mainly been given over to friendly matches. However the competition only lasted for two seasons. Clubs involved in critical positions in the Football League were reluctant to risk their leading players in these matches. In both seasons, Notts finished bottom of their section and in fact won only one match out of 13.

WATNEY CUP
A pre-season tournament played between 1970 and 1973. Notts played one game in 1972, losing to Sheffield United. The Watney Cup was the first sponsored tournament in English soccer, and it introduced the penalty shoot-out to the game.

WORLD WARS
During both World Wars the Football League competition was abandoned. One season was played at the beginning of World War I (season 1914/15), but at the beginning of World War II the competition was immediately abandoned with the Magpies having played two games of the new season.

In World War I, the Football League carried on with regional competitions and the Magpies took part in the Midland Section which was divided into a Principal Tournament and a Subsidiary Tournament.

The latter was run towards the end of the season when the Principal Tournament had been completed. The Magpies' season-by-season records in the Midland Section are as follows:

Principal Tournament	P	W	D	L	F	A	Pts	Position
1915/16	26	10	6	10	39	36	26	8th of 14
1916/17	30	13	6	11	47	52	32	7th of 16
1917/18	28	7	9	12	43	54	23	10th of 15
1918/19	30	16	9	5	65	38	41	3rd of 16
Subsidiary Tournament								
1915/16: Southern Div.	10	5	3	2	16	12	13	2nd of 6
1916/17: Group Four	6	1	2	3	9	12	4	4th of 4
1917/18: Group C	6	4	0	2	19	2	8	1st of 4
1918/19: Group B	6	2	0	4	13	13	4	3rd of 4

A system of Regional League football was also adopted during World War II. The F.A.Cup was cancelled until 1945/46. However a League Cup competition was organised, split into separate South and North events from 1942/43. The Magpies' season-by-season records in the various Regional Leagues follow. They did not compete during season 1941/42 because of bomb damage to Meadow Lane.

East Midlands Regional

1939/40	20	6	2	12	40	57	14	11th of 11

South Regional

1940/41	21	8	3	10	42	66	0.636	(30th of 34)

(goal average and not points decided the positions this season)

North Regional

The first championship ended on Dec. 25th and the second started on Dec. 26th.

1942/43 (1)	18	7	2	9	34	57	16	29th of 48
(2)	20	9	6	5	37	34	24	12th of 54
1943/44 (1)	18	4	3	11	26	53	11	47th of 50
(2)	20	3	0	17	23	68	6	54th of 56
1944/45 (1)	18	2	1	15	19	62	5	54th of 54
(2)	21	4	0	17	29	62	8	59th of 60

Division Three South (Northern Section)

1945/46	20	8	4	8	39	47	20	6th of 11

Division Three South Cup (Northern Section)

1945/46	16	5	0	11	17	31	10	11/11

Jimmy Cantrell was the Magpies leading scorer in the Midland Section matches for every season during World War I. He totalled 63 goals as follows; 1915/16 - 11; 1916/17 - 12; 1917/18 - 18, 1918/19 - 22. He also scored 13 goals in subsidiary tournament matches and two in friendlies, bringing his aggregate to 78. Leading scorer in World War II was a guest player, Colin Collindridge with 20 (12 in the League and 8 in the cups).

The biggest win in WWI was an 8-0 victory at home to Grimsby Town in the Midland Section on December 22nd, 1917. In the Second World War, Northampton Town were beaten 7-1 on October 13th 1945. Notts lost 4-11 at Walsall on November 9th, 1940, and 1-9 at home to Leicester City on October 30th, 1943.

Most appearances in WWI were by Jimmy Cantrell (127), WA Flint (101), S Richards (99) and Albert Iremonger (93). These figures are for the Midland Section Principal Tournament and the Subsidiary tournaments 1915-19. In WW2, much greater use was made of guest players, and tracking appearances is quite difficult! In 1943/44 for instance, more than 120 players appeared for the club, but only ten of these reached ten games. Regular players throughout the Second War were W.G. Corkhill (81) and A.A. Southwell (66). Notable first appearances for the club included Freddie Steele (39/40), Andy Beattie and Frank Broome (40/41), Colin Collindridge, Leon Leuty, Billy Wright and Tommy Lawton (42/43), Ian McPherson and Jackie Sewell (44/45) and Jesse Pye (45/46).

Statistical Introduction

1. The Players (pages 90 - 104)

The main part of this chapter lists all 832 players who have played in the Football League to the end of season 1994/95. The "first" and "last" seasons are the first year of each season; thus a player with the entry "1923   1929" appeared between seasons 1923/24 and 1929/30 inclusive. An entry in the first column only indicates that the player only appeared in a single season. "Two line" entries show that a player had two separate spells at the club, but his appearances and goal totals are combined.

The "appearances and goals" columns have headings for the Football League, the F.A. Cup, the Football League Cup and miscellaneous games. The latter column includes test matches, play-offs, the Third Division Cup, Watney Cup, Full and Associate Members Cups, Anglo-Scottish and Anglo-Italian Cups. I have not included the United Counties League as many reserve players were used for these fixtures.

Players with League appearances in the early years often have disproportionately large F.A. Cup appearance totals. This is due to their Cup appearances occurring over a much longer period than their League career.

Shorter lists of players comprise:
      (i)   Those who appeared in the F.A. Cup but made no League appearances (before 1888 and in 1945/46)
      (ii)   Those who played only in the League Cup or the miscellaneous tournaments
      (iii) Those who played only in the two expunged games from 1939/40
      (iv) All players who appeared in the two World Wars. For guest players, their club is noted where known.

2. Season by Season Statistics (pages 105 - 266)

No attempt has been made to specify line up details until 1879/80. From that year onwards, players numbered 1 to 11 have appeared in the following "traditional" positions:
1 Goal keeper.   2, 3 Right full back and left full back.   4, 6 Right and left half back, known as wing halves.
5 Centre half. Until the 1930s, this player often played in front of the wing halves.   7,11 Right and left wingers.
8, 10 Right and left inside forwards.   9 Centre forward.

From 1888/89 onwards, the grids show the results of all games in the Football League, F.A. Cup, Football League Cup and other competitive games played by the first team. Games which were expunged from the records because of the resignation of a club are not included. Attendances since 1925 are taken from the official Football League records; prior to 1925, estimated attendances from newspaper reports have been used.

The identification of goal scorers in early seasons is somewhat problematic. Reports often speak of the ball *"forced over the line in a scrimmage"*. The count of Harry Cursham's F.A. Cup goals is important as he is the record holder; all 49 have been checked with the local paper (but we have only the reporter's word for it of course). A continuing problem with goal scoring records is whether "own goals" should sometimes be credited to the player who made the shot; again, the report of the game has usually been used to try to decide where the credit should lie. The scorers of penalty goals are given when known, but it should be noted that there may be other instances that are not recorded.

Substitutes are shown with the numbers 12, 13 and 14. 12 is used if only one substitute is used, disregarding his actual shirt number. The players who came off have their numbers underlined. 13 is only used once in the book (1994/95 Anglo-Italian Cup Final). Cup round numbers (left of tables) are indicated thus: R = Round (R3 = 3rd round, R2/1 = 2nd round 1st leg, SF2 = Semi-final 2nd leg, etc.) rep = Replay. r2 = 2nd replay. Pr = Prel. round.

3. Other Games: Friendlies and The County Cup (Pages 267 - 270)

All non-cup games were "friendlies" of course until the formation of the Football League. Some of these traditional fixtures continued after the formation of the Football League, such as Boxing Day meetings with Nottingham Forest. Increasing financial pressures then caused tours to be undertaken to earn revenue, notably in April 1890. Testimonial and charity games have been a continuing tradition.

The Notts County Cup has provided regular competitive fixtures with Mansfield Town and Nottingham Forest; these games are indicated with "CC" after the result.

"Warm up" games have become a common pre-season activity in recent years. It is sometimes difficult to decide if these should be classified as "friendlies" or should just be regarded as practice games, especially since some are played behind closed doors.

NOTTS' LEAGUE RECORD AGAINST OTHER CLUBS

Present day club names are used throughout.

	P	W	D	L	F	A	W	D	L	F	A	F	A	% WON
			Home:					**Away:**				**Total Goals:**		
Accrington	10	4	1	0	22	4	2	0	3	14	11	36	15	60.00
Accrington Stanley	2	0	1	0	1	1	0	0	1	0	3	1	4	0.00
Aldershot	36	12	2	4	35	14	8	5	5	18	17	53	31	55.56
Arsenal	44	14	2	6	48	36	6	5	11	19	30	67	66	45.45
Aston Villa	66	13	8	12	52	49	3	7	23	29	83	81	132	24.24
Barnsley	58	14	3	12	59	46	3	13	13	28	46	87	92	29.31
Barrow	10	2	1	2	10	8	2	0	3	7	9	17	17	40.00
Birmingham C	52	13	8	5	48	26	5	6	15	25	44	73	70	34.62
Blackburn R	86	19	15	9	80	49	12	7	24	54	91	134	140	36.05
Blackpool	42	9	4	8	33	29	6	7	8	27	34	60	63	35.71
Bolton Wanderers	74	14	13	10	48	44	9	7	21	39	75	87	119	31.08
Bournemouth	38	10	2	7	34	30	3	6	10	16	29	50	59	34.21
Bradford City	44	11	7	4	35	21	10	3	9	36	40	71	61	47.73
Bradford Park Avenue	38	8	5	6	37	29	5	7	7	32	39	69	68	34.21
Brentford	46	13	5	5	38	21	3	8	12	19	40	57	61	34.78
Brighton & Hove Albion	38	10	3	6	31	22	6	6	7	28	34	59	56	42.11
Bristol City	80	21	10	9	65	37	8	8	24	42	71	107	108	36.25
Bristol Rovers	64	21	6	5	77	39	5	16	11	39	55	116	94	40.62
Burnley	42	15	4	2	60	17	2	6	13	12	34	72	51	40.48
Burton Utd.	8	4	0	0	22	4	2	2	0	8	3	30	7	75.00
Burton Wan.	6	2	0	1	8	4	2	0	1	6	2	14	6	66.67
Bury	82	23	10	8	69	48	9	10	22	36	70	105	118	39.02
Cambridge U	10	3	2	0	8	2	3	0	2	7	8	15	10	60.00
Cardiff City	48	13	5	6	43	28	9	4	11	35	36	78	64	45.83
Carlisle Utd.	14	6	0	1	11	6	3	0	4	8	11	19	17	64.29
Charlton Athletic	30	7	7	1	29	16	1	5	9	13	34	42	50	26.67
Chelsea	32	9	4	3	30	15	3	4	9	22	34	52	49	37.50
Chester City	24	6	5	1	22	13	5	2	5	18	20	40	33	45.83
Chesterfield	34	12	3	2	31	14	5	6	6	16	24	47	38	50.00
Colchester U	16	6	1	1	21	5	2	2	4	11	20	32	25	50.00
Coventry City	30	10	3	2	28	14	5	3	7	22	26	50	40	50.00
Crewe Alexandra	24	8	2	2	35	7	4	1	7	13	21	48	28	50.00
Crystal Palace	42	7	6	8	30	26	6	5	10	24	32	54	58	30.95
Darlington	20	6	4	0	26	10	3	1	6	18	27	44	37	45.00
Darwen	8	4	0	0	15	2	1	0	3	5	8	20	10	62.50
Derby Co.	54	10	9	8	39	35	4	9	14	25	48	64	83	25.93
Doncaster R	34	7	3	7	33	34	5	3	9	27	31	60	65	35.29
Everton	66	9	11	13	37	44	7	2	24	31	82	68	126	24.24
Exeter City	30	8	5	2	35	12	4	8	3	23	20	58	32	40.00
Fulham	56	12	10	6	52	28	4	3	21	32	78	84	106	28.57
Gainsborough Trinity	2	1	0	0	2	0	0	0	1	2	3	4	3	50.00
Gateshead	12	6	0	0	18	2	1	2	3	3	9	21	11	58.33
Gillingham	18	5	2	2	16	10	2	1	6	10	17	26	27	38.89
Glossop	4	0	2	0	2	2	1	1	0	1	0	3	2	25.00
Grimsby T	54	16	3	8	48	28	3	9	15	31	48	79	76	35.19
Halifax T	22	5	4	2	25	13	5	2	4	13	16	38	29	45.45
Hartlepool U	14	5	1	1	10	3	1	1	5	9	17	19	20	42.86
Hereford U	2	1	0	0	3	2	1	0	0	4	1	7	3	100.00
Huddersfield	20	6	2	2	16	8	2	2	6	6	16	22	24	40.00
Hull City	54	15	8	4	56	23	7	6	14	24	48	80	71	40.74
Ipswich T	22	5	0	6	20	23	5	2	4	15	10	35	33	45.45
Leeds City	2	1	0	0	4	0	1	0	0	4	2	8	2	100.00
Leeds Uunited	32	8	3	5	25	20	1	3	12	7	40	32	60	28.12
Leicester C	42	5	8	8	35	30	6	4	11	29	39	64	69	26.19
Leyton Orient	54	16	5	6	48	23	8	8	11	33	35	81	58	44.44
Lincoln C	44	14	7	1	41	14	10	5	7	30	31	71	45	54.55

	Home:						Away:					Total Goals:		
	P	W	D	L	F	A	W	D	L	F	A	F	A	% WON
Liverpool	60	12	7	11	46	41	2	5	23	17	69	63	110	23.33
Loughborough	4	2	0	0	5	1	2	0	0	4	1	9	2	100.00
Luton Town	50	7	9	9	31	38	2	5	18	23	62	54	100	18.00
Manchester City	56	14	7	7	43	25	3	4	21	17	61	60	86	30.36
Manchester Utd.	48	10	5	9	33	33	4	9	11	27	41	60	74	29.17
Mansfield T	22	7	3	1	22	10	4	3	4	13	17	35	27	50.00
Middlesbrough	54	15	7	5	50	34	4	2	21	23	64	73	98	35.19
Midlsbrough Ironopolis	2	1	0	0	3	0	0	1	0	0	0	3	0	50.00
Millwall	46	6	8	9	31	33	6	6	11	26	46	57	79	26.09
Newcastle U	60	12	7	11	37	39	5	8	17	34	75	71	114	28.33
Newport Co.	40	16	3	1	76	17	4	5	11	21	35	97	52	50.00
Northampton	34	14	1	2	36	16	5	5	7	21	29	57	45	55.88
Northwich Victoria	2	1	0	0	6	1	1	0	0	1	0	7	1	100.00
Norwich C	22	5	4	2	23	12	4	3	4	17	25	40	37	40.91
Nottm Forest	86	14	15	14	66	64	14	8	21	41	56	107	120	32.56
Oldham Ath.	62	20	7	4	51	27	6	8	17	37	62	88	89	41.94
Oxford United	16	4	3	1	12	5	1	3	4	10	16	22	21	31.25
Peterborough	16	5	3	0	17	6	1	3	4	6	12	23	18	37.50
Plymouth Argyle	30	12	0	3	30	11	7	5	3	26	22	56	33	63.33
Port Vale	74	21	9	7	88	44	12	10	15	43	55	131	99	44.59
Portsmouth	20	4	2	4	15	12	2	4	4	10	19	25	31	30.00
Preston North End	70	14	11	10	52	47	6	6	23	29	77	81	124	28.57
Queen's Park Rangers	36	6	7	5	23	21	5	3	10	22	31	45	52	30.56
Reading	42	13	6	2	38	16	5	4	12	28	47	66	63	42.86
Rochdale	18	4	5	0	17	8	3	5	1	12	9	29	17	38.89
Rotherham Town	6	2	1	0	8	4	2	0	1	4	2	12	6	66.67
Rotherham United	32	11	1	4	29	16	5	6	5	18	19	47	35	50.00
Scunthorpe Utd.	8	4	0	0	9	1	2	0	2	5	5	14	6	75.00
Sheffield Utd.	68	14	5	15	55	55	7	4	23	33	70	88	125	30.88
Sheffield Wednesday	56	13	7	8	42	33	5	8	15	20	47	62	80	32.14
Shrewsbury T	20	6	1	3	18	14	0	6	4	11	23	29	37	30.00
Southampton	42	6	6	9	33	31	2	4	15	20	50	53	81	19.05
Southend U	50	14	6	5	47	30	6	2	17	28	48	75	78	40.00
Southport	10	2	1	2	8	5	2	1	2	5	4	13	9	40.00
Stockport County	18	6	2	1	20	7	3	2	4	8	10	28	17	50.00
Stoke City	66	15	8	10	56	38	8	10	15	26	48	82	86	34.85
Sunderland	74	20	12	5	69	36	6	10	21	35	85	104	121	35.14
Swansea	60	15	5	10	56	40	3	10	17	25	58	81	98	30.00
Swindon T	36	10	4	4	25	11	4	3	11	21	38	46	49	38.89
Thames	2	1	0	0	4	0	0	1	0	0	0	4	0	50.00
Torquay United	30	7	6	2	22	8	5	6	4	25	22	47	30	40.00
Tottenham Hotspur	34	7	6	4	27	16	3	2	12	18	36	45	52	29.41
Tranmere Rovers	22	6	3	2	20	10	4	0	7	16	22	36	32	45.45
Walsall	40	15	4	1	50	16	3	6	11	29	36	79	52	45.00
Watford	46	13	1	9	37	32	7	3	13	31	45	68	77	43.48
West Bromwich Albion	60	17	7	6	54	29	4	9	17	41	74	95	103	35.00
West Ham United	52	12	8	6	42	23	6	3	17	27	59	69	82	34.62
Wigan Athletic	10	2	3	0	9	6	1	1	3	4	7	13	13	30.00
Wimbledon	4	0	1	1	3	4	0	0	2	2	5	5	9	0.00
Wolves	66	15	11	7	71	40	5	8	20	32	67	103	107	30.30
Workington	10	2	2	1	6	6	3	1	1	6	6	12	12	50.00
Wrexham	28	8	5	1	28	14	1	2	11	13	35	41	49	32.14
York City	26	9	3	1	28	10	4	5	4	21	23	49	33	50.00

Player		Date of Birth	Place of Birth	Died	First League Season	Last League Season	Previous Club	Next Club	Appearances				Goals			
									League	FAC	FLC	Other	League	FAC	FLC	Oth.
ABRAHAMS J	James				1891				4				1			
ABTHORPE J	John	19/01/1933	Mansfield		1955			Wolves	5				3			
ADAMSON H	Henry	27/06/1924	Kelty, Fife		1947	1955	Jeanfield Swifts	Gainsborough Trin.	233	16			5			
AGANA PAO	Tony	02/10/1963	Bromley		1991	1993	Sheffield United		93	5	6	12	10	1	2	3
AGNEW DY	David	04/08/1939	Kilwinning		1962	1966	Scunthorpe United	Ilkeston T	85	4	2		1			
ALLAN J	John				1894	1897	Derby County	Heanor T	79	5		8	28	2		
ALLEN H	Herbert		Wellington		1923		Wellington St.George		1							
ALLEN HA	Anthony	27/10/1924	Beeston, Notts		1951	1953	Nottm. Forest	Corby Town	30							
ALLEN RHA	Robert	05/12/1916	Shepton Mallet		1946			Bristol City	1							
ALLIN T	Thomas			1931	1888		Boston		6				2			
ALLSEBROOK R	Richard	25/09/1892	Newstead	1961	1912	1919	Newstead	Ebbw Vale	97	3			2			
ALLSOPP E	Elijah				1893	1896		Bury	59	3		2	19	2		1
ANDERSON J					1904			Port Glasgow Ath.	9							
ANDREWS H	Harold	13/08/1903	Lincoln	1988	1927	1931	Lincoln City	Barnsley	134	6			55	3		
ARMSTRONG KC	Ken	31/01/1959	Bridgnorth		1983		Southampton (loan)		10							
ARNOTT W	Walter	12/05/1863	Pollokshields	1931	1894		Newcastle West End		1	1						
ASHER T	Tom	21/12/1936	Dunscroft, Yorks		1957	1958	Wath Wan.	Ilkeston Town	31				4			
ASHURST W	Bill	04/05/1894	Willington	1947	1920	1926	Lincoln City	West Bromwich A.	200	22						
ASTLE J	Jeff	13/06/1942	Eastwood		1961	1964	John Player	West Bromwich A.	103	5	8		31	1	9	
ASTLEY JE	Joseph	1899	Cradley Heath	1969	1928		Manchester Utd.	Northwich Victoria	4							
AVRAMOVIC R	Raddy	29/11/1949	Croatia		1979	1982	NK Rijeka	Coventry City	149	3	14	15				
BAGNALL R	Reg	22/11/1926	Brinsworth		1946	1947	Rotherham United		9	1						
BAGSHAW JJ	Jimmy	25/12/1885	Derby	1966	1919	1920	Derby County	Watford	24							
BAILEY LF					1888				1				1			
BAKEWELL GH	George				1891			Derby County	5	1			1			
BALL GH	Geoff	02/11/1944	Nottingham		1967	1971	Nottm. Forest	Ilkeston T	112	5	3					
BALL WH	William	1876	W Derby, Liverpool		1899	1900	Everton	Blackburn Rovers	65	5			2			
BARBER MJ	Mike	24/08/1941	Kensington		1963	1964	QPR		33	2	4		3			
BARKER RJ	Richie	23/12/1939	Loughborough		1968	1971	Derby County	Peterborough Utd.	112	5	4		36		1	
BARLEY HF	Harry	1905	Grimsby	1958	1933		New Brighton	Scunthorpe U	11				1			
BARNES PL	Paul	16/11/1967	Leicester		1985	1989		Stoke City	53	1		13	14			5
BARRY LJ	Len	27/10/1901	Sneinton	1974	1920	1927	RAF Cranwell	Leicester City	146	7			10	1		
BARTLETT KF	Kevin	12/10/1962	Portsmouth		1989	1992	West Bromwich A.	Cambridge United	99	6	7	8	33	1	3	3
BASSETT EJ	Ted	01/01/1889	Deptford	1970	1913	1914	Millwall	Watford	44	1			5			
BATES AN	Anthony	06/04/1938	Blidworth		1958			Sutton Town	1							
BATES BF	Brian	04/12/1944	Beeston		1963	1968		Mansfield Town	128	2	7		24	1		
BAXTER WA	William	06/09/1917	Nottingham	1992	1946	1953	Nottm. Forest	Grantham Town	140	13						
BEAVER D	David	04/04/1966	Kirkby-in-Ashfield		1984				1	1						
BEAVON DG	David	08/12/1961	Nottingham		1980		Nottm. Schools	Lincoln City	5	1						
BEAVON MS	Stuart	30/11/1958	Wolverhampton		1979		Tottenham H. (loan)		6							
BEEBY O	Oliver	02/10/1934	Whetstone, Leics		1959		Leicester City	Oxford United	13	2						
BEECH A	Albert	24/09/1912	Fenton (Stoke)		1937		Huddersfield T		13			1				
BELFORD D	Dale	11/07/1967	Burton-on-Trent		1987		Sutton Coldfield		1							
BELL E	Ernest				1891				5	1						
BEMMENT F	Fred	1883	Lowestoft	1957	1907		Norwich City	Chesterfield	9							
BENJAMIN T	Tristan	01/04/1957	St Kitts, WI		1974	1986		Chesterfield	311	17	29	28	4			1
BENSKIN DW	Dennis	28/05/1947	Nottingham		1965				4				1			
BERESFORD JW	John	25/01/1946	Sheffield		1965	1966	Chesterfield	Hartlepool U	50	1	2		13	1		
BERESFORD R	Reg	29/06/1924	Chesterfield		1946		Hardwick Col.		9	4			1			
BETTISON FL					1910				1							
BILLINGTON B	Brian	28/04/1951	Leicester		1969		Leicester City	Enderby T	7							
BIRCHENALL AJ	Alan	22/08/1945	East Ham		1975		Leicester City (loan)		33	3		2				
					1977		San Jose	Memphis								
BIRCUMSHAW A	Tony	08/02/1945	Mansfield		1960	1965		Hartlepool United	148	6	11		1			
BIRCUMSHAW PB	Peter	29/08/1938	Mansfield		1956	1961		Bradford City	72	6	1		40	7	1	
BIRD WS	Walter	1891	Hugglescote, Leics.	1965	1912	1914	Coalville Swifts	Grimsby Town	10				2			
BIRTLES G	Garry	27/07/1956	Nottingham		1987	1988	Nottm. Forest	Grimsby Town	63	4	6	9	9	1	1	1
BISBY CC	Charlie	10/09/1904	Mexborough		1926	1931	Denaby U	Coventry City	206	9			1			
BLOCKLEY JP	Jeff	12/09/1949	Leicester		1978	1979	Leicester City	Enderby T	59	3	6	6	5			1
BLOOD JF	Jack	02/10/1914	Nottingham	1992	1938			Exeter City	8	3						
BLY TG	Terry	22/10/1935	Fincham		1963	1964	Coventry City	Grantham T	29	2	2		4	1		
BLYTH G	George	1911	Motherwell	1984	1935	1937	Hibernian		99	3		4				
BOLTON IR	Ian	13/07/1953	Leicester		1971	1976	Birmingham City	Watford	70	3	5		4			
BOREHAM RW	Reginald	27/05/1896	High Wycombe	1976	1920		Wycombe Wan.	Wycombe Wan.	3							
BOUCHER T	Tom	1873			1896	1898	Stourbridge	Bedminster	79	4		4	32	1		1
BOWERS JA	John	14/11/1939	Leicester		1966			Derby County	5							
BOYES WE	Wally	05/01/1913	Killamarsh	1960	1949		Everton	Scunthorpe United	3				1			
BRADD LJ	Les	06/11/1947	Buxton		1967	1977	Rotherham United	Stockport County	394	22	17	8	125	4	7	1
BRADLEY G	Gordon	20/05/1925	Scunthorpe		1950	1957	Leicester City	Cambridge United	192	10			1			
BRADLEY H	Herbert		Padiham		1910		Bury	Preston North End	3							
BRAILSFORD JR	James	1877	Lincoln		1897		Lincoln City		1							
BRAMHAM A	Albert		West Melton		1934	1935		Rotherham United	18			1	10			1
BRAMLEY C	Charles	1870	Nottingham	1916	1891	1897	Notts Rangers		126	13		12	8			
BRANNON MK	Michael		Wombwell		1937			Barnsley	3			2				
BREALEY H					1894	1895		Hucknall St.Johns	8			2	3			1
BREARLEY J	John	1875	West Derby, L'pool		1897	1900		Millwall Athletic	9							
BRINDLEY JC	John 'Bill'	29/01/1947	Nottingham		1970	1975	Nottm. Forest	Gillingham	223	12	14	1				
BROADBENT AH	Albert	20/08/1934	Dudley		1953	1954	Dudley Town	Sheffield Wed.	31	4			11	2		
BRODIE GW	George		Castle Douglas		1922		Wigan Borough	Darlington	1							

PLAYER		Date of Birth	Place of Birth	Died	First League Season	Last League Season	Previous Club	Next Club	Appearances				Goals			
									League	FAC	FLC	Other	League	FAC	FLC	Oth.
BROOK G	Gary	09/05/1964	Dewsbury		1990		Blackpool (loan)		1							
BROOME FH	Frank	11/06/1915	Berkhamsted	1994	1949	1952	Derby County	Brentford	105	9			35	6		
BROUGHTON M	Matthew	08/10/1880	Grantham		1904		Grantham	Grantham	2				1			
BROWN AW	Alan	26/08/1914	Corbridge		1948		Burnley		13	2						
BROWN C	Cyril	25/05/1918	Ashington		1946		Sunderland	Boston U	13	1			5			
BROWN D	David	26/11/1887	Dundee		1921		Stoke City	Kilmarnock	14				7			
BROWN GH	George				1888		Nottm. Forest	Nottm. Forest	19	5			1			
BROWN HT	Harry	09/04/1924	Kingsbury, London	1982	1946	1948	QPR	Derby County	93	9						
BROWN JA					1888				1	3				1		
BROWN K	Keith	01/01/1942	Hucknall		1958			Rotherham United	8				4			
BROWN R	Ralph	26/02/1944	Ilkeston		1962		Aston Villa	Nuneaton Borough	18	1			3	1		
BROWN RE	Roy	05/10/1945	Hove		1970	1974	Reading	Mansfield Town	113	9	10	1				
BROWN RM	Ray	11/02/1928	Carlisle		1951		Queen's Park		7							
BROWN W	William				1894		Nottm. Forest		1			1				
BRUCE D	Daniel	20/10/1870	Bonhill	1931	1892	1895	Glasgow Rangers	Birmingham City	89	9		11	47	3		2
BRUNT GR	Geoff	24/11/1926	Nottingham		1949	1953		Heanor Town	29	1			1			
BULCH RS	Robert	01/01/1933	Newcastle		1955	1957	Washington	Darlington	27				1			
BULL W	Walter	19/12/1874	Nottingham	1952	1894	1903	St. Andrews, Nottm.	Tottenham H.	282	18		6	53	5		
BURDITT FCK	Ken	12/11/1906	Ibstock	1977	1937	1938	Millwall	Colchester United	20			1				
BURGON FA	Archie	28/03/1912	Nottingham	1994	1932	1933	Newark T	Tottenham H.	26	1			7			
BURKE J	Jimmy				1892		Newark T	Lincoln City	15	2		2	4	1		
BURKE SJ	Steve	29/09/1960	Nottingham		1984		QPR (loan)		5		2					
BURNS JA	James	20/6/1865	Rainham, Essex	1957	1891		West Bromwich A.	South Weald	1							
BURNS K	Kenny	23/09/1953	Glasgow		1984		Derby County (loan)		2							
BURROWS W	William				1893				1			1				
BUSBY MG	Martyn	24/03/1953	Slough		1976	1977	QPR	QPR	37	1	1	5	4			
BUTLER JH	John	10/03/1937	Birmingham		1958	1961	Bestwood Col.	Chester	109	3	3					
BUTLER PJF	Peter	27/08/1966	Halifax		1994		West Ham United		20	2	2	3				
BUTLER PL	Peter	03/10/1942	Nottingham		1961	1965		Bradford City	44	3	3					
BUTLIN BD	Barry	09/11/1949	Rolleston		1968	1969	Derby County (loan)		30	1			13			
BUXTON IR	Ian	17/04/1938	Cromford		1969		Luton Town	Port Vale	5	1			1			
CALDERHEAD D	David	19/06/1864	Hurlford, Ayr	1938	1889	1899	Queen o' South Wan.	Lincoln City	278	25		15	12			
CALE F	Fred				1895				1							
CALLADINE CF	Charles				1907				3							
CAMPBELL DA	David	02/06/1965	Derry		1986		Nottm. Forest (loan)		18				2			
CANTRELL J	Jimmy	07/05/1882	Chesterfield	1960	1907	1912	Aston Villa	Tottenham H.	131	5			64	1		
CARGILL JG	Jim	22/09/1945	Alyth, Perth		1966		Nottm. Forest		10							
CARLIN W	Willie	06/10/1940	Liverpool		1971	1973	Leicester City	Cardiff City	60	5	2		2	1		
CARTER AB	Alfred	1876			1896	1898			20	1			5			
CARTER SC	Steve	23/04/1953	Great Yarmouth		1971	1978	Manchester City	Derby County	188	9	13	11	21		3	2
CARTWRIGHT M	Mick	09/10/1946	Birmingham		1967	1968	Coventry City	Rochdale	16		1					
CARVER GF	Gerry	27/06/1935	Worcester		1953	1965	Boldmere St.Michaels		280	12	5		10			
CASHMORE AA	Arthur	30/10/1893	Birmingham		1921		Cardiff City	Darlaston	14	4			6			
CATLIN R	Bob	22/06/1965	London		1992	1993	Marconi (Aust.)		3		1	1				
CHADBURN J	John	1873	Mansfield	1924	1894	1896	Lincoln City	Wolves	50	2		7	15			
CHALMERS J	James	03/12/1877	Old Luce		1899		Preston North End	Watford	25	3			2	1		
CHALMERS L	Len	04/09/1936	Corby		1966	1967	Leicester City	Dunstable T	51	1	2		1			
CHALMERS T	Thomas	1882	Beith, Ayrshire		1905	1908	Beith		18	1			1			
CHALMERS W	William	1913	Bellshill, Lanark		1936	1937	Bury	Aldershot	65	1		4	17	1		
CHANDLER ACH	Arthur	27/11/1895	Paddington	1984	1935		Leicester City	Leicester City	10	2		1	6			1
CHAPMAN GA	Gary	01/05/1964	Bradford		1989	1990	Bradford City	Exeter C	25			3	4			
CHAPMAN H	Harry	04/03/1921	Liverpool		1948	1950	Aston Villa		53	3			5			
CHAPMAN HG	Herbert	19/01/1878	Kiveton Park	1934	1903		Sheffield United	Northampton T	7				1			
CHAPMAN RD	Bob 'Sammy'	18/08/1946	Wednesbury		1977		Nottm. Forest	Shrewsbury Town	42	3	2	7		1		1
CHARLESWORTH G	George		Bolsover		1919		Sutton Junction	Sutton Town	30				4			
CHATHAM RH	Ray	20/07/1924	Wolverhampton		1953	1958	Wolves	Margate	127	3			4			
CHERRY SR	Steve	05/08/1960	Nottingham		1988	1993	Plymouth Argyle		266	14	17	31				
CHIEDOZIE JO	John	18/04/1960	Owerri, Nigeria		1981 1989	1983	Leyton Orient	Tottenham H.	112	8	11		16	2	2	
CHILDS H	Henry	1906	Sunderland		1928		West Stanley	Halifax Town	1							
CHIPPERFIELD JJ	Jimmy	04/03/1894	Bethnal Green	1966	1921		Tottenham H.	Northfleet	18	6			2	3		
CHRISTIE TJ	Trevor	28/02/1959	Cresswell, Northumb.		1979	1983	Leicester City	Nottm. Forest	186	10	20	10	63	3	10	3
CLAMP AF	Arthur	01/05/1884	Sneinton	1918	1906	1914	Sneinton		275	14			3			
CLARE WE	Edwin	1884			1903	1904	Mansfield Woodhouse	Brighton	6							
CLARKE D	David	25/09/1946	Derby		1966		Nottm. Forest		24	1	2					
CLARKE DA	David	03/12/1964	Nottingham		1982	1986		Lincoln City	123	13	10	3	8	1	2	
CLARKE GW	William				1933	1935	West Bromwich A.		37	2		1	1			
CLAYTON S	Stanley	1916	Castleford		1937	1938	Upton Col.		31	5			3	1		
CLEMENTS JE	John				1888	1889	St. Saviours, Nottm.	Manchester Utd.	14	4						
CLIFF E	Eddie	30/09/1951	Liverpool		1973		Burnley	Chicago Sting	5							
CLINCH T	Thomas	1876			1904		Reading		6							
COATES DP	David	11/04/1935	Newcastle		1964	1966	Mansfield Town		66	2	3		1			
COCK DJ	Donald	08/07/1896	Hayle	1974	1922	1924	Fulham	Arsenal	85	7			32	2		
COGLIN S	Steve	14/10/1903	Willenhall		1931		Grimsby Town	Worcester C	13	1			3			
COLES FG	Gordon	1875	Nottingham	1947	1895			Nottm. Forest	1			2				
COLLIER G	Geoff	25/07/1950	Blackpool		1973		Macclesfield T	Macclesfield T	3							
CONNELL A	Archibald				1927		Queen of the South		4				1			
CONNOR JH	Henry	1875	Barnsley		1895			Newark	17	2						
COOK J	Jack	27/07/1891	Sunderland		1919	1923	Middlesbrough	Northampton T	98	19			11	5		
COOK T					1888				1							

PLAYER		Date of Birth	Place of Birth	Died	First League Season	Last League Season	Previous Club	Next Club	Appearances				Goals			
									League	FAC	FLC	Other	League	FAC	FLC	Oth.
COOKE JR	James		Sunderland		1919		Mansfield Mechanics	Ilkeston U	12				2			
COOKSON AE	Alfred		Nottingham		1896				3							
COOLE W	Billy	27/01/1925	Manchester		1953	1955	Mansfield Town	Barrow	42	1			5			
COOPER E	Edward	1891	Walsall		1920		Newcastle United		4							
COOPER J	Joe	1899	Newbold, Derbys	1959	1922	1923	Chesterfield	Grimsby Town	31	2			4			
COOPER S	Sedley	1914	Garforth		1936	1938	Huddersfield T		56	3			14	2		
COOPER T	Terry	11/03/1950	Croesyceiliog		1971	1972	Newport County	Lincoln City	9			1				
COPE HW	Horace	24/05/1899	Treeton	1961	1920	1926	Treeton Works	Arsenal	125	5			6			
CORKHILL WG	Billy	23/04/1910	Belfast	1978	1931	1938	Marine	Cardiff C	264	20		4	9	2		
					1946	1951	Cardiff C	Scunthorpe Utd.								
CORNWELL R	Ralph	07/09/1901	Nottingham		1923	1925	Sneinton Institute	Norwich City	42	4						
COULSTON W	Walter		Warwell		1938		Barnsley		1							
COX PR	Paul	01/01/1972	Nottingham		1991	1993			44	2	3	3	1		1	
COZENS JW	John	14/05/1946	Hammersmith		1970	1972	Hillingdo Borough	Peterborough Utd.	44	7	3		13	4	3	
CRANK J	Joseph				1896				1							
CRAPPER J	Joseph		Sheffield		1921			Huddersfield T	2							
CRAYTHORNE R	Reuben	21/01/1882	Small Heath		1904	1913	Coventry City	Darlington	282	14			12			
CRESSWELL F	Frank	05/09/1908	South Shields	1979	1933		Chester	Chester	16				4			
CRICHTON PA	Paul	03/10/1965	Pontefract		1986		Nottm. Forest (loan)		5							
CRICKMORE CA	Charlie	11/02/1942	Hull		1969	1971	Norwich City		59	4	1		11	2		
CRISPIN T	Tim	07/06/1948	Leicester		1966	1967		Lincoln City	8							
CRONE R	Robert	1870	Belfast	1943	1896	1897	Burton Swifts	Bedminster	32	3		4				
CROOKES RE	Robert	29/02/1924	Retford		1949	1955	Retford T	Worksop T	177	8			45	1		
CRUICKSHANK FJ	Frank	20/11/1931	Falkirk		1953	1959	Nuneaton Borough	Cheltenham T	151	4			5			
CUMNER HR	Horace	31/03/1918	Aberdare		1946	1947	Arsenal	Watford	66	8			11	2		
CURRIE JB	James		Galston		1919		Kilmarnock		8				1			
CURSHAM HA	Harry	27/11/1859	Wilford	1941	1888	1890			9	36			2	49		
DAFT HB	Harry	05/04/1866	Radcliffe-on-Trent	1945	1888	1892		Nottm. Forest	137	33		6	58	19		3
					1893	1894	Nottm. Forest	Newark								
DAINTY HC	Herbert	02/06/1879	Rushton	1961	1903		Northampton T	Southampton	20	1						
DALE GH	George	02/05/1883	Nottingham		1914		Millwall	Chelsea	18	1			5			
DALTON RT	Tim	14/10/1965	Waterford		1985		Coventry City	Boston U	1							
DALY J	Joseph	28/12/1899	Lancaster		1920	1926	Cliftonville	Northampton T	139	15			12			
DANIEL RC	Ray	10/12/1964	Luton		1994		Portsmouth (loan)		5			1				
DAVIES JG	John	18/11/1959	Llandyssil		1985		Hull City (loan)		10							
DAVIES W	Willie	16/02/1900	Troedyrhiwfuwch	1953	1927	1929	Cardiff City	Tottenham H.	71	2			9			
DAVIS AG	Arthur	1900	Birmingham	1955	1923	1927	QPR	Crystal Palace	140	6			51	3		
DAVIS DJ	Darren	05/02/1967	Sutton-in-Ashfield		1983	1987		Lincoln City	92	6	6	7	1	1		
DAVIS SM	Steve	30/10/1968	Hexham		1990		Southampton (loan)		2							
DAVISON AJ	Aidan	11/05/1968	Sedgefield		1988		Billingham Synthonia	Bury	1							
DAWS A	Tony	10/09/1966	Sheffield		1984	1985		Sheffield United	8				1			
DAYKIN RB	Brian	04/08/1937	Long Eaton		1962		Derby County	Corinthians(Sydney)	3							
DEAN RJ	Jerry	13/02/1881	Wellington		1904	1911	Wellington T		254	14			49	3		
DEAN WR	Bill 'Dixie'	22/01/1907	Birkenhead	1980	1937	1938	Everton	Sligo Rovers	9				3			
DEANS T	Tom	07/01/1922	Shieldhill		1949	1955	Clyde	Boston U	239	13						
DEATH WG	Billy	13/11/1900	Rotherham	1984	1920	1922	Rotherham Town	Sunderland	21	2			4			
DEIGHTON AD	Alex	1877			1897		Rock Ferry		10	1			1			
DEVEY W	Will	12/04/1865	Perry Barr	1935	1896	1897	Burton Wanderers	Walsall	14				3			
DEVLIN PJ	Paul	14/04/1972	Birmingham		1991	1993	Stafford Rangers		115	5	10	15	19	1		4
DEWICK JA	John	28/11/1919	Rotherham		1946				1							
DICKSON W	Bill	15/04/1923	Lurgan, Co. Armagh		1946	1947	Glenavon	Chelsea	21				2			
DIJKSTRA M	Meindert	28/02/1967	Eindhoven		1992	1993	Willem II(Holland)		29	3	2	8	1			
DINSDALE N	Norman	20/06/1898	Hounslet	1970	1920	1927	Anston United	Coventry City	267	27			11			
DIXON H	Harry				1893		Kettering T		3							
DOBSON CF	Charles	09/09/1862	Basford	1939	1888				1	29				6		
DOCHERTY A					1892		Partick Thistle		6				1			
DOCHERTY B	Bernard	11/08/1941	Bellshill		1964		Cambuslang Rgrs.		25	2	3		2			
DODD GF	George	07/02/1885	Whitchurch		1907	1910	Workington	Chelsea	91	1			20			
DOHERTY JG	Jim	31/01/1957	Douglas		1979	1980	Cumnock Juniors	Motherwell	8			1				
DOLPHIN A	Alf		Redditch		1920		Oldham Athletic	Darlington	24				3			
DONALDSON J	Joseph				1898				3							
DONNELLY S	Sam		Annbank		1893	1894	Annbank	Blackpool	32	6		10	7	2		
DOWALL W	Bill		Thornliebank		1938		Ballymena		6							
DOWNING KG	Keith	23/07/1965	Oldbury		1984	1986	Mile Oak Rov.	Wolves	23				1			
DOWSEY J	John	1905	Gateshead	1942	1928	1931	Sunderland	Northampton T	98	5			4			
DRAPER MA	Mark	11/11/1970	Derby		1988	1993		Leicester City	222	10	15	23	41	2	2	5
DRYDEN RA	Richard	14/06/1969	Stroud		1991	1992	Exeter City	Plymouth Argyle	31	3	2	2	1			
DYER PD	Paul	24/01/1953	Leicester		1972	1973		Colchester United	7							
EARLE HT	Henry				1904		Clapton		23	1						
EDGE DJ	Declan	18/09/1965	Malacca		1985		Gisbourne C (NZ)	Gisbourne C (NZ)	10	3		2	2			
EDWARDS JW	Jack	23/02/1924	Manchester	1978	1952	1953	Kidderminster Harr.	King's Lynn	25				3			
EDWARDS RT	Dick	20/11/1942	Kirkby-in-Ashfield		1959	1966	East Kirkby	Mansfield Town	221	10	14		20		1	
ELLEMAN AR	Allan		Ashington		1891		West Bromwich A.	Grimsby Town	6				2			
ELLIOTT JW	John	23/12/1946	Ashington		1967	1968	Ashington		64	2	2		7			
ELLIOTT SD	Sid	1910	Sunderland		1931	1933	Bristol City	Bradford City	51	2			15			
EMBERTON FP	Fred 'Teddy'	1884	Thryston	1957	1904	1914	Stafford Rangers		365	17			2	1		
EMENALO M	Michael	14/07/1965	Aba, Nigeria		1994		RWD Molenbeek		7			4				
EMMITT HW	Herbert	06/08/1857	Nottingham	1901	1888			Nottm. Forest	4	27				4		
EVANS FJ	Fred	20/05/1923	Petersfield		1947	1950	Portsmouth	Crystal Palace	39				14			
EVANS WE	Billy	05/09/1921	Birmingham	1960	1949	1952	Aston Villa	Gillingham	96	7			14			

PLAYER		Date of Birth	Place of Birth	Died	First League Season	Last League Season	Previous Club	Next Club	Appearances				Goals			
									League	FAC	FLC	Other	League	FAC	FLC	Oth.
FAIRCLOUGH WR	Wayne	27/04/1968	Nottingham		1985	1989		Mansfield Town	71	3	3	13				
FALLON WJ	William	14/01/1912	Larne, Ireland	1989	1933	1937	Dolphin	Sheffield Wed.	135	10		3	23	3		1
					1946		Sheffield Wed.	Exeter City								
FARINA F	Frank	05/09/1964	Australia		1991			Bari (loan)	3							
FARMER RJ	Ron	06/03/1936	Guernsey		1967	1968	Coventry City	Grantham T	69	2			5			
FASHANU JS	Justin	19/02/1961	Hackney		1982	1984	Nottm. Forest	Brighton & Hove Alb.	64	2	8		20	2	1	
FAWELL DS	Derek	22/03/1944	Hartlepool		1964		Spennymoor U	Lincoln City	1							
FEATHERBY LW	Len	28/07/1905	King's Lynn	1972	1935		Plymouth Argyle	King's Lynn	3		1					
FEEBERY A	Alf	10/09/1909	Hucknall	1989	1929	1938	Hucknall Congs.	Bristol Rovers	221	7		4	1			
FEENEY TW	Tom	26/08/1910	Grangetown	1973	1932		Newcastle United	Lincoln City	17				2			
FENNER T	Tom	12/05/1904	Warrington		1927	1933	Wigan Borough	Bradford City	158	5			70	1		
FENWICK R	Bob	29/09/1894	Walker		1922	1924	Lincoln City	Lincoln City	6							
FERGUSON A	Alex	1903	Glasgow	1894	1889	1890	Rangers	Newark	22	5						
FERGUSON C	Charlie	22/11/1910	Dunfermline		1936		Middlesbrough	Luton Town	22	1		2	8			2
FERGUSON JS	James		Airdrie		1927	1931	Brentford		158	6						
FERRIER J					1894				2							
FISHER F	Fred	11/04/1910	Hucknall		1929		Newark T	Torquay United	3				1			
FLANAGAN DC	Daniel	24/11/1924	Dublin		1946		Dundalk	Shelbourne	2				2			
FLEMING JG	Gary	17/02/1967	Derry		1989		Manchester C (loan)		3		1					
FLETCHER F	Frederick				1894	1895	Derby County		9		3		3			
FLETCHER HH	Harry	13/06/1873	Birmingham	1923	1897	1899	Grimsby Town	Grimsby Town	60	5			17	1		
FLINT WA	Billy	21/03/1890	Underwood	1955	1908	1925	Eastwood Rgs.		376	32			40	1		
FLOWER AJ	Tony	02/02/1945	Carlton		1961	1966		Halifax Town	129	5	6		17			
FLOWER T	Thomas	1916			1938		Liverpool		36	4		1				
FORREST JR	Bobby	13/05/1931	Rossington		1958	1961	Leeds United	Weymouth	117	6	3		37		1	
FORSYTH ME	Mike	20/03/1966	Liverpool		1994		Derby County		7							
FOSTER CJ	Colin	16/07/1964	Chislehurst		1993		West Ham U (loan)		9		2					
FOSTER JH	John	1894	Wombwell		1919		Worksop T	Luton Town	32	3			1			
FOUNTAIN R	Richard	1883	Scarborough		1905			Accrington Stanley	1							
FRASER J	Jack	10/11/1876	Dumbarton	1952	1897	1898	Motherwell	Newcastle United	41	2			5			
FREEMAN A	Anthony	29/08/1928	Melton Mowbray		1946	1949	Melton Town	Boston U	44	6			2	1		
FROGGATT F	Frank	21/03/1898	Sheffield	1944	1927	1930	Sheffield Wed.	Chesterfield	115	3			1			
FROGGATT JL	John	13/12/1945	Stanton Hill		1963	1964	East Kirkby MW	Boston Utd.	4		1				1	
FRY KF	Keith	11/04/1941	Cardiff		1961	1963	Newport County	Merthyr Town	73	4	6		9	3		
GADSBY MD	Mick	01/08/1947	Oswestry		1967		Ashbourne	York City	11							
GALBRAITH					1888				1							
GALLACHER HK	Hughie	02/02/1903	Bellshill	1957	1936	1937	Derby County	Grimsby Town	45	1		1	32			
GALLAGHER J	Jimmy	02/09/1911	Bury		1937	1938	Bury	Exeter City	23	2		1	2	1		
GALLAGHER TD	Tommy	25/08/1974	Nottingham		1993				20			7				
GALLOWAY MA	Mick	13/10/1974	Nottingham		1994				7							
GANNON E	Eddie	03/01/1921	Dublin	1989	1946	1948	Shelbourne	Sheffield Wed.	107	11			2			
GANNON JP	Jim	07/09/1968	Southwark		1993		Stockport Co. (loan)		2							
GARNER WD	Bill	14/12/1947	Leicester		1966			Bedford Town	2							
GARRETT FH	Fred	1889	Stanton Hill		1909	1911		Stockport County	8							
GAUGHRAN BM	Benny	29/09/1915	Dublin	1977	1938			Dundalk	2		1		1			
GEE E	Ellis	15/06/1878	Grassmoor		1900	1906	Everton	Reading	214	14			21	2		
GIBBON H	Harry		Sunderland		1927		Sunderland		3							
GIBSON APS	Alex	28/11/1939	Kirkconnel		1959	1968	Auchinleck	Boston Utd.	347	10	16		10			
GIBSON T	Tommy	23/10/1888	Maxwelltown		1919	1922	Nottm. Forest	Southend United	63	6			5	1		
GIBSON W	William	1869			1896	1897	Sunderland	Lincoln City	41	3		4				
GISSING JWD	John	24/11/1938	Stapleford		1957	1960	Stapleford B.C.	Chesterfield	22				1			
GLEN A	Alex	11/12/1878	Kilsyth		1903		Grimsby Town	Tottenham H.	20	1			3			
GOATER LS	Shaun	25/05/1970	Bermuda		1993		Rotherham Utd. (loan)		1							
GOOCH PG	Percy	01/09/1882	Lowestoft	1956	1907		Birmingham City	Norwich City	3				1			
GOODWIN MA	Mark	20/02/1960	Sheffield		1980	1986	Leicester City	Walsall	237	15	20	10	23		3	
GOSS W	William		Nottingham		1899		Heanor T	Portsmouth	16	3			1	1		
GOUCHER GH	George	18/05/1902	Shirebrook		1926		Shirebrook	Nottm. Forest	1							
GOULD G	Geoff	07/01/1945	Blackburn		1969		Bradford PA		1							
GRAY AM	Andy	30/11/1955	Glasgow		1987		Aston Villa (loan)		4	2					1	
GREATOREX L	Laurie	1902	Huthwaite		1924		Dronfield	Southend U	4							
GREEN AW	Arthur	12/05/1881	Aberystwyth	1966	1902	1906	Walsall	Nottm. Forest	134	8			56	3		
GREEN R	Rick	23/11/1952	Scunthorpe		1978		Chesterfield	Scunthorpe United	9	4		2		1		
GREEN RCG	Ronnie	12/03/1912	Frampton Cotterell	1979	1934	1935	Arsenal	Charlton Athletic	36			1	5			1
GRICE F	Frank	13/11/1908	Derby	1988	1931	1935	Linby	Tottenham H.	102	5		2	4	1		
GRICE R	Reuben	1886	Ruddington		1910	1911		Burnley	4							
GRIFFITHS A	Arthur	16/03/1879	Aston		1903	1911	Bristol Rovers		163	8			1			
GROOME PB	Pat	16/03/1934	Nottingham		1952	1957	Bonsall	Skegness T	40	1						
GUNN W	William	04/12/1858	Nottingham	1921	1888	1892	Nottm. Forest		3	20			1	13		
GUTTRIDGE FH	Frank	12/04/1866	Nottingham	1918	1888	1894		Southampton	18	1						
HADEN S	Sampson	17/01/1902	Royston, Yorks	1935	1927		Arsenal	Peterborough Utd.	289	11		1	36	2		
HADLEY A	Arthur	1877	Reading		1898	1901	Reading	Leicester Fosse	76	6			22			
HAIG P	Paul		Nottingham		1913		Leicester Fosse		1							
HALL GW	Willie	12/03/1912	Newark	1967	1930	1932	Ransome & Marles	Tottenham H.	34	1			7	1		
HALL WH	William				1894				2							
HALTON RL	Reg	11/07/1916	Buxton	1988	1937		Manchester Utd.	Bury	6	1		2				1
HAMILTON W	Billy	24/10/1904	Musselburgh	1984	1930		Accrington Stanley	Alloa	2							
HAMMOND L	Leonard	12/09/1901	Rugby	1983	1933		Northampton T		26	1						
HAMPSON T	Tommy	02/05/1898	Bury		1929		Cardiff City		1							
HAMPTON IK	Ivan	15/10/1942	Kimberley		1960	1966	Rotherham United	Halifax Town	141	3	12		1			
HANDLEY G	George				1895			Derby County	1							

PLAYER		Date of Birth	Place of Birth	Died	First League Season	Last League Season	Previous Club	Next Club	Appearances				Goals			
									League	FAC	FLC	Other	League	FAC	FLC	Oth.
HANNAH GL	George	11/12/1928	Liverpool	1990	1964	1965	Manchester City	Bradford City	25		1		1			
HANNIGAN R	Richard				1898		Morton	Arsenal	15	1			2			
HARBOTTLE MS	Mark	26/09/1968	Nottingham		1985				4		1		1			
HARDING PJ	Paul	06/03/1964	Mitcham		1990	1992	Barnet	Birmingham C	54	6	1	8	1			2
HARKER E	Edward				1888				2	12				2		
HARKIN JT	Terry	14/09/1941	Derry		1966		Cardiff City	Southport	28	1			10			
HARKOUK RP	Rachid	19/05/1956	Chelsea		1980	1985	QPR		144	11	12	7	39	5	5	3
HARPER RG	Rowland	4/1881	Lichfield	1949	1907	1908	Aston Villa	Mansfield Invicta	10				1			
HARPER T	Theo "Fay"	1868	Annesley		1892	1893	Mansfield Town		46	6		5				
HARRIS GT	George	1898	High Wycombe		1922	1923	Southend United	QPR	2							
HARRIS NL	Neil	30/10/1894	Tollcross, Glasgow	1941	1925	1926	Newcastle United	Oldham Athletic	49	3			23	2		
HARRISON A	Albert				1905				3							
HARRISON AE	Alfred				1894			Nottm. Forest	1							
HART PA	Paul	04/05/1953	Golborne		1987		Birmingham City	Chesterfield	23	2		4				
HATELEY A	Tony	13/06/1941	Derby		1958	1962	Normanton Sports	Aston Villa	188	13	6		109	4	1	
					1970	1971	Birmingham C	Oldham Ath.								
HATTON C	Cyril	14/09/1918	Grantham	1987	1936	1938	Grantham Co-op	QPR	62	3		2	15			
HEATHCOTE J	James	17/11/1894	Bolton		1922		Blackpool	Pontypridd	12				1			
HENDRY J	Jack				1890	1895	Glasgow Rangers	Heanor Town	163	18		11	1			
HENDRY R	Robert	1876			1897		Eevrton	Morton	7							
HENRYS A	Arthur				1896		Leicester Fosse		7							
HENSHALL HV	Horace	14/06/1889	Hednesford	1951	1912	1921	Aston Villa	Sheffield Wed.	164	16			27	2		
HESFORD I	Iain	04/03/1960	Noola, Kenya		1985		Sheffield Wed. (loan)		10			1				
HIGGINS A	Andy	26/04/1909	Gartsherrie	1966	1934		Newport County	Lille	10				2			
HILL H	Harold	24/09/1899	Blackwell, Derbys		1919	1924	New Hucknall Col.	Sheffield Wed.	151	19			50	6		
HILLHOUSE JT	John		Kilmarnock		1926			Rochdale	4							
HILLS WJ	Walter		Nottingham		1924	1926	Meadow Thursday		3							
HILTON F	Fred	08/07/1903	Sheffield		1924	1928	Grimsby Town	Scunthorpe United	109	5			3			
HINDMARSH JS	John		Ashington		1937	1938	Burnley		57	5		3				
HOBSON J	John	01/06/1946	Barnsley		1969	1970	Barnsley		49	1	1		6			
HODDER W	William				1888				20	2			3			
HODSON SP	Simeon	05/03/1966	Lincoln		1983	1984		Charlton Athletic	27	3						
HOGG GJ	Graeme	17/06/1964	Aberdeen		1994		Portsmouth		17			1				
HOLD O	Oscar	19/10/1918	Carlton, West Yorks		1948		Norwich City	Chelmsford City	19	4			9			
HOLDER DJ	David	15/12/1943	Cheltenham		1963		Cardiff City	Barrow	8	1	2					
HOLDER SW	Steve	21/04/1952	Nottingham		1969				1							
HOLLAND JH	John	1863			1888			Nottm Forest	9	9						
HOLMES WH	Harry	1908	Ambergate		1933		Heanor T	Heanor T	2							
HOOKS P	Paul	30/05/1959	Wallsend		1976	1982	Aston Villa	Derby County	173	9	15	19	30	1	6	4
HOOLEY A					1891				3				1			
HOOPER WG	William	20/02/1884	Lewisham	1952	1912		Nottm. Forest	New Brompton	16	1			1			
HOPKINS GH	George		Sheffield		1926	1927	Newark Town		28							
HOROBIN R	Roy	10/03/1935	Brownhills		1958	1961	West Bromwich A.	Peterborough Utd.	123	7	2		37	2		
HOTEN RV	Ralph	27/12/1896	Pinxton	1978	1919	1920	Pinxton FC	Portsmouth	4				1			
HOUGHTON R	Roy		Spalding		1937	1938		Boston T	8			3				
HOUGHTON WE	Eric	29/06/1910	Billingborough		1946	1948	Aston Villa		55	5			10			
HOULT A	Aubrey	09/07/1915	Ashby-de-la-Zouch		1934	1935	Oaks Parish Church	Northampton T	8			1				
HOWE HA	Bert	01/04/1916	Rugby		1947	1948	Leicester City		52	7						
HOYLE CR	Colin	15/01/1972	Wirksworth		1994		Bradford City		3			1				
HUBBARD J	John	24/03/1925	Wath-on-Dearne		1946			Scarborough	13	6			2	1		
HULME J	John	06/02/1945	Mobberley		1971		Bolton Wan. (loan)		8							
HUMPHREYS P	Percy	03/12/1880	Cambridge	1959	1901	1906	QPR	Leicester Fosse	189	13			66	7		
HUNT D	David	17/04/1959	Leicester		1977	1986	Derby County	Aston Villa	336	22	28	21	28	2	5	2
INNES R	Bob	23/07/1878	Lanark		1901	1902	New Brompton	Nottm. Forest	48	3						
IREMONGER A	Albert	15/06/1884	Norton, Yorks	1958	1904	1925	Notts Jardines	Lincoln City	564	37						
JACKSON C	Craig	15/09/1968	Newark		1985	1986			5	1						
JACKSON H	Harry	1864			1888		Sneinton Wan.	Nottm. Forest	5	21			3	19		
JACKSON J	James	26/03/1931	Glasgow		1948		Mapperley Celtic		113	9			47	3		
					1951	1957		Headington Utd.								
JAKEMAN GW	George	1899	Small Heath	1970	1929	1932	Aston Villa	Kidderminster Harr.	70	1						
JAMES L	Lance	1890	Nottingham		1910	1913			6							
JAMES WB	Wilf	19/02/1907	Cross Keys		1928	1929	Owston Park	West Ham United	16				5			
JARDINE RJ	Robert				1941	1888		Heanor T	18			1	9			
JARVIS H	Harry	08/10/1928	Maltby		1952	1954	Worksop T	Nottm Forest	29	1						
JAYES AG	Gordon	26/09/1923	Leicester		1946	1947	Leicester City	Nuneaton Borough	27	3			7	1		
JEMSON NB	Nigel	10/08/1969	Preston		1994		Sheffield Wed.		11		2	1	1		2	
JENNINGS W	Bill	25/02/1891	Bulwell		1913	1914		Norwich City	42	1						
JOHNSON J	Joseph		Stanford		1919			Watford	10							
JOHNSON MO	Michael	04/07/1973	Nottingham		1991	1993			107	4	9	16				
JOHNSON T	Tommy	15/01/1971	Newcastle		1988	1991		Derby County	118	5	9	17	47	1	5	4
JOHNSTON TD	Tom	30/12/1918	Berwick-on-Tweed		1948	1956	Nottm. Forest	Birmingham (coach)	267	18			88	4		
JONES AF	Fred	25/12/1888	Newstead		1907	1910	Sutton Town	Coventry City	86	5			27	4		
					1912		Coventry City	Coventry City								
JONES AT	Albert	06/02/1883	Talgarth	1963	1905	1906	Nottm. Forest	Norwich City	30	1						
JONES B	Barrie	31/10/1938	Barnsley		1961	1963	Barnsley	King's Lynn	42	2	6		15		2	
JONES JW	Jimmy	1897	Warsop		1919	1920	Welbeck Col.	Alfreton	11							
JONES M	Mick	24/03/1947	Sunderland		1969	1972	Derby County	Peterborough Utd.	100	8	6	1	1			
JONES MR	Mark	21/12/1965	Mansfield		1983	1984			6							
JONES, AARON	Aaron	1884	Rotherham	1950	1906	1907	Birmingham City		22	4			6	2		
JONES, FRED	Fred				1934		Swansea Town		1							

PLAYER		Date of Birth	Place of Birth	Died	First League Season	Last League Season	Previous Club	Next Club	Appearances				Goals			
									League	FAC	FLC	Other	League	FAC	FLC	Oth.
JOYCE C	Chris	19/04/1933	Dumbarton		1959	1961	Nottm. Forest	Nuneaton Borough	62	1	1		18			
JOYNES RA	Dickie	1880			1901	1902	Newark	Brighton & Hove Alb.	46	1			3			
JULIAN W	Walter	1914			1934	1937		Crewe Alexandra	14			3				
KAVANAGH E	Edward	20/07/1941	Glasgow		1964		Cambuslang Rgrs.	Boston U	25	2	3		4	1		
KAVANAGH T	Terrence	1912	Dublin		1936		Everton	Exeter City	2			1				
KEARTON JB	Jason	09/07/1969	Ipswich, Australia		1994		Everton (loan)		10			2				
KEEBLE FW	Fred	30/08/1919	Coventry		1947		Grimsby Town		4				1			
KEELING P	Percy	1903	Alfreton		1924		Alfreton T		6							
KEETLEY T	Tom	16/11/1898	Derby	1958	1929	1932	Doncaster Rovers	Lincoln City	103	7			94	4		
KELLY EP	Eddie	07/02/1951	Glasgow		1980		Leicester City	Bournemouth	27	1	5	7	1		2	
KELLY P	Peter	20/03/1901	Tyldesley	1950	1925	1927	New Brighton	New Brighton	69	1			19			
KELLY W	William	1879			1903		West Ham United	Brighton & Hove Alb.	2							
KEMP H	Haydn	17/01/1897	Sheffield	1982	1920	1930	Chesterfield	Thames	286	26			6			
KERR G	George				1893		Kilmarnock		23	1		5	6			1
KEVAN DJ	David	31/08/1968	Wigtown		1985	1989		Stoke City	89	6	4	9	3	1		
KIDDIER JF	James				1895				15				4			
KILCLINE B	Brian	07/05/1962	Nottingham		1979	1983		Coventry City	158	10	15	9	9	2	1	1
KILFORD JD	John	08/11/1938	Derby		1958		Derby Corinthians	Leeds United	26	1						
KING JD	Jeff	09/11/1953	Fauldhouse		1975		Derby County (loan)		3							
KING LH					1892	1893			3			1				
KING PG	Phil	28/12/1967	Bristol		1993		Sheffield Wed. (loan)		6			2				
KING TP	Thomas		Belvoir		1934	1993		Bournemouth	2							
KINSEY G	George	20/06/1866	Burton-on-Trent	1911	1896		Derby County	Bristol Rovers	4							
KIRK JJ	James	1882			1902			Lincoln City	1							
KIRKHAM R	Royce	17/10/1937	Ollerton		1956		Ollerton Colliery	Workington	1							
KIRKUP FW	Frank	12/01/1939	Spennymoor		1965		Carlisle United	Workington	29	1	2		3			
KNOX T	Thomas	1909	Ushaw Moor		1933	1935	Hartlepools United	Crystal Palace	72	5		1				
KUHL M	Martin	10/01/1965	Frimley		1994		Derby County (loan)		2							
LADD IM	Ian	22/11/1958	Peterborough		1977			Cambridge U	1							
LAHTINEN AA	Aki	31/10/1958	Finland		1981	1984	Oulu Palloseura		45	3	5		2			
LAIRD A	Alex	02/06/1926	Newmains		1953			Chelsea	1							
LAMB J	John	1893			1913	1914	Worcester City		8				3			
LANE F	Frank	20/07/1948	Wallasey		1975		Liverpool	Kettering T	2							
LANE JG	John	10/11/1931	Birmingham		1956	1958	Birmingham City	Hinckley Ath.	57	3			19			
LANGFORD JW	John	04/08/1937	Kirkby-in-Ashfield		1958		Nottm. Forest		16							
LANGHAM W	Billy	1876	Nottingham		1896	1897	South Shore	Bristol City	47	3		4	15			1
LAW N	Nicky	08/09/1961	Greenwich		1988	1989	Plymouth Argyle	Rotherham U	47	1	4	4	4			
LAWLESS JPH	Henry				1929				2							
LAWRENCE E	Eddie	24/08/1907	Cefn Mawr		1931	1935	Clapton Orient	Bournemouth	138	4		1	2			
LAWTON T	Tommy	06/10/1919	Bolton		1947	1951	Chelsea	Brentford	151	15			90	13		
LEE GM	Garnet	07/06/1887	Calverton	1976	1910				4							
LEGG A	Andy	28/07/1966	Neath		1993		Swansea City		64	5	7	11	5			3
LEONARD J	John				1897		Derby County	Bristol Rovers	1				1			
LEONARD MC	Mick	09/05/1959	Carshalton		1979	1988	Halifax Town	Chesterfield	204	20	15	15				
LEUTY LH	Leon	23/10/1920	Meole Brace	1955	1950	1955	Bradford Park Ave.		188	12			3	1		
LEVERTON R	Roland "Tot"	08/05/1926	Whitwell		1953	1955	Nottm. Forest	Walsall	45	5			5			
LEWIS G	George	1876	Chasetown		1897	1901	Wellingborough	Bristol City	129	8			1	1		
LEWIS HH	Harry	25/10/1910	Merthyr Tydfil		1933	1934	Southend United	West Ham United	32	1			7			
LINDLEY T	Tinsley	27/10/1865	Nottingham	1940	1889		Nottm. Forest	Nottm. Forest	2	1						
LINTON JA	James	02/12/1930	Glasgow		1952	1958	Kirkintilloch	Watford	114	6						
LISTER E	Eric	13/08/1933	Willenhall		1954	1956	Wolves	Boston U	8							
LOCKER W	Billy	16/2/1866	Long Eaton	1952	1890		Long Eaton Rgs.	Derby County	21	6			12	2		
LOCKIE AJ	Alex	11/04/1915	South Shields		1946		Sunderland		23	3						
LOGAN J	James	24/06/1870	Troon	1900	1900	1904	Aston Villa	Dundee	41	7		8	31	6		
LOGAN P	Peter		Glasgow		1898		Motherwell	Arsenal	16	1			6			
LOVATT HA	Harry	1906	Audley		1930	1931	Leicester City	Northampton T	9	2			3			
LOVELL FW	Fred	18/06/1929	Crewe		1952	1953			7				2			
LOWE E	Eddie	11/07/1925	Halesowen		1963	1964	Fulham		9							
LOXLEY H	Bert	03/02/1934	Bonsall		1954	1963	Bonsall FC	Mansfield Town	245	13	8		9	1	1	
LUND GJ	Gary	13/09/1964	Grimsby		1987	1993	Lincoln City		248	16	18	34	62	4	5	8
LUNN H	Harry	20/03/1925	Lurgan		1946		Glenavon	Portsmouth	24	3			5			
LYLE D	David				1890				2							
LYMAN CC	Colin	09/03/1914	Northampton	1986	1947		Nottm. Forest		21				5			
MABBOTT J	John				1892	1893			2							
MACARTNEY CW	Charles	04/02/1910	Stamford		1932	1934	Stamford T	Wrexham	50	1			19			
MACDONALD JS	John	23/09/1922	Edinburgh		1948		Carshalton Ath.	QPR	1							
MACHIN P	Prestwood	01/07/1892	Nottingham		1913			Nottm Forest	1							
MACKAY JA	James	1898	Ryton		1923		Carlisle United	Lincoln City	3				1			
MACLACHLAN J	Jimmy				1893		Derby County	Derby County	2							
MACONNACHIE A	Alexander				1898	1900	Derby County	Third Lanark	76	5			26	2		
MADDISON F	Frank	06/05/1934	Worksop		1956	1957			15							
MAIDMENT JHC	Jimmy	28/09/1901	Monkwearmouth	1977	1931	1932	Lincoln City	Accrington Stanley	44	1						
MAINMAN HL	Harry	1880	Liverpool	1953	1901	1906	Reading		130	7						
MAIR G	Gordon	18/12/1958	Coatbridge		1976	1983		Lincoln City	131	4	14	6	18		2	1
MANN AF	Arthur	23/01/1948	Burntisland		1972	1978	Man. City	Shrewsbury Town	253	14	16	9	21	1	2	1
MANN RH	Ron	08/10/1932	Doncaster		1950		Meadows Boys Club	Aldershot	1							
MANNS PH	Paul	15/04/1961	Stafford		1979	1980	Cardiff City	Chester City	7	1	1	7	1	1		1
MANSLEY A	Allan	31/08/1946	Liverpool		1971		Fulham (loan)		11	1			2			
MARDON HJ	Harry	08/06/1914	Cardiff	1981	1936	1937	Hereford U	Bournemouth	22	1		4	8			5
MARRIOTT F	Frank	26/10/1893	Sutton-in-Ashfield		1919	1922	Sutton Junction	Swansea Town	96	16			1			

PLAYER		Date of Birth	Place of Birth	Died	First League Season	Last League Season	Previous Club	Next Club	Appearances League	FAC	FLC	Other	Goals League	FAC	FLC	Oth.
MARSDEN C	Chris	03/01/1969	Sheffield		1994		Wolves		7			1				1
MARSH I	Ike				1899			Doncaster Rovers	3							
MARSH JK	Jack	08/10/1922	Mansfield		1946	1948	Mansfield Boys Club	Coventry City	42	5			18	3		
MARSHALL SK	Stan	20/04/1946	Goole		1966	1967	Middlesbrough		49	1	2		17	1		
MARTIN DK	Davy 'Boy'	01/02/1914	Belfast	1991	1938		Nottm. Forest	Glentoran	26	4			16	1		
MASSON DS	Don	26/08/1946	Banchory		1968	1974	Middlesbrough	QPR	401	16	23	13	92	3	1	1
					1978	1981	Derby Co.									
MATTHEWS CH	Cyril	01/12/1901	Cowes	1973	1927	1929	Bury	Stockport County	15							
MATTHEWS R	Rob	14/10/1970	Slough		1991	1993		Luton Town	44	5	2	7	10	2		
MATTHEWS W	Billy	1880	Derby	1916	1906	1911	Aston Villa	Derby County	177	11			37	6		
MAW AW	Arthur	29/12/1909	Scunthorpe	1964	1928	1931	Scunthorpe United	Leicester City	35	1			11			
MAY E	Ted	1865			1888	1889			29	7			4	5		
MAY W	William	1865		1936	1888		Long Eaton Rgs.		4							
MAYS AW	Billy	12/03/1902	Ynyshir	1959	1929		Wrexham	Burnley	8				4			
MCCAIRNS T	Tommy	22/12/1873	Dinsdale	1932	1899		Bristol Rovers	Lincoln City	4							
MCCALL J	John	1880			1903		Bristol Rovers		3							
MCCALLUM CJ	Neil	03/07/1868	Bonhill	1920	1895		Nottm. Forest	Heanor T	13	2			3			
MCCAPPIN S	Sam		London		1899				7							
MCCAVANA WT	William	24/01/1921	Belfast		1948		Coleraine	Coleraine	3							
MCCLELLAND J	John	07/12/1955	Belfast		1991		Leeds United (loan)		6							
MCCORMACK JC	Cecil	15/02/1922	Newcastle	1995	1951	1955	Barnsley	King's Lynn	82	3			35	1		
MCCULLOCH G	Gordon	1888	Hinckley		1911			Lincoln City	1							
MCCULLOCH I	Iain	28/12/1954	Kilmarnock		1978	1983	Kilmarnock		215	11	16	17	51	2	1	
MCDERMENT WS	Billy	05/01/1943	Paisley		1969		Luton Town	Morton	3	1						
MCDONAGH JM	Jim	06/10/1952	Rotherham		1983	1984	Bolton Wanderers	Wichita Wings	35	4	7					
MCDONALD E	Ted	1876	Newcastle-under-Lyme		1899	1903	Burslem Pot Vale	Portsmouth	139	13			3			
MCGORIAN IM	Isaac	19/10/1901	Durham		1928		Sunderland	Carlisle United	1							
MCGOVERN PM	Pat	14/05/1948	Edinburgh		1967				3	1						
MCGRATH, JAMES	James	04/03/1907	Washington, Co.Durm.		1934		Port Vale	Bradford PA	11				3			
MCGRATH, JOHN	John	21/03/1932	Tidworth		1955	1957	Aldershot	Darlington	54	3			5			
MCGREGOR AC	Andrew				1890	1892	Wishaw Thistle		44	7			11	5		
MCINNES T	Thomas	22/3/1870	Glasgow		1889	1892		Everton	73	13		1	20	7		
MCINTYRE JA	Jim	1881	Darlaston		1902		Walsall Swifts	Northampton T	9				3			
MCLEAN T	Thomas	1866	Alexandria	1936	1888	1891		Derby County	66	10		2				
MCLENAHAN H	Hugh	23/03/1909	Manchester	1988	1936	1938	Manchester Utd.		54	2		2	1			
MCLEOD W	Billy	1887	Hebburn		1919	1920	Leeds City	Doncaster Rovers	40	3			10	2		
MCMAIN J	Joseph	1875	Preston		1899		Wolves		26	3			13	2		
MCMANUS CE	Eric	14/11/1950	Limavady		1972	1978	Coventry City	Stoke City	229	9	13	14				
MCMILLAN J	James				1889		Queen o'South Wan.		22	3						
MCMORRAN JW	Jimmy	29/10/1942	Muirkirk		1969		Walsall	Halifax Town	6							
MCNAMEE P	Peter	20/03/1935	Glasgow		1965		Peterborough Utd.		3							
MCPARLAND IJ	Ian	04/10/1961	Edinburgh		1980	1988	Ormiston Primrose	Hull City	221	17	16	13	69	9	5	7
MCPHERSON IB	Ian	26/07/1920	Glasgow	1983	1951	1952	Arsenal	Brentford	50	4			7	3		
MCPHERSON K	Ken	25/03/1927	West Hartlepool		1950	1952	Horden Colliery	Middlesbrough	26	4			10	4		
MCPHERSON L	Lachlan	01/07/1900	Cambuslang		1921	1923	Cambuslang	Swansea Town	32				5			
MCSTAY W	Willie	26/11/1961	Hamilton		1987	1989	Huddersfield T	Kilmarnock	45		4	7	1			
MCSWEGAN GJ	Gary	24/09/1970	Glasgow		1993		Glasgow Rangers		59	5	6	6	21	1	3	1
MCVAY DR	David	05/03/1955	Workington		1973	1978	Fairham School	Peterborough U	113	4	8	5	2		1	
MELLORS M	Mark	30/04/1880	Basford	1961	1902	1903	Nottm. Forest	Brighton & Hove Alb.	9							
MEADS T	Tommy	02/11/1900	Grassmoor	1983	1935		Tottenham H.		18	2		1	2			
MERRITT R	Dicky	22/07/1897	Shiney Row, Durham	1978	1929		York City		1							
MILLINGTON J	John	1916	Bolton		1935	1936	Clapton Orient	Birmingham	15			1	2			
MILLS BR	Bertie	23/02/1900	Multan, India		1925	1928	Hull City	Birmingham	76	3			34	1		
MILLS GR	Gary	11/11/1961	Northampton		1987	1988	Nottm. Forest	Leicester City	109	7	9	14	8		1	
					1994		Leicester City									
MILLS PC	Percy	10/01/1909	Barton-on-Humber	1967	1927	1938	Barton T		407	20		7	22			
MIMMS RA	Bobby	12/10/1963	York		1985		Everton (loan)		2			1				
MITCHELL A	Arnold	01/12/1929	Rotherham		1951		Nottm. Forest	Exeter City	1							
MITCHELL M	Michael	1904	Glasgow		1924		Burnbank		5							
MOLLOY P	Peter	1911	Rossendale	1993	1947		Distillery		1							
MOLLOY W	William				1931				2				1			
MONTGOMERY J	John	18/06/1876	Chryston	1940	1898	1910	Tottenham H.		316	23			2			
MOORE AE	Albert	1863			1888				10	17			3	6		
MOORE B	Brian	24/12/1938	Hemsworth		1961	1962	Mansfield Town	Doncaster Rovers	27	1	1		3		1	
MOORE GW	George	1888	Newport, Salop		1907		Stafford Rangers		1							
MOORE H	Harry	05/08/1896			1984	1921	Worksop T	Worksop Congs.	16							
MORLEY H	Herbert	1882	Kiveton Park	1957	1906	1914	Grimsby Town		258	11						
MORLEY HA	Haydon	26/11/1863	Derby	1953	1888		Derby County	Derby County	2	7						
MORRAD FG	Frank	28/02/1920	Brentford		1946			Leyton Orient	1							
MORRIS JJ	Jack	1876			1900	1902	Blackpool	Bristol City	77	5			30	3		
MOSLEY AE	Andrew	1883	Sneinton		1906	1909	Sneinton		11							
MOULDEN A	Tony	28/08/1942	Farnworth		1965		Peterborough Utd.	Rochdale	23		1		1			
MOULSON C	Con	03/09/1906	Fethard	1989	1936	1938	Lincoln City		97	6		3				
MOWL JW	William	23/06/1922	Bulwell		1948			Mansfield Town	3	1						
MUIR R	Robert	1880	Kilmarnock		1904		Bristol Rovers	Norwich City	19	1						
MUNRO D	David	1880			1907		Third Lanark		12	2			1			
MURPHY S	Shaun	05/11/1970	Sydney		1992	1993	Perth Italia		54	3	4	7	2			1
MURPHY, F. JOHN	John	16/08/1949	Edinburgh		1967	1968	Edina Boys Club		19				2			
MURPHY, JAMES B	Jim	29/11/1942	Glasgow		1967	1968	Raith Rovers	Raith Rovers	33	2			7			
MURPHY, JOHN	John	1874			1924	1896	1897	Hucknall St.Johns	Bristol City	37	2		4	24		

PLAYER		Date of Birth	Place of Birth	Died	First League Season	Last League Season	Previous Club	Next Club	Appearances				Goals			
									League	FAC	FLC	Other	League	FAC	FLC	Oth.
NEEDHAM DW	Dave	21/05/1949	Leicester		1965	1976	Blaby Youth Club	QPR	429	17	21	4	32	2	1	
NELSON GP	Garry	16/01/1961	Braintree		1990		Brighton (loan)		2							
NEWSHAM S	Stan	24/03/1931	Farnworth		1957	1961	Bournemouth		99	4			44			
NEWTON J	John	19/01/1940	Edinburgh		1958	1960	Craiglea Thistle	York City	5							
NICOL S	Steve	11/12/1961	Irvine		1994		Liverpool		19							
NIXON JC	Jon	20/01/1948	Ilkeston		1969	1974	Ilkeston T	Peterborough Utd.	179	12	8		32	3	3	
NOON H	Harold	06/10/1937	Sutton-in-Ashfield		1957	1961	Bentinck Meths.	Bradford City	122	6	3				1	
NORRIS SM	Steve	22/09/1961	Coventry		1989		Scarborough (loan)		1	1						
NORTON DW	David	03/03/1965	Cannock		1988	1990	Aston Villa	Hull City	27		4	5	1			
NOTLEY W	Wilfred	1913			1935		Bourne T		20	3			9			
NUGENT J	John				1904				3							
O'BRIEN RC	Ray	21/05/1951	Dublin		1973	1982	Manchester Utd.	Boston U	323	11	24	27	31		4	4
O'DONNELL D	Dennis	1880	Willington Quay		1907			Bradford PA	18	1			4			
O'NEILL MHM	Martin	01/03/1952	Kilrea		1983	1984	Norwich City		64	7	10		5		2	
O'RIORDAN DJ	Don	14/04/1957	Dublin		1988	1992	Grimsby Town	Torquay U	109	6	6	18	5	2	1	1
OAKES DR	Dennis	10/04/1946	Bedworth		1967	1970	Coventry City	Peterborough Utd.	120	3	3					
OLDERSHAW H	Harry				1921				1							
ORGILL H	Harry	01/10/1920	Hucknall	1980	1947		Nottm. Forest		2							
OSBORNE AW	Archie				1890	1893	Vale of Leven Ath.	Clyde	46	6		5	1			
OSWALD, JAMES	James	03/01/1868	Greenock	1948	1889	1892	Third Lanark	St. Bernards	95	11		1	55	9		
OSWALD, JOHN	John		Greenock		1889		Third Lanark	Burnley	22	3			6	4		
OWEN HG	Hugh	19/05/1859	Bath	1912	1888				1							
PACE DJ	Derek	11/03/1932	Bloxwich	1989	1964	1965	Sheffield United	Walsall	29	1			15			
PACEY H	Herbert		Nottingham		1910	1911			3							
PALMER CA	Charlie	10/07/1963	Aylesbury		1988	1993	Hull City	Walsall	182	10	9	20	7			2
PAPE AA	Albert	1897	Wath-on-Dearne	1955	1923		Rotherham County	Clapton Orient	6	2			2	1		
PARIS AD	Alan	15/08/1964	Slough		1990	1991	Leicester City	Slough Town	42	4	2	5	1			
PARKE J					1892		Jordanhill		1							
PARKS A	Albert	09/02/1926	Lurgan		1946	1947	Glenavon	Glenavon	30				4			
PARRY C	Cyril	13/12/1937	Derby		1957	1958	Derby County		12				2			
PAXTON JW	John	24/03/1928	Wolverhampton		1950		Wolves		2							
PEART JG	Jack	03/10/1888	South Shields	1948	1912	1919	Newcastle United	Birmingham City	82	2			51	1		
PEMBLETON A	Arthur	25/01/1895	Palterton	1976	1919	1921	Woodhouse Exchange	Millwall	71	9						
PENNINGTON H	Harry	21/04/1880	Salford		1900	1904	Brentford		126	10						
PEPPER FW					1909	1911			5							
PERRY J	Joe	1893	Brierley Hill		1914		Stourbridge	Ebbw Vale	18							
PIKE GA	Geoff	28/09/1956	Clapton		1987	1988	West Ham United	Leyton Orient	82	5	6	8	17	2	1	
PIMBLEY DW	Doug	19/06/1917	Birmingham		1947	1949	Birmingham City	Hereford United	23				1			
PLACKETT S	Syd	21/09/1898	Sawley	1950	1926	1929	Derby County		84	1						
PLATNAUER NR	Nicky	10/06/1961	Leicester		1989	1990	Cardiff City	Leicester C	57	1	6	10	1			
PLATTS R	Robert	1901	Sheffield		1920	1924	Anston United	Southend United	50	3			3			
POOLE W	William	16/09/1900	Keyworth		1919		Boots Athletic	Coventry City	1							
POPE FH	Frankie	1880	Brierley Hill		1906		Wolves	Walsall	2							
POPPITT J	James	1879		1930	1905	1906	Swindon Town	Lincoln City	15				2			
POSKETT TW	Tom	26/12/1909	Esh Winning	1972	1934		Lincoln City	Tranmere Rovers	10							
POTTER A	Arthur	1874	Nottingham		1897			Bristol City	2							
POVEY VR	Vic	15/03/1944	Wolverhampton		1963	1964	Wolves		35				3			
PRASKI J	Josef	22/01/1926	France		1948		Jeanfield Swifts		3							
PRESCOTT TG	Thomas	08/01/1875	Attercliffe	1957	1896	1904	L'pool South End	QPR	212	14		4	1			
PRICE LP	Llewellyn	12/08/1896	Caersws	1969	1922	1927	Aston Villa	QPR	66	4			6	1		
PRING KD	Keith	11/03/1943	Newport		1967	1968	Rotherham United	Southport	44	1	2		2			
PRITCHARD RT	Roy	09/05/1925	Dawley	1993	1957		Aston Villa	Port Vale	18	1				1		
PROBERT EW	Eric	17/02/1952	South Kirkby		1973	1976	Burnley	Darlington	122	3	9	5	13			
PROTHEROE S	Sydney	1914	Douglas		1938		Rochdale		2							
PROUDFOOT J	James	31/01/1906	Chester-le-Street		1932		Barnsley	Southend United	10							
PURVIS B	Bartholomew	15/10/1921	Gateshead		1948	1950	Plymouth Argyle	Carlisle United	25	2						
RANDALL K	Kevin	20/08/1945	Ashton-under-Lyne		1972	1975	Chesterfield	Mansfield Town	121	7	7		39	4	4	
RANKIN JP	Johnnie		Coatbridge		1934	1935	Chelsea	Burton Town	25	1			2			
RAWSON K	Ken	18/09/1931	Ripley		1954	1960	Ripley	Ilkeston Town	34							
RAYNER JP	Jim	31/03/1935	Cornsay		1964		Grantham T	Ilkeston Town	32	2	2		13	1		
READ CW	Charles	21/03/1912	Holbeach	1964	1938		Mansfield T		36	3			2			
REECE PJ	Paul	16/07/1968	Nottingham		1994		Oxford United		11		1	3				
REEVES D	David	19/11/1967	Birkenhead		1992	1993	Bolton Wanderers	Carlisle United	13		2		2			
REGIS DR	Dave	03/03/1964	Paddington		1990	1991	Barnet	Plymouth Argyle	46		2	6	15			2
REID J	Jimmy	1880	Bellshill		1903	1904	Gainsborough Trin.	Watford	16	1			2			
REID P	Peter	20/06/1956	Huyton		1993		Southampton	Bury	5							
REILLY MM	Matt	22/03/1874	Donnybrook	1954	1905		Dundee	Tottenham H.	16							
RICHARDS LG	Lloyd	11/02/1958	Jamaica		1975	1977		York City	9		2	2				
RICHARDS P	Pedro	01/11/1956	Edmonton		1974	1985		Boston U	399	19	38	28	5		1	
RICHARDS S	Sam	1889	Bulwell		1910	1921	Bulwell		179	6			69	2		
RICHARDSON J	John	20/04/1945	Worksop		1971		Derby County	King's Lynn	2		1					
RICKARDS CT	Tom 'Tex'	1914	Giltbrook		1932	1937	Johnson & Barnes	Cardiff City	112	7		5	22	2		2
RIDEOUT PD	Paul	14/08/1964	Bournemouth		1991		Southampton	Glasgow Rangers	11	1	2	2	3			
RIDGWAY I	Ian	28/12/1975	Nottingham		1994				1							
RIGBY NE	Norman	23/05/1923	Newark		1947	1950	Newark T	Peterborough Utd.	46	3						
RILEY H	Harry	22/11/1909	Hollinwood	1982	1933		Lincoln City	Cardiff City	16				3			
RILEY J	Joe	1913	Sheffield		1937		Bournemouth		7				1			
RIMMER SA	Stuart	12/10/1964	Southport		1988		Watford	Walsall	4	2		3	2			
ROBERTSON S	Samuel	1882	Cowdenbeath		1905		Dundee		2							
ROBINSON DA	David	14/01/1965	Middlesbrough		1992	1993	Peterborough Utd.		3		1		1		1	

PLAYER		Date of Birth	Place of Birth	Died	First League Season	Last League Season	Previous Club	Next Club	Appearances League	FAC	FLC	Other	Goals League	FAC	FLC	Oth.
ROBINSON GF	George	17/06/1925	Melton Mowbray		1946		Holwell Works		29	5						
ROBINSON LJ	Len	01/10/1946	Nottingham		1963	1964	Nottm. Forest		4							
ROBINSON MJ	Mark	26/11/1960	Nottingham		1984	1985	Ilkeston T	Shepshed	26	1	1	1	1			
ROBINSON P	Peter	29/01/1922	Manchester		1949	1952	Chesterfield	King's Lynn	82	2			1			
ROBINSON PJ	Phil	06/01/1967	Stafford		1989	1991	Wolves	Huddersfield T	66	2	6	10	5		2	
ROBLEDO EO	Ted	26/07/1928	Chile	1970	1957		Colo Colo (Chile)		2							
ROBY D	Don	15/11/1933	Wigan		1950	1960	Orrell Bisphan Meths.	Derby County	226	6	1		37			
ROEDER GV	Glenn	13/12/1955	Woodford		1983		QPR (loan)		4	3						
ROSE MJ	Mike	22/07/1943	New Barnet		1966	1969	Charlton Athletic	Mansfield T	109	3	4					
ROSS I	Ian	26/11/1947	Glasgow		1976		Aston Villa (loan)		4				1			
ROSS W	William	1874	Kiveton Park		1900	1903	Reading	Grimsby Town	110	8			28	1		
ROY JR	Jack	23/03/1914	Southampton	1980	1937	1938	Sheffield Wed.	Tranmere Rovers	15		1					
RUSHTON BWE	Brian	21/10/1943	Sedgley		1967		Birmingham City		3	1						
RUSSELL DK	David	06/04/1868	Shots, Airdrie	1918	1895				9							
RUSSELL ET	Eddie	15/07/1928	Cranwell		1958		Leicester City		9							
RUSSELL KJ	Kevin	06/12/1966	Portsmouth		1994		Bournemouth		11							
RUSSELL PW	Peter	16/01/1935	Gornal		1955	1958	Wolves	Hereford United	106	4			6			
RUSSELL RI	Bobby	27/12/1919	Aberdour		1948		Chelsea	Leyton Orient	2							
RYAN JO	John	28/10/1944	Liverpool		1969		Luton Town	Altrincham	24	1	1		1			
SANDERSON E	Edgar	16/03/1874			1897	1898			34	2						
SANDS JI	Joseph				1903			Nottm. Forest	2							
SCANLON I	Ian	13/07/1952	Stirling		1972	1977	East Stirling	Aberdeen	111	1	10	9	31		3	1
SEWELL J	Jackie	24/01/1927	Whitehaven		1946	1950	Kells Centre	Sheffield Wed.	178	15			97	7		
SHARMAN J					1897	1899	Beeston Humber	Grimsby Town	2							
SHARPE JW	John	09/12/1866	Ruddington	1936	1889				3							
SHAW AF·	Arthur	01/08/1869	Basford		1888	1889		Nottm. Forest	4							
SHAW TF	Frederick	27/03/1909	Hucknall		1934	1936	Birmingham	Mansfield Town	56	1		2	20			1
SHELTON A	Alfred	11/09/1865	Nottingham	1923	1888	1895	Notts Rangers	Loughborough	195	26		10	5	1		
SHELTON C	Charles	22/01/1864	Nottingham	1899	1888	1891	Notts Rangers		20	3			1	1		
SHELTON G	Gary	21/03/1958	Nottingham		1979		Aston Villa (loan)		8							
SHEPPERSON G	George				1893	1895	Northwich Victoria		5			4				1
SHERIDAN J	John	25/05/1938	Ramsgate		1957	1965	Linby Col.	Hartlepool United	287	11	10		9	1	2	
SHERLOCK PG	Paul	17/11/1973	Wigan		1993			Mansfield Town	12	2	1	3	1			
SHERWIN M	Mordecai	26/02/1851	Greasley	1910	1888				1	11						
SHIELS DP	Dennis	24/08/1938	Belfast		1965		Peterborough Utd.	Retford Town	29	1	1		6			
SHOOTER A	Francis A.	1906	Worksop		1930		Ransome & Marles	Mansfield Town	2							
SHORT, CHRIS	Christian	09/05/1970	Munster		1990	1993	Scarborough		92	5	5	7	2			1
SHORT, CRAIG	Craig	25/06/1968	Bridlington		1989	1992	Scarborough	Derby County	128	8	6	16	6	1	1	2
SHREWSBURY P	Philip	25/03/1947	Langley Mill		1966		Nottm. Forest		2							
SHUFFLEBOTTOM J		1888			1904		Loughborough	Small Heath	1							
SIMCOE KE	Ken	14/02/1937	Nottingham		1960		Coventry City	Heanor T	2							
SIMPSON A	Alex	24/11/1924	Glasgow		1949	1952	Wolves	Southampton	74	2			6	1		
SIMPSON M	Michael	28/02/1974	Nottingham		1993		Nottm Forest		24		3	7	3			
SIMPSON T	Tom	13/08/1879	Keyworth	1961	1899	1901		Leicester Fosse	7							
SIMS J	John	14/08/1952	Belper		1975	1977	Derby Co.	Exeter City	61	1	4	8	13		1	3
SIMS SF	Steve	02/07/1957	Lincoln		1984	1986	Watford	Watford	85	7	9	3	5		1	
SISSON T	Tom	19/10/1894	Basford	1976	1914		Rigley's Athletic	Gillingham	3							
SLAWSON SM	Steve	13/11/1972	Hucknall		1991	1993			38	3	2	7	4			1
SMALLEY PT	Paul	17/11/1966	Nottingham		1985	1987		Scunthorpe United	118	10	4	12				
SMITH AW	Albert	23/07/1890	Nottingham	1921			Nottm Forest	Nottm Forest	4							
SMITH D	David	25/06/1961	Sidcup		1992		Plymouth Argyle		37	1	2	2	8			
SMITH DA	David		Nottingham		1900			Middlesbrough	5							
SMITH DF	Dave	11/03/1956	Nottingham		1975	1977		Torquay United	50	2	5	6				1
SMITH G	George	1901	Glasgow		1924	1927	Strathclyde	West Ham United	83	3						
SMITH GH	George	13/04/1936	Nottingham		1955	1966	Dale Rovers	Hartlepool United	323	15	14					
SMITH GWC	Graham	02/11/1947	Liverpool		1968		Loughborough Cols.	Colchester United	10							
SMITH HR	Harold		Wealdstone		1930	1934	Wealdstone	Cardiff City	117	5						
SMITH JW	Joseph				1932		Barnsley		23	1						
SMITH KW	Keith	15/09/1940	Woodville		1967	1969	Leyton Orient	Tamworth	89	3	4		7			
SMITH MC	Mark	21/03/1960	Sheffield		1992		Barnsley	Lincoln C	5							
SMITH RL	Roy	22/09/1916	Shirebrook		1948	1952	Sheffield Wed.		110	5						
SMITH WA	William	29/09/1901	Bath		1923	1926	Bath City	West Ham United	41	4			4			
SMITH, JACK	Jack	24/04/1936	Hartlepool		1966	1968	Brighton & Hove Alb.	Margate	78	2	3		12			
SMITH, JAMES	Jimmy	12/03/1902	Old Kilpatrick	1975	1936		Newport County	Dumbarton	4				1			
SMITH, WALTER	Walter				1899		South Liverpool		2							
SMITH, WILLIAM	"Tich"	10/11/1871	Sawley	1907	1889			Nottm. Forest	23	1			11			
					1896		Long Eaton Rgs	Nottm Forest								
SNOOK HD	Herbert	23/12/1867		1947	1888				1	3						
SOUTAR HW	Harry	1905	Invergowrie		1930		Accrington Stanley	Rotherham United	7	2						
SOUTHWELL AA	Aubrey	21/08/1921	Grantham		1946	1956	Nottm. Forest	Boston United	328	29			2			
SPENCER F	Fred	1873			1901		Nottm. Forest		15	1			2			
STABB GH	George	26/09/1912	Paignton		1934		Torquay U	Port Vale	24	1			6			
STANIFORTH C	Chris	26/09/1897	Carrington	1954	1924	1925	Mansfield Town	Mansfield Town	66	1			22			
					1927		Mansfield Town	Mansfield Town								
STANT PR	Phil	13/10/1962	Bolton		1989		Hereford United	Fulham	22	1	2	5	6		1	
STEELE E	Ernest	18/06/1908	Middleton	1972	1934	1935	Torquay United	Bath City	54	4		1	9	1		
STEELE MA	Murray	7/1891	Mansfield	1922	1912		Mansfield Mechanics	Mansfield Mechanics	3							
STEVENS S	Sammy	18/11/1890	Netherton		1920		Hull City	Coventry City	22	3			9	2		
STEVENSON AE	Alfred		Asfordby		1926			Newark Town	3							
STEWART A	Alex	1869	Greenock		1896	1897	Nottm. Forest	Bedminster	35	1		4	3			

PLAYER		Date of Birth	Place of Birth	Died	First League Season	Last League Season	Previous Club	Next Club	Appearances League	FAC	FLC	Other	Goals League	FAC	FLC	Oth.
STILL RG	Ron	10/06/1943	Aberdeen		1965	1966	Arsenal	Brentford	46	3			15			
STIMPSON GH	George	25/01/1910	Giltbrook	1983	1930	1933	Kimberley Ams.	Rhyl	90	3						
STOAKES JH	James	17/12/1895	Newark	1979	1919			Norwich City	2							
STOKES A	Alfred	1903	West Bromwich		1926	1928	Allen & Everitt	Coventry City	13							
STONE G	Geoff	10/04/1924	Mansfield		1948	1949	Beeston Boys Club	Darlington	4							
STONE M	Mike	23/05/1938	Hucknall		1958		Linby Col.	Sutton Town	7							
STOTHERT J	James		Blackburn		1894	1895	Lincoln City	Bacup	23			6				
STREETS GH	George	05/04/1893	Nottingham	1958	1919	1927	Sheffield Wed.	Boston Town	133	9						
STUBBS BH	Brian	08/02/1950	Keyworth		1968	1979	Loughborough U	Grantham T	426	22	23	16	21	1	4	1
SULLIVAN JA	James	14/11/1904	Burnley		1925	1927	Crewe Alex.	Grantham	22	2			10			
SUTER ER	Bob	10/07/1878	Epperstone		1898	1906	Newark T	Halifax Town	42	5						
SWIFT GH	George	03/02/1870	Wellington St George	1942	1902		Leicester Fosse	Leeds City	16							
TAIT BS	Barry	30/06/1938	York		1964		Crewe Alexandra		3							
TAIT RJ	Robert	04/10/1938	Edinburgh		1962	1963	Aberdeen	Barrow	60	4	5		11	2	2	
TARPLIN W	Walter	1884	Small Heath		1903	1907	Coventry C	Reading	97	6			25	2		
TASKER E	Ernest				1919				1							
TAYLOR GA	George	1916	Boston		1938		Boston United		6							
TAYLOR GT	George	12/12/1907	Walsall		1925	1933	Stourbridge	Bolton Wanderers	265	12			46	3		
TAYLOR JE	John	11/09/1924	Newcastle		1953	1956	Wolves	Bradford PA	53	1			19			
TAYLOR T	Tommy				1938			Walsall	25	3			1			
TEWKESBURY KC	Ken	10/04/1909	Hove	1970	1932		Aston Villa	Walsall	7							
THOMAS DR	Dean	19/12/1961	Bedworth		1989	1993	Northampton T		134	6	11	14	8			
THOMPSON DS	David	27/05/1962	Manchester		1986	1987	Rochdale	Wigan Athletic	55	3	4	2	8			
THOMPSON TW	Terry	25/12/1946	Barlestone		1965	1967	Wolves		66	2	3		3			
THORNE T	Terry	02/02/1947	Kirton-in-Lindsey		1966		Ipswich Town		2							
THORPE A	Adrian	25/11/1963	Chesterfield		1987	1988	Bradford City	Walsall	59	4	3	8	9	1	1	2
THORPE AE	Albert	14/07/1910	Pilsley	1971	1931		Mansfield Town	Norwich City	1							
THRAVES J	Jimmy	1870	Stapleford	1936	1890	1891	Leicester Fosse	Leicester Fosse	4	5						
THURMAN H					1898		Gedling Grove		2							
TOMLINSON T	Tom	1890	Sheffield		1912		Mexborough	Newport Co.	7							
TOONE G	George	10/06/1868	Nottingham	1943	1889	1898	Notts Rangers	Bristol City	265	22		18				
					1901		Bristol City									
TOONE G(JR)	George, Jr.				1913			Mansfield Mechanics	1							
TOSER EW	Ernie	30/11/1913	London		1946		Millwall		2							
TOWLER BE	Bernard	13/03/1912	Ipswich	1992	1938		Lincoln City		22				9			
TUCKER K	Ken	02/10/1925	Poplar		1956	1957	West Ham United	Margate	28	2			5	1		
TURNER GW	George	1911			1930		Sneinton	Luton Town	3				1			
TURNER P	Phil	12/02/1962	Sheffield		1988	1993	Leicester City		225	13	17	34	15	3		3
TURNER RP	Robbie	18/09/1966	Littlethorpe		1992		Plymouth Argyle	Exeter C	8	1			1			
TWIGG RL	Richard	10/09/1939	Barry		1958		Barry Town		2							
UPTON F	Frank	18/10/1934	Ainsley Hill		1966		Derby County	Worcester C	34	1			3			
VALLANCE R	Robert				1929		Grantham T	Grantham T	8							
VASEY RH	Bob	16/12/1907	Consett		1936	1937	Nottm Forest	Brighton & Hove A.	27	1		3	1			
VINCENT R	Robert	29/05/1949	Leicester		1965				1							
VINTER M	Mick	23/05/1954	Boston		1972	1978	Boston United	Wrexham	166	8	10	10	54	5	1	3
WADE A	Allen	19/07/1926	Scunthorpe		1952	1955			9							
WAINWRIGHT T	Thomas	1880	Nantwich		1904	1905	Wellington		8							
WAITT MH	Mick	25/06/1960	Hexham		1984	1986	Keyworth U	Lincoln City	82	10	5	5	27	4	1	
WALKER A	Arthur	1888	Ripley		1908	1911	QPR		53	3			9			
WALKER G	George	24/05/1909	Musselburgh		1933	1935	St. Mirren	Crystal Palace	100	4		1	1			
WALKER JA	John	1871			1891	1892	Derby County		4							
WALKER JH	Harry	1891	Wirksworth	1934	1920		Derby County	Fulham	5							
WALKER RN	Richard	09/11/1971	Derby		1992	1993		Mansfield T	40		6	6	4			
WALKERDINE GC	Garnet				1903			Gainsborough Trin.	1							
WALKERDINE H	Harry				1889			Gainsborough Trin	38	2		1	16	1		
					1891	1892	Gainsborough Trin.									
WALL TH	Thomas	19/05/1909	Millwall		1932			Tottenham H	3							
WARBURTON BF	Ben				1888				2	2						
WARD A	Alfred	1883	Eastwood	1926	1903		Clowne White Star	Brighton & HA	7	1						
WARD J	John	18/01/1948	Mansfield		1965				5							
WARDLE ES					1888				2	4					1	
WARNER A	Alf	1879	Nottingham		1899	1901		Tottenham H.	56	3			15	1		
					1907		Luton Town									
WATERALL A	Albert	01/03/1887	Nottingham	1963	1910	1912	Sneinton	Stockport County	26	1			1			
WATERALL I	Isaac "Ike"	03/10/1888	Nottingham	1970	1906			Rotherham County	184	7			12	1		
					1909	1919	Rotherham County	Millwall								
WATERALL T	Tom	1885	Radford	1951	1905	1907	Radford	Bradford PA	28	4			5			
WATHEY F	Frank				1912		Mexborough		7							
WATLING BJ	Barry	16/07/1946	Walthamstow		1969	1971	Bristol City	Hartlepool United	66	4	1					
WATSON AEC	Arthur	1868	Hucknall	1937	1893	1894	Mansfield	Mansfield	22	5		2	13	1		
WATSON CR	Charles	10/03/1949	Newark		1967				1							
WATSON DV	Dave	05/10/1946	Stapleford		1966	1967		Rotherham United	50	1	2		2			
					1984		Derby Co.	Kettering T								
WATSON J	Joseph				1932	1933	Derby Wednesday		10							
WATSON JB	Jimmy	1914	Durham	1979	1938		Gillingham	Bristol Rovers	17				4			
WATSON N	Norman	21/12/1899	Sunderland		1932		Leicester City	Wigan Athletic	5							
WATTS AE	Ernie	1872	Woolhampton		1898		Reading	Reading	17	1						
WATTS TH					1906				3							
WEAVER E	Eric	01/07/1943	Rhymney		1967		Swindon Town	Northampton T	17	1			4			
WEIGHTMAN F	Fred				1888				1				1			

PLAYER		Date of Birth	Place of Birth	Died	First League Season	Last League Season	Previous Club	Next Club	Appearances				Goals			
									League	FAC	FLC	Other	League	FAC	FLC	Oth.
WELLS M	Mark	15/10/1971	Leicester		1991	1992		Huddersfield T	2			1				
WEST, ABE	Abe				1912				1							
WEST, ALF	Alf	15/12/1881	Nottingham		1911	1914	Liverpool	Mansfield T	130	4			4			
WHITCOMBE GC	George				1930		Port Vale	Ashton National	7	1						
WHITE DW	Devon	02/03/1964	Nottingham		1994		QPR		20	2		3	7	1		1
WHITELAW A	Andrew	09/05/1865	Jamestown	1938	1891	1892	Vale of Leven	Heanor T	41	3		1				
WHITTAKER FJ	Fred	12/10/1923	Canada		1946		Vancouver		10				2			
WHYTE P	Peter				1902				3	4						
WIDDOWSON ALBERT	Albert				1891				3							
WIDDOWSON TH					1888				12	2						
WIDDOWSON, ALF	Alf	16/09/1900	Keyworth	1970	1919	1927	Boots Ath.	Coventry City	141	16			39	7		
WILEMAN RA	Richard	04/10/1947	Breedon		1966				2							
WILKINSON F	Frank				1889	1893			9	1		5				
WILKINSON JW	John	10/1883	Hucknall Torkard		1904	1905		Tottenham H.	7							
WILLIAMS A	Andy	29/07/1962	Birmingham		1991	1993	Leeds U	Rotherham U	39	1	3		2			
WILLIAMS D	David		Liverpool		1912	1913	Glossop	Luton Town	31	1			5			
WILLIAMS JN	John	11/05/1968	Birmingham		1994		Coventry City (loan)		5				2			
WILLIAMSON A	Albert				1891			Derby County	2							
WILLS GF	Gordon	24/04/1934	West Bromwich		1953	1957	Wolves	Leicester City	154	7			46	1		
WILSON AP	Andrew	13/10/1947	Maltby		1968			Rotherham U (loan)	1							
WILSON KJ	Kevin	18/04/1961	Banbury		1991	1993	Chelsea	Walsall	69	2	4	6	3			
WITHE C	Chris	25/09/1962	Liverpool		1987	1988	Bradford City	Bury	80	5	4	12	3			1
WITHERS A	Alan	20/10/1930	Bulwell		1958	1962	Lincoln City	Wisbech T	121	6	4		22	2		
WOOD GT	Gary	02/12/1955	Corby		1977	1980	Kettering T	Kettering T	11	1	2	4				
WOODFIELD T	Terry	21/01/1946	Nottingham		1963				5							
WOODFORD RM	Robert	06/12/1943	Keyworth		1961				3							
WOODLAND A	Arthur		Nottingham		1919	1921	Norwich City	Southend United	48	1			1			
WOOLLEY J	James		Keyworth		1912	1914	Keyworth		3							
WOOLLEY RA	Robert	29/12/1947	Nottingham	1971	1963	1965	Greenwood School		9				2			
WORTHINGTON N	Nigel	04/11/1961	Ballymena		1981	1983	Ballymena U	Sheffield Wed.	67	4	11	3	4			
WORTHINGTON PR	Bob	22/04/1947	Halifax		1968	1973	Middlesbrough	Southend United	232	14	10		1			
WREN JE	Jack	1894	Bristol		1922	1925	Bristol C	Southport	63	4						
WRIGHT BAW	Bernard	19/09/1923	Walthamstow		1946				2							
WRIGHT F	Fred	1908	Ruddington		1928		Ruddington	Hull City	1							
WRIGHT JE	John		North Winsford		1931			Matlock Town	1				1			
WYLIE RM	Ron	06/08/1933	Glasgow		1951	1958	Clydesdale	Aston Villa	227	10			35	3		
WYLLIE J	John	1914			1938			Lincoln City	1			1				
WYNESS GD	George		Sunderland		1936		Rochdale	Gateshead	10							
YATES DR	Dean	26/10/1967	Leicester		1984	1993		Derby County	314	20	24	36	33			4
YEOMANS K	Kelvin	25/08/1947	Nottingham		1967		Beeston	Ilkeston T	1							
YOUNG A	Archibald	1915	Paisley		1938			Portsmouth	11							
YOUNG AF	Alan	26/10/1955	Kirkcaldy		1984	1985	Brighton & Hove Albion	Rochdale	43	5	6		12	1	2	
YOUNG RA	Richard	18/10/1968	Nottingham		1986			Southend United	35	3	2	2	5	1		

OTHER NOTTS' PLAYERS

Played in F.A. Cup but made no League appearances

		First season	Last season	Date of birth	Place of Birth	Died	Previous Club	Next Club
BAUSOR T		1881						
BROWN GN	Noel	1888						
BROWN HH	Henry	1888						
BURTON FE	Frank	1886		18/03/1865		1948		
CHAPMAN H		1880	1885					
COTTERILL WH		1886	1888					
COULBY GA	George	1884		1866				
CURSHAM AW	Alfred	1878	1883	14/03/1853	Wilford	1884		
CURSHAM CL	Charles	1877	1881	1858		1923		
DIXON JA	John	1883	1884	27/05/1861	Grantham	1931		
DOBSON ATC	Alfred	1881	1884	28/3/1859	Sherwood, Notts	1932		
GILLETT LF	Leonard	1882		21/1/1861	Derby			
GREENHALGH EH	Ernest	1877	1882	3/1849	Mansfield	1922		
GREENHALGH H	Harold	1877	1880					
GREENHALGH RJ	Richard	1877	1878	1856		1936		
HARRIS K	Kevin	1945		20/02/18	Dublin	1984		Brentford
HENFREY AG	Arthur	1893		1868	Wellingborough	1929		
HIBBERT C		1889						
JESSOP E		1879						
JESSOP H	Henry	1877	1882			1914		
KEELY EM	Erasmus	1877						
KEELY SH		1877						
KIRBY A	Alan	1945		19/12/26	Barrow			Barrow
MACRAE S	Stuart	1879	1886	1857	Port Bannatyne	1927		
MALTBY CL	Charles	1880		1858	Farndon	1936		
MARSHALL AT		1884					Nottm. Mellors	
MARSHALL JT		1888						
MEREDITH RD	Robert	1945						
MOORE HT	Harry	1881	1887	27/6/1861	Nottingham	1939		
MORGAN JR	John	1879		1855	Pengwern	1937		
MORSE H	Harold	1878						
OLIVER TA	Thomas	1877	1879					
OWEN REV. JRB	John	1878		1848	Reading	1921		
PALMER S		1880						
PARKER A	Albert	1945						
PEACOCK E	Ernest	1945		11/12/24	Bristol	1966		Bristol C
PEARSON WA		1877						
PYE J	Jesse	1945		22/12/21	Treeton	1984	Sheff. Utd.	Wolves
RATCLIFFE P	Patrick	1945		31/12/19	Dublin		Bohemians	Wolves
SEALS G	George	1877	1882					
SMITH SG	Stuart	1882	1883				Manchester	
SMYTHE EM		1879						
SNOOK FW	Frederick	1888		1864		1904		
SNOOK JB	James	1883	1883					
SNOOK PW	Percy	1888		1870		1955		
STANCER LB	Leslie	1945						
STEVENS H		1888						
WIDDOWSON SW	Sam Weller	1877		16/04/1851	Hucknall Torkard	1927		
WOOLLEY E		1883						

Played in Football League Cup Only

KING C	Colin	1979		1958	Edinburgh		Clydebank	Mansfield T

Played in Miscellaneous Games Only

SISSONS HP	Henry	1894			Worksop		Burton Swifts	Mansfield T
ROBERTS D	Dennis	1936		05/02/18	Bretton			Bristol City
DALLMAN W	William	1938		08/08/18	Mansfield		Rufford Col.	Mansfield Town

Another 13 players only appeared in the United Counties League:
Askew, Broughton, Dean, Dugard, I Gadsby, W Garrett, F Haslam, Howkins, J McGinn, Mounteney, WL Murray, W Oldershaw and Smith.

Made debut in 1939/40 League Matches

CHESTER TH	Thomas	1939			Glasgow		Burnley	
KNOX JP	James	1939		1913	Glasgow		St. Mirren	
MACKENZIE J	James	1939		1916	Sudbrook		Cardiff C	
RAYNER FW	Frank	1939		1913	Goldthorpe		Burnley	
RINGROSE A	Alfred	1939		18/11/1916	Edmonton	1968	Tottenham H	
WEIGHTMAN E	Eric	1939		1913	York		Chesterfield	

World War One Players

The following players made appearances during World War One. The clubs of guest players are given when known.

	Apps	Gls	Guest From:		Apps	Gls	Guest From:
Allsebrook R	27	1		Lilley B	1		
Atkin J	1		Derby County	Loversuch A	1		
Bache JW	19	6	Aston Villa	Mann J	1	1	
Bacon T	1			Marriott F	45		
Bagshaw JJ	86	3	Derby County	McNeal R	10		West Bromwich Alb.
Barraclough	1			Mee GW	11	1	
Bartrop W	1			Morley H	43		
Bell	1			Morris W	1		
Bell JJ	1		Nottm. Forest	Neal G	7		
Bird W	31	4		Newman GW	3	2	
Blackburn G	1			Orme JH	1		
Bowser S	14		West Bromwich Alb.	Parrish J	4	2	
Boyne R	1			Peart JG	1		
Branston JT	25			Pennington J	25		West Bromwich Alb.
Brooks	1			Perry J	30		
Brownlow W	1			Plant	1		
Bryan JJ	31			Poole WS	1		
Cantrell J	127	29	Tottenham Hotspur	Price W	1		
Charles F	1			Pykett B	4		
Charlesworth G	51	3		Reider J	1		
Clamp A	11			Richards S	100	50	
Clarke	1			Robson M	2		
Clay T	21	3	Tottenham Hotspur	Sambrooke C	6		
Cook J	7	3		Sankey T	1		
Cooke JR	5	1		Scrimshaw A	16	1	
Crossley CH	1			Scrimshaw H	5		
Cumming J	19	2		Sheldon L	34	1	
Dale GH	3	2		Short J	42	20	Lincoln City
Davis	1			Sissons W	1		
Davis F	1			Smith G	5		
Dexter F	2			Smith J	4		West Bromwich Alb.
Dexter G	2			Starkey G	1		
Driver T	1			Steele MA	6		
Dunn R	23	3		Storer H	1	1	
Edleston	1			Storey	1		
Fearnley	1	1		Tattershall W	2		
Feebery J	3		Bolton Wanderers	Thompson	1		
Flint WA	100	13		Thurman M	1		
Foster JH	19	1		Timmins W	24		
Foster WH	3			Tinsley W	1	1	
Goodman T	1			Toone G (Jr)	3		
Graham DC	2			Tremelling S	2	1	
Hasell AA	2			Turner H	1		
Hawley F	12	1		Walker JH	39	8	Derby County
Hayes J	2			Walkerdine	1		
Henshall HV	63	15		Waterall A	10		Stockport County
Hill H	1			Waterall I	72	6	
Housley H	12	6	Mansfield Town	Waterall T	16		Watford
Iremonger A	93			West, Alf	5		
James W	6	1		White	1		
Jennings W	46	2		White J	1		
Johnson H (Jr)	1			White T	15		
Johnson J	19			Wield T	2		
Jones B	1			Willis AS	1		
Kay H	1			Wilson J	1		
Keeling S	2			Woodlands A	15		
Kemp H	3	1		Woods J	2	1	
Laxton LE	4			Woolley J	2		
Leafe D	1			Wright H	5		
Leatherland J	1			Yates A	1		
Leonard H	1	2	Derby County				

World War Two Players

The following players appeared during World War Two. The clubs of guest players are given when known. Other guest players are marked with a *.

Name	Apps	Gls	Guest from:	Name	Apps	Gls	Guest from:	Name	Apps	Gls	Guest from:
Airlie S	2	1	*	Coen L	15	2	Coventry C	Hazel	1	0	
Akers W	1	0	Mansfield T	Coleman E	1	0	Norwich City	Hepworth R	36	2	Bradford PA
Alderton JH	1	0	Wolves	Collindridge C	35	20	Sheff. Utd.	Hewitt H	1	0	Northampton
Alexander T	3	0		Collins AD	3	0	Chesterfield	Higson S	1	0	
Allen RHA	21	0		Connor	1	0		Hilliard G	1	0	*
Allen W	2	1		Cooper EJ	6	0		Hinchcliffe T	1	0	Derby Co.
Anderson J	1	1	Queen o' South	Cooper S	6	0		Hinsley G	5	2	Bradford City
Andrews G	1	0		Corkhill WG	83	1	Cardiff C	Hinton E	1	0	Lincoln City
Antonio GR	24	7	Stoke C	Coulston W	8	0		Hodgkins JS	1	0	
Ashton P	3	0	Nottm. Forest	Crisp GH	1	0	Nottm. Forest	Hogg F	20	0	Luton T
Ashworth	1	0	Blackpool	Crooks SD	38	16	Derby Co.	Hollis KB	1	0	Nottm. Forest
Bacuzzi J	4	0	Fulham	Davidson DBL	15	0	Bradford PA	Holmes E	2	1	
Bagnall R	3	1		Davidson RT	2	0	Coventry C	Houghton WE	3	0	
Bailey L	2	0	*	Davie J	13	6	Brighton & HA	Howard	1	0	
Baker D	12	1	Sheff. Utd.	Davies RG	1	0	Nottm. Forest	Howarth G	2	0	
Ball E	1	0		Davies W	4	0	*	Hoyle D	3	0	
Ball WJE	1	0		Davis RD	2	2	Sunderland	Hubbard J	27	4	
Barke JL	15	0	Mansfield T	Dean	1	0		Hughes A	1	0	*
Barker JW	8	0	Derby Co.	DeLisle	1	0		Hughes S	11	0	Brighton &HA
Barnard CH	2	0	*	Dickson W	1	0		Hunter J	3	2	Preston NE
Barsby CF	1	0		Dimond S	5	3	Man. Utd.	Huntley	1	0	
Barton P	8	0		Dixon W	1	0		Hutchinson J	4	0	
Bartram S	2	0	Charlton Ath.	Donaldson HA	6	0		Iceton OL	1	0	Preston NE
Baxter WE	1	0	Nottm. Forest	Drinkwater	1	0		Iddon H	1	0	Preston NE
Beattie A	20	1	Preston NE	Drury GB	2	2	Arsenal	Iverson RT	4	0	Aston Villa
Beattie R	1	0	Preston NE	Drysdale J	1	0	*	Jackson H	4	0	
Becci A	1	0	Arbroath	Duggan	1	0	Bradford PA	James J (1)	1	0	
Bell T	1	0	*	Duncan D	39	10	Derby Co.	James J (2)	1	0	
Bellis A	1	0	Port Vale	Duns L	5	1	Sunderland	Jepson A	4	0	Port Vale
Benner R	23	0		Edwards GR	16	6	Aston Villa	Jessop W	3	0	Preston NE
Beresford R	28	10		Edwards WJ	3	0		Johnson J	1	0	*
Berry	1	0		Elliott CS	4	0	Coventry C	Johnson JT	9	0	*
Bicknell R	5	0	Wolves	Ellmer FB	7	0		Johnson JW	4	1	Huddersfield T
Bingham	1	0		Everett HP	13	0		Johnston TD	1	0	Nottm. Forest
Blagg EA	1	0	Nottm. Forest	Fell J	1	0	*	Jones A	1	0	
Bland P	1	0	*	Fenton M	2	1	*	Jones B	1	0	
Blood JF	3	0	Exeter City	Findlay PA	1	0		Jones DO	13	0	Leicester C
Bloomfield W	1	0		Flaherty E	2	1		Jones H	2	0	Burton T
Boileau HA	4	0	Coventry C	Fletcher	1	0	Blackpool	Jones JT	2	0	
Booth LJ	7	2		Flint K	14	1		Jones LJ	50	11	Arsenal
Bowers J	16	8	Leicester C	Flintson	1	0		Keen E	4	0	Derby Co.
Brader FW	5	2		Flower T	9	0		Kingwell LE	1	0	Torquay Utd.
Bradley G	2	0	Leicester C	Foster J	1	0		Kirby N	9	0	
Bradshaw	2	0		Gallacher P	2	0	Stoke City	Kirkham R	1	0	
Bramley E	4	0	Mansfield T	Gallago	1	0		Kirkpatrick S	2	0	
Bridges	1	0	Sheffield Utd.	Gardner	1	0		Kirton J	25	0	Stoke City
Briggs R	1	0		Gascoigne D	1	0		Knott H	1	1	Hull City
Brook R	2	0	Bristol City	Gascoigne D	2	2		Knowles C	1	1	
Brookbanks E	2	0		Gilson H	1	0		Knox JP	2	1	
Brooks	5	0	Burnley	Girdham A	3	0		Lager EW	2	2	Coventry C
Broome FH	20	15	Aston Villa	Glover P	3	0	*	Lamb W	1	0	
Brown AW	4	1	Burnley	Godfrey L	10	0	Aston Villa	Lambe	1	0	
Brown E	4	0		Goodman	1	0		Lambert R	1	0	
Brown GR	10	0	QPR	Goodwin FN	2	0		Lane H	4	1	*
Brown M	1	0		Graham R	1	0	Leicester C	Lawton T	1	0	Everton
Brunt GR	2	0		Grant AF	1	0	Leicester C	Ledger JK	16	2	
Buckley FL	14	3		Grant EA	1	0		Leuty LH	12	0	
Burgess R	16	0	Tottenham H	Gray R	25	2	Oldham Ath.	Lewis G	6	2	Crystal P.
Butler S	2	0	West Brom.	Greaves	1	0		Liddle D	12	4	Leicester C
Bye JH	1	0	Birmingham C	Green T	3	0	Coventry C	Lilley K	1	0	
Cairns WH	3	0	Newcastle U	Gregory H	1	0		Long D	3	0	
Carrick R	1	0	*	Griffiths J	9	0	Man. Utd.	Lovering W	2	0	*
Carter	1	0		Griffiths K	1	0		Lunn	1	0	
Carter HS	1	0	Sunderland	Groves A	5	2	Portsmouth	Lyman CC	2	1	Tottenham H
Carter J	2	0		Guttridge R	5	0	Aston Villa	Mackenzie J	14	6	
Challinor C	1	0		Hague JK	3	0	Southend U	Major L	1	0	Leicester C
Challinor J	6	0	Stoke City	Haines J	5	0	*	Marsh JK	5	5	
Chapman RJF	1	0	QPR	Haines JTW	4	1	Swansea T	Marshall JG	20	0	Burnley
Chester TH	4	0		Hall B	11	0		Martin DK	4	3	
Clack FE	5	0	Brentford	Hann R	19	0	Derby Co.	Martin EJ	1	0	
Clarke GA	14	1		Harris K	18	1		Martin FA	1	1	
Clayton S	7	2		Harrison R	5	2	*	Mason J	5	0	
Clements	1	0		Hatfield B	3	1	Bradford PA	Massie A	9	0	Aston Villa
Clift BC	3	1	West Brom.	Hatton C	16	8		Maund JH	2	1	Nottm. Forest
Clover G	1	1		Haycock F	1	0	Aston Villa	McEwan F	1	0	QPR

Name	Apps	Gls	Guest from:
McMullen J	2	0	*
McNaughton GN	2	0	
McPherson IB	41	12	Glasgow Rgs
Melling F	1	0	
Meredith RD	10	2	
Middleton L	2	0	
Mills A	1	0	*
Mills PC	27	2	
Moran A	2	0	
Morby JH	8	0	Aston Villa
Mordue J	1	0	
Morgan	1	0	
Morley J	3	0	
Morrad FG	20	6	
Moss G	10	3	
Moulson C	14	0	
Mowl WJ	10	0	
Munks JA	5	0	
Murphy G	2	0	Bradford C
Musson WU	5	0	Derby County
Mynard LD	1	0	Wolves
Newman	1	2	
Nicholas J	1	0	
Nicholas JT	43	2	Derby Co.
Nicholls H	13	0	Northampton
Nugent S	1	0	
O'Donnell F	3	1	
O'Neill T	6	0	
Oakley JC	4	0	Chesterfield
Openshaw	1	0	
Padman	1	0	
Page D	1	0	
Parker A	8	1	
Parkin FW	4	0	
Parks A	15	2	
Parr J	3	0	Derby Co.
Pavlov M	1	0	Lincoln City
Peacock E	15	0	
Pettitt	1	0	
Piercy C	5	0	Chester
Pithie DS	1	0	*
Pomphrey EA	10	0	
Potts	1	0	
Pritchard R	1	0	*
Probert	1	0	
Pye J	30	16	
Ramage PMF	5	0	Derby Co.
Ratcliffe PC	19	0	
Rawcliffe F	16	5	Wolves
Rayner F	6	1	
Read CW	7	2	
Renshaw	1	0	
Rhodes K	1	0	
Rickards CT	20	9	Cardiff City
Rigby NE	11	0	
Ringrose A	1	0	
Rist FH	1	0	Charlton Ath.
Roberts D	3	0	Wolves
Robinson GF	5	0	
Robinson GH	1	1	Charlton Ath.
Robinson P	1	0	
Rollett E	3	0	
Rollinson	1	0	
Ross J	1	0	*
Rossington K	1	0	*
Rothwell E	2	0	Bolton Wan.
Rowley W	1	0	
Ruecroft EJ	1	0	Halifax T
Russell D	1	0	*
Sail GH	1	0	
Sewell J	28	8	
Sharman F	22	0	Leicester C
Sheen J	4	0	Sheff. Utd.
Shell FH	2	0	Aston Villa
Siddons F	2	1	
Sidlow C	7	0	Wolves
Simpson C	2	1	
Skidmore W	2	0	Wolves
Slack L	1	0	Derby Co.
Smallwood E	1	0	
Smeeton J	1	0	
Smith J	4	0	
Smith JT	4	0	*
Smith L	7	0	*
Smith R	1	0	
Sneddon T	1	0	Rochdale
Southwell AA	66	1	
Sparrow	2	0	
Stancer LB	19	0	
Stanowski	1	0	
Steele FC	7	3	Stoke City
Steen AW	3	0	Wolves
Stephenson R	7	0	
Stewart R	1	0	*
Stillyards G	1	0	Lincoln C
Strain N	14	4	
Streten BR	19	0	
Somerfield AG+.	1	0	Wolves
Summers	1	0	
Sweet	2	0	
Swinburne TA	1	0	Newcastle U
Tapping FH	4	0	Blackpool
Taylor	1	0	
Taylor GT	5	0	Coventry C
Taylor JL	3	0	
Taylor WB	1	0	Grimsby T
Thorne	1	0	
Thorpe A	4	0	
Toothill R	4	0	
Towler BE	43	15	
Townrow RF	1	0	*
Trim RF	1	0	Nottm. Forest
Tweed GE	1	0	*
Tyroll	1	0	
Unwin S	6	0	
Vallance	4	1	
Van Gelden J	2	0	
Vause PG	1	0	Rochdale
Vincent NE	3	0	Grimsby T
Waite JH	1	0	
Wakeman A	2	0	
Walker E	3	1	Bradford
Walsh W	14	2	Derby Co.
Walters H	8	0	Wolves
Warburton A	3	1	
Ward TV	11	0	Derby Co.
Waterall K	2	0	
Weaver S	1	1	Chelsea
Weightman E	5	0	
Wheldon E	2	0	
White A	3	0	
Whitehead J	2	0	
Wilcox GE	10	0	Derby Co.
Wildgoose C	1	0	
Wilkinson N	40	0	Stoke City
Wilson	1	1	
Windle R	5	0	
Wiseman G	20	0	
Wood CC	1	0	
Woodcock E	2	0	
Woolacott H	1	0	*
Wright	2	0	
Wright H	1	0	*
Wright J	2	3	
Wright WA	5	1	Wolves

Appendix

Seasonal Statistics and Team Groups
1864/65 - 1994/95

1864/65

1	Dec	8	TRENT VALLEY	0-0	
2	Jan	2	SHEFFIELD	0-1	J Patterson (capt.), T Elliott, W Elliott, R Fountain, H Moody, R Daft, CF Daft, G Parr, John Parr, H Parr, JW Thackery, JB Gibson, EB Steegman, A Scrimshaw, W Goddard, H Simons, JS Wright, W Wright
3	Mar	9	Lincoln	0-0	J Patterson (capt.), H Simons, JB Gibson, E Steegman, W Wright, F Wright, B Bradley, CF Daft, S Scrimshaw, E Bradley, H Moody, W Elliott, J Hack, J Hodges, WA Hodges
4	Mar	23	Sheffield	0-1	J Patterson (capt.), H Simons, CF Daft, T Bignall, W Elliott, J Wright, H Moody, J Hack, J Hodges, T Elliott, FB Gibson, Allott, B Bradley

Home games at the Meadows Cricket Ground

1865/66

1	Jan	25	SHEFFIELD	1-2	Packer	J Patterson, FC Smith, A Deedes, JS Wright, JB Gibson, AB Baillon, G Packer, H Browne, W Elliott, S Scrimshaw, H Rastall, WA Hodges, JC Hodges, J Hack, C Steegman
2	Mar	15	Sheffield	0-1		J Patterson (capt.), AB Baillon, H Moody, G Packer, W Elliott, J Hack, W Birkin, J Shaw, W Lymbery, H Browne, CF Daft, HH Herbert, G Steegman, JM Astill, J Wilkinson
3	Mar	22	Nottm. Forest	0-0		EB Steegman, J Hack (capt.), AB Baillon, W Elliott, T Elliott, W Ward, JC Hodges, H Browne, W Goddard, B Bradley, J Wilkinson
4	Apr	19	NOTTM. FOREST	0-0		EB Steegman, J Hack, AB Baillon, W Elliott, W Ward, CS Wardle, Lees, J Wilkinson, Wright, S Scrimshaw, Stranger

Home games at the Meadows Cricket Ground

1866/67

1	Dec	13	Practice			FC Smith with A Deedes, G Pym, WA Hodges, JC Hodges, W Ward, W Bury, G Fellows. EB Steegman with H Simons, W Goddard, R Daft, J Hack, AB Baillon, HW Chambers
2	Dec	20	NOTTM. FOREST	1-1	Hack	A Deedes (capt), WA Birkin, AB Baillon, J Hack, TP Keely, JC Hodges, FC Smith, WA Hodges, W Ward, W Goddard, EB Steegman, CS Wardle, A Waring, G Baillon, W. Browne
3	Feb	7	PUBLIC SCHOOLS	1-0	WA Hodges	AB Baillon, WS Birkin, W Goddard, J Hack, WA Hodges, JC Hodges, F Newsome, EB Steegman, H Simons, W Ward, CS Wardle
4	Feb	14	Sheffield	1-0	Rothera (and a rouge)	A Deedes (capt.), EB Steegman, JC Hodges, John Lambert, C Rothera, CS Wardle, W Goddard, J Hack, AB Baillon, W Lymbery, TP Keely
5	Feb	28	Nottm. Forest	1-0	WA Hodges	FC Smith (capt.), AB Baillon, T Keely, JC Hodges, WA Hodges, T Elliott, J Lambert, J Hack, W Ward (2 short)
6	Mar	14	SHEFFIELD	1-0	JC Hodges	A Deedes (capt.), WA Hodges, JC Hodges, J Hack, W Goddard, T Keeley, J Lambert, C Rothera, FC Smith, CS Wardle, AB Baillon

Game 1 at Bramcote, 2 and 3 at the Meadows, game 6 at Trent Bridge

1867/68

1	Nov	21	Robin Hood Rifles	1-0	JC Hodges	AB Baillon, F Baillon, B Richard, CF Elliott, JS Shaw, CS Wardle, C Rothera, G Hine, WA Hodges (capt), JC Hodges, W Ward(absent)
2	Nov	28	Sheffield			No details available
3	Dec	12	Practice Match			11 of the Town (capt. A Deedes) v. 11 of the County (capt. R Daft)
4	Dec	26	Nottm. Forest (Practice)			No details available
5	Jan	23	ROBIN HOOD RIFLES	0-0		JC Hodges, WA Hodges, AB Baillon, RF Baillon, C Rothera, J Rothera, L Melville, A Lambert, W Bell, W Ward, JH Stafford, CS Wardle
6	Feb	6	PUBLIC SCHOOLS	0-0		No details available
7	Feb	20	PUBLIC SCHOOLS	1-0	WA Hodges	WA Hodges (capt.), JC Hodges, J Hack, CH Stafford, CS Wardle, W Ward, AB Baillon, F Baillon, R Rothera, H Simons

Home games at the Meadows Cricket Ground

1868/69

Home games at the Meadows

#	Date	Opponent	Score	Scorers	Baillon AB	Hodges WA	Hodges JC	Lambert J	Barks A	Rothera FW	Williams H	Daft R	Stafford CH	Greenhalgh EH	Hack J	Wardle CS	Forman A	Elliott W	Wilde C	Beckett E	Rothera CL	Steegman EB	Hine A	Morse H
1	Jan 28	ROBIN HOOD RIFLES	0-0		x	x	x			x	x	x	x			x					x		x	x
2	Feb 26	Newark	0-2		x		x	x		x	x				x	x	x	x		x				
3	Mar 4	NEWARK	2-1 Unknown		x	x	x			x	x				x	x	x	x		x				
4	Mar 11	ROBIN HOOD RIFLES			x					x	x	x	x			x			x	x	x	x	x	x
5	Mar 18	SOUTH DERBYSHIRE			x	x	x	x	x	x	x	x	x	x	x	x	x	x	x	x				

1869/70

Home games at the Meadows except 10 (on the Forest)
Played in game 3: FC Smith. In game 5: Palethorpe. In game 7: S Morse. In game 9: EB Steegman

#	Date	Opponent	Score	Scorers	Wardle CS	Rothera FW	Baillon AB	Daft R	Forman A	Rothera CL	Keely GP	Lambert J	Greenhalgh EH	Baillon FJ	Elliott WJ	Hack J	Keely EM	Stafford CH	Hodges JC	Enfield H	Revis WH	Bonifant RH	Edwards W	Hodges WA	Jones E	Keely T	Lambert T	McCraith JW
1	Nov 11	NEWARK	3-0	AB Baillon, Daft, CL Rothera	x	x	x	x	x	x	x			x		x	x							x	x			
2	Nov 13	Nottm. Forest	0-0		x	x	x		x	x	x		x	x	x		x										x	
3	Nov 18	South Derbyshire	3-2	CL Rothera 3	x	x	x	x	x	x	x	x		x	x	x			x									x
4	Dec 2	ROBIN HOOD RIFLES	4-0	AB Baillon, CL Rothera, EH Greenhalgh	x	x	x	x	x	x	x		x				x	x										x
5	Dec 16	Sheffield	0-1		x	x	x	x	x	x	x	x	x		x													
6	Jan 20	Lincoln	1-0	Daft	x		x	x		x	x	x			x		x		x						x			
7	Jan 29	SHEFFIELD	0-0		x	x	x	x	x		x	x				x		x		x								
8	Feb 3	Newark	1-0	Daft	x	x	x	x	x		x		x		x				x		x							
9	Feb 26	SOUTH DERBYSHIRE	0-0		x	x		x		x	x	x		x		x	x			x								
10	Mar 12	LINCOLN	1-0	EM Keely	x	x	x	x	x		x	x	x	x		x										x		
11	Mar 17	Chesterfield	3-1	CH Stafford 2, unknown	x	x			x		x	x	x	x		x				x								

1870/71

All home games at the Meadows Cricket Ground except 3, Trent Bridge
Played in game 9: WS Beckett, JP Donovan, L Dooney. In game 8: Fisher, J Rothera, CH Stafford.
Played in game 10: Diamond, A Hine

#	Date	Opponent	Score	Scorers	Baillon AB	Dewner W	Elliott WJ	Forman A	Greenhalgh EH	Hack J	Hodges JC	Keely EM	Lambert J	Rothera FW	Wardle CS	Hodges WA	Lambert T	Shuttleworth H	Enfield H	Keely GP	Shuttleworth J	Forman J	Hodges G	Daft R	Richards	Steegman EB	Johnson WJ	Marriott W	Parr G	Leipman L
1	Nov 17	NEWARK	0-0		x	x									x															
2	24	Nottm. Law Club	0-1		x	x		x	x	x	x	x				x	x	x	x											
3	Dec 3	SHEFFIELD			x	x						x	x	x	x	x		x	x	x	x									
4	15	Lincoln	2-0	Wardle, FW Rothera							x	x	x	x	x	x		x	x			x	x							
5	Feb 9	NOTTM. LAW CLUB	1-1 Unknown		x	x		x		x	x				x		x							x	x	x				
6	16	Newark	1-0	J Lambert	x	x		x	x		x		x	x	x													x	x	x
7	23	Chesterfield	0-0			x		x		x		x	x	x	x														x	x
8	Mar 4	LINCOLN	1-0 Unknown		x		x	x					x		x		x										x			
9	9	Sheffield	0-0		x	x					x			x	x	x										x			x	
10	Nov 9	NEWARK			x	x	x	x	x	x	x	x	x	x	x	x														

1871/72

All home games at the Meadows Cricket Ground
Played in game 2: L Leipman. In game 3: R Daft, J Hack. In game 5: H Williams. In game 6: H Morse, S Smith, S Windley.
Played in game 7: Jones. In game 8: C Browne, JW Rothera.
Played in game 9: Browne, Carlisle, Muir, Padley, JH Richardson, Riggall, H Wyles (all of Lincoln). In game 10: MJ Ellison, Wake.

#	Date	Opponent	Score	Scorers	Forman A	Baillon AB	Greenhalgh EH	Parr J	Rothera FW	Wardle CS	Keely EM	Lambert J	Lambert T	Pearson AH	Curstam AW	Lambert AW	Parr G	Rothera CL	Crawford D	Johnson WG	Morse S	Robinson H	Ashwell AT	Forman J	Forman JR	Hodges JC	Kirk JP	Morse E	Spencer CJ	Steegman EB
1	Oct 28	LINCOLN	1-0	Baillon	x	x	x		x	x	x		x		x			x		x										
2	Nov 9	NOTTM. LAW CLUB	1-0	CL Rothera	x	x	x			x		x	x	x				x								x				
3	16	South Derbyshire	1-4					x	x	x		x	x	x		x			x										x	
4	25	NEWARK	1-0	AW Lambert	x	x	x	x			x	x	x		x		x	x									x			
5	Dec 28	Newark	2-1	Wardle, S Morse				x		x						x			x	x	x	x		x	x					
6	Jan 4	PUBLIC SCHOOLS	0-0		x						x			x			x			x						x				
7	11	NOTTM LAW CLUB	0-0		x	x	x			x			x	x				x			x			x	x	x				
8	25	Sheffield	0-1				x	x		x	x	x	x		x		x	x												
9	Feb 8	Lincoln	0-1							x					x	x														
10	13	NOTTM. FOREST	0-1		x	x		x	x			x			x	x				x							x			
11	24	Nottm. Forest	1-2	J Parr	x	x		x	x		x			x	x					x	x					x				x
12	Mar 16	SHEFFIELD	0-1		x	x	x	x	x					x		x	x		x		x							x		

1872/73

#	Date		Opponent	Score	Scorers	Greenhalgh EH	Cursham AW	Revis WH	Spencer CJ	Widdowson SW	Parr J	Seals G	Robinson WM	Wake RG	Mason W	Marriott F	Bright A	Ashwell AT	Wardle CS	Forman A	Pearson AH	Hayes G	Kirk JJP	Tomlinson J	Bright J	Hack J	Davies H	Johnson WG	Owen JRB	Greenhalgh A	Jones E	Keely EM
1	Oct	31	NOTTM. LAW CLUB	1-0	EH Greenhalgh	x		x	x		x								x	x	x									x	x	x
2	Nov	14	SOUTH DERBYSHIRE	1-0	Revis	x	x	x	x						x				x	x	x				x		x					x
3	Dec	7	Nottm. Forest	0-1		x	x					x	x		x			x	x	x	x				x				x			
4		12	OCKBROOK	4-0	Owen 2, Cursham, unknown	x	x	x										x	x	x					x	x			x		x	
5	Jan	4	NOTTM. FOREST	0-0		x	x		x			x				x	x	x							x							
6		16	Sheffield	2-3	Widdowson 2		x	x	x	x			x	x		x	x	x					x		x							
7	Feb	15	SHEFFIELD	1-0	Owen	x	x	x	x	x	x	x	x	x											x				x			
8		22	LINCOLN	4-0	Cursham, Revis, Widdowson 2	x	x	x	x	x			x	x	x									x	x				x			
9	Mar	17	LONDON	0-0		x	x	x	x	x	x		x			x	x	x				x										
10		27	NOTTM. LAW CLUB	0-0		x		x			x		x	x						x	x	x			x		x	x				

All home games at Meadows Cricket Ground except 9, Trent Bridge
Played in game 1: J Ward, AB Baillon. In game 3: W Whiteley. In game 4 CH Stafford.
Played in game 5: S Morse, E Morse, H Greenhalgh, F Rayner

Standing: Marriott, Mason, Revis
Sitting: Parr, Widdowson, A.Bright, Robinson
Front: A.Cursham, Hayes, E.H.Greenhalgh, Spencer

1873/74

#		Date	Match	Score	Scorers	Baillon AB	Greenhalgh EH	Revis WH	Seals G	Spencer CJ	Parr J	Robinson WM	Bright A	Widdowson SW	Marriott F	Pearson AH	Cursham AW	Bright J	Rothera CL	Ashwell F	Johnson WG	Rothera FW	Greenhalgh A	Steegman EB	Wake RG	Owen JRB
1	Oct	25	STOKE	2-0	Widdowson 2	x	x	x	x	x				x	x	x	x			x				x		
2	Nov	1	Lincoln	0-0			x		x		x	x									x				x	
3		6	South Derbyshire	3-4	AW Cursham 2, Spencer	x		x	x			x	x		x	x	x	x								
4		20	NOTTM. LAW CLUB	0-2		x	x	x											x	x				x	x	
5		29	LONDON	2-0	Spencer, Robinson	x	x	x	x	x	x	x	x	x				x								x
6	Dec	18	SAWLEY ATHLETIC	0-0		x	x	x			x		x		x	x		x				x				
7		20	Newark	2-0	Spencer, one og	x		x	x		x		x						x	x						
8		27	Nottm. Forest	1-1	EH Greenhalgh	x	x				x				x	x		x	x				x			
9	Jan	15	Sheffield	0-2		x		x				x	x	x		x			x	x			x			
10	Feb	7	NOTTM. FOREST	0-0		x		x				x	x	x			x	x					x		x	
11		16	London	0-4		x	x	x	x	x		x	x	x			x		x		x					
12		18	London	1-1	Widdowson	x	x	x	x	x		x	x	x			x		x							

Home games at Trent Bridge except 4, 6 at the Meadows
Played in game 2: Allen, FC Cursham, CH Stafford, J Johnson, CS Wardle.
Played in game 4: Norris, AJ Bates. In game 6, JC Hodges, Forman. In game 7: AG Ashwell, J Forman, JR Forman.
Played in game 8: J Lambert, S Morse, E Morse. In game 11: T Lambert. In game 12: W Mason, H Davies.

1874/75

#		Date	Match	Score	Scorers	Greenhalgh H	Widdowson SW	Jessop H	Baillon AB	Greenhalgh EH	Revis WH	Cursham AW	Spencer CJ	Seals G	Robinson WM	Rothera FW	Chapman W	Bright J	Smith JH	Wake RG	Hadden JH	Hadden WJ	Rothera CL
1	Nov	14	NOTTM. FOREST	0-0		x				x		x			x	x	x	x	x	x			
2		21	SHEFFIELD	0-3			x	x	x	x	x	x			x	x			x	x	x		
3	Jan	14	Sheffield	2-1	EH Greenhalgh, Cursham	x	x			x	x	x	x	x			x						
4		21	Newark	7-0	EH Greenhalgh 2, Widdowson 2, Revis, Spencer, H Greenhalgh	x	x	x	x	x	x	x				x						x	x
5		30	Queen's Park	0-6		x	x	x		x	x	x	x	x	x					x			
6	Feb	6	SHEFFIELD	1-0	og	x	x	x	x	x	x	x			x	x	x		x				
7		9	Nottm. Forest	1-5	Parr	x		x	x	x						x		x				x	x
8	Mar	8	QUEEN'S PARK	1-1	Widdowson		x	x	x	x	x	x	x			x	x		x				

Home games at Trent Bridge except 1, Meadows
Played in game 1; Bethel, Freeman, WG Johnson. In game 3: B Ashwell, T Lambert, J Whyat, AW WInfield.
Played in game 5; Roberts. In game 7, AC Goodyer, GE Power, J Parr.

1875/76

#		Date	Match	Score	Scorers	Greenhalgh H	Greenhalgh RJ	Rothera FW	Greenhalgh EH	Revis WH	Hadden WJ	Ellis D	Seals G	Jessop H	Cursham AW	Dodson AT	Chapman W	Ashwell HG	Dobson WH	Keely A	Lambert J	Parr J	Power GE	Ashwell AT	Widdowson SW	Lambert T	Keely EM
1	Nov	13	Nottm. Forest	0-2																							
2		27	SHEFFIELD	0-0			x	x	x	x		x			x			x						x		x	x
3	Dec	11	Derbyshire	1-1	Hadden		x	x	x	x	x	x	x			x	x	x	x								
4		16	Grantham	0-0		x	x	x		x							x										
5	Jan	6	GRANTHAM	2-0	Revis, HG Ashwell	x	x	x	x	x			x		x	x	x					x					
6	Feb	10	Sheffield	2-7	Ellis 2	x	x	x		x	x		x		x	x	x		x					x			
7		17	Derby Grammar School	1-0	Cursham		x		x		x				x	x			x		x						
8		24	Cambridge University	0-0		x	x	x	x	x	x	x	x		x	x				x							
9		29	NOTTM. FOREST	1-0	Cursham	x	x	x	x		x	x	x	x	x	x					x						

Home games at Trent Bridge except 5, Meadows
Played in game 7: AJ Bates, CJ Caborn, EB Steegman, one unknown

1876/77

#		Date	Match	Score	Scorers	Greenhalgh H	Baillon AB	Jessop H	Greenhalgh RJ	Greenhalgh EH	Keely EM	Oliver TA	Hadden WJ	Cursham AW	Seals G	Cursham CL	Rothera FW	Dobson AT	Ashwell F	Widdowson SW	Wake WR	Keely ER	Davies W	Potter S	Keely S	Dobson WH	Pearson WA	Parr G
1	Oct	7	Queen's Park	1-5	og	x	x	x	x	x	x	x	x	x	x		x				x	x						
2	Nov	18	Nottm. Forest	2-0	AW Cursham, one og	x	x	x	x	x	x	x	x	x	x		x											
3	Dec	16	NEWARK	4-1	Unknown		x	x		x		x	x	x	x	x		x			x	x	x	x				
4	Jan	27	MANCHESTER	2-0	RJ Greenhalgh, AW Cursham	x	x	x	x	x	x	x	x	x	x				x									
5	Feb	1	Sheffield	3-7	AW Cursham 2, Oliver	x			x	x	x	x	x	x	x	x		x	x							x		
6		8	NOTTM. FOREST	1-1	Oliver	x	x	x	x	x	x	x	x	x	x	x												x
7		24	Derby Grammar School	0-2		x	x	x	x	x	x	x	x	x	x	x												
8	Mar	17	SHEFFIELD	2-0	Hadden, H Greenhalgh	x		x	x	x	x	x	x	x	x					x	x							

Home games at Trent Bridge except 6, Meadows

1877/78

					Greenhalgh H	Greenhalgh EH	Cursham HA	Greenhalgh RJ	Keely EM	Oliver TA	Cursham AW	Dobson AT	Keely SH	Seals G	Jessop H	Widdowson SW	Cursham CL	Keely ER	Pearson AH	Butler H	Reckless S	Baillon AB	Corfield HA
1	Oct	13	STOKE	4-1	HA Cursham 3, RJ Greenhalgh	X	X	X	X	X	X	X		X	X		X				X			
2		25	NOTTM. LAW CLUB	5-6	Unknown	X	X		X	X				X	X					X		X	X	
3	Nov	17	Queen's Park	1-6	EM Keely	X	X	X	X	X	X	X		X	X	X				X				
4	Dec	6	Soutwell	1-10	Reckless		X	X	X													X		
5		15	Manchester	6-0	HA Cursham 5, EM Keely	X	X	X	X	X		X		X				X	X		X			
6		20	Sheffield	1-2	HA Cursham	X	X	X	X	X	X	X	X	X				X	X					
7		22	Derbyshire	4-0	Unknown	X	X	X	X	X		X	X	X	X	X			X					
8	Jan	12	SOUTHWELL	4-0	Unknown	X	X	X	X	X		X	X	X			X	X	X					
9		19	QUEEN'S PARK	1-2	AW Cursham	X	X	X	X	X		X	X	X			X	X	X					
10	Feb	2	Stoke	1-0	Corfield	X	X	X	X			X	X	X			X	X	X					X
11		9	Manchester	4-1	CL Cursham. RJ Greenhalgh, HA Cursham, H Greenhalgh	X	X	X	X		X		X		X	X		X				X	X	
12		20	DERBY GRAMMAR SCHOOL	8-2	HA Cursham 4, Oliver, Seals, CL Cursham, AW Cursham	X	X	X			X	X	X		X		X	X	X		X			
13		23	SHEFFIELD	7-0	CL Cursham 3, AW Cursham 2, HA Cursham, RJ Greenhalgh	X	X	X	X		X	X	X		X		X	X	X		X			
14		28	NOTTM LAW CLUB	2-8	Dobson, Corfield		X						X							X			X	X

Home games at Beeston except 9 (Trent Bridge).
Played in game 2: AH Pearson. In game 3: FW Rothera
Played in game 4: Hill, Jones, Warner, Oldini, Johnson
Played in game 12: WH Scottorn. In game 14: Harrison, Haughton, Neale, Russell, Smith

F.A. Cup

						Greenhalgh H	Greenhalgh EH	Cursham HA	Greenhalgh RJ	Keely EM	Oliver TA	Cursham AW	Dobson AT	Keely SH	Seals G	Jessop H	Widdowson SW	Cursham CL	Keely ER	Pearson AH
R1	Nov	3	SHEFFIELD	1-1	HA Cursham	1500	X	X	X	X	X	X			X	X	X	X			X
rep	Dec	1	Sheffield	0-3		1500	X	X	X	X	X			X	X	X	X				

Home game at Trent Bridge.
Played in the replay: E Jessop

Back: E.Keely, Rothera, Ashwell(Umpire), H.Greenhalgh, H.Cursham, Seals
Middle: R.Greenhalgh, A.Cursham, E.Greenhalgh, Oliver, S.Keely
Front: Jessop

1878/79

#	Date		Opponent	Score	Scorers	Greenhalgh H	Greenhalgh EH	Dobson AT	Seals G	Morse H	Cursham AW	Greenhalgh RJ	Cursham CL	Owen Rev. JRB	Cursham HA	Oliver TA	Jessop AE	Britten TJ	Widdowson SW	Jarrett RJ	Pearson AH	Woodcock A	Ashwell F	Grace GF	Smythe A
1	Oct	5	Stoke	0-1		x	x	x		x	x	x	x		x	x					x				
2		19	SHEFFIELD	8-0	RJ Greenhalgh 3, CL Cursham 2, HA Cursham 2, Seals	x	x	x	x	x		x	x		x	x	x			x					
3	Nov	9	Queen's Park	0-4		x	x	x	x	x	x	x	x			x	x		x						
4		23	Derby Grammar School	8-0		x	x	x	x	x	x	x	x		x	x	x								
5		30	DERBYSHIRE	1-0	Oliver	x	x	x		x	x	x	x		x	x		x	x						
6	Dec	5	DERBYSHIRE	6-1	AW Cursham 2, HA Cursham 2, CL Cursham, E Jessop	x	x	x		x	x	x	x		x	x	x			x					
7		7	NEWARK	4-1	RJ Greenhalgh 2, Corfield 2		x					x	x			x	x				x		x		
8	Feb	1	QUEEN'S PARK	0-2		x	x		x	x	x	x	x		x	x			x				x		
9		8	GREY FRIARS	2-3	CL Cursham, Rev. JRB Owen	x			x	x		x	x	x		x	x							x	x
10		20	Sheffield	4-2	Britten, Woodcock, unknown 2	x	x	x		x	x	x	x			x	x	x				x			
11	Mar	8	STOKE	1-0	AW Cursham	x	x	x		x	x	x	x		x		x				x				

Games 2, 5, 8 and 9 at Trent Bridge. Games 6, 7 and 11 at the Meadows. Game 5 played under floodlights.
Played in game 7: H Corfield, CJ Lewis, R Baillon, W Davies. In game 3: J. Lindon. In game 11: H Jessop.

F.A. Cup

	Date		Opponent	Score	Scorers	Att	Greenhalgh H	Greenhalgh EH	Dobson AT	Seals G	Morse H	Cursham AW	Greenhalgh RJ	Cursham CL	Owen Rev. JRB	Cursham HA	Oliver TA	Jessop AE
R1	Nov	16	NOTTM FOREST	1-3	Rev. JRB Owen	500	x	x	x	x	x	x	x	x	x	x	x	x

Played at Beeston Cricket Ground

1879/80

#	Date		Opponent	Score	Scorers	Greenhalgh H	Greenhalgh EH	Jessop H	Dobson AT	Morse H	Jessop E	Cursham AW	Cursham CL	Seals G	Cursham HA	Oliver TA	Greenhalgh RJ	Morgan JR	Dobson CF	Horsley A	Pearson WA	Pearson D	Smythe EM	Baillon JC	Bennett FT	Butler H	Chapman H	Everall J	Lounds J
1	Oct	11	Derby Grammar School	2-0	Unknown	1			4	6	7		8	9	10	11					2	3							
2		25	Derbyshire	3-4	Unknown	1	2	3		6	7	8		9	10	11	9				4								
3	Nov	1	Sheffield	0-5		1	2	3		6	7		8	9	10	11				9									
4		15	Queen's Park	1-4	HA Cursham	9	3	4		6	7	8			10	11			2					5					
5	Jan	17	Nottm. Forest	1-7	CL Cursham		2	3	4	6	7		8	1	10	11												9	
6	Feb	28	SHEFFIELD	2-3	CL Cursham, unknown	1	2			6	7	8	9	9						11		3					4		
7	Mar	6	GREY FRIARS	3-3	E Jessop 2, CL Cursham		2		4	6	11		9	1			9	3	8							7			10
8		12	DERBY GRAMMAR SC.	2-2	RJ Greenhalgh, Bennett					9	6	5			2		10		3						4	7			

The players' positions were still somewhat flexible; thus two number 9s will be found in some of the games.
Home games at Trent Bridge except number 6, Beeston.
Played in game 1: Richards. One unknown player in game 3. Goalkeeper in game 4: SG Smith.
Played in game 5: V. Smith. Played in game 6: J Smith. Goalkeeper unknown in game 8. Played in game 8: A Orton (8), CL Maltby (11).

F.A. Cup

	Date		Opponent	Score		Att	Greenhalgh H	Greenhalgh EH	Jessop H	Dobson AT	Morse H	Jessop E	Cursham AW	Cursham CL	Seals G	Cursham HA	Oliver TA	Greenhalgh RJ	Morgan JR	Dobson CF	Horsley A	Pearson WA	Pearson D	Smythe EM	Baillon JC
R1	Nov	8	Nottm. Forest	0-4		2000	1	9	3		6	7			9	10	11			2					4

Played at Trent Bridge. Played at no. 5: S Macrae.

1880/81

#	Date		Opponent	Score	Scorers	Greenhalgh H	Dobson AT	Jessop H	Palmer S	Macrae S	Chapman H	Cursham AW	Cursham CL	Morse H	Cursham HA	Greenhalgh EH	Dobson CF	Bourne A	Ellis D	Everall J	Greenhalgh RJ	Jessop E	Lewis CJ	Malby CL
1	Oct	16	Nottm. Forest	0-4				3	8	6		7	10	4	11	3						5		
2	Nov	6	QUEEN'S PARK	3-4	AW Cursham 2, HA Cursham	1	2		4	5	6	7	8	9	10					3				
3	Dec	11	SHEFFIELD	8-1	HA Cursham 5, Morse 3	1	2	3	5		6	7	8	9	10	4								
4		18	STAVELEY	3-2	CL Cursham, HA Cursham, Morse	1	2	3	4	5	6	7	8	9	10	11								
5	Jan	8	NEWARK	15-1	HA Cursham 5, EH Greenhalgh 3, Morse 2, CL Cursham, 2 og	1	2	3	5		6	7	8	9	10	11				4				
6		15	Blackburn Rovers	1-3	Morse	1	2	3	5		6	7	8	9	10	11								
7	Feb	5	BLACKBURN ROVERS	3-7	CL Cursham, HA Cursham 2	1	2		4	5	6	7	8	9	10	11		3						
8		19	Sheffield	4-2	AW Cursham, CL Cursham, Morse, one og		2	3			6	7	8	9	10	11		4		5				
9	Mar	5	NOTTM. FOREST	1-0	AW Cursham		2	3	4	5	6	7	8	9	10	11								
10		14	Staveley	1-1	CF Dobson		2	3	5		6	7	8		10	11	4	9					1	

Home games at the Castle Cricket Ground
Played in game 1: WA Pearson (1), Rev. AC Ratcliffe (9). In game 2, TA Oliver (11).
Played in game 3: W Willis. In game 6, W Standing.
Goalkeeper in game 8: WH Stacey. In game 9, W Sorby

F.A. Cup

	Date		Opponent	Score	Scorers	Att	Greenhalgh H	Dobson AT	Jessop H	Palmer S	Macrae S	Chapman H	Cursham AW	Cursham CL	Morse H	Cursham HA	Greenhalgh EH	Malby CL
R1	Nov	4	DERBYSHIRE	4-4	AW Cursham, HA Cursham 2, one unknown		1	2		9	5	6	7	8	9	11	4	10
rep.		27	Derbyshire	4-2	HA Cursham 2, EH Greenhalgh, Morse		1	2	3	4	5	6	7	8	9	10	11	
R3	Feb	12	ASTON VILLA	1-3	CL Cursham	4000	1	2	3	4	5	6	7	8	9	10	11	

Home games at Trent Bridge.
Game 2 after extra time. Notts had a bye in round 2.

1881/82

#	Date		Opponent	Score	Scorers	Jessop H	Dobson AT	Moore HT	Fletcher H	Chapman H	Dobson CF	Cursham CL	Cursham AW	Bausor T	Greenhalgh EH	Cursham HA	Emmitt HW	Maltby CL	Bourne B	Morse H	Danks T	Gunn W	Wilks J	Oliver TA
1	Oct	1	Derby Midland	1-1	AW Cursham		2				6	7	8			11							10	
2		8	Stoke	4-1	Unknown																			
3		22	Blackburn Rovers	1-10	Bausor		2			5	6	7	8		9	11				10				4
4	Nov	10	GRANTHAM	13-0	Unknown	1	2	3	4	5	6	7	8	9	10	11								
5		12	STAVELEY	7-0	HA Cursham 4, CL Cursham 2, Bausor	1	2	3	4	5	6	7	8	9	10	11								
6		26	Queen's Park	1-10	CL Cursham	1	2	3	4	5		7	8	9	10	11			6					
7	Dec	3	Aston Villa	2-2	HA Cursham, unknown	1	2	3		5	6	7	8	9	10	11								4
8		17	Nottm. Forest	5-0	Bausor 2, HA Cursham 2, Greenhalgh	1	2	3	4	5	6	7	8	9	10	11								
9	Jan	5	OLD CARTHUSIANS	5-1	Bausor 3, HA Cursham 2	1	2	3		5		7	8	9	10	11	4		6					
10		26	SHEFFIELD	5-1	HA Cursham 2, Bausor 2, Greenhalgh	1	2	3		5		7	8	9	10	11			6					
11		28	DERBY MIDLAND	7-2	HA Cursham 4, AW Cursham, Bausor, Greenhalgh	1		3		5		7	8	9	10	11		4			2			
12	Feb	4	Pilgrims	5-1	HA Cursham 4, Bausor	1	2	3		5		7	8	9	10	11					4			
13		6	Old Carthusians	0-4		1	2	3		5		7	8	9	10	11			6					
14		11	NOTTM. FOREST	1-2	CL Cursham	1	2	3		5	6	7	8	9	10	11					4			
15		18	STOKE	4-3	Bausor 2, Emmitt, Danks			3		5	6		8	9	10		4	1		11	2	7		
16		21	Sheffield	5-0	Bausor, HA Cursham, 3 unknown	1		3		5	6		8	9	10	11	2			7				
17		25	QUEEN'S PARK	1-4	HA Cursham	1	2	3		5	6				9	10	11	4				7		

Home games at the Castle Cricket Ground
Played in game 1: Biddell, R Cursham, Dexter, Gowthorne, Simpkin. In game 3, CJ Lewis (1), G Beardshaw (3). In game 10: W Sherlock (4).
Played in game 11: C Matthews (6). In game 12: ED Ellis (6). In game 13: JG Thompson (4). In game 16: H Shelton (4). In game 17: E Jessop (8).

F.A. Cup

	Date		Opponent	Score	Scorers	Att	Jessop H	Dobson AT	Moore HT	Fletcher H	Chapman H	Dobson CF	Cursham CL	Cursham AW	Bausor T	Greenhalgh EH	Cursham HA	Emmitt HW
R2	Nov	24	WEDNESBURY STROLLERS	5-3	AW Cursham 2, HA Cursham 2, Knowles (og)		1	2	3	4	5	6	7	8	9	10	11	
rep	Dec	10	Wednesbury Strollers	11-1	HA Cursham 6, AW Cursham 2, CF Dobson, CL Cursham, Bausor		1	2	3		5	6	7	8	9	10	11	4
R3		31	Aston Villa	2-2	Bausor 2	7000	1	2	3	4	5	6	7	8	9	10	11	
rep	Jan	7	ASTON VILLA	2-2	Chapman, AW Cursham	7000	1	2	3	4	5	6	7	8	9	10	11	
rep		14	Aston Villa	1-4	HA Cursham	12000	1	2	3	4	5	6	7	8	9	10	11	

Round 1: Drawn v. Calthorpe; walk over.
Round 2 at the Castle Ground. Replayed at Derby Cricket Ground, after protest
First game with Aston Villa after extra time (at 90 mins, 2-2).
First replay at the Castle, also after extra time (at 90 mins, 1-1)

1882/83

#		Date	Opponent	Score	Scorers	Jessop H	Dobson AT	Moore HT	Dobson CF	Macrae S	Chapman H	Smith SG	Cursham AW	Cursham HA	Gunn W	Greenhalgh EH	Gillett LF	Harker E	Bausor T	Emmitt HW	Moore AE	Seals G	Billyeald H	Cursham CL
1	Oct	5	LOCAL CLUBS XI	10-1	HA Cursham 6, Bausor 2, Gunn	1	2	3	4		6				7	10			11	5				
2		7	Aston Villa	2-1	HA Cursham 2	1	2	3	4		6	10	8	9	7	5			11					
3		14	SHEFFIELD	8-1	Smith 2, HA Cursham 2, Gunn 2, AW Cursham	1	2	3	4		6	7	8	9	10	5			11					
4		21	STOKE	5-0	HA Cursham 4, CF Dobson		2	3	4		6	7	8	9	10	5			11					
5		28	LIVERPOOL RAMBLERS	3-1	HA Cursham 2, AW Cursham	1	2	3	4	5	6	7	8	9	10	11								
6	Nov	11	BLACKBURN ROVERS	7-1	AW Cursham 3, Smith 2, Gunn, Greenhalgh		2	3	4	5	6	7	8	9	10	11								
7		18	WALSALL	7-2	HA Cursham 2, Gunn 2, Smith, AW Cursham, CF Dobson	1	2	3	4	5	6	7	8	9	10	11								
8		25	QUEEN'S PARK	1-3	Gunn	1	2	3	4	5	6	7	8	9	10			11						
9	Dec	2	Wednesbury Old Athletic	1-5	Unknown		2	3	4	5	6	7	8	9				11						10
10		23	OLD CARTHUSIANS	2-0	Smith, HA Cursham		2	3	4	5	6	7	8	9	10	11	1							
11		30	POLLOKSHIELDS ATH.	5-2	AW Cursham 2, Greenhalgh 2, E Jessop		2	3	4		6	7	8		10	11		5					1	
12	Jan	13	WEDNESBURY OLD ATH.	6-1	HA Cursham 2, Gunn, AW Cursham, Smith, HT Moore		2	3	4	5	6	7	8	9	10	11	1							
13		20	Nottm. Forest	1-1	HA Cursham		2	3	4	5	6	7	8	9	10	11						1		
14		27	Queen's Park	4-5	AW Cursham 3, unknown		2	3	4		6	7	8	9	10	11	1			5				
15	Feb	6	Sheffield	8-2	HA Cursham 4, Gunn, Beardshaw(og), Marsden(og), Wake(og)		2	3	4		6		8	9	10	11	1		7		5			
16		17	MITCHELL'S ST. GEORGE'S	10-0	HA Cursham 3, Gunn 2, Greenhalgh, CF Dobson, Smith, AW Cursham		2	3	4	5	6	7	8	9	10	11								
17		24	DERBY MIDLAND	3-0	AE Moore, Smith, Snook	1	2		4		6	7			10	11					5		8	
18	Mar	24	Stoke	5-1	Unknown							7		9	11	3			10				8	

Home games at the Castle except 5 (Meadows), 6, 8 and 11 (Trent Bridge). Game 13 also at Trent Bridge.
Team details incomplete for game 18. Unknown scorers in games 1, 3 and 16.
Played in game 1: W Walker (8). In game 4: H Morse (1). In game 9: J Handford (1). In game 11: E Jessop(9). In game 17: JB Snook (9), T Fiddler (3).
Played in game 6: J Everall (1). In game 16: T Bloom (1).

F.A. Cup

		Date	Opponent	Score	Scorers	Jessop H	Dobson AT	Moore HT	Dobson CF	Macrae S	Chapman H	Smith SG	Cursham AW	Cursham HA	Gunn W	Greenhalgh EH	Gillett LF	Harker E	Bausor T	Emmitt HW	Moore AE	Seals G	Billyeald H	Cursham CL
R1	Nov	4	SHEFFIELD	6-1	AW Cursham 3, HA Cursham 2, Smith	1	2	3	4	5	6	7	8	9	10	11								
R3	Dec	27	PHOENIX BESSEMER	4-1	Gunn 2, AW Cursham, HA Cursham		2	3	4	5	6	7	8	9	10	11							1	
R4	Feb	12	Sheffield Wednesday	4-1	AW Cursham 2, HA Cursham, Smith		2	3	4	5	6	7	8	9	10	11	1							
R5	Mar	3	ASTON VILLA	4-3	HA Cursham 3, Gunn		2	3	4	5	6	7	8	9	10	11	1							
SF		17	Old Etonians	1-2	HA Cursham		2		4	5	6	7	8	9	10	11	1		3					

Bye in round 2
Semi final played at Kennington Oval
R1 and R5 at Castle ground, R3 at the Meadows (Castle ground flooded).

1883/84

Player columns (left→right): Sherwin M · Dobson AT · Moore HT · Emmitt HW · Macrae S · Chapman H · Cursham AW · Gunn W · Dobson CF · Dixon JA · Cursham HA · Smith SG · Harker H · Woolley E · Moore AE · Jessop H · Scotton WH · Snook JB · Fidler A · Brown H · Shelton C · Snook FW

#	Date	Opponent	Res	Scorers	She	DoAT	MoHT	Emm	Mac	Cha	CuAW	Gunn	DoCF	Dix	CuHA	Smi	Har	Woo	MoAE	Jes	Sco	SnJB	Fid	Bro	Shel	SnFW
1	Sep 22	Stoke	1-1	Gunn	1	2	3	4	5	6	7	11	9		10	8										
2	29	WALSALL SWIFTS	4-2	AW Cursham, Gunn, CF Dobson, HA Cursham	1	2		3	5		7	11	4	10	9	8	6									
3	Oct 4	ATTERCLIFFE	6-2	HA Cursham 3, AT Dobson, AW Cursham, Gunn	1	2		3	5		7	11	4		9	8	6									
4	6	WEDNESBURY OLD ATH.	3-0	Gunn, HA Cursham, Smith	1	2		3	5	6	7	11	4		9	8	10									
5	13	Blackburn Rovers	0-4		1	2		3	5	6		11	4		7	8	9				10					
6	20	Nottm. Forest	0-0		1	2		3	5		7	11	4		9	8	6		10							
7	27	SOUTH OF ENGLAND	6-1	Dixon 2, CF Dobson, HA Cursham 2, JB Snook	1	2		3	5	6	7		4	10	11		8					9				
8	Nov 3	BLACKBURN OLYMPIC	3-2	AW Cursham 2, Gunn	1	2			5	6	9	7	4	10	11	8				3						
9	5	Aston Villa	1-2	CF Dobson	1	2			5	6	9	7	4	10	11					3						
10	17	BRENTWOOD	3-2	HA Cursham 3	1	2	3	4	5		8	7	9	10	11		6									
11	24	SHEFFIELD	4-1	AW Cursham, CF Dobson, HA Cursham, one og	1	2	3	4	5		8	7	9	10	11											
12	Dec 15	PADIHAM	5-1	HA Cursham 4, CF Dobson	1	2	3		5	6	8	7	9		11			4	10							
13	17	Sheffield	1-1	HA Cursham	1		3		5	6	8	7			11			10					4	2		
14	22	LOCKWOOD BROS.	1-1	CF Dobson		2	3		5		8	7	9	10	11		1						4	6		
15	26	NOTTM. FOREST	5-1	CF Dobson 2, Dixon, HA Cursham, Hancock (og)	1	2	3	4		6	8	7	9	10	11										5	
16	Jan 5	DERBY MIDLAND	3-3	AW Cursham 2, CF Dobson		2	1	3	5	6	8	7	9	10	11				4							
17	12	BOLTON ASSOC.	7-1	AW Cursham 2, Gunn 2, Macrae, Dixon, HA Cursham	1	2	3	4	5	6	8	7	9	10	11											
18	14	WEDNESBURY TOWN	4-0	Emmitt 2, Dixon, HA Cursham	1	2		3	5	6	8	7	9	10	11		4									
19	26	Sheffield Wednesday	0-0				3	5		6			9	10			8	11	7							2
20	Feb 16	STOKE	4-1	AW Cursham, Gunn, Dixon, HA Cursham			3	5		6	8	7	9	10	11						1				4	2
21	23	ASTON VILLA	2-0	Emmitt, Chapman	1			3	4	6	8	11	9	10											5	2
22	26	GREAT LEVER	4-1	HA Cursham 2, Gunn, CF Dobson	1	2	3			6	8	7	9	10	11		4								5	
23	Mar 8	Walsall Swifts	1-2	Unknown			3		5	6	8	7					4	11	8				2			
24	26	Attercliffe	0-2				3			6		7			4						8					
25	Apr 3	QUEEN'S PARK	0-3		1		3	4	5	6	8	7	9	10	11							2				
				App	19	18	16	22	14	20	20	24	23	16	21	6	12	6	4	4	3	2	2	2	3	3

All games at Trent Bridge except 25, Castle Ground (AW Cursham's benefit). Played in game 3: Wilson (10).
Played in game 9: OG Wall (no. 8). In game 13: EH Greenhalgh (9).
Played in game 19: A Malpas (1), J Smith (4). In game 21: E Jessop (7). In game 23: G Turner (1).
Played in games 23 and 24: H Jackson (9), JA Brown (10). Played in game 24: A Huskinson (1), J Everall (2), T Charles (5), H Matthews (11).

F.A. Cup

Rd	Date	Opponent	Res	Scorers	Att	She	DoAT	MoHT	Emm	Mac	Cha	CuAW	Gunn	DoCF	Dix	CuHA	Smi	Har	Woo
R1	Nov 10	SHEFFIELD HEELEY	3-1	HA Cursham 3	4000	1	2		3	5	6		9		4	10	11	8	7
R2	Dec 1	NOTTM. FOREST	3-0	AW Cursham, CF Dobson, Dixon	10000	1	2	3	4	5	6	8	7	9	10	11			
R3	20	Grantham	4-1	HA Cursham 2, Macrae, AW Cursham	600	1	2	3	4	5	6	8	7		10	11			
R4	Jan 19	BOLTON WANDERERS	2-2	Macrae, AW Cursham	12000	1	2	3	4	5	6	8	7	9	10	11			
rep	Feb 2	Bolton Wanderers	2-1	CF Dobson 2	14496	1	2	3	4	5	6	8	7	9	10	11			
R5	9	SWIFTS	1-1	HA Cursham	11000	1	2	3	4	5	6	8	7	9	10	11			
rep	14	Swifts	1-0	HA Cursham	2500	1	2	3	4	5	6	8	7	9	10	11			
SF	Mar 1	Blackburn Rovers	0-1		15000	1	2	3	4	5	6	7	11	8	10	9			

Home games at Trent Bridge. Semi-final at Aston Lower Grounds, Birmingham. Round 4 and round 5 ties after extra time.

Back: Ashwell(Umpire), Dixon, Emmitt, W.Gunn, H.Moore, A.Dobson
Middle: Sherwin, A.Cursham, Macrae
Front: C.Dobson, H.Cursham, Chapman

1884/85

#		Date	Opponent	Score	Scorers	Att	Sherwin M	Dobson AT	Moore HT	Dobson CF	Emmitt HW	Chapman H	Gunn W	Moore AE	Jackson H	Dixon JA	Cursham HA	Marshall AT	Macrae S	Snook FW	Brown JA	Coulby GA	Shelton C	Danks T	Harker E	Brown HH	Cotterill WH	Fidler T	Daft HB	Woolley E
1	Oct	2	DERBY COUNTY	3-1	Gunn, Dixon, Cursham	1500	1		3		5	6	7		9	10	11				2			8	4					
2		4	SHEFFIELD	6-2	Jackson 3, Cursham 2, Gunn	1500	1		3		5	6	7		9		11				2		4	8						
3		11	Blackburn Olympic	0-3		4000			3		5	6	7		8	9					2	11	4							
4		18	SHEFFIELD WEDNESDAY	0-0		2000	1	2	3	4	5	6	7		9	10								8		11				
5		25	DARWEN	2-0	Jackson, Danks	3000	1	2	3	4	5	6	7		9	10	11							8						
6	Nov	1	Sheffied Wednesday	1-0	AE Moore	2000			2	4		5		8		10	3				11	9		7						
7		13	CORINTHIANS	7-1	Marshall 3, Gunn 2, Jackson, Cursham		1	2	3	4	5	6	7		9	10	11	8												
8		15	BRENTWOOD	3-0	Jackson, Cursham, Marshall	2000	1	2	3	4	5	6	7		9	10	11	8												
9		22	NOTTS RANGERS	6-2	AE Moore 2, Cursham 2, Jackson, Marshall	2000		2	3	4	5	6	7	10	9		11	8												
10		27	Oxford University	2-1	Gunn 2		1	2	3		4	6	7	8	9	10	11						5							
11		29	BLACKBURN ROVERS	2-3	Gunn, Dixon	8000	1	2	3	4		6	7		9	10	11	8	5											
12	Dec	20	DERBY MIDLAND	8-0	Cursham 4, Jackson 2, Marshall 2	1000	1		3	4	5	6	7	10	9		11	8		2										
13		22	CORINTHIANS	3-2	Cursham 2, Jackson	2000	1		3	4	5	6	7		9	10	11	8		2										
14		26	NOTTM. FOREST	0-3		10000	1		3	4		6	7		9	10	11	8	5	2										
15		27	ACTON	5-0	Jackson 2, AE Moore, Cursham, Fidler	1000	1		3			6		8	9	10	11			2								5		
16		29	HENDON	8-2	* See below	1000	1		3		4	6	7	8		10	5	9			11							2		
17	Jan	10	WEDNESBURY OLD ATH.	5-0	JA Brown 2, Gunn, AE Moore, Cursham	1000	1		3	4	5		7	8		10	9			2	11									
18		17	BLACKBURN OLYMPIC	1-1	Gunn	6000	1		3	4	5	6	2	8	9	10				7	11									
19		31	Preston North End	2-3	Hay (og), Dixon	8000			3	4	5	6	7	8	9	10			11			1						2		
20	Feb	7	PRESTON NORTH END	2-1	AE Moore, Dixon	8000		2	3	4		6	7	8	9	10	11					1								
21		14	SWIFTS	3-1	Jackson, Dixon, Cursham	3000		2	3	4		6	7	8	9	10	11			5		1								
22	Mar	7	Sheffield	3-0	HH Brown, E Woolley, HB Daft					5		6		7							10					11	2	3	9	8
23		14	Bolton Wanderers	2-4	Jackson, E Woolley	8000				4	5	6	8		9			7								11	3			10
24		21	Blackburn Rovers	0-2		2000		2	3	4		6		7	8			5								11			9	
25		28	Notts Rangers	2-1	Gunn, Cursham	3000			3	4	5	6	7	8		10	9			2	11	1								
26	Apr	11	PRESTON NORTH END	1-2	Jackson	3000			3	4		6	7		9	10	11		5		8	1	2							
27		18	NOTTM. FOREST	3-2	Cursham 2, Gunn	6000			3	4	2		7		9	10	11		5			1	6							
28		25	Derby County						3	4	2		7			10					11		5						6	
			Apps				16	10	26	22	25	19	24	18	21	22	22	10	6	9	10	8	6	5	2	3	3	4	2	2
			Goals										11	6	15	7	19	8			3			1		1		1	1	2

Home games at Trent Bridge except 26 and 27 at the Castle Ground.
Game 25 was a Notts F.A. Cup semi final.. Forest scratched from final..
Scorers in game 16: AE Moore 3, Dixon 2, Gunn, Marshall, JA Brown
Played in game 2: B Wright of Glasgow Rangers (10). In game 6: WV Machin, J Stennet. In games 15 (at 6) and 22 (4): AE Scott. In 22, 23 and 28: J Woolley (1).
In game 9, R Simpkin (1). Only 10 men in game 17 (AT Marshall did not arrive). Played in game 23, W Topham (2). In game 28, JB Snook (9), CF Daft (8).

F.A. Cup

#		Date	Opponent	Score	Scorers	Att	Sherwin M	Dobson AT	Moore HT	Dobson CF	Emmitt HW	Chapman H	Gunn W	Moore AE	Jackson H	Dixon JA	Cursham HA	Marshall AT	Macrae S	Snook FW	Brown JA	Coulby GA	Shelton C	Danks T	Harker E	Brown HH	Cotterill WH	Fidler T	Daft HB	Woolley E
R1	Nov	8	NOTTS OLYMPIC	2-0	Dixon, Emmitt	2000	1	2	3	4	5	6	7		9	10	11								8					
R2	Dec	6	Staveley	2-0	Gunn, Cursham	2500	1	2	3	4		6	7		9	10	11	8	5											
R3	Jan	3	SHEFFIELD	5-0	*see below	5000	1		3	4		6	7		9	10	11	8	5	2										
R4		24	Walsall Swifts	4-1	Jackson 2, Gunn, JA Brown	5000	1		3	4	5	6	7	8	9	10					11									
R6	Feb	21	QUEEN'S PARK	2-2	Gunn, Cursham	17000		2	3	4		6	7	8	9	10	11						5							1
rep		28	Queen's Park	1-2	Jackson	10000		2	3	4		6	7	8	9	10	11						5							1

R6 replay at Derby Cricket Ground. Home games at Trent Bridge. Scorers in R3: CF Dobson, Gunn, Jackson, Cursham, Marshall. Played in R4: F Johnson (2). Bye in R5.

Back: Macrae, C.Dobson, W.Gunn, Dixon
Middle: H.Cursham, A.Dobson, H.Moore
Front: A.Moore, Coulby, Jackson

1885/86

No	Date		Opponent	Score	Scorers	Att	Sherwin M	Snook FW	Moore HT	Dobson CF	Emmitt HW	Chapman H	Gunn W	Moore AE	Jackson H	Cursham HA	Daft HB	Coulby GA	Marshall AT	Macrae S	Harker E	Brown JA	Turner G	Huskinson CJ	Peters A	Cotterill WH	Shelton G	Lindley T	Wilson J	Butler F	Shelton C	Brown HH
1	Sep	19	Lincoln	4-0	Cursham 2, Daft, Gunn			2	3	6	4		7	8	11	10	9	1		5												
2		26	Derby County	3-0	Jackson 2, Gunn	5000		2	3	6	4		7	8	9	10	11	1		5												
3	Oct	1	SHEFFIELD WEDNESDAY	6-1	AE Moore 3, Jackson 2, Daft	4000		2	3	6	4		7	8	9	10	11	1		5												
4		3	BRENTWOOD	3-0	AE Moore, Daft, Jackson	4000		2	3	6	4		7	8	9	10	11	1		5												
5		10	Queen's Park	1-5	Daft	5000		2				6			9	3	8	7			4	10				5						11
6		10	WALSALL SWIFTS	0-1		1500	1		3	2	5		7	8										9								
7		17	PRESTON NORTH END	0-4		5000		2	3	6	4		7	8	9	10	11	1		5												
8		31	Blackburn Rovers	3-1	Jackson, Turner (og), Gunn	600	1		3		5	6	7	8	9	10	11								2	4						
9	Nov	7	BLACKBURN OLYMPIC	4-0	Cursham, AE Moore, Jackson 2	4000	1	2	3	4	5	6	7	8	9	10	11															
10		14	WEST BROMWICH ALB.	4-3	Cursham 3, Gunn	2000	1	2	3	4	5	6	7	8	9	10	11															
11		28	Nottm. Forest	4-1	Daft 2, Cursham, Jackson	8000	1	2	3	4	5		7	8	9	10	11			5												
12	Dec	5	OXFORD UNIVERSITY	6-0	Jackson 2, Daft 2, Cursham, Gunn	2000	1	2	3	4	5		7	8	9	10	11			5												
13		19	Sheffield	6-1	Jackson 3, JA Brown, Robinson (og)		1			4	6				9						7	10				5	8					11
14		26	BOLTON WANDERERS	3-3	Cursham 2, Gunn	10000	1	2	3	6	5		7	8		10	11					9				4						
15		28	GREAT LEVER	1-3	Gunn	8000	1	2	3	6	5		7	8		10	11					9				4						
16	Jan	2	Preston North End	2-8	Jackson 2	7000	1	2	3	6	5		7	8	9	10	11									4						
17		9	BLACKBURN ROVERS	4-0	Daft 2, Jackson	4000	1	2	3		4		7	8	9	10	11			5					6							
18		16	NOTTM. FOREST	5-0	Cursham 3, Jackson, AE Moore	9000	1	2	3	6	4		7	8	9	10	11			5												
19		30	DERBY COUNTY	7-3	*See below	2000	1		3	6	5			8	9		11				7				2	4	10					
20	Feb	4	Wellingborough GS	11-3	Jackson 8, unknown 3				3		4	6			9	2			5				11	8								11
21		6	Blackburn Olympic	0-0		2000			3	6	5		7	8	9		11								2	4	10					
22		13	ASTON VILLA	3-5	Gunn, Jackson, Jones (og)				3		5		7	8	9		11	6							2	4	10					
23		20	QUEEN'S PARK	1-0	Jackson					4		6		8	9	3	11		2	5	7			1				10				
24		20	Walsall Swifts	0-5					3		5	2														4			9	8		
25		27	ACCRINGTON	3-2	Cursham 2, Jackson	2000			3					8	9	11				5	7			1	10	3					6	
26	Mar	6	Corinthians	0-7		2000			3	6	5			8	9	10	11		2		7				1	4						
27		9	Aston Villa	2-3	Dawson (og), one unknown				3	8	5				9	2	11				7				10	4						
28		13	Accrington	1-2	Jackson	2000			3		5	6			9											4	2			8	11	
29		20	West Bromwich Alb.	0-3					3	6	5			8	9	2	11				7				10	4						
30		27	Sheffield Wednesday	1-1	Wilson (og)				3	6	5				9		11				7					2						
31	Apr	3	Bolton Wanderers	1-6	Jackson				3	6	5				9	2	7	1							11			10		8		
32		15	Derby County	1-4	Jackson				3	6	5			8	9	10	7	1	2		4											
			Apps				13	15	29	24	30	6	20	24	28	24	26	10	3	11	10	5	3	6	11	11	5	2	2	3	2	2
			Goals										8	8	34	15	11				1	1					1					

Home games at Trent Bridge. Game 32 for the Derby County Charity Cup.
Scorers in game 19: AE Moore 2, Jackson 2, Daft, Harker, G Shelton.
Played in game 6: T Danks (10), AE Scott (4), PH Richards (6), E Woolley (11)
Played in game 13: C West (2), J Bentley (3)
Played in game 20: GN Brown (10), JR Sands (1)
Played in games 23, 25 and 26: G Turner (at 1). In games 27 to 30 inclusive: J Slater (at 1).
Played in game 24: Rose (11), Thompson (10), HJ Moore (6), CF Daft (7). In game 27: HA Morley (6)
Played in game 28: Dicks (7), Maltby (10). In game 30, J Housley (4). In game 31, Hibbert (4)

Five own goals, four unknown

F.A. Cup

No	Date		Opponent	Score	Scorers	Att	Sherwin M	Snook FW	Moore HT	Dobson CF	Emmitt HW	Chapman H	Gunn W	Moore AE	Jackson H	Cursham HA	Daft HB	Coulby GA	Marshall AT	Macrae S
R1	Oct	24	ROTHERHAM TOWN	15-0	*See below	1500	1	2	3	4	5	6	7	8	9	10	11			
R2	Nov	21	SHEFFIELD	8-0	Gunn 3, Jackson 3, Cursham, Daft	3000	1	2	3	4	5	6	7	8	9	10	11			
R3	Dec	12	Notts Rangers	3-1	Cursham 3	3000	1	2	3	6	4		7	8	9	10	11			5
R4	Jan	23	South Shore	1-2	Emmitt	3000	1	2	3	6	4		7	8	9	10	11			5

Scorers in R1: Cursham 4, Jackson 3, AE Moore 2, Daft 2, Dobson, Emmitt, Gunn, Brown (og)

1886/87

#		Date	Opponent	Score	Scorers	Att	Holland JH	Marshall AT	Morley HA	Emmitt HW	Macrae S	Dobson CF	Moore AE	Harker E	Jackson H	Cursham HA	Daft HB	Burton FE	May W	Brown GH	Spibey J	May E	Cotterill WH	Peters A	Spibey G	Morley W	Dixon JA	Brown JA
1	Oct	2	BRENTWOOD	2-0	Jackson, Harker	1000	1	2		5			8	7	9	3	11			6			4					
2		7	WALSALL TOWN	4-4	Moore, Jackson, Daft, W May		1	2		5			8		9	3	11		7	10			6	4				
3		9	STOKE	1-2	W May	1500	1	2	3	4			8		9	5	11		7	10	6							
4		16	SHEFFIELD	9-1	Jackson 4, Harker 2, Moore 2, Daft	1000	1	2	3	5		6	8	7	9	10	11						4					
5		23	DERBY COUNTY	3-6	Harker, Jackson, Daft	3000	1	2	3	4	5	6	8	7	9	10	11											
6		25	Blackburn Olympic	3-4	Cursham 2, one unknown		1		3	5			8		9	10				6					4	11		
7	Nov	6	Preston North End	0-14			1	2	3	5			8		9	10			7				6	4				11
8		27	Accrington	0-8	2000		1			5										7			6	4	3	11		
9	Dec	4	DERBY MIDLAND	3-2	Cursham, Daft, Burton		1	2	3	5		6	8	4	9	10	11	7										
10		16	CORINTHIANS	1-1	Emmitt	2000	1		3	4	5	6	8	7			10	11	9							2		
11		18	WOLVES	3-1	Daft 2, Jackson	3000	1	2	3	5		6	8	7	9		10	11					4					
12		27	NOTTM. FOREST	0-2			1	2	3	4	5	6	8	7	9		10	11										
13	Jan	15	LOCKWOOD BROS.	11-0	* See below	1500	1	2	3	5		6	8	7	9		10	11					4					
14		22	WEST BROMWICH ALB.	3-1	Jackson 2, Emmitt	4000	1	2	3	5		6	8	7	9		10	11					4					
15	Feb	5	MITCHELLS ST. GEORGES	5-0	Cursham 3, Harker, Morley	2000	1	2	3	5		6	8	7	9		10	11					4					
16		12	Nottm. Forest	2-1	Cursham 2	10000	1	2	3	4	5	6	8	7	9		10	11										
17		22	BLACKBURN ROVERS	2-2	Moore, Jackson	2000	1		3	5		6	8	7	9		10	11					4			2		
18		26	ASTON VILLA	1-3	Moore	3000	1	2	3	5		6	10	4			11	9		7								
19	Mar	7	Derby County	3-3	Cursham, Daft, W May		1		2	5				4			11	9		7			6	8		3		
20		12	Stoke	1-4	W May		1		2	5				4			11	9	10	7			6	8		3		
21		19	NOTTM. FOREST	1-1	Cursham	3000	1	2	3	5		6		7			10	9	8				4					
22		21	Sheffield	4-1	Burton, W May, GN Brown, one unknown		1		2	5							3		9	7	4		8					11
23		26	Queen's Park	2-5	Cursham, Daft		1	2	3	5				4			10	9		7	6		8					
24		28	Hibernian	0-6			1	2	3	5				4				9		7	6		8					
25		31	PRESTON NORTH END	2-3	Burton, Bakewell		1		3	4	5	6					9	11					10			2	8	
26	Apr	2	Wolves	0-2			1	2		4		6									7			3				9
27		9	Derby County	0-3			1		3	5								9			4	8			6	11		
28		11	Aston Villa	1-10	Maltby		1	3		4							10		11	7			6		2			
29		16	Nottm. Forest	1-3	Daft	2000	1	2	3	5	9	6	10	7			11	8					4					
			Apps				29	20	24	29		6	16	18	19	15	23	21	12	11	7	10	8	5	7	5	3	2	3
			Goals						1	2			5	6	14	15	11	3		1			5					

One own goal, two unknown, three by players below

All games at Trent Bridge except game 21, Castle Ground.
Games 21 and 29 were the Notts F.A. Cup semi-final.

Scorers in game 13: Jackson 3, Cursham 2, Daft 2, Dobson, Harker, Spibey and Salkeld (og)
Played in game 1: Wilson (3). In game 6, Warrell (7). In game 8: Oliver (2), Spencer (8), Webb (9).
Played in game 6: J Carlin (2).
Played in games 8 and 24: Reddish (at 10).
Played in game 18, A Gill (8). In game 20, F Geary (10). In game 21, C Huskinson (11)
Played in game 22, A Shepherd (6), GN Brown (10). In game 25, GH Bakewell (7). In game 26, Stevens (10), Thorpe (11), Rouse (8)
Played in game 27, A Shaw (10), ES Wardle (7), L Wright (2). In games 23 and 24: A Shulcer (at 11).
Played in game 28: A Shepherd (5), JT Marshall (8), Maltby (9)

F.A. Cup

	Date	Opponent	Score	Scorers	Att	Holland JH	Marshall AT	Morley HA	Emmitt HW	Macrae S	Dobson CF	Moore AE	Harker E	Jackson H	Cursham HA	Daft HB	Burton FE	May W	Brown GH	Spibey J	May E	Cotterill WH	Peters A
R1	Oct 30	BASFORD ROVERS	13-0	Daft 5, Burton 5, Jackson, Cursham, Slater(og)	800	1	2		5		6	8	4	9	10	11	7		3				
R2	Nov 13	NOTTS RANGERS	3-3	Jackson, Cursham, Burton		1	2	3	5			8	6	9	10	11	7						4
rep	20	NOTTS RANGERS	5-0	Cursham 3, Jackson, Burton	5000	1	2	3	5		6	8	4	9	10	11	7						
R3	Dec 11	Staveley	3-0	Jackson 2, Cursham	3000	1	2	3	4	5	6	8	7	9	10	11							
R5	Jan 29	GREAT MARLOW	5-2	Cursham 3, Jackson, Speller (og)	8000	1	2	3	4	5	6	8	7	9	10	11							
R6	Feb 19	WEST BROMWICH ALB.	1-4	Cursham	15067	1	2	3	4	5	6	8	7	9	10	11							

Bye in Round 4

1887/88

#	Date		Opponent	Res	Scorers	Att	Holland JH	Morley HA	Moore HT	Harker E	Emmitt HW	Dobson CF	Gunn W	Cursham HA	Jackson H	Brown JA	Daft HB	Brown GH	Warburton BF	Marshall JT	Dixon JA	Stevens H	Brown HH	Snook HD	Wardle ES	Moore AE	Shepherd A	Brown GN	Clements J	Lovegrove WF	May W
1	Sep	17	Walsall Town	0-4			1		3		5				9	10							11	7	8						4
2		24	Stoke	1-3	Dixon		1	2	3		4	6	7	10	9		11				8										
3	Oct	1	LEEK	8-1	JA Brown 4, Jackson 2, Gunn, Daft	good	1	2	3	4	5	6	7		9	10	11										8				
4		3	West Bromwich Albion	1-5	Jackson		1	2	3		5		7		9	10											8				11
5		6	MITCHELLS ST. GEORGES	5-2	Jackson 3, Gunn, Daft	fair	1	2	3	4	5		7		9		11	6									8				10
6		8	EVERTON	1-1	Jackson	1500	1		3	4	5		7		9	10		6					11				8				
7		22	ASTON VILLA	8-2	JA Brown 4, Jackson 2, Gunn, Emmitt	3000	1	2	3	4	5		7	8	9	10	11	6													
8		29	Blackburn Rovers	4-4	Wilkinson 2, Jackson, Daft		1	2	3	8	4		7		10		11	6									5				
9	Nov	5	PRESTON NORTH END	2-3	Jackson, JA Brown	7000	1	2	3	4	5		7		9	10	11	6			8										
10		19	GRIMSBY TOWN	4-0	Cursham 2, Gunn, Daft	2000	1	2	3		5	4	7	8	9	10	11	6													
11	Dec	3	Nottm. Forest	1-0	Daft	good	1		3	4	5		7	2	9	10	11	6			8										
12		10	BLACKBURN ROVERS	4-2	Jackson 3, Gunn	2000	1	2		8	4		7	3	9	10	11	6												5	
13		12	Mitchell's St. George's	0-10			1				5		7	2	9	10	11					8						6	3		
14		17	Preston North End	2-5	Daft, JA Brown	4000			3		4		7	2	9	10	11	6										8	5		
15		17	Leek	1-2	Marshall																										
16		22	CORINTHIANS	1-4	Daft	fair	1		3	4			7	2	9	10	11	6			8										
17		26	NOTTM. FOREST	0-0		12000	1		3	4			7	2	9	10	11	6			8										
18		31	WALSALL SWIFTS	4-0	Daft 2, Ackroyd, Sheriston	1000	1		3		4		7	2	9		11	6			8										
19	Jan	7	Grimsby Town	3-4	Daft 2, Lovegrove	4000	1	2	3		4		7				11	6			8									9	
20		14	WEST BROMWICH ALB.	3-3	Daft 2, Jackson		1			4				3	9		11	6			8	7									
21		21	NOTTS RANGERS	0-8		2000	1			4				3	9		11	6			8							7			
22		28	CHURCH	6-0	Jackson 3, Gunn 2, Dixon		1				5		7	3	9				4	8	10			2				7			
23	Feb	4	STOKE	2-1	Jackson, Daft		1				5			3	9		11	6	4	8		7		2						10	
24		11	HALLIWELL	1-4	Wardle	small																	11	3	7		8			9	
25		11	Queen's Park	2-2	Harker, Gunn	1000	1		3	8			7	2	9		11	6	5	8											
26		14	BOLTON WANDERERS	0-3		4000	1		3	7	5		10		9			6	4	8		11		2							
27		18	DERBY COUNTY	2-3	Emmitt, Marshall	good	1				5		7	3	9			6	4	8		11	10	2							
28	Mar	5	Sheffield Wednesday	4-3	Geary 2, Daft, Hodder	1500	1	2			4		7		8		11				5							6	3		
29		10	Everton	1-3	Gunn		1		3		4		7		9	10	11					8						5	6		
30		17	Long Eaton Rangers	1-5	Harker	1000	1	3		10	6		7	2	9		11			4							8	5			
31		24	Halliwell	0-7		3500	1		3		5		7		9		11	6				8	10				8				
32		31	Derby County	0-3		2000	1	3		10	6		7	2	9		11		5	4							8				
33	Apr	7	Aston Villa	3-3	Wardle 2, Weightman		1				4			10	2	9		6									7	5			
			Apps				30	13	20	16	26	3	27	19	30	14	24	21	10	9	7	6	5	5	5	4	6	4	5	3	3
			Goals								2	2	9	2	19	10	15				2				3						1

Eight goals scored by players below

All home games at Trent Bridge.
Played in game 1: Maltby (6). In game 2, H Knight (5)
Played in games 1 and 6 (at 2) and 4 (at 4): A Peters.
Line up unknown for game 15.
Played in game 5, FE Burton (8). In game 8: Wilkinson (9). In game 13, EC Princip (4). In game 14: M Sherwin (1).
Played in 16: W Sadler (5). In game 17: C Shelton (5). In games 20 and 21: AT Marshall (2). In game 22, J Plackett (6).
Played in games 18 to 21 inclusive: W Sheriston (at 5), J Ackroyd (at 10).
Played in game 24: W Sadler (5), M Sherwin (1), WH Cotterill (4), A Shelton (6), W Topham (2), Oliver (10).
Played in game 25: T Robertson, of Cowlairs (4). In game 28, F Geary (9), W Hodder (10). In game 29; Oliver (2).
Played in game 31: F Spibey(2), J Spibey(4). In game 33, EC Princip (8), FH Guttridge (3), Weightman (11)

F.A. Cup

#	Date		Opponent	Res	Scorers	Att	Holland JH	Morley HA	Moore HT	Harker E	Emmitt HW	Dobson CF	Gunn W	Cursham HA	Jackson H	Brown JA	Daft HB	Brown GH	Warburton BF	Marshall JT	Dixon JA	Stevens H	Brown HH	Snook HD	Wardle ES	Moore AE	Shepherd A	Brown GN	Clements J	Lovegrove WF	May W
R1	Oct	15	LINCOLN RAMBLERS	9-0	AE Moore 3, Daft 3, Jackson 2, Gunn		1	2	3	4	5	6	7		9	10	11									8					
R2			Basford Rovers	wo																											
R3	Nov	26	Nottm. Forest	1-2	Gunn	11500	1	2	3	6	4		7	8	9	10	11		5												

R1 played at Trent Bridge by arrangement.

League Tables 1888/89 to 1898/99

1888/89

1	Preston North End	22	10	1	0	39	7	8	3	0	35	8	40
2	Aston Villa	22	10	0	1	44	16	2	5	4	17	27	29
3	Wolverhampton Wan.	22	8	2	1	30	14	4	2	5	20	23	28
4	Blackburn Rovers	22	7	4	0	44	22	3	2	6	22	23	26
5	Bolton Wanderers	22	6	0	5	35	30	4	2	5	28	29	22
6	West Bromwich Alb.	22	6	2	3	25	24	4	0	7	15	22	22
7	Accrington	22	5	3	3	26	17	1	5	5	22	31	20
8	Everton	22	8	0	3	24	17	1	2	8	11	29	20
9	Burnley	22	6	3	2	21	19	1	0	10	21	43	17
10	Derby County	22	5	1	5	22	20	2	1	8	19	41	16
11	NOTTS COUNTY	22	4	2	5	25	32	1	0	10	15	41	12
12	Stoke	22	3	4	4	15	18	1	0	10	11	33	12

1889/90

1	Preston North End	22	8	1	2	41	12	7	2	2	30	18	33
2	Everton	22	8	2	1	40	15	6	1	4	25	25	31
3	Blackburn Rovers	22	9	0	2	59	18	3	3	5	19	23	27
4	Wolverhampton Wan.	22	6	3	2	28	14	4	2	5	23	24	25
5	West Bromwich Alb.	22	8	1	2	37	20	3	2	6	10	30	25
6	Accrington	22	6	4	1	33	25	3	2	6	20	31	24
7	Derby County	22	8	2	1	32	13	1	1	9	11	42	21
8	Aston Villa	22	6	2	3	30	15	1	3	7	13	36	19
9	Bolton Wanderers	22	6	1	4	37	24	3	0	8	17	41	19
10	NOTTS COUNTY	22	4	3	4	20	19	2	2	7	23	32	17
11	Burnley	22	3	1	7	20	21	1	4	6	16	44	13
12	Stoke	22	2	3	6	18	20	1	1	9	9	49	10

1890/91

1	Everton	22	9	0	2	39	12	5	1	5	24	17	29
2	Preston North End	22	7	3	1	30	5	5	0	6	14	18	27
3	NOTTS COUNTY	22	9	1	1	33	11	2	3	6	19	24	26
4	Wolverhampton Wan.	22	8	1	2	23	8	4	1	6	16	42	26
5	Bolton Wanderers	22	9	0	2	36	14	3	1	7	11	20	25
6	Blackburn Rovers	22	7	1	3	29	19	4	1	6	23	24	24
7	Sunderland	22	7	2	2	31	13	3	3	5	20	18	23
8	Burnley	22	7	1	3	33	24	2	2	7	19	39	21
9	Aston Villa	22	5	4	2	29	18	2	0	9	16	40	18
10	Accrington	22	5	1	5	19	19	1	3	7	9	31	16
11	Derby County	22	6	1	4	38	28	1	0	10	9	53	15
12	West Bromwich Alb.	22	3	1	7	17	26	2	1	8	17	31	12

1891/92

1	Sunderland	26	13	0	0	55	11	8	0	5	38	25	42
2	Preston North End	26	12	0	1	42	8	6	1	6	19	23	37
3	Bolton Wanderers	26	9	2	2	29	14	8	0	5	22	23	36
4	Aston Villa	26	10	0	3	63	23	5	0	8	26	33	30
5	Everton	26	8	2	3	32	22	4	2	7	17	27	28
6	Wolverhampton Wan.	26	8	2	3	34	15	3	2	8	25	31	26
7	Burnley	26	9	1	3	34	14	2	3	8	15	31	26
8	NOTTS COUNTY	26	9	3	1	41	12	2	1	10	14	39	26
9	Blackburn Rovers	26	8	3	2	39	26	2	3	8	19	39	26
10	Derby County	26	6	3	4	28	18	4	1	8	18	34	24
11	Accrington	26	7	3	3	24	20	1	1	11	16	58	20
12	West Bromwich Alb.	26	6	3	4	37	24	0	3	10	14	34	18
13	Stoke	26	5	0	8	19	19	0	4	9	19	42	14
14	Darwen	26	4	1	8	31	43	0	2	11	7	69	11

1892/93 Division 1

1	Sunderland	30	13	2	0	58	17	9	2	4	42	19	48
2	Preston North End	30	11	2	2	34	10	6	1	8	23	29	37
3	Everton	30	9	3	3	44	17	7	1	7	30	34	36
4	Aston Villa	30	12	1	2	50	24	4	2	9	23	38	35
5	Bolton Wanderers	30	12	1	2	43	21	1	5	9	13	34	32
6	Burnley	30	10	2	3	37	15	3	2	10	14	29	30
7	Stoke	30	8	2	5	33	16	4	3	8	25	32	29
8	West Bromwich Alb.	30	9	2	4	35	17	3	3	9	23	52	29
9	Blackburn Rovers	30	5	8	2	29	24	3	5	7	18	32	29
10	Nottingham Forest	30	7	2	6	30	27	3	6	6	18	25	28
11	Wolverhampton Wan.	30	11	2	2	32	17	1	2	12	15	51	28
12	Sheffield Wed.	30	8	2	5	34	28	4	1	10	21	37	27
13	Derby County	30	5	6	4	30	28	4	3	8	22	36	27
14	NOTTS COUNTY	30	8	3	4	34	15	2	1	12	19	46	24
15	Accrington	30	5	5	5	29	34	1	6	8	28	47	23
16	Newton Heath	30	6	3	6	39	35	0	3	12	11	50	18

1893/94 Division 2

1	Liverpool	28	14	0	0	46	6	8	6	0	31	12	50
2	Small Heath	28	12	0	2	68	19	9	0	5	35	25	42
3	NOTTS COUNTY	28	12	1	1	55	14	6	2	6	15	17	39
4	Newcastle United	28	12	1	1	44	10	3	5	6	22	29	36
5	Grimsby Town	28	11	1	2	47	16	4	1	9	24	42	32
6	Burton Swifts	28	9	1	4	52	26	5	2	7	27	35	31
7	Burslem Port Vale	28	10	2	2	43	20	3	2	9	23	44	30
8	Lincoln City	28	5	4	5	31	22	6	2	6	28	36	28
9	Woolwich Arsenal	28	9	1	4	33	19	3	3	8	19	36	28
10	Walsall Town Swfts	28	8	1	5	36	23	2	2	10	15	38	23
11	Middlsbro Irnoplis	28	7	4	3	27	20	1	0	13	10	52	20
12	Crewe Alexandra	28	3	7	4	22	22	3	0	11	20	51	19
13	Ardwick	28	6	1	7	32	20	2	1	11	15	51	18
14	Rotherham Town	28	5	1	8	28	42	1	2	11	16	49	15
15	Northwich Victoria	28	3	3	8	17	34	0	0	14	13	64	9

1894/95 Division 2

1	Bury	30	15	0	0	48	11	8	2	5	30	22	48
2	NOTTS COUNTY	30	12	2	1	50	15	5	3	7	25	30	39
3	Newton Heath	30	9	6	0	52	18	6	2	7	26	26	38
4	Leicester Fosse	30	11	2	2	45	20	4	6	5	27	33	38
5	Grimsby Town	30	14	0	1	51	16	4	1	10	28	36	37
6	Darwen	30	13	1	1	53	10	3	3	9	21	33	36
7	Burton Wanderers	30	10	3	2	49	9	4	4	7	18	30	35
8	Woolwich Arsenal	30	11	3	1	54	20	3	3	9	21	38	34
9	Manchester City	30	9	3	3	56	28	5	0	10	26	44	31
10	Newcastle United	30	11	1	3	51	28	1	2	12	21	56	27
11	Burton Swifts	30	9	2	4	34	20	2	1	12	18	54	25
12	Rotherham Town	30	10	0	5	37	22	1	2	12	18	40	24
13	Lincoln City	30	8	0	7	32	27	2	0	13	20	65	20
14	Walsall Town Swfts	30	8	0	7	35	25	2	0	13	12	67	20
15	Burslem Port Vale	30	6	3	6	30	23	1	1	13	9	54	18
16	Crewe Alexandra	30	3	4	8	20	34	0	0	15	6	69	10

1895/96 Division 2

1	Liverpool	30	14	1	0	65	11	8	1	6	41	21	46
2	Manchester City	30	12	3	0	37	9	9	1	5	26	29	46
3	Grimsby Town	30	14	1	0	51	9	6	1	8	31	29	42
4	Burton Wanderers	30	12	1	2	43	15	7	3	5	26	25	42
5	Newcastle United	30	14	0	1	57	14	2	2	11	16	36	34
6	Newton Heath	30	12	2	1	48	15	3	1	11	18	42	33
7	Woolwich Arsenal	30	11	1	3	42	11	3	3	9	16	31	32
8	Leicester Fosse	30	10	0	5	40	16	4	4	7	17	28	32
9	Darwen	30	9	4	2	55	22	3	2	10	17	45	30
10	NOTTS COUNTY	30	8	1	6	41	22	4	1	10	16	32	26
11	Burton Swifts	30	7	2	6	24	26	3	2	10	15	43	24
12	Loughborough	30	7	3	5	32	25	2	2	11	8	41	23
13	Lincoln City	30	7	1	7	36	24	2	3	10	17	51	22
14	Burslem Port Vale	30	6	4	5	25	24	1	0	14	18	54	18
15	Rotherham Town	30	7	2	6	27	26	0	1	14	7	71	17
16	Crewe Alexandra	30	5	2	8	22	28	0	1	14	8	67	13

1896/97 Division 2

1	NOTTS COUNTY	30	12	1	2	60	18	7	3	5	32	25	42
2	Newton Heath	30	11	4	0	37	10	6	1	8	19	24	39
3	Grimsby Town	30	12	2	1	44	15	5	2	8	22	30	38
4	Small Heath	30	8	3	4	36	23	8	2	5	33	24	37
5	Newcastle United	30	13	1	1	42	13	4	0	11	14	39	35
6	Manchester City	30	10	3	2	39	15	2	5	8	19	35	32
7	Gainsborough Trin.	30	10	2	3	35	16	2	5	8	15	31	31
8	Blackpool	30	11	3	1	39	16	2	2	11	20	40	31
9	Leicester Fosse	30	11	2	2	44	20	2	2	11	15	37	30
10	Woolwich Arsenal	30	10	1	4	42	20	3	3	9	26	50	30
11	Darwen	30	13	0	2	54	16	1	0	14	13	45	28
12	Walsall	30	8	2	5	37	25	3	2	10	17	44	26
13	Loughborough	30	10	0	5	37	14	2	1	12	13	50	25
14	Burton Swifts	30	7	4	4	33	20	2	2	11	13	41	24
15	Burton Wanderers	30	8	1	6	22	22	1	1	13	9	45	20
16	Lincoln City	30	4	2	9	17	27	1	0	14	10	58	12

1897/98 Division 1

1	Sheffield United	30	9	4	2	27	14	8	4	3	29	17	42
2	Sunderland	30	12	2	1	27	8	4	3	8	16	22	37
3	Wolverhampton Wan.	30	10	4	1	36	14	4	3	8	21	27	35
4	Everton	30	11	3	1	33	12	2	6	7	15	27	35
5	Sheffield Wed.	30	12	0	3	39	15	3	3	9	12	27	33
6	Aston Villa	30	12	1	2	47	21	2	4	9	14	30	33
7	West Bromwich Alb.	30	8	5	2	25	16	3	5	7	19	29	32
8	Nottingham Forest	30	7	5	3	30	19	4	4	7	17	30	31
9	Liverpool	30	7	4	4	27	16	4	2	9	21	29	28
10	Derby County	30	10	3	2	40	19	1	3	11	17	42	28
11	Bolton Wanderers	30	9	2	4	18	13	2	2	11	10	28	26
12	Preston North End	30	7	5	3	26	15	1	3	11	9	28	24
13	NOTTS COUNTY	30	4	6	5	23	23	4	2	9	13	23	24
14	Bury	30	8	3	4	25	19	0	5	10	14	32	24
15	Blackburn Rovers	30	4	7	4	20	22	3	3	9	19	32	24
16	Stoke	30	8	3	4	21	14	0	5	10	14	41	24

1898/99 Division 1

1	Aston Villa	34	15	2	0	58	13	4	5	8	18	27	45
2	Liverpool	34	12	3	2	29	10	7	2	8	20	23	43
3	Burnley	34	11	5	1	32	15	4	4	9	13	32	39
4	Everton	34	10	2	5	25	13	5	6	6	23	28	38
5	NOTTS COUNTY	34	9	6	2	33	20	3	7	7	14	31	37
6	Blackburn Rovers	34	9	5	3	41	23	5	3	9	19	29	36
7	Sunderland	34	11	3	3	26	10	4	3	10	15	31	36
8	Wolverhampton Wan.	34	9	5	3	30	13	5	2	10	24	35	35
9	Derby County	34	11	5	1	46	19	1	6	10	16	38	35
10	Bury	34	9	5	3	31	18	5	2	10	17	31	35
11	Nottingham Forest	34	6	6	5	22	18	5	5	7	20	24	33
12	Stoke	34	10	4	3	29	17	3	3	11	18	35	33
13	Newcastle United	34	9	3	5	33	18	2	5	10	16	30	30
14	West Bromwich Alb.	34	11	1	5	28	9	1	5	11	14	48	30
15	Preston North End	34	10	4	3	29	14	0	5	12	15	33	29
16	Sheffield United	34	7	8	2	31	20	2	3	12	14	31	29
17	Bolton Wanderers	34	6	5	6	24	21	3	2	12	13	30	25
18	Sheffield Wed.	34	8	2	7	26	24	0	6	11	6	37	24

1888/89 — 11th in The Football League

#	Mon	Date	Opponent	Score	Scorers	Att	Holland JH	Guttridge FH	McLean T	Brown GH	Warburton BF	Shelton A	Hodder W	Harker E	Jardine R	Moore AE	Wardle ES	Shelton C	Jackson H	Daft HB	Allin T	Cursham HA	Clements JE	Sherwin M	May W	Widdowson TH	Snook HD	Dobson CF	Shaw AF	Galbraith	May E	Emmitt HW
1	Sep	15	Everton	1-2	Moore	6000	1	2	3	4	5	6	7	8	9	10	11															
2		22	Stoke	0-3		3000	1	3	2	4		6	7		9	10		5	11	8												
3		29	Aston Villa	1-9	Coulton(og)	4000	1	2	3	4		6	7			9		5		8												
4	Oct	6	BLACKBURN ROVERS	3-3	Daft, Jardine, Moore	4000	1	3		4		6	7		11	8		5		10	9	2										
5		13	EVERTON	3-1	Daft, Jardine, Moore	4000	1	3		4		6	7		11	8		5		10	9	2										
6		20	West Bromwich Alb.	2-4	Allin 2	3448	1	3		4	5	6	7		11	8				10	9	2										
7		27	BURNLEY	6-1	Jardine 5, Daft	5000	1	2		4		6	7		11	8		5		10	9		3									
8	Nov	3	PRESTON NORTH END	0-7		7000		2		4		6	7		11	8		5		10	9		3									
9		10	ACCRINGTON	3-3	Daft, Jardine, C Shelton	8000		3				6	7	4	11	8		5		10		2		1	9							
10		24	STOKE	0-3		2000	1	3		4		6	7		11	8		5		10		2			9							
11	Dec	8	ASTON VILLA	2-4	Jardine, Weightman	2000			6	4					11						9					1	3	5	8			
12		15	Blackburn Rovers	2-5	Brown, Hodder	4000		2	5	4		6	7							11		3			8	1				9	10	
13		22	Derby County	2-3	Daft, Hodder	2500		2		4		6	7					5		10		9	3		8	1					11	
14		29	Burnley	0-1		0			3	5		6	7	8					9	10						1					11	4
15	Jan	5	Preston North End	1-4	Daft	4000		9	2			6	7	8				5		10			3			1					11	4
16		12	WEST BROMWICH ALB.	2-1	Cursham, Hodder	1500			2	4		6	7	8				5		10		9	3			1					11	
17		19	WOLVERHAMPTON W.	3-0	May 2, Cursham	3000			2	4		6	7	8				5		10		9	3			1					11	
18		26	Accrington	2-1	Daft, McLennan(og)	5000		9	2	4		6	7	8				5		10			3			1					11	
19	Feb	23	Wolverhampton Wand.	1-2	Jackson	4000	10		2	4		6	7	8							9		3			1					11	5
20	Mar	5	BOLTON WANDERERS	0-4		3000		2		4		6	7	8				5		9			3			1			10		11	
21		9	Bolton Wanderers	3-7	Jackson, May, ANO	3000		2		4		6	7	8						10	9		3			1					11	5
22		16	DERBY COUNTY	3-5	Bailey, Daft, Jackson	5000			2	4		6					7	5	8	11			3			1					10	
			Apps				9	17	12	19	2	21	20	2	18	10	2	15	5	19	6	8	12	1	4	12	1	1	2	1	11	4
			Goals						1				3		9	3		1	3	8	2	2									3	

Games 20 and 22 played at the Castle Ground.

Two own goals, one unknown, two by players below.

Played in game 3: W Gunn (no. 7), JA Brown (11). Played in game 8: HG Owen (1).
Played in game 11: T Cooke (7), F Weightman (10, one goal). In game 22: F Bailey (9, one goal).
Played in games 11 and 14: HA Morley (2).

F.A. Cup

#	Mon	Date	Opponent	Score	Scorers	Att	Holland JH	Guttridge FH	McLean T	Brown GH	Warburton BF	Shelton A	Hodder W	Harker E	Jardine R	Moore AE	Wardle ES	Shelton C	Jackson H	Daft HB	Allin T	Cursham HA	Clements JE	Sherwin M	May W	Widdowson TH	Snook HD	Dobson CF	Shaw AF	Galbraith	May E	Emmitt HW
Q1	Oct	6	ECKINGTON	4-1	Jackson, Emmitt, Marshall 2	good				2		4		7					9							1	3	6				5
Q2		27	BEESTON ST. JOHN'S	4-2	Harker, HH Brown 2, Marshall					5			10	7												1	2	6				
Q3	Nov	17	DERBY MIDLAND	2-1	Daft, Harker		1			4		6		11	8	7				9	10	2					3					5
Q4	Dec	8	Staveley	3-1	Cursham, Daft, Wardle			2				6			8	7		5		10		9	3			1					11	4
R1	Feb	2	OLD BRIGHTONIANS	2-0	C Shelton, Moore				2	4		6	7	8				5		10			3			1					11	
R2		16	Sheffield Wednesday	2-3	A Shelton, FW Snook	10000			2	4		6	7					5	9	10			3			1					11	

Played in game Q1: JT Marshall (no. 8, 2 goals), H Stevens (10), HH Brown (11).
Played in game Q2: H Stevens (3), WH Cotterill (4), JT Marshall (8, 1goal), GN Brown (9), HH Brown (11, 2 goals)
Q1 and Q2 games played by the reserve team before the League game on the same day.
FW Snook played in Round 1 (at 9) and Round 2 (at 8).

1889/90 — 10th in The Football League

#	Date	Opponent	Res	Scorers	Att	Toone G	Clements JE	McMillan G	Ferguson A	McLean T	Shelton A	Smith, William	Oswald, John	Oswald, James	May E	Daft HB	Calderhead D	Sharpe JW	Lindley T	Shaw AF	McInnes T	Walkerdine H	Wilkinson F	Smith AW
1	Sep 7	Wolverhampton Wand.	0-2		4000	1	2	3	4	5	6	7	8	9	10	11								
2	14	Aston Villa	1-1	James Oswald	6500	1		3	4	2	6	7	8	9	10	11	5							
3	21	WEST BROMWICH ALB.	1-2	W Smith	6200	1		3	4	2	6	7	8	9	10	11	5							
4	28	Derby County	0-2		3000	1		3	4	2	6	7	8	9		11	5	10						
5	Oct 5	STOKE	3-1	James Oswald 2, Daft	3000	1		3	4	2	6	7	10	9	8	11	5							
6	12	Accrington	8-1	* see below	1500	1		3	4	2	6	7	10	9	8	11	5							
7	19	EVERTON	4-3	W Smith 2, May, James Oswald	6000	1		3	4	2	6	7	10	9	8	11	5							
8	26	Bolton Wanderers	4-0	James Oswald 2, John Oswald, OG	5000	1		3	4	2	6	7	10	9	8	11	5							
9	Nov 2	BURNLEY	1-1	James Oswald	1000	1		3	4	2	6	7	10	9	8	11	5							
10	9	ASTON VILLA	1-1	Daft	4000	1		3	4	2	6	7	10		8	11	5	9						
11	16	Blackburn Rovers	1-9	John Oswald	6000	1	9	3	4	2	6	7	10		8	11	5							
12	Dec 7	Everton	3-5	Daft, James Oswald, W Smith	5000	1		3	4	2	6	7	10	9	8	11	5							
13	14	WOLVERHAMPTON W.	0-2		3000	1		3	4	2	6		10	9		11	5			7	8			
14	21	DERBY COUNTY	3-1	James Oswald 2, John Oswald	3000	1		3	4	2	6		10	9		11	5			7	8			
15	Jan 4	West Bromwich Alb.	2-4	Daft, McInnes	4700	1		3	4	2	6		10	9		11	5				8	7		
16	11	BOLTON WANDERERS	3-5	Daft 2, James Oswald	4000	1		3	4	2	6		10	9		11					8	7	5	
17	Feb 18	BLACKBURN ROVERS	1-1	John Oswald	4000	1		3		2	6		10	8	7	11	5	9						4
18	Mar 1	Preston North End	3-4	Calderhead 2, James Oswald	3000	1		3		2	6	7	10	9	8	11	5							4
19	13	ACCRINGTON	3-1	Daft, W Smith 2	2000	1		3	4	2	6	7	10	9	8	11	5							
20	15	Burnley	0-3		0	1		3	6	2			10	9	8		5		11		7			4
21	24	Stoke	1-1	James Oswald	2500	1		3	6	2			10	9	8		5		11		7			4
22	27	PRESTON NORTH END	0-1		0	1		3	4	2	6	7	10	9	11		5				8			
		Apps				22	2	22	20	22	20	15	22	19	18	19	20	3	2	2	7	2	1	4
		Goals										7	6	15	1	10	2				1			

Games 3, 19, 22 at the Castle Ground

*Scorers in game 6: James Oswald 2, Daft 3, John Oswald 2, W Smith

F.A. Cup

#	Date	Opponent	Res	Scorers	Att	Toone G	Clements JE	McMillan G	Ferguson A	McLean T	Shelton A	Smith, William	Oswald, John	Oswald, James	May E	Daft HB	Calderhead D	Sharpe JW	Lindley T	Shaw AF	McInnes T	Walkerdine H	Wilkinson F	Smith AW
R1	Jan 18	Birmingham St. George's	4-4	John Oswald 2, Daft, McInnes	12000	1		3	4	2	6		10	9	8	11	5				7			
rep	Jan 25	BIRM. ST. GEORGE'S	6-2	McInnes 2, May 2, Daft, John Oswald	large	1		3	4	2	6		10	9	8	11	5				7			
R2	Feb 1	ASTON VILLA	4-1	May 3, James Oswald	large	1		3	4	2	6		10	9	8	11	5				7			
R3	Feb 15	Sheffield Wednesday	0-5			1		3	4	2	6		10	9	8	11	5				7			
rep	Feb 22	Sheffield Wednesday	3-2	Daft, John Oswald, W Smith	14000	1		3	4	2	6		10	9	8	11	5				7			
r2	Mar 3	Sheffield Wednesday	1-2	McInnes	8000	1		3	4	2	6	10			8	11			9		7			

Played in R3 rep. 2: C Hibbert (no. 5)

R3 and R3 replay both replayed after protest. R3 rep. 2 at Derbyshire Cricket Ground.

1890/91 3rd in The Football League

#		Date	Opponent	Score	Scorers	Att	Toone G	McLean T	Hendry J	Osborne AW	Calderhead D	Shelton A	McGregor AC	McInnes T	Oswald, James	Locker W	Daft HB	Shelton C	Ferguson A	Gunn W	Lyle D	Thraves J	Cursham HA
1	Sep	6	Bolton Wanderers	2-4	McInnes, ANO	6000	1	2	3	4	5	6	7	8	9	10	11						
2		13	Aston Villa	2-3	Locker, McGregor	6000	1	2	3	4	5	6	7	8	9	10	11						
3		20	ACCRINGTON	5-0	Oswald 3, Locker, Shelton	0	1	2	3	4	5	6	7	8	9	10	11						
4		22	Wolverhampton Wand.	1-1	Osborne	4000	1	2	3	4	5	6	7	8	9	10	11						
5		27	DERBY COUNTY	2-1	McGregor, McInnes	7500	1	2	3	4	5	6	7	8	9	10	11						
6	Oct	2	BOLTON WANDERERS	3-1	Calderhead, McInnes, Oswald	6000	1	2	3	4	5	6	7	8	9	10	11						
7		11	WEST BROMWICH ALB.	3-2	Daft, McGregor, Oswald	4900	1	2	3	4	5	6	7	8	9	10	11						
8		18	West Bromwich Alb.	1-1	McInnes	7367	1		3	4	5	6	7	8	9	10	11	2					
9		25	Accrington	2-3	Locker, Daft	0	1		3	4	5	6	7	8	9	10	11	2					
10	Nov	1	EVERTON	3-1	Daft, McGregor, McInnes	13000	1	2	3	4	5	6	7	8	9	10	11						
11		8	Preston North End	0-0		4000	1	2	3	4	5	6	7	8	9	10	11						
12		15	BLACKBURN ROVERS	1-2	Oswald	11000	1	2	3	4	5	6	7	8	9	10	11						
13		22	WOLVERHAMPTON W.	1-1	Locker	3000	1	2	3	4	5		7	8	9	10	11			6			
14		29	ASTON VILLA	7-1	Locker 3, Oswald 3, McInnes	4000	1	2	3	4		6	7	8	9	10	11	5					
15	Dec	6	PRESTON NORTH END	2-1	Locker, Oswald	10000	1	2	3	4	5	6	7	8	9	10	11						
16		15	SUNDERLAND	2-1	Daft, Locker	8000	1	2	3	4	5	6	7	8	9	10	11						
17		20	Burnley	1-0	Oswald	5000	1	2	3	4	5	6	7	8	9	10	11						
18		27	Derby County	1-3	Locker	5000	1	2	3	4	5	6	7	8	9	10	11						
19	Jan	3	Everton	2-4	Locker, one og	12000	1		3	4	5	6	7	8	9	10	11			2			
20		24	Sunderland	0-4		5000	1		3	4	2	6	7	8	9		11	5			10		
21	Feb	10	BURNLEY	4-0	McGregor 2, McInnes, Oswald	4000			3	4	5	6	7	8	9		11				10	1	2
22	Mar	14	Blackburn Rovers	7-1	Daft 2, McGregor 2, Oswald 2, Locker	7000			3	4	5	6	7	8	9	10	11			2		1	
				Apps			20	16	22	22	21	21	22	22	22	21	21	4	2	1	2	2	1
				Goals						1	1		8	7	14	12	6	1					

Game 3 at the Castle Ground

One own goal, one unknown

F.A. Cup

		Date	Opponent	Score	Scorers	Att	Toone G	McLean T	Hendry J	Osborne AW	Calderhead D	Shelton A	McGregor AC	McInnes T	Oswald, James	Locker W	Daft HB	Shelton C	Ferguson A	Gunn W	Lyle D	Thraves J	Cursham HA
R1	Jan	17	Sheffield United	9-1	McGregor 4, Oswald 2, Daft, Locker, McInnes	9000	1	2	3	4	5	6	7	8	9	10	11						
R2	Jan	31	BURNLEY	2-1	Daft 2	good			3	4	5	6	7	8	9	10	11			2		1	
R3	Feb	14	STOKE	1-0	Locker	12000		2	3	4	5	6	7	8	9	10	11					1	
SF	Feb	28	Sunderland	3-3	McGregor, McInnes, Oswald	25000			3	4	5	6	7	8	9	10	11					1	2
rep	Mar	11	Sunderland	2-0	Oswald 2	16000		2	3	4	5	6	7	8	9	10	11					1	
F	Mar	21	Blackburn Rovers	1-3	Oswald	23000			3	4	5	6	7	8	9	10	11			2		1	

SF and replay at Bramall Lane, Final at Kennington Oval

1891/92 — 8th in The Football League

#	Mon	Date / Opponent	Score	Scorers	Att	Toone G	Whitelaw A	Hendry J	Osborne AW	Calderhead D	Shelton A	Bakewell GH	McInnes T	Oswald, James	Walkerdine H	Daft HB	McLean T	Bramley C	Thraves J	Elleman AR	Burns J	Bell E	Williamson A	Abrahams J	Walker JA	Shelton C	Wilkinson F	Hooley A	Widdowson, Albert
1	Sep	5 PRESTON NORTH END	2-0	Daft 2	10000	1	2	3	4	5	6	7	8	9	10	11													
2		12 Blackburn Rovers	4-5	Oswald 2, Walkerdine, Forbes(og)	7000	1	2	3	4	5	6	7	8	9	10	11													
3		19 Derby County	0-3		8000	1	2	3	4	5	6	7	8	9	10	11													
4		26 STOKE	1-1	Walkerdine	6000	1		3		5	6	7	8	9	10	11	2	4											
5	Oct	1 BOLTON WANDERERS	2-0	Daft, Bakewell	3000	1		3		5	6	7	8	9	10	11	2	4											
6		10 WEST BROMWICH ALB.	4-0	McInnes 2, Elleman, Walkerdine	4000			3		5	6		8	9	10	11	2	4	1	7									
7		17 Wolverhampton Wand.	1-2	Elleman	900			3		5	6		8	9	10	11	2	4	1	7									
8		24 DARWEN	5-0	Daft 2, Oswald 2, Walkerdine	4000	1		3		5	6		8	9	10	11	2	4		7									
9		31 West Bromwich Alb.	2-2	McInnes 2	5200	1		3		5	6		8	9	10	11	2	4		7									
10	Nov	7 Aston Villa	1-5	Walkerdine	3000	1		3		5	6		7	9	10	11	2	4					8						
11		14 WOLVERHAMPTON W.	2-2	Daft, Walkerdine	3000	1		3		5	6		8	9	10	11	2	4		7									
12		21 Accrington	0-2		1000	1		3		5	6		8		10	11	2	4		7		9							
13		28 ACCRINGTON	9-0	* See below	3000	1		3		5	6		8	9	10	11	2	4					7						
14	Dec	5 Sunderland	0-4		0	1		3		5	6			9	10	11	2	4			8			7					
15		12 Preston North End	0-6		300	1		3		5	6		8	9	10	11	2	4						7					
16		19 BLACKBURN ROVERS	2-2	Abrahams, Walkerdine	6000	1		3		5	6		8	9	10	11	2	4						7					
17	Jan	2 ASTON VILLA	5-2	Daft 3, Oswald 2	3000	1		3		5	6		8	9		11	2	4						7	10				
18		9 EVERTON	1-3	Walkerdine	4000	1		3		5	6		8	9	7	11	2	4				10							
19	Feb	6 Stoke	3-1	Daft 2, Walkerdine	4000	1	2	3		5	6		8	9	7	11		4				10							
20		20 DERBY COUNTY	2-1	Oswald 2	3000	1	2	3		5	6		8	9	7	11		4				10							
21		27 Darwen	3-2	Oswald 2, McInnes	3000	1	2	3		5			8	9	7	11	4					10				6			
22	Mar	1 BURNLEY	5-1	Oswald 3, Hooley, Walkerdine	2000	1	2	3		5	6		8	9	10	11											4	7	
23		26 Bolton Wanderers	0-2		6000	1	2	3		5	6		8	9	10			4										7	11
24	Apr	9 SUNDERLAND	1-0	Oswald	10000	1	2	3	4	5	6		8	9	10	11												7	
25		15 Burnley	0-1		10000	1	2	3	4	5	6		8	9	10	11													7
26		16 Everton	0-4		10000	1	2	3		5	6		8	9	10			4							7				11
		Apps				24	11	26	5	26	25	5	25	24	25	24	16	19	2	6	1	5	2	4	3	1	1	3	3
		Goals								1		1	6	15	13	13				2				1				1	

Games 1, 24 at the Castle Ground

* Scorers in game 13: Walkerdine 3, Daft 2, Calderhead, McInnes, Oswald, one unknown

One own goal, one unknown

F.A. Cup

	Mon	Date / Opponent	Score	Att	Toone G	Whitelaw A	Hendry J	Osborne AW	Calderhead D	Shelton A	Bakewell GH	McInnes T	Oswald, James	Walkerdine H	Daft HB	McLean T	Bramley C	Thraves J	Elleman AR	Burns J	Bell E	Williamson A	Abrahams J	Walker JA	Shelton C	Wilkinson F	Hooley A	Widdowson, Albert
R1	Jan	16 Sunderland	0-3	16000	1	2	3	4	5	6		8	9		11								10					
rep	Jan	23 Sunderland	0-4	12000	1	2	3		5	6	7	8	9		11	4							10					

First game declared void after protest. Played in first game: W Locker (no. 7).

Back: Kirk(Trainer), Bramley, Calderhead, Toone, Hendry, A.Shelton
Front: McLean, Burns, McInnes, Oswald, Walkerdine, Daft

1892/93 — 14th in Division One (Relegated)

#	Date	Opponent	Score	Scorers	Att	Toone G	Whitelaw A	Hendry J	Parke J	Calderhead D	Shelton A	McGregor AC	Docherty A	Oswald James	Walkerdine H	Daft HB	Bramley C	Walker JA	Bruce D	McInnes T	Burke J	Harper T	Wilkinson F	King LH	Gunn W	Mabbott J
1	Sep 3	SHEFFIELD WEDNESDAY	0-1		10000	1	2	3	4	5	6	7	8	9	10	11										
2	10	Sunderland	2-2	Bramley, Walkerdine	10000	1	2	3		5	6	7	8	9	10	11	4									
3	17	DERBY COUNTY	1-1	Walkerdine	12000	1	2	3		5	6	7	8	9	10	11	4									
4	24	Wolverhampton Wand.	0-3		4000	1	2	3		5	6	7		9	10	11	4	8								
5	Oct 1	PRESTON NORTH END	3-1	Daft, Docherty, McGregor	8000	1	2	3		5	6	7	8	9	10	11	4									
6	6	BOLTON WANDERERS	2-2	Bramley, Daft	8000	1	2	3		5	6	7		8	10	11	4		9							
7	8	NOTTM. FOREST	3-0	Walkerdine, Daft, Bruce	18000	1	2	3		5	6	7		8	10	11	4		9							
8	19	Derby County	5-4	Bruce 2, Daft 2, McGregor	5000	1	2	3		5	6	7		8	10	11	4		9							
9	22	Burnley	0-3		7000	1	2	3		5	6	7	10		4	11			9	8						
10	29	West Bromwich Alb.	2-4	Burke, Bruce	3000	1	2	3		5	6	7			4	11			9	8	10					
11	Nov 5	STOKE	0-1		10000	1	2	3		5	6	7			4	11			9	8	10					
12	12	Newton Heath	3-1	Burke, McInnes, Oswald	8000	1	2	3		5	6	7		9			4		11	8	10					
13	19	WEST BROMWICH ALB.	8-1	Daft 3, Oswald 3, Bruce 2	8000	1	2	3		5	6	7		9		11	4		10	8						
14	26	SUNDERLAND	3-1	Daft, McGregor, McInnes	8000	1	2	3		5	6	7		9		11	4		10	8						
15	Dec 8	BURNLEY	3-1	McInnes, Oswald, Hillman(og)	4000	1	2	3		5	6	7		9		11	4		10	8						
16	10	Accrington	2-4	Daft, Oswald	1500	1	2	3		5	6	7		9		11	4		10	8						
17	17	EVERTON	1-2	Oswald	10000	1	2	3		5	6	7		9		11	4		10	8						
18	24	Blackburn Rovers	0-1		5000	1	2	3		5	6	7	4	8		11			9	10						
19	31	ASTON VILLA	1-4	Bruce	4000	1	2	3		5	6	7		8		11	4		9	10						
20	Jan 7	Everton	0-6		8000	1	2	3			6	7		9					10	11		4	5	8		
21	14	BLACKBURN ROVERS	0-0		3000	1	2	3			6			9	8		4		10	11			5	7		
22	26	NEWTON HEATH	4-0	Bruce, Oswald, Gunn, Burke	1000	1	2	3		5	6			9			4		10	8	11				7	
23	Feb 11	ACCRINGTON	2-0	Bruce, McInnes	4000	1	2	3		5	6		7	9			4		11	8	10	4				
24	25	Nottm. Forest	1-3	Bruce	15000	1	2	3			6	7		9			4		11	8	10	5				
25	Mar 11	Stoke	0-1		6000	1	2	3		5	6		7	9			4		11	8	10					
26	18	Aston Villa	1-3	McInnes	4000	1	2	3		5	6			9			4		11	8	10					7
27	25	Bolton Wanderers	1-4	McInnes	4000	1	2	3		5	6	7		9			4		11	8	10					
28	31	Preston North End	0-4		6000		2	1		5	6			7			4		11	8	10	3				
29	Apr 3	Sheffield Wednesday	2-3	Oswald 2	1000	1	2	6		5	11			7			4		9	8	10	3				
30	8	WOLVERHAMPTON W.	3-0	Bruce, Burke, Oswald	2500	1	2	3		5	11			7			4		9	8	10	6				
		Apps				29	30	30	1	27	30	22	6	30	11	18	23	1	25	19	15	4	4	2	1	1
		Goals										3	1	11	3	10	2		11	6	4				1	

One own goal

Games 1, 3 and 30 at Castle Ground
Game 28: Only 10 men.

Test Match

Date	Opponent	Score	Scorers	Att	Toone	Whitelaw	Hendry		Calderhead	Shelton			Oswald		Daft	Bramley		Bruce	McInnes	Burke
Apr 22	Darwen	2-3	Kenyon (og), Bruce	3000	1	2	3		5	6			9	7		4		11	8	10

Played at Hyde Road, Manchester

F.A. Cup

	Date	Opponent	Score	Scorers	Att	Toone	Whitelaw	Hendry	Calderhead	Shelton	McGregor	Oswald	Bramley	Bruce	McInnes	Burke	King
R1	Jan 21	SHANKHOUSE	4-0	Oswald 3, McInnes	good	1	2	3		6	7	9	4	11	8	10	5
R2	Feb 4	Middlesbro' Ironopolis	2-3	Burke, Walkerdine	10000	1	2	3	5	6	7	9	4	11	8	10	

Standing: Thomas(Director), Harris(Secretary), McInnes, Hendry, Calderhead, Toone, Shelton, Kirk(Trainer)
Sitting: McGregor, Oswald, Bruce, Walkerdine, Daft
Front: Bramley, Whitelaw

1893/94 — 3rd in Division Two

#	Date	Opponent	Score	Scorers	Att	Toone G	Harper T	Hendry J	Osborne AW	Calderhead D	Shelton A	Watson AE	Donnelly S	Bruce D	Kerr G	Dixon H	Bramley C	Daft HB	Mabbott J	Logan J	MacLachlan J	Burrows W	Wilkinson F	King LH	Allsopp E	Shepperson G
1	Sep 2	Crewe Alexandra	2-0	Bruce, Watson	2000	1	2	3	4	5	6	7	8	9	10	11										
2	9	WOOLWICH ARSENAL	3-2	Bruce 2, Watson	6000	1	2	3	4	5	6	7	8	9	10	11										
3	11	Northwich Victoria	1-0	Bruce	1000	1	2	3	4	5	6	7	8	9	10	11										
4	16	Rotherham Town	2-0	Bramley, Daft	1000	1	2	3	4	5	6	7		9	10		8	11								
5	30	LIVERPOOL	1-1	Watson	6000	1	2	3	4	5	6	7		9	10			11	8							
6	Oct 5	GRIMSBY TOWN	3-0	Logan 2, Bruce	4000	1	2	3	4	5	6	7		8	10			11		9						
7	14	NEWCASTLE UNITED	3-1	Daft, Logan, Watson	3000	1	2	3	4	5	6	7	10					11		9	8					
8	21	Grimsby Town	2-5	Logan, Higgins(og)	3000	1	2	3	4	5	6	7		10	8			11		9						
9	26	PORT VALE	6-1	Logan 3, Daft, Kerr, Watson	3000	1	2	3		5	6	7		10	8		4	11		9						
10	28	Ardwick	0-0		4000	1	2	3		5	6	7		10	8		4	11		9						
11	Nov 4	MIDDLESBRO' IRON.	3-0	Watson, Logan, Daft	5000	1	2	3		5	6	7		10	8		4	11		9						
12	16	LINCOLN CITY	1-2	Bruce	2000	1	2	3		5	6			10	7		4	11		9	8					
13	18	Liverpool	1-2	Bruce	8000	1	2	3	4	5	6	7		10	8			11		9						
14	23	NORTHWICH VIC.	6-1	Logan 3, Bruce 2, Watson	1000	1	2	3	4	5	6	7		10	8			11		9						
15	25	Port Vale	0-1		1000	1	2	3	4	5	6	7		10	8			11		9						
16	30	BURTON SWIFTS	6-2	Kerr 3, Logan, Daft, Watson	2000	1		3	5	2	6	7		10	8		4	11		9						
17	Dec 9	Newcastle United	0-3		3000	1	2	3		5	6		7	8	10		4	11		9						
18	16	Middlesbro' Ironopolis	0-0		2000		2	3		5	6			8			11			9		1	4	7		
19	30	Burton Swifts	2-0	Logan 2	0	1	2	3	5				7	10	8		4	11		9			6			
20	Jan 11	ROTHERHAM TOWN	4-2	Bruce 3, Kerr	1500	1		3	5		2		7	10	8		4	11		9			6			
21	20	WALSALL	2-0	Bruce, Shelton	2000	1		3	5	2	6	7	8	9	10		4	11								
22	Feb 3	SMALL HEATH	3-1	Logan, Watson, Jenkyns(og)	6000	1		3	5	2	6	7		8	10		4	11		9						
23	17	CREWE ALEXANDRA	9-1	Watson 4, Bruce 2, Logan 2, Daft	300	1	2		5	3	6	7		8	10		4	11		9						
24	Mar 12	Walsall	1-2	Logan	2000	1	2	3	5		6			8	10	7	4	11		9						
25	15	ARDWICK	5-0	Logan 2, Allsopp, Bruce, Kerr	2500	1	2	3		5	6			10	8		4	11		9					7	
26	23	Lincoln City	2-0	Bruce, Daft	6000	1	2	3		5	6	7		8	10		4	11		9						
27	24	Woolwich Arsenal	2-1	Bruce, Logan	13000	1	2	3		5	6			8	10		4	11		9						7
28	Apr 7	Small Heath	0-3		8500	1	2	3		5	6	7	8	9	10		4	11								
		Apps				27	24	27	19	26	25	20	15	26	23	3	18	24	1	21	2	1	3	1	1	1
		Goals									1	13		18	6		1	7		21					1	

Game 2 at Castle Ground

Two own goals

Test match

	Date	Opponent	Score		Att	Toone G	Harper T	Hendry J	Osborne AW	Calderhead D	Shelton A	Watson AE	Donnelly S	Bruce D	Kerr G	Dixon H	Bramley C	Daft HB	Mabbott J	Logan J	MacLachlan J	Burrows W	Wilkinson F	King LH	Allsopp E	Shepperson G
	Apr 28	Preston North End	0-4		8000	1	2		3		6	7	8	10			4	11		9			5			

Played at Olive Grove, Sheffield

F.A. Cup

	Date	Opponent	Score	Scorers	Att	Toone G	Harper T	Hendry J	Osborne AW	Calderhead D	Shelton A	Watson AE	Donnelly S	Bruce D	Kerr G	Dixon H	Bramley C	Daft HB	Mabbott J	Logan J
R1	Jan 27	BURNLEY	1-0	Logan	8000	1	2	3		5	6	7		10			4	11		9
R2	Feb 10	Burton Wanderers	2-1	Donnelly, Logan(p)	6000	1	2	3		5	6		8	10	7		4	11		9
R3	Feb 24	Nottm. Forest	1-1	Bruce	15000	1	2	3		5	6	7	8	10			4	11		9
rep	Mar 3	NOTTM. FOREST	4-1	Bruce 2, Donnelly, Logan	12000	1	2	3		5	6	7	8	10			4	11		9
SF	Mar 10	BLACKBURN ROVERS	1-0	Daft	20000	1	2	3		5	6	7	8	10			4	11		9
F	Mar 31	BOLTON WANDERERS	4-1	Logan 3, Watson	37000	1	2	3		5	6	7	8	10			4	11		9

Round 3 first game after extra time.
SF at Bramall Lane, Final at Goodison Park
Played in Round 1: AG Henfrey (at no. 8). Calderhead sent off.

United Counties League (East Midlands Division)

#	Date	Opponent	Score	Scorers	Att	Toone G	Harper T	Hendry J	Osborne AW	Calderhead D	Shelton A	Watson AE	Donnelly S	Bruce D	Kerr G	Dixon H	Bramley C	Daft HB	Mabbott J	Logan J	MacLachlan J	Burrows W	Wilkinson F	King LH	Allsopp E	Shepperson G
1	Dec 2	SHEFFIELD UNITED	0-0		good	1	2	3		5	6		8	10	7		4	11		9						
2	Jan 6	Nottm. Forest	0-1		4000	1	2	3	5				7	10	8		4	11		9			6			
3	13	Derby County	1-8	Kerr		1		3	5		2		7	10	8		4	11		9			6			
4	Mar 17	SHEFFIELD WEDNESDAY	2-1	Daft, Shepperson	3000	1	2	3		5	6	7		10			4	11		9						8
5	26	DERBY COUNTY	0-4		4000				4						6						1	5	7			8
6	Apr 9	Sheffield Wednesday	0-4		1000	1		3	5	2				8	11	10	4			9			6			
7	19	NOTTM. FOREST	3-4	Bruce, Daft 2	3000	1	2	3		5	6	7		8	10		4	11		9						

Games 4 and 5 at Castle Ground, game 7 at Town Ground. Return game with Sheffield United not played.
Played in game 5: Askew (3), Dean (10), Murray (2), H Sissons (9), J Burke (11).
Played in game 6: Gadsby (7)

- 1893/94 Season -

Back: Harris (Secretary), Donnelly, Harper, Toone, Calderhead, Hendry, Bramley (Director), Featherstone (Director)
Middle: Watson, Kerr, Logan, Bruce, Daft
Front: Bramley, Osborne

- 1894/95 Season -

Back: Harris(Secretary), Chadburn, Donnelly, W.Gunn(Director), Fletcher, Allsopp, Goode(Trainer)
Front: Hendry, Shelton, Bramley, Calderhead, Bruce, Harrison, Stothert

1894/95 — 2nd in Division Two

#		Date	Opponent	Res	Scorers	Att	Toone G	Harper T	Hendry J	Bramley C	Calderhead D	Shelton A	Chadburn J	Allsopp E	Logan J	Bruce D	Daft HB	Donnelly S	Bull W	Shepperson G	Brown W	Harrison AE	Fletcher F	Stothert J	Watson AE	Allan J	Guttridge FH	Hall WH	Arnott W	Ferrier J	Brealey H
1	Sep	15	DARWEN	2-1	Calderhead, Chadburn	10000	1	2	3	4	5	6	7	8	9	10	11														
2		17	Burslem Port Vale	3-0	Allsopp 2, Bramley	1000	1	2	3	4	5	6	7	8	9	10	11														
3		22	Newcastle United	2-2	Daft, Chadburn	3000	1	2	3	4	5	6	7	8	9	10	11														
4		29	LINCOLN CITY	3-0	Bruce, Daft, Logan	7000	1	2	3	4	5	6	7	8	9	10	11														
5	Oct	4	GRIMSBY TOWN	3-2	Chadburn, Daft, Logan	5000	1	2	3	4	5	6	7	8	9	10	11														
6		6	LEICESTER FOSSE	3-0	Allsopp 2, Daft	0	1	2	3	4	5	6	7	8	9	10	11														
7		13	MANCHESTER CITY	1-3	Logan	6000	1	2	3	4	5	6	7	8	9	10	11														
8		27	WOOLWICH ARSENAL	2-2	Chadburn, Logan	2000	1	2	3	4	5	6	7		9	10	11	8													
9	Nov	3	Woolwich Arsenal	1-2	Logan	11000	1	2	3	4	5	6	7		9	10	11	8													
10		5	Rotherham Town	2-1	Allsopp, Bruce	0	1		3	4	5	6	7	9		10	11		2	8											
11		10	CREWE ALEXANDRA	5-1	Bruce 2, Allsopp, Donnelly, Shelton	3500			3	4	5	6		9		11		8		2	1										
12		24	BURY	2-1	Allsopp 2(1p)	10000		2	3	4	5	6	7	10	9			8				1	11								
13	Dec	1	Leicester Fosse	1-5	Fletcher	6000	1	2	3	4	5	6		8	9		11	10					7								
14		8	Burton Wanderers	0-1		3000	1		3	4	5			10	6	9		8					11	2	7						
15		15	NEWTON HEATH	1-1	Bruce	3000	1	2	3	4	5	6		10	9		11	8							7						
16		22	Burton Swifts	2-2	Allsopp 2	0	1	2	3	4	5	6	7	10	9		11	8													
17		25	WALSALL	5-0	Logan 3, Calderhead, Donnelly	4000	1	2	3	4	5	6	7		9		11	8								10					
18	Jan	1	Bury	1-2	Allsopp	12000	1	2	3	4	5	6		7	9		11	8								10					
19		5	BURTON WANDERERS	2-0	Bramley, Hendry	3000	1	2	3	4	5			7	9		11	8						6		10					
20		12	BURTON SWIFTS	5-1	Allsopp 2, Donnelly 2, Allan	1500	1	2	3	4	5	6		7	9			8					11			10					
21		16	Crewe Alexandra	3-0	Logan 2, Allan	100	1	2	3	4	5			7	9		11	8						6		10					
22		26	Darwen	1-2	Bramley	4000	1		3	4	5		7		9		11	8						6		10	2				
23	Feb	5	Grimsby Town	1-0	Allsopp	4000	1		3	4	5	6	7	11	9	2		8						6		10					
24		26	BURSLEM PORT VALE	10-0	* See below	1500	1		3	4	5			7		9		8	11					6		10			2		
25	Mar	9	Manchester City	1-7	Bruce	7000	1		3	4	5	6	7			9		8	11							10		2			
26		16	ROTHERHAM TOWN	4-2	Bull 3, Donnelly	2000	1		3	4	5		7			9		8	11					6		10		2			
27		23	NEWCASTLE UNITED	2-1	Bruce, Bull	4000	1		3	4	5	6	7			9		8	11							10				2	
28		25	Walsall	1-2	Bruce	1500	1			4	5	6	7			9	11	8						3		10				2	
29	Apr	12	Lincoln City	3-1	Allsopp, Bruce, Bull	5000	1		3	4	5	6		8		9			10					2		7					11
30		20	Newton Heath	3-3	Chadburn 2, Bruce	12000	1		3	4	5	6	7	8		10			11					2		9					

Game 1 at the Castle Ground
*Scorers in game 24: Bruce 5, Donnelly 2, Allsopp, Bull, Allan

	Toone G	Harper T	Hendry J	Bramley C	Calderhead D	Shelton A	Chadburn J	Allsopp E	Logan J	Bruce D	Daft HB	Donnelly S	Bull W	Shepperson G	Brown W	Harrison AE	Fletcher F	Stothert J	Watson AE	Allan J	Guttridge FH	Hall WH	Arnott W	Ferrier J	Brealey H
Apps	28	18	29	30	27	27	17	25	20	29	12	17	10	2	1	1	5	9	2	14	1	2	1	2	1
Goals			1	3	2	1	6	16	10	15	4	7	6				1			3					

Test Match

	Date	Opponent	Res	Scorers	Att	Toone G	Hendry J	Bramley C	Calderhead D	Shelton A	Chadburn J	Allsopp E	Fletcher F	Stothert J	Allan J
	Apr 27	Derby County	1-2	Fletcher	8000	1	3	4	5	6	7	8	11	2	9

Played at Filbert Street, Leicester
Played at no. 10: H Sissons

F.A. Cup

	Date	Opponent	Res	Scorers	Att	Toone G	Hendry J	Bramley C	Calderhead D	Shelton A	Allsopp E	Logan J	Daft HB	Donnelly S	Allan J	Arnott W
R1	Feb 2	Sheffield Wednesday	1-5	Allsopp(p)	7000	1	3	4	5	6	7	9	11	8	10	2

United Counties League (East Midlands Division)

#		Date	Opponent	Res	Scorers	Att	Toone G	Harper T	Hendry J	Bramley C	Calderhead D	Shelton A	Chadburn J	Allsopp E	Logan J	Bruce D	Donnelly S	Bull W	Shepperson G	Brown W	Harrison AE	Fletcher F	Stothert J	Allan J	Brealey H
1	Feb	9	SHEFFIELD WEDNESDAY	0-2		1000	1		3	4	5		7		9	2	8	11					6	10	
2	Mar	4	Sheffield Wednesday	2-5	Allsopp, Chadburn	fair		2			5	6	10	11	9		8			1			3		
3	Mar	14	LEICESTER FOSSE	0-2		700	1			4	5		7					10	9	8		11	6		
4	Mar	30	Nottm. Forest	0-3		3000	1				5	6			9							11	8	3	10
5	Apr	13	Leicester Fosse	1-2	Garrett	4500	1				4	11											2		7
6	Apr	29	NOTTM. FOREST	0-1		1000	1		3	4	5		7										6	2	9

Game 6 played at the Town Ground.
Played in game 2: Smith (7). Only 10 men. In game 3: J McGinn (2), J Mounteney (6), T McLean (3).
Played in game 4: T McLean (2), F Coles (4). In game 5: Broughton (9), Garrett (8), Haslam (3), Howkins (6), Oldershaw (5). F Coles(10).
Played in game 6: Dugard (10), Garrett(8), R Jardine (11).

1895/96 — 10th in Division Two

No	Date		Opponent	Score	Scorers	Att	Toone G	Stothert J	Hendry J	Bramley C	Calderhead D	Shelton A	Chadburn J	Allsopp E	Allan J	Bruce D	Bull W	Russell D	McCallum N	Brealey H	Connor JH	Cale F	Shepperson G	Kiddier JF	Fletcher F	Handley G	Coles F
1	Sep	7	LIVERPOOL	2-3	Allsopp, Calderhead	7000	1	2	3	4	5	6	7	8	9	10	11										
2		14	Burslem Port Vale	4-0	Allan 2, Bruce, Allsopp	2000	1	2	3	4	5	6	7	8	9	10	11										
3		21	Newcastle United	1-5	Bruce	7000	1	2	3	4	5	6	7		9	10	11		8								
4		28	DARWEN	4-1	Bull 2, Allan, Brealey	5000	1	2	3		5	6	7		9		10	4		8	11						
5	Oct	3	GRIMSBY TOWN	5-3	Allan 2, Bruce, Bull, Brealey	3500	1	2	3		5	6	7		9	8	10	4		11							
6		5	Crewe Alexandra	1-5	Chadburn	500	1	2	3		5	6	7		9	8	10	4			11						
7		19	LINCOLN CITY	2-0	Allan, Bull	3000	1	2			4	6	7	11	9		10	5	8		3						
8		26	Liverpool	0-3		8000	1	2	3	4		6	7	11	9	8	10	5									
9	Nov	2	WOOLWICH ARSENAL	3-4	Chadburn, Shelton, Calderhead	8000	1	2	3		4	6	7		8	9	10	5			11						
10		9	BURTON WANDERERS	1-4	Chadburn	3000	1	2	3		4	6	7		9	10	11	5	8								
11		16	Rotherham Town	0-1		500	1	2	3	4	5	6		8	9		10				11						
12		23	NEWTON HEATH	0-2		3000	1	2	3	4	5	6	7	11	8		9					10					
13		30	ROTHERHAM TOWN	0-0		1500	1	2	3	4	5	11	7	6			9						8	10			
14	Dec	7	BURSLEM PORT VALE	7-2	Bull 2, Fletcher 2, Allan, Calderhead, Kiddier	1000	1		3	4	5		7	6	8		11				2			10	9		
15		14	Newton Heath	0-3		3000	1		3	4	5		7	8	9		11		6		2			10			
16		25	LOUGHBOROUGH	2-0	Bull, Chadburn	3000	1		3	4	5	6	7		8		10			11	2			9			
17		28	Loughborough	3-1	Brealey, Calderhead, Chadburn	1500	1		3		5	6	7	4	8		10			11	2			9			
18	Jan	1	Darwen	0-2		0	1		3		5	6	7	4	10		11				2				9	8	
19		11	Leicester Fosse	1-2	Bull	6000	1		3	4	5	6	7		8		10				2			9	11		
20		18	Burton Swifts	0-0		2000	1		3		5	6	7	4	8		10				2			9	11		
21	Feb	8	LEICESTER FOSSE	1-2	Bull	4000	1		3	4	5	6	7		9	10	11		8		2						
22		22	BURTON SWIFTS	5-0	Allan 2, McCallum 2, Bramley	2000	1		3	4	5		7		10		11		8		2			9			6
23		29	MANCHESTER CITY	3-0	Bull, Kiddier, Allan	4000	1		3	4	5	6	7		10		11		8		2			9			
24	Mar	7	Woolwich Arsenal	0-2		6000	1		3	4	5	6	7		10		11		8		2			9			
25		14	NEWCASTLE UNITED	0-1		2000	1		3	4	5	6	7		10		11		8		2		9				
26		21	Grimsby Town	0-3		3000	1	2	3	4	5	6	7		10		11		8					9			
27	Apr	3	Lincoln City	3-2	Bull, Kiddier, Allan	4000	1		3	4	5	6	7		10		11		8		2			9			
28		4	CREWE ALEXANDRA	6-0	Bull 2, Chadburn, Kiddier, McCallum, Shelton	1000	1		3	4	5	6	7		10		11		8		2			9			
29		6	Burton Wanderers	3-1	Chadburn, Bull 2	3000	1		3	4	5	6	7		10		11		8		2			9			
30		8	Manchester City	0-2		6000	1		3	4	5	6	7		10		11		8		2			9			
			Apps				30	14	29	21	29	26	29	14	29	9	30	9	13	7	17	1	2	15	4	1	1
			Goals							1	4	2	7	2	11	3	15		3	3				4	2		

Game 1 at the Town Ground

F.A.Cup

No	Date		Opponent	Score	Scorers	Att	Toone G	Stothert J	Hendry J	Bramley C	Calderhead D	Shelton A	Chadburn J	Allsopp E	Allan J	Bruce D	Bull W	Russell D	McCallum N	Brealey H	Connor JH	Cale F	Shepperson G	Kiddier JF	Fletcher F	Handley G	Coles F
R1	Feb	1	Wolverhampton Wand.	2-2	Bull 2	9300	1		3	4	5	6	7	9	10		11		8		2						
rep	Feb	5	WOLVERHAMPTON W.	3-4	Allan, Allsopp, Bull	8000	1		3	4	5	6	7	9	10		11		8		2						

1896/97 — Top of Division Two: Promoted

#	Date	Opponent	Score	Scorers	Att	Toone G	Prescott TG	Gibson W	Allsopp E	Calderhead D	Henrys A	Chadburn J	Smith William	Boucher T	Murphy John	Bull W	Langham W	Allan J	Bramley C	Cookson AE	Crone R	Carter AB	Stewart A	Kinsey G	Devey W	Crank J
1	Sep 5	LOUGHBOROUGH	3-1	Chadburn 2, Smith	1000	1	2	3	4	5	6	7	8	9	10	11										
2	12	Leicester Fosse	3-2	Murphy, Smith, Bull	5000	1	2	3	4	5	6	7	8	9	10	11										
3	19	NEWCASTLE UNITED	3-1	Murphy, Bull, Langham	6000	1	2	3	4	5	6		8	9	10	11	7									
4	26	Woolwich Arsenal	3-2	Smith, Boucher 2	9000	1	2	3	4	5	6		8	9	10	11	7									
5	Oct 1	GRIMSBY TOWN	1-3	Murphy	10000	1	2	3	4	5	6		8	9	10	11	7									
6	3	Burton Wanderers	3-0	Murphy 2, Boucher	1000	1	2	3	4	5	6	7	8	9	10	11										
7	10	MANCHESTER CITY	3-3	Murphy, Bull, Calderhead	7000	1	2	3	4	5	6			9	10	11	7	8								
8	17	LEICESTER FOSSE	6-0	Allan 2, Murphy 2, Bull, Calderhead	5000	1	2	3	6	5				9	10	11	7	8	4							
9	24	Loughborough	1-0	Boucher	2000	1	2	3	6	5				9	10	11	7	8	4							
10	31	Manchester City	4-1	Murphy 2, Bramley, Langham	12000	1	2	3	6	5				9	10	11	7	8	4							
11	Nov 7	WOOLWICH ARSENAL	7-4	Bull 3, Allan, Allsopp, Langham, Murphy	3000	1	2	3	6	5				9	10	11	7	8	4							
12	14	WALSALL	5-2	Boucher, Murphy 2, Bull	5000	1	2	3	6	5				9	10	11	7	8	4							
13	21	Grimsby Town	1-3	Boucher	7000	1	2	3	6	5			8	9	10	11	7		4							
14	28	Blackpool	2-3	Boucher, Bull	2500	1	2	3	6	5				9	10	11	7	8	4							
15	Dec 5	BURTON SWIFTS	6-1	Boucher 2, Langham 2, Murphy, Allan	4000	1	2	3	6	5				9	10	11	7	8	4							
16	12	Newcastle United	2-2	Allan, Bull	14000	1	2	3		5				9	10	11	7	8	4		6					
17	19	NEWTON HEATH	3-0	Allan, Langham, Murphy	5000	1	2	3		5				9	10	11	7	8	4		6					
18	Jan 2	Burton Swifts	4-1	Boucher 3, Langham	2000	1	2	3		5				9	10	11	7	8	4		6					
19	9	GAINSBORO' TRINITY	2-0	Allan, Boucher	1000	1	2		6	5				9	10	11	7	8	4		3					
20	16	Walsall	3-1	Murphy 2, Bull	3000	1	2	3		5				9	10	11	7	8	4		6					
21	23	LINCOLN CITY	8-0	Bull 3, Boucher 2, Murphy 2, Allan	2000	1	2	3	4	5				9	10	11	7	8			6					
22	Feb 6	DARWEN	4-0	Boucher 2, Allan, Langham	4000	1		3	6	5			11	9	10		7	8	4		2					
23	27	Darwen	1-2	Bull	4000	1	2	3	4	5				9	10	11	7	8			6					
24	Mar 6	Gainsborough Trinity	2-3	Boucher, Murphy	3000	1	2	3	4	5				9	10	11	7				6	8				
25	13	BURTON WANDERERS	5-0	Bull 2, Boucher, Carter, Smith	6000	1	2	3		5			7	9	10	11			4		6	8				
26	20	BLACKPOOL	3-1	Boucher, Langham, Murphy	7000	1	2	3		5				9	10	11	7				6	8	4			
27	27	Newton Heath	1-1	Devey	10000	1	2	3		5				9	10	11		8					4	6	7	
28	31	Lincoln City	1-1	Murphy	0	1	2	3						9	10	11		8		5			4	6	7	
29	Apr 3	SMALL HEATH	1-2	Boucher	4000	1	2	3		5				9	10	11	7						4	6	8	
30	10	Small Heath	1-3	Langham	7000	1		3						9		11	7	8		6			4	5	10	2
	Apps					30	28	29	19	28	7	4	8	30	28	30	25	19	14	3	11	3	5	4	4	1
	Goals								1	2		2	4	22	22	17	10	9	1			1			1	

Games 1 and 3 at the Town Ground

Test matches

#	Date	Opponent	Score	Scorers	Att	Toone G	Prescott TG	Gibson W	Calderhead D	Boucher T	Murphy John	Bull W	Langham W	Allan J	Bramley C	Crone R
1	Apr 17	SUNDERLAND	1-0	Langham	7000	1	2	3	5	9	10	11	7	8	4	6
2	Apr 19	Sunderland	0-0		10000	1	2	3	5	9	10	11	7	8	4	6
3	Apr 24	BURNLEY	1-1	Boucher (p)	15000	1	2	3	5	9	10	11	7	8	4	6
4	Apr 26	Burnley	1-0	Brealey	11000	1	2	3	5	9	10		7	8	4	6

Game 3 at the Town Ground   Played in game 4: H Brealey (at no. 11)

F.A. Cup

#	Date	Opponent	Score	Scorers	Att	Toone G	Prescott TG	Gibson W	Calderhead D	Boucher T	Murphy John	Bull W	Langham W	Allan J	Bramley C	Crone R
R1	Jan 30	Small Heath	2-1	Allan, Boucher	10000	1	2	3	5	9	10	11	7	8	4	6
R2	Feb 13	Aston Villa	1-2	Bull	4000	1	2	3	5	9	10	11	7	8	4	6

Back: Not known, Bramley, W.Smith, Prescott, Toone, Allsopp, Gibson, not known
Middle: Langham, Allen, Calderhead, Murphy, Bull, Goode(Trainer)
Front: Boucher

1897/98   13th in Division One

No		Date	Opponent	Score	Scorers	Att	Toone G	Prescott TG	Gibson W	Crone R	Calderhead D	Stewart A	Langham W	Allan J	Boucher T	Devey W	Bull W	Murphy, John	Braisford JR	Deighton AD	Carter AB	Hendry R	Brearley J	Bramley C	Lewis G	Sharman J	Potter A	Fraser J	Sanderson E	Leonard J	Fletcher H
1	Sep	2	Stoke	0-2		3500	1	2	3	4	5	6	7	8	9	10	11														
2		4	Nottm. Forest	1-1	Bull	15000	1	2	3	4	5	6		8	9	7	11	10													
3		11	ASTON VILLA	2-3	Langham, Murphy	6000	1	2	3	4	5	6	7	8	9		11	10													
4		18	Bolton Wanderers	0-1		9000	1	2	3	4	5	6	7	8	9		11	10													
5		25	DERBY COUNTY	1-1	Bull	12000	1	2	3	4	5	6		8	9	7	11	10													
6	Oct	2	Sheffield Wednesday	1-3	Boucher	12000	1	2		3	5	6		8	9	7	11	10		4											
7		7	PRESTON NORTH END	1-1	Langham	11000	1	2	3	4	5	6	7	8	9		11				10										
8		9	NOTTM. FOREST	1-3	Allan	15000	1	2	3	4	5	6	7	10	9		11				8										
9		16	Aston Villa	2-4	Carter, Stewart(p)	10000	1	2		4	5	3	7	10	9	6	11				8										
10		23	STOKE	4-0	Devey 2, Allan, Stewart	6000	1	2		3	5	6	7	10	9	4	11				8										
11		30	Wolverhampton Wand.	1-3	Carter	7000	1	2		4	5	6	7	10			3				8	9	11								
12	Nov	6	BOLTON WANDERERS	1-2	Langham	8000	1	2			5	6	7	10		11	3				8	9		4							
13		27	Bury	0-0		2000	1	2		4	5	6	7	10			3			11	8	9									
14	Dec	4	SHEFFIELD WEDNESDAY	0-0		3000	1	2	3	4	5	6	7	10						11	8	9									
15		11	Everton	0-1		5000	1	2	3	4	5	6	7	10						11	8	9									
16		18	WOLVERHAMPTON W.	2-2	Carter, Deighton	4000	1	2	3	4	5	6	7	10			9			11	8										
17		25	Derby County	2-1	Bull, Langham	11000	1	2	3	4	5	6	7	10			9			11	8										
18	Jan	1	SHEFFIELD UNITED	1-3	Stewart(p)	11000	1	2		4	5	6	7	10			9			11	8				3						
19		3	Sunderland	0-2		3000	1	2	3		5	6	7	10			9			11	8				4						
20		15	EVERTON	3-2	Boucher 2, Langham	8000		2		4	5	6	7	10			9			11	8				3	1					
21	Feb	5	SUNDERLAND	0-1		10000	1	2		4	5	6	7	10			9								3		8	11			
22		19	Sheffield United	1-0	Murphy	7500	1	2			5	6	7	10			4	9			8				3			11			
23		26	BURY	2-1	Fraser, Carter	7000	1	2			5	6	7	10			4	9			8				3			11			
24	Mar	5	BLACKBURN ROVERS	0-0		16000	1	2		4	5	6	7	10				9			8				3			11			
25		12	Liverpool	0-2		8000	1	2			5	6		8	9					10					3		7	11	4		
26		19	WEST BROMWICH ALB.	2-2	Boucher, Fraser	3600	1	2			5	6		8	9					10		7			3			11	4		
27	Apr	2	LIVERPOOL	3-2	Boucher 2, Leonard	8000	1	2			5	6		8	9										3			11	4	7	10
28		4	West Bromwich Alb.	3-0	Allan, Boucher, Fletcher	4000	1	2			5	6		8	9		7								3			11	4		10
29		8	Preston North End	1-3	Allan	9000	1	2			5	6		8	9		7								3			11	4		10
30		9	Blackburn Rovers	1-0	Fletcher	6000	1	2			5	6	7	8			4					9			3			11			10
			Apps				29	30	12	21	29	30	22	17	26	10	23	9	1	10	16	7	1	1	13	1	2	10	5	1	4
			Goals									3	5	4	7	2	3	2		1	4							2		1	2

F.A. Cup

No		Date	Opponent	Score	Scorers	Att	Toone G	Prescott TG	Gibson W	Crone R	Calderhead D	Stewart A	Langham W	Allan J	Boucher T	Devey W	Bull W	Murphy, John	Braisford JR	Deighton AD	Carter AB	Hendry R	Brearley J	Bramley C	Lewis G	Sharman J	Potter A	Fraser J	Sanderson E	Leonard J	Fletcher H
R1	Jan	29	WOLVERHAMPTON W.	0-1		15000	1	2	3	4	5	6	7	10	9					11	8										

1898/99 — 5th in Division One

Player columns (left to right): Toone G, Prescott TG, Lewis G, Bull W, Calderhead D, Sanderson E, Hannigan R, Maconnachie A, Boucher T, Fletcher H, Fraser J, Hadley A, Montgomery J, Logan P, Carter AB, Thurman H, Watts A, Suter ER, Donaldson J

#	Date	Opponent	Score	Scorers	Att	Toone	Prescott	Lewis	Bull	Calderhead	Sanderson	Hannigan	Maconnachie	Boucher	Fletcher	Fraser	Hadley	Montgomery	Logan	Carter	Thurman	Watts	Suter	Donaldson
1	Sep 3	Burnley	1-1	Maconnachie	6000	1	2	3	4	5	6	7	8	9	10	11								
2	10	SHEFFIELD UNITED	2-2	Fletcher 2	15000	1	2	3	4	5	6	7	8	9	10	11								
3	17	Newcastle United	2-1	Hadley, Maconnachie	25000	1	2	3	4	5	6		8	9	10	11	7							
4	24	PRESTON NORTH END	1-0	Fraser	12000	1	2	3	4	5	6		8	9	10	11	7							
5	Oct 1	Liverpool	0-0		12000	1	2	3	4	5	6		8	9	10	11	7							
6	8	NOTTM. FOREST	2-2	Hadley, Maconnachie(p)	20000	1	2	3	4	5	6		8	9	10	11	7							
7	15	Bolton Wanderers	1-0	Maconnachie	5000	1	2	3	4	5	6		8	9	10	11	7							
8	22	DERBY COUNTY	2-2	Hadley, Maconnachie	15000	1	2	3	4	5	6		8	9	10	11	7							
9	29	West Bromwich Alb.	0-2		4286	1	2	3	4	5	6	7	8	9	10	11								
10	Nov 5	BLACKBURN ROVERS	5-3	*See below	6000	1	2		4	5	6	7	8		10	11		3	9					
11	12	Sheffield Wednesday	1-1	Fraser	10000	1	2	3	4	5	6	7	8		10	11			9					
12	19	SUNDERLAND	5-2	Fletcher 2, Logan 2, Maconnachie	17000	1	2	3	4	5	6		8		10	7	11		9					
13	26	Wolverhampton Wand.	0-1		4800	1	2	3	4	5	6		8		10	7	11		9					
14	Dec 3	EVERTON	0-1		10000	1	2		4	5	6		8		10	7	11	3	9					
15	10	BURY	4-1	Boucher, Fletcher, Fraser, Logan	8000	1	2	3		5	6			8	10	7	11		9	4				
16	17	Stoke	1-1	Fletcher	5000	1	2	3		5	6		8		10	11	7		9		4			
17	24	ASTON VILLA	1-0	Maconnachie	20000	1	2	3		5	6		8		10	11	7		9		4			
18	27	LIVERPOOL	1-1	Fletcher(p)	16000	1	2	3		5	6		8	9	10	11	7					4		
19	31	BURNLEY	2-2	Maconnachie 2	12000	1	2	3		5	6	7	8	9	10	11						4		
20	Jan 2	Blackburn Rovers	0-6		4000	1	2	3		5	6	7	8	9	10	11						4		
21	7	Sheffield United	2-2	Hannigan, Maconnachie	8000	1	2	3		5	6	7	8		10	11			9			4		
22	14	NEWCASTLE UNITED	3-1	Fletcher, Logan, Maconnachie	7000	1	2	3		5	6	7	8		10	11			9			4		
23	Feb 4	Nottm. Forest	0-0		16000	1	2	3		5	6		8		10	11	7		9			4		
24	18	Derby County	2-4	Fletcher, Hadley	8000		2	3	4	5			8	9	10	11	7					6	1	
25	Mar 9	WEST BROMWICH ALB.	0-0		2488		2		4	5	10	7	8	9		11		3				6	1	
26	11	SHEFFIELD WEDNESDAY	1-0	Fletcher	8000		2		4	5		7	8		10	11		3	9			6	1	
27	18	Sunderland	1-1	Maconnachie	6000		2		4	5		7	8		10			3	9			6		1
28	20	Preston North End	0-2		3000		2		4	5		7	8		10			3	9			6		1
29	25	WOLVERHAMPTON W.	0-2		4000			2	4	5		7	8		10	11		3	9			6		1
30	Apr 1	Everton	2-1	Boucher, Fletcher	12000			3	2	5	6		8	9	10	11	7					4	1	
31	3	BOLTON WANDERERS	2-1	Fletcher, Hadley	8000			3	2	5	6		8	9	10	11	7					4	1	
32	8	Bury	0-2		5000			3	2	5	6		8	9	10	11	7					4	1	
33	15	STOKE	2-0	Maconnachie, Fletcher	5000			3	2	5	6		8	9	10	11	7					4	1	
34	22	Aston Villa	1-6	Bull	8000			3	2	5	4		8	9	10	11	7					6	1	
		Apps				23	28	28	25	34	29	15	33	23	32	31	19	7	16	1	2	17	8	3
		Goals							1			2	14	3	13	3	5		6					

Game 33 at the City Ground

Scorers in game 10: Logan 2, Boucher, Hannigan, Maconnachie

F.A. Cup

#	Date	Opponent	Score	Scorers	Att	Toone	Prescott	Lewis	Bull	Calderhead	Sanderson	Hannigan	Maconnachie	Boucher	Fletcher	Fraser	Hadley	Montgomery	Logan	Carter	Thurman	Watts	Suter	Donaldson
R1	Jan 28	KETTERING	2-0	Fletcher, Maconnachie	7000	1	2	3	4	5	6	7	8		10	11			9					
R2	Feb 11	SOUTHAMPTON	0-1		18000	1	2	3		5	6		8	9	10	11	7					4		

Back: Callan(Director), Prescott, Bull, Calderhead, Sanderson, Lewis, Goode(Trainer)
Middle: Harris(Secretary), Hannigan, MaConnachie, Fletcher, Fraser, Toone
Front: Boucher

League Tables 1899/1900 to 1907/08

	1899/00 Division 1	P	W	D	L	F	A	W	D	L	F	A	Pts
1	Aston Villa	34	12	4	1	45	18	10	2	5	32	17	50
2	Sheffield United	34	11	5	1	40	11	7	7	3	23	22	48
3	Sunderland	34	12	2	3	27	9	7	1	9	23	26	41
4	Wolverhampton Wan.	34	8	4	5	28	16	7	5	5	20	21	39
5	Newcastle United	34	10	5	2	34	15	3	5	9	19	28	36
6	Derby County	34	11	2	4	32	15	3	6	8	13	28	36
7	Manchester City	34	10	3	4	33	15	3	5	9	17	29	34
8	Nottingham Forest	34	12	3	2	42	16	1	5	11	14	39	34
9	Stoke	34	9	5	3	24	15	4	3	10	13	30	34
10	Liverpool	34	9	4	4	31	19	5	1	11	18	26	33
11	Everton	34	11	1	5	30	15	2	6	9	17	34	33
12	Bury	34	12	2	3	29	14	1	4	12	11	30	32
13	West Bromwich Alb.	34	8	6	3	27	11	3	2	12	16	40	30
14	Blackburn Rovers	34	12	2	3	38	22	1	2	14	11	39	30
15	NOTTS COUNTY	34	5	7	5	29	22	4	4	9	17	38	29
16	Preston North End	34	9	3	5	28	20	3	1	13	10	28	28
17	Burnley	34	10	2	5	28	17	1	3	13	6	37	27
18	Glossop	34	4	6	7	19	22	0	4	13	12	52	18

	1900/01 Division 1	P	W	D	L	F	A	W	D	L	F	A	Pts
1	Liverpool	34	12	2	3	36	13	7	5	5	23	22	45
2	Sunderland	34	12	3	2	43	11	3	10	4	14	15	43
3	NOTTS COUNTY	34	13	2	2	39	18	5	2	10	15	28	40
4	Nottingham Forest	34	10	4	3	32	14	6	3	8	21	22	39
5	Bury	34	11	3	3	31	10	5	4	8	22	27	39
6	Newcastle United	34	10	5	2	27	13	4	5	8	15	24	38
7	Everton	34	10	4	3	37	17	6	1	10	18	25	37
8	Sheffield Wed.	34	13	2	2	38	16	0	8	9	14	26	36
9	Blackburn Rovers	34	9	4	4	24	18	3	5	9	15	29	33
10	Bolton Wanderers	34	10	5	2	21	12	3	2	12	18	43	33
11	Manchester City	34	12	3	2	32	16	1	3	13	16	42	32
12	Derby County	34	10	4	3	43	18	2	3	12	12	24	31
13	Wolverhampton Wan.	34	6	10	1	21	15	3	3	11	18	40	31
14	Sheffield United	34	8	4	5	22	23	4	3	10	13	29	31
15	Aston Villa	34	8	5	4	32	18	2	5	10	13	33	30
16	Stoke	34	8	3	6	23	15	3	2	12	23	42	27
17	Preston North End	34	6	4	7	29	30	3	3	11	20	45	25
18	West Bromwich Alb.	34	4	4	9	21	27	3	4	10	14	35	22

	1901/02 Division 1	P	W	D	L	F	A	W	D	L	F	A	Pts
1	Sunderland	34	12	3	2	32	14	7	3	7	18	21	44
2	Everton	34	11	2	4	31	11	6	5	6	22	24	41
3	Newcastle United	34	11	3	3	41	14	3	6	8	7	20	37
4	Blackburn Rovers	34	12	2	3	36	16	3	4	10	16	32	36
5	Nottingham Forest	34	11	4	2	32	13	2	5	10	11	30	35
6	Derby County	34	11	5	1	26	10	2	4	11	13	31	35
7	Bury	34	11	5	1	31	9	2	3	12	13	29	34
8	Aston Villa	34	9	5	3	27	13	4	3	10	15	27	34
9	Sheffield Wed.	34	9	5	3	30	14	4	3	10	18	38	34
10	Sheffield United	34	10	5	2	38	13	3	2	12	15	35	33
11	Liverpool	34	8	3	6	28	16	2	9	6	14	22	32
12	Bolton Wanderers	34	10	6	1	38	17	2	2	13	13	39	32
13	NOTTS COUNTY	34	12	2	3	44	19	2	2	13	7	38	32
14	Wolverhampton Wan.	34	12	3	2	32	13	1	3	13	14	44	32
15	Grimsby Town	34	11	3	3	33	16	2	3	12	11	44	32
16	Stoke	34	10	4	3	31	12	1	5	11	14	43	31
17	Small Heath	34	8	5	4	31	14	3	3	11	16	31	30
18	Manchester City	34	10	3	4	28	17	1	3	13	14	41	28

	1902/03 Division 1	P	W	D	L	F	A	W	D	L	F	A	Pts
1	Sheffield Wed.	34	12	3	2	31	7	7	1	9	23	29	42
2	Aston Villa	34	11	3	3	43	18	8	0	9	18	22	41
3	Sunderland	34	10	5	2	27	11	6	4	7	24	25	41
4	Sheffield United	34	11	0	6	36	22	6	5	6	22	22	39
5	Liverpool	34	11	3	3	48	21	6	1	10	20	28	38
6	Stoke	34	11	2	4	29	11	4	5	8	17	27	37
7	West Bromwich Alb.	34	10	2	5	37	27	6	2	9	17	26	36
8	Bury	34	14	1	2	41	14	2	2	13	13	29	35
9	Derby County	34	13	2	2	34	11	3	1	13	16	36	35
10	Nottingham Forest	34	10	3	4	33	22	4	4	9	16	25	35
11	Wolverhampton Wan.	34	12	2	3	34	17	2	3	12	14	40	33
12	Everton	34	10	2	5	28	18	3	4	10	17	29	32
13	Middlesbrough	34	10	3	4	27	16	4	1	12	14	34	32
14	Newcastle United	34	12	1	4	31	11	2	3	12	10	40	32
15	NOTTS COUNTY	34	8	5	4	25	16	4	2	11	16	33	31
16	Blackburn Rovers	34	9	2	6	27	24	3	3	11	17	39	29
17	Grimsby Town	34	6	5	6	28	22	2	4	11	15	40	25
18	Bolton Wanderers	34	6	2	9	18	20	2	1	14	19	53	19

	1903/04 Division 1	P	W	D	L	F	A	W	D	L	F	A	Pts
1	Sheffield Wed.	34	14	3	0	34	10	6	4	7	14	18	47
2	Manchester City	34	10	4	3	35	19	9	2	6	36	26	44
3	Everton	34	13	0	4	36	12	6	5	6	23	20	43
4	Newcastle United	34	12	3	2	31	13	6	3	8	27	32	42
5	Aston Villa	34	13	1	3	41	16	4	6	7	29	32	41
6	Sunderland	34	12	3	2	41	15	5	2	10	22	34	39
7	Sheffield United	34	9	6	2	40	21	6	2	9	22	36	38
8	Wolverhampton Wan.	34	10	6	1	29	23	4	2	11	15	43	36
9	Nottingham Forest	34	7	3	7	29	26	4	6	7	28	31	31
10	Middlesbrough	34	9	3	5	30	17	0	9	8	16	30	30
11	Small Heath	34	8	5	4	25	19	3	3	11	14	33	30
12	Bury	34	6	8	3	25	20	1	7	9	15	33	29
13	NOTTS COUNTY	34	9	3	5	27	26	3	2	12	10	35	29
14	Derby County	34	7	3	7	41	33	2	7	8	17	27	28
15	Blackburn Rovers	34	7	5	5	29	23	4	1	12	19	37	28
16	Stoke	34	9	2	6	45	26	1	5	11	9	31	27
17	Liverpool	34	7	5	5	24	20	2	3	12	25	42	26
18	West Bromwich Alb.	34	4	8	5	19	19	3	2	12	17	41	24

	1904/05 Division 1	P	W	D	L	F	A	W	D	L	F	A	Pts
1	Newcastle United	34	14	1	2	41	12	9	1	7	31	21	48
2	Everton	34	14	2	1	36	11	7	3	7	27	25	47
3	Manchester City	34	14	3	0	46	17	6	3	8	20	20	46
4	Aston Villa	34	11	2	4	32	15	8	2	7	31	28	42
5	Sunderland	34	11	3	3	37	19	5	5	7	23	25	40
6	Sheffield United	34	13	0	4	39	20	6	2	9	25	36	40
7	Small Heath	34	11	1	5	32	17	6	4	7	22	21	39
8	Preston North End	34	9	5	3	28	13	4	5	8	14	24	36
9	Sheffield Wed.	34	10	3	4	39	22	4	2	11	22	35	33
10	Woolwich Arsenal	34	9	5	3	19	12	3	4	10	17	28	33
11	Derby County	34	9	4	4	29	19	3	4	10	8	29	32
12	Stoke	34	10	3	4	26	18	3	1	13	14	40	30
13	Blackburn Rovers	34	9	3	5	28	18	2	2	13	12	33	27
14	Wolverhampton Wan.	34	10	2	5	30	23	1	2	14	17	50	26
15	Middlesbrough	34	7	3	7	21	24	2	5	10	15	32	26
16	Nottingham Forest	34	5	3	9	24	28	4	4	9	16	33	25
17	Bury	34	8	2	7	34	26	2	2	13	13	41	24
18	NOTTS COUNTY	34	1	7	9	16	33	4	1	12	20	36	18

	1905/06 Division 1	P	W	D	L	F	A	W	D	L	F	A	Pts
1	Liverpool	38	14	3	2	49	15	9	2	8	30	31	51
2	Preston North End	38	12	5	2	36	15	5	8	6	18	24	47
3	Sheffield Wed.	38	12	5	2	40	20	6	3	10	23	32	44
4	Newcastle United	38	12	4	3	49	23	6	3	10	25	25	43
5	Manchester City	38	11	2	6	46	23	8	3	8	27	31	43
6	Bolton Wanderers	38	13	1	5	51	22	4	6	9	30	45	41
7	Birmingham	38	14	2	3	49	20	3	5	11	16	39	41
8	Aston Villa	38	13	2	4	51	19	4	4	11	21	37	40
9	Blackburn Rovers	38	10	5	4	34	18	6	3	10	20	34	40
10	Stoke	38	12	5	2	41	15	4	2	13	13	40	39
11	Everton	38	12	1	6	44	30	3	6	10	26	36	37
12	Woolwich Arsenal	38	12	4	3	43	21	3	3	13	19	43	37
13	Sheffield United	38	10	4	5	33	23	5	2	12	24	39	36
14	Sunderland	38	13	2	4	40	21	2	3	14	21	49	35
15	Derby County	38	10	5	4	27	16	4	2	13	12	42	35
16	NOTTS COUNTY	38	8	9	2	34	21	3	3	13	21	50	34
17	Bury	38	8	5	6	30	26	3	5	11	27	48	32
18	Middlesbrough	38	10	4	5	41	23	0	7	12	15	48	31
19	Nottingham Forest	38	11	2	6	40	27	2	3	14	18	52	31
20	Wolverhampton Wan.	38	7	5	7	38	28	1	2	16	20	71	23

	1906/07 Division 1	P	W	D	L	F	A	W	D	L	F	A	Pts
1	Newcastle United	38	18	1	0	51	12	4	6	9	23	34	51
2	Bristol City	38	12	3	4	37	18	8	5	6	29	29	48
3	Everton	38	16	2	1	50	10	4	3	12	20	36	45
4	Sheffield United	38	13	4	2	36	17	4	7	8	21	38	45
5	Aston Villa	38	13	4	2	51	19	6	2	11	27	33	44
6	Bolton Wanderers	38	10	4	5	35	18	8	4	7	24	29	44
7	Woolwich Arsenal	38	15	1	3	38	15	5	3	11	28	44	44
8	Manchester United	38	10	6	3	33	15	7	2	10	20	41	42
9	Birmingham	38	13	5	1	41	17	2	3	14	11	35	38
10	Sunderland	38	10	4	5	42	31	4	5	10	23	35	37
11	Middlesbrough	38	11	2	6	33	21	4	4	11	23	42	36
12	Blackburn Rovers	38	10	3	6	40	25	4	4	11	16	34	35
13	Sheffield Wed.	38	8	5	6	33	26	4	6	9	16	34	35
14	Preston North End	38	13	4	2	35	19	1	3	15	9	38	35
15	Liverpool	38	9	2	8	45	32	4	5	10	19	33	33
16	Bury	38	9	4	6	30	23	4	2	13	28	45	32
17	Manchester City	38	7	7	5	29	25	3	5	11	24	52	32
18	NOTTS COUNTY	38	6	9	4	31	18	2	6	11	15	32	31
19	Derby County	38	8	6	5	29	19	1	3	15	12	40	27
20	Stoke	38	7	6	6	27	22	1	4	14	14	42	26

	1907/08 Division 1	P	W	D	L	F	A	W	D	L	F	A	Pts
1	Manchester United	38	15	1	3	43	19	8	5	6	38	29	52
2	Aston Villa	38	9	6	4	47	24	8	3	8	30	35	43
3	Manchester City	38	12	5	2	36	19	4	6	9	26	35	43
4	Newcastle United	38	11	4	4	41	24	4	8	7	24	30	42
5	Sheffield Wed.	38	14	0	5	50	25	5	4	10	23	39	42
6	Middlesbrough	38	12	2	5	32	16	5	5	9	22	29	41
7	Bury	38	8	7	4	29	22	6	4	9	29	39	39
8	Liverpool	38	11	2	6	43	24	5	4	10	25	37	38
9	Nottingham Forest	38	11	6	2	42	21	2	5	12	17	41	37
10	Bristol City	38	8	7	4	29	21	4	5	10	29	40	36
11	Everton	38	11	4	4	34	24	4	2	13	24	40	36
12	Preston North End	38	9	7	3	33	18	3	5	11	14	35	36
13	Chelsea	38	8	3	8	30	35	6	5	8	23	27	36
14	Blackburn Rovers	38	10	7	2	35	23	2	5	12	16	40	36
14	Woolwich Arsenal	38	9	8	2	32	18	3	4	12	19	45	36
16	Sunderland	38	11	2	6	53	31	5	1	13	25	44	35
17	Sheffield United	38	8	6	5	27	22	4	5	10	25	36	35
18	NOTTS COUNTY	38	9	3	7	24	19	4	5	10	15	32	34
19	Bolton Wanderers	38	10	3	6	35	26	4	2	13	17	32	33
20	Birmingham	38	6	6	7	22	28	3	6	10	18	32	30

1899/1900   15th in Division One

#	Date	Opponent	Score	Scorers	Att	Suter ER	Prescott TG	Lewis G	Bull W	Calderhead D	Ball WH	Hadley A	Maconnachie A	McMain J	Fletcher H	Chalmers J	Goss W	Montgomery J	McCairns T	Sharman J	McCappin S	McDonald E	Warner A	Marsh I	Simpson T	Smith Walter
1	Sep 2	Derby County	1-0	Maconnachie	15000	1	2	3	4	5	6	7	8	9	10	11										
2	9	BURY	2-2	Bull, Maconnachie	10000	1	2	3	4	5	6	7	8	9	10	11										
3	16	WOLVERHAMPTON W.	0-0		5000	1	2	3	4	5	6	7	8	9	10	11										
4	23	Manchester City	1-5	Maconnachie	22000	1	2	3	4	5	6	7	9	8	10			11								
5	30	SHEFFIELD UNITED	1-2	Fletcher	9500	1		2	4	5	6	7	8	9	10	11			3							
6	Oct 5	LIVERPOOL	2-1	Maconnachie(p), Hadley	10000	1		2	4	5	6	7	8	9	10	11			3							
7	7	Newcastle United	0-6		20000	1		2	4	5	6		8	7	10	11			3	9				-		
8	14	ASTON VILLA	1-4	Ball	10000		2	3	4	5	6	7	8		10			11	9		1					
9	21	Liverpool	1-3	Ball	10000	1	2	3	4	5	6	7	8	9	10			11								
10	28	BURNLEY	6-1	Maconnachie 2. McMain 2, Bull, Hadley	10000		2	3	4	5	6	7	8	9	10	11					1					
11	Nov 4	Preston North End	3-4	Maconnachie 2, Hadley	4000		2	3	4	5	6	7	8	9	10	11					1					
12	11	NOTTM. FOREST	1-2	McMain	12000		2	3	5		4	7	8	9	10	11					1	6				
13	18	Glossop	0-0		4000		2	3	5		4	7	8	9		11					1	6	10			
14	25	STOKE	1-3	Fletcher	12000		2	3	5		4	7	8	9	10	11					1	6				
15	Dec 2	Sunderland	0-5		10000		2		6		4	7	8	9	10	11		3			1				5	
16	9	WEST BROMWICH ALB.	1-2	Maconnachie(p)	4186	1	4	2	5		6	11	8	9	7			3				10				
17	16	Everton	2-0	Hadley, McMain	4000	1		2	5		4	7	8	9		11	10	3				6				
18	23	BLACKBURN ROVERS	5-1	Hadley 3, McMain 2	5000	1		2	5		4	7	8	9		11	10	3				6				
19	30	DERBY COUNTY	0-0		8000	1		2	5		4	7	8	9		11	10	3				6				
20	Jan 6	Bury	1-0	McMain	1000	1		2	5		4	7	8	9		11	10	3				6				
21	13	Wolverhampton Wand.	2-2	Chalmers, Goss	4500	1		2	5		4	7	8	9		11	10	3				6				
22	20	MANCHESTER CITY	1-1	Bull	8000	1		2	5		4	7	8	9		11	10	3				6				
23	Feb 3	Sheffield United	1-1	McMain	6000			2	5		4	7	8	9		11	10	3			1	6				
24	17	Aston Villa	2-6	Hadley 2	22000	1		2	5		4	7	8	9	10	11		3				6				
25	Mar 3	Burnley	0-3		5000	1		2	5		4	7	8		9		10	3				6		11		
26	10	PRESTON NORTH END	3-0	McMain 2, Warner	10000	1		2	5		4	7	8	9		11		3				6	10			
27	17	Nottm. Forest	3-0	Maconnachie(p), Hadley, Chalmers	18000	1		2	5		4	7	8	9		11		3				6	10			
28	24	GLOSSOP	0-0		5000	1		2	5		4	7	8			11		3				10	6			9
29	31	Stoke	0-1		7000	1		2	5		4	7	8		10	11		3				9	6			
30	Apr 7	SUNDERLAND	3-1	McMain 2, Maconnachie	6000	1		2	5		4		8	9	7	11		3				6	10			
31	14	West Bromwich Alb.	0-0		3254	1		2	5		4		8		7	11	10	3				6	9			
32	16	NEWCASTLE UNITED	0-0		10000	1		2	5		4		8	9	7	11		3				6	10			
33	21	EVERTON	2-2	Maconnachie, McMain	6000	1		2	5		4		8	9	7	11		3				6	10			
34	28	Blackburn Rovers	0-2		5000	1	2		5		4				7	11	10	3				6	8			9
	Apps					26	14	32	34	11	34	28	33	26	24	25	16	23	4	1	7	20	10	3	1	2
	Goals								3		2	10	13	12	2	2	1						1			

Games 32,33 at the City Ground

F.A. Cup

#	Date	Opponent	Score	Scorers	Att	Suter ER	Prescott TG	Lewis G	Bull W	Calderhead D	Ball WH	Hadley A	Maconnachie A	McMain J	Fletcher H	Chalmers J	Goss W	Montgomery J	McCairns T	Sharman J	McCappin S	McDonald E	Warner A	Marsh I	Simpson T	Smith Walter
R1	Jan 27	CHORLEY	6-0	McMain 2, Bull, Chalmers, Goss, Maconnachie	6000	1		2	5		4	7	8	9		11	10	3				6				
R2	Feb 10	BURY	0-0		10000	1		2	5		4	7	8	9		11	10	3				6				
rep	Feb 14	Bury	0-2		3000	1		2	5		4	7	8	9		11	10	3				6				

Standing: Bramley(Treasurer), Harris(Secretary), Prescott, Suter, Lewis, Ball, Shelton(Director), Goode(Trainer)
Sitting: Hadley, Maconnachie, Calderhead, Fletcher, Chalmers, Thomas(Director)
Front: Bull, McMain

1900/01 — 3rd in Division One

#	Mon	Date	Opponent	Res	Scorers	Att	Suter ER	Lewis G	Montgomery J	Smith DA	Bull W	McDonald E	Morris JJ	Maconnachie A	Ross W	Warner A	Gee E	Pennington H	Ball WH	Hadley A	Brearley J	Prescott TG	Simpson T	Spencer F
1	Sep	1	SUNDERLAND	2-2	Bull, Warner	12000	1	2	3	4	5	6	7	8	9	10	11							
2		3	Wolverhampton Wand.	2-3	Ross 2	5000	1	2	3	4	5	6	7	8	9	10	11							
3		8	Derby County	1-2	Hadley	10000		2	3		5	6		8	9		11	1	4	7		10		
4		10	Stoke	1-1	Morris	2500		2	3		5	6	10	8	9		11	1	4	7				
5		15	BOLTON WANDERERS	3-1	Gee, Morris, Hadley	10000		2			5	6	10	8	9		11	1	4	7		3		
6		22	Sheffield Wednesday	1-4	Hadley	18000		2			5	6	10	8	9		11	1	4	7		3		
7		29	Preston North End	1-0	Morris	6000		2			5	6	10	8	9		11	1	4	7		3		
8	Oct	6	WOLVERHAMPTON W.	4-1	Warner 3, Ross	12000		2			5	6	10		9	8		1	4	7		3		11
9		13	Aston Villa	2-1	Gee, Morris	15000		2			5	6	10	8	9		11	1	4	7		3		
10		20	LIVERPOOL	3-0	Ross, Morris, Bull	18000		2			5	6	10	8	9		11	1	4	7		3		
11		27	Newcastle United	0-2		12000		2			5	6	10	8	9		11	1	4	7		3		
12	Nov	3	SHEFFIELD UNITED	2-4	Morris, Ross	12000		2			5	6	10		9	8	11	1	4	7		3		
13		5	West Bromwich Alb.	0-1		10492		2		5		6	10		9	8		1	4	7		3	11	
14		10	Manchester City	0-2		16000		2		4	5	6	10		9	8	11	1		7		3		
15		17	BURY	1-0	Ross	7000		2			5	6	10		9	8	11	1	4	7		3		
16		24	Nottm. Forest	0-5		18000		2			5	6	10		9	8		1	4	7		3	11	
17	Dec	1	BLACKBURN ROVERS	2-1	Ross, Morris	6000				3	5	6	10		9	8	11	1	4	7		2		
18		15	WEST BROMWICH ALB.	1-0	Warner	6500		2			5	6	10		9	8	11	1	4	7		3		
19		22	Everton	1-0	Spencer	12000		2			5	6	10		9	8	11	1	4			3		7
20		26	NOTTM. FOREST	1-0	Ross	20000		2			5	6	10		9	8	11	1	4			3		7
21		29	Sunderland	1-1	Warner	10000		2			5	6	10		9	8	11	1	4			3		7
22	Jan	5	DERBY COUNTY	2-1	Gee, Ross	15000		2			5	6	10		9	8	11	1	4			3		7
23		19	SHEFFIELD WEDNESDAY	2-0	Warner, Morris	6000		2			5	6	10		9	8	11	1	4			3		7
24	Feb	16	ASTON VILLA	2-0	Warner, Ross	15000		2			5	6	10		9	8	11	1		7	4	3		
25	Mar	2	NEWCASTLE UNITED	3-1	Gee, Morris, Warner	4000		2			5		10		9	8	11	1	4	7	6	3		
26		9	Sheffield United	2-4	Warner 2	15000		2			5	6	10		9	8	11	1	4	7		3		
27		16	MANCHESTER CITY	0-0		5000		2				6	10		9	8	11	1	4	7	5	3		
28		23	Bury	0-1		8000		2			5	6	10		9	8	11	1	4	7		3		
29		27	PRESTON NORTH END	6-1	Ross, Warner, Morris 2, Gee, Hadley	1500		2			5	6	10		9	8	11	1	4	7		3		
30	Apr	5	Bolton Wanderers	1-0	Hadley	18000		2			5	6	10		9	8	11	1	4	7		3		
31		6	Blackburn Rovers	2-0	Morris, Hadley	6000		2	3		5	6	10		9	8	11	1	4	7				
32		8	Liverpool	0-1		15000		2	3		5	6	10		9	8	11	1	4	7				
33		9	EVERTON	3-2	Morris 2, Ross	9000		2	3		5	6	10		9	8	11	1	4	7				
34		13	STOKE	2-4	Morris 2	6000		2	3		5	6	10		9	8	11	1	4	7				
Apps							2	33	8	5	32	32	33	10	34	27	30	32	31	24	8	24	2	7
Goals											2		16		12	12	5			6				1

Games 1, 33, 34 at the City Ground

F.A. Cup

#	Mon	Date	Opponent	Res	Scorers	Att	Suter ER	Lewis G	Montgomery J	Smith DA	Bull W	McDonald E	Morris JJ	Maconnachie A	Ross W	Warner A	Gee E	Pennington H	Ball WH	Hadley A	Brearley J	Prescott TG	Simpson T	Spencer F
R1	Feb	9	LIVERPOOL	2-0	Morris 2	18000		2			5	6	10		9	8	11	1	4	7		3		
R2	Feb	23	WOLVERHAMPTON W.	2-3	Morris, Warner	17000		2			5	6	10		9	8	11	1	4	7		3		

Back: Bramley(Treasurer), Prescott, Harris(Secretary), Pennington, Spencer(Director), Lewis, Callan
Middle: MaConnachie, Ball, Bull, McDonald, Montgomery
Front: Hadley, Warner, Ross, Morris, Gee, Goode(Trainer)

1901/02   13th in Division One

#	Date	Opponent	Score	Scorers	Att	Pennington H	Prescott TG	Lewis G	Innes R	Bull W	McDonald E	Hadley A	Warner A	Ross W	Morris JJ	Gee E	Humphreys P	Mainman HL	Spencer F	Simpson T	Suter ER	Montgomery J	Toone G	Joynes R
1	Sep 7	Derby County	0-2		12000	1	2	3	4	5	6	7	8	9	10	11								
2	Sep 9	Aston Villa	0-2		12000	1	2	3	4	5	6	7	8	9	10	11								
3	Sep 14	SHEFFIELD WEDNESDAY	6-1	Morris 3, Gee 2, Humphreys	12000	1	2	3	4	5	6		8	7	10	11	9							
4	Sep 21	GRIMSBY TOWN	3-0	Morris, McDonald, Humphreys	7000	1	2	3	4	5	6			7	9	10	11	8						
5	Sep 28	Bolton Wanderers	1-1	Morris	11000	1	2	3		5	6			7	9	10	11	8						
6	Oct 3	NEWCASTLE UNITED	0-2		10000	1	2	3		5	6			7	9	10	11	8	4					
7	Oct 5	MANCHESTER CITY	2-0	Ross, Warner	12000	1	2	3		5	6		8	9	10	11			4	7				
8	Oct 12	Wolverhampton Wand.	1-3	Morris	5000	1	2	3		5	6		8		10	11	9		4	7				
9	Oct 19	LIVERPOOL	2-2	Humphreys 2	10000	1	2	3		5	6		8		10	11	9		4	7				
10	Oct 26	Newcastle United	0-8		16000	1	2	3		5	6		8		10	11	9		4	7				
11	Nov 2	ASTON VILLA	0-3		10000		2	3	4	5	6			9	10	11	8		7		1			
12	Nov 9	Sheffield United	0-3		10865		2		4	3	6				10	11	9	5	7	8	1			
13	Nov 16	NOTTM. FOREST	3-0	Ross 2, McDonald	12000	1	2	3	4	5	6			9	10	11		8	7					
14	Nov 23	Bury	0-3		4000	1	2	3	4	5	6			9	10	11		8	7					
15	Nov 30	BLACKBURN ROVERS	3-0	Gee, Humphreys, Hadley	7000	1	2	3	4	5	6	7		9	10	11	8							
16	Dec 7	Stoke	0-3		7000	1	2	3	4	5	6	7		9	10	11	8							
17	Dec 14	EVERTON	0-2		4000	1			2	4	5	6	7	8	9	11	10					3		
18	Dec 21	Sunderland	1-2	Spencer	7249	1		2		4	6			9	10	11	8	5	7			3		
19	Dec 26	Nottm. Forest	0-1		17000	1		2		4	6			9	10	11	8	5	7			3		
20	Dec 28	SMALL HEATH	6-1	Morris 3(1p), Humphreys, Lewis, Bull	8000			2		4	6			9	10	11	8	5				3	1	7
21	Jan 4	DERBY COUNTY	3-2	Joynes, Bull, Humphreys	7000			2		4	6			9	10	11	8	5				3	1	7
22	Jan 11	Sheffield Wednesday	0-4		10000			2		4	6			9	10	11	8	5				3	1	7
23	Jan 18	Grimsby Town	0-1		7000	1		2		4	6			9	10	11	8	5				3		7
24	Feb 1	Manchester City	0-1		20000	1		2	4	5	6			9	10	11	8					3		7
25	Feb 15	Liverpool	1-0	Ross	10000	1	2		4	5	6			9	10	11	8					3		7
26	Mar 8	SHEFFIELD UNITED	4-0	Morris 2, Ross, Joynes	10000	1	2		4	5	6			9	10	11	8					3		7
27	Mar 22	BURY	2-1	Ross 2	8000	1	2		4	5	6			9	10	11	8					3		7
28	Mar 28	WOLVERHAMPTON W.	5-3	Humphreys 3, Ross 2	12000	1	2		4	5	6			9	10	11	8					3		7
29	Mar 29	Blackburn Rovers	2-4	McDonald, Bull	6000	1	2		4	5	6			9	10	11	8					3		7
30	Mar 31	BOLTON WANDERERS	2-1	Humphreys, Morris	15000	1	2		4	5	6			9	10	11	8					3		7
31	Apr 5	STOKE	1-1	Bull	4000	1	2		4	5	6			9	10	11	8					3		7
32	Apr 12	Everton	1-0	Humphreys	15000	1	2		4	5	6			9	10	11	8					3		7
33	Apr 19	SUNDERLAND	2-0	Humphreys 2	10000	1	2		4	5	6			9	10	11	8					3		7
34	Apr 26	Small Heath	0-0		20000	1	2		4	5	6			9	10	11	8					3		7
		Apps				29	26	23	29	34	34	5	12	23	33	33	31	12	8	4	2	18	3	15
		Goals						1		4	3		1	9	12	3	14		1					2

Game 33 at the City Ground

F.A. Cup

#	Date	Opponent	Score	Scorers	Att	Pennington H	Prescott TG	Lewis G	Innes R	Bull W	McDonald E	Hadley A	Warner A	Ross W	Morris JJ	Gee E	Humphreys P	Mainman HL	Spencer F	Simpson T	Suter ER	Montgomery J	Toone G	Joynes R
R1	Jan 25	READING	1-2	Lewis	10000	1		2		4	6		8	9	10	11		5	7			3		

Back: Bramley (Treasurer), Prescott, Suter, Harris (Sec), Pennington, Lewis, Montgomery, H.Spencer
Middle: F.Spencer, Innes, Bull, Pollock, Mainman, Goode (Trainer)
Front: Warner, Humphreys, Ross, Morris, Gee

1902/03 15th in Division One

#	Date	Opponent	Res	Scorers	Att	Pennington H	Prescott TG	Montgomery J	Innes R	Bull W	McDonald E	Joynes R	Humphreys P	Ross W	Morris JJ	Gee E	McIntyre JA	Green AW	Swift G	Mainman HL	Whyte P	Kirk JJ	Mellors M
1	Sep 6	WEST BROMWICH ALB.	3-1	Ross, Joynes, Gee	12339	1	2	3	4	5	6	7	8	9	10	11							
2	13	Derby County	1-4	Humphreys	12000	1	2	3	4	5	6	7	8	9	10		11						
3	15	Stoke	2-0	Humphreys, Green	8000	1	2	3	4	5	6	7	8	11	10			9					
4	20	Bolton Wanderers	1-0	Bull	6000	1	2	3	4	5	6	7	8	11	10			9					
5	27	MIDDLESBROUGH	2-0	Humphreys, Ross	10000	1	2	3	4	5	6	7	8	11	10			9	2				
6	Oct 3	SHEFFIELD WEDNESDAY	0-3		6000	1	2	3	4	5	6	7	8	11	10			9					
7	4	Newcastle United	1-6	Green	10000	1	2	3		5	6	7	8	10		11		9		4			
8	11	WOLVERHAMPTON W.	0-0		7000	1	2	3	4	5		7	8	10		11		9		6			
9	18	Liverpool	2-0	Ross, Green	16000	1	2	3		5	6	7	8	10		11		9		4			
10	25	SHEFFIELD UNITED	1-1	Green	11000	1	2	3		5	6	7	8	10		11		9		4			
11	Nov 1	Grimsby Town	1-1	Humphreys	3000	1	2	3		5	6	7	8	10		11		9		4			
12	8	ASTON VILLA	2-1	Green 2	7000	1	2	3	4	5		7	8	10		11		9		6			
13	15	Nottm. Forest	0-0		15000	1	2	3		5	6	7	8	10		11		9		4			
14	22	BURY	1-0	Green(p)	7000	1	2			5	6	7	8	10		11		9	3	4			
15	29	Blackburn Rovers	2-1	Humphreys, Green(p)	5000	1	2		4	5		7	8	10		11		9	3	6			
16	Dec 6	SUNDERLAND	0-0		7000	1	2		4	5		7	8	10		11		9	3	6			
17	20	EVERTON	2-0	Humphreys, Green	8000	1	2		4		6	7	8	10		11		9	3	5			
18	26	NOTTM. FOREST	1-1	Green	18000	1	2			5	6	7	8	10		11		9	3	4			
19	27	Sheffield Wednesday	0-2		20000	1	2		4	5	6	7	8	10		11		9	3				
20	Jan 3	West Bromwich Alb.	2-3	Green 2	16785	1	2			5	6	7	8	11	10			9	3	4			
21	10	DERBY COUNTY	2-1	Humphreys, Morris	16000	1			4	2	6	7	8	11	10			9	3	5			
22	17	BOLTON WANDERERS	1-3	Ross	6000	1			4	2	6	7	8	11	10			9	3	5			
23	24	Middlesbrough	1-2	Morris	10000	1	2			5	6		8		10		11	9	3	4	7		
24	31	NEWCASTLE UNITED	2-2	Humphreys 2	10000	1	2	3		5	6		8	10		11		9		4	7		
25	Feb 14	LIVERPOOL	1-2	Bull	8000	1	2	3		5	6		8	10		11		9		4	7		
26	28	GRIMSBY TOWN	0-1		7000	1		3	4	5		7	8	10		11		9	2			6	
27	Mar 26	Bury	1-3	Humphreys	2000	1	2	3	4	11	6	7	8				10	9		5			
28	28	BLACKBURN ROVERS	4-0	McIntyre, Humphreys 2, Green	2000	1	2	3		5	6	7	8				11	10	9	5			
29	Apr 4	Sunderland	1-2	McIntyre	7000	1		3	4	5	6	7	8				11	10	9	2			
30	10	Sheffield United	0-3		8000		2	3		5	6	7	8				11	10	9	4			1
31	11	STOKE	3-0	Humphreys 2, Green(p)	6000	1	2	3		5	6	7	8				11	10	9	4			
32	13	Wolverhampton Wand.	0-2		3000		2	3	4	5	6	7	8				11	10		9			1
33	15	Aston Villa	1-2	McIntyre	20000	1		3	4	2	6	7	8		5		11	10		9			
34	18	Everton	0-2		6000	1			4	5	6	7	8	2			11	10	2	3			
			Apps			32	27	21	19	33	28	31	33	27	11	24	9	32	16	25	3	1	2
			Goals							2		1	14	4	2	1	3	14					

Game 1 at the City Ground

F.A. Cup

Rd	Date	Opponent	Res	Scorers	Att	Pennington H	Prescott TG	Montgomery J	Innes R	Bull W	McDonald E	Joynes R	Humphreys P	Ross W	Morris JJ	Gee E	McIntyre JA	Green AW	Swift G	Mainman HL	Whyte P	Kirk JJ	Mellors M
R1	Feb 7	SOUTHAMPTON	0-0		15000	1	2	3		5	6	7	8	10		11		9		4			
rep	Feb 11	Southampton	2-2	Gee 2	16734	1	2	3		5	6		8	10		11		9		4	7		
rep2	Feb 16	SOUTHAMPTON	2-1	Humphreys, Green	18000	1	2	3	4	5	6		8	10		11		9		5	7		
R2	Feb 21	Grimsby Town	2-0	Green, Humphreys	9000	1	2	3	4	5	6		8	10		11		9			7		
R3	Mar 7	Bury	0-1		20000	1	2	3		5	6		8	10		11		9		4	7		

R1 replay and replay 2 after extra time. Replay 2 at Villa Park.

Back: Spencer (Director), Prescott, Montgomery, Pennington, Harris (Secretary), Swift, Gee, Bramley (Director)
Middle: Thomas (kneeling, Director), Joynes, Innes, Bull, McDonald, Ross, Goode (Trainer)
Front: Humphreys, Green, Morris

1903/04 — 13th in Division One

#	Date	Opponent	Res	Scorers	Att	Pennington H	Prescott TG	Montgomery J	Mainman HL	Bull W	McDonald E	McCall J	Humphreys P	Green AW	Glen A	Gee E	Reid J	Dainty HC	Ross W	Chapman HG	Griffiths A	Mellors M	Kelly W	Ward A	Walkerdine G	Sands J	Clare WE	Tarplin W
1	Sep 1	Sunderland	1-4	Glen	15000	1	2	3	4	5	6	7	8	9	10	11												
2	Sep 5	Everton	1-3	Humphreys	20000	1	2	3	4	5	6	7	8	9	10	11												
3	Sep 12	STOKE	1-0	Green	12000	1	2	3	4	5	6	7	8	9		11	10											
4	Sep 19	Derby County	1-0	Humphreys	15000	1	2		4	3	6		8	9		11	10	5	7									
5	Sep 26	MANCHESTER CITY	0-3		15000	1	2		4	3	6		8	9		11	10	5	7									
6	Oct 1	LIVERPOOL	4-2	Green 2, Humphreys, Chapman	7000	1	2	3	4		6		8	9		11	10	5		7								
7	Oct 3	WOLVERHAMPTON W.	0-2		12000	1	2	3	4		6		8	9		11	10	5		7								
8	Oct 10	Sheffield United	1-3	Green(p)	18000	1	2		4		6		8	9	10	11		5		7	3							
9	Oct 17	NEWCASTLE UNITED	3-2	Prescott, Green, Ross	9000		2		5	3			8	9		11		6	7	10		1	4					
10	Oct 24	Aston Villa	0-4		16000		2		5	3	6		8	9		11		4	10	7		1						
11	Oct 31	MIDDLESBROUGH	3-2	Humphreys, Green 2	8000		2		5	3	6		8	9		11		4	10			1		7				
12	Nov 7	Liverpool	1-2	Humphreys	10000		2		5	3	6		8	9		11		4	10			1		7				
13	Nov 14	BURY	0-0		8000		2		5	3	6		8	9		11		4	10			1		7				
14	Nov 21	Blackburn Rovers	0-3		6000		2		5	3			8	9	10	11		4	7		6	1						
15	Nov 28	NOTTM. FOREST	1-3	Green	6000		2	3	4	5			7	9		11		6	10	8		1						
16	Dec 12	SUNDERLAND	2-1	Montgomery, Green(p)	6000	1	2	3	4	5			7	9	10	11		6		8								
17	Dec 19	West Bromwich Alb.	0-0		8188	1	2	3	4	5			7	8	10	11		6	9									
18	Dec 25	Nottm. Forest	1-0	Ross	15000	1	2	3	4	5			7	8	10	11		6	9									
19	Dec 26	SMALL HEATH	2-0	Humphreys, Green	16000	1	2	3	4	5			7	8	10	11		6	9									
20	Jan 1	Bury	0-3		10000	1	2	3	4	5	6		7	8	10	11			9									
21	Jan 2	EVERTON	0-3		6000	1	2	3		5	6		7	8	10	11			9		4							
22	Jan 9	Stoke	2-0	Green 2(1p)	6000	1	2	3		5	6		8	9		11			10		4			7				
23	Jan 16	DERBY COUNTY	2-2	Green(p), Humphreys	16000	1	2	3		5	6		8	9		11			10		4			7				
24	Jan 23	Manchester City	0-3		15000	1	2	3		5	6		8			11			9		4			7	10			
25	Jan 30	Wolverhampton Wand.	1-1	Glen	4500	1	2	3		5	6		8		10	11			9		4			7				
26	Feb 13	Newcastle United	1-4	Humphreys	12000	1	2			5	6		8	9	10	11		4	7		3							
27	Feb 20	WEST BROMWICH ALB.	2-3	Glen, Green(p)	5991	1	2			5	6		8	9	10	11		4	7		3							
28	Feb 22	Sheffield Wednesday	0-2		7000	1	2			3	6		8		10	7		4	9				5			11		
29	Feb 27	Middlesbrough	0-1		6000	1	2			5	6		8		10	7		4	9		3					11		
30	Mar 19	BLACKBURN ROVERS	4-2	Green 4(2p)	7000	1	2	3		5	6		8	9	10	11			7		4							
31	Apr 1	ASTON VILLA	0-0		15000	1	2	3	6	5			8	9	10	11			7		4							
32	Apr 2	SHEFFIELD WEDNESDAY	1-0	Humphreys	12000	1	2	3	6	5			8	9	10	11			7		4							
33	Apr 4	SHEFFIELD UNITED	2-1	Ross, Green	16000	1	2	3	4	5	6		8	9	10	11			7									
34	Apr 23	Small Heath	0-2		8000	1		3	4	5	6		8	9	10	11											2	7
		Apps				27	33	21	24	31	25	3	34	30	20	34	5	20	26	7	13	7	2	7	1	2	1	1
		Goals					1	1					9	19	3				3	1								

F.A. Cup

#	Date	Opponent	Res	Scorers	Att	Pennington H	Prescott TG	Montgomery J	Mainman HL	Bull W	McDonald E	McCall J	Humphreys P	Green AW	Glen A	Gee E	Reid J	Dainty HC	Ross W	Chapman HG	Griffiths A	Mellors M	Kelly W	Ward A	Walkerdine G	Sands J	Clare WE	Tarplin W
R1	Feb 6	MANCHESTER UTD.	3-3	Ross, Humphreys 2	12000	1	2	3		5	6		8	9		11			10		4			7				
rep	Feb 10	Manchester Utd.	1-2	Green (p)	15000	1	2			3	6		8	9	10	11		5	7		4							

Back: Dainty, Montgomery, MacDonald, not known
Middle: Not known, Prescott, Harris(Sec), Mainman, Griffiths, Ross, Bull, not known, Gee, Swift (Trainer), Humphreys
Front: Chapman, not known, Green, Pennington, not known, not known

1904/05   18th in Division One

#		Date	Opponent	Score	Scorers	Att	Earle HT	Prescott TG	Montgomery J	Anderson J	Mainman HL	Griffiths A	Muir R	Humphreys P	Green AW	Reid J	Gee E	Pennington H	Clare WE	Dean RJ	Craythorne R	Clinch T	Wilkinson JW	Emberton FP	Tarplin W	Shufflebottom J	Wainwright T	Broughton M	Nugent J	Iremonger A
1	Sep	3	EVERTON	1-2	Reid	12000	1	2	3	4	5	6	7	8	9	10	11													
2		5	Sunderland	0-5		8000		2	3	4	5	6	7	8	9	10	11	1												
3		10	Small Heath	2-1	Dean, Craythorne	12500	1		3	4	5	6	7		9		11		2	8	10									
4		17	MANCHESTER CITY	1-1	Dean	10000	1			4	5	6	7		9		11		2	8	10	3								
5		24	Stoke	2-0	Green, Dean	6000	1		3	4	5	6	7		9		11			8	10	2								
6	Oct	1	Sheffield United	1-2	Green	12500	1		3	4	5	6	7		9		11			8	10	2								
7		8	NEWCASTLE UNITED	0-3		12000	1		3	4	5	6	7		9		11			8	10		2							
8		15	Preston North End	1-3	Green	10000	1		3		5	6	7	8	9				2	11	10			4						
9		22	MIDDLESBROUGH	0-0		7000	1		3		5	6	7	8	9				2	11				4			10			
10		29	Wolverhampton Wand.	1-3	Craythorne	6000	1		3	6	5		7	8	9		11		2		10			4						
11	Nov	5	BURY	0-1		7000	1		3			6	7	8	9		11				10	2		4		5				
12		12	Aston Villa	2-4	Griffiths, Green	15000	1		3		6	2		8	9		11			7	10			4		5				
13		19	BLACKBURN ROVERS	2-1	Dean, Crompton(og)	5000	1		3		6	2	7	5	9		11			8	10			4						
14		26	Nottm. Forest	1-2	Craythorne	10000	1		3		6	2	7	5	9		11			8	10			4						
15	Dec	3	SHEFFIELD WEDNESDAY	2-2	Dean, Broughton	8000	1		3		6			5	9		11			8	10	2		4			7			
16		17	WOOLWICH ARSENAL	1-5	Green	15000	1		3		6			5	9		11			8	10	2		4			7			
17		24	Derby County	1-1	Gee	8000			3		6	2	7	5			11	1		8	10			4	9					
18		31	Everton	1-5	Humphreys	14000	1		3			2	7	5		10	11			8	6			4	9					
19	Jan	2	Newcastle United	0-1		20000	1		3			2	7	5	8	10	11			7	6			4	9					
20		7	SMALL HEATH	0-0		6000	1		3		5	2	7			10	11			8	6			4	9					
21		14	Manchester City	1-2	Tarplin	10000	1		3		6	2	7	5			11			8	10			4	9					
22		21	STOKE	0-0		8000	1		3		6	2	7	5			11			8	10			4	9					
23		28	SHEFFIELD UNITED	1-5	Humphreys(p)	10000	1		3	6	5	2		8	9		11			7	10			4						
24	Feb	11	PRESTON NORTH END	1-3	Dean	6000	1		3			2	7	5		10	11			8	6			4	9					
25		18	DERBY COUNTY	0-0		8000			3			2	7	5	10		11			8	6			4	9				1	
26		25	WOLVERHAMPTON W.	3-4	Dean(p), Tarplin, Craythorne	4000			3			2	7	5		10	11			8	6			4	9				1	
27	Mar	11	ASTON VILLA	1-2	Tarplin	10000			3		6	2		5	9		11	1		7	10			4	8					
28		18	Blackburn Rovers	0-1		7000			3			2		5	9	10		1		7	11			4	8		6			
29		25	NOTTM. FOREST	1-2	Reid	10000			3			2		9		10	11	1		7	6			4	8		5			
30	Apr	1	Sheffield Wednesday	0-1		5000			3		4	2		9		10	11			7	6				8		5			1
31		8	SUNDERLAND	2-2	Humphreys, Tarplin	3000	1		3		4	2		8		10	11			7	6				9		5			
32		15	Woolwich Arsenal	2-1	Green, Humphreys	12000			3		5	2		8	9		11			7	6			4	10				1	
33		21	Bury	0-2		10000			3		5	2		8	9		11	1		7	6			4	10					
34		24	Middlesbrough	5-2	Humphreys 2, Dean, Green 2	10000			3		5	2		8	9		11			7	6			4	10					1

Games 1 and 31 at the City Ground

	Earle HT	Prescott TG	Montgomery J	Anderson J	Mainman HL	Griffiths A	Muir R	Humphreys P	Green AW	Reid J	Gee E	Pennington H	Clare WE	Dean RJ	Craythorne R	Clinch T	Wilkinson JW	Emberton FP	Tarplin W	Shufflebottom J	Wainwright T	Broughton M	Nugent J	Iremonger A
Apps	23	2	33	9	26	31	19	28	27	11	30	6	5	30	31	6	1	25	18	1	5	2	3	2
Goals							1	6	8	2	1			8	4				4					

One own goal

F.A. Cup

		Date	Opponent	Score		Att	Earle HT		Montgomery J		Mainman HL	Griffiths A	Muir R	Humphreys P		Reid J	Gee E			Dean RJ				Emberton FP	Tarplin W					
R1	Feb	4	Bury	0-1		12000	1		3		6	2	7	5		10	11			8				4	9					

Back: Clinch, Spencer (Director), Clare, Lawrence, Earl, Harris (Sec.), Wainwright, Montgomery,
Clare, Griffiths, Shufflebottom, Smith (Asst.Trainer), Alcock (Res.Sec.)
Middle: Swift (kneeling, Trainer), Dean, Anderson, Mainmam, Green, Gee, Reid (kneeling),
Front: Muir, Wilkinson, Worton, Craythorne

1905/06 — 16th in Division One

No	Date	Opponent	Score	Scorers	Att	Reilly M	Robertson S	Montgomery J	Emberton FP	Mainman HL	Craythorne R	Dean RJ	Humphreys P	Green AW	Fountain R	Gee E	Tarplin W	Griffiths A	Iremonger A	Wainwright T	Harrison A	Poppitt J	Wilkinson JW	Jones AT	Chalmers T	Waterall T
1	Sep 2	Stoke	0-3		7000	1	2	3	4	5	6	7	8	9	10	11										
2	9	BOLTON WANDERERS	3-3	Humphreys, Tarplin, Dean	4000	1	2	3	4	5	6	7	8	9		11	10									
3	16	Woolwich Arsenal	1-1	Gee	16000	1		3	4	5	6	7	8	9		11	10	2								
4	23	BLACKBURN ROVERS	1-1	Dean(p)	8000	1		3	4	5	6	7	8	9		11	10	2								
5	30	Sunderland	3-1	Craythorne, Dean(p), Green	7000	1		3	4	5	6	7	8	9		11	10	2								
6	Oct 5	WOLVERHAMPTON W.	5-2	Green, Tarplin 2, Humphreys 2	4500			3	4	5	6	7	8	9		11	10	2	1							
7	7	BIRMINGHAM	0-0		6500			3	4	5	6	7	8	9		11	10	2	1							
8	14	Everton	2-6	Gee, Dean	14000			3	4		6		8	9		11	10	2	1	5	7					
9	21	DERBY COUNTY	1-0	Green	14500			3	4	5	6	7	8	9		11	10	2	1							
10	28	Sheffield Wednesday	1-3	Gee	12000	1			4	5	6	7	8			11	9	2				10	3			
11	Nov 4	NOTTM. FOREST	1-1	Tarplin	12000	1			4	5	6	7	8			11	9	2				10	3			
12	11	Manchester City	1-5	Dean(p)	14000	1			4		6	7	8			11	9	2		5		10	3			
13	18	Bury	2-2	Dean, Humphreys	0	1		3	4	5	6	7	8			11	9	2				10				
14	25	Middlesbrough	1-4	Green	8000	1			4		6	7	5	9		11	8	2				10	3			
15	Dec 2	PRESTON NORTH END	2-2	Tarplin, Gee	8000	1			4		6	7	5	9		11	10	2				8	3			
16	9	Newcastle United	1-3	Tarplin	18000	1		3	4		6	8	5	9		11	10				7			2		
17	16	ASTON VILLA	2-1	Dean, Green	14000	1		3	4	5	6	7	8	9		11	10							2		
18	23	Liverpool	0-2		10000	1		3	4	5	6	7	8	9		11	10							2		
19	25	Nottm. Forest	2-1	Dean(p), Green	18000	1		3	4	5	6	7	8	9		11	10							2		
20	26	SHEFFIELD UNITED	2-3	Gee, Green	16000	1		3	4	5	6	7	8	9		11	10	2								
21	27	SUNDERLAND	4-1	Tarplin 2, Poppitt, Green	8000			3		5	6	7		9		11	10	2	1	4		8				
22	30	STOKE	1-1	Dean(p)	10000			3	4	5	6	7		9		11	10		1			8		2		
23	Jan 1	Sheffield United	0-1		17000				4	5	6	7		9		11	10		1			8	3	2		
24	20	WOOLWICH ARSENAL	1-0	Tarplin	5000				4	5	6	7	8	9		11	10	3	1					2		
25	27	Blackburn Rovers	3-1	Tarplin 2, Humphreys	14000				4	5	6	7	8	9		11	10	3	1					2		
26	Feb 3	Bolton Wanderers	0-2		10000				4	5	6	7	8	9		11	10	3	1					2		
27	10	Birmingham	2-4	Tarplin 2	12000			3	4	5	6	7	8	9		11	10		1					2		
28	17	EVERTON	0-0		10000			3	4	5	6	7	8	9		11	10		1					2		
29	24	Derby County	1-1	Humphreys	6000			3	4	5	6	7	8	9		11	10		1					2		
30	Mar 3	SHEFFIELD WEDNESDAY	1-3	Humphreys	10000			3	4		6	7	8	9		11	10		1	5				2		
31	17	MANCHESTER CITY	3-0	Green(p), Dean, Humphreys	12000			3	4	5	6	7	8	9		11	10		1					2		
32	21	LIVERPOOL	3-0	Dean, Green, Humphreys	8000			3	4	5	6	7	8	9		11	10	2	1							
33	24	Bury	0-0		6000			3	4		6	7	8	9		11	10	2	1						5	
34	31	MIDDLESBROUGH	1-5	Humphreys	15000			3	4		6	7	8	9		11	10	2	1						5	
35	Apr 7	Preston North End	1-4	Chalmers	7000			3	4		6	7	8	9		11	10	2	1						5	
36	14	NEWCASTLE UNITED	1-0	Green	16000			3	4	5	6	7	8	9		11	10	2	1							
37	16	Wolverhampton Wand.	1-6	Green	4000			3	4	5	6	7	8	9			10	2	1							11
38	21	Aston Villa	1-2	Green	5000			3	4		6	7	8	9		11	10		1					2	5	
	Apps					16	2	29	37	28	38	38	34	34	1	37	36	26	22	3	3	9	6	14	4	1
	Goals										1	11	10	13		5	13					1			1	

Game 36 at the City Ground

F.A. Cup

No	Date	Opponent	Score	Scorers	Att	Reilly M	Robertson S	Montgomery J	Emberton FP	Mainman HL	Craythorne R	Dean RJ	Humphreys P	Green AW	Fountain R	Gee E	Tarplin W	Griffiths A	Iremonger A	Wainwright T	Harrison A	Poppitt J	Wilkinson JW	Jones AT	Chalmers T	Waterall T
R1	Jan 13	Sunderland	0-1		20000			3	4	5	6	7	8	9		11	10		1					2		

Dean, Humphreys, Mainman, Green, Emberton, Reilly, Griffiths, Tarplin, Montgomery, Craythorne, Gee

1906/07   18th in Division One

#		Date	Opponent	Score	Scorers	Att	Iremonger A	Jones AT	Montgomery J	Emberton FP	Mainman HL	Craythorne R	Dean RJ	Humphreys P	Green AW	Tarplin W	Gee E	Poppitt J	Chalmers T	Griffiths A	Waterall T	Pope FH	Watts TH	Matthews W	Jones, Aaron	Suter ER	Clamp A	Mosley A	Morley H	Waterall I
1	Sep	1	BOLTON WANDERERS	0-0		5000	1	2	3	4	5	6	7	8	9	10	11													
2		8	Manchester Utd.	0-0		20000	1	2	3	4	5	6	7	8	9	10	11													
3		15	STOKE	2-2	Humphreys, Poppitt	11000	1	2	3	4	5	6	7	8		10	11	9												
4		17	Everton	2-2	Tarplin, Humphreys	10000	1	2	3	4		6	7	8	9	10	11				5									
5		22	Blackburn Rovers	2-0	Gee, Green	11000	1	2	3	4		6	7	8	9	10	11				5									
6		29	SUNDERLAND	0-0		20000	1		3	4	5	6	7	8		10	11	9			2									
7	Oct	6	Birmingham	0-2		10000	1	2	3	4	5	6	7	8	9	10						11								
8		13	EVERTON	0-1		10000	1	2	3	4	5		7	8		10	11			6		9								
9		20	Woolwich Arsenal	0-1		25000	1		3	4	5		7	8		10	11			2		9								
10		27	SHEFFIELD WEDNESDAY	2-2	Dean, Gee	14000	1		3	4	5	6	7	8		10	11			2			9							
11	Nov	3	Bury	0-3		7000	1		3	4	5	6	7	8		10	11	9		2										
12		10	MANCHESTER CITY	0-0		10000	1		3	4	5	6	7	8	9		11			2			10							7
13		17	Middlesbrough	0-2		12000	1	2	3	4	5			8	9	10	11			6										7
14		24	PRESTON NORTH END	0-0		8000	1		3	4	5	6		8	9	10	11			2										7
15	Dec	1	Newcastle United	3-4	Dean, Green, Gee	28000	1	2	3	4	5	10	7		9	8	11			6										
16		8	ASTON VILLA	1-1	Dean(p)	12000	1	2	3	4	5		7	8	9	10	11			6										
17		15	Liverpool	1-5	Waterall	5000	1	2	3	4	5	10	7	8	9					6	11									
18		22	BRISTOL CITY	2-3	Jones, Gee	10000	1		3	4		6	7	8			11			2		5	10	9						
19		24	Derby County	0-3		8000	1		3	4			7	5		10	11		6	2			8	9						
20		26	Sheffield United	1-2	Humphreys	14419		2	3	4	1				9	10	11		5	6				8						7
21		29	Bolton Wanderers	0-0		6000		2							9	10	11		5	3				8						7
22	Jan	5	MANCHESTER UTD.	3-0	Gee(p), Matthews, Humphreys	10000			3	4		6			9	10	11		5	2				8						
23		19	Stoke	1-1	Craythorne	4000		2		4		6	7		9	10	11		5	3				8		1				
24		26	BLACKBURN ROVERS	1-2	Gee	8000		2		4		6	10				11		5	3				8	9	1				7
25	Feb	9	BIRMINGHAM	2-2	Matthews, Jones	8000	1		3	4		6	7		9					2	11			8	10	5				
26	Mar	2	Sheffield Wednesday	3-1	Humphreys, Matthews 2	10000	1		3	4		6	7		9					2	11			8	10	5				
27		13	BURY	1-2	Humphreys	7000	1	2		4		6	7	8	9					3	11				10		5			
28		16	Manchester City	1-2	Craythorne	18000	1			4		10	7	8			11		5	3				9			6	2		
29		29	DERBY COUNTY	4-0	Humphreys 3, Waterall	16000	1			4		6	7	9					3		11			8	10		5		2	
30		30	Preston North End	0-0		8000	1			4		6	7	9						3	11			8	10		5		2	
31	Apr	1	SHEFFIELD UNITED	4-0	Humphreys 2, Dean, Matthews	18000	1			4		6	7	9	10				5	3	11			8						
32		6	NEWCASTLE UNITED	1-0	Jones	12000	1			4		6	7	9			11		5	3				8	10					
33		10	MIDDLESBROUGH	2-2	Tarplin, Matthews	6000	1			4		6	7		9	11				3				8	10		5		2	
34		13	Aston Villa	0-0		14000	1		3	4		6	7		9					3				8	10		5		2	
35		17	WOOLWICH ARSENAL	4-1	Clamp, Humphreys 2, Waterall	3000	1			4		6	7	9						3	11			8	10		5		2	
36		20	LIVERPOOL	2-0	Tarplin, Jones	1000	1			4		6	7			8	10			3	11				9		5		2	
37		24	Sunderland	1-3	Jones	3000	1			4		6	7			8	10			3	11				9		5		2	
38		27	Bristol City	0-1		12000	1			4		6	7			8	10			3	11				9		5		2	
			Apps				33	16	24	38	15	33	35	29	11	27	26	6	12	29	12	2	3	16	16	4	13	2	10	6
			Goals									2	4	13	2	3	6	1			3			6	5		1			

Games 1, 32, 33, 35 and 36 at the City Ground.

F.A. Cup

		Date	Opponent	Score	Scorers	Att	Iremonger A	Jones AT	Montgomery J	Emberton FP	Mainman HL	Craythorne R	Dean RJ	Humphreys P	Green AW	Tarplin W	Gee E	Poppitt J	Chalmers T	Griffiths A	Waterall T	Pope FH	Watts TH	Matthews W	Jones, Aaron	Suter ER	Clamp A	Mosley A	Morley H	Waterall I
R1	Jan	12	PRESTON NORTH END	1-0	Matthews	15000			3	4		6	7	9		10	11		5	2				8		1				
R2	Feb	2	Burslem Port Vale	2-2	Humphreys, Matthews	9000			3	4		6	7	9						2	11			8	10	1	5			
rep	Feb	6	BURSLEM PORT VALE	5-0	*see below	10000	1		3	4		6	7	9						2	11			8	10		5			
R3	Feb	23	TOTTENHAM HOTSPUR	4-0	Dean 2, Humphreys, Matthews	25000	1		3	4		6	7	9						2	11			8	10		5			
R4	Mar	9	West Bromwich Albion	1-3	Jones	27474	1		3	4		6	7	9						2	11			8	10		5			

*Scorers in R2 replay: Matthews 2, Jones, Humphreys, Emberton.

Back: Mr Burton, Emberton, A.T.Jones, Iremonger, Montgomery, Harris(Secretary), Green, Prescott(Trainer)
Front: Dean, Humphreys, Tarplin, Mainman, Poppitt, Craythorne, Gee

1907/08 — 18th in Division One

No		Date	Match	Score	Scorers	Att	Iremonger A	Morley H	Griffiths A	Emberton FP	Clamp A	Craythorne R	Dean RJ	Munro D	O'Donnell D	Matthews W	Jones, Aaron	Waterall T	Bemment F	Tarplin W	Warner A	Jones AF	Montgomery J	Dodd GF	Moore GW	Calladine CF	Chalmers T	Gooch PG	Cantrell J	Harper R
1	Sep	2	Woolwich Arsenal	1-1	Munro	10000	1	2	3	4	5	6	7	11	9	8	10													
2		4	Newcastle United	1-1	Aaron Jones	25000	1	2	3	4	5	6	7	11	9	8	10													
3		7	Sunderland	3-4	O'Donnell 2, Waterall	18000	1	2	3	4	5	6	7		9	8	10	11												
4		14	WOOLWICH ARSENAL	2-0	Matthews, Waterall	10000	1	2	3	4	5	6	7		9	8	10	11												
5		21	Sheffield Wednesday	0-2		16000	1	2	3	4		6	7		9	8	10	11	5											
6		28	BRISTOL CITY	3-1	Dean(p), O'Donnell, Craythorne	14000	1	2	3	4		6	7		9	8	10	11	5											
7	Oct	3	BURY	2-1	Matthews, Emberton	10000	1	2	3	4		6	7		9	8		11	5			10								
8		5	NEWCASTLE UNITED	0-1		16000	1	2	3	4		6	7		9	8		11	5			10								
9		12	Manchester City	1-2	Tarplin	10000	1	2	3	4		6	7		10	8		11	5	9										
10		19	PRESTON NORTH END	0-1		8000	1	2	3	4	5	6	7		9			11		10	8									
11		26	Bury	0-0		8000	1	2	3	4	5	9	7			8		11	6			10								
12	Nov	2	ASTON VILLA	0-3		12000	1	2	3	4	5	6	7		9	8		11				10								
13		9	Liverpool	0-6		18000	1	2	3	8	5	6	7		9			11			4	10								
14		16	MIDDLESBROUGH	2-0	AF Jones 2	8000	1	2		4	5	6	7	11	9	8						10	3							
15		23	Sheffield United	1-0	O'Donnell	7000	1	2		4	5	6	7	11	9	8						10	3							
16		30	CHELSEA	2-0	Warner, AF Jones	10000	1	2		4	5	6	7		9			11			8	10	3							
17	Dec	7	Nottm. Forest	0-2		20000	1	2		4	5	6	7		9	8						10	11	3						
18		14	MANCHESTER UTD.	1-1	AF Jones	8000	1	2		4	5	6	7	11		8					9	10	3							
19		21	Blackburn Rovers	1-1	AF Jones	10000	1	2		4	5	6	7	11		8					9	10	3							
20		25	EVERTON	2-1	Tarplin 2	14000	1	2		4	5	6	7	11						9		10	3	8						
21		26	Birmingham	0-0		25000	1	2		4	5	6	7	11						9		10	3	8						
22		27	BIRMINGHAM	0-0		5000	1	2		4	5	6	7	11						9		10	3	8						
23		28	BOLTON WANDERERS	0-1		6000	1	2		4	5	6						11				9	3	10				8	7	
24	Jan	4	SUNDERLAND	4-0	Dean(p), Tarplin 2, Dodd	5000	1	2		4	5	6	7	11						9		10	3	8						
25		18	SHEFFIELD WEDNESDAY	1-2	AF Jones	10000	1	2		4	5	6	7	11	9	8						10	3							
26		25	Bristol City	1-2	Dean(p)	12000	1	2		4	5	6	7	11		8					9	10	3							
27	Feb	8	MANCHESTER CITY	1-0	Clamp	8000	1	2		4	5	6	7			8					9	11	3	10						
28		15	Preston North End	0-1		8000	1	2		4	5	6	7			8					9	11	3	10						
29	Mar	2	Aston Villa	1-5	Dean	8000	1	2		4	5	6	7			8					11	10	3	9						
30		7	LIVERPOOL	2-2	Dodd(p), Matthews	10000	1	2		4	5	6		11		8					9		3	10	7					
31		14	Middlesbrough	1-3	Dodd	15000	1	2		4								11	6	8		10	3	9		7	5			
32		21	SHEFFIELD UNITED	0-3		12000	1	2		4	5					8			6				3	11				9	10	7
33	Apr	4	NOTTM. FOREST	2-0	Cantrell, Gooch	15000	1	2		4	5	6				8							3	11				9	10	7
34		11	Manchester Utd.	1-0	Dodd	10000	1	2		4	5	6				8							3	11				9	10	7
35		18	BLACKBURN ROVERS	0-2		12000	1	2		4	5	6				8					9		3	11					10	7
36		20	Everton	0-1		10000	1	2		4	5	6				8					11	10	3	9						7
37		25	Bolton Wanderers	1-0	Cantrell	15000	1	2	6	4	5					8						10	3	11					9	7
38		29	Chelsea	2-1	Harper, Dodd(p)	10000	1	2	6	4	5					8						10	3	11					9	7
Apps							38	38	18	34	33	34	28	12	18	28	6	15	9	15	7	22	25	16	1	3	1	3	7	7
Goals										1	1	1	4	1	4	3	1	2		5	1	6		5				1	2	1

Game 35 at the City Ground

F.A. Cup

		Date	Match	Score	Scorers	Att	Iremonger A	Morley H	Griffiths A	Emberton FP	Clamp A	Craythorne R	Dean RJ	Munro D	O'Donnell D	Matthews W	Jones, Aaron	Waterall T	Bemment F	Tarplin W	Warner A	Jones AF	Montgomery J	Dodd GF	Moore GW	Calladine CF	Chalmers T	Gooch PG	Cantrell J	Harper R
R1	Jan	11	MIDDLESBROUGH	2-0	AF Jones 2	16000	1	2		4	5	6	7	11		8					9	10	3							
R2	Feb	1	BOLTON WANDERERS	1-1	Tarplin	18000	1	2		4	5	6	7	11		8				9		10	3							
rep	Feb	5	Bolton Wanderers	1-2	Tarplin	17441	1	2		4	5	6	7			8		11		9		10	3							

R2 replay after extra time

Back: Mr Sandbrook, Morley, Suter, Harris (Secretary), Emberton, Clamp, Montgomery, Bemment, Chalmers, Griffiths
Middle: Dean, Tarplin, O'Donnell, A.Jones, Munro, T.Waterall, Prescott (Trainer)
Front: Moore, Craythorne

League Tables 1908/09 to 1914/15

1908/09 Division 1

		P	W	D	L	F	A	W	D	L	F	A	Pts
1	Newcastle United	38	14	1	4	32	20	10	4	5	33	21	53
2	Everton	38	11	3	5	51	28	7	7	5	31	29	46
3	Sunderland	38	14	0	5	41	23	7	2	10	37	40	44
4	Blackburn Rovers	38	6	6	7	29	26	8	7	4	32	24	41
5	Sheffield Wed.	38	15	0	4	48	24	2	6	11	19	37	40
6	Woolwich Arsenal	38	9	3	7	24	18	5	7	7	28	31	38
7	Aston Villa	38	8	7	4	31	22	6	3	10	27	34	38
8	Bristol City	38	7	7	5	24	25	6	5	8	21	33	38
9	Middlesbrough	38	11	2	6	38	21	3	7	9	21	32	37
10	Preston North End	38	8	7	4	29	17	5	4	10	19	27	37
11	Chelsea	38	8	7	4	33	22	6	2	11	23	39	37
12	Sheffield United	38	9	5	5	31	25	5	4	10	20	34	37
13	Manchester United	38	10	3	6	37	33	5	4	10	21	35	37
14	Nottingham Forest	38	9	2	8	39	24	5	6	8	27	33	36
15	NOTTS COUNTY	38	9	4	6	31	23	5	4	10	20	25	36
16	Liverpool	38	9	5	5	36	25	6	1	12	21	40	36
17	Bury	38	9	6	4	35	27	5	2	12	28	50	36
18	Bradford City	38	7	6	6	27	20	5	4	10	20	27	34
19	Manchester City	38	12	3	4	50	23	3	1	15	17	46	34
20	Leicester Fosse	38	6	6	7	32	41	2	3	14	22	61	25

1909/10 Division 1

		P	W	D	L	F	A	W	D	L	F	A	Pts
1	Aston Villa	38	17	2	0	62	19	6	5	8	22	23	53
2	Liverpool	38	13	3	3	47	23	8	3	8	31	34	48
3	Blackburn Rovers	38	13	6	0	47	17	5	3	11	26	38	45
4	Newcastle United	38	11	3	5	33	22	8	4	7	37	34	45
5	Manchester United	38	14	2	3	41	20	5	5	9	28	41	45
6	Sheffield United	38	10	5	4	42	19	6	5	8	20	22	42
7	Bradford City	38	12	3	4	38	17	5	5	9	26	30	42
8	Sunderland	38	12	3	4	40	18	6	2	11	26	33	41
9	NOTTS COUNTY	38	10	5	4	41	26	5	5	9	26	33	40
10	Everton	38	8	6	5	30	28	8	2	9	21	28	40
11	Sheffield Wed.	38	11	4	4	38	28	4	5	10	22	35	39
12	Preston North End	38	14	2	3	36	13	1	3	15	16	45	35
13	Bury	38	8	3	8	35	30	4	6	9	27	36	33
14	Nottingham Forest	38	4	7	8	19	34	7	4	8	35	38	33
15	Tottenham Hotspur	38	10	6	3	35	23	1	4	14	18	46	32
16	Bristol City	38	9	5	5	28	18	3	3	13	17	42	32
17	Middlesbrough	38	8	4	7	34	36	3	5	11	22	37	31
18	Woolwich Arsenal	38	6	5	8	17	19	5	4	10	20	48	31
19	Chelsea	38	10	4	5	32	24	1	3	15	15	46	29
20	Bolton Wanderers	38	7	2	10	31	34	2	4	13	13	37	24

1910/11 Division 1

		P	W	D	L	F	A	W	D	L	F	A	Pts
1	Manchester United	38	14	4	1	47	18	8	4	7	25	22	52
2	Aston Villa	38	15	3	1	50	18	7	4	8	19	23	51
3	Sunderland	38	10	6	3	44	22	5	9	5	23	26	45
4	Everton	38	12	3	4	34	17	7	4	8	16	19	45
5	Bradford City	38	13	1	5	33	16	7	4	8	18	26	45
6	Sheffield Wed.	38	10	5	4	24	15	7	3	9	23	33	42
7	Oldham Athletic	38	13	4	2	30	12	3	5	11	14	29	41
8	Newcastle United	38	8	7	4	37	18	7	3	9	24	25	40
9	Sheffield United	38	8	3	8	27	21	7	5	7	22	22	38
10	Woolwich Arsenal	38	9	6	4	24	14	4	6	9	17	35	38
11	NOTTS COUNTY	38	9	6	4	21	16	5	4	10	16	29	38
12	Blackburn Rovers	38	12	2	5	40	14	1	9	9	22	40	37
13	Liverpool	38	11	3	5	38	19	4	4	11	15	34	37
14	Preston North End	38	8	5	6	25	19	4	6	9	15	30	35
15	Tottenham Hotspur	38	10	5	4	40	23	3	1	15	12	40	32
16	Middlesbrough	38	9	5	5	31	21	2	5	12	18	42	32
17	Manchester City	38	7	5	7	26	26	2	8	9	17	32	31
18	Bury	38	8	9	2	27	18	1	2	16	16	53	29
19	Bristol City	38	8	4	7	23	21	3	1	15	20	45	27
20	Nottingham Forest	38	5	4	10	28	31	4	3	12	27	44	25

1911/12 Division 1

		P	W	D	L	F	A	W	D	L	F	A	Pts
1	Blackburn Rovers	38	13	6	0	35	10	7	3	9	25	33	49
2	Everton	38	13	5	1	29	12	7	1	11	17	30	46
3	Newcastle United	39	10	1	0	07	10	8	4	7	27	25	44
4	Bolton Wanderers	38	14	2	3	35	15	6	1	12	19	28	43
5	Sheffield Wed.	38	11	3	5	44	17	5	6	8	25	32	41
6	Aston Villa	38	12	2	5	48	22	5	5	9	28	41	41
7	Middlesbrough	38	11	6	2	35	17	5	2	12	21	28	40
8	Sunderland	38	10	6	3	37	14	4	5	10	21	37	39
9	West Bromwich Alb.	38	10	6	3	23	15	5	3	11	20	32	39
10	Woolwich Arsenal	38	12	3	4	38	19	3	5	11	17	40	38
11	Bradford City	38	12	3	4	31	15	3	5	11	15	35	38
12	Tottenham Hotspur	38	10	4	5	35	20	4	5	10	18	33	37
13	Manchester United	38	9	5	5	29	19	4	6	9	16	41	37
14	Sheffield United	38	10	4	5	47	29	3	6	10	16	27	36
15	Manchester City	38	10	5	4	39	20	3	4	12	17	38	35
16	NOTTS COUNTY	38	9	4	6	26	20	5	3	11	20	43	35
17	Liverpool	38	8	4	7	27	23	4	6	9	22	32	34
18	Oldham Athletic	38	10	3	6	32	19	2	7	10	14	35	34
19	Preston North End	38	8	4	7	26	25	5	3	11	14	32	33
20	Bury	38	6	5	8	23	25	0	4	15	9	34	21

1912/13 Division 1

		P	W	D	L	F	A	W	D	L	F	A	Pts
1	Sunderland	38	14	2	3	47	17	11	2	6	39	26	54
2	Aston Villa	38	13	4	2	57	21	6	8	5	29	31	50
3	Sheffield Wed.	38	12	4	3	44	23	9	3	7	31	32	49
4	Manchester United	38	13	3	3	41	14	6	5	8	28	29	46
5	Blackburn Rovers	38	10	5	4	54	21	6	8	5	25	22	45
6	Manchester City	38	12	3	4	34	15	6	5	8	19	22	44
7	Derby County	38	10	2	7	40	29	7	6	6	29	37	42
8	Bolton Wanderers	38	10	6	3	36	20	6	4	9	26	43	42
9	Oldham Athletic	38	11	7	1	33	12	3	7	9	17	43	42
10	West Bromwich Alb.	38	8	7	4	30	20	5	5	9	27	30	38
11	Everton	38	8	2	9	28	31	7	5	7	20	23	37
12	Liverpool	38	12	2	5	40	24	4	3	12	21	47	37
13	Bradford City	38	10	5	4	33	22	2	6	11	17	38	35
14	Newcastle United	38	8	5	6	30	23	5	3	11	17	24	34
15	Sheffield United	38	10	5	4	36	24	4	1	14	20	46	34
16	Middlesbrough	38	6	9	4	29	22	5	1	13	26	47	32
17	Tottenham Hotspur	38	9	3	7	28	25	3	3	13	17	47	30
18	Chelsea	38	7	2	10	29	40	4	4	11	22	33	28
19	NOTTS COUNTY	38	6	4	9	19	20	1	5	13	9	36	23
20	Woolwich Arsenal	38	1	8	10	11	31	2	4	13	15	43	18

1913/14 Division 2

		P	W	D	L	F	A	W	D	L	F	A	Pts
1	NOTTS COUNTY	38	16	2	1	55	13	7	5	7	22	23	53
2	Bradford Park Ave.	38	15	1	3	44	20	8	2	9	27	27	49
3	Woolwich Arsenal	38	14	3	2	34	10	6	6	7	20	28	49
4	Leeds City	38	15	2	2	54	16	5	5	9	22	30	47
5	Barnsley	38	14	1	4	33	15	5	6	8	18	30	45
6	Clapton Orient	38	14	5	0	38	11	2	6	11	9	24	43
7	Hull City	38	9	5	5	29	13	7	4	8	24	24	41
8	Bristol City	38	12	5	2	32	10	4	4	11	20	40	41
9	Wolverhampton Wan.	38	14	1	4	33	16	4	4	11	18	36	41
10	Bury	38	12	6	1	30	14	3	4	12	9	26	40
11	Fulham	38	10	3	6	31	20	6	3	10	15	23	38
12	Stockport County	38	9	6	4	32	18	4	4	11	23	39	36
13	Huddersfield Town	38	8	4	7	28	22	5	4	10	19	31	34
14	Birmingham	38	10	4	5	31	18	2	6	11	17	42	34
15	Grimsby Town	38	10	4	5	24	15	3	4	12	18	43	34
16	Blackpool	38	6	10	3	24	19	3	4	12	9	25	32
17	Glossop	38	8	3	8	32	24	3	3	13	19	43	28
18	Leicester Fosse	38	7	2	10	29	28	4	2	13	16	33	26
19	Lincoln City	38	8	5	6	23	23	2	1	16	13	43	26
20	Nottingham Forest	38	7	7	5	27	23	0	2	17	10	53	23

1914/15 Division 1

		P	W	D	L	F	A	W	D	L	F	A	Pts
1	Everton	38	8	5	6	44	29	11	3	5	32	18	46
2	Oldham Athletic	38	11	5	3	46	25	6	6	7	24	31	45
3	Blackburn Rovers	38	11	4	4	51	27	7	3	9	32	34	43
4	Burnley	38	12	1	6	38	18	6	6	7	23	29	43
5	Manchester City	38	9	7	3	29	15	6	6	7	20	24	43
6	Sheffield United	38	11	5	3	28	13	4	8	7	21	28	43
7	Sheffield Wed.	38	10	7	2	43	23	5	6	8	18	31	43
8	Sunderland	38	11	3	5	46	30	7	2	10	35	42	41
9	Bradford Park Ave.	38	11	4	4	40	20	6	3	10	29	45	41
10	West Bromwich Alb.	38	8	7	4	31	9	4	5	10	18	34	40
11	Bradford City	38	11	7	1	40	18	2	7	10	15	31	40
12	Middlesbrough	38	10	6	3	42	24	3	6	10	20	50	38
13	Liverpool	38	11	5	3	45	34	3	4	12	20	41	37
14	Aston Villa	38	10	5	4	39	32	3	6	10	23	40	37
15	Newcastle United	38	8	4	7	29	23	3	6	10	17	25	32
16	NOTTS COUNTY	38	8	7	4	28	18	1	6	12	13	39	31
17	Bolton Wanderers	38	8	5	6	35	27	3	3	13	33	57	30
18	Manchester United	38	8	6	5	27	19	1	6	12	19	43	30
19	Chelsea	38	8	6	5	32	25	0	7	12	19	40	29
20	Tottenham Hotspur	38	7	7	5	30	29	1	5	13	27	61	28

1908/09   15th in Division One

#	Date	Opponent	Score	Scorers	Att	Iremonger A	Morley H	Montgomery J	Emberton FP	Clamp A	Craythorne R	Walker A	Harper R	Cantrell J	Matthews W	Dodd GF	Dean RJ	Mosley A	Jones AF	Griffiths A	Flint WA	Chalmers T
1	Sep 5	WOOLWICH ARSENAL	2-1	Cantrell, Matthews	15000	1	2	3	4	5	6	9	7	10	8	11						
2	12	Sheffield Wednesday	0-2		20000	1	2	3	4	5	6	9	7	10	8	11						
3	19	Newcastle United	0-1		35000	1	2	3	4	5	6	9	7	10	8	11						
4	26	BRISTOL CITY	0-1		13000	1	2	3	4	5	6			10	8	11	7					
5	Oct 3	Preston North End	0-0		9000	1		3	4	5	6			9	8	11	7	2	10			
6	10	MIDDLESBROUGH	3-2	Cantrell 2, Matthews	8000	1	2	3	4	5	6			9	8	11	7		10			
7	17	Manchester City	0-1		28000	1		3	4	5	6			9	8	11	7	2	10			
8	24	LIVERPOOL	1-2	Walker	10000	1		3	4	5	6	10		9	8	11	7	2				
9	31	Bury	1-3	Walker	7000	1		3	4	5	6	10		9	8	11	7	2				
10	Nov 7	SHEFFIELD UNITED	3-1	Cantrell, Dodd, Walker	8000	1	2		4	5	6	11		9	8	10	7	3				
11	14	Aston Villa	1-1	Dodd	15000	1		3	4	5	6	11		9	8	10	7	2				
12	21	NOTTM. FOREST	3-0	Dodd 2(1p), Dean	14000	1	2	3	4	5	6	11		9	8	10	7					
13	28	Sunderland	1-0	Dean	10000	1	2	3	4	5	6	11		9	8	10	7					
14	Dec 5	CHELSEA	3-0	Cantrell, Craythorne, Dean	14000	1	2	3	4	5	6	11		9	8	10	7					
15	12	Blackburn Rovers	2-0	Dodd, Walker	10000	1	2	3	4	5	6	11		9	8	10	7					
16	19	BRADFORD CITY	1-1	Matthews	12000	1	2	3	4	5	6	11		9	8	10	7					
17	25	Everton	1-0	Walker	35000	1	2	3	4	5	6	11		9	8	10	7					
18	26	EVERTON	0-0		25000	1	2	3	4	5		11		9	8	10	7			6		
19	Jan 1	Manchester Utd.	3-4	Dodd 2, Dean	20000	1	2	3	4	5	6	11		9	8	10	7					
20	2	Woolwich Arsenal	0-1		13000	1	2	3	4	5	6	11		9	8	10	7					
21	9	SHEFFIELD WEDNESDAY	1-0	Walker	12000	1	2	3	4	5	6	11		9	8	10	7					
22	23	NEWCASTLE UNITED	0-4		12000	1	2	3	4	5	6	11		9	8	10	7					
23	30	Bristol City	0-1		10000	1	2	3	4	5	6	11		9	8	10	7					
24	Feb 13	Middlesbrough	2-1	Cantrell 2	12000	1	2	3	4	5	6	11		9	8	10	7					
25	20	MANCHESTER CITY	5-1	Cantrell 4, Walker	4000	1	2	3	4	5	6	11		9	8	10	7					
26	27	Liverpool	1-1	Matthews	12000	1	2	3	4	5	6	11		9	8	10	7					
27	Mar 10	PRESTON NORTH END	1-0	Matthews	4500	1	2	3	4	5	6	11		9	8	10	7					
28	13	Sheffield United	2-3	Matthews, Cantrell	12000	1	2	3	4	5	6	11		9	8	10	7					
29	20	ASTON VILLA	1-1	Dodd	5000	1	2	3	4	5	6	11		9	8	10	7					
30	24	BURY	3-2	Dean(p), Cantrell 2	2000	1	2	3	4	5	6	11		9	8	10	7					
31	27	Nottm. Forest	0-1		14000	1	2	3	4	5	6	11		9	8	10	7					
32	Apr 3	SUNDERLAND	0-0		10000	1		3	4	5	6	11		9	8		7			2	10	
33	9	LEICESTER FOSSE	2-3	Cantrell 2	16000	1	2	3	4	5		11		9	8		7			6	10	
34	10	Chelsea	2-3	Matthews, Birnie (og)	30000	1	2	3	4	5		11		9	8	10	7			6		
35	12	Leicester Fosse	2-0	Dodd, Cantrell	8000	1		3	4	5	6	11		9	8	10	7			2		
36	13	MANCHESTER UTD.	0-1		7000	1	2	3	4	5		11		9	8	10	7					6
37	17	BLACKBURN ROVERS	2-3	Cantrell, Jones	6000	1	2	3	4	5	6			9	8	11	7		10			
38	24	Bradford City	2-2	Dean 2(1p)	18000	1	2	3	4	5	6	11		9	8		7		10			
		Apps				38	31	37	38	38	34	34	3	38	38	35	35	6	5	5	2	1
		Goals									1	7		18	7	9	7		1			

Games 1, 33, 36 and 37 at the City Ground

One own goal

F.A. Cup

	Date	Opponent	Score		Att	Iremonger A	Morley H	Montgomery J	Emberton FP	Clamp A	Craythorne R	Walker A	Harper R	Cantrell J	Matthews W	Dodd GF	Dean RJ	Mosley A	Jones AF	Griffiths A	Flint WA	Chalmers T
R1	Jan 16	BLACKBURN ROVERS	0-1		13700	1	2	3	4	5	6	11		9	8	10	7					

Back: A.Jones, Morley, Chalmers, Mosley, Cantrell, Harris (Secretary), Montgomery, Dodsley, Prescott (Trainer)
Middle: Emberton, Dean, Matthews, Walker, Dodd, Craythorne, Gooch
Front: Moore, Clamp, Nichol

1909/10 — 9th in Division One

No		Date	Opponent	Score	Scorers	Att	Iremonger A	Morley H	Montgomery J	Emberton FP	Clamp A	Craythorne R	Dean RJ	Matthews W	Cantrell J	Walker A	Dodd GF	Griffiths A	Jones AF	Waterall I	Flint WA	Mosley A	Garrett FH	Pepper FW
1	Sep	1	Chelsea	2-2	Dean(p), Cantrell	10000	1	2	3	4	5	6	7	8	9	11	10							
2		4	Nottm. Forest	1-2	Walker	18000	1	2	3	4	5	6	7	8	9	11	10							
3		6	Manchester Utd.	1-2	Jones	5000	1	2	3	4	5		7	8			11	9	6	10				
4		11	SUNDERLAND	1-1	Jones	5000	1	2	3	4	5		7	8			11		6	10				
5		18	Everton	0-2		25000	1	2	3	4	5	6		8	9		11		10	7				
6		25	MANCHESTER UTD.	3-2	Jones, Waterall, Matthews	12000	1	2	3	4	5	6		8	9		11		10	7				
7	Oct	2	Bradford City	1-2	Cantrell	24000	1	2	3	4	5	6		8	9		11		10	7				
8		7	WOOLWICH ARSENAL	5-1	Cantrell 3, Jones, Clamp	10000	1	2	3	4	5	6	7	8	9		11		10					
9		9	SHEFFIELD WEDNESDAY	0-0		16000	1	2	3	4	5	6	7	8	9		11		10					
10		16	Bristol City	1-3	Cantrell	12000	1	2	3	4	5				9	8	11	6	10	7				
11		18	Sheffield United	2-2	Cantrell, Dodd	10000	1	2	3	4	5		7	8	9		11	6	10					
12		23	BURY	3-1	Jones, Cantrell, Dean	7000	1	2	3	4	5		7	8	9		11	6	10					
13		30	Tottenham Hotspur	3-1	Cantrell 2, Matthews	25000	1	2	3	4	5		7	8	9		11	6	10					
14	Nov	6	PRESTON NORTH END	3-1	Dodd(p), Dean, Jones	10000	1	2	3	4	5		7	8	9		11	6	10					
15		13	MIDDLESBROUGH	2-1	Matthews, Cantrell	9000	1	2	3	4	5	6	7	8	9	11			10					
16		20	Newcastle United	3-1	Jones, Cantrell, Dean	20000	1	2		4	5	6	7	8	9	11		3	10					
17		27	LIVERPOOL	3-1	Jones 2, Cantrell	5000	1	2		4	5	6	7	8	9	11		3	10					
18	Dec	4	Aston Villa	1-1	Matthews	8000	1	2		4	5	6	7	8	9	11		3	10					
19		11	SHEFFIELD UNITED	1-2	Dean(p)	9000	1	2	3	4	5	6	7	8	9	11			10					
20		18	Woolwich Arsenal	2-1	Jones, Cantrell	10000	1	2	3	4	5	6	7	8	9	11			10					
21		25	CHELSEA	2-1	Jones, Cantrell	14000	1	2	3	4	5	6	7	8	9	11			10					
22		28	BLACKBURN ROVERS	2-2	Matthews, Cantrell	18000	1	2	3	4	5	6	7	8	9	11			10					
23	Jan	1	Bolton Wanderers	4-3	Flint 2, Dean, Cantrell	20000	1	2	3	4	5	6	7		9	11			10		8			
24		8	NOTTM. FOREST	4-1	Cantrell 2, Jones, Walker	15000	1	2	3	4	5	6	7	8	9	11			10					
25		22	Sunderland	3-0	Matthews, Cantrell, Jones	5000	1	2	3	4	5	6	7	8	9	11			10					
26	Feb	12	BRADFORD CITY	3-2	Matthews, Jones 2	12000	1		3	4	5	6	7	8	9	11			10			2		
27		19	Sheffield Wednesday	0-0		8000	1		3	4	5	6	7	8	9	11			10					
28		26	BRISTOL CITY	0-2		8000	1	2	3		5	6	7	8		11			10			9	4	
29	Mar	5	Bury	1-1	Dodd	10000	1	2	3		5	6		8			11	9	4	10	7			
30		12	TOTTENHAM HOTSPUR	3-0	Dodd, Flint, Jones	8000	1	2	3		5	6					11	9	4	10	7	8		
31		19	Preston North End	0-4		7000	1	2	3						9		11	4	10	7	8			
32		25	Blackburn Rovers	0-2		12000	1		3	4	5	6	7	8	9	2			10	11				
33		26	Middlesbrough	0-2		12000	1		3		5			8			11	9	10	7		2	4	
34		28	BOLTON WANDERERS	0-0		9000	1		3	4	5	6		8			11	2	10	7		9		
35	Apr	2	NEWCASTLE UNITED	2-2	Dodd(p), Matthews	9000	1		3	4	5	6		8	9		11	2	10	7				
36		9	Liverpool	1-2	Cantrell	15000	1	2	3	4	5			8	9		11	6	10	7				
37		13	EVERTON	2-3	Matthews, Cantrell	3000	1		3	4	5			8	9		11	6	10	7		2		
38		16	ASTON VILLA	2-3	Waterall, Jones	13000	1			4	5			8	9		11	3	10	7		2		6
Apps							38	31	34	33	38	29	25	35	29	15	31	20	36	14	5	3	1	1
Goals											1		6	9	22	2	5		17	2	3			

F.A. Cup

No		Date	Opponent	Score	Scorers	Att	Iremonger A	Morley H	Montgomery J	Emberton FP	Clamp A	Craythorne R	Dean RJ	Matthews W	Cantrell J	Walker A	Dodd GF	Griffiths A	Jones AF	Waterall I	Flint WA	Mosley A	Garrett FH	Pepper FW
R1	Jan	15	Bradford City	2-4	Jones 2	17000	1	2	3	4	5	6	7	8	9	11			10					

Notts sold ground rights for £1000

Back: Bramley (Treasurer), Emberton, Harris (Secretary), Morley, Iremonger, Suter, Clamp, T.Griffiths,
Prescott (Trainer),McLean (Asst.Trainer), Sandbrook
Middle: Craythorne, Dean, Matthews, Montgomery, Cantrell, Dodd, Walker
Front: I.Waterall, F.Jones, Mosley

1910/11 — 11th in Division One

#		Date	Opponent	Score	Scorers	Att	Iremonger A	Griffiths A	Montgomery J	Emberton FP	Clamp A	Craythorne R	Dean RJ	Matthews W	Cantrell J	Bradley H	Jones AF	Dodd GF	Flint WA	Richards S	Waterall I	Garrett FH	Bettison F	Lee GM	Pacey H	Morley H	Walker A	Waterall A	Grice R	James L
1	Sep	1	Blackburn Rovers	1-1	Dean	17000	1	2	3	4	5	6	7	8	9	11	10													
2		3	NOTTM. FOREST	1-1	Matthews	28000	1	2	3	4	5	6	7	8	9		10	11												
3		10	Manchester City	1-0	Richards	30000	1	2	3	4	5	6	7	8					9	10	11									
4		17	EVERTON	0-0		15000	1	2	3	4	5	6	7	8	9					10	11									
5		24	Sheffield Wednesday	3-1	Richards 2, Flint	12000	1	2	3	4	5	6	7	8					9	10	11									
6	Oct	1	BRISTOL CITY	2-0	Richards, Waterall	14000	1	2	3	4	5	6	7	8					9	10	11									
7		8	Newcastle United	0-2		30000	1	2	3	4	5	6	7	8					9	10	11									
8		15	TOTTENHAM HOTSPUR	1-0	Matthews	14000	1	2	3	4	5	6	7	8	9					10	11									
9		22	Middlesbrough	1-4	Cantrell	17000	1	2	3	4	5	6	7	8	9					10	11									
10		29	PRESTON NORTH END	3-3	Matthews, Waterall, Cantrell	10000	1	2	3	4	5		7	8	9					10	11	6								
11	Nov	5	Oldham Athletic	1-2	Cantrell	15000	1		3	4	5		7	8	9					10	11	6	2							
12		12	Manchester Utd.	0-0		16000	1		3	4	5	6		8		11		10	9	7						2				
13		19	LIVERPOOL	1-0	Richards	10000	1	6	3	4	5			8		11			9	10	7					2				
14		26	Bury	0-0		5000	1		3	4	5			8				11	9	10	7				6	2				
15	Dec	3	SHEFFIELD UNITED	0-3		9000	1		3	4	5		7	8					9	10	11				6	2				
16		10	Aston Villa	1-3	Cantrell	12000	1		3	4	5	6	7		9			10	8		11					2				
17		17	SUNDERLAND	1-1	Richards	7000	1		3	4	5	6	7		9				8	10	11					2				
18		24	Woolwich Arsenal	1-2	Cantrell	8000	1	2	3	4	5	6	7		9				8	10	11									
19		26	BRADFORD CITY	1-1	Dean(p)	25000	1	2	3	4	5	6	7	8	9			10			11									
20		31	Nottm. Forest	2-0	Cantrell 2	15000	1		3	4	5	6	7	8	9			10			11					2				
21	Jan	7	MANCHESTER CITY	0-1		10000	1	2	3	4	5	6	7	8					9	10	11									
22		21	Everton	0-5		14000	1		3	4	5	6			9				8	10	11					2				
23		28	SHEFFIELD WEDNESDAY	2-0	Dodd, Matthews	12000	1		3	4	5	6	7	8	9			11	10							2				
24	Feb	4	Bristol City	0-1		6000	1		3	4		6		8	9			11	10	7		5				2				
25		11	NEWCASTLE UNITED	2-2	Cantrell 2	12000	1		3	4		6		8	9			11		7		5				2		10		
26		18	Tottenham Hotspur	0-3		25000	1		3	4	5	6		8	9			11		7						2		10		
27	Mar	4	Preston North End	0-2		5000	1		3	4	5	6	7	8	9				10		11					2				
28		11	OLDHAM ATHLETIC	1-0	Matthews	10000	1		3	4	5	6	7	8	9				10		11					2				
29		18	MANCHESTER UTD.	1-0	Cantrell	14000	1		3	4	5	6	7	8	9				10		11					2				
30		25	Liverpool	1-2	Waterall	10000	1		3	4	5	6	7	8	9				10		11					2				
31	Apr	1	BURY	1-0	Craythorne	6000	1	2	3	4	5	6	7	8	9				10		11									
32		8	Sheffield United	2-0	Craythorne, Cantrell	5000	1	2	3	4	5	6		8	9				10	7	11									
33		14	BLACKBURN ROVERS	2-0	Montgomery(p), Dean	20000	1		3	4	5	6	7	8	9				10		11					2				
34		15	ASTON VILLA	1-2	Dean(p)	20000	1	2	3	4	5	6	7		9				10		11						8			
35		17	Bradford City	1-0	Cantrell	15000	1		3	4	5	6			9					10	7						8		11	2
36		18	MIDDLESBROUGH	1-0	Richards	8000	1		3	4	5	6	7		9					10	11						8			2
37		22	Sunderland	1-1	Cantrell	10000	1	2	3	4	5		7		9					10	11						8	6		
38		29	WOOLWICH ARSENAL	0-2		6500	1		3		4	5	6	7						9	10	11					2	8		
						Apps	38	20	36	37	36	33	30	29	28	3	3	9	25	20	35	4	1	4	2	14	3	5	1	2
						Goals		1			2	4	5	13					1	1	7	3								

First season at Meadow Lane

F.A. Cup

R		Date	Opponent	Score	Scorers	Att	Iremonger A	Montgomery J	Emberton FP	Clamp A	Craythorne R	Dean RJ	Cantrell J	Flint WA	Waterall I	Morley H	Walker A
R1	Jan	14	Swindon Town	1-3	Dean(p)	12332	1	3	4	5	6	7	9	8	11	2	10

Back: Harris (Secretary), Emberton, Hughes, Morley, Heath (Director), Suter, McLean (Asst. Trainer), Prescott(Trainer)
Middle: I.Waterall, Dean, Matthews, Cantrell, Craythorne, Bradley, Griffiths
Front: Dodd, Birch

No		Date	Opponent	Score	Scorers	Att	Iremonger A	Morley H	West, Alf	Emberton FP	Clamp A	Craythorne R	Dean RJ	Matthews W	Cantrell J	Richards S	Waterall I	Flint WA	Waterall A	Walker A	Garrett FH	Griffiths A	Pacey H	Grice R	Pepper FW	McCulloch G
1	Sep	2	West Bromwich Alb.	1-2	Richards	26638	1	2	3	4	5	6	7	8	9	10	11									
2		9	SUNDERLAND	3-1	Craythorne, Matthews, Richards	12000	1	2	3	4	5	6	7	8	9	10	11									
3		16	Blackburn Rovers	0-0		16568	1	2	3	4	5	6	7	8	9	10	11									
4		23	SHEFFIELD WEDNESDAY	1-0	Matthews	12000	1	2	3	4	5	6	7	8	9	10	11									
5		30	Bury	1-0	Richards	8000	1	2	3	4	5	6	7	8	9	10	11									
6	Oct	5	BRADFORD CITY	0-0		11000	1	2	3	4	5	6	7	8	9		11	10								
7		7	MIDDLESBROUGH	2-1	Cantrell, Matthews	21000	1	2	3	4	5	6	7	8	9		11	10								
8		14	PRESTON NORTH END	1-2	Flint	10000	1	2	3	4	5	6	7	8			11	9	10							
9		21	Tottenham Hotspur	2-2	Matthews, Cantrell	25000	1	2	3	4	5	6	7	8	9	10	11									
10		28	MANCHESTER UTD.	0-1		14000	1	2	3	4	5	6	7	8	9	10	11									
11	Nov	4	Liverpool	0-3		15000	1	2	3	4	5	6	7	8		10	11	9								
12		18	Newcastle United	2-3	Dean 2	20000	1	2	3	4	5	6	7	8		10	11	9								
13		25	SHEFFIELD UNITED	2-0	Cantrell, Richards	5000	1	2	3	4	5	6	7	8	9	10	11									
14	Dec	2	Oldham Athletic	2-1	Richards 2	8000	1	2	3	4	5	6	7	8		10	11	9								
15		9	BOLTON WANDERERS	3-2	Flint 2, Matthews	12000	1	2	3	4	5	6	7	8		10	11	9								
16		16	Bradford City	3-2	Flint, Richards, Dean	15000	1	2	3	4	5	6	7	8		10	11	9								
17		23	WOOLWICH ARSENAL	3-1	Flint, Matthews, Richards	6000	1	2	3	4	5	6	7	8		10	11	9								
18		25	MANCHESTER CITY	0-1		15000	1	2	3	4	5	6	7	8		10	11			9						
19		26	Manchester City	0-4		35000	1	2	3	4			7	8		10	11	9			5	6				
20		30	WEST BROMWICH ALB.	2-0	Richards, Waterall	10000	1	2	3	4	5		7	8		10	11	9			6					
21	Jan	6	Sunderland	0-5		10000	1	2	3	4	5		7	8		10	11	9					6			
22		20	BLACKBURN ROVERS	1-3	Cantrell	3000	1	2	3	4	5	6		8	9	10	11	7								
23		27	Sheffield Wednesday	0-3		8000	1	2	3	4	5	6		8	9	10	11	7								
24	Feb	10	Middlesbrough	0-4		9714	1	2	3		5	6	7	4	9	10	11	8								
25		14	BURY	2-0	Flint 2	4000	1	2	3	4	5	6		8	11	10	7	9								
26		17	Preston North End	1-2	Waterall	5000	1	2	3	4	5		7	6	8	10	11	9								
27		24	TOTTENHAM HOTSPUR	2-2	Cantrell, West(p)	12000	1	2	3	4	5	6		8	10		7	9						11		
28	Mar	2	Manchester Utd.	0-2		7000	1	2	3	4	5	6	7		9	10		8						11		
29		9	LIVERPOOL	0-0		15000	1	2	3		5			8		10	7	9			6			11	4	
30		13	ASTON VILLA	2-0	Flint, Matthews	6000	1	2	3		5	6	7	8	9		11	10							4	
31		16	Aston Villa	1-5	Cantrell	15000	1	2	3		5	6	7	8	9		11	10							4	
32		23	NEWCASTLE UNITED	1-4	Cantrell	8000	1	2	3		5	6	7	8	9		11	10							4	
33		30	Sheffield United	3-1	Richards 2, Dean	7000	1	2	3	4	5	6	7		9	10	11	8								
34	Apr	5	EVERTON	0-1		15000	1	2	3	4	5	6	7		9	10	11	8								
35		6	OLDHAM ATHLETIC	1-1	Flint	7500	1	2	3	4	5	6	7			10	11	9								8
36		8	Everton	1-1	Richards	16000	1	2	3	4	5	6	7			10	11	9	8							
37		13	Bolton Wanderers	0-3		13000	1	2	3	4	5	6	7			10	11	9	8							
38		27	Woolwich Arsenal	3-0	Cantrell, Dean, Richards	10000	1	2	3	4	5	6	7		9	10	11	8								
Apps							38	38	38	33	37	33	33	31	23	31	37	29	3	1	3	1	1	3	4	1
Goals									1			1	5	7	8	13	2	9								

F.A. Cup

No		Date	Opponent	Score	Scorers	Att	Iremonger A	Morley H	West, Alf	Emberton FP	Clamp A	Craythorne R	Dean RJ	Matthews W	Cantrell J	Richards S	Waterall I	Flint WA
R1	Jan	13	Luton Town	4-2	Cantrell, Matthews, Richards, I.Waterall	8000	1	2	3	4	5	6		8	9	10	11	7
R2	Feb	3	Swindon Town	0-2		13780	1	2	3	4	5	6	7	8	10		11	9

Back: Prescott(Trainer), Emberton, Iremonger, Morley, Suter, Craythorne, Pepper, McLean(Assistant Trainer)
Middle: Clamp, Dean, Matthews, Cantrell, Richards, I.Waterall, Griffiths, Montgomery
Front: Flint, Walker, A.Waterall, West

1912/13
19th in Division One (Relegated)

#		Date	Opponent	Score	Scorers	Att	Iremonger A	Morley H	West, Alf	Emberton FP	Clamp A	Craythorne R	Jones AF	Flint WA	Cantrell J	Tomlinson T	Waterall I	Wathey F	Richards S	Waterall A	Hooper W	Steele MA	Williams D	West, Abe	Henshall HV	Allsebrook R	James L	Woolley J	Peart JG	Bird W
1	Sep	2	MANCHESTER CITY	0-1		12000	1	2	3	4	5	6	10	8	9	11	7													
2		7	WEST BROMWICH ALB.	1-1	Flint	13000	1	2	3	4	5	6	10	8	9	11	7													
3		14	Everton	0-4		25000	1	2	3	4	5	6	10	8	9	11	7													
4		21	SHEFFIELD WEDNESDAY	1-2	Cantrell	12000	1	2	3	4	5	6		8	9		11	7	10											
5		28	Blackburn Rovers	1-2	West(p)	20104	1	2	3	4	5	6	10	9	11		7						8							
6	Oct	5	DERBY COUNTY	0-1		30000	1	2	3	4	5	6	10	9	11		7						8							
7		19	MIDDLESBROUGH	1-3	Richards	10000	1	2	3	4	5	6		9			11		8	10	7									
8		26	Sunderland	0-4		8000		2	3	4	5	6		9			11	7		10			8	1						
9	Nov	2	Manchester Utd.	1-2	West(p)	12000		2	3	4	5	6	10	8			11				7			1	9					
10		4	Tottenham Hotspur	3-0	West(p), Flint, Waterall	12000		2	3	4	5	6	10	8			11				7				9	1				
11		9	ASTON VILLA	1-1	Williams	20000	1	2	3	4	5	6	10	8			7								9	11				
12		16	Liverpool	0-0		15000	1	2	3	4	5	6	10	8			7								9	11				
13		23	BOLTON WANDERERS	1-0	Henshall	8000	1	2	3	4	5	6	10	8			7								9	11				
14		30	Sheffield United	0-2		7000	1	2	3	4	5		10	6					8		7				9	11				
15	Dec	7	NEWCASTLE UNITED	0-1		10000	1	2	3	4	5		10	6					8		7				9	11				
16		14	Oldham Athletic	0-4		8000	1	2	3	4	5		6							10	8	7			9	11				
17		21	CHELSEA	0-0		12000	1	2	3	4	5		9							10	7		8		11	6				
18		25	Woolwich Arsenal	0-0		7000	1	2	3	4	5		10				11				7		8		9	6				
19		26	WOOLWICH ARSENAL	2-1	Jones 2	12000	1	2	3		5		10	4			11				7		8		9	6				
20		28	West Bromwich Alb.	0-2		21041	1		3		5		10	4			11				7		8		9	6	2			
21	Jan	2	Manchester City	0-4		22000	1		3		5		10	4			11				7		8		9	6		2		
22		4	EVERTON	0-1		5000	1	2	3		5		10	4			11				7		8		9	6				
23		18	Sheffield Wednesday	1-3	Williams	15000	1	2	3		5		10	4			11	7					8		9	6				
24		25	BLACKBURN ROVERS	3-1	Williams, Jones, Henshall	15000	1	2	3		5		10	4			7						8		9	6				
25	Feb	8	Derby County	0-1		12000	1	2	3		5		10	4			7						8		9	6				
26		15	TOTTENHAM HOTSPUR	0-1		10000	1	2	3		5		10	4		11					7		8			6			9	
27	Mar	1	SUNDERLAND	2-1	Flint, Peart	10000	1	2	3		5			4		11				10	7		8			6			9	
28		8	MANCHESTER UTD.	1-2	Flint(p)	10000	1	2	3		5			4		11				10	7		8			6			9	
29		15	Aston Villa	0-1		20000	1	2	3		5			4			7			10	8				9	6				
30		21	Bradford City	0-1		12000	1	2	3		5			4			7			10			8		9	6				
31		22	LIVERPOOL	3-0	Peart 3	7000	1	2	3	4	5						7			10	8				11	6			9	
32		24	BRADFORD CITY	1-1	Richards	15000	1	2	3	4	5						7			10	8				11	6			9	
33		29	Bolton Wanderers	0-0		17000	1	2	3	4	5					11		7		10	8		9			6				
34	Apr	2	Middlesbrough	1-1	Peart	6000	1	2	3	4	5		7							10	8				11	6			9	
35		5	SHEFFIELD UNITED	0-1		9000	1	2	3	4	5		8			7				10					11	6			9	
36		12	Newcastle United	0-0		10000	1	2	3	4	5		7							10	8				11	6			9	
37		19	OLDHAM ATHLETIC	2-1	Waterall, Peart(p)	6000	1	2	3	4	5		7			11				10	8					6			9	
38		26	Chelsea	2-5	Hooper, Peart	15000	1		3	4	5		6			11				10	7							2	9	8
			Apps				34	35	38	26	38	13	20	35	6	7	19	7	18	18	16	3	24	1	24	21	1	2	11	1
			Goals						3				3	4	1		2			2			1		3	2			7	

F.A. Cup

#		Date	Opponent	Score		Att	Iremonger A	Morley H	West, Alf	Emberton FP	Clamp A	Craythorne R	Jones AF	Flint WA	Cantrell J	Tomlinson T	Waterall I	Wathey F	Richards S	Waterall A	Hooper W	Steele MA	Williams D	West, Abe	Henshall HV	Allsebrook R	James L	Woolley J	Peart JG	Bird W
R1	Jan	11	Bristol Rovers	0-2		11000	1	2	3		5		10	4			11				7		8		9	6				

Back: Bramley(Treasurer), A.Waterall, Harris (Secretary), Morley, Iremonger, Emberton, Steele, Montgomery, McLean(Asst Trainer)   Middle: Wathey, Bird, Clamp, Richards, West (Alf)
Front: I.Waterall, Craythorne, Cantrell, F.Jones, Tomlinson, Prescott (Trainer)

1913/14 — Top of Division Two (Promoted)

#		Date	Opponent	Score	Scorers	Att	Iremonger A	Morley H	West, Alf	Emberton FP	Clamp A	Allsebrook R	Waterall I	Flint WA	Peart JG	Richards S	Williams D	Bird W	Machin P	Craythorne R	Bassett E	Haig P	Henshall HV	Toone G. Jr	Jennings W	Lamb J	James L
1	Sep	6	Grimsby Town	0-0		5000	1	2	3	4	5	6	7	8	9	10	11										
2		13	BIRMINGHAM	5-1	Waterall 2, Flint 2, Williams	12000	1	2	3	4	5	6	7	8	9	10	11										
3		15	Woolwich Arsenal	0-3		20000	1	2	3	4	5	6	7	8		10	11	9									
4		20	Bristol City	1-1	Bassett	14000	1		3	4	5			8		10	11	9		2	6	7					
5		24	BLACKPOOL	2-0	Richards, Williams	5000	1	2	3	4	5			8		10	11	9		6	7						
6		27	LEEDS CITY	4-0	Richards 2, Flint, Bassett	12000	1	2	3	4	5	6		8	9	10	11				7						
7	Oct	2	LINCOLN CITY	2-1	Richards, Henshall	12000	1	2	3	4	5	6		8	9	10					7		11				
8		4	Clapton Orient	0-1		12000	1	2	3	4			11	8		10				6	7			9	5		
9		11	GLOSSOP	2-2	Richards 2	10000	1	2	3	4	5	6		8	9	10	11				7						
10		18	Stockport County	2-1	Peart, Richards	8000	1	2	3	4		6		8	9	10					7		11		5		
11		25	BRADFORD PARK AVE.	2-3	Peart 2	10000	1	2	3	4		6		8	9	10					7		11		5		
12	Nov	1	FULHAM	4-0	Peart 3, Flint	12000	1	2	3	4		6		8	9	10					7		11		5		
13		8	Leicester Fosse	2-0	Peart, Richards	12000	1	2	3	4		6		8	9	10					7		11		5		
14		15	WOLVERHAMPTON W.	2-0	Henshall, Richards	7000	1	2	3	4		6		8	9	10					7		11		5		
15		22	Hull City	0-2		10000	1	2	3	4		6		8	9	10					7		11		5		
16		29	BARNSLEY	3-1	Richards, Flint, Peart	10000	1	2	3	4		6		8	9	10					7		11		5		
17	Dec	6	Bury	3-3	Richards, Peart, Flint	5000	1	2	3	4		6		8	9	10					7		11		5		
18		13	HUDDERSFIELD T	3-0	Peart 2, Richards	12000	1	2	3	4		6		8	9	10					7		11		5		
19		20	Lincoln City	0-0		5000	1	2	3	4		6		8	9	10					7		11		5		
20		25	NOTTM. FOREST	2-2	Peart 2	17000	1	2	3	4		6		8	9	10					7		11		5		
21		26	Nottm. Forest	0-1		22500	1	2	3	4		6		8	9	10					7		11		5		
22		27	GRIMSBY TOWN	4-0	Peart 3, Flint	14000	1	2	3	4	5			8	9	10				6	7		11				
23	Jan	1	WOOLWICH ARSENAL	1-0	Flint	7000	1	2	3	4	5	6		8	9	10					7		11				
24		3	Birmingham	1-2	Richards	10000	1	2	3	4	5	6		8		10			9		7		11				
25		17	BRISTOL CITY	4-0	Richards 2, Peart, Bassett	10000	1	2	3	4	5	6	11	8	9	10					7						
26		24	Leeds City	4-2	Flint 3, Richards	25000	1	2	3	4	5	6		8	9	10					7		11				
27	Feb	7	CLAPTON ORIENT	3-0	Richards, Henshall, Peart	9000	1	2	3	4	5	6		8	9	10					7		11				
28		14	Glossop	1-0	Peart	2000	1	2	3	4		6		8	9	10					7		11		5		
29		21	STOCKPORT COUNTY	2-1	Peart, Bassett	12000	1	2	3	4		6		8	9	10					7		11		5		
30		28	Bradford Park Ave.	3-0	Richards 2, Peart	25000	1	2	3	4	5	6		8	9	10					7		11				
31	Mar	7	Fulham	2-1	Henshall, Peart	18000	1	2	3	4	5	6		8	9	10					7		11				
32		14	LEICESTER FOSSE	4-1	Peart 2, Flint, Richards	14000	1	2	3	4	5	6		8	9	10					7		11				
33		21	Wolverhampton Wand.	1-4	Flint	13000	1	2	3	4	5	6		8	9						7		11			10	
34		28	HULL CITY	4-1	Peart 2, Allsebrook, Bassett	25000	1	2	3	4		6		8	9						7		11		5	10	
35	Apr	4	Barnsley	1-0	Flint	13000	1	2		4		6		8	9	10					7		11		5		3
36		11	BURY	2-0	Richards, Peart	10000	1	2		4		6		8	9	10					7		11		5		3
37		13	Blackpool	0-0		8000	1		3	4		6	11	8	9	10					7				5		2
38		18	Huddersfield T	1-2	Peart	9000	1	2	3	4		6		8	9	10					7		11		5		
Apps							38	36	36	38	18	34	7	38	30	36	7	3	1	4	35	1	30	1	20	2	3
Goals												1	2	14	28	21	2				5		4				

F.A. Cup

| R1 | Jan | 10 | Sheffield Wednesday | 2-3 | Flint, Peart(p) | 27600 | 1 | 2 | 3 | 4 | 5 | 6 | | 8 | 9 | 10 | | | | | 7 | | 11 | | | | |

Back: McLean (Asst. Trainer), Tuke, Clamp, Iremonger, Steele, Emberton, Peart, I.Waterall, Prescott(Trainer)
Middle: Allsebrook, Bassett, Flint, Richards, Morley, West, Jennings, Henshall, Perry
Front: Dale, Lamb

1914/15 — 16th in Division One

#		Date	Opponent	Score	Scorers	Att	Iremonger A	Morley H	West Alf	Emberton FP	Jennings W	Allsebrook R	Waterall I	Flint WA	Peart JG	Richards S	Lamb J	Dale G	Clamp A	Bassett E	Henshall HV	Perry J	Bird W	Sisson T	Woolley J
1	Sep	2	Aston Villa	1-2	Lamb	10000	1	2	3	4	5	6	7	8	9	10	11								
2		5	Liverpool	1-1	Lamb	15000	1	2	3	4	5	6	11	7	9		10	8							
3		12	BRADFORD PARK AVE.	1-2	Allsebrook	9000	1	2	3	4	5	6	11	7	9		10	8							
4		19	Oldham Athletic	0-2		8900	1	2	3		4	6	11	9			10		8	5	7				
5		26	MANCHESTER UTD.	4-2	Peart 2(1p), Flint, Richards	12000	1	2	3	4		6	7	8	9	10				5	11				
6	Oct	3	Bolton Wanderers	2-1	Peart 2	14000	1	2	3	4		6	7	8	9	10				5	11				
7		10	BLACKBURN ROVERS	1-1	Flint	14000	1		3	4		6	7	8	9	10				5	11	2			
8		17	MANCHESTER CITY	0-2		14000	1		3	4		6	7	8	9	10				5	11	2			
9		24	Sunderland	1-3	Peart	10000	1		3	4		6	11	8	9	10				5	7	2			
10		31	SHEFFIELD WEDNESDAY	1-2	Waterall	10000	1		3	4		6	11		9	10				5	7	2	8		
11	Nov	7	West Bromwich Alb.	1-4	Flint	10368	1	2	3	4		6	7	8	9	10				5	11				
12		14	EVERTON	0-0		10000	1	2		4		6	7	8	9	10				5	11			3	
13		21	Chelsea	1-4	Emberton	15000	1	2		4		6	7	8	9	10				5	11			3	
14		28	BRADFORD CITY	0-0		7000	1	2			5	6	7	4	9	10	8				11			3	
15	Dec	5	Burnley	0-0		9000	1	2			5	6	7	4	9	10			8		11				3
16		12	TOTTENHAM HOTSPUR	1-2	Richards	7000	1	2			4	6	7	8	9	10				5	11	3			
17		19	Newcastle United	1-1	Lamb	10000	1	2		3	5	6	7	4	9	10	8				11				
18		25	Middlesbrough	0-1		9000	1	2		3	5	6	7	4	9	10	8				11				
19		26	MIDDLESBROUGH	5-1	Dale 2, Richards 2, Henshall	14000	1	2		3	5	6	7	4	9	10		8			11				
20		28	Sheffield United	0-1		15000	1	2		3	5	6	7	4	9	10		8			11				
21	Jan	2	LIVERPOOL	3-1	Peart, Richards, Dale	8000	1			3	5	6	7	4	9	10		8			11	2			
22		16	Bradford Park Ave.	1-3	Dale	7000	1	2	3	5	9	6	7	4		10		8			11				
23		23	OLDHAM ATHLETIC	2-2	Bird, Richards	7000	1	2	3		5	6		4		10			8	7	11		9		
24		30	Manchester Utd.	2-2	Dale, Bird	10000	1	2	3		5	6		4				10	8	7	11		9		
25	Feb	13	Blackburn Rovers	1-5	Henshall	3000	1	2	3		5	6	7	4				10	8		11		9		
26		20	Tottenham Hotspur	0-2		12000	1			3	2	6	7	4	9				8	5	11			10	
27		22	Manchester City	0-0		20000	1			3	4	6	7		9				8	5	11	2		10	
28		27	SUNDERLAND	2-1	Richards, Scott(og)	8000	1			3		6	7	4	9	10			8	5	11	2			
29	Mar	6	Sheffield Wednesday	0-0		12000	1			3	4	6	7		9	10			8	5	11	2			
30		13	WEST BROMWICH ALB.	1-1	Peart	10000	1			3		6	7	4	9	10			8	5	11	2			
31		17	BOLTON WANDERERS	0-0		4000	1			3		6	7	4	9	10			8	5	11	2			
32		20	Everton	0-4		10000	1			3		6	7	4	9	10			8	5	11	2			
33	Apr	2	SHEFFIELD UNITED	3-1	Henshall, Flint, Peart	9000	1	2		4		6	7	8	9	10				5	11	3			
34		3	Bradford City	1-3	Peart	8000	1	2		4		6	11	8	9	10				5	7	3			
35		5	ASTON VILLA	1-1	Peart	12000	1		2	4		6		8	9	10			5	7	11	3			
36		10	BURNLEY	0-0		9000	1	2		4		6		8	9	10			7	5	11				
37		24	NEWCASTLE UNITED	1-0	Henshall	11000	1	2		4		6		8	9	10			7	5	11	3			
38		28	CHELSEA	2-0	Peart, Richards	9000	1	2		4		6	7	8	9	10				5	11	3			
			Apps				38	25	18	26	22	38	33	36	32	34	6	18	24	9	31	18	6	3	1
			Goals							1		1	1	4	11	8	3	5			4		2		

One own goal

F.A. Cup

#		Date	Opponent	Score	Scorers	Att	Iremonger A	Morley H	West Alf	Emberton FP	Jennings W	Allsebrook R	Waterall I	Flint WA	Peart JG	Richards S	Lamb J	Dale G	Clamp A	Bassett E	Henshall HV	Perry J	Bird W	Sisson T	Woolley J
R1	Jan	9	Bolton Wanderers	1-2	Richards	17870	1	2		3	5	6	7	4	9	10			8		11				

Back: McLean(Asst. Trainer), I.Waterall, Emberton, Clamp, Craythorne
Standing: Fisher(Sec/Man), Goddard(Dir), Morley, Jennings, Iremonger, Allsebrook, West, Prescott(Train), Bramley(Dir)
Sitting: Newton(Director), Bird, Flint, Peart, Richards, Henshall, Godfrey(Director
Front: Bassett, Williams

1915/16

#		Date	Opponent	Score	Scorers	Att.	1	2	3	4	5	6	7	8	9	10	11
1	Sep	4	HULL CITY	2-0	Cantrell, Henshall	6000	Iremonger A	Morley H	Perry J	Jennings W	Clamp A	Allsebrook	Waterall I	Flint WA	Cantrell J	Lilley B	Henshall HV
2		11	Nottm. Forest	5-3	Henshall 4 (2p), Flint	12000	Iremonger A	Morley H	Perry J	Bird W	Jennings W	Allsebrook	Waterall I	Flint WA	Cantrell J	Parrish J	Henshall HV
3		18	BARNSLEY	1-0	Flint	4000	Iremonger A	Morley H	Perry J	Jennings W	Clamp A	Allsebrook	Waterall I	Flint WA	Bird W	Parrish J	Henshall HV
4	Oct	2	SHEFFIELD UNITED	3-0	Flint 2, Cantrell	3000	Iremonger A	Morley H	Perry J	Jennings W	Clamp A	Allsebrook	Waterall I	Flint WA	Cantrell J	Richards S	Henshall HV
5		9	Bradford City	2-1	Cantrell, Parrish	5000	Iremonger A	Morley H	Perry J	Bagshaw JJ	Jennings W	Allsebrook	Waterall I	Flint WA	Cantrell J	Parrish J	Henshall HV
6		16	HUDDERSFIELD T	1-1	Parrish	6000	Iremonger A	Morley H	Perry J	Toone G (Jr	Jennings W	Allsebrook	Waterall I	Flint WA	Cantrell J	Parrish J	Henshall HV
7		23	Grimsby Town	2-2	Cantrell, Flint	4000	Iremonger A	Morley H	Perry J	Jennings W	Toone G (Jr	Allsebrook	Waterall I	Flint WA	Cantrell J	Richards S	Henshall HV
8		30	Lincoln City	0-3		4000	Iremonger A	Morley H	Perry J	Bagshaw JJ	Clamp A	Allsebrook	Waterall I	Flint WA	Cantrell J	Bache JW	Dunn R
9	Nov	6	DERBY COUNTY	5-0	Cantrell 3, Bache, Flint	7000	Iremonger A	Morley H	Perry J	Bagshaw JJ	Clamp A	Allsebrook	Waterall I	Flint WA	Cantrell J	Bache JW	Henshall HV
10		13	Sheffield Wednesday	1-4	Cantrell	5000	Iremonger A	Morley H	Perry J	Jennings W	Toone G (Jr	Bagshaw JJ	Plant	Flint WA	Cantrell J	Bache JW	Henshall HV
11		20	BRADFORD PARK AVE.	3-0	Bache, Cantrell, Henshall (p)	4000	Iremonger A	Morley H	Perry J	Jennings W	Bowser S	Bagshaw JJ	Wright H	Flint WA	Cantrell J	Bache JW	Henshall HV
12		27	Leeds City	4-0	Bache 2, Bagshaw, Cantrell	4000	Iremonger A	Morley H	Perry J	Jennings W	Clamp A	Bagshaw JJ	Wright H	Flint WA	Cantrell J	Bache JW	Henshall HV
13	Dec	4	Hull City	0-3		1000	Iremonger A	Morley H	Perry J	Jennings W	Clamp A	Bagshaw JJ	Wright H	Flint WA	Cantrell J	Bache JW	Leatherland J
14		11	NOTTM. FOREST	0-0		7000	Iremonger A	Morley H	Perry J	Jennings W	Bowser S	Bagshaw JJ	Wright H	Flint WA	Cantrell J	Bache JW	Henshall HV
15		18	Barnsley	0-1		5000	Iremonger A	Morley H	Perry J	Flint WA	Jennings W	Bagshaw JJ	Waterall I	Richards S	Cantrell J	Bache JW	Henshall HV
16		25	LEICESTER FOSSE	1-2	Henshall	4000	Iremonger A	Morley H	Johnson J	Flint WA	Clamp A	Bagshaw JJ	Waterall I	Richards S	Cantrell J	Bache JW	Henshall HV
17		27	Leicester Fosse	1-2	Henshall (p)	3000	Iremonger A	Sissons W	Perry J	Jennings W	Clamp A	Bagshaw JJ	Waterall I	Flint WA	Cantrell J	Bache JW	Henshall HV
18	Jan	1	Sheffield United	1-1	Flint	5500	Steele MA	Morley H	Perry J	Jennings W	Bagshaw JJ	Allsebrook	Waterall I	Flint WA	Cantrell J	Bache JW	Henshall HV
19		8	BRADFORD CITY	1-0	Cantrell	5000	Iremonger A	Morley H	Perry J	Bagshaw JJ	Bowser S	Allsebrook	Waterall I	Flint WA	Cantrell J	Bache JW	Henshall HV
20		15	Huddersfield Town	1-2	Henshall (p)	4000	Iremonger A	Morley H	Perry J	Bagshaw JJ	Bowser S	Allsebrook	Waterall I	Flint WA	Cantrell J	Bache JW	Henshall HV
21		22	GRIMSBY TOWN	1-2	Bache	3000	Steele MA	Perry J	Feebery J	Bagshaw JJ	Clamp A	Allsebrook	Waterall I	Flint WA	Cantrell J	Bache JW	Henshall HV
22		29	LINCOLN CITY	2-1	Bache, Ward (og)	4000	Steele MA	Morley H	Feebery J	Robson M	Jennings W	Allsebrook	Waterall I	Thurman M	Cantrell J	Bache JW	Henshall HV
23	Feb	5	Derby County	0-2		2000	Iremonger A	Morley H	Feebery J	Robson M	Bagshaw JJ	Allsebrook	Richards S	Sankey T	Cantrell J	Bache JW	Henshall HV
24		12	SHEFFIELD WEDNESDAY	1-1	Allsebrook	4000	Iremonger A	Morley H	Perry J	Flint WA	Jennings W	Allsebrook	Waterall I	Bird W	Cantrell J	Bache JW	Henshall HV
25		19	Bradford Park Avenue	0-4		4000	Steele MA	Morley H	Johnson J	Flint WA	Jennings W	Allsebrook	Waterall I	Bird W	Cantrell J	Bache JW	Henshall HV
26	Apr	21	LEEDS CITY	1-1	Foster	3000	Iremonger A	Morley H	Johnson J	Flint WA	Foster JH	Bagshaw JJ	Waterall I	Bird W	Cantrell J	Richards S	Henshall HV
27	Mar	4	Leicester Fosse	0-0		3000	Iremonger A	Morley H	Johnson J	Bagshaw JJ	Jennings W	Allsebrook	Waterall I	Bird W	Flint WA	Bache JW	Henshall HV
28		11	CHESTERFIELD	1-1	Bird	1500	Iremonger A	Johnson J	Bagshaw JJ	Jennings W	Bowser S	Allsebrook	Waterall I	Bird W	Flint WA	Richards S	Henshall HV
29		18	DERBY COUNTY	3-1	Henshall, Richards, Waterall (p)	2000	Iremonger A	Morley H	Johnson J	Jennings W	Bowser S	Allsebrook	Waterall I	Bird W	Flint WA	Richards S	Henshall HV
30		25	Stoke	0-3		4000	Iremonger A	Morley H	Perry J	Flint WA	Bowser S	Jennings W	Waterall I	Bird W	Cantrell J	Richards S	Henshall HV
31	Apr	1	NOTTM. FOREST	2-0	Cantrell, Richards	6000	Iremonger A	Morley H	Johnson J	Flint WA	Foster JH	Allsebrook	Waterall I	Bird W	Cantrell J	Richards S	Henshall HV
32		8	LEICESTER FOSSE	1-1	Bird	3000	Iremonger A	Morley H	Johnson J	Jennings W	Foster JH	Bagshaw JJ	Flint WA	Bird W	Cantrell J	Richards S	Henshall HV
33		15	Chesterfield	1-0	Henshall	4000	Iremonger A	Morley H	Johnson J	Jennings W	Foster JH	Bagshaw JJ	Waterall I	Bird W	Cantrell J	Richards S	Henshall HV
34		22	Derby County	3-2	Bird, Cantrell, Waterall (p)	4000	Iremonger A	Jennings W	Johnson J	Flint WA	Foster JH	Bagshaw JJ	Waterall I	Bird W	Cantrell J	Richards S	Henshall HV
35		24	Nottm. Forest	2-4	Cantrell, Richards	9000	Iremonger A	Morley H	Johnson J	Flint WA	Foster JH	Bagshaw JJ	Jennings W	Bird W	Cantrell J	Richards S	Henshall HV
36		29	STOKE	3-0	Richards 2, Bird	3000	Iremonger A	Morley H	Johnson J	Blackburn G	Foster JH	Bagshaw JJ	Wright H	Bird W	Cantrell J	Richards S	Henshall HV

Games 1 - 26: League, Midland Section
Games 27 - 36: Subsidiary Competition

1916/17

#		Date	Opponent	Score	Scorers	Att	1	2	3	4	5	6	7	8	9	10	11
1	Sep	2	Nottm. Forest	3-4	Cantrell, Henshall, Walker		Iremonger A	Morley H	Pennington J	Flint WA	Foster JH	Bagshaw JJ	Pykett B	Bird W	Cantrell J	Walker JH	Henshall HV
2		9	BARNSLEY	1-1	Walker		Iremonger A	Perry J	Pennington J	Bowser S	Foster JH	Bagshaw JJ	Bartrop W	Bird W	Cantrell J	Walker JH	Henshall HV
3		16	Leeds City	0-5		3000	Neal G	Jennings W	Pennington J	Walker JH	Foster JH	Bagshaw JJ	Laxton LE	Flint WA	Cantrell J	Housley H	Henshall HV
4		23	SHEFFIELD UNITED	2-0	Cantrell, Mann	3000	Iremonger A	Morley H	Pennington J	Walker JH	Jennings W	Bagshaw JJ	Laxton LE	Mann J	Cantrell J	Housley H	Henshall HV
5		30	Bradford City	2-1	Cantrell 2	2000	Iremonger A	Morley H	Pennington J	Flint WA	Foster JH	Jennings W	Laxton LE	Walker JH	Cantrell J	Housley H	Henshall HV
6	Oct	7	LEICESTER FOSSE	5-1	Cantrell 3, Housley 2	3000	Iremonger A	Morley H	Pennington J	Flint WA	Foster JH	Bagshaw JJ	Tattershall W	Walker JH	Cantrell J	Housley H	Henshall HV
7		14	Grimsby Town	3-3	Flint, Housley, Jennings	2000	Neal G	Bagshaw JJ	Dexter G	Flint WA	Jennings W	Graham DC	Laxton LE	Pykett B	Cantrell J	Housley H	Henshall HV
8		21	CHESTERFIELD	1-4	Walker	4000	Iremonger A	Morley H	Pennington J	Flint WA	Foster JH	Jennings W	Walker JH	Pykett B	Cantrell J	Housley H	Henshall HV
9		28	ROTHERHAM COUNTY	2-2	Dunn, Housley	2000	Iremonger A	Morley H	Pennington J	Flint WA	Bowser S	Woodlands A	Scrimshaw A	Turner H	Housley H	Walker JH	Dunn R
10	Nov	4	Huddersfield T	0-1		3000	Iremonger A	Morley H	Pennington J	Flint WA	Bowser S	Woodlands A	Scrimshaw A	Walker JH	Cantrell J	Housley H	Brownlow W
11		11	LINCOLN CITY	0-4		2500	Iremonger A	Charlesworth G	Dexter G	Flint WA	Foster JH	Woodlands A	Scrimshaw A	Clarke	Cantrell J	Walker JH	Dunn R
12		18	Sheffield Wednesday	0-2		2000	Iremonger A	Perry J	Pennington J	Flint WA	Bowser S	Bagshaw JJ	Foster WH	Walker JH	Cantrell J	Richards S	Reider J
13		25	BRADFORD PARK AVE.	2-1	Cantrell, Cooke	3000	Iremonger A	Perry J	Pennington J	Flint WA	Bowser S	Walker JH	Cooke JR	Cantrell J	Sambrooke C	Richards S	Henshall HV
14	Dec	2	Birmingham	0-4			Neal G	Perry J	Pennington J	Flint WA	Bowser S	Walker JH	Cooke JR	Cantrell J	Sambrooke C	Richards S	Hayes J
15		9	NOTTM. FOREST	2-2	Cantrell, Richards	3000	Neal G	Perry J	Kay H	Flint WA	Woodlands A	Bird W	Cooke JR	Housley H	Sambrooke C	Richards S	Hayes J
16		16	Barnsley	0-4		500	Iremonger A	Morley H	Perry J	Bowser S	Foster JH	Walker JH	James W	Housley H	Cantrell J	Richards S	Foster WH
17		23	LEEDS CITY	1-0	Housley	2000	Edleston	Bagshaw JJ	Woolley J	Flint WA	Woodlands A	Walker JH	James W	Housley H	Cantrell J	Richards S	Henshall HV
18		25	Hull City	0-2		5000	Iremonger A	Bagshaw JJ	Woolley J	Flint WA	Woodlands A	Walker JH	Cooke JR	Housley H	Cantrell J	Richards S	Foster WH
19		26	HULL CITY	7-1	Richards 3, Cantrell 2, Dunn, Walker	7000	Iremonger A	Clay T	Walker JH	Flint WA	Woodlands A	Bagshaw JJ	James W	Housley H	Cantrell J	Richards S	Dunn R
20		30	Sheffield United	1-0	James	2000	Iremonger A	Wilson J	Pennington J	Flint WA	Woodlands A	Charles F	Johnson H (Jr)	James W	Cantrell J	Bird W	Dunn R
21	Jan	6	BRADFORD CITY	1-0	Richards	1600	Neal G	Morley H	Pennington J	Flint WA	Woodlands A	Walker JH	Bird W	Cantrell J	Sambrooke C	Richards S	Dunn R
22		13	Leicester Fosse	1-0	Walker (p)	1200	Neal G	Morley H	White T	Flint WA	Woodlands A	Walker JH	James W	Bird W	Cantrell J	Richards S	Dunn R
23		20	GRIMSBY TOWN	2-3	Dunn, Walker	2500	Branston JT	White T	Pennington J	Bird W	Woodlands A	James W	Walker JH	Housley H	Cantrell J	Richards S	Dunn R
24		27	Chesterfield	1-3	Housley	4500	Branston JT	White T	Pennington J	Flint WA	Woodlands A	James W	Scrimshaw A	Davis F	Cantrell J	Housley H	Dunn R
25	Feb	3	Rotherham County	3-0	Cantrell, Richards, Scrimshaw	1500	Branston JT	White T	Pennington J	Flint WA	Jennings W	Walker JH	Scrimshaw A	Bird W	Cantrell J	Richards S	Dunn R
26		10	HUDDERSFIELD T	2-1	Flint, Richards		Branston JT	Dexter F	Pennington J	Flint WA	Jennings W	Walker JH	Scrimshaw A	Bird W	Cantrell J	Richards S	Dunn R
27		17	Lincoln City	2-1	Flint, Richards	3000	Branston JT	White T	Dexter F	Flint WA	Jennings W	Walker JH	Scrimshaw A	Bird W	Cantrell J	Richards S	Dunn R
28		24	SHEFFIELD WEDNESDAY	1-0	Richards	2500	Branston JT	White T	Pennington J	Flint WA	Jennings W	Walker JH	Scrimshaw A	Bird W	Cantrell J	Richards S	Dunn R
29	Mar	3	Bradford Park Avenue	1-1	Feamley	2000	Branston JT	Barraclough	Pennington J	Flint WA	Woodlands A	Jennings W	Scrimshaw A	Bird W	Cantrell J	Feamley	Dunn R
30		10	BIRMINGHAM	1-1	Woods	2000	Branston JT	White T	Pennington J	Flint WA	Woodlands A	Walker JH	Scrimshaw A	Woods J	Cantrell J	Richards S	Dunn R
31	Mar	24	NOTTM. FOREST	2-2	Flint, Walker (p)	4000	Branston JT	White T	Pennington J	Flint WA	Woodlands A	Walker JH	Scrimshaw A	Woods J	Cantrell J	Richards S	Dunn R
32		31	Birmingham	1-1	Walker (p)		Branston JT	White T	Pennington J	Flint WA	Jennings W	Walker JH	Scrimshaw A	Bird W	Cantrell J	Driver T	Dunn R
33	Apr	7	Leicester Fosse	1-2	Cantrell		Branston JT	White T	Walker JH	Starkey G	Woodlands A	Flint WA	Scrimshaw A	Bird W	Cantrell J	Richards S	Dunn R
34		9	LEICESTER FOSSE	2-3	Cantrell, Richards	3000	Branston JT	White T	Walker JH	Flint WA	Hawley F	Jennings W	Scrimshaw A	Bird W	Cantrell J	Richards S	Dunn R
35		14	Nottm. Forest	3-2	Flint 2, Cantrell		Iremonger A	Morley H	Pennington J	White T	Woodlands A	Jennings W	Scrimshaw A	Bird W	Flint WA	Walker JH	Cantrell J
36		21	BIRMINGHAM	0-2			Iremonger A	White T	Pennington J	Flint WA	Woodlands A	Walker JH	Scrimshaw A	Bird W	Cantrell J	Richards S	Dunn R

Games 1 - 30: League, Midland Section
Games 31 - 36: Subsidiary Competition

1917/18

#	Date	Opponent	Att	Score	Scorers											
						Iremonger A	Smith J	Smith G	Bryan J	Tremelling S	McNeal R	Waterall I	Flint WA	Cantrell J	Richards S	Jones B
1	Sep 1	LEICESTER FOSSE		2-1	Richards, Tremelling	Iremonger A	Smith J	Smith G	Bryan J	Tremelling S	McNeal R	Waterall I	Flint WA	Cantrell J	Richards S	Jones B
2	8	Leicester Fosse		0-1		Iremonger A	Bagshaw JJ	Smith G	Bryan J	Tremelling S	McNeal R	Scrimshaw H	Flint WA	Cantrell J	Richards S	Waterall I
3	15	HULL CITY		2-2	Cantrell, Richards	Branston JT	Clay T	Charlesworth G	Flint WA	Hawley F	McNeal R	Scrimshaw H	Pykett B	Cantrell J	Richards S	Waterall I
4	22	Hull City		2-1	Cumming, Hawley	Branston JT	Charlesworth G	Loversuch A	Flint WA	Hawley F	Bagshaw JJ	Scrimshaw H	Cumming J	Cantrell J	Richards S	Waterall I
5	Oct 13	Barnsley		0-0		Branston JT	Clay T	Charlesworth G	Bryan J	Hawley F	McNeal R	Sheldon L	Cumming J	Cantrell J	Richards S	Waterall I
6	20	BARNSLEY		4-2	Cantrell 2, Sheldon, Day(og)	Branston JT	Smith G	Charlesworth G	Bryan J	Hawley F	McNeal R	Sheldon L	Cumming J	Cantrell J	Richards S	Waterall I
7	27	Bradford Park Avenue	3000	0-1		Branston JT	Smith G	Charlesworth G	Bryan J	Hawley F	Bagshaw JJ	Sheldon L	Cumming J	Cantrell J	Richards S	Jennings W
8	Nov 3	BRADFORD PARK AVE.	2000	0-1		Iremonger A	Charlesworth G	Smith G	Bryan J	Hawley F	Bagshaw JJ	Laxton LE	Cumming J	Cantrell J	Richards S	Waterall I
9	10	Sheffield United	6000	1-6	Cantrell	Iremonger A	Smith J	Charlesworth G	Bryan J	Hawley F	McNeal R	Sheldon L	Cumming J	Boyne R	Richards S	Cantrell J
10	17	SHEFFIELD UNITED		0-6		Iremonger A	Smith J	Charlesworth G	Bryan J	Hawley F	McNeal R	Sheldon L	Cumming J	Cantrell J	Richards S	Dunn R
11	24	Leeds City	2000	0-2		Branston JT	Charlesworth G	Yates A	Cumming J	Hawley F	McNeal R	Sheldon L	Leafe D	Cantrell J	Richards S	Dunn R
12	Dec 1	LEEDS CITY	3000	2-4	Cumming, Richards	Branston JT	Charlesworth G	Marriott F	Bryan J	Hawley F	McNeal R	Sheldon L	Cumming J	Cantrell J	Richards S	Waterall I
13	8	LINCOLN CITY		1-1	Cantrell	Branston JT	Smith J	Charlesworth G	Bryan J	Hawley F	Cumming J	Sheldon L	Goodman T	Cantrell J	Richards S	Dunn R
14	15	Lincoln City		2-1	Richards 2	Branston JT	Charlesworth G	Marriott F	Bryan J	Bagshaw JJ	Wield T	Cumming J	Sheldon L	Cantrell J	Richards S	Waterall I
15	22	GRIMSBY TOWN		8-0	Cantrell 5, Richards 2, Henshall (p)	Branston JT	Charlesworth G	Marriott F	Bryan J	Bagshaw JJ	Wield T	Waterall I	Cumming J	Cantrell J	Richards S	Henshall HV
16	25	NOTTM. FOREST		0-1		Branston JT	Clay T	Charlesworth G	Flint WA	Bagshaw JJ	Waterall A	Sheldon L	Cumming J	Cantrell J	Richards S	Waterall I
17	26	Nottn. Forest		0-0		Iremonger A	Charlesworth G	Clay T	Bryan J	Bagshaw JJ	Waterall A	Sheldon L	Flint WA	Cantrell J	Richards S	Waterall I
18	29	Grimsby Town		0-2		Iremonger A	Charlesworth G	White J	Bryan J	Flint WA	Graham DC	Sheldon L	Short J	Cantrell J	Richards S	Waterall I
19	Jan 5	BIRMINGHAM		3-3	Cantrell, Richards, Short	Branston JT	Charlesworth G	Atkin J	Bryan J	Bagshaw JJ	Marriott F	Sheldon L	Short J	Cantrell J	Richards S	Waterall I
20	12	Birmingham		2-7	Richards 2	Branston JT	Perry J	Charlesworth G	Bell JJ	Bagshaw JJ	Bryan J	Sheldon L	Short J	Cantrell J	Richards S	Crossley CH
21	19	BRADFORD CITY		2-2	Cantrell, Richards	Iremonger A	Charlesworth G	Marriott F	Bryan J	Bagshaw JJ	Cumming J	Sheldon L	Short J	Cantrell J	Richards S	Willis AS
22	26	Bradford City		0-0		Iremonger A	Charlesworth G	Marriott F	Bryan J	Bagshaw JJ	Cumming J	Sheldon L	Short J	Cantrell J	Poole WS	Timmins W
23	Feb 2	HUDDERSFIELD T	2000	3-2	Cantrell 2, Richards	Branston JT	Charlesworth G	Marriott F	Bryan J	Bagshaw JJ	Cumming J	Sheldon L	Short J	Cantrell J	Richards S	Timmins W
24	16	SHEFFIELD WEDNESDAY		3-0	Waterall 2, Short	Iremonger A	Charlesworth G	Marriott F	Timmins W	Bagshaw JJ	Bryan J	Sheldon L	Short J	Cantrell J	Richards S	Waterall I
25	23	Sheffield Wednesday		1-2	Richards	Iremonger A	Charlesworth G	Marriott F	Bryan J	Bagshaw JJ	Timmins W	Sheldon L	Short J	Cantrell J	Richards S	Mee GW
26	Mar 2	ROTHERHAM COUNTY		2-2	Cantrell, Richards	Iremonger A	Charlesworth G	Marriott F	Bryan J	Bagshaw JJ	Timmins W	Sheldon L	Short J	Cantrell J	Richards S	Mee GW
27	9	Rotherham County	4000	2-2	Cantrell 2	Iremonger A	Charlesworth G	Marriott F	Bryan J	Bagshaw JJ	Timmins W	Sheldon L	Short J	Cantrell J	Richards S	Waterall I
28	Apr 2	Huddersfield Town		1-2	Cantrell	Keeling S	Clay T	Charlesworth G	Bryan J	Bagshaw JJ	Timmins W	Waterall I	Short J	Cantrell J	Richards S	Mee GW
29	Mar 16	LEICESTER FOSSE		5-0	Short 2, Cantrell, Charlesworth(p), Richards	Iremonger A	Charlesworth G	Marriott F	Bryan J	Bagshaw JJ	Timmins W	Sheldon L	Short J	Cantrell J	Richards S	Brooks
30	23	Leicester Fosse		1-3	Cantrell	Iremonger A	Charlesworth G	Pennington J	Bryan J	Bagshaw JJ	Timmins W	Sheldon L	Short J	Cantrell J	Richards S	Mee GW
31	28	NOTTM. FOREST		3-1	Flint, Short, Waterall	Iremonger A	Clay T	Flint WA	Flint WA	Bagshaw JJ	Timmins W	Scrimshaw H	Short J	Cantrell J	Richards S	Waterall I
32	30	BIRMINGHAM		5-1	Cantrell 2, Richards 2, Mee	Iremonger A	Clay T	Charlesworth G	Bryan J	Bagshaw JJ	Timmins W	Sheldon L	Short J	Cantrell J	Richards S	Mee GW
33	Apr 1	Nottm. Forest		3-0	Richards 2, Cantrell	Iremonger A	Clay T	Charlesworth G	Flint WA	Bagshaw JJ	Timmins W	Waterall I	Short J	Cantrell J	Richards S	Mee GW
34	6	Birmingham		2-3	Cantrell 2	Iremonger A	Charlesworth G	Keeling S	Short J	Bagshaw JJ	Timmins W	Sheldon L	Scrimshaw H	Cantrell J	Richards S	Mee GW

Games 1 - 28: League, Midland Section
Games 29 - 34: Subsidiary Competition

1918/19

No	Mth	Date	Opponent	Att	Res	Scorers	1	2	3	4	5	6	7	8	9	10	11
1	Sep	7	Leeds City	5000	1-4	Short	Johnson J	Clay T	Marriott F	Waterall A	Bagshaw JJ	Timmins W	Sheldon L	Cumming J	Short J	Richards S	Waterall I
2		14	LEEDS CITY	7000	5-2	Cantrell 2, Clay (p), Richards, Short	Johnson J	Clay T	Marriott F	Waterall A	Bagshaw JJ	Timmins W	Sheldon L	Short J	Cantrell J	Richards S	Waterall I
3		21	Sheffield United	10000	2-2	Cantrell, Richards	Johnson J	Clay T	Marriott F	Waterall A	Bagshaw JJ	Timmins W	Sheldon L	Short J	Cantrell J	Richards S	Waterall I
4		28	SHEFFIELD UNITED	6000	5-2	Short 3, Cantrell 2	Johnson J	Clay T	Marriott F	Waterall A	Bagshaw JJ	Timmins W	Sheldon L	Short J	Cantrell J	Richards S	Waterall I
5	Oct	5	Bradford Park Avenue	3000	0-0		Johnson J	Charlesworth G	Marriott F	Waterall A	Bagshaw JJ	Timmins W	Sheldon L	Short J	Cantrell J	Walker JH	Mee GW
6		12	BRADFORD PARK AVE.	7000	4-1	Cantrell 2, Richards 2	Johnson J	Clay T	Marriott F	Flint WA	Bagshaw JJ	Timmins W	Walker JH	Short J	Cantrell J	Richards S	Waterall I
7		19	HULL CITY		1-0	Cantrell	Iremonger A	Clay T	Marriott F	Bryan J	Bagshaw JJ	Timmins W	Sheldon L	Short J	Cantrell J	Richards S	Waterall I
8		26	Hull City		1-1	Cantrell	Iremonger A	Charlesworth G	Marriott F	Bryan J	Bagshaw JJ	Timmins W	Sheldon L	Hill H	Cantrell J	White	Waterall I
9	Nov	2	COVENTRY CITY		4-0	Bagshaw, Charlesworth(p), Short, Tinsley	Iremonger A	Charlesworth G	Marriott F	Bryan J	Bagshaw JJ	Waterall A	Sheldon L	Short J	Cantrell J	Tinsley W	Waterall T
10		9	Coventry City		1-5	Storer	Iremonger A	Charlesworth G	Marriott F	Bryan J	Bagshaw JJ	Timmins W	Waterall I	Storer H	Cantrell J	Richards S	Waterall T
11		16	BARNSLEY		4-4	Clay 2 (2p), Kemp, Short	Iremonger A	Clay T	Marriott F	Kemp H	Bagshaw JJ	Timmins W	Waterall I	Short J	Cantrell J	Richards S	Waterall T
12		23	Barnsley		0-1		Iremonger A	Clay T	Marriott F	Cumming J	Bagshaw JJ	Waterall T	Waterall I	Storey	Price W	Richards S	Timmins W
13		30	LEICESTER FOSSE		1-0	Short	Iremonger A	Clay T	Marriott F	Flint WA	Bagshaw JJ	Waterall A	Waterall I	Short J	Cumming J	Richards S	Kemp H
14	Dec	7	Leicester Fosse		0-3		Orme JH	Charlesworth G	Marriott F	Waterall A	Bagshaw JJ	Waterall T	Cooke JR	Short J	Kemp H	Richards S	Waterall I
15		14	Lincoln City		1-0	Short	Iremonger A	Charlesworth G	Marriott F	Flint WA	Bagshaw JJ	Jennings W	Waterall I	Short J	Cantrell J	Richards S	Waterall T
16		21	LINCOLN CITY		2-1	Cantrell 2	Iremonger A	Clay T	Marriott F	Flint WA	Bagshaw JJ	Waterall T	Waterall I	Short J	Cantrell J	Richards S	Henshall HV
17		25	Nottm. Forest		0-2		Iremonger A	Clay T	Marriott F	Flint WA	Bagshaw JJ	Waterall T	Waterall I	Short J	Cantrell J	Richards S	Henshall HV
18		26	NOTTM. FOREST		1-1	Richards	Hasell AA	Clay T	Marriott F	Flint WA	Bagshaw JJ	Waterall T	Waterall I	Short J	Cantrell J	Richards S	Henshall HV
19		28	Rotherham County		1-0	Cantrell	Hasell AA	Bagshaw JJ	Marriott F	Flint WA	Jennings W	Waterall T	Waterall I	Short J	Cantrell J	Richards S	Mee GW
20	Jan	4	ROTHERHAM COUNTY		2-0	Richards, Cantrell	Iremonger A	Bagshaw JJ	Marriott F	Flint WA	Jennings W	Waterall T	Waterall I	Short J	Cantrell J	Richards S	Mee GW
21		11	Birmingham		7-0	Cantrell 3, Richards 2, Short 2	Iremonger A	Charlesworth G	Marriott F	Flint WA	Bagshaw JJ	Waterall T	Waterall I	Short J	Cantrell J	Richards S	Henshall HV
22		18	BIRMINGHAM		2-0	Cantrell, Richards	Iremonger A	Charlesworth G	Marriott F	Flint WA	Bagshaw JJ	Waterall T	Waterall I	Short J	Cantrell J	Richards S	Henshall HV
23		25	Bradford City		6-3	Short 3, Leonard 2, Richards	Iremonger A	Charlesworth G	Marriott F	Flint WA	Bagshaw JJ	Waterall T	Waterall I	Leonard H	Cantrell J	Richards S	Henshall HV
24	Feb	1	BRADFORD CITY		2-0	Richards 2	Iremonger A	Charlesworth G	Marriott F	Flint WA	Bagshaw JJ	Waterall T	Waterall I	Short J	Cantrell J	Richards S	Henshall HV
25		8	Huddersfield T		1-1	Jennings	Iremonger A	Charlesworth G	Marriott F	Flint WA	Bagshaw JJ	Waterall T	Waterall I	Jennings W	Cantrell J	Richards S	Henshall HV
26		15	HUDDERSFIELD T		6-2	Cantrell 4, Bagshaw, Charlesworth(p)	Iremonger A	Charlesworth G	Marriott F	Flint WA	Bagshaw JJ	Morris W	Waterall I	Short J	Cantrell J	Richards S	Henshall HV
27		22	Sheffield Wednesday		2-2	Waterall, Newman	Iremonger A	Charlesworth G	Marriott F	Flint WA	Bagshaw JJ	Short J	Waterall I	Bell	Newman GW	Richards S	Henshall HV
28	Mar	1	SHEFFIELD WEDNESDAY		0-0		Iremonger A	Charlesworth G	Marriott F	Flint WA	Bagshaw JJ	Johnson J	Waterall I	Short J	Cantrell J	Richards S	Henshall HV
29		8	Grimsby Town		0-0		Iremonger A	Charlesworth G	Marriott F	Flint WA	Jennings W	Walker JH	Sheldon L	Newman GW	Cantrell J	Richards S	Henshall HV
30		15	GRIMSBY TOWN		3-1	Cantrell, Cook, Newman	Iremonger A	Charlesworth G	Marriott F	Flint WA	Bagshaw JJ	Jennings W	Cook J	Newman GW	Cantrell J	Richards S	Henshall HV
31	Mar	22	Leicester Fosse		1-5	Cook	Iremonger A	Bacon T	Walkerdine	Flint WA	Foster JH	Allsebrook R	Cook J	Jennings W	Davis	Richards S	Henshall HV
32		29	LEICESTER FOSSE		5-0	Richards 2, Cantrell, Dale, Henshall	Iremonger A	West, Alf	Marriott F	Flint WA	Foster JH	Allsebrook R	Cook J	Dale G	Cantrell J	Richards S	Henshall HV
33	Apr	5	Birmingham		3-0	Dale, Henshall, Richards	Iremonger A	West, Alf	Marriott F	Flint WA	Foster JH	Allsebrook R	Cook J	Dale G	Cantrell J	Richards S	Henshall HV
34		12	BIRMINGHAM		1-2	Short	Iremonger A	West, Alf	Marriott F	Flint WA	Foster JH	Allsebrook R	Cook J	Short J	Cantrell J	Richards S	Henshall HV
35		18	Nottm. Forest		2-3	Cantrell, Cook	Steele MA	Charlesworth G	West, Alf	Flint WA	Foster JH	Allsebrook R	Cook J	Thompson	Cantrell J	Richards S	Henshall HV
36		21	NOTTM. FOREST		1-3	Richards	Steele MA	Charlesworth G	West, Alf	Flint WA	Jennings W	Allsebrook R	Cook J	Dale G	Peart JG	Richards S	Mee GW

Games 1 - 30: League, Midland Section
Games 31 - 36: Subsidiary Competition

- 1918/19 Season -

Back: Fisher (Sec.Manager), Newton (Director), White (Director), Bagshaw, A.Iremonger,
not known, J.Iremonger (Trainer), Charlesworth, I.Waterall, Bramley (Director), Godfrey (Director)
Middle: J.R.Cooke, Newman, Cantrell, Richards, Henshall
Front: Jennings, Flint, Marriott

- 1919/20 Season -

Back: Gibson, Flint, Foster, Pembleton, Iremonger, Streets, Woodland, Bagshaw, Marriott
Front: Waterall, Hill, McLeod, Cook, Henshall

#	Date	Opponent	Score	Scorers	Att	Iremonger A	Charlesworth G	Johnson J	Flint WA	Pembleton A	Allsebrook R	Waterall I	Cook J	Peart JG	Richards S	Henshall HV	Cooke JR	Foster JH	Currie JB	Streets GH	Marriott F	Hill H	Tasker E	McLeod W	Gibson T	Woodland A	Bagshaw JJ	Hoten RV	Stoakes JH	Jones JW	Widdowson Alf
1	Aug 30	BURNLEY	2-0	Richards, Henshall	14000	1	2	3	4	5	6		7	8	9	10	11														
2	Sep 1	Sheffield United	0-3		15000	1	2	3	4	5	6		7	10	9	11		8													
3	Sep 6	Burnley	1-2	Peart	12000	1	2	3	4	5			7	10	9	11		6	8												
4	Sep 13	Sheffield Wednesday	0-0		4000		2		4	5				10	9	11		7	6	8	1	3									
5	Sep 20	SHEFFIELD WEDNESDAY	3-1	Henshall, Charlesworth(p), Peart	11000		2		4	5				10	9	11		7	6	8	1	3									
6	Sep 27	Manchester City	1-4	Currie	20000	1	2		4	5				10		11		7	6	8		3		9							
7	Oct 2	SHEFFIELD UNITED	2-2	Henshall, Peart	7000	1	2		8	5	6		7		9	11		4	10			3									
8	Oct 4	MANCHESTER CITY	4-1	Charlesworth(p), Cook 2, Peart	14000	1	2		4	5			7	8	9	11		6				3		10							
9	Oct 11	Derby County	1-3	Peart	15000	1	2		4	5			7	8	9	11		6				3		10							
10	Oct 18	DERBY COUNTY	2-2	Henshall, Charlesworth(p)	25000	1	2		4	5			7	8	9	10	11	6				3									
11	Oct 25	West Bromwich Alb.	0-8		36086	1			4	5		6	8			11		7				3		10	2	9					
12	Nov 1	WEST BROMWICH ALB.	2-0	Hill 2	12050		2		4	5		11	8					7	6		1	3		10		9					
13	Nov 8	Sunderland	1-3	Cook	20000		2		4	5		11	8					7	6		1	3		10		9					
14	Nov 15	SUNDERLAND	2-2	Hill, Richards	14000		2		4	5			7		10	11		6			1	3		8		9					
15	Nov 22	Arsenal	1-3	Hill	25000		2		4	5				10		11		7	6		1	3		8		9					
16	Nov 29	ARSENAL	2-2	Richards, McLeod	6000		2		4	6			7		10	11				5	1	3		8		9					
17	Dec 6	Everton	2-1	Hill, McLeod	16000		2		4	6			7		10	11				5	1	3		8		9					
18	Dec 13	EVERTON	1-1	Charlesworth(p)	16000		2	3	4	6			7		10	11				5	1			8		9					
19	Dec 20	Bradford City	4-3	Henshall, Hill 2, McLeod	16000			3	4	6			7	8		11				5	1	10		9	2						
20	Dec 25	BLACKBURN ROVERS	5-0	McLeod 2, Foster, Richards 2	18000				4	6			7		8	11		10		5	1	3		9	2						
21	Dec 27	BRADFORD CITY	5-2	Hill, Richards 2, Henshall, Gibson(p)	25000				4	5		6	7		10	11				8	1	3		9	2						
22	Jan 1	Blackburn Rovers	1-1	Cook	30000				4	6			7	8		11		5	10		1	3		9	2						
23	Jan 3	Bolton Wanderers	0-1		25000				4	6			8			11		5	7	3	1	10		9	2						
24	Jan 17	BOLTON WANDERERS	2-2	McLeod, Hill	22000				4	6			7		10	11		5		8	1	3		9	2						
25	Jan 24	PRESTON NORTH END	1-2	McLeod	15000		2		4	6			7		10	11		5		8	1			9		3					
26	Feb 7	BRADFORD PARK AVE.	0-2		20000							6	7	10		11		4		8	1	3		9	2	5					
27	Feb 14	Bradford Park Ave.	1-0	Cook	18000	1			4				8	10		11		7				3		9	2	6	5				
28	Feb 26	LIVERPOOL	1-0	Hill	10000	1			4				8	10		11		7				3		9	2	6	5				
29	Feb 28	Liverpool	0-3		35000		2						8			11		7	6		1	3		10		9		4	5		
30	Mar 4	Preston North End	0-2		12000		9	3								11		7	6	8	1	10			2			4	5		
31	Mar 13	CHELSEA	0-1		16000	1	2			9			8			11		4	6			3	7	10			5				
32	Mar 17	Chelsea	0-2		20000	1	2						7	8				6	10			4		9		3	5			11	
33	Mar 20	Newcastle United	1-2	Hill	35000	1	2			6			7			10			4			3		8		9	5			11	
34	Mar 27	NEWCASTLE UNITED	0-0		16000	1	2			6			7			10			4					8		3	5			11	9
35	Apr 2	MIDDLESBROUGH	1-1	Hill	20000	1	2	10		6			7			11		4				3		8		9	5				
36	Apr 3	Aston Villa	1-3	Waterall	35000	1	2	10				6	7					4				3		8		9	5			11	
37	Apr 5	Middlesbrough	2-5	McLeod, Holmes(og)	20000	1	2			6			7			10						3		9			5		4	11	
38	Apr 10	ASTON VILLA	2-1	Henshall, McLeod	18000	1	2			6			7			10		4				3		8		9	5			11	
39	Apr 17	Oldham Athletic	0-0		17892	1	2			6			7			10		4				3		8		9	5			11	
40	Apr 24	OLDHAM ATHLETIC	2-1	Henshall 2	15000	1	2			6			7			10		4				3		8		9	5			11	
41	Apr 26	Manchester Utd.	0-0		18000	1	2			6			7			10		4				3		8		9	5			11	
42	May 1	MANCHESTER UTD.	0-2		23000	1	2			6			7			10		4				3		8		9	5			11	
		Apps				21	30	10	27	35	4	33	21	9	11	32	12	32	8	21	27	33	1	30	23	10	16	2	2	10	1
		Goals					4					1	5	5	7	9		1	1			12		9	1						

Played in game 37: W Poole (8).

One own goal

F.A. Cup

Rd	Date	Opponent	Score	Scorers	Att	Flint WA	Pembleton A	Cook J	Peart JG	Henshall HV	Foster JH	Marriott F	Hill H	McLeod W	Gibson T	Woodland A	Hoten RV
R1	Jan 10	MILLWALL	2-0	Hill, McLeod	30000	4	6	7	8	11	5	1	3	10	2	9	
R2	Jan 31	MIDDLESBROUGH	1-0	John Cook	28000	4	6	7	10	11	5	1	3	8	2	9	
R3	Feb 21	BRADFORD PARK AVE.	3-4	Gibson(p), Henshall, McLeod	36246	4		7	8	11	5	1	3	10	2	9	6

		P	W	D	L	F	A	W	D	L	F	A	Pts
1	West Bromwich Alb.	42	17	1	3	65	21	11	3	7	39	26	60
2	Burnley	42	13	5	3	43	27	8	4	9	22	32	51
3	Chelsea	42	15	3	3	33	10	7	2	12	23	41	49
4	Liverpool	42	12	5	4	35	18	7	5	9	24	26	48
5	Sunderland	42	17	2	2	45	16	5	2	14	27	43	48
6	Bolton Wanderers	42	11	3	7	35	29	8	6	7	37	36	47
7	Manchester City	42	14	5	2	52	27	4	4	13	19	35	45
8	Newcastle United	42	11	5	5	31	13	6	4	11	13	26	43
9	Aston Villa	42	11	3	7	49	36	7	3	11	26	37	42
10	Arsenal	42	11	5	5	32	21	4	7	10	24	37	42
11	Bradford Park Ave.	42	8	6	7	31	26	7	6	8	29	37	42
12	Manchester United	42	6	8	7	20	17	7	6	8	34	33	40
13	Middlesbrough	42	10	5	6	35	23	5	5	11	26	42	40
14	Sheffield United	42	14	5	2	43	20	2	3	16	16	49	40
15	Bradford City	42	10	6	5	36	25	4	5	12	18	38	39
16	Everton	42	8	6	7	42	29	4	8	9	27	39	38
17	Oldham Athletic	42	12	4	5	33	19	3	4	14	16	33	38
18	Derby County	42	12	5	4	36	18	1	7	13	11	39	38
19	Preston North End	42	9	6	6	35	27	5	4	12	22	46	38
20	Blackburn Rovers	42	11	4	6	48	30	2	7	12	16	47	37
21	NOTTS COUNTY	42	9	8	4	39	25	3	4	14	17	49	36
22	Sheffield Wed.	42	6	4	11	14	23	1	5	15	14	41	23

1920/21 — 6th in Division Two

#	Date	Opponent	Score	Scorers	Att	Iremonger A	Ashurst W	Gibson T	Flint WA	Woodland A	Walker JH	Dolphin A	Hill H	Stevens S	McLeod W	Henshall HV	Marriott F	Pembleton A	Cooper E	Boreham RW	Cook J	Bagshaw JJ	Kemp H	Dinsdale N	Richards S	Widdowson Alf	Streets GH	Death WG	Cope HW	Hoten RV	Daly J	Barry LJ
1	Aug 28	Bristol City	1-0	Woodland	25600	1	2	3	4	5	6	7	8	9	10	11																
2	30	BARNSLEY	1-0	Stevens	18000	1	2	3	4	5	6	7	8	9	10	11																
3	Sep 4	BRISTOL CITY	2-2	Stevens, Flint	17000	1	2		4	5				9		11	3	6	7	8	10											
4	6	Barnsley	2-2	Henshall, Stevens	10000	1	2		4		6			9		11	3		7		10	5	8									
5	11	Nottm. Forest	0-1		25000	1	2	3	4		6			9		11		7	10	8		5										
6	18	NOTTM. FOREST	2-0	Stevens 2	25000	1	2		4	5			10	9		11	3	6	7		8											
7	25	Fulham	1-3	Hill	20000	1	2		4	5		7	10	9		11	3			6	8											
8	Oct 2	FULHAM	2-1	Kemp, Dolphin	14000	1	2		4	5		7		9		11	3	6			8		10									
9	9	Stoke	0-1		10000	1	2		4	5		7		9		11	3	6			10		8									
10	16	STOKE	3-0	Stevens 2, Dolphin	14000	1	2		4	6		7		9		11	3				10		8	5								
11	23	CARDIFF CITY	1-2	Henshall	22000	1	2		4	6		7		9		11	3				8			5	10							
12	30	Cardiff City	1-1	Stevens	30000	1	2		4	6		7		9	10	11	3				8			5								
13	Nov 6	COVENTRY CITY	1-1	McLeod	19000	1	2			6	4	7		9	10	11	3				8			5								
14	13	Coventry City	1-1	Richards	22000	1	2			6		7	8	9			3	4						5	10							
15	20	LEICESTER CITY	1-1	Richards	18000	1	2			6		7	8	9		11	3	4						5	10							
16	27	Leicester City	3-0	Richards, Henshall, Hill	22000	1	2		4			7	8	9		11	3	6						5	10							
17	Dec 4	LEEDS UNITED	1-2	Dinsdale	12000	1	2		4			7	8	9		11	3	6						5	10							
18	11	Leeds United	0-3		17000	1	2	3	9	4		7				11		6			8			5	10							
19	18	Blackpool	2-0	Dolphin, Widdowson	9000	1	2	3	4			7				11		6			8			5	10	9						
20	25	Sheffield Wednesday	1-1	Richards	27000	1	2	3	4			7				11		6			8			5	10	9						
21	27	SHEFFIELD WEDNESDAY	3-0	Cook, Richards 2	30578	1	2	3	4	6		7				11					8			5	10	9						
22	Jan 1	BLACKPOOL	1-2	Gibson(p)	15000		2	3	4	6		7				11					8			5	10	9	1					
23	15	Rotherham County	0-0		10000		2		4	6				9		11	3				8		7	5	10		1					
24	22	ROTHERHAM COUNTY	1-0	Stevens	10000		2		4					9		11	3	6			8		7	5	10		1					
25	Feb 5	Birmingham	1-2	Barton(og)	40000		2		4	5		7		9	10		3	6			8						1	11				
26	12	Port Vale	2-1	Hill 2	14000		2		4			7	8	9			3	6						5	10		1	11				
27	16	BIRMINGHAM	0-0		14000				4			7	8	9	10		3	6						5			1	11	2			
28	19	Port Vale	0-1		12000				4			7	8	9	10		3	6					11	5			1		2			
29	26	South Shields	0-1		15000	1		2	4	6		7	8	9		11	3							5						10		
30	Mar 5	SOUTH SHIELDS	2-0	Gibson 2(2p)	12000	1		2	4	6		7		9			3				8			5	10			11				
31	12	Hull City	1-1	Gibson(p)	8000	1		2	4	6			8	9			3							5	10			11			7	
32	19	HULL CITY	4-1	Hill 2, Henshall, Richards	12000	1		2	4				8	9		11	3	6						5	10						7	
33	25	West Ham United	2-0	Hill, Richards	28000	1		2	4				8	9		11	3	6						5	10						7	
34	26	WOLVERHAMPTON W.	2-1	Hill 2	16000	1		2	4				8	9			3	6						5	10						7	11
35	28	WEST HAM UNITED	1-1	Hoten	22000		2		4					9		11	3	6			8			5			1			10	7	
36	Apr 2	Wolverhampton Wand.	0-1		15984	1		2	4					9			3	6			8			5	10						7	11
37	9	STOCKPORT COUNTY	3-0	Henshall, Hill 2	7000	1		2	3	4			8	9		11		6						5	10						7	
38	16	Stockport County	0-1		7000	1		2	3	4				9		11		6			8			5	10						7	
39	23	CLAPTON ORIENT	3-1	Flint, Cook, Richards	10000		2		4	5						11		6			8				10	9	1		3		7	
40	30	Clapton Orient	0-3		20000	1		2	4					9		11	3	6			8			5	10						7	
41	May 2	BURY	2-1	Henshall, Widdowson	12000		2	3	4							10		6			8			5		9	1	11			7	
42	7	Bury	1-0	Widdowson	6000	1		2	3	4						10		6			8			5		9		11				
		Apps				32	28	24	38	23	5	24	22	22	10	33	29	23	4	3	26	8	11	30	23	7	10	7	3	2	11	2
		Goals						4	2	1		3	11	9	1	6					2		1	1	9	3				1		

Played in game 14: JW Jones (11). In game 42: R Platts (7).

One own goal

F.A. Cup

Rnd	Date	Opponent	Score	Scorers	Att	Ashurst W	Flint WA	Stevens S	Henshall HV	Marriott F	Pembleton A	Cook J	Kemp H	Dinsdale N	Richards S	Streets GH
R1	Jan 8	WEST BROMWICH ALB.	3-0	Stevens 2, Cook	32995	2	4	9	11	3	6	8	7	5	10	1
R2	Jan 29	ASTON VILLA	0-0		45014	2	4	9	11	3	6	8	7	5	10	1
rep	Feb 2	Aston Villa	0-1		49491	2	4		9	11				7	5	10	1

	P	W	D	L	F	A	W	D	L	F	A	Pts
1 Birmingham	42	16	4	1	55	13	8	6	7	24	25	58
2 Cardiff City	42	13	5	3	27	9	11	5	5	32	23	58
3 Bristol City	42	14	3	4	35	12	5	10	6	14	17	51
4 Blackpool	42	12	3	6	32	19	8	7	6	22	23	50
5 West Ham United	42	13	5	3	38	11	6	5	10	13	19	48
6 NOTTS COUNTY	42	12	5	4	36	17	6	6	9	19	23	47
7 Clapton Orient	42	13	6	2	31	9	3	7	11	12	33	45
8 South Shields	42	13	4	4	41	16	4	6	11	20	30	44
9 Fulham	42	14	4	3	33	12	2	6	13	10	35	42
10 Sheffield Wed.	42	9	7	5	31	14	6	4	11	17	34	41
11 Bury	42	10	8	3	29	13	5	2	14	16	36	40
12 Leicester City	42	10	8	3	26	11	2	8	11	13	35	40
13 Hull City	42	7	10	4	24	18	3	10	8	19	35	40
14 Leeds United	42	11	5	5	30	14	3	5	13	10	31	38
15 Wolverhampton Wan.	42	11	4	6	34	24	5	2	14	15	42	38
16 Barnsley	42	9	10	2	31	17	1	6	14	17	33	36
17 Port Vale	42	7	6	8	28	19	4	8	9	15	30	36
18 Nottingham Forest	42	9	6	6	37	26	3	6	12	11	29	36
19 Rotherham County	42	8	9	4	23	21	4	3	14	14	32	36
20 Stoke	42	9	5	7	26	16	3	6	12	20	40	35
21 Coventry City	42	8	6	7	24	25	4	5	12	15	45	35
22 Stockport County	42	8	6	7	30	24	1	6	14	12	51	30

- 1920/21 Season -

Back: Flint, Streets, Walker, Foster, Ashurst, Iremonger
Third Row: McLeod, Cook, Marriott, Hill, Henshall, Stevens, Bagshaw
Second Row: Charlesworth, Cooper, Widdowson, Kemp, Jones, Cope
Front: Pembleton, Woodland, Dolphin

- 1921/22 Season -

Back: Brown, Little, Fisher, Ashurst, Woodlands, Flint
Standing: McLean (Asst. Trainer), J.Iremonger (Trainer), Henshall, Cope, Dinsdale, A.Iremonger, Pembleton, McPherson, Gibson, Fisher (Sec.Manager)
Sitting: Widdowson, Platts, Hill, Kemp, Death   Front: Richards, Cook, Daly, Marriott

1921/22 — 13th in Division Two

#	Date		Opponent	Score	Scorers	Att.	Iremonger A	Cope HW	Gibson T	Flint WA	Woodland A	Pembleton A	Daly J	Cook J	Hill H	Brown D	Death WG	Streets GH	Ashurst W	Dinsdale N	Marriott F	McPherson L	Platts R	Widdowson Alf	Moore H	Henshall HV	Richards S	Cashmore AA	Kemp H	Chipperfield JJ	Crapper J
1	Aug	27	BRISTOL CITY	0-2		12000	1	2	3	4	5	6	7	8	9	10	11														
2		29	Wolverhampton Wand.	2-1	Hill, Death	12000			3	4			7	8	9	10	11	1	2	5											
3	Sep	3	Bristol City	2-2	Daly, McPherson	20000	1			4		6	7		10	9	11		2	5	3	8									
4		5	WOLVERHAMPTON W.	4-0	Death 3, Hill	12000	1			4		6	7		10	9	11		2	5	3	8									
5		10	SHEFFIELD WEDNESDAY	2-0	Brown 2	15000	1			4		6	7		10	9	11		2	5	3	8									
6		17	Sheffield Wednesday	0-2		12000	1			4		6	7		10	9	11		2	5	3	8									
7		24	FULHAM	3-0	Brown, Flint, McPherson	16000	1			4		6			10	9	11		2	5	3	8	7								
8	Oct	1	Fulham	0-4		20000	1			4		6			10	9	11		2	5	3	8	7								
9		6	BARNSLEY	1-4	Daly	12000	1			4		6	7		9		11		2	5	3	8		10							
10		8	BLACKPOOL	2-1	Brown, Dinsdale	14000	1		2	4			7			9				5		8		11	10	6					
11		15	Blackpool	2-1	Widdowson, Brown	9000	1		3	4						9				5				8	7	10	6	11			
12		22	CLAPTON ORIENT	0-0		8000	1		3	4			7			9			2	5				8		10	6	11			
13		29	Clapton Orient	1-2	Widdowson	15000	1		3	4			7	8					2	5				9			6	11	10		
14	Nov	5	NOTTM. FOREST	1-1	Widdowson	26000	1			4			7	8					2	5	3			11	10	6			9		
15		14	Nottm. Forest	0-0		16000	1			4	5			8			11		2		3		7		10	6			9		
16		19	Stoke	0-0		12000	1			4	5			8			11		2		3		7		10	6			9		
17		26	STOKE	0-0		14000	1						7	8					2	5	3				10	6			9	4	
18	Dec	3	LEEDS UNITED	4-1	Henshall, Cashmore 2, Marriott(p)	12000	1						7	8					2	5	3					6	11	10	9	4	
19		10	Leeds United	1-1	Henshall	15000	1		2				7	8						5	3					6	11	10	9	4	
20		17	Hull City	0-2		14000	1	2						8	9					5	3		7			6	11	10		4	
21		24	HULL CITY	2-0	Richards 2	18000	1			4				8					2	5	3			7		10	9	6	11		
22		26	Crystal Palace	0-1		18000	1			4	6			8					2	5	3			10		7		9	11		
23		27	CRYSTAL PALACE	3-2	Cashmore 2, Dinsdale(p)	22000	1			4		6		8	10				2	5	3			7				9	11		
24		31	BRADFORD PARK AVE.	3-0	Cook, Brown 2	12000	1			4		6		8	10	9			2	5	3			7					11		
25	Jan	21	SOUTH SHIELDS	2-0	Cashmore 2	9000	1			4		6		8	10				2	5	3			7				9	11		
26	Feb	4	PORT VALE	1-2	Dinsdale	6000	1			4				8					2	5	3		7			11	10	9	6		
27		11	Port Vale	0-0		8000	1			4					10				2	5	3		8	7	9	11			6		
28		25	West Ham United	1-2	Cook	20000	1		2	4			5	7	8	10				3					9				6		11
29		28	Bradford Park Ave.	1-2	McPherson	7000	1		2		4		5	7						3		10			9				8	6	11
30	Mar	11	Bury	0-1		10000	1	2	3				4	7		10				5					9				8	6	11
31		15	South Shields	0-0		10000	1			4				7	8				2	5	3				9			10	6	11	
32		18	Leicester City	0-3		14000	1			4				7	8	10			2	5	3				9				6	11	
33		29	WEST HAM UNITED	1-1	Cook	7000				4				7	8	10			1	2	5	3			9		11		6		
34	Apr	1	Derby County	1-1	Chipperfield	12000				4			5	7	8	10			1	2		3			9				6	11	
35		5	BURY	1-1	Hill	5000				4				7	8	10			1	2		3			9				6	11	
36		8	DERBY COUNTY	1-2	Hill	6500			3	4				7	8	10			1	2	5				9				6	11	
37		14	ROTHERHAM COUNTY	2-0	Widdowson, Chipperfield	12000	1	3	2	4					8	10				5				7	9	6				11	
38		15	COVENTRY CITY	1-1	Widdowson	7000		3	2	4					8	10		1		5				7	9	6				11	
39		17	Rotherham County	0-3		12000		3	2	4			4		8	10		11	1	2	5			7	9	6				11	
40		22	Coventry City	2-4	Hill 2	11000	1	3		4					8	10			2	5					9	6				11	7
41		26	LEICESTER CITY	0-0		5000	1	3		4		6			8	10			2	5					9					11	7
42		29	Barnsley	0-3		15000	1	3				4				10			2	5				8	7	9	6			11	
			Apps				35	10	12	30	15	13	23	25	28	14	12	7	33	36	29	13	14	26	16	14	6	14	16	18	2
			Goals							1			2	3	6	7	4			3	1	3		5		2	2	6		2	

Played in game 17: H Oldershaw (11)

F.A. Cup

	Date		Opponent	Score	Scorers	Att.	Iremonger A	Cope HW	Gibson T	Flint WA	Woodland A	Pembleton A	Daly J	Cook J	Hill H	Brown D	Death WG	Streets GH	Ashurst W	Dinsdale N	Marriott F	McPherson L	Platts R	Widdowson Alf	Moore H	Henshall HV	Richards S	Cashmore AA	Kemp H	Chipperfield JJ	Crapper J
R1	Jan	7	Grimsby Town	1-1	Hill	12000	1			4		6		8	10				2	5	3					7		9		11	
rep	Jan	12	GRIMSBY TOWN	3-0	Cook, Henshall, Hill	16381	1			4		6	7	8	10				2	5	3					11		9			
R2	Jan	28	Bradford City	1-1	Widdowson	18752	1			4		6			10				2	5	3			9		7		8		11	
rep	Jan	1	BRADFORD CITY	0-0		20108	1			4		6		8	10				2	5	3					7		9		11	
r2	Feb	6	BRADFORD CITY	1-0	Widdowson	29882	1			4				8	10				2	5	3		7	9		11			6		
R3	Feb	18	West Bromwich Albion	1-1	Widdowson	43853	1			4			7	8	10				2	5	3			9		11			6		
rep	Feb	22	WEST BROMWICH ALB.	2-0	Cook, Hill	24278	1		2	4			7	8	10					5	3			9					6	11	
R4	Mar	4	ASTON VILLA	2-2	Chipperfield 2	35551	1			4			7	8	10				2	5	3			9					6	11	
rep	Mar	8	Aston Villa	4-3	Chipperfield, Hill, Widdowson, Cook	40161	1		3	4			7	8	10				2	5				9					6	11	
SF	Mar	25	Huddersfield T	1-3	Hill	46323	1			4			7	8	10				2	5	3			9		11			6		

R2 replay after extra time. R2 replay 2 at Bramall Lane.
R4 replay after extra time. Semi-final at Turf Moor, Burnley

		P	W	D	L	F	A	W	D	L	F	A	Pts
1	Nottingham Forest	42	13	7	1	29	9	9	5	7	22	21	56
2	Stoke	42	9	11	1	31	11	9	5	7	29	33	52
3	Barnsley	42	14	5	2	43	18	8	3	10	24	34	52
4	West Ham United	42	15	3	3	39	13	5	5	11	13	26	48
5	Hull City	42	13	5	3	36	13	6	5	10	15	28	48
6	South Shields	42	11	7	3	25	13	6	5	10	18	25	46
7	Fulham	42	14	5	2	41	8	4	4	13	16	30	45
8	Leeds United	42	10	8	3	31	12	6	5	10	17	26	45
9	Leicester City	42	11	6	4	30	16	3	11	7	9	18	45
10	Sheffield Wed.	42	12	4	5	31	24	3	10	8	16	26	44
11	Bury	42	11	3	7	35	19	4	7	10	19	36	40
12	Derby County	42	11	3	7	34	22	4	6	11	26	42	39
13	NOTTS COUNTY	42	10	7	4	34	18	2	8	11	13	33	39
14	Crystal Palace	42	9	6	6	28	20	4	7	10	17	31	39
15	Clapton Orient	42	12	4	5	33	18	3	5	13	10	32	39
16	Rotherham County	42	8	9	4	17	7	6	2	13	15	36	39
17	Wolverhampton Wan.	42	8	7	6	28	19	5	4	12	16	30	37
18	Port Vale	42	10	5	6	28	19	4	3	14	15	38	36
19	Blackpool	42	11	1	9	33	27	4	4	13	11	30	35
20	Coventry City	42	8	5	8	31	21	4	5	12	20	39	34
21	Bradford Park Ave.	42	10	5	6	32	22	2	4	15	14	40	33
22	Bristol City	42	10	3	8	25	18	2	6	13	12	40	33

1922/23 Champions of Division Two (Promoted)

	Date		Opponent	Score	Scorers	Att	Iremonger A	Ashurst W	Cope HW	Dinsdale N	Wren JE	Kemp H	Daly J	Cook J	Hill H	Heathcote J	Price LP	Marriott F	Brodie G	Flint WA	Cock DJ	Streets GH	McPherson L	Platts R	Barry LJ	Widdowson Alf	Gibson T	Fenwick R	Harris G	Cooper J	Death WG
1	Aug	26	Coventry City	2-1	Hill 2	20000	1	2	3	4	5	6	7	8	9	10	11														
2		28	SOUTH SHIELDS	2-0	Hill 2	12000	1	2	3	4	5	6	7	8	9	10	11														
3	Sep	2	COVENTRY CITY	2-0	Cope, Cook	14000	1	2	3	4	5	6	7	8	9	10	11														
4		4	South Shields	0-1		12000	1	2	3	4	5	6	7	8	9	10	11														
5		9	HULL CITY	0-1		12000	1	2		4	5	6	7		9	10	11	3	8												
6		16	Hull City	2-0	Price, Daly	9000	1	2	3	5	6		7	8	9	10	11			4											
7		23	Sheffield Wednesday	1-0	Cook	20000	1	2	3	5	6		7	8	9	10	11			4											
8		30	SHEFFIELD WEDNESDAY	1-0	Heathcote	15000	1	2	3	5	6		7	8	9	10	11			4											
9	Oct	7	Barnsley	0-1		12000	1		3	5	6		7	8		10	11	2		4	9										
10		14	BARNSLEY	1-0	Daly	15000		2	3	5	6		7	8		10	11			4	9	1									
11		21	Port Vale	0-0		6000		2	3	5	6		7	8	10		11			4	9	1									
12		28	PORT VALE	1-0	Hill	12000		2	3	5	6		7		10		11			4	9	1	8								
13	Nov	4	BLACKPOOL	2-0	Hill, Daly	12000		2	3	5	6		7		10		11			4	9	1	8								
14		11	Blackpool	1-1	Cock	12000		2	3	5	6		7		10		11			4	9	1	8								
15		18	WOLVERHAMPTON W.	4-1	Cock 2, McPherson, Daly	14000		2	3	5	6		7		10		11			4	9	1	8								
16		25	Wolverhampton Wand.	0-1		17262	1	2	3	5	6		7		10		11			4	9		8								
17	Dec	2	BRADFORD CITY	0-0		12000	1	2	3	5	6				10		11			4	9		8	7							
18		9	Bradford City	2-1	Cock 2	12000	1	2	3	5		6	7			10	11			4	9		8								
19		16	SOUTHAMPTON	1-0	Cock	10000	1	2	3	5		6	7	10			11			4	9		8								
20		23	Southampton	1-0	Hill	9000	1	2		5	6	11	7		10			3		4	9		8								
21		25	FULHAM	1-0	McPherson	14000	1	2		5	6		7		10			3		4	9		8		11						
22		26	Fulham	1-2	Cock	25000	1	2		5	6		7		10			3		4	9		8		11						
23		30	Derby County	0-0		22500		2		5	6		7		10			3		4		1	8		11	9					
24	Jan	6	DERBY COUNTY	1-2	Dinsdale (p)	26000		2		5	6		7		10			3		4	9	1			11	8					
25		20	Leicester City	1-2	Daly	22000		2		5	6	4	7	8		10	11				9	1					3				
26		27	LEICESTER CITY	1-0	Dinsdale	28000	1	2		5	6	4	7	8							9		10		11		3				
27	Feb	10	MANCHESTER UTD.	1-6	Cock	11000	1	2	3	5	6		7	8						4	9		10		11						
28		17	Bury	2-2	Price, Cock	12000		2	3	5			6		8	7				4	10	1			9						
29		21	Manchester Utd.	1-1	Widdowson	18000		2			6	7		8			11	3		4	10	1			9		5				
30	Mar	3	Rotherham County	0-1		10000		2		5		6		8	7		11	3		4	10	1			9						
31		10	ROTHERHAM COUNTY	2-0	Cook, Cock	12000		2	3			4	7	8	10		11				9	1						5	6		
32		17	CLAPTON ORIENT	3-1	Hill, Platts, Cooper	14000		2	3	5	6	4			10		11				9	1		7						8	
33		21	BURY	1-0	Hill	9000		2	3	5		6			10		7				9	1			11			4	8	
34		24	Clapton Orient	1-2	Cock	17000		2	3	5	6	4	7		10		11				9	1							8	
35		30	Crystal Palace	1-0	Hill	9000		2	3	5		6			10		11			4	9	1		7					8	
36		31	STOCKPORT COUNTY	2-0	Hill, Dinsdale	14000		2		5	6			8	10		11	3		4	9	1		7						
37	Apr	2	CRYSTAL PALACE	0-4		20000		2		5		6		8	10		11	3		4	9	1		7						
38		7	Stockport County	0-0		12000		2		5		6			10					4	9	1		7	11		3		8	
39		14	LEEDS UNITED	1-0	Dinsdale	13000		2		5		6		8	10					4	9	1		7	11		3			
40		18	WEST HAM UNITED	2-0	Cock 2	15000		2	3	5		6		8	10					4	9	1		7						11
41		21	Leeds United	0-3		8000		2	3	5		6		8	10					4	9	1		7						11
42	May	5	West Ham United	1-0	Hill	26000	1	2	3	5	6				10		11			4	9			7					8	

	Apps	19	41	28	40	29	23	29	22	35	12	31	11	1	31	33	23	14	10	9	5	4	3	1	6	2
	Goals		1	4				5	3	12	1	2				13		2	1		1					1	

F.A. Cup

	Date		Opponent	Score	Att	Iremonger A	Ashurst W	Cope HW	Dinsdale N	Wren JE	Kemp H	Daly J	Cook J	Hill H	Heathcote J	Price LP	Marriott F	Brodie G	Flint WA	Cock DJ										Death WG
R1	Jan	13	Plymouth Argyle	0-0	27000	1	2	3	5	6		7	8	10					4	9										11
rep	Jan	17	PLYMOUTH ARGYLE	0-1	16000	1	2		5	6	10	7	8				3		4	9										11

- 1922/23 Season -

Back: McPherson, Bell (Coach), Cope, J.Iremonger (Trainer), Platts, Marriott, Cook, Heathcoat, A.Iremonger, Ashurst, McLean(Ass. Trainer), Death
Middle: Daly, Widdowson, Flint, Hill, Dinsdale, Wren, Gibson, Ashford, Harris
Front: Shepherd, Kirkwood

- 1923/24 Season -

Back: Wren, Dinsdale, Ashurst, J.Iremonger (Trainer), W.Smith, A.Iremonger, Fisher(Sec/Man.), Cope, McClean (Asst. Train), Fenwick
Middle: Widdowson, Hill, Kemp, Cook, Flint, Brodie, Harris, Pape
Front: Price, McPherson, Platts, Cock, Daly, Cornwall

1923/24 — 10th in Division One

#		Date	Opponent	Score	Scorers	Att	Iremonger A	Ashurst W	Cope HW	Flint WA	Dinsdale N	Kemp H	Cooper J	Mackay JA	Cock DJ	Hill H	Price LP	Cornwell R	McPherson L	Daly J	Barry LJ	Wren JE	Platts R	Cook J	Widdowson Alf	Pape A	Streets GH	Fenwick R	Allen H	Harris G	Davis AG	Smith WA
1	Aug	25	BURNLEY	2-1	Hill 2	25000	1	2	3	4	5	6	8	7	9	10	11															
2		29	Middlesbrough	3-2	Cooper, Cock, Mackay	10000	1	2		4	5	6	8	7	9	10	11	3														
3	Sep	1	Burnley	1-1	Cock	18000	1	2	3		5	6	8	7	9	10	11		4													
4		8	HUDDERSFIELD T	1-0	Hill	20000	1	2	3	4	5	6	8		9	10	11			7												
5		15	Huddersfield T	0-0		16000	1	2	3	4	5	6	8		9	10				7		11										
6		22	NOTTM. FOREST	2-1	Cock 2	30000	1	2	3	4	5	6	8		9	10				7		11										
7		29	Nottm. Forest	0-1		32000	1		2	4	5		8		9	10		3		7		11	6									
8	Oct	4	MIDDLESBROUGH	1-0	Hill	12000	1	2	3	4	5	6	8		9	10				7		11										
9		6	TOTTENHAM HOTSPUR	0-0		25000	1	2		4	5	6	8		9	10		3		7		11										
10		13	Tottenham Hotspur	3-1	Cock, Cooper, Hill	35000	1	2			5	6	8		9	10		3	4	7		11										
11		20	EVERTON	1-1	Cock	18000	1	2	3		5	6	8		9	10			4	7		11										
12		27	Everton	0-3		30000	1	2	3		5	6	8		9	10			4	7		11										
13	Nov	3	Aston Villa	0-0		35000	1	2	3		5	6	8		9	10					11	4	7									
14		10	ASTON VILLA	0-1		12000	1	2	3	4	5	6			9	10				7		11	8									
15		17	Birmingham	0-0		15000	1	2	3	4	5	6	8		9	7						11					10					
16		24	BIRMINGHAM	1-1	Pape	8000	1	2	3	4	5	6	8		9	7						11				10						
17	Dec	1	Manchester City	0-1		22990	1	2		4	5	6	8		10	7		3				11			9							
18		8	MANCHESTER CITY	2-0	Cock, Pape	12000		2		4	5				9	10	11	3					6	7		8	1					
19		15	Bolton Wanderers	1-7	Cock	16000		2		4					9	10	11	3					6	7		8	1	5				
20		22	BOLTON WANDERERS	1-1	Cock	10000	1	2	3			6			9	10	11						4	7		8		5				
21		26	ARSENAL	1-2	Cock	14000	1		2		5	6			9	10						11	4	7	8							
22		27	Arsenal	0-0		16000	1		2		5	6	8		9	10	11	3		7			4									
23		29	Sunderland	1-1	Cope	8000	1		2		5	6	8		9	10	11	3		7			4									
24	Jan	1	Blackburn Rovers	1-4	Daly	18000	1		2		5	6	8		9	10	11	3		7			4									
25		5	SUNDERLAND	1-2	Cooper	16000	1	2	3		5	6	8		9	10	11			7			4									
26		19	PRESTON NORTH END	0-0		12000		2	3		5	6	8		9		11			7									1	10	4	
27		26	Preston North End	1-2	Hill	12000		2	3	4	5	6	8		9	10	11			7										1		
28	Feb	9	Chelsea	6-0	Widdowson 2, Price 2, Davis 2	15000	1	2		4	5	6					11	3		7			8		9						10	
29		16	NEWCASTLE UNITED	1-0	Platts	14000	1	2		4	5	6	8				11	3					7		9						10	
30	Mar	1	WEST HAM UNITED	1-1	Widdowson	10000	1		3	4	5	6					11					8	7		9						10	2
31		5	CHELSEA	0-0		8000	1	2	3	4	5	6					11					7	8		9						10	
32		8	West Ham United	1-1	Widdowson	20000	1		3	4	5	6	8				11						7		9						10	2
33		15	Cardiff City	2-0	Davis, Blair(og)	18000	1		3	4	5	6			9		11	2		7					8						10	
34		19	Newcastle United	2-1	Cock, Davis	10000	1		3	4	5	6			9		11	2		7					8						10	
35		22	CARDIFF CITY	1-0	Davis	20000	1	2	3	4	5	6			9					7		11			8						10	
36	Apr	5	SHEFFIELD UNITED	0-2		15000	1	2	3	4	5	6			9		11			7					8						10	
37		7	Sheffield United	1-3	Davis	11000	1	2		4	5	6			9			3		7		11			8						10	
38		12	West Bromwich Alb.	0-5		8003	1	2	3		5	6	8						4	7		11			9						10	
39		18	BLACKBURN ROVERS	3-0	Hill 2, Widdowson	16000		2	3		5	6				8	11			7		4			9				1		10	
40		19	WEST BROMWICH ALB.	1-0	Davis	20000		2	3		5	6				8				7		11	4		9				1		10	
41		26	Liverpool	0-1		15000		2	3	4	5	6				8	11			7					9				1		10	
42	May	3	LIVERPOOL	1-2	Widdowson	20000		2		4	5	6				8	11	3					7		9				1		10	
			Apps				34	33	32	26	40	38	25	3	32	30	24	17	5	26	11	14	17	4	16	6	8	2	1	1	15	2
			Goals						1				3	1	11	8	2			1			1		6	2					7	

F.A. Cup

	Date	Opponent	Score	Scorers	Att	Iremonger A	Ashurst W	Cope HW	Flint WA	Dinsdale N	Kemp H	Cooper J	Mackay JA	Cock DJ	Hill H	Price LP	Cornwell R	McPherson L	Daly J	Barry LJ	Wren JE	Platts R	Cook J	Widdowson Alf	Pape A	Streets GH	Fenwick R	Allen H	Harris G	Davis AG	Smith WA
R1	Jan 12	Queens Park Rangers	2-1	Pape, Price	13000	1	2	3		5	6	8				10	11		7		4			9							
R2	Feb 2	Crystal Palace	0-0		19500	1	2		4	5	6	8		9	11		3		7						10						
rep	Feb 6	CRYSTAL PALACE	0-0		20600	1	2		4	5	6			10	11	2			7					8	9						
r2	Feb 11	Crystal Palace	0-0		16440	1	2		4	5	6			10	11	2			7					8	9						
r3	Feb 18	Crystal Palace	1-2	Widdowson	10259	1	2		4	5	6			9	10	11	2					7		8							

R2 replay and replay 2 after extra time. Replays 2 and 3 at Villa Park

		P	W	D	L	F	A	W	D	L	F	A	Pts
1	Huddersfield Town	42	15	5	1	35	9	8	6	7	25	24	57
2	Cardiff City	42	14	5	2	35	13	8	8	5	26	21	57
3	Sunderland	42	12	7	2	38	20	10	2	9	33	34	53
4	Bolton Wanderers	42	13	6	2	45	13	5	8	8	23	21	50
5	Sheffield United	42	12	5	4	39	16	7	7	7	30	33	50
6	Aston Villa	42	10	10	1	33	11	8	3	10	19	26	49
7	Everton	42	13	7	1	43	18	5	6	10	19	35	49
8	Blackburn Rovers	42	14	5	2	40	13	3	6	12	14	37	45
9	Newcastle United	42	13	5	3	40	21	4	5	12	20	33	44
10	NOTTS COUNTY	42	9	7	5	21	15	5	7	9	23	34	42
11	Manchester City	42	11	7	3	34	24	4	5	12	20	47	42
12	Liverpool	42	11	5	5	35	20	4	6	11	14	28	41
13	West Ham United	42	10	6	5	26	17	3	9	9	14	26	41
14	Birmingham	42	10	4	7	25	19	3	9	9	16	30	39
15	Tottenham Hotspur	42	9	6	6	30	22	3	8	10	20	34	38
16	West Bromwich Alb.	42	10	6	5	43	30	2	8	11	8	32	38
17	Burnley	42	10	5	6	39	27	2	7	12	16	33	36
18	Preston North End	42	8	4	9	34	27	4	6	11	18	40	34
19	Arsenal	42	8	5	8	25	24	4	4	13	15	39	33
20	Nottingham Forest	42	7	9	5	19	15	3	3	15	23	49	32
21	Chelsea	42	7	9	5	23	21	2	5	14	8	32	32
22	Middlesbrough	42	6	4	11	23	23	1	4	16	14	37	22

1924/25 9th in Division One

#		Date	Opponent	Score	Scorers	Att	Iremonger A	Ashurst W	Cope HW	Flint WA	Dinsdale N	Kemp H	Daly J	Widdowson, Alf	Cock DJ	Davis AG	Barry LJ	Wren JE	Hill H	Greatorex L	Cornwell R	Streets GH	Mitchell M	Platts R	Fenwick R	Keeling P	Hills WJ	Smith WA	Staniforth C	Smith G	Hilton F
1	Aug	30	West Bromwich Alb.	2-1	Daly, Davis	21572	1	2	3	4	5	6	7	8	9	10	11														
2	Sep	1	LEEDS UNITED	1-0	Widdowson	16000	1	2	3	4	5	6	7	8	9	10	11														
3		6	TOTTENHAM HOTSPUR	0-0		20000	1	2	3	4	5		7		9	10	11	6	8												
4		10	Leeds United	1-1	Cope	18000	1	2	3	4			7	8		10	11	6		9											
5		13	Bolton Wanderers	0-1		15000	1		3	4	5		7	8		10	11	6		9	2										
6		15	Birmingham	0-1		20000			3	4	5	6	7	8	9	10	11						2	1							
7		20	NOTTM. FOREST	0-0		25000		2	3	4	5	6	7		9	10	11		8					1							
8		27	EVERTON	3-1	Hill, Barry, Davis	12000	1	2	3	4	5	6	7		9	10	11		8												
9	Oct	4	Sunderland	1-0	Davis	25000	1	2	3	4	5	6	7	8	9	10	11														
10		11	CARDIFF CITY	3-0	Cope(p), Cock, Widdowson	20000	1	2	3		5	6	7	8	9	10	11					4									
11		18	Preston North End	1-0	Barry	15000	1	2			5	6	7	8	9	10	11				3	4									
12		25	Bury	1-2	Cock	20000	1	2		4	5	6	7	8	9	10	11				3										
13	Nov	1	MANCHESTER CITY	2-0	Cock, Barry	12000		2		4	5	6	7	8	9	10	11				3		1								
14		8	Arsenal	1-0	Cock	35000		2		4	5	6	7	8	9	10	11				3		1								
15		15	ASTON VILLA	0-0		25000		2	3	4	5	6	7	8	9	10	11						1								
16		22	Huddersfield T	0-0		12300		2			5	6	7	8	9	10	11			4	3		1								
17		29	BLACKBURN ROVERS	0-0		15000		2			5	6	7	8		10	11			4	3		1		9						
18	Dec	6	West Ham United	0-3		18000	1	2		4	5		7		9	10	11	6			3				8						
19		13	SHEFFIELD UNITED	2-0	Cock 2	12000	1	2	3	4	5			8	9		11	6			10			7							
20		20	Newcastle United	0-1		20000	1	2		4	5	6		8	9	10	11				3			7							
21		25	LIVERPOOL	1-2	Davis	18000	1	2		4	5	6		8	9	10	11				3			7							
22		26	Liverpool	0-1		30000		2		4		6			9	10	11				3		1			5	7	8			
23		27	WEST BROMWICH ALB.	0-2		12000	1				5	6			9	10	11			8	3			4	7				2		
24	Jan	3	Tottenham Hotspur	1-1	Platts	30000	1	2			5	6			9	10	11				3		4	7					8		
25		17	BOLTON WANDERERS	0-1		14000	1	2	3		5	6			9	10	11						4	7					8		
26		24	Nottm. Forest	0-0		15000	1	2	3		5	6	7		9	10	11												8		
27	Feb	7	SUNDERLAND	4-1	Widdowson, Cock 2, Davis	16000	1	2	3	4	5	6	7	8	9	10	11														
28		14	Cardiff City	1-1	Davis	25000	1	2		4	5	6	7	8		10	11				3								9		
29		28	BURY	1-1	Dinsdale	9000	1		3	4	5		7	8		10	11	6											9	2	
30	Mar	7	Manchester City	1-2	Barry	25000	1		3	4	5	6		8		10	11									7			9	2	
31		14	ARSENAL	2-1	Staniforth, Widdowson	12000	1	2	3	4	5	6		8	9		11									7			10		
32		18	Everton	0-1		25000		2	3						9	10	11	6		4			1			7			8		5
33		21	Aston Villa	0-0		15000	1				5	6		8	9		11			4	3					7			10	2	
34	Apr	1	PRESTON NORTH END	1-0	Widdowson	4000	1		3	4	5	6		8	9		11									7			10	2	
35		4	Blackburn Rovers	2-0	Widdowson, Davis	8000	1		3	4	5	6	7		9	10	11												8	2	
36		10	Burnley	1-1	Staniforth	17000	1		3	4		6	7		9	10	11												8	2	5
37		11	WEST HAM UNITED	4-1	Widdowson 2, Davis, Flint	10000			3	4	5	6	7		9	10	11						1						8	2	
38		13	BURNLEY	2-0	Widdowson, Davis	8000	1		3	4	5	6	7		9	10	11												8	2	
39		18	Sheffield United	0-2		15000	1		3	4	5	6	7		9	10	11												8	2	
40		25	NEWCASTLE UNITED	2-0	Davis, Widdowson	7000	1	2	3	4	5	6	7		9	10	11												8		
41		29	HUDDERSFIELD T	1-1	Kemp	8000	1	2	3	4	5	6	7		9	10	11												8		
42	May	2	BIRMINGHAM	0-1		8000	1	2	3		5	6	7		9	10	11	4											8		
			Apps				32	30	28	31	39	35	30	39	20	41	42	11	3	4	16	10	5	8	1	6	1	1	18	9	2
			Goals						2	1	1	1	1	10	8	10	4		1					1					2		

F.A. Cup

#		Date	Opponent	Score	Scorers	Att	Iremonger A	Ashurst W	Cope HW	Flint WA	Dinsdale N	Kemp H	Daly J	Widdowson, Alf	Cock DJ	Davis AG	Barry LJ	Wren JE	Hill H	Greatorex L	Cornwell R	Streets GH	Mitchell M	Platts R	Fenwick R	Keeling P	Hills WJ	Smith WA	Staniforth C	Smith G	Hilton F
R1	Jan	10	Coventry City	2-0	Cock, Davis	21736		2	3		5	6		8	9	10	11	4					1	7							
R2	Jan	31	NORWICH CITY	4-0	Davis 2, Cock, Barry	21061	1	2	3	4	5	6	7	8	9	10	11														
R3	Feb	21	CARDIFF CITY	0-2		39000	1	2	3	4	5	6	7	8	9	10	11														

		P	W	D	L	F	A	W	D	L	F	A	Pts
1	Huddersfield Town	42	10	8	3	31	10	11	8	2	38	18	58
2	West Bromwich Alb.	42	13	6	2	40	17	10	4	7	18	17	56
3	Bolton Wanderers	42	18	2	1	61	13	4	9	8	15	21	55
4	Liverpool	42	13	5	3	43	20	7	5	9	20	35	50
5	Bury	42	13	4	4	35	20	4	11	6	19	31	49
6	Newcastle United	42	11	6	4	43	18	5	10	6	18	24	49
7	Sunderland	42	13	6	2	39	14	6	4	11	25	37	48
8	Birmingham	42	10	8	3	27	17	7	4	10	22	36	46
9	NOTTS COUNTY	42	11	6	4	29	12	5	7	9	13	19	45
10	Manchester City	42	11	7	3	44	29	6	2	13	32	39	43
11	Cardiff City	42	11	5	5	35	19	5	6	10	21	32	43
12	Tottenham Hotspur	42	9	8	4	32	16	6	4	11	20	27	42
13	West Ham United	42	12	7	2	37	12	3	5	13	25	48	42
14	Sheffield United	42	10	5	6	34	25	3	8	10	21	38	39
15	Aston Villa	42	10	7	4	34	25	3	6	12	24	46	39
16	Blackburn Rovers	42	7	6	8	31	26	4	7	10	22	40	35
17	Everton	42	11	4	6	25	20	1	7	13	15	40	35
18	Leeds United	42	9	8	4	29	17	2	4	15	17	42	34
19	Burnley	42	7	8	6	28	31	4	4	13	18	44	34
20	Arsenal	42	12	3	6	33	17	2	2	17	13	41	33
21	Preston North End	42	8	2	11	29	35	2	4	15	8	39	26
22	Nottingham Forest	42	5	6	10	17	23	1	6	14	12	42	24

- 1924/25 Season -

Back: Fisher (Sec.Manager), Wren, J.Iremonger(Trainer), Ashurst, Dinsdale, A.Iremonger, Price, McLean (Asst. Trainer)
Middle: Davis, Barry, Hill, Flint, Kemp, Widdowson, Cornwell, Cope
Front: Platts, Daly, Cock

- 1925/26 Season -

Back: Cope, Cornwell, W.Smith, Wren, Price, Dinsdale, Davis, Allen
Middle: Taylor, Mitchell, Flint, Dukes, Crapper, Kemp, Barry, Staniforth
Front: Hills

1925/26 22nd in Division One (Relegated)

#	Date	Opponent	Res	Scorers	Att	Iremonger A	Cornwell R	Cope HW	Flint WA	Dinsdale N	Kemp H	Daly J	Staniforth C	Widdowson Alf	Davis AG	Barry LJ	Streets GH	Taylor GT	Hilton F	Ashurst W	Wren JE	Smith WA	Sullivan JA	Harris N	Smith G	Kelly P	Mills BR	Price LP
1	Aug 29	LEEDS UNITED	1-0	Davis	18155	1	2	3	4	5	6	7	8	9	10	11												
2	Sep 2	Liverpool	0-2		19616		2	3	4	5	6	7	8	9	10	11	1											
3	Sep 5	Newcastle United	3-6	Widdowson, Staniforth 2	33264	1	2	3	4	5	6		8	9	10	11		7										
4	Sep 7	Burnley	0-0		13561	1	2	3	4	5			8	9	10	11		7	6									
5	Sep 12	BOLTON WANDERERS	3-0	Staniforth 2, Widdowson	18587	1		3		5			8	9	10	11		7	4	2	6							
6	Sep 19	Birmingham	1-0	Staniforth	3977	1		3		5			8	9	10	11		7	6	2	4							
7	Sep 21	BURNLEY	0-1		8363	1		3		5			8	9	10	11		7	6	2	4							
8	Sep 26	Aston Villa	1-2	Widdowson	22382	1		3		5	4		8	9	10	11		7	6	2								
9	Oct 1	LIVERPOOL	1-2	Widdowson	9802	1		3		5			8	9	10	11		7	6	2								
10	Oct 3	LEICESTER CITY	2-2	Davis, Newton(og)	34508	1		3	4	5			8	9	10	11		7	6	2								
11	Oct 10	West Ham United	0-1		21401	1		3		5	4		8	9	10	11		7	6	2								
12	Oct 17	BURY	4-1	Widdowson 2, Davis, Cope(p)	15312	1		3		5	4		8	9	10	11		7	6	2								
13	Oct 24	Blackburn Rovers	1-4	Davis	10096	1		3		5	4		8		10	11		7	6	2			9					
14	Oct 31	SHEFFIELD UNITED	2-0	Sullivan 2	13343	1		3	4	5			8		10	11		7	6	2			9					
15	Nov 7	West Bromwich Alb.	4-4	Sullivan 3, Davis	17186	1		3	4	5			8		10	11		7	6	2			9					
16	Nov 14	EVERTON	0-3		14962	1		3	4	5					10	11		7	6	2			9	8				
17	Nov 21	Manchester City	1-1	Davis	16837	1			4	5				9	10	11		7	6	2		3		8				
18	Nov 28	TOTTENHAM HOTSPUR	4-2	Davis 3, Harris	12191	1			4	5				9	10	11		7	6	2		3		8				
19	Dec 5	Cardiff City	1-2	Davis	17856	1			4	5				9	10			7	6	2		3		8				11
20	Dec 12	SUNDERLAND	2-0	Widdowson, Dinsdale	20583	1		3	4	5				9	10	11		7	6	2				8				
21	Dec 19	Huddersfield T	0-2		7972	1		3	4	5				9	10	11		7	6	2				8				
22	Dec 25	Arsenal	0-3		33398	1		3	4	5				9	10	11		7	6	2				8				
23	Dec 26	ARSENAL	4-1	Harris 4	32045	1		3	4	5				9	10	11		7	6	2				8				
24	Jan 2	Leeds United	1-2	Harris	14615	1		3		5	4				10	11		7	6	2				8	9			
25	Jan 16	NEWCASTLE UNITED	1-3	Sullivan	10700	1				5	4	7			10	11			6			3	9	8	2			
26	Jan 23	Bolton Wanderers	1-2	Sullivan	15507	1			4	5		7			10	11			6			3	9	8	2			
27	Feb 6	ASTON VILLA	1-0	Flint	18426	1			4	5	6				10	11		7				3	9	8	2			
28	Feb 13	Leicester City	0-1		30938	1			4	5	6			9	10	11		7				3		8	2			
29	Feb 27	Bury	1-3	Kelly	14480			3	4	5	6				10	11	1	7					9		2	8		
30	Mar 3	BIRMINGHAM	3-0	Barry, Harris, Kelly	8131				4	5	6				10	11	1	7				3	9			8		
31	Mar 6	BLACKBURN ROVERS	1-1	Cope	10658			3	4	5	6				10	11	1	7				2	9			8		
32	Mar 13	Sheffield United	0-3		16507			3	4	5	6				10	11	1	7				2	9			8		
33	Mar 20	WEST BROMWICH ALB.	0-0		14888	1		3		5	6				10	11		7			4				2	8	9	
34	Mar 22	WEST HAM UNITED	1-1	Mills	4278	1		3		5	6				10	11		7			4				2	8	9	
35	Mar 27	Everton	1-1		16877	1		3		5	6				10	11		7			4				2	8	9	
36	Apr 2	MANCHESTER UTD.	0-3		18453	1				5	4	7		9	10	11			6			3		8	2			
37	Apr 3	MANCHESTER CITY	1-0	Daly	16266	1					4	7			10	11			5	6	3			8	2	9		
38	Apr 5	Manchester Utd.	1-0	Smith W(p)	19606	1					4	7			10	11			5	6		3		8	2	9		
39	Apr 10	Tottenham Hotspur	0-4		17892	1			4		6			9	10	11		7	5			3			2	8		
40	Apr 17	CARDIFF CITY	2-4	Staniforth, Davis	8712	1			4		6		8	9	10	11		7	5			3			2	8		
41	Apr 24	Sunderland	1-3	Taylor	8262	1				5	6			9		11				4	3			8	2	10		
42	May 1	HUDDERSFIELD T	4-2	Davis 3, Daly	4715	1				5	4	7		9	10	11			6			3			2	8		
		Apps				34	9	23	23	39	27	7	21	20	36	41	8	35	29	19	9	17	9	22	16	14	3	1
		Goals						2	1	1		2	6	7	14	1		1				1	7	7		2	1	

One Own Goal

F.A. Cup

#	Date	Opponent	Res	Scorers	Att	Iremonger A	Cornwell R	Cope HW	Flint WA	Dinsdale N	Kemp H	Daly J	Staniforth C	Widdowson Alf	Davis AG	Barry LJ	Streets GH	Taylor GT	Hilton F	Ashurst W	Wren JE	Smith WA	Sullivan JA	Harris N	Smith G	Kelly P	Mills BR	Price LP
R3	Jan 9	LEICESTER CITY	2-0	Widdowson, Taylor	33495	1				5	4			9	10	11		7	6	2		3		8				
R4	Jan 30	NEW BRIGHTON	2-0	Harris 2	18944	1			4	5	6				10	11		7				3	9	8				
R5	Feb 20	FULHAM	0-1		33000	1			4	5					10	11		7	6			3	9	8	2			

First and Second Division Clubs exempt to R3
Played in game 2: WJ Hills (at no. 2)

Division One final table

		P	W	D	L	F	A	W	D	L	F	A	Pts
1	Huddersfield Town	42	14	6	1	50	17	9	5	7	42	43	57
2	Arsenal	42	16	2	3	57	19	6	6	9	30	44	52
3	Sunderland	42	17	2	2	67	30	4	4	13	29	50	48
4	Bury	42	12	4	5	55	34	8	3	10	30	43	47
5	Sheffield United	42	15	3	3	72	29	4	5	12	30	53	46
6	Aston Villa	42	12	7	2	56	25	4	5	12	30	51	44
7	Liverpool	42	9	8	4	43	27	5	8	8	27	36	44
8	Bolton Wanderers	42	11	6	4	46	31	6	4	11	29	45	44
9	Manchester United	42	12	4	5	40	26	7	2	12	26	47	44
10	Newcastle United	42	13	3	5	59	33	3	7	11	25	42	42
11	Everton	42	9	9	3	42	26	3	9	9	30	44	42
12	Blackburn Rovers	42	11	6	4	59	33	4	5	12	32	47	41
13	West Bromwich Alb.	42	13	5	3	59	29	3	3	15	20	49	40
14	Birmingham	42	14	2	5	35	25	2	6	13	31	56	40
15	Tottenham Hotspur	42	11	4	6	45	36	4	5	12	21	43	39
16	Cardiff City	42	8	5	8	30	25	8	2	11	31	51	39
17	Leicester City	42	11	3	7	42	32	3	7	11	28	48	38
18	West Ham United	42	14	2	5	45	27	1	5	15	18	49	37
19	Leeds United	42	11	5	5	38	28	3	3	15	26	48	36
20	Burnley	42	7	7	7	43	35	6	3	12	42	73	36
21	Manchester City	42	8	7	6	48	42	4	4	13	41	58	35
22	NOTTS COUNTY	42	11	4	6	37	26	2	3	16	17	48	33

1926/27　16th in Division Two

No	Date	Opponent	Score	Scorers	Att	Streets GH	Ashurst W	Smith WA	Widdowson Alf	Dinsdale N	Hilton F	Daly J	Mills BR	Sullivan JA	Davis AG	Barry LJ	Kemp H	Kelly P	Harris N	Smith G	Bisby CC	Price LP	Hills WJ	Cope HW	Stevenson AE	Hopkins GH	Stokes A	Plackett S	Taylor GT	Hillhouse JT	Goucher GH
1	Aug 28	South Shields	0-5		6835	1	2	3	4	5	6	7	8	9	10	11															
2	30	Preston North End	1-4	Mills	15289	1	2	3	4	5	6	7	8	9	10	11															
3	Sep 4	HULL CITY	1-0	W Smith	9629	1	2	3		5	4		7		9			10	11	6	8										
4	6	Chelsea	0-2		15572	1	2	3		5	4		7		9			10	11	6	8										
5	11	Wolverhampton Wand.	1-0	Harris	14390	1	2	3		5	4		8					10	11	6	7	9									
6	13	CHELSEA	5-0	Barry, W Smith(p), Harris, Mills, Davis	9094	1	2	3		5	4		8					10	11	6	7	9									
7	18	NOTTM. FOREST	1-2	Harris	18539	1	2	3		5	4		8					10	11	6	7	9									
8	25	CLAPTON ORIENT	3-1	Harris, Davis 2	8804	1	2	3		5			8					10	11	6	7	9			4						
9	Oct 2	Middlesbrough	2-4	Davis, W Smith	15386	1	2	3		5			8					10	11	6	7	9			4						
10	9	PORT VALE	2-1	Kelly, Harris	11838	1	2	3		5			8					10	11	6	7	9			4						
11	16	Reading	1-7	Dinsdale	12936	1	2		4	5			8					10	11	6	7	9			3						
12	23	SWANSEA TOWN	1-3	Davis	11634	1	2	3		5			8		10			6	11	4	9				7						
13	30	Barnsley	4-4	Davis 4	4671	1	2		9	5		7	4		10		6		11		8				3						
14	Nov 6	MANCHESTER CITY	1-0	Sullivan(p)	5953	1	2			5		7	4	9	10		6		11		8				3						
15	13	Darlington	2-4	Davis, Barry	5038	1	2			5		7	4	9	10		6		11		8				3						
16	20	PORTSMOUTH	2-3	Harris, Kelly	7974	1	2		9	5			4		10				11	7	8		6		3						
17	27	Oldham Athletic	2-5	Harris, Davis	11886	1			9	5			4		10				11	7	8	2	6		3						
18	Dec 4	FULHAM	4-0	Harris 2, Kelly 2	9486	1				5	6	7	4		10				11	8	9		3		2						
19	18	BLACKPOOL	2-3	Davis, Harris	8108	1				5	6	7	4		10				11	8	9	2	3								
20	25	SOUTHAMPTON	0-1		11373	1				5			4	9	10	11				6	8	9	2	3							
21	27	Southampton	0-2		19120	1		3		5		7	4				6	8	9		2		11		10						
22	Jan 1	PRESTON NORTH END	1-1	Widdowson	10006	1		3	9	5	6		10			4		7	8		2		11								
23	15	SOUTH SHIELDS	4-1	Harris 2, Mills, Kelly	8717	1	2			5	6		9		10	11	4	7	8		3							1			
24	22	Hull City	0-2		8891	1		3		5	6		9		10	11	4	7	8	2								1			
25	29	Grimsby Town	4-1	Widdowson 2, Kelly, Harris	9347	1		2	9	5	6				10	11		7	8		3							1	4		
26	Feb 5	Nottm. Forest	0-2		25518	1		2	9	5	4				10	11	6	7	8		3							1			
27	9	WOLVERHAMPTON W.	2-2	Kelly, Harris	5106	1		2	9						10	11	6	7	8		3							1	4		
28	12	Clapton Orient	1-2	Davis	10846	1		2		5					10	11	4	8	9		3							1		6	7
29	23	MIDDLESBROUGH	2-2	Harris, Barry	12042	1		2		5					10	11		8	9		3									6	7
30	26	Port Vale	2-6	Davis, Barry	9638	1				5		4			10	11		8	9	2	3									6	7
31	Mar 12	Swansea Town	1-0	Taylor	13026	1				5	4		9	10		11		8		2	3								6	7	
32	16	READING	2-0	Kelly, Sullivan	8880	1				5	4		9	10		11		8		2	3								6	7	
33	19	BARNSLEY	1-1	Sullivan	15327	1				5	4		9		10	11		8		2	3								6	7	
34	26	Manchester City	1-4	Widdowson	17242	1			9	5	4					11		8	10	2	3								6	7	
35	Apr 2	DARLINGTON	3-1	Davis 2, Kelly	8138	1			9	5	4				10	11		8		2	3								6	7	
36	9	Portsmouth	1-9	Kelly	15768	1				5					10			8		2	3	11				9			6	7	4
37	16	OLDHAM ATHLETIC	1-2	Price(p)	8497	1				5	4				10			8	9	2	3	11							6	7	
38	18	BRADFORD CITY	4-0	Kelly 2, Daly, Harris	7988	1			10	5	4	7						8	9	2	3	11							6		
39	19	Bradford City	2-1	Kelly, Price(p)	13046	1			10	5		7						8	9	2	3	11							6		4
40	23	Fulham	0-3		12643	1			10	5		7						8		2	3	11				9			6		4
41	30	GRIMSBY TOWN	3-0	Barry, Kelly, Widdowson	9196	1			10	5	4			9		11	6	8			3							1		7	
42	May 7	Blackpool	0-5		5651	1			10	5				9		11	6	8			3							1		7	2

	Streets GH	Ashurst W	Smith WA	Widdowson Alf	Dinsdale N	Hilton F	Daly J	Mills BR	Sullivan JA	Davis AG	Barry LJ	Kemp H	Kelly P	Harris N	Smith G	Bisby CC	Price LP	Hills WJ	Cope HW	Stevenson AE	Hopkins GH	Stokes A	Plackett S	Taylor GT	Hillhouse JT	Goucher GH
Apps	34	16	21	17	38	26	13	27	11	32	35	22	40	27	20	28	8	2	1	3	8	2	14	12	4	1
Goals			3	5	1		1	3	3	16	5		14	16		2								1		

F.A. Cup

Rd	Date	Opponent	Score	Scorers	Att	Streets GH	Ashurst W	Smith WA	Widdowson Alf	Dinsdale N	Hilton F	Daly J	Mills BR	Sullivan JA	Davis AG	Barry LJ	Kemp H	Kelly P	Harris N	Smith G	Bisby CC	Price LP
R3	Jan 8	Newcastle United	1-8	Widdowson	32564	1		3	9	5	6	7	10			11		4	8			2

		P	W	D	L	F	A	W	D	L	F	A	Pts
1	Middlesbrough	42	18	2	1	78	23	9	6	6	44	37	62
2	Portsmouth	42	14	4	3	58	17	9	4	8	29	32	54
3	Manchester City	42	15	3	3	65	23	7	7	7	43	38	54
4	Chelsea	42	13	7	1	40	17	7	5	9	22	35	52
5	Nottingham Forest	42	14	6	1	57	23	4	8	9	23	32	50
6	Preston North End	42	14	4	3	54	29	6	5	10	20	43	49
7	Hull City	42	13	4	4	43	19	7	3	11	20	33	47
8	Port Vale	42	11	6	4	50	26	5	7	9	38	52	45
9	Blackpool	42	13	5	3	65	26	5	3	13	30	54	44
10	Oldham Athletic	42	12	3	6	50	37	7	3	11	24	47	44
11	Barnsley	42	13	5	3	56	23	4	4	13	32	64	43
12	Swansea Town	42	13	5	3	44	21	3	6	12	24	51	43
13	Southampton	42	9	8	4	35	22	6	4	11	25	40	42
14	Reading	42	14	1	6	47	20	2	7	12	17	52	40
15	Wolverhampton Wan.	42	10	4	7	54	30	4	3	14	19	45	35
16	NOTTS COUNTY	42	11	4	6	45	24	1	1	16	25	72	35
17	Grimsby Town	42	6	7	8	39	39	5	5	11	35	52	34
18	Fulham	42	11	4	6	39	31	2	4	15	19	61	34
19	South Shields	42	10	8	3	49	25	1	3	17	22	71	33
20	Clapton Orient	42	9	3	9	37	35	3	4	14	23	61	31
21	Darlington	42	10	3	8	53	42	2	3	16	26	56	30
22	Bradford City	42	6	4	11	30	28	1	5	15	20	60	23

- 1926/27 Season -

Back: W.A.Smith, Ashurst, Hilton, Streets, Price, Lowe, Dinsdale, Hyde
Middle: Kemp, Widdowson, Green, Hills, Stevenson, Bisby, G.Smith, Daly
Front: Rhodes, Barry, Davis, Harris, B.B.Mills, Kelly

- 1927/28 Season -

Back: Stevenson, Davis, Stokes, Hopkins, McLean (Asst. Trainer), Hyde, Chamberlain, Price
Standing: Mellors (Trainer), P.C.Mills, Wise, Widdowson, Gibbons, Kemp, Goucher, C.Smith
Sitting: Hilton, Plackett, Bisby, Staniforth, G.Smith, Taylor
Front: B.B.Mills, Dinsdale, Kelly

1927/28 15th in Division Two

#	Date		Opponent	Score	Scorers	Att	Hopkins GH	Smith G	Bisby CC	Hilton F	Dinsdale N	Plackett S	Kelly P	Mills BR	Staniforth C	Davis AG	Barry LJ	Taylor GT	Widdowson Alf	Gibson H	Andrews H	Connell A	Davies W	Fenner T	Ferguson JS	Froggatt F	Haden S	Kemp H	Matthews CH	Mills PC	Stokes A	Streets GH
1	Aug	27	BRISTOL CITY	1-2	Staniforth	15302	1	2	3	4	5	6	7	8	9	10	11															
2	Sep	3	Stoke City	0-3		22236	1	2	3	5		6	8	4	9		11	7	10													
3		7	Chelsea	0-5		18416	1	2	3	5		6	8	4	9		11	7	10													
4		10	SOUTHAMPTON	0-0		9673	1	2	3	5		6		8			11		10	7											4	
5		17	Nottm. Forest	1-2	BR Mills	21957	1	2	3	5		6	8	9	10		11	7									4					
6		24	Oldham Athletic	0-0		12417	1	2	3	5		6		9	10	8	11	7									4					
7	Oct	1	GRIMSBY TOWN	3-2	Davis 2, Staniforth	7174	1	2	3	5		6		9	10	8		7									4					
8		6	CHELSEA	0-1		9127	1	2	3	5		6	8	9	10			7									11	4				
9		8	Reading	2-2	BR Mills, Staniforth	11978	1	2	3	5		6	8	9	10			7									11	4				
10		15	BLACKPOOL	3-1	Taylor, Davis, Staniforth	11885	1	2	3	5		6	8	9	10			7									11	4				
11		22	PORT VALE	2-4	Connell, Staniforth	9053	1	2	3	5		6		9	10			7				8					11	4				
12		29	South Shields	3-2	Staniforth 2, Kelly	6379		2	3	6	5		8		9	10		7									11	4				1
13	Nov	5	LEEDS UNITED	2-2	Staniforth, Hilton(p)	9866		2	3	6	5		8		9	10		7									11	4				1
14		12	Wolverhampton Wand.	2-2	Davis, Kelly	16100		2	3	6	5		8		9	10		7									11	4				1
15		19	BARNSLEY	9-0	BR Mills 5, Staniforth 3, Haden	9382		2	3	6				9	8	10		7								5	11	4				1
16		26	Preston North End	0-4		16041		2	3	6				9	8	10		7								5	11	4				1
17	Dec	3	SWANSEA TOWN	2-0	Taylor, BR Mills	11618		2	3	6				9	8	10		7								5	11	4				1
18		10	Fulham	1-2	Staniforth	11562		2	3	6				9	8	10		7								5	11				4	1
19		17	HULL CITY	1-1	BR Mills	8758		2	3	6				9	8	10		7								5	11	4				1
20		24	Manchester City	1-3	BR Mills	18362		2	3	6				9				7	10			8				5	11	4				1
21		26	West Bromwich Alb.	2-2	BR Mills, Kemp	14642	1	2	3	6				9				7	10			8				5	11	4				
22		27	WEST BROMWICH ALB.	3-0	Widdowson 2, BR Mills	17755		2	3	6		4		9				7	10			8				5	11					1
23		31	Bristol City	2-1	BR Mills 2	6476		2	3	6				9	8			7	10							5	11	4				1
24	Jan	7	STOKE CITY	1-2	Haden	13365		2	3	6				9	8			7	10							5	11	4				1
25		21	Southampton	1-5	BR Mills	10002	1	2	3	6	5			9				7	8								11	4				
26	Feb	4	OLDHAM ATHLETIC	2-1	Kemp, Kelly	8678	1	2	3	6			8	9				7	10							5	11	4				
27		11	Grimsby Town	0-1		7666	1	2	3	6			8	9		10		7								5	11	4				
28		18	READING	1-1	Fenner	8034	1	2	3	6				9	10					7				8		5	11	4				
29		22	NOTTM. FOREST	1-2	BR Mills	13241	1	2	3	6				9	10			7						8		5	11	4				
30		25	Blackpool	3-3	BR Mills, Staniforth 2	9423	1	2	3	6				9	10					7				8		5	11	4				
31	Mar	3	Port Vale	0-3		9644	1	2	3	5		6		9	10									8			7	4				
32		10	SOUTH SHIELDS	4-1	BR Mills 2, Hilton(p), Taylor	8117	1	2	3	6				9	10						8			7		5	11	4				
33		17	Leeds United	0-6		17643		2	3	6				9	10								7		1		5	11	4	8		
34		24	WOLVERHAMPTON W.	1-2	Haden	13617		2	3	6				9					8				11		1		5	10	4	7		
35		31	Barnsley	0-0		5619			3	5		6	8	9							10				1	7	11				2	4
36	Apr	6	CLAPTON ORIENT	3-0	BR Mills, Haden, Hilton(p)	13924			3	5		6	8	9							10				1	7	11				2	4
37		7	PRESTON NORTH END	6-2	Davies 2, Taylor 3, Haden	16226			3			6	8					9			10		7		1		5	11			2	4
38		9	Clapton Orient	1-0	Taylor	10166		2	3			6	8					9			10		7		1		5	11				4
39		14	Swansea Town	1-1	Taylor	11566		2	3			6	8					9			10		7		1		5	11				4
40		21	FULHAM	0-1		7655		2	3			6	8					9			10		7		1		5	11				4
41		28	Hull City	1-1	Wilson(og)	5284		2	3	4		6						9			10		7	8	1		5	11				
42	May	5	MANCHESTER CITY	2-1	Fenner, Taylor	9907			3	4		6						9			10		7	8	1		5	11			2	

LP Price played in games 7 (at 11) and 31 (11).
JA Sullivan played in games 4 (at 9) and 25 (10).

	Hopkins GH	Smith G	Bisby CC	Hilton F	Dinsdale N	Plackett S	Kelly P	Mills BR	Staniforth C	Davis AG	Barry LJ	Taylor GT	Widdowson Alf	Gibson H	Andrews H	Connell A	Davies W	Fenner T	Ferguson JS	Froggatt F	Haden S	Kemp H	Matthews CH	Mills PC	Stokes A	Streets GH
Apps	20	38	42	38	5	21	15	31	27	16	6	34	10	3	8	4	9	7	10	24	35	28	3	4	8	12
Goals				3			3	20	14	4		9	2			1	2	2			5	2				

One own goal

F.A. Cup

	Date		Opponent	Score	Scorers	Att	Hopkins GH	Smith G	Bisby CC	Hilton F	Dinsdale N	Plackett S	Kelly P	Mills BR	Staniforth C	Davis AG	Barry LJ	Taylor GT	Widdowson Alf	Gibson H	Andrews H	Connell A	Davies W	Fenner T	Ferguson JS	Froggatt F	Haden S	Kemp H	Matthews CH	Mills PC	Stokes A	Streets GH
R3	Jan	14	SHEFFIELD UNITED	2-3	BR Mills, Taylor	28232		2	3	6				9	8			7	10							5	11	4				1

		P	W	D	L	F	A	W	D	L	F	A	Pts
1	Manchester City	42	18	2	1	70	27	7	7	7	30	32	59
2	Leeds United	42	16	2	3	63	15	9	5	7	35	34	57
3	Chelsea	42	15	2	4	46	15	8	6	7	29	30	54
4	Preston North End	42	15	3	3	62	24	7	6	8	38	42	53
5	Stoke City	42	14	5	2	44	17	8	3	10	34	42	52
6	Swansea Town	42	13	6	2	46	17	5	6	10	29	46	48
7	Oldham Athletic	42	15	3	3	55	18	4	5	12	20	33	46
8	West Bromwich Alb.	42	10	7	4	50	28	7	5	9	40	42	46
9	Port Vale	42	11	6	4	45	20	7	2	12	23	37	44
10	Nottingham Forest	42	10	6	5	54	37	5	4	12	29	47	40
11	Grimsby Town	42	8	6	7	41	41	6	6	9	28	42	40
12	Bristol City	42	11	5	5	42	18	4	4	13	34	61	39
13	Barnsley	42	10	5	6	43	36	4	6	11	22	49	39
14	Hull City	42	9	8	4	25	19	3	7	11	16	35	39
15	NOTTS COUNTY	42	10	4	7	47	26	3	8	10	21	48	38
16	Wolverhampton Wan.	42	11	5	5	43	31	2	5	14	20	60	36
17	Southampton	42	11	3	7	54	40	3	4	14	14	37	35
18	Reading	42	9	8	4	32	22	2	5	14	21	53	35
19	Blackpool	42	11	3	7	55	43	2	5	14	28	58	34
20	Clapton Orient	42	9	7	5	32	25	2	5	14	23	60	34
21	Fulham	42	12	7	2	46	22	1	0	20	22	67	33
22	South Shields	42	5	5	11	30	41	2	4	15	26	70	23

1928/29   5th in Division Two

#	Date		Opponent	Score	Scorers	Att	Ferguson JS	Mills PC	Bisby CC	Hilton F	Froggatt F	Plackett S	Davies W	Fenner T	Taylor GT	Andrews H	Haden S	Kemp H	Matthews CH	Mills BR	Stokes A	Astley J	Dowsey J	McGorian IM	James W	Maw AW	Childs H	Wright F
1	Aug	25	Millwall	1-0	Fenner	27221	1	2	3	4	5	6	7	8	9	10	11											
2		27	WEST BROMWICH ALB.	3-1	Taylor, Andrews, Haden	10395	1	2	3	4	5	6	7	8	9	10	11											
3	Sep	1	PORT VALE	3-0	Haden 2, Fenner	15314	1	2	3	4	5	6	7	8	9	10	11											
4		3	West Bromwich Alb.	3-1	Andrews 3	9541	1	2	3	4	5	6	7	8	9	10	11											
5		6	Hull City	1-1	Andrews	14790	1	2	3	4	5	6	7	8	9	10	11											
6		15	TOTTENHAM HOTSPUR	2-0	Fenner 2	23304	1	2	3	4	5	6	7	8	9	10	11											
7		22	Reading	2-1	Taylor, Davis	12165	1	2	3	4	5	6	7	8	9	10	11											
8		29	PRESTON NORTH END	0-1		19380	1	2	3	4	5	6	7	8	9	10	11											
9	Oct	6	Middlesbrough	1-3	Davis	16984	1	2	3	4	5	6	7	8	9	10	11											
10		13	OLDHAM ATHLETIC	2-0	Haden, Andrews	11957	1	2	3	4	5	6	7	8	9	10	11											
11		20	NOTTM. FOREST	1-1	Fenner	22249	1	2	3		5	6	7	8	9	10	11	4										
12		27	Bristol City	4-0	Andrews 2, BR Mills 2	8496	1	2	3		5	6		8		10	11	4	7	9								
13	Nov	3	BARNSLEY	4-1	BR Mills, Andrews 2, Fenner	16917	1	2	3		5	6	7	8		10	11	4		9								
14		10	Clapton Orient	2-2	Andrews, PC Mills	9746	1	2	3		5	6	7	8		10	11			9	4							
15		17	BLACKPOOL	3-1	BR Mills 2, Fenner	13987	1	2	3		5	6		8		10	11	4	7	9								
16		24	Swansea Town	0-1		10498	1	2	3		5	6	7	8		10	11	4		9								
17	Dec	1	BRADFORD PARK AVE.	3-3	Davis, Fenner, BR Mills	14875	1	2	3		5	6	7	8		10	11	4		9								
18		8	Grimsby Town	2-2	Haden, Fenner	12381	1	2	3		5	6	7	8		10	11	4		9								
19		15	STOKE CITY	1-0	BR Mills	10166	1	2	3		5	6	7	8		10	11	4		9								
20		22	Chelsea	1-1	BR Mills	19560	1	2	3		5	6	7	8		10	11	4		9								
21		25	SOUTHAMPTON	1-1	Andrews	21865	1	2	3		5	6	7	8		10	11	4		9								
22		26	Southampton	0-4		20441	1	2	3	6	5			8	9	10	11		7		4							
23		29	MILLWALL	4-5	Fenner 2, Andrews, Froggatt	12727	1	2	3		5	6	7	8		10	11	4		9								
24	Jan	5	Port Vale	0-3		7475	1	2		4	5	6	7	8		10	11			9		3						
25		19	HULL CITY	6-0	Andrews, BR Mills 3, Fenner 2	13271	1	2	3	5		6	7	8		10	11	4		9								
26		26	Tottenham Hotspur	0-3		16946	1	2	3	5		6	7	8		10	11	4		9								
27	Feb	2	READING	1-1	Andrews	9807	1	2	3		5	6		8		10	11	4	7	9								
28		9	Preston North End	1-0	Taylor	15666	1	2	3		5	6	7	8	9	10	11	4										
29		16	MIDDLESBROUGH	0-3		11534	1	2	3		5	6	7	8	9		11	4						10				
30		23	Oldham Athletic	2-3	Andrews, Fenner	10947	1	2	3		5		7	8		10	11	4						9	6			
31	Mar	2	Nottm. Forest	2-1	Dowsey, Fenner	18438	1	2	3		5	6	7	8		10	11	4						8				
32		9	BRISTOL CITY	2-0	Fenner, PC Mills	13001	1	2	3		5	6	7	8		10	11	4						8				
33		13	CHELSEA	4-3	Fenner 2, Andrews, Haden(p)	11235	1	2	3		5	6	7	8		10	11	4						8				
34		16	Barnsley	0-2		7518	1	2	3		5	6	7	8		10	11	4						8				
35		23	CLAPTON ORIENT	2-0	Haden, Andrews	10965	1	2			5	6	7	8		10	11	4					3	8				
36		30	Blackpool	2-3	Taylor 2	16049	1	2	3		5	6	7			9	10	11	4					8				
37	Apr	1	WOLVERHAMPTON W.	3-0	Bisby, Davis, James	16373	1	2	3		5	6	7	8	9		11	4							10			
38		2	Wolverhampton Wand.	1-3	Kemp	12060	1	2	3		5				9		11	6	7		4				10	8		
39		6	SWANSEA TOWN	5-1	Dowsey 2, James, Andrews, Haden(p)	9429	1		3		5	6			9	11	4	7				3	8		10			
40		13	Bradford Park Ave.	2-2	Andrews, Haden	15104	1		3		5	6	7		9	11	4					3	8		10			
41		20	GRIMSBY TOWN	1-2	James	28139	1	2	3		5	6	7		9	11	4						8		10			
42		27	Stoke City	0-5		8165	1				5	6	7		9	11	4						8		10		2	3
			Apps				42	39	39	14	40	39	36	36	17	39	42	29	6	15	3	4	12	1	6	1	1	1
			Goals					2	1		1		4	18	5	20	9	1		11			3		3			

F.A. Cup

#	Date		Opponent	Score	Scorers	Att	Ferguson JS	Mills PC	Bisby CC	Hilton F	Froggatt F	Plackett S	Davies W	Fenner T		Andrews H	Haden S			Mills BR								
R3	Jan	12	Derby County	3-4	Haden 2, Andrews	21318	1	2	3	4	5	6	7	8		10	11			9								

		P	W	D	L	F	A	W	D	L	F	A	Pts
1	Middlesbrough	42	14	4	3	54	22	8	7	6	38	35	55
2	Grimsby Town	42	16	2	3	49	24	8	3	10	33	37	53
3	Bradford Park Ave.	42	18	2	1	62	22	4	2	15	26	48	48
4	Southampton	42	12	6	3	48	22	5	8	8	26	38	48
5	NOTTS COUNTY	42	13	4	4	51	24	6	5	10	27	41	47
6	Stoke City	42	12	7	2	46	16	5	5	11	28	35	46
7	West Bromwich Alb.	42	13	4	4	50	25	6	4	11	30	54	46
8	Blackpool	42	13	4	4	49	18	6	3	12	43	58	45
9	Chelsea	42	10	6	5	40	30	7	4	10	24	35	44
10	Tottenham Hotspur	42	16	3	2	50	26	1	6	14	25	55	43
11	Nottingham Forest	42	8	6	7	34	33	7	6	8	37	37	42
12	Hull City	42	8	8	5	38	24	5	6	10	20	39	40
13	Preston North End	42	12	6	3	58	27	3	3	15	20	52	39
14	Millwall	42	10	4	7	43	35	6	3	12	28	51	39
15	Reading	42	12	3	6	48	30	3	6	12	15	56	39
16	Barnsley	42	12	4	5	51	28	4	2	15	18	38	38
17	Wolverhampton Wan.	42	9	6	6	41	31	6	1	14	36	50	37
18	Oldham Athletic	42	15	2	4	37	24	1	3	17	17	51	37
19	Swansea Town	42	12	3	6	46	26	1	7	13	16	49	36
20	Bristol City	42	11	6	4	37	25	2	4	15	21	47	36
21	Port Vale	42	14	1	6	53	25	1	3	17	18	61	34
22	Clapton Orient	42	10	4	7	29	25	2	4	15	16	47	32

- 1928/29 Season -

Back: Andrews, Astley, Hilton, C.G.Smith, Hamilton, B.B.Mills
Standing: Fenner, Ratcliffe (Trainer), Holdsworth, Robertson, Wilson, Ferguson, P.C.Mills,
Henshall (Sec/Man.), Plackett   Sitting: Davies, Kemp, Childs, Bisby, Taylor, Haden
Front: Stokes, Keeling, Kerry, Matthews

- 1929/30 Season -

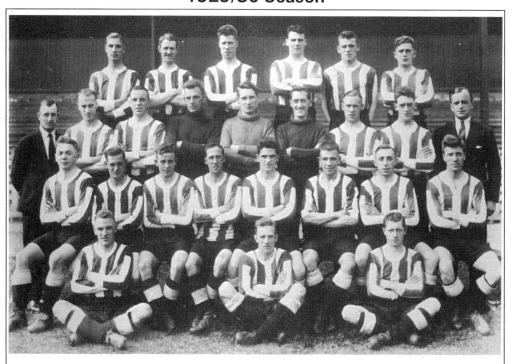

Back: Fisher, Plackett, Mills, Hilton, Robinson, James
Standing: Banks (Asst.Trainer), Fenner, McGorian, Ferguson, Robertson, Hampson, Froggatt, Feebury,
Ratcliffe (Trainer)   Sitting: Dowsey, Davies, Maw, Merritt, Keetley, Taylor, Andrews, Matthews
Front: Bisby, Haden, Kemp

1929/30 22nd in Division Two (Relegated)

#	Date	Opponent	Score	Scorers	Att	Ferguson JS	Jakeman GW	Bisby CC	Kemp H	Froggatt F	Plackett S	Davies W	Dowsey J	Keetley T	Andrews H	Haden S	Mills PC	Fenner T	James W	Vallance R	Maw AW	Taylor GT	Matthews CH	Fisher F	Merritt R	Hampson T	Feebery A	Lawless H	Mays AW
1	Aug 31	BRISTOL CITY	3-1	Keetley 3	12259	1	2	3	4	5	6	7	8	9	10	11													
2	Sep 2	Bradford City	0-2		20366	1	4	3		5	6	7	8	9	10	11	2												
3	7	Nottm. Forest	1-1	Keetley	18230	1	2	3	6	5		7	4	9	10	11		8											
4	9	BRADFORD CITY	2-0	Keetley 2	8890	1	2	3	6	5		7	4	9	10	11		8	10										
5	14	Reading	0-2		13957	1	2	3	6	5		7	4	9	10	11		8											
6	16	Cardiff City	1-3	Maw	11533	1	2	3	4	5		7				11			10	6	8	9							
7	21	CHARLTON ATHLETIC	4-0	Andrews 2, Keetley 2(1p)	12213	1	2	3		5		7	4	9	10	11				6	8								
8	25	CARDIFF CITY	2-1	Fenner 2	7778	1	2	3		5		7	4	9	10	11		8		6									
9	28	Hull City	0-0		8680	1		3		5	6	7	4	9	10	11	2	8											
10	Oct 5	STOKE CITY	3-3	Andrews 2, Fenner	18129	1	2	3		5		7	4	9	10	11		8		6									
11	12	Wolverhampton Wand.	1-5	Andrews	19939	1	2	3	6	5		7	4		10	11		9		8									
12	19	CHELSEA	2-2	Davies, Fenner	13878	1	2	3	6	5		7	4		10	11		9		8									
13	26	Bury	0-2		8691	1	2			6	5		4		10	11	3			8	9	7							
14	Nov 2	BLACKPOOL	0-2		13282	1	2			4	5	7	8	9		11	3		10	6									
15	9	Barnsley	2-2	Keetley, Andrews	5116	1	2			4	5	7	8	9	10	11	3			6									
16	16	BRADFORD PARK AVE.	1-1	Haden	8034	1		3	6	5		7	4	9	10	11	2				8								
17	23	West Bromwich Alb.	2-4	Fisher, Taylor	15118	1		3	4			7	5		10	11	2			6		9		8					
18	30	TOTTENHAM HOTSPUR	0-1		10294	1		3	4	5	6	7	8		10		2					9				11			
19	Dec 7	Southampton	2-2	Davies, Keetley	9235	1		3	4		6	7	5	9		11	2		10					8					
20	14	MILLWALL	1-1	Keetley	8776	1		3	4		6	7	5	9		11	2		10					8					
21	21	Oldham Athletic	2-2	Andrews, Keetley	13172	1		3		5	6	7	4	9	10	11	2				8								
22	25	Swansea Town	2-3	Andrews, Taylor	7148	1		3		5	6	7	4		10	11	2				8	9							
23	26	SWANSEA TOWN	0-0		19284	1		3		5	6	7	4	9	10	11	2				8								
24	28	Bristol City	0-0		8520	1		3	6	5		7	4	9	10	11	2				8								
25	Jan 4	NOTTM. FOREST	0-0		20917	1		3	6	5		7	4	9	10	11	2				8								
26	18	READING	3-0	James, Andrews, Davies	10614	1		3	6	5		7	4		10	11	2		9		8								
27	Feb 1	HULL CITY	4-1	Andrews 2, James, Haden	11747	1		3	6	5			4		9	11	2		10		8	7							
28	8	Stoke City	1-1	Andrews	8689	1		3	6	5		7	4		9	11	2		10		8								
29	15	Wolverhampton W.	0-3		11268			3	6	5			4		9	11	2		10		8	7			1				
30	22	Chelsea	1-3	Taylor	37103	1			6				4		9	11	2				10	8	7				3	5	
31	Mar 1	BURY	1-3	Andrews	7016	1			6				4		10	11	2				8	9	7				3	5	
32	8	Blackpool	2-1	Andrews, Maw	13233	1		3	6	5			4		10	11	2				8	7							9
33	15	BARNSLEY	3-0	Mays, Henderson(og), Maw	6006	1		3	6	5			4		10	11	2				8	7							9
34	22	Bradford Park Ave.	3-3	Andrews 2, Maw	10535	1		3	6	5			4		10	11	2				8	7							9
35	29	WEST BROMWICH ALB.	2-1	Mays 2	10026	1		3	6	5			4		10	11	2				8	7							9
36	Apr 5	Tottenham Hotspur	0-2		17848	1		3	6	5			4		10	11	2				8	7							9
37	7	Charlton Athletic	0-1		3801	1		3	6	5			4		10	11	2	8						7					9
38	12	SOUTHAMPTON	1-2	Andrews	7632	1		3	6	5			4		10	11	2			9	8	7							
39	18	Preston North End	1-3	Mays	10592	1		3	6	5	4		8		10	11	2					7							9
40	19	Millwall	0-2		10029	1		3	6	5			4	9	10	11	2	8				7							
41	22	PRESTON NORTH END	0-3		10002	1		3		5			4	9	10	11	2	8		6		7							
42	26	OLDHAM ATHLETIC	1-1	Mills	9945	1			6	5			4		10	11	2	8				7					3		9
	Apps					41	14	36	33	37	10	26	41	20	38	40	32	12	10	8	15	25	6	3	1	1	3	2	8
	Goals											3		12	17	2	1	4	2		4	3	1						4

One own goal

F.A. Cup

	Date	Opponent	Score	Att	Ferguson JS	Jakeman GW	Bisby CC	Kemp H	Froggatt F	Plackett S	Davies W	Dowsey J	Keetley T	Andrews H	Haden S	Mills PC	Fenner T	James W	Vallance R	Maw AW	Taylor GT	Matthews CH	Fisher F	Merritt R	Hampson T	Feebery A	Lawless H	Mays AW
R3	Jan 11	West Ham United	0-4	28384	1		3	6	5		7	4	9	10	11	2				8								

		P	W	D	L	F	A	W	D	L	F	A	Pts
1	Blackpool	42	17	1	3	63	22	10	3	8	35	45	58
2	Chelsea	42	17	3	1	49	14	5	8	8	25	32	55
3	Oldham Athletic	42	14	5	2	60	21	7	6	8	30	30	53
4	Bradford Park Ave.	42	14	5	2	65	28	5	7	9	26	42	50
5	Bury	42	14	2	5	45	27	8	3	10	33	40	49
6	West Bromwich Alb.	42	16	1	4	73	31	5	4	12	32	42	47
7	Southampton	42	14	6	1	46	22	3	5	13	31	54	45
8	Cardiff City	42	14	4	3	41	16	4	4	13	20	43	44
9	Wolverhampton Wan.	42	14	3	4	53	24	2	6	13	24	55	41
10	Nottingham Forest	42	9	6	6	36	28	4	9	8	19	41	41
11	Stoke City	42	12	4	5	41	20	4	4	13	33	52	40
12	Tottenham Hotspur	42	11	8	2	43	24	4	1	16	16	37	39
13	Charlton Athletic	42	10	6	5	39	23	4	5	12	20	40	39
14	Millwall	42	10	7	4	36	26	2	8	11	21	47	39
15	Swansea Town	42	11	5	5	42	23	3	4	14	15	38	37
16	Preston North End	42	7	7	7	42	36	6	4	11	23	44	37
17	Barnsley	42	12	7	2	39	22	2	1	18	17	49	36
18	Bradford City	42	7	7	7	33	30	5	5	11	27	47	36
19	Reading	42	10	7	4	31	20	2	4	15	23	47	35
20	Bristol City	42	11	4	6	36	30	2	5	14	25	53	35
21	Hull City	42	11	3	7	30	24	3	4	14	21	54	35
22	NOTTS COUNTY	42	8	7	6	33	26	1	8	12	21	44	33

1930/31 — Champions of Division Three (South) - Promoted

#	Date	Opponent	Score	Scorers	Att	Ferguson JS	Mills PC	Bisby CC	Dowsey J	Froggatt F	Kemp H	Taylor GT	Fenner T	Keetley T	Andrews H	Haden S	Feebery A	Jakeman GW	Maw AW	Smith HR	Shooter A	Whitcombe GC	Soutar HW	Lovatt H	Turner GW	Stimpson GH	Hamilton W	Hall GW
1	Aug 30	Coventry City	2-1	Watson(og), Keetley	17915	1	2	3	4	5	6	7	8	9	10	11												
2	Sep 3	THAMES	4-0	Andrews, Taylor, Keetley 2	10125	1	2	3	4	5	6	7	8	9	10	11												
3	6	FULHAM	6-1	Keetley 4, Andrews, Fenner	10167	1	2	3	4	5	6	7	8	9	10	11												
4	8	Norwich City	2-2	Fenner, Taylor	10985	1	2		4	5	6	7	8	9	10	11	3											
5	13	Swindon Town	2-1	Andrews, Taylor	6797	1	2		4	5	6	7	8	9	10	11	3											
6	20	BOURNEMOUTH	2-0	Fenner 2	9579	1	2		4	5	6	7	8	9	10	11	3											
7	24	Brentford	2-2	Keetley 2	9999	1	2		4		6	7	8	9	10	11	3	5										
8	27	Watford	1-0	Fenner	12000	1	2		4	5	6	7	8	9	10	11	3											
9	Oct 2	NORWICH CITY	4-0	Keetley 2, Mills(p), Fenner	6987	1	2	3	4	5	6	7	8	9		11			10									
10	4	BRISTOL ROVERS	3-0	Fenner 2, Maw	11929	1	2	3	4	5	6	7	8	9		11			10									
11	11	CLAPTON ORIENT	5-0	Keetley 3, Fenner 2	11106	1	2	3	4	5		7	8	9	10	11		6										
12	18	Newport County	3-2	Keetley 3	5245	1	2	3	4	5	6	7	8	9	10	11												
13	25	GILLINGHAM	2-1	Andrews, Fenner	11740	1	2	3		5	6	7	8	9	10	11			4									
14	Nov 1	Exeter City	3-3	Maw 2, Andrews	7315	1	2	3		5	6	7	8	9		11			4	10								
15	8	BRIGHTON & HOVE ALB.	2-2	Keetley, Andrews	12362	1	2	3		5	6	7	8	9	10	11			4									
16	15	Torquay United	4-1	Andrews, Keetley 3	6730	1	2	3	4		6	7	8	9	10	11			5									
17	22	NORTHAMPTON T	2-2	Andrews, Keetley	21329	1	2	3	4		6	7	8	9	10	11			5									
18	Dec 6	CRYSTAL PALACE	2-2	Fenner, Keetley	11935	1	2	3	4		6	7	8	9		11			10	5								
19	17	Southend United	1-2	Kemp	4827	1	2				6	7	8	9		11	3		10	5								
20	20	LUTON TOWN	1-0	Fenner	11307	1	2	3	4			7	8			11		6	10	5	9							
21	25	Queens Park Rangers	1-4	Maw	14501	1	2	3	4		6	7			10	11			8		9	5						
22	26	QUEENS PARK RANGERS	2-0	Keetley 2	13696		2	3	4		6	7		9	10	11			8			5	1					
23	27	COVENTRY CITY	4-1	Keetley 2, Andrews, Lovatt	16803		2	3	4		6	7		9	10	11						5	1	8				
24	Jan 3	Fulham	1-3	Andrews	11606		2	3	4			7		9	10	11					6	5	1	8				
25	17	SWINDON TOWN	2-0	Keetley, Haden	11448		2	3	4			7		9	10	11					6	5	1	8				
26	28	Bournemouth	1-2	Turner	4778		2		4			7	8		10		3				6	5	1		9	11		
27	31	WATFORD	1-0	Andrews	11705		2		4			7	8	9	10		3				6	5	1			11		
28	Feb 7	Bristol Rovers	2-2	Fenner, Keetley	11552		2		4			7	8	9	10		3					5	1			11		
29	14	Clapton Orient	4-1	Fenner, Keetley 2, Taylor	6245	1	2	3	4			7	8	9	10	11						5				6		
30	21	NEWPORT COUNTY	5-0	Fenner 2, Keetley 2, Dowsey	11913	1	2	3	4			7	8	9	10	11						5				6		
31	28	Gillingham	5-0	Andrews 2, Haden(p), Keetley, Fenner	8264	1		3	4		6		8	9	10							5				2	7	
32	Mar 7	EXETER CITY	1-2	Keetley	12781	1		3	4		6		8	9	10							5				2		
33	14	Brighton & Hove Alb.	3-1	Keetley 2, Andrews	14037	1	2	3	4			7	8	9	10	11						5				6		
34	21	TORQUAY UNITED	2-0	Haden(p), Fenner	11951	1	2	3	4			7	8	9	10	11						5				6		
35	28	Northampton T	0-0		14284	1	2	3	4			7	8	9	10	11						5				6		
36	Apr 3	WALSALL	6-1	Andrews 3, Fenner 2, Keetley	11858	1	2	3	4			7	8	9	10	11						5				6		
37	4	BRENTFORD	1-0	Keetley	14759	1	2	3	4			7	8	9	10	11						5				6		
38	6	Walsall	1-2	Maw	5187	1	2	3	5	4		7	8	9		11			10							6		
39	11	Crystal Palace	1-1	Taylor	19638	1	2	3	4			7	8			11		6	10			5			9			
40	18	SOUTHEND UNITED	1-1	Haden	11919	1	2	3	4			7	8	9		11		6	10			5						
41	25	Luton Town	0-3		7312	1	2	3	4			7				11		6	10			5			9		8	
42	May 2	Thames	0-0		3731	1	2	3	4			7				11		6	8			5			9			10
		Apps				35	40	33	39	14	24	41	35	34	33	39	9	12	13	21	2	7	7	7	3	11	2	1
		Goals					1		1		1	5	21	39	17	4			5					1	1			

F.A. Cup

#	Date	Opponent	Score	Scorers	Att	Ferguson JS	Mills PC	Bisby CC	Dowsey J	Froggatt F	Kemp H	Taylor GT	Fenner T	Keetley T	Andrews H	Haden S	Feebery A	Jakeman GW	Maw AW	Smith HR	Shooter A	Whitcombe GC	Soutar HW	Lovatt H	Turner GW	Stimpson GH	Hamilton W	Hall GW
R1	Nov 29	Chesterfield	2-1	Fenner, Taylor	13401	1	2	3	4		6	7	8	9	10	11						5						
R2	Dec 13	Doncaster Rovers	1-0	Bowman(og)	17763	1	2	3	4		6	7	8	9		11			10			5						
R3	Jan 10	SWANSEA TOWN	3-1	Andrews 2, Keetley	23802		2	3	4			7		9	10	11					6	5	1	8				
R4	Jan 24	Sheffield United	1-4	Keetley	42178		2	3	4		6	7		9	10	11						5	1	8				

One own goal

		P	W	D	L	F	A	W	D	L	F	A	Pts
1	NOTTS COUNTY	42	16	4	1	58	13	8	7	6	39	33	59
2	Crystal Palace	42	17	2	2	71	20	5	5	11	36	51	51
3	Brentford	42	14	3	4	62	30	8	3	10	28	34	50
4	Brighton & Hove A.	42	13	5	3	45	20	4	10	7	23	33	49
5	Southend United	42	16	0	5	53	26	6	5	10	23	34	49
6	Northampton Town	42	10	6	5	37	20	8	6	7	40	39	48
7	Luton Town	42	15	3	3	61	17	4	5	12	15	34	46
8	Queen's Park Rgs.	42	15	0	6	57	23	5	3	13	25	52	43
9	Fulham	42	15	3	3	49	21	3	4	14	28	54	43
10	Bournemouth	42	11	7	3	39	22	4	6	11	33	51	43
11	Torquay United	42	13	5	3	56	26	4	4	13	24	58	43
12	Swindon Town	42	15	5	1	68	29	3	1	17	21	65	42
13	Exeter City	42	12	6	3	55	35	5	2	14	29	55	42
14	Coventry City	42	11	4	6	55	28	5	5	11	20	37	41
15	Bristol Rovers	42	12	3	6	49	36	4	5	12	26	56	40
16	Gillingham	42	10	6	5	40	29	4	4	13	21	47	38
17	Walsall	42	9	5	7	44	38	5	4	12	34	57	37
18	Watford	42	9	4	8	41	29	5	3	13	31	46	35
19	Clapton Orient	42	12	3	6	47	33	2	4	15	16	58	35
20	Thames	42	12	5	4	34	20	1	3	17	20	73	34
21	Newport County	42	10	5	6	45	31	1	1	19	24	80	28
22	Norwich City	42	10	7	4	37	20	0	1	20	10	56	28

- 1930/31 Season -

Back: Hamilton, Banks (Trainer), Froggatt, Turner, Ferguson, Wightman (Coach), Soutar, H.Smith, P.C.Mills,
Henshall (Sec.Manager), Stimpson   Middle: Fenner, Feebury, Bisby, Kemp, Keetley, Andrews, Haden, Lovatt
Front: Jakeman, Taylor, Maw, Shooter, Dowsey

- 1931/32 Season -

Back: Dowsey, Bycroft, Corkhill, H.R.Smith, Grice, Raven, M.Smith
Standing: Andrews, Taylor, Stimpson, Thorpe, Feebury, Jones, Wright
Sitting: Murphy, Sheldon, Lawrence, Ferguson, Bisby, Maidment, Lovatt, Coglin, Haden
Front: Mills, Jakeman, Fenner, Keetley, Maw, Hall

1931/32　16th in Division Two

Results & Line-ups

No	Date	Opponent	Score	Scorers	Att
1	Aug 29	MILLWALL	2-0	Haden, Keetley	15464
2	Sep 2	Bristol City	2-3	Keetley, Mills	8552
3	5	Bradford City	2-0	Taylor, Keetley	13731
4	12	LEEDS UNITED	1-1	Keetley	12630
5	14	Oldham Athletic	2-5	Andrews, Keetley	7117
6	19	Swansea Town	1-5		10933
7	23	OLDHAM ATHLETIC	1-0	Wright	7068
8	26	BARNSLEY	2-3	Lovatt 2	11700
9	Oct 3	Nottm. Forest	1-2	Haden	20703
10	10	Plymouth Argyle	4-3	Keetley 3, Fenner	22655
11	17	TOTTENHAM HOTSPUR	3-1	Keetley, Fenner, Taylor	13397
12	24	Manchester Utd.	3-3	Keetley 3	6694
13	31	BRADFORD PARK AVE.	0-2		12687
14	Nov 7	Chesterfield	4-1	Keetley 3, Fenner	10303
15	14	CHARLTON ATHLETIC	2-2	Keetley, Haden	11681
16	21	Stoke City	2-2	Hall, Keetley	10816
17	28	SOUTHAMPTON	5-0	Keetley 3(1p), Fenner 2	10307
18	Dec 5	Preston North End	0-0		6320
19	12	BURNLEY	5-0	Fenner 3, Grice, Haden	13198
20	19	Wolverhampton Wand.	0-0		16291
21	25	PORT VALE	4-2	Keetley 3, Coglin	21367
22	26	Port Vale	0-2		13463
23	Jan 2	Millwall	3-4	Keetley 2, Coglin	13752
24	16	BRADFORD CITY	1-1	Taylor	10693
25	23	Leeds United	2-2	Taylor, Maw	14562
26	30	SWANSEA TOWN	1-2	Maw	10628
27	Feb 6	Barnsley	1-1	Fenner	5188
28	13	NOTTM. FOREST	2-6	Haden, Taylor	18199
29	20	PLYMOUTH ARGYLE	3-0	Hall 2, Fenner	11434
30	27	Tottenham Hotspur	0-2		20481
31	Mar 5	MANCHESTER UTD.	1-2	Mellor (og)	10817
32	12	Bradford Park Ave.	1-1	Grice	12185
33	19	CHESTERFIELD	1-1	Elliott	14507
34	25	Bury	1-2	Haden	7482
35	26	Charlton Athletic	1-3	Mills(p)	15356
36	28	BURY	0-1		11706
37	Apr 2	STOKE CITY	2-1	Haden, Taylor	10839
38	9	Southampton	1-3	Molloy	7332
39	16	PRESTON NORTH END	1-4	Keetley	5872
40	23	Burnley	1-1	Keetley	5604
41	30	WOLVERHAMPTON W.	3-1	Taylor, Haden, Fenner	12000
42	May 7	BRISTOL CITY	3-0	Fenner, Coglin, Mills(p)	5773

Player appearances (shirt numbers)

No	Ferguson JS	Mills PC	Bisby CC	Dowsey J	Smith HR	Jakeman GW	Taylor GT	Fenner T	Keetley T	Andrews H	Haden S	Stimpson GH	Lawrence E	Lovatt HA	Maw AW	Grice F	Hall GW	Wright JE	Coglin S	Feebery A	Maidment JHC	Corkhill WG	Elliott SD	Molloy W	Thorpe AE
1	1	2	3	4	5	6	7	8	9	10	11														
2	1	2	3	4	5	6	7	8	9	10	11														
3	1	2			5	6	7	8	9	10	11	3	4												
4	1	2			5	6	7		9	10	11	3	4	8											
5	1	2	3	4			7		9	10	11	5	6		8										
6	1	2	3	4	5		7		9	10	11		6		8										
7	1	2	3	4			7				11	6				5	8	9	10						
8	1	2		4			7			10	11	6		8		9	5			3					
9	1	2			5		7	8	9		11		4			6			10	3					
10	1	2			5		7	8	9		11		4			6			10	3					
11		2			5		7	8	9		11		4			6			10	3	1				
12	1	2			5		7	8	9		11		4			6			10	3					
13	1		3		5	6	7	8	9		11	2	4						10						
14			3		5	6	7	8	9		11	2	4						10		1				
15			3		5	6	7	8	9		11	2	4						10		1				
16			3			6	7	8	9		11	2	4				5		10		1				
17	1		3			6	7	8	9		11	2	4				5		10						
18	1		3			6	7	8	9		11	2	4				5		10						
19	1		3			6	7	8	9		11	2	4			5			10						
20	1		3			6	7	8	9		11	2	4			5			10						
21	1		3			6	7	8	9		11	2	4			5			10						
22	1		3			6	7	8	9		11	2	4			5			10						
23	1	2	3			6	7	8	9		11		4			5			10						
24	1	2				6	7		9		11	3	4			5	8		10						
25	1	2	3			6	7		9	10	11		4		8	5									
26	1	2	3			6	7		9	10	11		4		8	5									
27		2	3		5	6	7	8	9		11								10		1	4			
28		2	3		5	6	7	8	9		11								10		1	4			
29	1					6	7	8	9		11	2	4			5	10			3					
30	1					6	7	8	9		11	2	4			5	10			3					
31	1					6	7	8	9		11	2	4			5	10			3					
32	1	2	3		5	6	7	8			11		4			9	10								
33	1	2	3		5	6	7	8			11		4				10						9		
34	1		3		5	6	7	8			11	2	4				10						9		
35	1	2			5	6	7			10	11	3	4		8								9		
36	1	2	3		5	6	7	8			11		4				10						9		
37			3			6	7	8			11	2	4			5			10		1			9	
38			3			6	7	8			11	2	4			5			10		1			9	
39			3			6	7	8	9		11	2	4			5			10		1				
40		2			5	6	7		9		11		4						10	3	1		8		
41		2			5	6	7	8	9		11		4						10	3	1				
42		2			5	6	7	8	9		11								10	3	1				4
Apps	30	24	28	6	26	30	42	32	29	16	41	23	39	2	6	20	21	1	13	11	12	2	5	2	1
Goals		3					7	12	28	1	8			2	2	2	3	1	3				1	1	

One own goal

F.A. Cup

Round	Date	Opponent	Score	Scorers	Att	Ferguson JS	Mills PC	Bisby CC	Smith HR	Jakeman GW	Taylor GT	Fenner T	Keetley T	Andrews H	Haden S	Stimpson GH	Lawrence E	Grice F	Hall GW	Coglin S
R3	Jan 9	BRISTOL CITY	2-2	Keetley 2	22761	1		3			7	8	9		11	2	6	5		10
rep	Jan 13	Bristol City	2-3	Hall, Grice	16065	1	2	3			7		9	10	11	4	6	5	8	

Division Two Final Table

		P	W	D	L	F	A	W	D	L	F	A	Pts
1	Wolverhampton Wan.	42	17	3	1	71	11	7	5	9	44	38	56
2	Leeds United	42	12	5	4	36	22	10	5	6	42	32	54
3	Stoke City	42	14	6	1	47	19	5	8	8	22	29	52
4	Plymouth Argyle	42	14	4	3	69	29	6	5	10	31	37	49
5	Bury	42	13	4	4	44	21	8	3	10	26	37	49
6	Bradford Park Ave.	42	17	2	2	44	18	4	5	12	28	45	49
7	Bradford City	42	10	7	4	53	26	6	6	9	27	35	45
8	Tottenham Hotspur	42	11	6	4	58	37	5	5	11	29	41	43
9	Millwall	42	13	3	5	43	21	4	6	11	18	40	43
10	Charlton Athletic	42	11	5	5	38	28	6	4	11	23	38	43
11	Nottingham Forest	42	13	4	4	49	27	3	6	12	28	45	42
12	Manchester United	42	12	3	6	44	31	5	5	11	27	41	42
13	Preston North End	42	11	6	4	37	25	5	4	12	38	52	42
14	Southampton	42	10	5	6	39	30	7	2	12	27	47	41
15	Swansea Town	42	12	4	5	45	22	4	3	14	28	53	39
16	NOTTS COUNTY	42	10	4	7	43	30	3	8	10	32	45	38
17	Chesterfield	42	11	3	7	43	33	2	8	11	21	53	37
18	Oldham Athletic	42	10	4	7	41	34	3	6	12	21	50	36
19	Burnley	42	7	8	6	36	36	6	1	14	23	51	35
20	Port Vale	42	8	4	9	30	33	5	3	13	28	56	33
21	Barnsley	42	8	7	6	35	30	4	2	15	20	61	33
22	Bristol City	42	4	7	10	22	37	2	4	15	17	41	23

1932/33   15th in Division Two

No		Date	Opponent	Score	Scorers	Att	Tewkesbury KC	Mills PC	Stimpson GH	Jakeman GW	Watson N	Lawrence E	Taylor GT	Fenner T	Keetley T	Proudfoot J	Haden S	Grice F	Hall GW	Smith HR	Elliott S	Maidment JHC	Feebery A	Feeney TW	Smith JW	Macartney CW	Burgon A	Corkhill WG	Watson J	Wall TH	Rickards T
1	Aug	27	LINCOLN CITY	1-1	Mills(p)	20987	1	2	3	4	5	6	7	8	9	10	11														
2		29	Bury	1-3	Keetley	8871	1		3	2	4	6	7		9	8	11	5	10												
3	Sep	3	West Ham United	1-1	Keetley	10656	1	3		2	4		7		9	10	11	6		5	8										
4		10	FULHAM	1-2	Keetley	10168	1	3		2	4		7		9	10	11	6		5	8										
5		17	Chesterfield	0-0		11049		2			4		7		9		11	6		5	8	1	3	10							
6		24	BRADFORD CITY	2-0	Haden, Elliott	13400		2		4			7				11	6			8	1	3	10	5	9					
7	Oct	1	Swansea Town	0-2		9636		2		4			7				11	6			8	1	3	10	5	9					
8		6	BURY	2-2	Macartney, Feeney	8044		2	3	4			7					6		5	8	1		10		9		11			
9		8	NOTTM. FOREST	2-4	Keetley, Taylor	16732		2	3				7		9	8		6	10	5		1						11			
10		15	PORT VALE	5-0	Keetley 2, Feeney, Hall, Haden	9217		2	3			6	7		9		11		10	5		1		8	4						
11		22	Charlton Athletic	3-3	Haden, Fenner, Taylor	10398		2	3			6	7	8	9		11		10	5		1			4						
12		29	STOKE CITY	3-4	Fenner, Keetley, Taylor	11358		2	3			6	7	8	9		11		10	5		1			4						
13	Nov	5	Manchester Utd.	0-2		24178		2	3			6	7	8	9		11		10	5		1			4						
14		12	PLYMOUTH ARGYLE	4-1	Elliott 2, Taylor, Hall	10479		2	3	4		6	7	8			11		10	5	9	1									
15		19	Preston North End	0-3		7298		2	3	5		6	7	8			11		10		9	1			4						
16		26	OLDHAM ATHLETIC	2-1	Taylor, Hall	8971	1	3		2		6	7	8			11	5	10		9				4						
17	Dec	3	Grimsby Town	1-1	Elliott	6065	1	3		2		6	7	8			11	5	10		9				4						
18		10	BURNLEY	4-2	Fenner 4	8216	1	3		2		6	7	8			11	5	10		9				4						
19		17	Bradford Park Ave.	4-3	Elliott 3, Hall	8792		3		2		6	7	8			11		10	5	9	1			4						
20		24	TOTTENHAM HOTSPUR	3-0	Taylor 2, Elliott	16355		3		2		6	7	8			11			5	9	1		10	4						
21		26	MILLWALL	1-0	Elliott	17627		3		2			7	8			11	6		5	9	1		10	4						
22		27	Millwall	1-1	Keetley	19958		3		2			7		9		11	6		5		1		10	4			8			
23		31	Lincoln City	1-1	Haden	9260		3		2			7	8			11	6		5	9	1		10	4						
24	Jan	7	WEST HAM UNITED	2-0	Smith JW, Haden	11437		3		2			7	8			11	6		5	9	1			4		10				
25		21	Fulham	4-3	Taylor 2, Keetley, Mills(p)	14795		3		2			7	8	9		11	6		5		1		10	4						
26	Feb	1	CHESTERFIELD	1-1	Keetley	4799		3		2			7	8	9		11	6		5		1		10	4						
27		4	Bradford City	2-1	Macartney, Corkhill	12755		3		2		4	7				11	6		5		1		10		9		8			
28		11	SWANSEA TOWN	1-2	Haden	12352		3		2		4	7				11	6		5	8	1		10		9					
29		18	Nottm. Forest	0-3		19846		3		2		10	7	8			11	6		5	9	1			4						
30	Mar	4	CHARLTON ATHLETIC	3-2	Pugsley(og), Burgon 2	8696		3		2		10	7				11	6		5	8	1			4		9				
31		11	Stoke City	2-0	Macartney, Haden	14376		3		2		4	7			10	11	6		5		1		8		9					
32		18	MANCHESTER UTD.	1-0	Keetley	13016		3		2		4	7		9	10	11	6		5		1		8							
33		20	Port Vale	0-4		5682		2				6	7		9	10	11			5		1		8	4				3		
34		25	Plymouth Argyle	2-0	Keetley 2	11609		2		4		6	7		9		11			5		1		10	8				3		
35	Apr	1	PRESTON NORTH END	0-0		9346		2		4		6	7		9		11			5	10	1			8				3		
36		8	Oldham Athletic	0-5		7257		2		4		6	7		9		11			5	10	1			8				3		
37		14	Southampton	2-6	Fenner, Taylor	8108		3		2			7	8		4	11	6		5		1		10		9					
38		15	GRIMSBY TOWN	1-3	Keetley	9230		3		2		4	7	8	9		11	6		5		1		10							
39		17	SOUTHAMPTON	1-2	Burgon	7588		2				4	7				11	6		5							9	10	3	1	
40		22	Burnley	1-2	Elliott	7665		3		2			7	8			11	6		5	9							4		1	10
41		29	BRADFORD PARK AVE.	1-4	Keetley	3306		3		2			7	8	9		11	6		5		1						4			10
42	May	6	Tottenham Hotspur	1-3	Grice	28015		2					7	8			11	6		5	9		3					4		1	10
			Apps				7	36	35	14	5	24	42	22	20	10	41	28	12	33	26	32	4	17	23	8	4	8	5	3	3
			Goals					2					10	6	15		7	1	4		11			2	1	3	3	1			

One own goal

F.A. Cup

No		Date	Opponent	Score	Scorers	Att	Mills PC	Stimpson GH	Jakeman GW	Taylor GT	Fenner T	Haden S	Grice F	Smith HR	Elliott S	Maidment JHC	Smith JW	Corkhill WG
R3	Jan	14	Tranmere Rovers	1-2	Corkhill	12420	3	2		7	8	11	6	5	9	1	4	10

		P	W	D	L	F	A	W	D	L	F	A	Pts
1	Stoke City	42	13	3	5	40	15	12	3	6	38	24	56
2	Tottenham Hotspur	42	14	7	0	58	19	6	8	7	38	32	55
3	Fulham	42	12	5	4	46	31	8	5	8	32	34	50
4	Bury	42	13	7	1	55	23	7	2	12	29	36	49
5	Nottingham Forest	42	9	8	4	37	28	8	7	6	30	31	49
6	Manchester United	42	11	5	5	40	24	4	8	9	31	44	43
7	Millwall	42	11	7	3	40	20	5	4	12	19	37	43
8	Bradford Park Ave.	42	13	4	4	51	27	4	4	13	26	44	42
9	Preston North End	42	12	2	7	53	36	4	8	9	21	34	42
10	Swansea Town	42	17	0	4	36	12	2	4	15	14	42	42
11	Bradford City	42	10	6	5	43	24	4	7	10	22	37	41
12	Southampton	42	15	3	3	48	22	3	2	16	18	44	41
13	Grimsby Town	42	8	10	3	49	34	6	3	12	30	50	41
14	Plymouth Argyle	42	13	4	4	45	22	3	5	13	18	45	41
15	NOTTS COUNTY	42	10	4	7	41	31	5	6	10	26	47	40
16	Oldham Athletic	42	10	4	7	38	31	5	4	12	29	49	38
17	Port Vale	42	12	3	6	49	27	2	7	12	17	52	38
18	Lincoln City	42	11	6	4	46	28	1	7	13	26	59	37
19	Burnley	42	8	9	4	35	20	3	5	13	32	59	36
20	West Ham United	42	12	6	3	56	31	1	3	17	19	62	35
21	Chesterfield	42	10	5	6	36	25	2	5	14	25	59	34
22	Charlton Athletic	42	9	3	9	35	35	3	4	14	25	56	31

- 1932/33 Season -

Back: Mills, Stimpson, J.W.Smith, Maidment, Grice, H.R.Smith, Elliott, Watson
Middle: Lawrence, Proudfoot, Jakeman, Keetley, Feeney, Hall, Fenner
Front: Taylor, Corkhill, Feebery, Haden

- 1933/34 Season -

Back: Mellors(Asst. Train), Lane, Feebury, Affleck, Hammond, Mills, Smith, Watson, A.Burgon, Banks (Trainer)
Standing: Jennings (Coach), Stimpson, Clarke, Corkhill, Grice, Elliott, Walker, Haden, Lawrence,
Henshall (Sec/Man.).   Sitting: Taylor, Jones, Fenner, H.Burgon, Macartney, Riley, Rickards, Lewis, Caiels
Front: Rowley, McAinsh

1933/34
18th in Division Two

#	Date	Opponent	Res	Scorers	Att	Hammond L	Stimpson GH	Feebery A	Smith HR	Walker G	Lawrence E	Taylor GT	Fenner T	Elliott S	Riley H	Haden S	Macartney CW	Lewis H	Grice F	Burgon A	Watson J	Mills PC	Rickards T	Corkhill WG	Holmes H	Cresswell F	Knox T	Clarke GW	Barley H	Fallon WJ
1	Aug 26	Hull City	1-0	Taylor	13441	1	2	3	4	5	6	7	8	9	10	11														
2	Sep 2	FULHAM	4-1	Macartney 2, Feebery(p), Fenner	14715	1	2	3	4	5	6	7	8			11	9			10										
3	4	Lincoln City	1-0	Taylor	8647	1	2	3	4	5	6	7	8			11	9			10										
4	9	Southampton	2-3	Fenner, Macartney	12237	1	2	3	4	5	6	7	8			11	9			10										
5	13	LINCOLN CITY	2-0	Taylor, Macartney	13709	1	2	3	4	5	6	7	8			11	9			10										
6	16	BLACKPOOL	1-1	Fenner	18957	1	2	3	4	5	6	7	8			11	9			10										
7	23	Bradford City	1-3	Fenner	11726	1	2	3	4		6	7	8			11	9			10	5									
8	30	Port Vale	3-2	Fenner 2, Macartney	15364	1	2	3	4	5	6	7	8				9			10		11								
9	Oct 7	Nottm. Forest	0-2		24452	1	2	3	4	5	6	7	8		10		9					11								
10	14	Swansea Town	1-1	Macartney	7715	1	2		4	5		7	8			11	9		6	10	3									
11	21	GRIMSBY TOWN	1-2	Macartney	16890	1	2		4	5		7	8			11	9		6	10	3									
12	28	Bradford Park Ave.	2-3	Macartney, Taylor	8997	1			4	5	10	7	8			11	9		6		3	2								
13	Nov 4	PRESTON NORTH END	2-2	Tremelling(og), Mills(p)	11445	1			4	5		7	8			11	9		6	10	3	2								
14	11	Oldham Athletic	0-2		6578	1			4	5		7	8			11	9		6	10	3	2								
15	18	BURNLEY	3-1	Lewis 2, Burgon	7938	1	2		4	5	6	7		8				10		11			3	9						
16	25	Brentford	2-2	Macartney, Taylor	12110	1	2		4	5	6	7		8			9	10		11			3							
17	Dec 2	BOLTON WANDERERS	1-2	Macartney	11279	1	2		4	5	6	7		8			9	10		11			3							
18	9	Manchester Utd.	2-1	Lewis, Haden	15564	1	2		4	5	6			8		11	9	10		7			3							
19	16	PLYMOUTH ARGYLE	2-1	Elliott, Macartney	7590	1	2		4	5	6			8		11	9	10		7			3							
20	23	West Ham United	3-5	Burgon 2, Elliott	16370	1	2		4	5	6			8		11	9	10		7			3							
21	25	MILLWALL	0-1		17298	1	2		4	5	6			8		11	9	10		7			3							
22	26	Millwall	2-3	Macartney, Hancock(og)	10172	1	2	3		5	6				10	11	9			7						8	4			
23	30	HULL CITY	0-0		9248	1	2	3		5	6				10	11	9								7	8	4			
24	Jan 1	Bury	1-3	Lewis	9886	1	2	3	8	5	6					11	9	10		7							4			
25	6	Fulham	0-3		15023	1		3		5	6			8		11	9	10		7						2	4			
26	20	SOUTHAMPTON	2-2	Cresswell, Lawrence	10942	1		3		5	6			8	10	11	9			7						2	4			
27	Feb 3	BRADFORD CITY	3-0	Riley 2, Burgon	10773			3		5	6			8	9					11		2				10	1	4	7	
28	7	Blackpool	1-2	Barley	10188			3		5	6			8		11	9					2				10	1	4	7	
29	10	Port Vale	0-0		10645			3		5	6			8			9			11		2				10	1	4	7	
30	17	NOTTM. FOREST	1-0	Cresswell	19643			3		5	6			8			9			11		2				10	1	4	7	
31	24	SWANSEA TOWN	1-1	Cresswell	10828			3		5	6			8			9			11		2				10	1	4	7	
32	Mar 3	Grimsby Town	2-2	Elliott, Riley	10918			3		5	6			8	9					11		2				10	1	4	7	11
33	17	Preston North End	0-2		10797			3		5	6			8	9					11		2				10	1	4	7	11
34	24	OLDHAM ATHLETIC	1-1	Cresswell	7897			3		5	6			8	9					11		2				10	1	4	7	11
35	30	BURY	2-1	Macartney 2	13382			3		5	6			8			9			11		2				10	1	4	7	11
36	31	Burnley	0-1		13971			3		5	6			8		11	9			7		2				10	1	4		
37	Apr 7	BRENTFORD	1-2	Macartney	11657			3		5	6			8		11	9			7		2				10	1	4		
38	14	Bolton Wanderers	0-1		11652			3	6	5	4			8		11	9					2				10	1		7	
39	16	BRADFORD PARK AVE.	1-0	Elliott	9141			3	6	5	4			8			9	7		11		2				10	1			
40	21	MANCHESTER UTD.	0-0		9645			3	6	5	4			8		11	9					2				10	1			
41	28	Plymouth Argyle	0-1		7465			3	6	5	4			8		11	9			7		2				10	1			
42	May 5	WEST HAM UNITED	1-2	Lewis	4436			3	4	5	6					11	9	10				2				8	1		7	
		Apps				26	21	30	28	41	38	17	14	20	16	27	34	21	6	22	5	28	4	4	2	16	16	11	11	4
		Goals						1			1	5	6	4	3	1	15	5		4		1				4			1	

Two own goals

F.A. Cup

Rd	Date	Opponent	Res		Att	Hammond L	Stimpson GH	Feebery A	Smith HR	Walker G	Lawrence E	Taylor GT	Fenner T	Elliott S	Riley H	Haden S	Macartney CW	Lewis H	Grice F	Burgon A	Watson J	Mills PC	Rickards T	Corkhill WG	Holmes H	Cresswell F	Knox T	Clarke GW	Barley H	Fallon WJ
R3	Jan 13	Swansea Town	0-1		13000	1		3		5	6			8		11	9	10		7						2	4			

		P	W	D	L	F	A	W	D	L	F	A	Pts
1	Grimsby Town	42	15	3	3	62	28	12	2	7	41	31	59
2	Preston North End	42	15	3	3	47	20	8	3	10	24	32	52
3	Bolton Wanderers	42	14	2	5	45	22	7	7	7	34	33	51
4	Brentford	42	15	2	4	52	24	7	5	9	33	36	51
5	Bradford Park Ave.	42	16	2	3	63	27	7	1	13	23	40	49
6	Bradford City	42	14	4	3	46	25	6	2	13	27	42	46
7	West Ham United	42	13	3	5	51	28	4	8	9	27	42	45
8	Port Vale	42	14	4	3	39	14	5	3	13	21	41	45
9	Oldham Athletic	42	12	5	4	48	28	5	5	11	24	32	44
10	Plymouth Argyle	42	12	7	2	43	20	3	6	12	26	50	43
11	Blackpool	42	10	8	3	39	27	5	5	11	23	37	43
12	Bury	42	12	4	5	43	31	5	5	11	27	42	43
13	Burnley	42	14	2	5	40	29	4	4	13	20	43	42
14	Southampton	42	15	2	4	40	21	0	6	15	14	37	38
15	Hull City	42	11	4	6	33	20	2	8	11	19	48	38
16	Fulham	42	13	3	5	29	17	2	4	15	19	50	37
17	Nottingham Forest	42	11	4	6	50	27	2	5	14	23	47	35
18	NOTTS COUNTY	42	9	7	5	32	22	3	4	14	21	40	35
19	Swansea Town	42	10	9	2	36	19	0	6	15	15	41	35
20	Manchester United	42	9	3	9	29	33	5	3	13	30	52	34
21	Millwall	42	8	8	5	21	17	3	3	15	18	51	33
22	Lincoln City	42	7	7	7	31	23	2	1	18	13	52	26

1934/35   22nd in Division Two (Relegated)

#	Mon	Date	Opponent	Res	Scorers	Att	Knox T	Mills PC	Feebery A	Lawrence E	Walker G	Clarke GW	McGrath, James	Rankin JP	Macartney CW	Lewis H	Haden S	Rickards T	Corkhill WG	Jones F	Fallon WJ	Higgins A	Smith HR	Poskett TW	Julian W	Steele E	Stabb GH	Grice F	Shaw F	Bramham A	Green RCG	King TP
1	Aug	25	Swansea Town	1-2	McGrath	11759	1	2	3	4	5	6	7	8	9	10	11															
2		27	Barnsley	1-1	Clarke	10338	1	2	3	4	5	6	7	8	9	10	11															
3	Sep	1	BURNLEY	1-0	McGrath	15363	1	2	3	4	5	6	7	8	9	10	11															
4		3	BARNSLEY	1-4	Macartney	8662	1	2	3	4	5	6		7	9	10	11	8														
5		8	Oldham Athletic	0-1		7350	1	2	3		5	6	7	10	9		11	8	4													
6		15	BOLTON WANDERERS	0-2		13783	1	2	3		5	6	7	10				8	4	9	11											
7		22	Southampton	1-1	Rickards	4850	1	2	3		5	6	7	10	9			8	4		11											
8		29	NOTTM. FOREST	3-5	McGrath, Higgins, Lewis	15294	1	2	3		5	6	7	10		9			4		11	8										
9	Oct	6	BRADFORD CITY	2-3	Lawrence(p), Rankin	13187	1	2	3	6			7	10	9		11		4			8			5							
10		13	Sheffield United	0-3		15173		2	3	6			7	10	9		11		4			8	1		5							
11		20	Brentford	1-4	Higgins	10409		2	3	6	5		7	10	9				4		11	8	1									
12		27	FULHAM	1-1	Fallon	11643		2	3	6	5			10					4		11	8	1			7	9					
13	Nov	3	Bradford Park Ave.	0-0		6831		2	3	6	5			10					4		11	8	1			7	9					
14		10	PLYMOUTH ARGYLE	1-3	Stabb	10927		2	3	6	5			10					4		11	8	1			7	9					
15		17	Norwich City	2-7	Lewis, Steele	11297		2	3	6						10	11		4			8	1			7	9	5				
16		24	NEWCASTLE UNITED	0-1		9616		2	3	6	5		11	10					4			8	1			7	9					
17	Dec	1	West Ham United	0-4		18390		2	3	6	5			10					4		11	8	1			7	9					
18		8	BLACKPOOL	3-2	Stabb 2, Steele	10067	1	2	3	6	5			8			11		4							7	9	10				
19		15	Bury	0-1		8346	1	2	3	6	5			8			11		4							7	9	10				
20		22	HULL CITY	1-1	Steele	5673	1	2	3		5			8		10			4		11					7	9	6				
21		25	Manchester Utd.	1-2	Steele	32965	1	2	3	6	5			8					4		11					7	9	10				
22		26	MANCHESTER UTD.	1-0	Stabb	24599	1	2	3	6	5			8					4		11					7	9	10				
23		29	SWANSEA TOWN	4-0	Shaw 3, Grice	13221	1	2	3	6	5								4		11					7	9	10	8			
24	Jan	5	Burnley	0-4		10409	1	2	3	6	5								4		11					7	9	10	8			
25		19	OLDHAM ATHLETIC	2-1	Stabb, Shaw	10984	1	2	3	6	5			8					4		11					7	9		10			
26		30	Bolton Wanderers	1-5	Steele	8220	1	2	3	6	5			8					4		11					7	9		10			
27	Feb	2	SOUTHAMPTON	3-1	Shaw 3	9240	1	2	3		5			8	9				4							7	11	6	10			
28		9	Nottm. Forest	3-2	Shaw, Bramham 2	19179	1	2	3	5	4			8												7	11	6	10	9		
29		16	Bradford City	0-2		2611	1	2	3	5	4			8												7	11	6	10	9		
30		23	SHEFFIELD UNITED	0-1		11724	1	2	3	5	4															7	10	6	8	9	11	
31	Mar	2	BRENTFORD	0-1		10252	1	2	3	4	5			8												7	9	6	10		11	
32		9	Fulham	0-7		8634	1	2	3	4	5			8												7	9	6	10		11	
33		16	BRADFORD PARK AVE.	1-1	Steele	9199			3					8					4				1	5		7	9	6	10		11	2
34		23	Plymouth Argyle	0-4		8691	1		3					8		10			4					5		7		6		9	11	2
35		30	NORWICH CITY	1-0	Bramham	7295	1	2	3					10					4					5		7		6	8	9	11	
36	Apr	6	Newcastle United	1-1	Bramham	12394	1	2	3					10					4					5		7		6	8	9	11	
37		13	WEST HAM UNITED	0-2		9721	1	2	3					10					4					5		7		6	8	9	11	
38		19	Port Vale	3-5	Rankin, Corkhill, Steele	9010	1	2	3					10					4					5		7		6	8	9	11	
39		20	Blackpool	1-3	Stabb	15434	1	2	3					10					4					5		7	9	6	8		11	
40		22	PORT VALE	3-2	Bramham 2, Shaw	6765	1	2	3					10					4					5		7		6	8	9	11	
41		27	BURY	1-2	Shaw	3448	1	2	3					8					4					5				6	10	9	11	
42	May	4	Hull City	1-5	Shaw	2721	1	2	3					10					4					5		7	9	6	8		11	
apps							32	40	39	27	34	8	11	23	8	11	19	9	32	1	14	10	9	10	2	30	24	24	20	9	13	2
Goals										1		1	3	2	1	2		1	1		1	2				7	5	1	12	6		

Played in game 41: A Hoult (7).

F.A. Cup

#	Mon	Date	Opponent	Res	Att	Knox T	Mills PC	Feebery A	Lawrence E	Walker G	Clarke GW	McGrath, James	Rankin JP	Macartney CW	Lewis H	Haden S	Rickards T	Corkhill WG	Jones F	Fallon WJ	Higgins A	Smith HR	Poskett TW	Julian W	Steele E	Stabb GH	Grice F	Shaw F	Bramham A	Green RCG	King TP
R3	Jan	12	Wolverhampton Wand.	0-4	26754	1	2	3	6	5			10					4		11					7	9		8			

	P	W	D	L	F	A	W	D	L	F	A	Pts
1 Brentford	42	19	2	0	59	14	7	7	7	34	34	61
2 Bolton Wanderers	42	17	1	3	63	15	9	3	9	33	33	56
3 West Ham United	42	18	1	2	46	17	8	3	10	34	46	56
4 Blackpool	42	16	4	1	46	18	5	7	9	33	39	53
5 Manchester United	42	16	2	3	50	21	7	2	12	26	34	50
6 Newcastle United	42	14	2	5	55	25	8	2	11	34	43	48
7 Fulham	42	15	3	3	62	26	2	9	10	14	30	46
8 Plymouth Argyle	42	13	3	5	48	26	6	5	10	27	38	46
9 Nottingham Forest	42	12	5	4	46	23	5	3	13	30	47	42
10 Bury	42	14	1	6	38	26	5	3	13	24	47	42
11 Sheffield United	42	11	4	6	51	30	5	5	11	28	40	41
12 Burnley	42	11	2	8	43	32	5	7	9	20	41	41
13 Hull City	42	9	6	6	32	22	7	2	12	31	52	40
14 Norwich City	42	11	6	4	51	23	3	5	13	20	38	39
15 Bradford Park Ave.	42	7	8	6	32	28	4	8	9	23	35	38
16 Barnsley	42	8	10	3	32	22	5	2	14	28	61	38
17 Swansea Town	42	13	5	3	41	22	1	3	17	15	45	36
18 Port Vale	42	10	7	4	42	28	1	5	15	13	46	34
19 Southampton	42	9	8	4	28	19	2	4	15	18	56	34
20 Bradford City	42	10	7	4	34	20	2	1	18	16	48	32
21 Oldham Athletic	42	10	3	8	44	40	0	3	18	12	55	26
22 NOTTS COUNTY	42	8	3	10	29	33	1	4	16	17	64	25

- 1934/35 Season -

Back: Lawrence, Feebury, Knox, Watson, Poskett, H.Smith, Julian, B.Jones
Middle: Fallon, Stimpson, Mills, Walker, Grice, M.Jones, Corkhill, F.Jones, Bramham
Front: McGrath, Rankin, Rickards, Macartney, C.Jones (Sec.Manager), Lewis, Hoult, Haden, Clarke

- 1935/36 Season -

Back: Feebury, Grice, Knox, Blyth, Mills, Chandler
Standing: Banks (Asst.Trainer), Walker, Clarke, Corkhill, Lawrence, Bramham, Featherby, Seddon(Trainer)
Sitting: Meads, Gillon, Millington, Smith (Sec/Man.), Barnes (Chairman), Godfrey (Treasurer), Rickards, Haden, Fallon
Front: Hoult, Green, Steele, Julian

1935/36   9th in Division Three (South)

Player columns (in order): Blyth G, Mills PC, Feebery A, Corkhill WG, Walker G, Meads T, Steele E, Featherby L, Chandler A, Green R, Millington J, Hoult A, Rickards T, Grice F, Bramham A, Haden S, Shaw F, Fallon WJ, Clarke GW, Notley W, Knox T, Rankin JP, Lawrence E, Julian W

#	Date	Opponent	Score	Scorers	Att	Bly	Mil	Fee	Cor	Wal	Mea	Ste	Fea	Cha	Gre	Min	Hou	Ric	Gri	Bra	Had	Sha	Fal	Cla	Not	Kno	Ran	Law	Jul
1	Aug 31	Bristol Rovers	0-0		15197	1	2	3	4	5	6	7	8	9	10	11													
2	Sep 4	GILLINGHAM	3-3	Green, Corkhill, Chandler	9863	1	2	3	4	5	6		8	9	10	11	7												
3	7	CLAPTON ORIENT	2-0	Rickards, Chandler	11966	1	2	3	4	5	6			9	10	11	7	8											
4	11	Gillingham	0-0		5162	1	2	3	4	5		7		9	10	11		8	6										
5	14	Southend United	0-0		11948	1	2	3	4	5	6	7		9	10	11		8											
6	18	BOURNEMOUTH	1-3	Mills(p)	7735	1	2	3	4	5	6	7			10	11		8			9								
7	21	NORTHAMPTON T	3-0	Bramham 2, Corkhill	8929	1	2	3	4	5	6					11		8		10	9	7							
8	28	Crystal Palace	0-0		16153	1	2	3	4	5	10					11		8	6		9	7							
9	Oct 5	READING	1-3	Mills(p)	10875	1	2	3	4	5	6					11		8			9	7	10						
10	12	Cardiff City	2-3	Meads, Chandler	11458	1	2	3	4	5	10			9					6			7	8	11					
11	19	QUEENS PARK RANGERS	3-0	Notley 2, Meads	7369	1	2	3	4		10								6			7	8	11	5	9			
12	26	Brighton & Hove Alb.	1-5	Notley	8158	1	2	3	4		10						7		6			8	11	5	9				
13	Nov 2	EXETER CITY	3-1	Shaw, Notley, Lawton(og)	7302		2	3	4			7			10				6			8	11	5	9	1			
14	9	Bristol City	1-1	Notley	12343		2	3	4			7			10				6			8	11	5	9	1			
15	16	COVENTRY CITY	2-1	Fallon, Green	17902		2	3	4			7			10				6			8	11	5	9	1			
16	23	Swindon Town	1-2	Notley	8233		2	3	4			7			10				6			8	11	5	9	1			
17	Dec 7	Torquay United	1-0	Rickards	3817		2	3	4			7						8	6				11	5	9	1	10		
18	18	MILLWALL	0-0		2325		2	3	4			7			10			8	6				11	5	9	1			
19	25	LUTON TOWN	0-3		12186		2	3				7						8	6				11	5	9	1	10	4	
20	26	Luton Town	0-1		17835		2	3	4	5	6			9	10		7	8					11			1			
21	28	BRISTOL ROVERS	6-0	Green 2, Chandler 2, Rickards, McLean(og)	8669		2	3	4	5	6			9	10		7	8					11			1			
22	Jan 4	Clapton Orient	2-0	Chandler, Rickards	9003		2	3	4	5	6			9	10		7	8					11			1			
23	18	SOUTHEND UNITED	1-2	Rickards	6584		2	3	4	5		7			10			8	6				11		9	1			
24	25	Northampton T	1-3	Shaw	6285		2	3	4	5			10	9				8	6			7	11			1			
25	Feb 1	CRYSTAL PALACE	3-1	Green, Bramham, Mills(p)	8385		2	3	4	5					10			8	6	9		7	11			1			
26	8	Reading	1-3	Fallon	7811		2	3	4	5					10			8	6		9	7	11			1			
27	12	ALDERSHOT	1-2	Fallon	2817		2	3	4	5	10							8	6		9	7	11			1			
28	15	CARDIFF CITY	2-0	Fallon, Shaw	4639		2	3	4								7	8	6			10	11	5	9	1			
29	22	Queens Park Rangers	2-2	Fallon, Steele	6497		2	3	4			7						8	6			10	11	5	9	1			
30	27	Newport County	2-1	Shaw, Corkhill	2818		2	3	4			7						8	6			10	11	5	9	1			
31	29	BRISTOL CITY	1-1	Mills(p)	3154		2	3	4			7			9			8	6			10	11	5		1			
32	Mar 7	Millwall	1-2	Shaw	8604		2	3	4			7						8	6			10	11	5	9	1			
33	14	BRIGHTON & HOVE ALB.	1-1	Rickards	5263			3	4			7						8	6		9	10	11	5		1			2
34	21	Coventry City	1-5	Steele	17145		2	3	4			7			10			8				9	11	5		1		6	
35	28	SWINDON TOWN	0-0		4798		2	3	8	5		7			9							10	11	4		1		6	
36	Apr 4	Aldershot	1-3	Shaw	3321		2	3	4			7										10	11	5	9	1		6	
37	10	Watford	2-1	Rickards, Bramham	10191	1	2	3	4	5		7						8		9		10	11					6	
38	11	TORQUAY UNITED	1-0	Notley	4445	1	2	3	4	5		7						8				10	11		9			6	
39	13	WATFORD	0-2		6343	1	2	3	4	5		7						8				10	11		9			6	
40	18	Exeter City	0-0		3888	1	2	3		5	6	7						8				10	11		9			4	
41	25	NEWPORT COUNTY	6-2	Notley 2, Walker, Shaw, Millington, Rickards	2180	1	2	3		5	6					7		8				10	11		9			4	
42	May 2	Bournemouth	1-0	Rickards	4872	1	2	3		5	6					11	7	8				10			9			4	
		Apps				18	42	41	38	25	18	24	3	10	23	8	7	33	24	9	5	27	32	18	20	24	2	10	1
		Goals					4		3	1	2	2		6	5	1		9		4		7	5		9				

Two own goals

F.A. Cup

	Date	Opponent	Score	Scorers	Att	Bly	Mil	Fee	Cor	Wal	Mea	Ste	Fea	Cha	Gre	Min	Hou	Ric	Gri	Bra	Had	Sha	Fal	Cla	Not	Kno	Ran	Law	Jul
R1	Nov 30	Grantham	2-0	Fallon, Green	8000		2	3	4			7			10			8	6				11	5	9	1			
R2	Dec 14	TORQUAY UNITED	3-0	Fallon, Rickards, Hunt(og)	13224		2	3	4			7			10			8	6				11	5	9	1			
R3	Jan 11	TRANMERE ROVERS	0-0		25153		2	3	4	5	6			9	10			8					11		7	1			
rep	Jan 15	Tranmere Rovers	3-4	Chandler, Rickards, Steele	15109		2	3	4	5	6	7		9	10			8					11			1			

Division Three (South) Cup

	Date	Opponent	Score	Scorers	Att	Bly	Mil	Fee	Cor	Wal	Mea	Ste	Fea	Cha	Gre	Min	Hou	Ric	Gri	Bra	Had	Sha	Fal	Cla	Not	Kno	Ran	Law	Jul
R1	Sep 25	WATFORD	2-1	Green, Chandler	3000	1	2	3	4	5		7		10	9	11		8	6										
R2	Oct 23	Swindon Town	3-4	Bramham, Shaw, Fallon	1814		2	5			10						7		6	9		8	11	5		1		4	

Division Three (South) — Final Table

		P	W	D	L	F	A	W	D	L	F	A	Pts
1	Coventry City	42	19	1	1	75	12	5	8	8	27	33	57
2	Luton Town	42	13	6	2	56	20	9	6	6	25	25	56
3	Reading	42	18	0	3	52	20	8	2	11	35	42	54
4	Queen's Park Rgs.	42	14	4	3	55	19	8	5	8	29	34	53
5	Watford	42	12	3	6	47	29	8	6	7	33	25	49
6	Crystal Palace	42	15	4	2	64	20	7	1	13	32	54	49
7	Brighton & Hove A.	42	13	4	4	48	25	5	4	12	22	38	44
8	Bournemouth	42	9	6	6	36	26	7	5	9	24	30	43
9	NOTTS COUNTY	42	10	5	6	40	25	5	7	9	20	32	42
10	Torquay United	42	14	4	3	41	27	2	5	14	21	35	41
11	Aldershot	42	9	6	6	29	21	5	6	10	24	40	40
12	Millwall	42	9	8	4	33	21	5	4	12	25	50	40
13	Bristol City	42	11	5	5	32	21	4	5	12	16	38	40
14	Clapton Orient	42	13	2	6	34	15	3	4	14	21	46	38
15	Northampton Town	42	12	5	4	38	24	3	3	15	24	66	38
16	Gillingham	42	9	5	7	34	25	5	4	12	32	52	37
17	Bristol Rovers	42	11	6	4	48	31	3	3	15	21	64	37
18	Southend United	42	8	7	6	38	21	5	3	13	23	41	36
19	Swindon Town	42	10	5	6	43	33	4	3	14	21	40	36
20	Cardiff City	42	11	5	5	37	23	2	5	14	23	50	36
21	Newport County	42	8	4	9	36	44	3	5	13	24	67	31
22	Exeter City	42	7	5	9	38	41	1	6	14	21	52	27

1936/37   2nd in Division Three (South)

No	Date	Opponent	Score	Scorers	Att	Blyth G	Mills PC	Feebery A	Corkhill WG	Wyness G	Vasey RH	Ferguson C	Chalmers W	Smith James	Shaw F	Fallon WJ	Julian W	Kavanagh T	Rickards T	Millington J	Mardon HJ	Gallacher HK	Moulson C	McLenahan H	Hatton C	Cooper S
1	Aug 29	EXETER CITY	3-1	Shaw, Ferguson 2	10216	1	2	3	4	5	6	7	8	9	10	11										
2	Sep 2	Crystal Palace	2-1	Fallon, Smith	11740	1	2	3	4	5	6	7	8	9	10	11										
3	Sep 5	Reading	1-4	Shaw	11189	1	2	3	4	5	6	7	8	9	10	11										
4	Sep 7	CRYSTAL PALACE	0-1		7042	1	2		4	5		7		9	10	11	3	6	8							
5	Sep 12	QUEENS PARK RANGERS	1-2	Mills(p)	5013	1	2	3	4	5					10	11		6	8	7	9					
6	Sep 19	Bristol City	1-1	Mills(p)	10330	1	2	3	4	5	6		8			11			10	7	9					
7	Sep 26	TORQUAY UNITED	2-0	Chalmers, Fallon	16021	1	2	3	4	5	6		8		10	11			7			9				
8	Oct 1	WALSALL	3-3	Gallacher 2, Mills(p)	10215	1	2	3	4		6		8		10				7		11	9	5			
9	Oct 3	Bournemouth	0-1		11974	1	2	3	4		6		8		10	11			7			9	5			
10	Oct 10	Clapton Orient	1-1	Fallon	10467	1		3	4		6		8		10	11	2		7			9	5			
11	Oct 17	NORTHAMPTON T	3-2	Gallacher 3(1p)	14557	1	2	3	4		6	10	8			11			7			9	5			
12	Oct 24	Bristol Rovers	3-2	Gallacher 2, Vasey	13187	1	2	3	4		6	10	8			11			7			9	5			
13	Oct 31	MILLWALL	1-1	Ferguson	14195	1	2	3	4		6	10	8			11			7			9	5			
14	Nov 7	Swindon Town	2-2	Mardon, Ferguson	10410	1	2	3	4		6	10				11			7		8	9	5			
15	Nov 14	ALDERSHOT	3-0	Gallacher(p), Rickards, Corkhill	13360	1	2	3	4		6	10	8			11			7			9	5			
16	Nov 21	Gillingham	0-3		12215	1	2	3	4		6	10	8			11			7			9	5			
17	Dec 5	Southend United	3-2	Chalmers, Rickards, Corkhill	6838	1	2	3	4			10	8			11	6		7			9	5			
18	Dec 12	WATFORD	2-1	Gallacher 2	8187	1	2	3	4			10	8			11	6		7			9	5			
19	Dec 19	Brighton & Hove Alb.	2-2	Ferguson, Gallacher	10989	1	2	3	4			10	8			11	6		7			9	5			
20	Dec 25	Luton Town	1-2	Ferguson	17569	1	2	3	4			10	8			11	6		7			9	5			
21	Dec 26	Exeter City	3-1	Fallon, Chalmers, Ferguson	11679	1	2	3	4		6	10	8			11			7			9	5			
22	Dec 28	LUTON TOWN	2-1	Chalmers, Mardon	16987	1	2	3	4		6		8			11			7		10	9	5			
23	Jan 2	READING	1-0	Mardon	15484	1	2	3	4		6		8			11			7		10	9	5			
24	Jan 9	Queens Park Rangers	2-0	Chalmers, Mardon	14938	1	2	3	4				8			11			7		10	9	5	6		
25	Jan 16	NEWPORT COUNTY	3-1	Fallon, Gallacher 2	10914	1	2	3	4				8			11			7		10	9	5	6		
26	Jan 23	BRISTOL CITY	1-0	Rickards	9033	1	2	3	4		6		8			11			7		10	9	5			
27	Jan 30	Torquay United	2-2	Gallacher(p), Rickards	2458	1	2	3	4		6	10	8			11			7			9	5			
28	Feb 6	BOURNEMOUTH	4-3	Chalmers 3, Gallacher	17695	1	2	3	4		6	10	8			11			7			9	5			
29	Feb 13	CLAPTON ORIENT	0-0		14316	1	2	3	4			10	8			11			7			9	5	6		
30	Feb 20	Northampton T	1-1	Hatton	18435	1	2	3	4				8			11			7		8	9	5	6	10	
31	Feb 27	BRISTOL ROVERS	4-3	Millington, Gallacher 3	13648	1	2	3	4		6		8			7				11	10	9	5			
32	Mar 8	Millwall	0-0		8644	1	2	3	4		6		8			7				11	10	9	5			
33	Mar 13	SWINDON TOWN	3-2	Gallacher, Cooper 2	16531	1	2	3	4		6		8			11			7			9	5			10
34	Mar 20	Aldershot	1-0	Fallon	5613	1	2	3	4				8			11						9	6	5	7	10
35	Mar 26	CARDIFF CITY	4-0	Gallacher 2, Chalmers, Ferguson	17664	1	2	3	4			10	8			11						9	6	5	7	
36	Mar 27	GILLINGHAM	2-0	Gallacher 2(1p)	20821	1	2	3	4			10	8			11			7			9	6	5		
37	Mar 29	Cardiff City	2-0	Rickards, Gallacher	20245	1	2	3	4			10	8			11			7			9	6	5		
38	Apr 3	Newport County	0-2		12324	1	2		4		6	10	8			11			7			9	3	5		
39	Apr 10	SOUTHEND UNITED	2-1	Mardon, Mills	15294	1		3	4				8			11	2		7			9	6	5		10
40	Apr 17	Watford	2-0	Rickards 2	10586	1		3	4				8			11	2		9				6	5	7	10
41	Apr 24	BRIGHTON & HOVE ALB.	0-1		29516	1	2	3	4				8			11			7			9	6	5		10
42	May 1	Walsall	1-2	Gallacher	5902	1	2	3	4				8			11			7			9	6	5		10

| | | | | Apps | | 42 | 41 | 38 | 41 | 10 | 22 | 22 | 38 | 4 | 9 | 41 | 8 | 2 | 33 | 7 | 14 | 32 | 31 | 17 | 4 | 6 |
| | | | | Goals | | | 4 | | 2 | | 1 | 8 | 9 | 1 | 2 | 6 | | | 7 | 1 | 5 | 25 | | | 1 | 2 |

F.A. Cup

	Date	Opponent	Score		Att	Blyth G	Mills PC	Feebery A	Corkhill WG	Wyness G	Vasey RH	Ferguson C	Chalmers W	Smith James	Shaw F	Fallon WJ	Julian W	Kavanagh T	Rickards T	Millington J	Mardon HJ	Gallacher HK	Moulson C
R1	Nov 28	Gateshead	0-2		11456	1	2	3	4		6	10				11			7		8	9	5

Division Three (South) Cup

	Date	Opponent	Score	Scorers	Att	Blyth G	Mills PC	Feebery A	Corkhill WG	Vasey RH	Ferguson C	Chalmers W	Shaw F	Fallon WJ	Julian W	Kavanagh T	Rickards T	Millington J	Mardon HJ	Gallacher HK	Moulson C	Cooper S
R2	Oct 21	READING	3-2	Mardon 2, Rickards	3212	1		3		6		8	10	11	2	4	7			9	5	
R3	Nov 11	Luton Town	4-2	Mardon 2, Ferguson 2	3000	1	2	3	4	6	10	8		11			7			9	5	
SF	Apr 26	WATFORD	1-1	Morgan (og)	1300	1		3	4	6	10	8				2	7	11		9	5	
rep	Sep 13	Watford	3-8	Mardon, Halton, Rickards	500							8				2				9		10

SF replay played in season 1937/38. Also played in this game: MK Brannon(1), J Gallager(3), JS Hindmarsh(4), Roberts(5), S Haden(6), RL Halton(7), R Houghton(11).

		P	W	D	L	F	A	W	D	L	F	A	Pts
1	Luton Town	42	19	1	1	69	16	8	3	10	34	37	58
2	NOTTS COUNTY	42	15	3	3	44	23	8	7	6	30	29	56
3	Brighton & Hove A.	42	15	5	1	49	16	9	0	12	25	27	53
4	Watford	42	14	4	3	53	21	5	7	9	32	39	49
5	Reading	42	14	5	2	53	23	5	6	10	23	37	49
6	Bournemouth	42	17	3	1	45	20	3	6	12	20	39	49
7	Northampton Town	42	15	4	2	56	22	5	2	14	29	46	46
8	Millwall	42	12	4	5	43	24	6	6	9	21	30	46
9	Queen's Park Rgs.	42	12	2	7	51	24	6	7	8	22	28	45
10	Southend United	42	10	8	3	49	23	7	3	11	29	44	45
11	Gillingham	42	14	5	2	36	18	4	3	14	16	48	44
12	Clapton Orient	42	10	8	3	29	17	4	7	10	23	35	43
13	Swindon Town	42	12	4	5	52	24	2	7	12	23	49	39
14	Crystal Palace	42	11	7	3	45	20	2	5	14	17	41	38
15	Bristol Rovers	42	14	3	4	49	20	2	1	18	22	60	36
16	Bristol City	42	13	3	5	42	20	2	3	16	16	50	36
17	Walsall	42	11	3	7	38	34	2	7	12	25	51	36
18	Cardiff City	42	10	5	6	35	24	4	2	15	19	63	35
19	Newport County	42	7	7	7	37	28	5	3	13	30	70	34
20	Torquay United	42	9	5	7	42	32	2	5	14	15	48	32
21	Exeter City	42	9	5	7	36	37	1	7	13	23	51	32
22	Aldershot	42	5	6	10	29	29	2	3	16	21	60	23

- 1936/37 Season -

Back: Wyness, Kavanagh, Chalmers, Blyth, Shaw, Vasey, Millington
Standing: Ratcliffe (Trainer), Julian, Mills, Feebury, Corkhill, Lowery, Walker, Rickards, Haden (Asst.Trainer)
Sitting: J.Smith, P.Smith (Sec/Man.), Hobson(Dir), Walker(Dir.), Barnes (Chair.), Towers (Dir.), Phillip (Dir.), Fallon
Front: Ferguson, Taylor, Stevens, Flewitt, Mardon

- 1937/38 Season -

Back: Rickards, Feebury, McLenahan, Fallon, Cooper, Vasey, Cottam
Standing: Ratcliffe(Trainer), Halton, Moulson, Corkhill, Brannon, Blyth, Mills, Chalmers, Roberts, Haden (Asst.Trainer)
Sitting: Mardon, H.Gallacher, Miller (Director), Barnes (Chairman), Towers (Director), Beech, Julian
Front: Hatton, Hindmarsh, Stevenson, R.Houghton

1937/38   11th in Division Three (South)

Scorers in game 19: Chalmers 2, Richards, Gallacher, Fallon

#		Date	Opponent	Score	Scorers	Att	Blyth G	Mills PC	Feebery A	Corkhill WG	McLenahan H	Beech A	Hatton R	Chalmers W	Gallacher HK	Cooper S	Fallon WJ	Mardon HJ	Hatton C	Rickards T	Clayton S	Gallagher J	Julian W	Vasey RH	Moulson C	Hindmarsh JS	Riley J	Brannon MK	Burditt K	Houghton R	Dean WR	Roy JR
1	Aug	28	SWINDON TOWN	3-0	Fallon, Corkhill, Chalmers	17313	1	2	3	4	5	6	7	8	9	10	11															
2	Sep	1	Exeter City	3-0	Gallacher, Corkhill, Angus(og)	8799	1	2	3	4	5	6	7	8	9	10	11															
3		4	Aldershot	1-0	Chalmers	7513	1	2	3	4	5	6	7	8		10	11	9														
4		8	EXETER CITY	0-0		17179	1	2	3	4	5	6	7	8	9		11		10													
5		11	MILLWALL	1-1	Mardon	15637	1	2	3	4	5	6					11	9	10	7	8											
6		18	Reading	2-0	Gallacher 2(1p)	14690	1	2	3	4	5	6		8	9	10	11			7												
7		22	BRISTOL CITY	2-0	Gallacher, Cooper	10937	1	2	3	4	5	6		8	9	10	11			7												
8		25	CRYSTAL PALACE	0-1		18164	1	2	3	4	5	6		8	9	10	11			7												
9	Oct	2	Cardiff City	2-2	Rickards, McLenahan	35468	1	2	3	4	5					10	11	9	8	7		6										
10		7	MANSFIELD TOWN	2-0	Fallon, Mardon	13632	1	2	3	4	5					10	11	9		7		6										
11		9	Newport County	0-3		11574	1		3	4	5	6		8		10	11	9		7			2									
12		16	BOURNEMOUTH	1-2	Mardon	15218	1	2	3	4					9		11	10	8	7					6							
13		23	Brighton & Hove Alb.	1-0	Marriott(og)	9231	1	2		4	5		11	8				9	10	7					6	3						
14		30	QUEENS PARK RANGERS	2-2	Chalmers, Hatton	11705	1	2		4	5			8			11	9	10	7					6	3						
15	Nov	6	Southend United	1-2	Fallon	8674	1	2		4	5		7	8			11		10	9					6	3						
16		13	CLAPTON ORIENT	1-0	Chalmers	11030	1	2		4	10			8	9		11			7		5				3	6					
17		20	Torquay United	3-0	Gallacher 2, Hatton	4286	1	2		4				8	9		11		7	10		5				3	6					
18	Dec	4	Bristol Rovers	1-1	O'Mahoney(og)	5572	1	2		4				8	9		11		7	10		5				3	6					
19		11	NORTHAMPTON T	5-0	*See below	9988	1	2		4	6			10	9		11		7	8		5				3						
20		18	Walsall	0-1		4483	1	2		4	6			10	9		11		7	8		5				3						
21		27	GILLINGHAM	1-0	Rickards	23337	1	2		4	6			10			11		7	8		5				3	9					
22	Jan	1	Swindon Town	0-1		9897	1	2		4	6			10			11		7	8		5				3	9					
23		15	ALDERSHOT	1-0	Chalmers	8125	1	2		4	5			10			11		7	8		9				3	6					
24		24	Millwall	0-5		12521	1	2		4	5			8			11		10	9						3	6					
25		29	READING	2-1	Hatton, Fallon	11046		2		4	5			8			11		10	7						3	6	1	9			
26	Feb	5	Crystal Palace	1-3	Fallon	16244	1				6		7				11		10			5			3	4			9	8		
27		12	CARDIFF CITY	2-0	Rickards, Fallon	13278	1	2		4	5			10			11		7	8						3	6		9			
28		19	NEWPORT COUNTY	1-1	Rickards	12843	1	2		4	5						11		10	9	7					3	6		8			
29		26	Bournemouth	1-1	Fallon	8599	1	2		4	5						11		10	9						3	6		8	7		
30	Mar	5	BRIGHTON & HOVE ALB.	0-3		14816	1	2	3	4							11		10						5		6		9	8	7	
31		12	Queens Park Rangers	1-2	Hatton	19078	1	2		4	5						11		10							3	6			8	9	
32		16	Gillingham	1-2	Chalmers	3949	1	2		4	5			8					10			6				3				7	9	11
33		19	SOUTHEND UNITED	0-2		12878	1	2		4	5						11		10	7	8				6	3					9	11
34		26	Clapton Orient	0-2		7483		2		4				8						7	5				3		6	9	1	10		11
35	Apr	2	TORQUAY UNITED	0-0		6470	1			4					10		11			8	5	2				3	6		9			7
36		9	Mansfield Town	2-1	Hatton, Gallagher	11190	1	2	3	4							11		10	8	9	5					6					7
37		15	Watford	0-2		14984	1	2	3	4							11		10	8	9	5					6					7
38		16	BRISTOL ROVERS	1-1	Cooper	3671		2	3	4						10				7		9					5	1	8			11
39		18	WATFORD	1-2	Gallagher	13820	1		3	4						10				7	8	9		2	5		6					11
40		23	Northampton T	0-2		11175	1	2	3	4	6					10			8	7		9			5							11
41		30	WALSALL	3-1	Hatton 2, Mills(p)	2828	1	2	3	4	6						11		10	8		5					9			7		
42	May	7	Bristol City	1-3	Riley(p)	13781	1	2	3	4							11			8		5					6	9		10		7
			Apps				39	40	19	41	29	13	6	27	13	17	29	8	21	30	15	21	3	5	30	18	7	3	12	4	3	9
			Goals					1		2	1			8	7	2	8	3	7	5		2					1					

Three own goals

F.A. Cup

		Date	Opponent	Score	Scorers	Att	Blyth G	Mills PC	Feebery A	Corkhill WG	McLenahan H	Beech A	Hatton R	Chalmers W	Gallacher HK	Cooper S	Fallon WJ	Mardon HJ	Hatton C	Rickards T	Clayton S	Gallagher J	Julian W	Vasey RH	Moulson C	Hindmarsh JS	Riley J	Brannon MK	Burditt K	Houghton R	Dean WR	Roy JR
R3	Jan	8	Aldershot	3-1	Chalmers, Gallagher, Rickards	9000	1	2		4	5			10			11			7	8	9				3	6					
R4	Jan	22	Huddersfield Town	0-1		29480	1	2		4	5			10			11			7	8	9				3	6					

Division Three (South) Cup

		Date	Opponent	Score		Att	Blyth G	Mills PC	Feebery A	Corkhill WG	McLenahan H	Beech A	Hatton R	Chalmers W	Gallacher HK	Cooper S	Fallon WJ	Mardon HJ	Hatton C	Rickards T	Clayton S	Gallagher J	Julian W	Vasey RH	Moulson C	Hindmarsh JS	Riley J	Brannon MK	Burditt K	Houghton R	Dean WR	Roy JR
R2	Nov	10	WATFORD	0-2		1000		2		4	5	10	11	8			9								3	6		1		7		

Division Three (South) final table

		P	W	D	L	F	A	W	D	L	F	A	Pts
1	Millwall	42	15	3	3	53	15	8	7	6	30	22	56
2	Bristol City	42	14	6	1	37	13	7	7	7	31	27	55
3	Queen's Park Rgs.	42	15	3	3	44	17	7	6	8	36	30	53
4	Watford	42	14	4	3	50	15	7	7	7	23	28	53
5	Brighton & Hove A.	42	15	3	3	40	16	6	6	9	24	28	51
6	Reading	42	17	2	2	44	21	3	9	9	27	42	51
7	Crystal Palace	42	14	4	3	45	17	4	8	9	22	30	48
8	Swindon Town	42	12	4	5	33	19	5	6	10	16	30	44
9	Northampton Town	42	12	4	5	30	19	5	5	11	21	38	43
10	Cardiff City	42	13	7	1	57	22	2	5	14	10	32	42
11	NOTTS COUNTY	42	10	6	5	29	17	6	3	12	21	33	41
12	Southend United	42	12	5	4	43	23	3	5	13	27	45	40
13	Bournemouth	42	8	10	3	36	20	6	2	13	20	37	40
14	Mansfield Town	42	12	5	4	46	26	3	4	14	16	41	39
15	Bristol Rovers	42	10	7	4	28	20	3	6	12	18	41	39
16	Newport County	42	9	10	2	31	15	2	6	13	12	37	38
17	Exeter City	42	10	4	7	37	32	3	8	10	20	38	38
18	Aldershot	42	11	4	6	23	14	1	7	13	16	45	35
19	Clapton Orient	42	10	7	4	27	19	3	0	18	15	42	33
20	Torquay United	42	7	5	9	22	28	2	7	12	16	45	30
21	Walsall	42	10	4	7	34	37	1	3	17	18	51	29
22	Gillingham	42	9	5	7	25	25	1	1	19	11	52	26

1938/39   11th in Division Three (South)

No	Date	Opponent	Res	Scorers	Att	Flower T	Mills PC	Moulson C	Young A	McLenahan H	Burditt K	Roy JR	Watson JB	Gaughran BM	Read CW	Protheroe S	Hatton C	Dean WR	Feebery A	Hindmarsh JS	Cooper S	Houghton R	Towler BE	Clayton S	Wyllie J	Dowall W	Martin DK	Taylor T	Blood JF	Taylor GA	Gallagher J	Coulston W
1	Aug 27	Swindon Town	1-4	Gaughran	13370	1	2	3	4	5	6	7	8	9	10	11																
2	31	CRYSTAL PALACE	0-1		10434	1	2	3	4	5	6	11	8		10		7	9														
3	Sep 3	TORQUAY UNITED	5-1	Dean 2, Watson 2, Head(og)	7698	1	2			5		7	8		6		10	9	3	4	11											
4	7	Bristol City	1-2	Cooper	17038	1	2			5		7	8		6		10	9	3	4	11											
5	10	Clapton Orient	1-1	Hatton	8573	1	2			5		11	8	9	6		10		3	4		7										
6	17	NEWPORT COUNTY	2-0	Dean, Cooper	10834	1	2			5			8		6	11	7	9	3	4	10											
7	24	Northampton T	1-2	Cooper	13949	1	2			5			8		6		7	9	3	4	10		11									
8	Oct 1	READING	2-0	Watson, Towler	10550	1	2			5			9		6		7		3	4	10		11	8								
9	8	ALDERSHOT	1-1	Cooper	13334	1	2	5					9		6		7		3	4	10		11	8								
10	15	Bristol Rovers	0-0		7872	1	2	5					9		6		7		3	4	10		11	8								
11	22	IPSWICH TOWN	2-1	Cooper, Towler	9918	1	2	5					9				7		3	4	10		11	8	6							
12	29	Bournemouth	2-3	Hatton, Towler	7585	1	2	5			6	7	9				8		3	4	10		11									
13	Nov 5	WALSALL	0-0		8811	1	2	5					8		6			9	3	4	10	7	11									
14	12	Mansfield Town	0-2		9852	1		5		9					6		10		3	4	11	7		8			2					
15	19	QUEENS PARK RANGERS	0-0		13363	1	2	5				7			6		10		3	4	11			8		9						
16	Dec 3	EXETER CITY	3-1	Martin 2, Clayton	10129	1	2	5		10		7					6		3	4	11			8		9						
17	17	BRIGHTON & HOVE ALB.	4-3	Martin 2, Towler, Hatton	8073	1	2	5							10		6		3	4			11	8			9	7				
18	24	SWINDON TOWN	2-0	Martin 2	9998	1	2	5							10		6		3	4			11	8			9	7				
19	26	Watford	1-0	Taylor	2522	1	2	5							10		6		3	4			11	8			9	7				
20	27	WATFORD	0-3		21208	1	2	5							10		6		3	4			11	8			9	7				
21	31	Torquay United	2-0	Hatton 2	2859	1	2	5							10		6			4		11		8			9	7	3			
22	Jan 14	CLAPTON ORIENT	1-0	Martin	10811	1	2	5			10						6			4		11		8			9	7	3			
23	28	NORTHAMPTON T	1-0	Clayton	10924	1	2	5							10		6			4		11		8			9	7	3			
24	Feb 2	Newport County	1-2	Watson	7010	1	2	5					8				6			4		11					9	7	3			
25	4	Reading	1-3	Martin	7342	1	2	5					8				6			4		11					9	7	3			
26	11	Aldershot	3-0	Martin 3	5634	1	2	5	4								8			6		11				3	9	7				
27	18	BRISTOL ROVERS	3-1	Cooper 2, Hatton	10229	1	2	5	4								8			6		11				3	9	7				
28	25	Ipswich Town	2-0	Martin, Cooper	10141	1	2	5	4								8			6		11				3	9	7				
29	Mar 4	BOURNEMOUTH	0-1		8539	1	2	5	4								8			6		11				3	9	7				
30	11	Walsall	3-3	Martin 2, Hatton	6465	1	2	5	4								8			6		11				3	9	7				
31	18	MANSFIELD TOWN	1-1	Cooper	11629	1	2	5	4								8		3	6		11					9	7				
32	25	Queens Park Rangers	1-0	Read	9164	1	2	5							6			8		4			11				9	7	3			
33	Apr 1	SOUTHEND UNITED	4-1	Towler 2, Mills(p), Clayton	9467	1	2	5							6					4			11	8			9	7	3			
34	7	Port Vale	1-3	Mills(p)	9658	1	2	5							6					4			11				9	7	3			
35	8	Exeter City	0-1		5916	1	2	5							6		10		3	4			11	8			9	7				
36	10	PORT VALE	4-0	Towler, Martin 2, Read	10401	1	2	5							6		8		3	4	10		11				9	7				
37	15	CARDIFF CITY	1-1		7640		2	5			6						8		3	4	10		11				9	7		1		
38	17	Cardiff City	1-4	Towler	5070		2	5			6						8		3	4	10		11				9	7		1		
39	22	Brighton & Hove Alb.	0-2		5508		2	5							6		8		3	4	10		11				9	7		1		
40	25	Southend United	0-1		2270		2	5					10				8		3	4	6		11				9	7		1		
41	29	Crystal Palace	1-5	Towler	6861		2	5			6		8				10		3				11					7		1	9	
42	May 6	BRISTOL CITY	0-0		4623		2	5								4	10		3		6	8	11							1	9	7

| Apps | | | | | | 36 | 41 | 36 | 11 | 8 | 8 | 6 | 17 | 2 | 36 | 2 | 37 | 6 | 27 | 39 | 33 | 4 | 22 | 16 | 1 | 6 | 26 | 25 | 8 | 6 | 2 | 1 |
| Goals | | | | | | | 2 | | | | | | 4 | 1 | 2 | | 7 | 3 | | | 10 | | 9 | 3 | | | 16 | 1 | | | | |

One own goal

F.A. Cup

No	Date	Opponent	Res	Scorers	Att	Flower T	Mills PC	Moulson C	Young A	McLenahan H	Burditt K	Roy JR	Watson JB	Gaughran BM	Read CW	Protheroe S	Hatton C	Dean WR	Feebery A	Hindmarsh JS	Cooper S	Houghton R	Towler BE	Clayton S	Wyllie J	Dowall W	Martin DK	Taylor T	Blood JF	Taylor GA	Gallagher J	Coulston W
R3	Jan 7	BURNLEY	3-1	Cooper 2, Clayton	14500	1	2	5									6			4		11		8			9	7	3			
R4	Jan 21	WALSALL	0-0		34462	1	2	5									6			4		11		8			9	7	3			
rep	Jan 26	Walsall	0-4		9563	1	2	5									6			4		11		8			9	7	3			

Division Three (South) Cup

No	Date	Opponent	Res	Scorers	Att	Flower T	Mills PC	Moulson C	Young A	McLenahan H	Burditt K	Roy JR	Watson JB	Gaughran BM	Read CW	Protheroe S	Hatton C	Dean WR	Feebery A	Hindmarsh JS	Cooper S	Houghton R	Towler BE	Clayton S	Wyllie J	Dowall W	Martin DK	Taylor T	Blood JF	Taylor GA	Gallagher J	Coulston W
R1	Oct 12	Mansfield Town	0-3		1616	1	2					9	11		10		8		3	4		7				6						

W Dallman played at no. 5

		P	W	D	L	F	A	W	D	L	F	A	Pts
1	Newport County	42	15	4	2	37	16	7	7	7	21	29	55
2	Crystal Palace	42	15	4	2	49	18	5	8	8	22	34	52
3	Brighton & Hove A.	42	14	5	2	43	14	5	6	10	25	35	49
4	Watford	42	14	6	1	44	15	3	6	12	18	36	46
5	Reading	42	12	6	3	46	23	4	8	9	23	36	46
6	Queen's Park Rgs.	42	10	8	3	44	15	5	6	10	24	34	44
7	Ipswich Town	42	14	3	4	46	21	2	9	10	16	31	44
8	Bristol City	42	14	5	2	42	19	2	7	12	19	44	44
9	Swindon Town	42	15	4	2	53	25	3	4	14	19	52	44
10	Aldershot	42	13	6	2	31	15	3	6	12	22	51	44
11	NOTTS COUNTY	42	12	6	3	36	16	5	3	13	23	38	43
12	Southend United	42	14	5	2	38	13	2	4	15	23	51	41
13	Cardiff City	42	12	1	8	40	28	3	10	8	21	37	41
14	Exeter City	42	9	9	3	40	32	4	5	12	25	50	40
15	Bournemouth	42	10	8	3	38	22	3	5	13	14	36	39
16	Mansfield Town	42	10	8	3	33	19	2	7	12	11	43	39
17	Northampton Town	42	13	5	3	41	20	2	3	16	10	38	38
18	Port Vale	42	10	5	6	36	23	4	4	13	16	35	37
19	Torquay United	42	7	5	9	27	28	7	4	10	27	42	37
20	Clapton Orient	42	10	9	2	40	16	1	4	16	13	39	35
21	Walsall	42	9	6	6	47	23	2	5	14	21	46	33
22	Bristol Rovers	42	8	8	5	30	17	2	5	14	25	44	33

- 1938/39 Season -

Back: McClenahan, Moulson, Dean, Feebury, Hatton
Standing: Mellors (Trainer), Roy, Mills, Flower, Blood, Taylor, O'Neill, Gallagher, England (Trainer)
Sitting: Hindmarsh, Burditt, Houghton, Parkes (Sec/Man.), Read, Watson, Protheroe
Front: Cooper, Wyllie, Young, Gaughran

- 1939/40 Season -

Back: Read, Cooper, Weightman, McNaughton, Mackenzie, Hargett
Standing: Tomkin (Coach), Chester, Moulson, Flower, Mills, Wheldon, Knox, Buckley, England(Trainer)
Sitting: Hatton, Houghton, Halford (Dir), Raynor (Dir), Barnes (Chair) Cottee (Treas), Hobson (Dir), Coulston, Rayner
Front: Martin, Wade

1939/40

League Jubilee Fund (Friendly Game)

No	Date	Opponent	Score	Scorers	Att	1	2	3	4	5	6	7	8	9	10	11
1	Aug 19	NOTTM. FOREST	1-1	Knox	6000	Wheldon E	Mills PC	Chester TH	Rayner F	Moulson C	Weightman E	Coulston W	Knox JP	Martin DK	Hatton C	Cooper S

Third Division (South)

No	Date	Opponent	Score	Scorers	Att	1	2	3	4	5	6	7	8	9	10	11
2	Aug 26	BOURNEMOUTH	2-1	Hatton, Martin	10772	Flower T	Mills PC	Ringrose A	Rayner F	Moulson C	Weightman E	Coulston W	Knox JP	Martin DK	Hatton C	Cooper S
3	Sep 2	Cardiff City	4-2	Martin 2, Hatton, Mackenzie	17324	Flower T	Mills PC	Chester TH	Rayner F	Moulson C	Weightman E	Coulston W	Mackenzie J	Martin DK	Hatton C	Cooper S

Friendlies

No	Date	Opponent	Score	Scorers	Att	1	2	3	4	5	6	7	8	9	10	11
4	Sep 23	Doncaster Rovers	2-4	Read, Bycroft (og)	3000	Flower T	Mills PC	McNaughton	Rayner F	Moulson C	Weightman E	Coulston W	Clayton S	Read CW	Hatton C	Cooper S
5	30	WOLVERHAMPTON W.	1-4	Rayner	5000	Flower T	Mills PC	Chester TH	Buckley FL	Barke JL	Weightman E	Houghton WE	Rayner F	Read CW	Cooper S	Towler BE
6	Oct 7	Northampton Town	0-6		3000	Wheldon E	Mills PC	Chester TH	Nicholas JT	Barker JW	Hann R	Walsh W	Crooks SD	Lambert R	England	Duncan D
7	14	Nottm. Forest	1-2	Crooks	4000	Wateman A	Mills PC	Wilcox GE	Nicholas JT	Barker JW	Hann R	Walsh W	Crooks SD	Hatton C	Houghton WE	Duncan D

League: East Midlands Region

No	Date	Opponent	Score	Scorers	Att	1	2	3	4	5	6	7	8	9	10	11
8	Oct 21	ROTHERHAM UNITED	2-0	Crooks, Harrison	2000	Hall B	Mills PC	Wilcox GE	Nicholas JT	Barker JW	Hann R	Crooks SD	Walsh W	Harrison R	McNaughton GN	Duncan D
9	28	Sheffield Wednesday	1-1	Duncan	3000	Hall B	Mills PC	Wilcox GE	Nicholas JT	Barker JW	Hann R	Walsh W	Crooks SD	Harrison R	Cooper S	Duncan D
10	Nov 11	Doncaster Rovers	1-2	Harrison	5479	Hall B	Mills PC	Wilcox GE	Nicholas JT	Barker JW	Hann R	Crooks SD	Walsh W	Harrison R	Jones H	Duncan D
11	18	CHESTERFIELD	1-4	Glover	5000	Hall B	Mills PC	Wilcox GE	Nicholas JT	Barker JW	Hann R	Crooks SD	Hilliard G	Glover P	Walsh W	Duncan D
12	25	Barnsley	1-2	Duncan	1500	Hall B	Mills PC	Wilcox GE	Nicholas JT	Barker JW	Hann R	Crooks SD	Coleman E	Glover P	Jones H	Duncan D
13	Dec 2	GRIMSBY TOWN	1-2	Crooks	7000	Hall B	Mills PC	Wilcox GE	Nicholas JT	Bailey L	Read CW	Crooks SD	Mackenzie J	Glover P	Jones B	Duncan D
14	9	Sheffield United	1-7	Crooks	3000	Hall B	Mills PC	Wilcox GE	Nicholas JT	Bailey L	Read CW	Crooks SD	Read CW	Harrison R	Hatton C	Duncan D
15	Jan 13	Mansfield Town	4-6	Towler 2, Buckley, Nicholas	2200	Hall B	Nicholas JT	Mason J	Ward TV	Hann R	Read CW	Crooks SD	Buckley FL	Mackenzie J	Towler BE	Duncan D
16	Mar 2	NOTTM. FOREST	4-3	Clayton, Crooks, Mackenzie, Towler	4000	Wilkinson N	Nicholas JT	Beattie A	Corkhill WG	Hann R	Ward TV	Crooks SD	Clayton S	Mackenzie J	Towler BE	Duncan D
17	9	DONCASTER ROVERS	4-0	Towler 2, Duncan, Steele	3000	Wilkinson N	Nicholas JT	Beattie A	Corkhill WG	Hann R	Ward TV	Crooks SD	Clayton S	Steele FC	Towler BE	Duncan D
18	16	Chesterfield	1-3	Crooks	6000	Wilkinson N	Nicholas JT	Beattie A	Corkhill WG	Hague JK	Ward TV	Crooks SD	Mackenzie J	Steele FC	Towler BE	Duncan D
19	22	MANSFIELD TOWN	2-2	Corkhill, Groves	4000	Wilkinson N	Nicholas JT	Beattie A	Corkhill WG	Hague JK	Ward TV	Crooks SD	Groves A	Mackenzie J	Towler BE	Duncan D
20	23	BARNSLEY	0-6		3000	Wilkinson N	Nicholas JT	Beattie A	Corkhill WG	Hague JK	Ward TV	Crooks SD	Clayton S	Brookbanks E	Read CW	Towler BE
21	25	Rotherham United	2-3	Read, Towler	2000	Wilkinson N	Nicholas JT	Beattie A	Corkhill WG	Barker JW	Ward TV	Clayton S	Rayner F	Read CW	Towler BE	Duncan D
22	30	Grimsby Town	2-3	Clayton, Hatton	2000	Hall B	Nicholas JT	Mason J	Corkhill WG	Baxter WE	Ward TV	Crooks SD	Clayton S	Mackenzie J	Hatton C	Duncan D
23	Apr 6	SHEFFIELD UNITED	3-0	Towler 2, Beattie	2500	Hall B	Griffiths J	Beattie A	Corkhill WG	Nicholas JT	Ward TV	Crooks SD	Groves A	Mackenzie J	Towler BE	Duncan D
24	May 4	Lincoln City	4-3	Mackenzie 2, Groves, Moss	2114	Flower T	Mills PC	Mason J	Corkhill WG	Nicholas JT	Munks JA	Crooks SD	Groves A	Mackenzie J	Moss G	Duncan D
25	18	SHEFFIELD WEDNESDAY	1-4	Moss		Waite JH	Mills PC	Mason J	Waterall K	Corkhill WG	Munks JA	Moss G	Groves A	Mackenzie J	Towler BE	Duncan D
26	25	Nottm. Forest	2-6	Duncan, PC Mills(p)	1771	Bartram S	Mills PC	Mason J	Waterall K	Corkhill WG	Munks JA	Crooks SD	Moss G	Mackenzie J	Mills A	Duncan D
27	Jun 1	LINCOLN CITY	3-0	Mackenzie 2, Crooks		Bartram S	Mills PC	Mason J	Corkhill WG	Davies RG	Munks JA	Brookbanks E	Crooks SD	Mackenzie J	Moss G	Duncan D

League Cup

No	Date	Opponent	Score	Scorers	Att	1	2	3	4	5	6	7	8	9	10	11
PR	Apr 13	Mansfield Town	5-3	Hatton 2, Crooks, Duncan, O'Donnell	4500	Wakeman A	Nicholas JT	Mills PC	Corkhill WG	Hann R	Ward TV	Crooks SD	Hatton C	O'Donnell F	Towler BE	Duncan D
R1/1	20	Arsenal	0-4		11521	Flower T	Lunn	Mills PC	Hann R	Nicholas JT	Ward TV	Crooks SD	Massie A	O'Donnell F	Towler BE	Duncan D
R1/2	27	ARSENAL	1-5	PC Mills (p)	14755	Flower T	Nicholas JT	Mills PC	Corkhill WG	Hann R	Ward TV	Crooks SD	Mackenzie J	O'Donnell F	Towler BE	Duncan D

1940/41

League South

#	Date	Opponent	Res	Scorers	Att	Sidlow C	Nicholas JT	Beattie A	Massie A	Iverson RT	Keen E	Crooks SD	Edwards GR	Broome FH	Fenton M	Duncan D
1	Aug 31	Stoke City	1-4	Crooks		Sidlow C	Nicholas JT	Beattie A	Massie A	Iverson RT	Keen E	Crooks SD	Edwards GR	Broome FH	Fenton M	Duncan D
2	Sep 7	STOKE CITY	3-2	Duncan, Fenton, McEwan	2000	Sidlow C	Sneddon T	Beattie A	Corkhill WG	Nicholas JT	Keen E	Crooks SD	Fenton M	McEwan F	Beattie R	Duncan D
3	28	Coventry City	1-1	Edwards	2000	Sidlow C	Smallwood E	Beattie A	Massie A	Iverson RT	Nicholas JT	Crooks SD	Smith JT	Broome FH	Edwards GR	Butler S
4	Oct 5	COVENTRY CITY	1-3	Crooks	2000	Sidlow C	Griffiths J	Beattie A	Massie A	Nicholas JT	Iverson RT	Crooks SD	Smith JT	Broome FH	Edwards GR	Duncan D
5	12	Walsall	2-3	Buckley, Crooks	3000	Sidlow C	Nicholas JT	Beattie A	Massie A	Lamb W	Iverson RT	Crooks SD	Buckley FL	Broome FH	Edwards GR	Duncan D
6	19	WALSALL	4-2	Broome 3, Nicholas (p)	1500	Sidlow C	Wilcox GE	Beattie A	Edwards GR	Nicholas JT	Massie A	Crooks SD	Smith JT	Broome FH	Duncan D	Butler S
7	26	West Bromwich Alb.	1-3	Edwards	2496	Sidlow C	Mills PC	Beattie A	Massie A	Nicholas JT	Buckley FL	Crooks SD	Smith JT	Broome FH	Edwards GR	Duncan D
8	Nov 2	West Bromwich Alb.	3-2	Broome, Buckley, Moss	2100	Mills PC	Findlay PA	Beattie A	Massie A	Nicholas JT	Buckley FL	Crooks SD	Cooper EJ	Broome FH	Moss G	Stein AW
9	9	Walsall	4-11	Broome 2, Crooks 2	400	Gilson H	Mills PC	Beattie A	Massie A	Nicholas JT	Buckley FL	Crooks SD	Cooper EJ	Broome FH	Moss G	Stein AW
10	16	WALSALL	2-1	Crooks 2	1000	Swinburne TA	Mills PC	Johnson JT	Beattie A	Nicholas JT	Buckley FL	Crooks SD	Cooper EJ	Broome FH	Gallacher P	Stein AW
11	30	BIRMINGHAM CITY	3-3	Broome, Duncan, one og	600	Streten BR	Mills PC	Middleton L	Ellmer FB	Nicholas JT	Munks JA	Buckley FL	Cooper EJ	Broome FH	Crisp GH	Duncan D
12	Dec 7	Leicester City	0-6		1500	Streten BR	Mills PC	Middleton L	Ellmer FB	Griffiths J	Buckley FL	Johnson JW	Crooks SD	Broome FH	Gallacher P	Duncan D
13	21	Northampton Town	1-2	Vallance	4500	Streten BR	Beattie A	Johnson JT	Jackson H	Nicholas JT	Buckley FL	Johnson JW	Cooper EJ	Broome FH	Vallance	Warburton G
14	25	Nottm. Forest	4-2	Broome, Johnson, Warburton, +1	2265	Streten BR	Griffiths J	Beattie A	Jackson H	Nicholas JT	Buckley FL	Johnson JW	Warburton G	Broome FH	Vallance	Duncan D
15	28	LEICESTER CITY	4-2	Broome 2, Duncan 2	2000	Streten BR	Beattie A	Johnson JT	Jackson H	Nicholas JT	Buckley FL	Johnson JW	Vallance	Broome FH	Warburton G	Duncan D
16	Jan 11	Wst Bromwich Alb.	1-8	Hinsley	1403	Streten BR	Griffiths J	Johnson JT	Vallance	Nicholas JT	Buckley FL	Taylor GT	Cooper EJ	Broome FH	Hinsley C	Duncan D
17	25	Stoke City	2-2	Broome 2	300	Streten BR	Griffiths J	Elliott CS	Vallance	Nicholas JT	Boileau HA	Taylor GT	Crooks SD	Broome FH	Green T	Duncan D
18	Feb 1	STOKE CITY	2-1	Broome, Duncan	1000	Streten BR	Griffiths J	Elliott CS	Hinsley C	Nicholas JT	Boileau HA	Taylor GT	Crooks SD	Broome FH	Green T	Duncan D
19	Mar 15	NOTTM. FOREST	0-4		2000	Streten BR	Parr J	Johnson JT	Musson WU	Nicholas JT	Ellmer FB	Crooks SD	Hinsley C	Harrison R	Carter HS	Vause PG
20	Apr 12	Nottm. Forest	3-1	Newman 2, Lyman	2000	Streten BR	Parr J	Brook R	Musson WU	Nicholas JT	Johnson JT	Lyman CC	Buckley FL	Broome FH	Wright	Newman
21	14	Chesterfield	0-3		1300	Streten BR	Brook R	Johnson JT	Bingham	Padman	Ellmer FB	Wright	Berry	Clements	Moss G	Lyman CC

Game 16 also counted for Midland Cup

League Cup

	Date	Opponent	Res	Scorers	Att											
R1/1	Feb 15	WEST BROMWICH ALB.	4-0	Broome 2, Crooks, Hinsley	2700	Streten BR	Elliott CS	Johnson JT	Taylor GT	Nicholas JT	Boileau HA	Crooks SD	Davidson RT	Broome FH	Hinsley C	Duncan D
R1/2	22	West Bromwich Alb.	0-5		2581	Streten BR	Elliott CS	Johnson JT	Hinsley C	Nicholas JT	Boileau HA	Taylor GT	Green T	Broome FH	Davidson RT	Duncan D

1941/42

No games played

- 1940/41 Season -

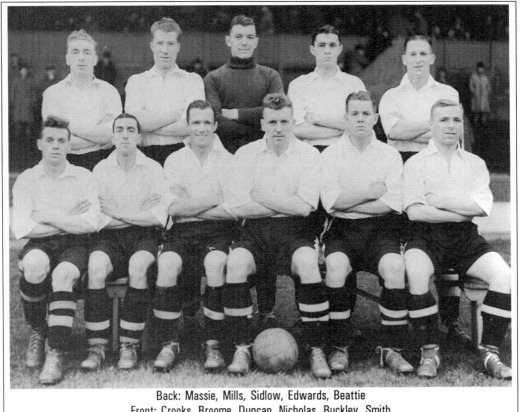

Back: Massie, Mills, Sidlow, Edwards, Beattie
Front: Crooks, Broome, Duncan, Nicholas, Buckley, Smith

- 1945/46 Season -

Back: Levey(Director), Poole(Trainer), Corkhill, Harris, Southwell, Wiseman, Hubbard, Allen, Drinkwater, Westcott,
Cottee(Director), Linnell(Director), Fisher(Secretary).   Front: Beresford, Peacock, Pye, McPherson

1942/43

League North First Championship

#	Date	Opponent	Score	Scorers	Att	1	2	3	4	5	6	7	8	9	10	11
1	Aug 29	DERBY COUNTY	1-6	Steele	3000	Flower T	Challiner J	Benner R	Corkhill WG	Sharman F	Jones LJ	Barsby CF	Cairns WH	Steele FC	Moss G	Jessop W
2	Sep 5	Derby County	0-2		8000	Wilkinson N	Corkhill WG	Jones DO	Burgess R	Sharman F	Kirton J	Antonio GR	Steele FC	Cairns WH	Jones LJ	Jessop W
3	Sep 12	Mansfield Town	1-0	L Jones (p)	2000	Wilkinson N	Corkhill WG	Benner R	Burgess R	Sharman F	Kirton J	Antonio GR	Steele FC	Cairns WH	Jones LJ	Jessop W
4	Sep 19	MANSFIELD TOWN	3-1	Antonio, L Jones, Weaver		Wilkinson N	Corkhill WG	Jones DO	Kirton J	Sharman F	Weaver S	Coulston W	Antonio GR	Bowers J	Jones LJ	Burgess R
5	Sep 26	CHESTERFIELD	2-0	Hatton (p), Liddle	3500	Wilkinson N	Corkhill WG	Kirton J	Clarke GA	Sharman F	Burgess R	Coulston W	Steele FC	Bowers J	Hatton C	Liddle D
6	Oct 3	Chesterfield	1-6	L Jones		Parkin FW	Corkhill WG	Jones DO	Clarke GA	Sharman F	Burgess R	Booth LJ	Haines JWT	Bowers J	Jones LJ	Liddle D
7	Oct 10	Leicester City	3-1	Liddle 2, Booth		Wilkinson N	Corkhill WG	Jones DO	Clarke GA	Sharman F	Burgess R	Booth LJ	Antonio GR	Bowers J	Jones LJ	Liddle D
8	Oct 17	LEICESTER CITY	1-1	Bowers	4000	Wilkinson N	Corkhill WG	Jones DO	Clarke GA	Sharman F	Kirton J	Booth LJ	Clayton S	Bowers J	Jones LJ	Robinson P
9	Oct 24	LINCOLN CITY	3-6	Marsh 2, Collindridge		Wilkinson N	Corkhill WG	Jones DO	Clarke GA	Sharman F	Burgess R	Antonio GR	Antonio GR	Marsh JK	Kirton J	Collindridge C
10	Oct 31	Lincoln City	1-8	Bowers		Wilkinson N	Ellmer FB	Sharman F	Ellmer FB	Fell J	Jones LJ	Brown E	Stillyards G	Bowers J	Bell T	Liddle T
11	Nov 7	Nottm. Forest	5-3	L Jones 2(1p), Bowers, Collindridge, Haines	5384	Wilkinson N	Jones DO	Benner R	Jones LJ	Sharman F	Kirton J	Booth LJ	Haines JWT	Bowers J	Liddle D	Collindridge C
12	Nov 14	NOT'M. FOREST	1-3	Antonio	4000	Wilkinson N	Benner R	Benner R	Antonio GR	Sharman F	Liddle D	Booth LJ	Haines JWT	Bowers J	Moss G	Collindridge C
13	Nov 21	SHEFFIELD WEDNESDAY	2-2	Booth, Collindridge		Wilkinson N	Jones DO	Benner R	Clarke GA	Sharman F	Booth LJ	Booth LJ	Antonio GR	Bowers J	Liddle D	Collindridge C
14	Nov 28	Sheffield Wednesday	1-3	Liddle	10000	Wilkinson N	Sharman F	Sharman F	Clarke GA	Hughes S	Ellmer FB	Ellmer FB	Jones LJ	Bowers J	Liddle D	Collindridge C
15	Dec 5	Northampton T	2-5	Brader, Collindridge	2000	Wilkinson N	Jones DO	Benner R	Clarke GA	Hughes S	Stancer LB	Coulston W	Antonio GR	Brader FW	Jones LJ	Liddle D
16	Dec 12	NORTHAMPTON T	2-0	Brader, L Jones(p)		Wilkinson N	Corkhill WG	Jones DO	Clarke GA	Sharman F	Hughes S	Coulston W	Antonio GR	Brader FW	Jones LJ	Liddle D
17	Dec 19	LINCOLN CITY	4-2	Collindridge 3, Clarke		Wilkinson N	Corkhill WG	Jones DO	Liddle D	Hughes S	Kirton J	Clarke GA	Antonio GR	Brader FW	Jones LJ	Collindridge C
18	Dec 25	Lincoln City	1-8	GH Robinson		Parkin FW	Blood JF	Benner R	Clarke GA	Lilley K	Stancer LB	Brown M	Hodgkins JS	Tweed GE	Robinson GH	Liddle D

League North Second Championship

#	Date	Opponent	Score	Scorers	Att	1	2	3	4	5	6	7	8	9	10	11
19	Dec 26	DERBY COUNTY	2-3	Antonio, Bowers	15000	Hall B	Corkhill WG	Benner R	Hann R	Sharman F	Wright WA	Rickards CT	Antonio GR	Bowers J	Ramage PMF	Collindridge C
20	Jan 2	Derby County	2-1	Collindridge, Marsh	7000	Wilkinson N	Corkhill WG	Benner R	Burgess R	Sharman F	Hann R	Rickards CT	Antonio GR	Marsh JK	Jones LJ	Collindridge C
21	Jan 9	Lincln City	2-0	Bowers, Collindridge		Ramage PMF	Corkhill WG	Benner R	Burgess R	Sharman F	Hann R	Rickards CT	Antonio GR	Bowers J	Jones LJ	Collindridge C
22	Jan 16	LINCOLN CITY	1-2	Bowers		Wilkinson N	Corkhill WG	Benner R	Burgess R	Sharman F	Jones LJ	Rickards CT	Antonio GR	Bowers J	Drury GB	Hinchcliffe T
23	Jan 23	SHEFFIELD UNITED	1-1	Marsh		Parkin FW	Corkhill WG	Marshall JG	Burgess R	Sharman F	Hughes S	Rickards CT	Jones LJ	Marsh JK	Ramage PMF	Jones LJ
24	Jan 30	Sheffield United	2-3	Bowers, Jones		Wilkinson N	Corkhill WG	Marshall JG	Antonio GR	Sharman F	Ramage PMF	Rickards CT	Jones LJ	Bowers J	Ramage PMF	Grant EA
25	Feb 6	Mansfield Town	4-2	Rawcliffe 2, Jones(p), Rickards		Ashton P	Trim RF	Benner R	Hollis KB	Hughes S	Kirton J	Clift BC	Jones LJ	Rickards CT	Rawcliffe F	Maund JH
26	Feb 13	MANSFIELD TOWN	2-0	Bowers, Maund		Wilkinson N	Benner R	Marshall JG	Hughes S	Leuty LH	Hughes S	Rickards CT	Jones LJ	Bowers J	Rawcliffe F	Maund JH
27	Feb 20	ROTHERHAM UNITED	4-0	Rickards 2, Antonio, Clift		Wilkinson N	Marshall JG	Benner R	Corkhill WG	Leuty LH	Hughes S	Clift BC	Antonio GR	Rickards CT	Rawcliffe F	Collindridge C
28	Feb 27	Rotherham United	2-2	Jones, Steele		Wilkinson N	Benner R	Marshall JG	Hann R	Leuty LH	Kirton J	Clift BC	Antonio GR	Steele FC	Rawcliffe F	Jones LJ
29	Mar 6	Derby County	3-1	Antonio, Rickards, Towler	10540	Wilkinson N	Corkhill WG	Benner R	Corkhill WG	Leuty LH	Kirton J	Antonio GR	Jones LJ	Rickards CT	Towler BE	Davies W
30	Mar 13	DER3Y COUNTY	2-2	Jones, Rickards	15100	Wilkinson N	Vincent NE	Corkhill WG	Barke JL	Leuty LH	Kirton J	Davies W	Jones LJ	Rickards CT	Towler BE	Collindridge C
31	Mar 20	Sheffield United	1-4	Collindridge (p)		Wilkinson N	Vincent NE	Corkhill WG	Barke JL	Leuty LH	Kirton J	Davies W	Jones LJ	Rickards CT	Towler BE	Collindridge C
32	Mar 27	SHEFFIELD UNITED	2-1	Rickards, Towler	12000	Wilkinson N	Bacuzzi J	Corkhill WG	Barke JL	Leuty LH	Kirton J	Davies W	Jones LJ	Rickards CT	Rawcliffe F	Towler BE
33	Apr 3	STOKE CITY	1-1	Rawcliffe		Wilkinson N	Corkhill WG	Benner R	Barke JL	Leuty LH	Kirton J	Duns L	Jones LJ	Bowers J	Rawcliffe F	Towler BE
34	Apr 10	Stoke City	1-1	Rickards	1000	Ashton P	Corkhill WG	Barke JL	Clarke GA	Leuty LH	Hughes S	Duns L	Jones LJ	Rickards CT	Rawcliffe F	Liddle D
35	Apr 17	Nottm. Forest	1-1	Duns	4443	Wilkinson N	Corkhill WG	Barke JL	Burgess R	Kirton J	Kirton J	Duns L	Jones LJ	Rickards CT	Towler BE	Collindridge C
36	Apr 24	NOTTM. FOREST	2-1	Jones, Rickards		Ashton P	Corkhill WG	Benner R	Rawcliffe F	Leuty LH	Barke JL	Duns L	Rickards CT	Rickards CT	Lawton T	Martin EJ
37	Apr 26	Coventry City	0-7		4384	Parkin FW	Corkhill WG	Benner R	Rigby NE	Hughes S	Barke JL	Brown GH	Rickards CT	Brader FW	Rawcliffe F	Parker A
38	May 1	COVENTRY CITY	2-1	Marsh, Towler(p)		Wilkinson N	Corkhill WG	Benner R	Burgess R	Leuty LH	Barke JL	Duns L	Rickards CT	Marsh JK	Jones LJ	Towler BE

Games 19 to 32 inclusive also counted for the League Cup
(Games 19 - 28 were a qualifying competition).

1943/44

League North First Championship

No	Date	Opponent	Att	Score	Scorers	1	2	3	4	5	6	7	8	9	10
1	Aug 28	Lincoln City		5-4	Rawcliffe 2, Lager 2, Antonio	Wilkinson N	Corkhill WG	Challinor J	Burgess R	Smith L	Kirton J	Antonio GR	Lager EW	Rawcliffe F	Towler BE
2	Sep 4	LINCOLN CITY	5000	0-0		Wilkinson N	Corkhill WG	Challinor J	Burgess R	Gray R	Kirton J	Antonio GR	Lager EW	Rawcliffe F	Collindridge C
3	Sep 11	DERBY COUNTY	5087	3-1	Drury 2, Anderson	Wilkinson N	Jones DO	Challinor J	Corkhill WG	Gray R	Kirton J	Anderson J	Jones LJ	Drury GB	Collindridge C
4	Sep 18	Derby County	8000	2-4	Collindridge 2 (1p)	Bloomfield W	Jones DO	Challinor J	Corkhill WG	Burgess R	Kirton J	Gray R	Rawcliffe F	Collindridge C	Marshall JG
5	Sep 25	Chesterfield	7000	0-3		Wilkinson N	Marshall JG	Challinor J	Corkhill WG	Gray R	Kirton J	Ross J	Brader FW	Jones LJ	Collins AD
6	Oct 2	CHESTERFIELD	4000	1-0	Hatfield	Donaldson HA	Corkhill WG	Marshall JG	Johnson J	Gray R	Keen E	Brunt GR	Hatfield B	Jones LJ	Flint K
7	Oct 9	MANSFIELD TOWN		0-2		Donaldson HA	Corkhill WG	Challinor J	Keen E	Gray R	Kirton J	Brunt GR	Hatfield B	Stancer LB	Collins AD
8	Oct 16	Mansfield Town	3500	0-4		Donaldson HA	Benner R	Russell D	Smith L	Gray R	Clarke GA	Jones LJ	Kirton J	Pettitt	Collindridge C
9	Oct 23	Leicester City		0-5		Donaldson HA	Corkhill WG	Marshall JG	Hann R	Sharman F	Gray R	Slack L	Jones LJ	Iddon H	Towler BE
10	Oct 30	LEICESTER CITY	5000	1-9	Antonio	Donaldson HA	Drysdale J	Corkhill WG	Unwin S	Gray R	Tower BE	Houghton WE	Rawcliffe F	Antonio GR	Roberts D
11	Nov 6	NOTTM. FOREST	6000	0-1		Donaldson HA	Corkhill WG	Marshall JG	Smith L	Gray R	Roberts D	Ball WJE	Hatfield B	Jones LJ	Collindridge C
12	Nov 13	Nottm. Forest	5300	4-0	Hunter 2, Walker, Collindridge(p)	Stretan BR	Corkhill WG	Bridges	Nicholls H	Gray R	Hunter J	Antonio GR	Walker E	Jones LJ	Collindridge C
13	Nov 20	Sheffield Wednesday		0-1		Jepsen A	Corkhill WG	Davidson DBL	Nicholls H	Gray R	Walters H	Hunter J	Walker E	James J(2)	Murphy G
14	Nov 27	SHEFFIELD WEDNESDAY		0-0		Jepsen A	Corkhill WG	Davidson DBL	Nicholls H	Gray R	Walters H	Antonio GR	Wright J	Jones LJ	Collindridge C
15	Dec 4	NORTHAMPTON T		2-5	Wright 2	Hinton E	Skidmore W	Davidson DBL	Nicholls H	Meling H	Walters H	Hewitt	Wright J	Wright J	Towler BE
16	Dec 11	Northampton T		1-1	Wright	Clack FE	Pritchard R	Davidson DBL	Nicholls H	Godfrey L	Alderton JH	Lane H	Jones LJ	Gardner	Summerfield A
17	Dec 18	Lincoln City		5-8	Ledger 3, Lane, Walsh	Rickards CT	Rigby NE	Davidson DBL	Nicholls H	Gray R	Jones LJ	Ledger JK	Vincent NE	Murphy G	Towler BE
18	Dec 25	LINCOLN CITY	1629	2-5	Walsh, Martin	Wilkinson N	Benner R	Davidson DBL	Ashworth	Rigby NE	Fletcher	Ledger JK	Walsh W	Lane H	Collindridge C

League North Second Championship

No	Date	Opponent	Att	Score	Scorers	1	2	3	4	5	6	7	8	9	10	11
19	Dec 27	LEICESTER CITY	10000	1-2	Edwards	Oakley JC	Gutteridge R	Davidson DBL	Nicholls H	Godfrey L	Gray R	Ledger JK	Edwards G	Walsh W	Towler BE	Collindridge C
20	Jan 1	Leicester City		2-7	Knott, Towler	Jepsen A	Gutteridge R	Marshall JG	Nicholls H	Godfrey L	Bye JH	Ledger JK	Lane H	Knott H	Walsh W	Towler BE
21	Jan 8	MANSFIELD TOWN		5-0	Dimond 2, Collindridge, Edwards, Ledger	Parr J	Nicholas J	Davidson DBL	Nicholls H	Smith L	Gray R	Ledger JK	Edwards G	Dimond S	Jones LJ	Collindridge C
22	Jan 15	Mansfield Town	3500	0-1		Graham R	Godfrey L	Davidson DBL	Musson WU	Gray R	Tower BE	Ledger JK	Edwards G	Dimond S	Jones LJ	Rothwell E
23	Jan 22	Nottm. Forest	6803	2-0	Dimond, Edwards	Stretan BR	Godfrey L	Davidson DBL	Nicholls H	Gray R	Musson WU	Ledger JK	Edwards G	Dimond S	Jones LJ	Smith J
24	Jan 29	NOTTM. FOREST	8000	0-3		Major L	Godfrey L	Gray R	Nicholls H	Walters H	Musson WU	Ledger JK	Edwards G	Dimond S	Jones LJ	Rothwell E
25	Feb 5	DERBY COUNTY	7000	0-2		Jones J	Gutteridge R	Godfrey L	Corkhill WG	Rist FH	Walters H	Edwards G	Haycock F	Dimond S	Jones LJ	Collins AD
26	Feb 12	Derby County	8000	3-7	Davis, Edwards, Flint	Jones J	Godfrey L	Gutteridge R	Godfrey L	Gray R	Walters H	Edwards G	Rawcliffe F	Davis RD	Towler BE	Flint K
27	Feb 19	Sheffield Wednesday	7000	0-2		Bradley G	Godfrey L	Gutteridge R	Walters H	Gray R	Tower BE	Ledger JK	Edwards G	Walsh W	Rawcliffe F	Collindridge C
28	Feb 26	SHEFFIELD WEDNESDAY	3000	1-5	Davis	Bradley G	Godfrey L	Davidson DBL	Rigby NE	Barke JL	Gray R	Edwards G	Ledger JK	Davis RD	Stancer LB	Collindridge C
29	Mar 11	Walsall		1-2	Rickards	Whitehead J	Becci A	Hepworth R	Rigby NE	Gray R	Rigby NE	Ledger JK	Edwards G	Stancer LB	Rickards CT	Flint K
30	Mar 18	NORTHAMPTON T		1-4	Gray	Whitehead J	Thorpe WF	Hepworth R	Rigby NE	Gray R	Marshall JG	Ledger JK	Brown E	Walsh W	Stancer LB	Flint K
31	Mar 25	Northampton T		1-4	Gray	Thorpe WF	James J(1)	Kirkpatrick S	Rigby NE	Marshall JG	Rigby NE	Ledger JK	Brown E	Walsh W	Stancer LB	Flint K
32	Apr 8	Doncaster Rovers		0-6		James J(1)	Kirkpatrick S	Marshall JG	Marshall JG	Southwell AA	Barke JL	Ledger JK	Higson S	Mordue J	Rollinson	Ledger JK
33	Apr 8	DONCASTER ROVERS		0-1		Thorpe WF	Davidson DBL	Davidson DBL	Southwell AA	Barke JL	Stancer LB	Ledger JK	Hogg F	Smith J	Openshaw	Ledger JK
34	Apr 10	Nottm. Forest		0-3		Thorpe WF	Davidson DBL	Davidson DBL	Kirkham R	Rigby NE	Greaves	DeLisle	Roberts D	Smith J	Flintson	Flint K
35	Apr 15	Mansfield Town	1000	0-5		Simpson C	Hepworth R	Everett HP	Unwin S	Southwell AA	Unwin S	Smeeton J	Gregory H	Stancer LB	Walker E	Griffiths K
36	Apr 22	MANSFIELD TOWN	1500	3-2	Allen, Simpson, Wilson	Thorpe WF	Everett HP	Hepworth R	Unwin S	Morley J	Morley J	Smeeton J	Simpson J	Allen W	Marsh JK	Wilson
37	Apr 29	COVENTRY CITY		1-4	Collindridge	Nugent S	Kirkpatrick S	Everett HP	Moran A	Barton P	Everett HP	Tyroll	Collindridge C	Potts	Morley J	Gascoigne D
38	May 6	Coventry City	1775	2-8	Gascoigne 2	Morgan	Everett HP	Moran A	Taylor JL	Barton P	Unwin S	Van Gelden J	Gascoigne D	Allen W	Renshaw	Drinkwater

Games 19 to 28 inclusive also counted for League Cup, 29 to 31 for the Midland Cup

League North First Championship

No	Date	Opponent	Score	Scorers	Att											
1	Aug 26	Lincoln City	2-4	Knowles, Morrad	3000	Clack FE	Hepworth R	Benner R	Hogg F	Barton P	Chapman RJF	Van Gelden J	Carrick R	Morrad FG	O'Neill T	Knowles C
2	Sep 2	LINCOLN CITY	4-5	Morrad 2, Davie, Hepworth	3000	Clack FE	Hepworth R	Barton P	Hogg F	Wright WA	Stancer LB	Dixon W	Morrad FG	Davie J	O'Neill T	Flint K
3	Sep 9	SHEF'IELD WEDNESDAY	2-0	Davie 2	6000	Carter J	Hepworth R	Pomphrey EA	Hogg F	Wright WA	Long D	Edwards WJ	Morrad FG	Davie J	O'Neill T	Flint K
4	Sep 16	Sheffield Wednesday	1-6	Morrad	10000	Morrad	Hepworth R	Pomphrey EA	Hogg F	Wright WA	Long D	Flint K	Stancer LB	Davie J	O'Neill T	Carter
5	Sep 23	Nottm. Forest	1-2	Hepworth (p)	10000	Clack FE	Hepworth R	Pomphrey EA	Long D	Barton P	Everett HP	Edwards WJ	Hogg F	Davie J	White A	Morrad FG
6	Sep 30	NOTTM. FOREST	0-0		9000	Clack FE	Hepworth R	Pomphrey EA	Southwell AA	Barton P	Baker D	White A	Hogg F	Davie J	Morrad FG	Flint K
7	Oct 7	BARNSLEY	0-3		5000	Streten BR	Hepworth R	Pomphrey EA	Southwell AA	Barton P	Baker D	White A	Morrad FG	Davie J	Stephenson R	Piercy C
8	Oct 14	Barnsley	2-6	Collindridge, Davie	5000	Streten BR	Hepworth R	Pomphrey EA	Hogg F	Southwell AA	Morrad FG	Piercy C	Wood CC	Davie J	O'Neill T	Collindridge C
9	Oct 21	Doncaster Rovers	1-3	Davie	4361	Streten BR	Hepworth R	Pomphrey EA	Southwell AA	Wright WA	Morrad FG	Piercy C	Sewell J	Davie J	Stephenson R	Piercy C
10	Oct 28	DONCASTER ROVERS	0-2		2000	Mowl WJ	Hepworth R	Pomphrey EA	Southwell AA	Moulson C	Morrad FG	Edwards WJ	Duggan	Sewell J	Stephenson R	Towler BE
11	Nov 4	DERBY COUNTY	1-4	Sewell	9000	Mowl WJ	Hepworth R	Pomphrey EA	Southwell AA	Moulson C	Morrad FG	Gascoigne D	Sewell J	Davie J	Hogg F	Collindridge C
12	Nov 11	Derby County	3-6	Coen 2, Sewell	10000	Mowl WJ	Hepworth R	Pomphrey EA	Southwell AA	Sparrow	Hogg F	Coen L	Sewell J	Davie J	Parker A	Piercy C
13	Nov 18	Sheffield United	0-6		8000	Mowl WJ	Hepworth R	Kingwell	Southwell AA	Bicknell R	Sparrow	Coen L	Sewell J	Davie J	Parker A	Stephenson R
14	Nov 25	SHEF'IELD UNITED	1-0	Airlie	2000	Mowl WJ	Bacuzzi J	Hepworth R	Southwell AA	Rigby NE	Hogg F	Coen L	Sewell J	Airlie S	Strain N	Towler BE
15	Dec 2	ROTHERHAM UNITED	0-2		4000	Mowl WJ	Rigby NE	Hepworth R	Southwell AA	Moulson C	Hogg F	Coen L	Sewell J	Windle R	Strain N	Flint K
16	Dec 9	Rotherham United	1-2	Davie	8000	Mowl WJ	Bacuzzi J	Hepworth R	Southwell AA	Bicknell R	Hogg F	Coen L	Sewell J	Davie J	McMullen J	Piercy C
17	Dec 16	CHESTERFIELD	0-3		3000	Southwell AA	Southwell AA	Brooks	Towler BE	Bicknell R	Sewell J	Strain N	Strain N	Morrad FG	McMullen J	Stancer LB
18	Dec 23	Chesterfield	0-8		7000	Bradshaw	Hepworth R	Skidmore W	Bicknell R	Southwell AA	Huntley	Strain N	Hughes A	Hughes A	Brooks	Towler BE

League North Second Championship

No	Date	Opponent	Score	Scorers	Att											
19	Dec 26	MANSFIELD TOWN	0-2			Oakley JC	Hepworth R	Marshall JG	Corkhill WG	Moulson C	Southwell AA	Sewell J	Hogg F	Brooks	Towler BE	Stephenson R
20	Dec 30	Mansfield Town	1-3	Towler	3000	Oakley JC	Southwell AA	Hepworth R	Pithie DS	Moulson C	Hogg F	Summers	Sewell J	Bicknell R	Towler BE	Mynard LD
21	Jan 6	Chesterfield	1-3	Collindridge	5000	Oakley JC	Hepworth R	Southwell AA	Taylor JL	Moulson C	Hogg F	Connor	Sewell J	Coen L	Towler BE	Collindridge C
22	Jan 13	CHESTERFIELD	1-3	Lewis	4000	Stanowski	Hepworth R	Southwell AA	Towler BE	Moulson C	Stancer LB	Sewell J	McPherson IB	Coen L	Lewis G	Pavlov M
23	Jan 20	Derby County	0-7		3500	Bradshaw	Griffiths J	Marshall JG	Southwell AA	Moulson C	Hogg F	Coen L	McPherson IB	Shell FH	Lewis G	Johnston TD
24	Jan 27	DERBY COUNTY	2-4	Collindridge, Lewis	6000	Bradshaw	Griffiths J	Marshall JG	Southwell AA	Barke JL	Hogg F	Coen L	McPherson IB	Collindridge C	Lewis G	Bellis A
25	Feb 3	LEICESTER CITY	1-4	Southwell	5000	Mowl WJ	Hepworth R	Allen RHA	Southwell AA	Moulson C	Everett HP	Coen L	McPherson IB	Shell FH	Strain N	Collindridge C
26	Feb 10	Leicester City	1-4	Wright	7500	Wiseman G	Hepworth R	Everett HP	Taylor JL	Southwell AA	Moulson C	Coen L	Sewell J	Brooks	McPherson IB	Wright H
27	Feb 17	Nottm. Forest	4-1	Collindridge 2, McPherson, Towler	8000	Wiseman G	Hepworth R	Allen RHA	Towler BE	Morby JH	Everett HP	Coen L	McPherson IB	Southwell AA	Sewell J	Collindridge C
28	Feb 24	NOTTM. FOREST	1-2	Morrad	10000	Streten BR	Hepworth R	Marshall JG	Towler BE	Morby JH	Everett HP	Coen L	McPherson IB	Morrad FG	Lewis G	Collindridge C
29	Mar 3	Lincoln City	2-3	Sewell 2	2500	Wiseman G	Hepworth R	Ball	Towler BE	Morby JH	Everett HP	Lambe	Sewell J	Townrow RF	Lewis G	Gallago
30	Mar 10	Coventry City	0-4		3166	Wiseman G	Marshall JG	Blood JF	Brooks	Morby JH	Everett HP	Lewis G	Lewis G	Hepworth R	Sewell J	Stephenson R
31	Mar 24	Coventry City	0-1		4339	Rollett E	Marshall JG	Blood JF	Baker D	Morby JH	Stancer LB	Akers W	McPherson IB	Hepworth R	Coen L	Flint K
32	Mar 31	COVENTRY CITY	1-2	Flaherty	2000	Rollett E	Southwell AA	Allen RHA	Stancer LB	Morby JH	Baker D	Windle R	McPherson IB	Hepworth R	Flaherty E	Towler BE
33	Apr 2	Nottm. Forest	0-6		6920	Taylor ?	Hepworth R	Everett HP	Unwin S	Peacock E	Stancer LB	Coen L	Hubbard J	Collindridge C	Flaherty E	Flint K
34	Apr 7	Port Vale	4-1	Strain 2, McPherson, Sewell	7000	Wiseman G	Bramley E	Everett HP	Southwell AA	Morby JH	Baker D	Windle R	McPherson IB	Strain N	Sewell J	Stephenson R
35	Apr 14	PORT VALE	2-1	Holmes, Strain	2000	Wiseman G	Bramley E	Allen RHA	Southwell AA	Morby JH	Baker D	Windle R	Hubbard J	Strain N	Sewell J	Holmes E
36	Apr 21	NOTTM. FOREST	1-3	Strain	4000	Andrews G	Southwell AA	Allen RHA	Foster J	Peacock E	Baker D	Windle R	Strain N	Strain N	Hubbard J	Holmes E
37	Apr 28	Nottm. Forest	5-2	McPherson 2, Sewell, Siddons, Toothill	3000	Wiseman G	Bramley E	Hutchinson J	Goodwin FN	Baker D	Hubbard J	Siddons F	McPherson IB	Parker A	Sewell J	Toothill R
38	May 5	Grimsby Town	1-3	Parker	4000	Kirby N	Hutchinson J	Hepworth R	Hubbard J	Probert	Hoyle D	Siddons F	McPherson IB	Parker A	Sewell J	Toothill R
39	May 12	GRIMSBY TOWN	1-3	McPherson	2000	Wiseman G	Bramley E	Allen RHA	Southwell AA	Baker D	Hoyle D	Wildgoose C	McPherson IB	Parker A	Sewell J	O'Neill T

Games 19 to 23 inclusive also counted for League Cup, 31, 32, 34 and 35 for the Midland Cup

1945/46

Third Division South (Northern Section)

#		Date	Opponents	Res	Scorers	Att	1	2	3	4	5	6	7	8	9	10	11
1	Sep	8	Ipswich Town	0-1		10605	Wiseman G	Southwell AA	Taylor WB	Goodman	Peacock E	McPherson IB	Hubbard J	Strain N	Hatton C	Pye J	Beresford R
2		12	Southend United	3-7	Pye 2, Beresford	4227	Wiseman G	Southwell AA	Allen RHA	Ellmer FB	Parker A	Stancer LB	Beresford R	Strain N	Pye J	McPherson IB	Morrad FG
3		15	IPSWICH TOWN	1-1	McPherson	9142	Wiseman G	Southwell AA	Allen RHA	Hubbard J	Blagg EA	Stancer LB	McPherson IB	Strain N	Sewell J	Pye J	Beresford R
4		19	PORT VALE	3-1	Beresford 2, McPherson	5857	Wiseman G	Southwell AA	Allen RHA	Hubbard J	Ruecroft EJ	Beresford R	McPherson IB	Woodcock E	McPherson IB	Sewell J	Meredith RD
5		22	NORWICH CITY	2-2	Pye (p), Sewell	10800	Wiseman G	Southwell AA	Allen RHA	Hubbard J	Harris K	Beresford R	McPherson IB	Sewell J	Pye J	McPherson IB	Toothill R
6		29	Norwich City	1-5	Pye	11692	Wiseman G	Corkhill WG	Allen RHA	Harris K	Southwell AA	Corkhill WG	Beresford R	Tapping FH	Tapping FH	McPherson IB	Alexander T
7	Oct	4	SOUTHEND UNITED	4-1	Pye 3, Beresford	4048	Wiseman G	Southwell AA	Allen RHA	Harris K	Peacock E	Peacock E	Beresford R	Tapping FH	Pye J	McPherson IB	Alexander T
8		6	Northampton T	2-1	Beresford, McPherson	7151	Wiseman G	Southwell AA	Allen RHA	Harris K	Peacock E	Peacock E	Beresford R	Hubbard J	Pye J	McPherson IB	Strain N
9		13	NORTHAMPTON T	7-1	*see below	12576	Wiseman G	Southwell AA	Hutchinson J	Harris K	Sweet	Peacock E	Beresford R	Hubbard J	Pye J	McPherson IB	Briggs R
10		20	MANSFIELD TOWN	1-0	Pye	17960	Wiseman G	Southwell AA	Hutchinson J	Harris K	Sweet	Peacock E	Beresford R	Hubbard J	Pye J	McPherson IB	Alexander T
11		27	Mansfield Town	3-2	Beresford, Harris, Pye	8794	Wiseman G	Southwell AA	Robinson GF	Harris K	Corkhill WG	Peacock E	Beresford R	Airlie S	McPherson IB	McPherson IB	Meredith RD
12	Nov	3	Queens Park Rangers	0-6		14527	Wiseman G	Southwell AA	Robinson GF	Harris K	Corkhill WG	Peacock E	Beresford R	Howarth G	McPherson IB	Pye J	Meredith RD
13		10	QUEENS PARK RANGERS	0-1		22286	Flower T	Southwell AA	Ratcliffe PC	Harris K	Corkhill WG	Read CW	Beresford R	Howarth G	McPherson IB	Pye J	Strain N
14	Dec	1	CLAPTON ORIENT	1-0	Meredith	13823	Kirby N	Southwell AA	Ratcliffe PC	Harris K	Corkhill WG	Peacock E	McPherson IB	Parker A	Pye J	McPherson IB	Meredith RD
15		15	Clapton Orient	3-3	McPherson 2, Pye		Thorne	Southwell AA	Ratcliffe PC	Harris K	Corkhill WG	Goodwin FN	McPherson IB	Iceton OL	McPherson IB	Pye J	Parks A
16		22	WALSALL	3-3	Parks, Pye, Sewell	3267	Kirby N	Southwell AA	Ratcliffe PC	Harris K	Corkhill WG	Rossington K	Hubbard J	Sewell J	Sewell J	Pye J	Rhodes K
17		24	WALSALL	2-0	Pye 2	11871	Kirby N	Southwell AA	Ratcliffe PC	Harris K	Corkhill WG	Peacock E	Sewell J	Sewell J	Parks A	Pye J	Parks A
18		25	WATFORD	2-7	Hubbard, Meredith	3589	Kirby N	Southwell AA	Ratcliffe PC	Harris K	Corkhill WG	Peacock E	Girdham A	Hubbard J	Pye J	Woodcock E	Meredith RD
19		26	WATFORD	1-2	McPherson	17374	Kirby N	Robinson GF	Robinson GF	Hubbard J	Corkhill WG	Peacock E	Beresford R	Woodcock E	Parks A	Pye J	Meredith RD
20		29	Port Vale	0-3	Pye	8000	Brown GR	Southwell AA	Allen RHA	Hubbard J	Corkhill WG	Hubbard J	Beresford R	Woollacott H	Pye J	Pye J	Meredith RD

Scorers in game 9: Hubbard 2, McPherson 2, Beresford, Briggs, Pye

Third Division South Cup (Northern Section) Qualifying Competition

#		Date	Opponents	Res	Scorers	Att	1	2	3	4	5	6	7	8	9	10	11
19	Jan	12	MANSFIELD TOWN	1-2	Pye	10796	Grant AF	Southwell AA	Allen RHA	Hubbard J	Peacock E	McPherson IB	Ratcliffe PC	Pye J	Hubbard J	Moss G	Meredith RD
20		19	Mansfield Town	0-2		4430	Rollett E	Allen RHA	Ratcliffe PC	Corkhill WG	Hoyle D	Beresford R	McPherson IB	Hubbard J	Jones A	Parks A	Parks A
21		26	Port Vale	1-2	Cumberledge (og)	2632	Wilkinson N	Southwell AA	Ratcliffe PC	Corkhill WG	Sheen J	Hubbard J	Dickson W	Sheen J	McPherson IB	McPherson IB	Beresford R
22	Feb	2	PORT VALE	3-2	Beresford, Parks, Sheen	7000	Bland P	Ratcliffe PC	Allen RHA	Corkhill WG	Southwell AA	Beresford R	Parks A	McPherson IB	Sheen J	Parks A	Meredith RD
23		9	Walsall	0-2		8088	Brown GR	Ratcliffe PC	Allen RHA	Southwell AA	Sheen J	Beresford R	McPherson IB	Parks A	Parks A	Parks A	Meredith RD
24		16	WALSALL	1-0	Hubbard	12109	Brown GR	Southwell AA	Ratcliffe PC	Corkhill WG	Hubbard J	Beresford R	Hatton C	Parks A	Pye J	Pye J	Hatton C
25		23	WATFORD	2-1	Beresford, O'Brien (og)	10921	Brown GR	Southwell AA	Ratcliffe PC	Baker D	Baker D	Baker D	Bagnall R	Smith R	Hatton C	Lovering W	Morrad FG
26	Mar	2	Watford	2-6	Beresford, Hatton	1500	Kirby N	Southwell AA	Allen RHA	Haines J	Haines J	Bagnall R	Haines J	Smith R	Lovering W	Smith R	Morrad FG
27		9	Northampton T	1-2	Lovering	7755	Brown GR	Ratcliffe PC	Allen RHA	Corkhill WG	Sheen J	Beresford R	Pye J	Lovering W	Lovering W	Lovering W	Morrad FG
28		16	NORTHAMPTON T	1-2	Pye	9925	Brown GR	Southwell AA	Ratcliffe PC	Haines J	Harris K	Girdham A	Hatton C	Haines J	Haines J	Hatton C	Morrad FG
29		23	IPSWICH TOWN	1-0	Haines	9966	Brown GR	Southwell AA	Ratcliffe PC	Harris K	Page D	Clover G	Bagnall R	Parks A	Rowley W	Haines J	Parks A
30		30	Ipswich Town	2-1	Hatton, Rowley	10474	Brown GR	Southwell AA	Ratcliffe PC	Corkhill WG	Corkhill WG	Parks A	Haines J	Haines J	Rowley W	Rowley W	Morrad FG
31	Apr	6	Queens Park Rangers	1-3	Ridyard (og)	13818	Brown GR	Southwell AA	Ratcliffe PC	Harris K	Harris K	Beresford R	McPherson IB	McPherson IB	Beresford R	Beresford R	Howard
32		13	QUEENS PARK RANGERS	0-3		9000	Brown GR	Southwell AA	Ratcliffe PC	Corkhill WG	Hubbard J	Dean	Pye J	Pye J	Bamard CH	Haines J	Morrad FG
33		19	NORWICH CITY	0-1		12000	Brown GR	Southwell AA	Robinson GF	Corkhill WG	Smith L	Beresford R	Pye J	Pye J	Bamard CH	Parks A	Toothill R
34		22	Norwich City	1-2	Pye	16000	Brown GR	Southwell AA	Robinson GF	Corkhill WG	Baker D	Sail GH	Sail GH	Pye J	Bamard CH	Pye J	Parks A

F.A. Cup

#		Date	Opponents	Res	Scorers	Att	1	2	3	4	5	6	7	8	9	10	11
R1/1	Nov	17	BRADFORD CITY	2-2	McPherson, Hubbard	20000	Flower T	Southwell AA	Robinson GF	Harris K	Corkhill WG	Peacock E	Beresford R	Pye J	Hubbard J	McPherson IB	Stancer LB
R1/2	Nov	24	Bradford City	2-1	McPherson, Parker	11000	Kirby N	Southwell AA	Robinson GF	Harris K	Corkhill WG	Peacock E	Beresford R	McPherson IB	Hubbard J	Pye J	Parker A
R2/1	Dec	8	Northampton T	1-3	McPherson	10000	Kirby N	Southwell AA	Ratcliffe PC	Harris K	Corkhill WG	Peacock E	Beresford R	McPherson IB	Hubbard J	Pye J	Meredith RD
R2/2	Dec	15	NORTHAMPTON T	1-0	Martin	18000	Kirby N	Southwell AA	Ratcliffe PC	Harris K	Corkhill WG	Peacock E	Beresford R	Pye J	Martin DK	Hubbard J	Meredith RD

Ties played over two legs in season 1945/46

1946/47   12th in Division Three (South)

#	Date		Opponent	Score	Scorers	Att	Brown HT	Corkhill WG	Robinson GF	Gannon E	Fallon WJ	Hubbard J	Beresford R	Brown C	Whittaker FJ	Cumner HR	Parks A	Toser E	Morrad FG	Bagnall R	Lockie AJ	Sewell J	Allen R	Baxter WE	Lunn H	Jayes AG	Southwell AA	Flanagan DC	Houghton WE	Wright BAW	Dickson W	Freeman A
1	Aug	31	BOURNEMOUTH	1-0	Brown C	26779	1	2	3	4	5	6	7	8	9	10	11															
2	Sep	7	Cardiff City	1-2	Lever(og)	24779	1	2	3	4	5	6	7	8	9	10	11															
3		11	BRISTOL CITY	0-3		17522	1	2	3	4		6	7	8		10	11	5	9													
4		14	NORWICH CITY	3-0	Sewell, Hubbard, Parks	18210	1	6	3	4		9		8		7	11			2	5	10										
5		21	Watford	2-2	Sewell, Hubbard	10100	1	2		4	11	9		8		7				6	5	10	3									
6		23	Port Vale	1-4	Cumner(p)	8574	1	2	3	4		6	9	8		7	11				5	10										
7		28	Northampton T	1-2	Beresford	11906	1	6	3	4			9	8		7	11			2	5	10										
8	Oct	3	PORT VALE	3-2	Brown C 2, Sewell	9542	1	6	3	4			9	8		7	11			2	5	10										
9		5	ALDERSHOT	2-0	Sewell 2	17298	1	2	3	4		6	7	8	9		11				5	10										
10		12	Brighton & Hove Alb.	2-3	Lunn, Sewell(p)	9419	1	2	3	4				8			11				5	10		6	7	9						
11		19	IPSWICH TOWN	1-2	Cumner	19886	1		3	4				8			11				5	10		6	7	9	2					
12		26	Leyton Orient	3-1	Jayes 2, Sewell	7613	1		3	4						11	8				5	10		6	7	9	2					
13	Nov	2	QUEENS PARK RANGERS	1-2	Sewell	27584	1		3	4						11	10				5	8		6	7	9	2					
14		9	Southend United	0-3		10100	1		3	4						11	10				5	8		6	7	9	2					
15		16	BRISTOL ROVERS	6-0	Jayes, Gannon, Lunn 2, Sewell 2	14390	1		3	4	11						8				5	10		6	7	9	2					
16		23	Mansfield Town	0-1		10899	1	4	3		11						8				5	10		6	7	9	2					
17	Dec	7	Crystal Palace	1-2	Jayes	12461	1		3	4	11						8				5	10		6	7	9	2					
18		21	Walsall	0-2		8801	1		3	4	11						8	10			5	9		6	7		2					
19		25	SWINDON TOWN	0-0		18439	1		3	4	11						8				5	10		6	7	9	2					
20		26	Swindon Town	2-4	Jayes, Brown C	17894	1		3	4	11	6		9							5				7	8	2					
21		28	Bournemouth	2-1	Brown C, Flanagan	13491	1		3	4		6		10			8				5				7	11	2	9				
22	Jan	4	CARDIFF CITY	1-1	Flanagan	28450	1		3	4		6		10			8				5				7	11	2	9				
23		18	Norwich City	2-2	Sewell, Lunn	16788	1	6	3	4		9					8				5	10			7		2		11			
24		23	TORQUAY UNITED	0-2		6295		6	3	4		9					8				5	10			7		2		11	1		
25		25	WATFORD	4-1	Cumner, Sewell, Houghton, Jayes	9511	1	6	3	4							8				5	10			7	9	2		11			
26	Feb	1	NORTHAMPTON T	1-0	Sewell	13096	1	4	3								8				5	10			7	9	2		11		6	
27		8	Aldershot	1-1	Cumner	2974	1	4	3								8				5	10			7	9	2		11		6	
28	Mar	8	Queens Park Rangers	1-4	Sewell	9455	1			4	11					3	8				5	10		6	7	9	2					
29		22	Bristol Rovers	1-4	Cumner	11888			3	4						8					5	10			7	9	2		11	1	6	
30		29	MANSFIELD TOWN	5-1	Fallon 2, Sewell 2, Houghton	12157	1		3	4	11						8				5	10				9	2		7		6	
31	Apr	4	EXETER CITY	0-0		15014	1		3	4	11						8				5	10				9	2		7		6	
32		5	Torquay United	2-1	Sewell 2	4064	1		3	4	11					9	8				5	10					2		7		6	
33		7	Exeter City	2-2	Sewell, Fallon	10796	1		3	4	11				9		8				5	10					2		7		6	
34		12	CRYSTAL PALACE	0-0		14890	1		3	4	11	9					8				5	10					2		7		6	
35		19	Reading	1-1	Parks	9446	1		3	4					9	11	8				5	10					2		7		6	
36		26	WALSALL	3-1	Whittaker, Dickson, Parks	10790	1		3	4					9		8				5	10				11	2		7		6	
37	May	3	Bristol City	1-1	Houghton	11834	1		3	4							8				5	10			7	9	2		11		6	
38		10	BRIGHTON & HOVE ALB.	2-0	Lunn, Whittaker(p)	12926	1		3	4					9		8				5	10			7		2		11		6	
39		17	Ipswich Town	2-1	Sewell 2	10229	1		3	4					9		8				5	10			7		2		11		6	
40		24	SOUTHEND UNITED	0-2		13901	1		3	4					9		8				5	10			7		2		11		6	
41		26	LEYTON ORIENT	1-2	Dickson	10689	1	4	3			9					8				5	10				11	2				6	7
42		29	READING	1-0	Jayes	6142	1		3	4							8				5	10				9	2		11		6	7
			Apps				36	29	29	38	15	13	9	13	10	35	17	2	1	6	23	37	1	25	24	26	32	2	18	2	15	2
			Goals							1	3	2	1	5	2	5	3					21			5	7		2	3		2	

One own goal

Played in game 13: JA Dewick (1).   In game 20: JK Marsh (10).

F.A. Cup

	Date		Opponent	Score	Scorers	Att	Brown HT	Corkhill WG	Robinson GF	Gannon E	Fallon WJ	Hubbard J	Beresford R	Brown C	Whittaker FJ	Cumner HR	Parks A	Toser E	Morrad FG	Bagnall R	Lockie AJ	Sewell J	Allen R	Baxter WE	Lunn H	Jayes AG	Southwell AA	Flanagan DC	Houghton WE	Wright BAW	Dickson W	Freeman A
R1	Nov	30	Leyton Orient	2-1	Jayes, Cumner	11800	1		3	4	11						8				5	10		6	7	9	2					
R2	Dec	14	SWINDON TOWN	2-1	Sewell, Fallon	18522	1		3	4	11						8				5	10		6	7	9	2					
R3	Jan	11	Luton Town	0-6		21820	1		3	4		6		10			8				5				7	9	2		11			

		P	W	D	L	F	A	W	D	L	F	A	Pts
1	Cardiff City	42	18	3	0	60	11	12	3	6	33	19	66
2	Queen's Park Rgs.	42	15	2	4	42	15	8	9	4	32	25	57
3	Bristol City	42	13	4	4	56	20	7	7	7	38	36	51
4	Swindon Town	42	15	4	2	56	25	4	7	10	28	48	49
5	Walsall	42	11	6	4	42	25	6	6	9	32	34	46
6	Ipswich Town	42	11	5	5	33	21	5	9	7	28	32	46
7	Bournemouth	42	12	4	5	43	20	6	4	11	29	34	44
8	Southend United	42	9	7	5	38	22	8	3	10	33	38	44
9	Reading	42	11	6	4	53	30	5	5	11	30	44	43
10	Port Vale	42	14	4	3	51	28	3	5	13	17	35	43
11	Torquay United	42	11	5	5	33	23	4	7	10	19	38	42
12	NOTTS COUNTY	42	11	4	6	35	19	4	6	11	28	44	40
13	Northampton Town	42	11	5	5	46	33	4	5	12	26	42	40
14	Bristol Rovers	42	9	6	6	34	26	7	2	12	25	43	40
15	Exeter City	42	11	6	4	37	27	4	3	14	23	42	39
16	Watford	42	11	4	6	39	27	6	1	14	22	49	39
17	Brighton & Hove A.	42	8	7	6	31	35	5	5	11	23	37	38
18	Crystal Palace	42	9	7	5	29	19	4	4	13	20	43	37
19	Leyton Orient	42	10	5	6	40	28	2	3	16	14	47	32
20	Aldershot	42	6	7	8	25	26	4	5	12	23	52	32
21	Norwich City	42	6	3	12	38	48	4	5	12	26	52	28
22	Mansfield Town	42	8	5	8	31	38	1	5	15	17	58	28

- 1946/47 Season -

Back: Cumner, Sewell, Allen, Lunn, Robinson, not known, not known, Bagnall, Adamson
Middle: C.Jackson, not known, Beresford, Hubbard, Southwell, Gannon, H.Brown, Morrad, not known, Cobley, not known, C.Brown
Front: Corkhill, Fisher(Sec), Hobson(Dir), Barnes(Chair), Cottee(Treas), Stollery(Man), Whittaker, Linnell(Dir), Fallon, Parks

- 1947/48 Season -

Back: Ratcliffe(Trainer), Gannon, Southwell, H.Brown, Howe, Baxter, F.Evans
Front: Freeman, Sewell, Lawton, Marsh, Parks, Corkhill

1947/48 6th in Division Three (South)

No	Date	Opponent	Score	Scorers	Att	Brown HT	Southwell AA	Howe HA	Gannon E	Baxter WE	Dickson W	Houghton WE	Lyman CC	Evans FJ	Sewell J	Jayes AG	Cumner HR	Corkhill WG	Parks A	Orgill H	Freeman A	Keeble FW	Marsh JK	Lawton T	Bagnall R	Pimbley DW	Rigby NE	Adamson H	Molloy P
1	Aug 23	Ipswich Town	0-2		14196	1	2	3	4	5	6	7	8	9	10	11													
2	28	BOURNEMOUTH	1-2	Sewell	14065	1	2	3	4	5	6	7	8	9	10		11												
3	30	BRISTOL CITY	3-1	Sewell, Houghton, Evans	18980	1	2	3	4	5				9	10		11	6	8										
4	Sep 3	Bournemouth	0-2		16885		3		4	5	6	7		9	10		11	2	8	1									
5	6	Reading	1-3	Sewell	11726	1	2		4	5	6		9	7	10		11	3	8										
6	11	QUEENS PARK RANGERS	1-1	Lyman	19335	1	2	3	4	5			9		10		11	6	8		7								
7	13	WALSALL	1-0	Cumner	20031	1	2	3	4	5			8	9	10		11	6			7								
8	18	Queens Park Rangers	1-4	Keeble	15708	1	2		4	5	6			9	10		11	3			7	8							
9	20	Leyton Orient	1-2	Sewell	11508	1	2	3	4	5			11		10			6	8		7	9							
10	27	EXETER CITY	1-1	Lyman	20851	1	2	3	4	5			8	9	10		11	6			7								
11	Oct 4	Newport County	1-3	Marsh	14015	1	2	3	4	5			9		10		11	6			7		8						
12	11	PORT VALE	2-1	Cumner, Gannon	20172	1	2	3	4	5			8		10		11	6			7		9						
13	18	Swindon Town	1-1	Marsh	18198	1	2	3	4	5			8		10		11	6			7		9						
14	25	TORQUAY UNITED	0-0		23155	1	2	3	4	5			8		10		11	6			7		9						
15	Nov 1	Crystal Palace	1-1	Marsh	16019	1	2	3	4	5					10		11	6			7	8	9						
16	8	ALDERSHOT	0-2		20827	1	2	3	4	5					10		11	6			7	8	9						
17	15	Northampton T	2-1	Lawton, Marsh	18272	1	2	3	4	5		7	8				11	6					10	9					
18	22	BRISTOL ROVERS	4-2	Lawton 2, Sewell 2	31450	1	2	3	4	5		7	8				11	6					10	9					
19	Dec 26	SWANSEA TOWN	5-1	Lawton 2, Freeman, Marsh, Sewell	45116	1	2	3	4				8				11	6			7		10	9	5				
20	27	Swansea Town	1-1	Marsh	23573		2	3	4		6		8				11	5	10	1	7		10	9					
21	Jan 3	Bristol City	0-1		35287	1	2	3	4		6			7	8		11	5					10	9					
22	17	READING	5-1	Sewell 3, Marsh, Lawton	34866	1	2	3			6				8		11	4			7		10	9	5				
23	31	Walsall	1-2	Lawton	20383	1	2	3	4				8				11	5			7		10	9					
24	Feb 7	LEYTON ORIENT	1-4	Lawton	28875	1	2	3	4		6		11						8		7		10	9	5				
25	14	Exeter City	1-0	Parks	16962	1	2	3	4		6		11					5	10		7		9						
26	21	NEWPORT COUNTY	4-1	Sewell 2, Lawton, Lyman	17762	1	2	3	4		6		11					5	10		7		9						
27	28	Port Vale	2-1	Lawton, Sewell	18147	1	2	3	4		6		11					5	10		7		9						
28	Mar 6	SWINDON TOWN	2-1	Marsh 2	27767	1	2	3	4				11					5	10		7		9			6			
29	13	Torquay United	2-2	Lyman, Marsh	8290	1	2	3		4			11					5	10		7		9			6			
30	20	CRYSTAL PALACE	1-0	Lyman	30558	1	2		4	3			11					5			7		10	9		6			
31	26	SOUTHEND UNITED	2-1	Lawton 2	35689	1	2	3					11					5			7		10	9		6			
32	27	Aldershot	0-1		12750	1	2	3					11				7	5					10	9		6			
33	29	Southend United	2-1	Cumner, Sheard(og)	17613	1	2	3	4	6					8		11	5			7		9			10			
34	Apr 3	NORTHAMPTON T	3-2	Lawton 2, Lowery(og)	30903	1	2	3	4						8		11	5			7		10	9		6			
35	7	Watford	3-1	Cumner, Sewell, Marsh	12532	1	2	3	4	6					8		11	5			7		9			10			
36	10	Bristol Rovers	0-2		12451	1	2	3	4	6					8		11	5	8		7		9			10			
37	15	IPSWICH TOWN	0-1		33505	1	2		4				8				11	5			7		10	9		6	3		
38	17	NORWICH CITY	1-2	Sewell	19183	1	2	3	4				8				11	5			7		9			10		6	
39	22	BRIGHTON & HOVE ALB.	4-0	Pimbley, Sewell, Marsh, Cumner	19585	1	2	3	4	6			8				11	5					7	9		10			
40	24	Brighton & Hove Alb.	3-1	Lawton 2, Cumner	19572	1	2	3	4				8				11	5			7		10	9		6			
41	28	Norwich City	1-0	Lawton	37863	1	2	3	4				8				11	6			7		10	9		6			
42	May 1	WATFORD	3-3	Lawton, Freeman, Sewell(p)	23174	1	2	3	4				8				11	6			7		10	9					5
	Apps					40	42	37	40	32	6	6	21	7	41	1	31	39	13	2	31	4	30	19	3	14	1	1	1
	Goals							1				1	5	1	17		6		1		2	1	12	18		1			

Two own goals

F.A. Cup

	Date	Opponent	Score	Scorers	Att	Brown HT	Southwell AA	Howe HA	Gannon E	Baxter WE	Dickson W	Lyman CC	Sewell J	Cumner HR	Corkhill WG	Freeman A	Marsh JK	Lawton T	Bagnall R
R1	Nov 29	HORSHAM	9-1	Lawton 3, Sewell 3, Marsh 2, Freeman	24815	1	2	3	4	5		8		11	6	7	10	9	
R2	Dec 13	STOCKTON	1-1	Sewell	30156	1	2	3	4	5		8		11	6	7	10	9	
rep	Dec 20	Stockton	4-1	Lawton 3, Cumner	34261	1	2	3	4			8		11	5	7	10	9	
R3	Jan 10	Birmingham City	2-0	Corkhill, Marsh	53000	1	2	3		6		8		11	4	7	10	9	5
R4	Jan 24	Swindon Town	0-1		27000	1	2	3	4	6		8		11	5	7	10	9	

R2 after extra time. R2 replay at Middlesbrough.
Played in R2 replay: J Hubbard (at no. 6)

	Team	P	W	D	L	F	A	W	D	L	F	A	Pts
1	Queen's Park Rgs.	42	16	3	2	44	17	10	6	5	30	20	61
2	Bournemouth	42	13	5	3	42	13	11	4	6	34	22	57
3	Walsall	42	13	5	3	37	12	8	4	9	33	28	51
4	Ipswich Town	42	16	1	4	42	18	7	2	12	25	43	49
5	Swansea Town	42	14	6	1	48	14	4	6	11	22	38	48
6	NOTTS COUNTY	42	12	4	5	44	27	7	4	10	24	32	46
7	Bristol City	42	11	4	6	47	26	7	3	11	30	39	43
8	Port Vale	42	14	4	3	48	18	2	7	12	15	36	43
9	Southend United	42	11	8	2	32	16	4	5	12	19	42	43
10	Reading	42	10	5	6	37	28	5	6	10	19	30	41
11	Exeter City	42	11	6	4	34	22	4	5	12	21	41	41
12	Newport County	42	9	8	4	38	28	5	5	11	23	45	41
13	Crystal Palace	42	12	5	4	32	14	1	8	12	17	35	39
14	Northampton Town	42	10	5	6	35	28	4	6	11	23	44	39
15	Watford	42	6	6	9	31	37	8	4	9	26	42	38
16	Swindon Town	42	6	10	5	21	20	4	6	11	20	26	36
17	Leyton Orient	42	8	5	8	31	32	5	5	11	20	41	36
18	Torquay United	42	7	6	8	40	29	4	7	10	23	33	35
19	Aldershot	42	5	10	6	22	26	5	5	11	23	41	35
20	Bristol Rovers	42	7	3	11	39	34	6	5	10	32	41	34
21	Norwich City	42	8	3	10	33	34	5	5	11	28	42	34
22	Brighton & Hove A.	42	8	4	9	26	31	3	8	10	17	42	34

1948/49   11th in Division Three (South)

#	Date	Opponent	Score	Scorers	Att	Brown HT	Southwell AA	Howe HA	Gannon E	Corkhill WG	Russell RI	Freeman A	Sewell J	Lawton T	Marsh JK	Johnston TD	Rigby NE	Baxter WE	Houghton WE	Adamson H	Evans FJ	Pimbley DW	Stone G	Brown AW	Hold O	Mowl JW	Smith RL	Purvis B	Chapman H	Praski J	McCavana WT
1	Aug 21	Torquay United	1-3	Sewell	10627	1	2	3	4	5	6	7	8	9	10	11															
2	26	WALSALL	2-0	Male(og), Johnston	35319	1	2	3	4	5	6	7	8	9	10	11															
3	28	BRISTOL ROVERS	4-1	Marsh, Sewell, Johnston, Lawton	33747	1	2		4	5		7	8	9	10	11	3	6													
4	Sep 2	Walsall	2-3	Sewell 2	14845	1	2		4	5		7	8	9	10	11	3	6													
5	4	Newport County	3-3	Sewell, Houghton, Marsh	16776	1	2	3	4	5			8	9	10	11		6	7												
6	9	IPSWICH TOWN	9-2	*See below	30985	1	2		4				8	9	10	11	3	5	7	6											
7	11	SWANSEA TOWN	1-1	Lawton	36471	1	2		4				8	9	10	11	3	5	7	6											
8	15	Ipswich Town	2-3	O'Mahoney(og), Lawton	21231	1	2		4	3			8	9	10	11		5	7	6											
9	18	Reading	4-1	Houghton, Evans 2, Johnston	23651	1	2		4				8	9		11		5	7	6	10										
10	23	SWINDON TOWN	1-2	Marsh	19527	1	2	3	4				8		10	11		5	7	6	9										
11	25	CRYSTAL PALACE	5-1	Johnston, Marsh 2, Sewell 2	24061	1	2	3	4				8		9	11		5	7	6	10										
12	Oct 2	Watford	1-1	Evans	22612	1	2	3	4				8	9		11		5	7	6	10										
13	9	Norwich City	0-3		29998	1	2	3	4				8	9	10	11			7	6				5							
14	16	EXETER CITY	9-0	Hold, Sewell 4, Lawton 4	36615	1	2	3	4				8	9		11			7	6				5	10						
15	23	Millwall	2-3	Sewell, Johnston	44627	1	2	3	4				8	9		11			7	6				5	10						
16	30	ALDERSHOT	2-0	Sewell, Johnston	35706	1	2	3	4			7	8	9		11				6				5	10						
17	Nov 6	Leyton Orient	1-3	Hold	16123	1	2	3	4			7	8			11				6	9			5	10						
18	13	PORT VALE	2-1	Johnston, Hold	29332		2	3	4				8	9		11		6	7					5	10	1					
19	20	Bristol City	1-3	Johnston	29663		2		4			7	8	9		11		6						5	10	1					
20	Dec 4	Brighton & Hove Alb.	2-3	Johnston, Hold	22994		2	3					8	9		11		4	7				6	5	10	1					
21	18	TORQUAY UNITED	5-0	Hold, Sewell 2, Johnston, Lawton	23007		2		4				8	9		11		5	7	6					10		1	3			
22	25	Northampton T	2-1	Johnston, Sewell	17724		2		4				8	9		11		5	7	6					10		1	3			
23	27	NORTHAMPTON T	2-0	Hold, Sewell	31171		2		4				8	9		11		5	7	6					10		1	3			
24	Jan 1	Bristol Rovers	2-3	Johnston, Hold	12617		2		4				8			11		5	7	6	10				9		1	3			
25	15	NEWPORT COUNTY	11-1	*See below	26843		2		4				8	9		11		5	7	6					10		1	3			
26	22	Swansea Town	1-3	Johnston	26493		2			4			8	9		11		5	7	6					10		1	3			
27	Feb 5	READING	1-0	Sewell	33165		2		4				8	9		11	5		7	6	10						1	3			
28	12	SOUTHEND UNITED	0-0		29290		2		4				8	9		11		5	7	6					10		1	3			
29	19	Crystal Palace	5-1	Johnston 3, Evans, Lawton	30925		2		4				8	9		11		5	7	6	10						1	3			
30	26	WATFORD	4-0	Johnston 3, Evans	31930		2		4				8	9		11		5	7	6	10						1	3			
31	Mar 5	NORWICH CITY	2-1	Lawton, Evans	34465		2		4				8	9		11		5	7	6	10						1	3			
32	12	Exeter City	1-3	Clark(og)	14374		2						8	9		11		5	7	6	10	4					1	3			
33	19	MILLWALL	1-3	Houghton	33818		2						8	9		11		5	10	6							1	3	4	7	
34	26	Aldershot	1-0	Johnston	9534		2						8	9		11		5	7	6	10						1	3	4		
35	Apr 2	LEYTON ORIENT	2-1	Houghton, Johnston	29287								8	9		11			7	6				5	10		1	3	4		2
36	9	Port Vale	0-1		12198								8	9		11			7	6				5	10		1	3	4		2
37	15	Bournemouth	1-2	Hold	24237							7	8			11		4		6				5	9		1	3	10		2
38	16	Bristol City	2-1	Sewell 2	27149		2						8			11		7					6	5	9		1	3	4	7	
39	18	BOURNEMOUTH	2-3	Evans, Lawton	28132		2						8	9		11				6	10			5			1	3	4	7	
40	23	Swindon Town	0-3		17716		2	3					8	9		11				6				5	10		1		4	7	
41	30	BRIGHTON & HOVE ALB.	1-1	Lawton	19478		2					7	8	9		11				6				5	10		1	3	4		
42	May 7	Southend United	2-3	Sewell, Hold	12256		2					7	8	9					11	6				5	10		1	3	4		
		Apps				17	39	15	29	7	2	10	42	36	11	41	5	27	31	33	10	8	3	13	19	3	22	21	10	3	3
		Goals											26	20	6	24			6		7				9						

Four own goals

*Scorers in game 6: Lawton 4, Sewell, Marsh, Houghton, Johnston, Bell(og). In game 25: Sewell 4, Johnston 2, Lawton 4, Houghton. Played in game 19: JS Macdonald (3). In game 38: J Jackson (10).

F.A. Cup

#	Date	Opponent	Score	Scorers	Att	Brown HT	Southwell AA	Howe HA	Gannon E	Freeman A	Sewell J	Lawton T	Johnston TD	Baxter WE	Houghton WE	Adamson H	Evans FJ	Brown AW	Hold O	Mowl JW	Smith RL	Purvis B
R1	Nov 27	PORT VALE	2-1	Lawton 2	36514		2	3	4		8	9	11	6	7			5	10	1		
R2	Dec 11	BARROW	3-2	Johnston 2, Lawton	36710	1	2	3	4		8	9	11	6	7			5	10			
R3	Jan 8	Plymouth Argyle	1-0	Sewell	40000		2		4		8	9	11	5	7	6	10				1	3
R4	29	Liverpool	0-1		61003		2		4		8	9	11	5	7	6	10				1	3

R3 after extra time

		P	W	D	L	F	A	W	D	L	F	A	Pts
1	Swansea Town	42	20	1	0	60	11	7	7	7	27	23	62
2	Reading	42	17	1	3	48	18	8	4	9	29	32	55
3	Bournemouth	42	15	2	4	42	17	7	6	8	27	31	52
4	Swindon Town	42	11	9	1	38	20	7	6	8	26	36	51
5	Bristol Rovers	42	13	5	3	42	23	6	5	10	19	28	48
6	Brighton & Hove A.	42	11	5	5	32	26	6	4	11	23	29	48
7	Ipswich Town	42	14	3	4	53	30	4	6	11	25	47	45
8	Millwall	42	12	7	2	42	23	5	4	12	21	41	45
9	Torquay United	42	12	5	4	45	26	5	6	10	20	44	45
10	Norwich City	42	11	6	4	32	10	5	6	10	35	39	44
11	NOTTS COUNTY	42	15	3	3	68	19	4	2	15	34	49	43
12	Exeter City	42	12	5	4	45	26	3	5	13	18	50	40
13	Port Vale	42	11	3	7	32	21	3	8	10	19	33	39
14	Walsall	42	9	5	7	34	28	6	3	12	22	36	38
15	Newport County	42	8	6	7	41	35	6	3	12	27	57	37
16	Bristol City	42	8	9	4	28	24	3	5	13	16	38	36
17	Watford	42	6	9	6	24	21	4	6	11	17	33	35
18	Southend United	42	5	10	6	18	18	4	6	11	23	28	34
19	Leyton Orient	42	9	6	6	36	29	2	6	13	22	51	34
20	Northampton Town	42	9	6	6	33	20	3	3	15	18	42	33
21	Aldershot	42	6	5	10	26	29	5	6	10	22	30	33
22	Crystal Palace	42	7	8	6	27	27	1	3	17	11	49	27

- 1948/49 Season -

Back: Purvis, Stone, Rigby, H.T.Brown, Mowl, Garneys, MacDonald, F.J.Evans
Standing: Ratcliffe(Trainer), Sewell, Howe, Johnston, Southwell, Pimbley, Hold, Baxter, Maltby(Trainer)
Sitting: Stollery(Manager), Corkhill, Lawton, Barnes(Chairman), A.W.Brown, Houghton, Fisher(Secretary)
Front: Jackson, Freeman, Lomas

- 1949/50 Season -

Back: Baxter, Deans, Southwell, R.Smith, Houghton(Manager), Rigby, Chapman, Adamson
Middle: Broome, Sewell, Lawton, W.Evans, Johnston
Front: F.Evans, Simpson

1949/50 — Champions of Division Three (South) - Promoted

#	Date		Opponent	Score	Scorers	Att	Smith RL	Southwell AA	Purvis B	Chapman H	Baxter WE	Adamson H	Evans FJ	Sewell J	Lawton T	Evans W	Johnston TD	Rigby NE	Stone G	Boyes WE	Crookes RE	Corkhill WG	Deans T	Broome FH	Simpson A	Pimbley DW	Brunt GR	Robinson P	Freeman A
1	Aug	20	SOUTHEND UNITED	2-0	FJ Evans, Sewell	33507	1	2	3	4	5	6	7	8	9	10	11												
2		24	Norwich City	3-4	Lawton, W Evans, Sewell	32131	1	2	3	4	5	6	7	8	9	10	11												
3		27	Bristol Rovers	3-0	Lawton 2, Johnston	24794	1	2		4	5	6	7	8	9	10	11	3											
4	Sep	1	NORWICH CITY	5-0	FJ Evans 2, W Evans, Lawton, Johnston	35149	1	2		4	5	6	7	8	9	10	11	3											
5		3	BOURNEMOUTH	2-0	Lawton 2	34606	1	2		4	5	6	7	8	9	10	11	3											
6		8	EXETER CITY	3-3	Johnston 2, Lawton	22287	1	2		4			7		9	10	6	3	5	8	11								
7		10	Crystal Palace	2-1	W Evans, Johnston	26847	1	2		4		6	7		9	10	11	3		8	5								
8		17	WATFORD	1-0	Sewell	33962	1	2		4	5	6	7	8	9	10	11	3											
9		24	Reading	1-0	W Evans	29091	1	2		4	5	6	7	8	9	10	11	3											
10	Oct	1	LEYTON ORIENT	7-1	Sewell 2, W Evans 2, Lawton 2, Johnston	36332	1	2		4	5	6	7	8	9	10	11	3											
11		8	Newport County	1-1	Sewell	21425	1			4	5	6	7	8	9	10	11	3					2						
12		15	BRISTOL CITY	4-1	Sewell 2, Southwell, Lawton	37978	1	7		4	5	6		8	9	10	11	3					2						
13		22	Brighton & Hove Alb.	3-2	Lawton 2(1p), Johnston	17222	1	2		4	5	6	7	8	9	10	11						3						
14		29	WALSALL	1-1	Lawton (p)	42676	1	2		4	5	6		8	9	10	11						3	7					
15	Nov	5	Millwall	3-1	Lawton, Sewell 2	19495	1	2		4	5	6		8	9	10	11						3	7					
16		12	SWINDON TOWN	3-0	Lawton 3 (2p)	37121	1			4	5	6		8	9	10	11	3					2	7					
17		19	Torquay United	0-0		13824	1			4	5	6		8	9	10	11	3					2	7					
18	Dec	3	Nottm. Forest	2-1	Lawton, Broome	37903	1			4	5	6		8	9	10	11	3					2	7					
19		17	Southend United	0-2		14628	1			4		6		8	9	10	11	3					2	7	5				
20		24	BRISTOL ROVERS	2-0	Broome, FJ Evans	31995	1			4	5	6	7	8	9	10		3					2	11					
21		26	IPSWICH TOWN	2-0	Sewell, Johnston	40192	1			4	5	6	7	8	9	10	11	3					2						
22		27	Ipswich Town	4-0	Sewell, Lawton 2, Johnston	22983	1			4	5	6	7	8	9	10	11	3					2						
23		31	Bournemouth	0-3		22585	1	2		4	5	6	7	8	9	10	11	3					2						
24	Jan	14	CRYSTAL PALACE	0-1		31303	1	2			5	6		8		10	11	3						7		4	9		
25		21	Watford	1-2	FJ Evans	17393	1	2		4		6	7	8		10	11	3						9	5				
26		28	ALDERSHOT	3-1	Broome, FJ Evans, Sewell	27024	1			4		6	9	8		10	11	3					2	7	5				
27	Feb	4	READING	4-0	Sewell, Broome, Lawton, Johnston	36183	1			4		6		8	9	10	11	3					2	7	5				
28		18	Leyton Orient	4-1	Sewell, Johnston 2, Broome	21633	1			4		6		8	9	10	11	3					2	7	5				
29		25	NEWPORT COUNTY	7-0	Sewell 3, Lawton 2(1p), Johnston, W Evans	28427	1			4		6		8	9	10	11	3					2	7	5				
30	Mar	4	Bristol City	0-4		29795	1			4		6		8	9	10	11	3					2	7	5				
31		11	BRIGHTON & HOVE ALB.	4-2	Tennant(og), Chapman, Lawton, Johnston	34322	1			8	5	6			9	10	11	3					2	7	4				
32		18	Walsall	3-3	Lawton, Johnston, Simpson	19589	1			8	5	6			9	10	11	3					2	7	4				
33		25	MILLWALL	2-0	Simpson 2	31024	1			4	5	6			9	10	11	3					2	7	8				
34	Apr	1	Swindon Town	1-1	Simpson	19876	1			4	5	6	7		9	10	11	3					2		8				
35		7	PORT VALE	3-1	Boyes, Lawton, Simpson	32021	1			4	5	6			9	10		3		11			2	7	8				
36		8	TORQUAY UNITED	1-1	Lawton	43906	1			4	5	6			9	10		3		11			2	7	8				
37		10	Port Vale	1-3	Lawton	15380	1	5	3		6	10	7		9								2	11	8			4	
38		15	Aldershot	0-2		9758	1			4	5	6		8	9	10	11	3					2	7					
39		22	NOTTM. FOREST	2-0	Sewell, Lawton	46000	1			4	5	6		8	9	10	11	3					2	7					
40		27	NORTHAMPTON T	2-0	Lawton 2	31843	1			4	5	6		8	9	10	11	3					2	7					
41		29	Northampton T	1-5	Broome	9940	1			4	5	6	9			10	11	3					2	7	8				
42	May	6	Exeter City	2-2	Broome, Crookes	10301	1			8	5	6				10		3			11		2	9				4	7
			Apps				42	18	3	39	33	42	20	32	37	41	37	36	1	3	3	1	29	24	16	1	1	2	1
			Goals					1		1			6	19	31	7	15			1	1			7	5				

One own goal

F.A. Cup

	Date		Opponent	Score	Scorers	Att	Smith RL	Southwell AA	Purvis B	Chapman H	Baxter WE	Adamson H	Evans FJ	Sewell J	Lawton T	Evans W	Johnston TD	Rigby NE	Stone G	Boyes WE	Crookes RE	Corkhill WG	Deans T	Broome FH	Simpson A	Pimbley DW	Brunt GR	Robinson P	Freeman A
R1	Nov	26	TILBURY	4-0	Broome 2, Lawton, Sewell	28584	1			4	5	6		8	9	10	11	3					2	7					
R2	Dec	10	Rochdale	2-1	Johnston, Lawton	24231	1			4		6		8	9	10	11	3					2	7	5				
R3	Jan	7	BURNLEY	1-4	Johnston	44000	1	2		4	5	6		8	9	10	11	3					2	7	5				7

League Table

		P	W	D	L	F	A	W	D	L	F	A	Pts
1	NOTTS COUNTY	42	17	3	1	60	12	8	5	8	35	38	58
2	Northampton Town	42	12	6	3	43	21	8	5	8	29	29	51
3	Southend United	42	15	4	2	43	15	4	9	8	23	33	51
4	Nottingham Forest	42	13	0	8	37	15	7	9	5	30	24	49
5	Torquay United	42	13	6	2	40	23	6	4	11	26	40	48
6	Watford	42	10	6	5	26	13	6	7	8	19	22	45
7	Crystal Palace	42	12	5	4	35	21	3	9	9	20	33	44
8	Brighton & Hove A.	42	9	8	4	32	24	7	4	10	25	45	44
9	Bristol Rovers	42	12	5	4	34	18	7	0	14	17	33	43
10	Reading	42	15	2	4	48	21	2	6	13	22	43	42
11	Norwich City	42	11	5	5	44	21	5	5	11	21	42	42
12	Bournemouth	42	11	6	4	38	19	5	4	12	19	37	42
13	Port Vale	42	12	6	3	33	13	3	5	13	14	29	41
14	Swindon Town	42	9	7	5	41	30	6	4	11	18	32	41
15	Bristol City	42	12	4	5	38	19	3	6	12	22	42	40
16	Exeter City	42	9	8	4	37	27	5	3	13	26	48	39
17	Ipswich Town	42	9	6	6	36	36	3	5	13	21	50	35
18	Leyton Orient	42	10	6	5	33	30	2	5	14	20	55	35
19	Walsall	42	8	8	5	37	25	1	8	12	24	37	34
20	Aldershot	42	10	5	6	30	16	3	3	15	18	44	34
21	Newport County	42	11	5	5	50	34	2	3	16	17	64	34
22	Millwall	42	11	1	9	39	29	3	3	15	16	34	32

1950/51   17th in Division Two

#		Date	Opponent	Score	Scorers	Att	Smith RL	Deans T	Rigby NE	Chapman H	Baxter WE	Adamson H	Broome FH	Sewell J	Simpson A	Evans W	Johnston TD	Paxton JW	Evans FJ	Crookes RE	Lawton T	Southwell AA	Robinson P	Bradley G	Corkhill WG	Leuty LH	McPherson K	Purvis B	Roby D	Mann R	Brunt GR
1	Aug	19	COVENTRY CITY	0-2		41023	1	2	3	4	5	6	7	8	9	10	11														
2		24	Queens Park Rangers	0-1		15962	1	2		4		6	7	8	5	10	11	3	9												
3		26	Cardiff City	0-2		36646	1	2		4		6	9		5	10	11	3	7	8											
4		31	QUEENS PARK RANGERS	3-3	W Evans, Crookes, Broome	33404	1	2	3	4		6	7		5	10	11			8	9										
5	Sep	2	BIRMINGHAM CITY	0-1		34648	1	3				6	7		5	10	11			8	9	2	4								
6		4	Leicester City	1-1	Johnston	37169	1	3				6	7	8	5	10	11			9		2	4								
7		9	Grimsby Town	4-1	Broome, Johnston, Sewell 2	21432		2				6	7	8			11				10	9	3	4	1	5					
8		16	DONCASTER ROV.	1-2	Broome	39381		2				6	7	8	5	10	11					9	3	4	1						
9		23	PRESTON NORTH END	1-3	Simpson	44195		2				6	7	8	10		11					9	3	4	1	5					
10		30	Bury	0-0		21328		2	3				7		6		11				10	9	4	1		5	8				
11	Oct	7	Sheffield United	2-1	Sewell 2	37569							7	8	6		11				10	9	4	1	2	5		3			
12		14	LUTON TOWN	2-2	Johnston, Sewell	34054							7	8	6		11				10	9	3	4	1	2	5				
13		21	Southampton	0-1		25905		2						8	6	7	10			11	9		3	4	1	5					
14		28	BARNSLEY	2-1	Johnston, Lawton	39335		2						8	6	7	10			11	9		4	3	1	5					
15	Nov	4	Brentford	3-1	Johnston, Broome 2	26999		2					7	8	6		10			11	9		4	3	1	5					
16		11	BLACKBURN ROVERS	1-1	Broome(p)	35487		2					7	8	6	10	11				9		4	3	1	5					
17		18	Leeds United	1-0	Sewell	29728		2					9	8	6	7	10			11			4	3	1	5					
18		25	WEST HAM UNITED	4-1	Lawton 2, Sewell, W Evans	27075		2					10	8	6	7	11				9		4	3	1	5					
19	Dec	2	Swansea Town	1-2	Broome	22457		2					10	8	6	7	11				9		4	3	1	5					
20		9	HULL CITY	2-2	Leuty, Lawton	32708		2				6	10	8		7	11				9		4	3	1	5					
21		16	Coventry City	2-1	Lawton 2	25114		2						8	6	7	10			11	9		4	3	1	5					
22		23	CARDIFF CITY	1-2	Johnston	27434		2						8	6	7	10			11	9		4	3	1	5					
23		25	Chesterfield	0-0		19148		2						8	6	7	10			11	9		4	3	1	5					
24		26	CHESTERFIELD	1-0	Leuty (p)	35035		2						8	6	7	10			11	9		4	3	1	5					
25		30	Birmingham City	4-1	Sewell 2, Crookes 2	33770		2					7	8	6		10			11	9		4	3	1	5					
26	Jan	13	GRIMSBY TOWN	3-2	Johnston, Broome, Sewell	24849		2					9	8	6	7	10			11			4	3	1	5					
27		20	Doncaster Rov.	2-3	Sewell, Johnston	26045	1	2			5		9	8	6	7	10			11			4	3							
28	Feb	3	Preston North End	1-3	Johnston	35597	1	2					7	8	6		10			11	9		4	3		5					
29		17	BURY	4-2	Lawton 2, W Evans, Johnston	21205	1						7	8	6	10	11				9	2	4	3		5					
30		24	SHEFFIELD UNITED	3-0	Sewell 2, Johnston	31290	1							8	6	10	11				9	2	4	3		5			7		
31	Mar	3	Luton Town	1-1	Crookes	17398	1							8	6	10	11			7		2	4	3		5	9				
32		10	SOUTHAMPTON	2-2	Sewell, Leuty	25712	1	3						8	6	10	11			7		2	4			5	9				
33		17	Barnsley	0-2		12932	1	3				6		8		10	11			7		2	4			5	9				
34		24	BRENTFORD	2-3	Broome, Johnston	24936	1	3					8		6	10	11			7	9	2	4			5					
35		26	Manchester City	0-0		31948	1	3						8	6	10	11			7	9	2	4			5					
36		31	Blackburn Rovers	0-0		17626	1	3						8	6	10	11			7	9	2	4			5					
37	Apr	7	LEEDS UNITED	0-0		23466	1	3						8	6	10	11			7	9	2	4			5					
38		14	West Ham United	2-4	Johnston 2	23226	1	3						8		10	11			7	9	2	4			5				6	
39		21	SWANSEA TOWN	3-2	Broome, Crookes, Adamson	17787	1	3				8	9		6	10				11		2	4			5					7
40		28	Hull City	0-1		24190	1	2	3			8	9		6	10				11			4			5					7
41		30	MANCHESTER CITY	0-0		13873		3				8			6	10				11		2	4		1	5	9				7
42	May	5	LEICESTER CITY	2-3	Crookes, Lawton	24092		3						8	6	10	11				9	2	4		1	5					7
Apps							20	37	4	4	2	14	33	26	39	35	37	2	2	31	30	20	38	22	21	33	5	1	1	1	4
Goals												1	10	14	1	3	14			6	9					3					

F.A. Cup

		Date	Opponent	Score	Scorers	Att	Smith RL	Deans T	Rigby NE	Chapman H	Baxter WE	Adamson H	Broome FH	Sewell J	Simpson A	Evans W	Johnston TD	Paxton JW	Evans FJ	Crookes RE	Lawton T	Southwell AA	Robinson P	Bradley G	Corkhill WG	Leuty LH	McPherson K	Purvis B	Roby D	Mann R	Brunt GR
R3	Jan	6	SOUTHAMPTON	3-4	Broome, Leuty(p), Simpson	29260		2					7	8	6		10			11	9		4	3	1	5					

		P	W	D	L	F	A	W	D	L	F	A	Pts
1	Preston North End	42	16	3	2	53	18	10	2	9	38	31	57
2	Manchester City	42	12	6	3	53	25	7	8	6	36	36	52
3	Cardiff City	42	13	7	1	36	20	4	9	8	17	25	50
4	Birmingham City	42	12	6	3	37	20	8	3	10	27	33	49
5	Leeds United	42	14	4	3	36	17	6	4	11	27	38	48
6	Blackburn Rovers	42	13	3	5	39	27	6	5	10	26	39	46
7	Coventry City	42	15	3	3	51	25	4	4	13	24	34	45
8	Sheffield United	42	11	4	6	44	27	5	8	8	28	35	44
9	Brentford	42	13	3	5	44	25	5	5	11	31	49	44
10	Hull City	42	12	5	4	47	28	4	6	11	27	42	43
11	Doncaster Rovers	42	9	6	6	37	32	6	7	8	27	36	43
12	Southampton	42	10	9	2	38	27	5	4	12	28	46	43
13	West Ham United	42	10	5	6	44	33	6	5	10	24	36	42
14	Leicester City	42	10	4	7	42	28	5	7	9	26	30	41
15	Barnsley	42	9	5	7	42	22	6	5	10	32	46	40
16	Queen's Park Rgs.	42	13	5	3	47	25	2	5	14	24	57	40
17	NOTTS COUNTY	42	7	7	7	37	34	6	6	9	24	26	39
18	Swansea Town	42	14	1	6	34	25	2	3	16	20	52	36
19	Luton Town	42	7	9	5	34	23	2	5	14	23	47	32
20	Bury	42	9	4	8	33	27	3	4	14	27	59	32
21	Chesterfield	42	7	7	7	30	28	2	5	14	14	41	30
22	Grimsby Town	42	6	8	7	37	38	2	4	15	24	57	28

- 1950/51 Season -

Back: Simpson, Houghton (Man.), Southwell, Smith, Fisher (Sec.), Chapman, Adamson, Moore (Trainer), Rigby
Middle: F.J.Evans, Broome, Sewell, Barnes (Chairman), Lawton, W.Evans, Johnston
Front: Baxter, Deans

- 1951/52 Season -

Back: Corkhill, Adamson, R.Smith, Bradley, K.McPherson, Baxter
Middle: Southwell, Robinson, Leuty, Simpson, Deans
Front: Houghton(Manager), I.McPherson, Broome, Lawton, W.Evans, Johnston, Moore(Trainer)

1951/52 15th in Division Two

League — Division Two

No	Date	Opponent	Score	Scorers	Att.
1	Aug 18	COVENTRY CITY	2-1	Crookes 2	34001
2	25	Swansea Town	1-1	Lawton	17905
3	30	BARNSLEY	4-0	Lawton(p), Broome 2, Johnston	15507
4	Sep 1	BURY	2-1	Lawton 2	30915
5	6	HULL CITY	4-0	Lawton, Broome, Johnston, McPherson	38203
6	8	Luton Town	0-6		24511
7	12	Barnsley	1-2	Crookes	16148
8	15	NOTTM. FOREST	2-2	Broome, Crookes	44087
9	20	Hull City	3-1	Lawton 2, Johnston	35499
10	22	QUEENS PARK RANGERS	0-0		23185
11	29	Blackburn Rovers	0-2		25560
12	Oct 6	Brentford	0-1		28214
13	13	DONCASTER ROV.	1-0	Crookes	23087
14	20	Everton	5-1	Jackson 4, Crookes	49604
15	27	SOUTHAMPTON	3-4	Jackson, Broome(p), Crookes	31540
16	Nov 3	Sheffield Wednesday	0-6		46570
17	10	LEEDS UNITED	1-2	Jackson	25307
18	17	Rotherham Utd.	0-2		20961
19	24	CARDIFF CITY	1-1	Jackson	19452
20	Dec 1	Birmingham City	0-2		26554
21	8	LEICESTER CITY	2-3	Crookes 2	27065
22	15	Coventry City	2-0	Broome, McCormack	20274
23	22	SWANSEA TOWN	2-0	Broome, McCormack	22175
24	25	SHEFFIELD UNITED	3-1	McCormack, Adamson, McPherson	30019
25	26	Sheffield United	0-1		39383
26	29	Bury	1-2	Broome	14942
27	Jan 5	LUTON TOWN	5-4	* See below	22808
28	19	Nottm. Forest	2-3	McCormack, Broome	40005
29	26	Queens Park Rangers	4-1	Lawton 2, McCormack, Crookes	18891
30	Feb 9	BLACKBURN ROVERS	0-1		26177
31	16	Brentford	5-2	* See below	22503
32	Mar 1	Doncaster Rov.	5-1	Lawton 2, Crookes 2, McPherson	22467
33	8	EVERTON	0-0		29380
34	15	Southampton	0-4		20604
35	22	SHEFFIELD WEDNESDAY	2-2	Crookes, Broome	32230
36	29	Leeds United	0-1		12867
37	Apr 5	ROTHERHAM UTD.	0-3		13161
38	11	West Ham United	1-2	Crookes	22859
39	12	Cardiff City	0-1		24178
40	14	WEST HAM UNITED	1-0	Robinson	16306
41	19	BIRMINGHAM CITY	5-0	Wylie 4, Adamson	24360
42	26	Leicester City	1-1	McPherson	21318

*Scorers in game 27: McCormack, McPherson, Crookes, Broome, Owen (og). In game 31: Broome 2 (1p), Lawton, Johnston, McPherson.

Player appearances (shirt numbers)

No	Smith RL	Southwell AA	Deans T	Robinson P	Leuty LH	Simpson A	McPherson I	Broome FH	Lawton T	Crookes RE	Johnston TD	Adamson H	Corkhill WG	Evans W	Brown RM	Baxter WE	Brunt GR	Mitchell A	Jackson J	Wylie RM	Bradley G	McCormack JC	Allen HA	McPherson K
1	1	2	3	4	5	6	7	8	9	10	11													
2	1	2	3	4	5	6	7	8	9	10	11													
3	1	2	3	4	5	6	7	8	9	10	11													
4	1	2	3	4	5	6	7	8	9	10	11													
5	1	2	3	4	5	6	7	8	9	10	11													
6	1	2	3	4	5		7	8	9	10	11	6												
7	1		3	4	5	6	7		9	8			2	10	11									
8	1	2	3	4			6		7	9	11	8		10			5							
9	1	2	3	4					7	9		10				11	5	8						
10	1	2	3	4				8	9			10				11	5	6	7					
11	1	2	3	4	5		10	8	9					7		11	6							
12	1	2	3	6	5		7		9		10	8				11	4							
13	1	2	3	6	5		7		9	11							4		8	10				
14	1	2	3	6	5		7		9	11							4		8	10				
15	1	2	3	6	5		7	9		11							4		8	10				
16		2	3	6	5		7		9	11							4		8	10	1			
17		2	3	6	5		7		9	11					10		4		8		1			
18		2	3	6	5		7		9	11					10		4		8		1			
19		2	3	4	5	6				11					10	7			8		1		9	
20	1	2	3		5	6		7	9	11	10						4		8					
21	1	2	3	4	5	6	7	8	9	10	11													
22			3	4	5	6	7	8	9	11											1	10	2	
23	1	2	3	4	5		7	10	9	11		6										8		
24	1	2	3	4	5		7	10	9	11		6										8		
25				4	3		7		9	10	11	6			5						1	8	2	
26	1	2		4	3		7	10	8	11		6			5							9		
27	1	2	3	4	5		7	10	8	11		6										9		
28		2	3	4	5		7	10	8	11		6									1	9		
29		2	3		5		7		9	11		6					4		10		1	8		
30			3		5		7		9	11		6					4		10		1	8	2	
31		2	3	4	5		7	8	9	10	11	6									1			
32		2	3	4	5		7	8	9	10	11	6									1			
33			3	4	5		7	8	9	10	11	6									1		2	
34		2	3	4	5		7	8		10	11	6									1	9		
35		2	3	4	5		8	7		10	11				6						1	9		
36			3	4	5		8	7		10	11				6						1		2	9
37			3	4	5		8	7		10	11				6						1		2	9
38			3	4	5	6	7			11				10					8		1	9	2	
39			3	4		6			7	11				10	5						1	9	2	
40			3	4	6	5			7	11				10							1	9	2	
41			3	4	5	6	7			11		8								10	1	9	2	
42			3	4	5	6	7					8					11			10	1	9	2	
Apps	23	32	40	38	38	17	34	32	29	38	20	17	1	7	7	10	11	1	11	7	19	17	11	2
Goals				1			6	13	12	15	4	2							7	4		6		

One own goal

F.A. Cup

Rd	Date	Opponent	Score	Scorers	Att.	Southwell AA	Deans T	Robinson P	Leuty LH	McPherson I	Broome FH	Lawton T	Crookes RE	Adamson H	Brown RM	Brunt GR	Jackson J	Bradley G	McCormack JC	Allen HA
R3	Jan 12	STOCKTON	4-0	Broome 2, Lawton, McCormack	22805	2	3	4	3	7	10	8	11	6	5			1	9	
R4	Feb 2	PORTSMOUTH	1-3	Lawton	46500	2	3		5	7		9	11	6		4	10	1	8	

Division Two — Final Table

	P	W	D	L	F	A	W	D	L	F	A	Pts
1 Sheffield Wed.	42	14	4	3	54	23	7	7	7	46	43	53
2 Cardiff City	42	18	2	1	52	15	2	9	10	20	39	51
3 Birmingham City	42	11	6	4	36	21	10	3	8	31	35	51
4 Nottingham Forest	42	12	6	3	41	22	6	7	8	36	40	49
5 Leicester City	42	12	6	3	48	24	7	3	11	30	40	47
6 Leeds United	42	13	7	1	35	15	5	4	12	24	42	47
7 Everton	42	12	5	4	42	25	5	5	11	22	33	44
8 Luton Town	42	9	7	5	46	35	7	5	9	31	43	44
9 Rotherham United	42	11	4	6	40	25	6	4	11	33	46	42
10 Brentford	42	11	7	3	34	20	4	5	12	20	35	42
11 Sheffield United	42	13	2	6	57	28	5	3	13	33	48	41
12 West Ham United	42	13	5	3	48	29	2	6	13	19	48	41
13 Southampton	42	11	6	4	40	25	4	5	12	21	48	41
14 Blackburn Rovers	42	11	3	7	35	30	6	3	12	19	33	40
15 NOTTS COUNTY	42	11	5	5	45	27	5	2	14	26	41	39
16 Doncaster Rovers	42	9	4	8	29	28	4	8	9	26	32	38
17 Bury	42	13	2	6	43	22	2	5	14	24	47	37
18 Hull City	42	11	5	5	44	23	2	6	13	16	47	37
19 Swansea Town	42	10	4	7	45	26	2	8	11	27	50	36
20 Barnsley	42	8	7	6	39	33	3	7	11	20	39	36
21 Coventry City	42	9	5	7	36	33	5	1	15	23	49	34
22 Queen's Park Rgs.	42	8	8	5	35	35	3	4	14	17	46	34

1952/53   19th in Division Two

#	Date	Opponents	Score	Scorers	Att.	Bradley G	Allen HA	Deans T	Robinson P	Leuty LH	Simpson A	McPherson I	Adamson H	McCormack JC	Wylie RM	Crookes RE	Johnston TD	Jackson J	Southwell AA	Baxter WE	Jarvis H	Broome FH	Smith RL	Groome PB	Wade A	Linton JA	McPherson K	Brunt GR	Edwards J	Evans W	Lovell FW
1	Aug 23	Leicester City	0-3		29584	1	2	3	4	5	6	7	8	9	10	11															
2	28	ROTHERHAM UTD.	2-1	Jackson, McCormack	23216	1	3	2		5		7	4	9	10	11	6	8													
3	30	NOTTM. FOREST	3-2	McCormack 2, Crookes	39920	1		2		5		7	4	9	10	11	6	8	3												
4	Sep 1	Rotherham Utd.	3-2	Broome, Crookes, McCormack	17043	1	3	2					4	9	10	11		8		5	6	7									
5	6	SOUTHAMPTON	1-2	Wylie	23160		3	2		5		7	4	9	10	11	6	8					1								
6	11	FULHAM	1-1	Jackson	19109	1		2		5			4	9	10	11	6	8				7		3							
7	13	Bury	1-0	Wylie	12445	1		2		5		7	4	9	10	11	6	8							3						
8	15	Fulham	0-6		14072	1		2		5		7	4	9	10	11	6	8	3												
9	20	BIRMINGHAM CITY	2-0	Crookes, Wylie	24538	1		2		5		7	4	9	10	11	6	8							3						
10	27	Luton Town	1-5	Johnston	13557	1		2		5		7	4	9	10	11	6	8							3						
11	Oct 4	LEEDS UNITED	3-2	McCormack 3	22836	1		2		5			4	9	10	11	6	8	3			7									
12	11	Everton	0-1		40626	1		2		5	8	7	4	9	10	11	6		3												
13	18	BRENTFORD	4-0	Jackson 2, I McPherson, Harper(og)	26033			2		5		7	4	9	10	11	6	8	3				1								
14	Nov 1	SWANSEA TOWN	3-4	McCormack, Johnston 2	21171			2		5		7	4	9	10	11	6	8	3				1								
15	8	Huddersfield T	0-1		28205			2		5		7	4	9	10	11	6	8	3						1						
16	15	SHEFFIELD UNITED	0-3		23889			2		5		7	4		10	11	6	8	3						1	9					
17	22	Barnsley	2-1	McCormack, Johnston	11626			2		5			4	9	8	11	10		3		6				1		7				
18	29	LINCOLN CITY	1-1	McCormack	18802	1		2		5			4	9	8	11	10		3		6						7				
19	Dec 6	Hull City	0-6		18333	1		2		5		11	4	9	7		8		3		6				1			10		
20	13	BLACKBURN ROVERS	5-0	K McPherson 4, Edwards	10222	1		2					4			11			3	5		7					9		10	8	
21	20	LEICESTER CITY	2-2	Evans, K McPherson	16168	1		2					4			11	6		3	5		7					9		10	8	
22	25	West Ham United	2-2	Broome(p), K McPherson	23614	1		3		2			4			11	6			5		7					9		10	8	
23	27	WEST HAM UNITED	1-1	Jackson	24189	1		3		2			4			11	6			5		7					9		10	8	
24	Jan 1	Blackburn Rovers	2-3	Broome(p), K McPherson	16147	1		3		2			4			11	6			5		7					9		10	8	
25	3	Nottm. Forest	0-1		37835	1		3	6	5		7	4			11				2							9		10	8	
26	17	Southampton	1-1	Evans	16262	1		3		5			4			11	6			2		7				1	9		10	8	
27	24	BURY	2-1	Johnston 2	18750	1		3		5			4		10		6			2		7				1	9		11	8	
28	Feb 7	Birmingham City	2-3	Evans, Jackson	24522		2	3	4			7				11	6	9		5						1			10	8	
29	19	LUTON TOWN	1-2	Broome(p)	8648	1		3		5			4		10		6			2		7					9		11	8	
30	21	Leeds United	1-3	Edwards	22922	1		3		5			4	7		11	6	8		2						1	9		10		
31	Mar 5	EVERTON	2-2	K McPherson, Edwards	7529	1		3	6	5			4		10			8		2		7					9		11		
32	7	Brentford	0-5		16147			3		5			4			11				2	6	7				1	9		10	8	
33	14	DONCASTER ROV.	4-3	K McPherson 2, Crookes 2	17115			3		5			4	7	8	11	6			2						1	9		10		
34	21	Swansea Town	1-5	McCormack	20304			3		5			4	7	8	11	6			2						1	9		10		
35	28	HUDDERSFIELD T	1-0	Wylie	15816	1		3		5			4	7	8	11	6			2							9		10		
36	Apr 3	PLYMOUTH ARGYLE	0-4		18322	1		3		5			4		8	11	6	9		2		7							10		
37	4	Sheffield United	1-2	Crookes	33603	1		3		5				7	8	11	6			2							9	4	10		
38	6	Plymouth Argyle	2-2	Adamson, Broome	18330	1		3		5			8	7		11	6			2		9						4		10	
39	11	BARNSLEY	1-0	Adamson	13855	1		3		5			8	7		11	6			2		9						4		10	
40	18	Lincoln City	0-3		14747	1		3		5				7		11	6	8		2								4		10	
41	22	Doncaster Rov.	0-2		10063	1	2	3		5		7			10		8	6	9									4	11		
42	25	HULL CITY	2-0	McCormack 2	11699	1		3		5				9	7	11	6	10	2									4			8
				Apps		28	6	42	4	38	2	16	37	25	32	38	37	21	28	8	5	16	3	1	3	11	19	7	21	13	1
				Goals								1	2	13	4	6	6	5				5					10		3	4	

One own goal

F.A. Cup

Rd	Date	Opponents	Score	Scorers	Att.	Bradley G	Allen HA	Deans T	Robinson P	Leuty LH	Simpson A	McPherson I	Adamson H	McCormack JC	Wylie RM	Crookes RE	Johnston TD	Jackson J	Southwell AA	Baxter WE	Jarvis H	Broome FH	Smith RL	Groome PB	Wade A	Linton JA	McPherson K	Brunt GR	Edwards J	Evans W	Lovell FW
R3	Jan 10	Leicester City	4-2	McPherson 2, Crookes, Broome(p)	30889			3		5			4		10	11	6			2		7				1	9			8	
R4	Jan 31	Bolton Wanderers	1-1	McPherson	40048			3		5			4		10	11	6			2		7				1	9			8	
rep	Feb 5	BOLTON WANDERERS	2-2	Jackson, McPherson	33669			3		5			4			11	6	10		2		7				1	9			8	
r2	Feb 9	Bolton Wanderers	0-1		23171			3		5			4		10	11	6			2		7				1	9			8	

R4 replay after extra time. Replay 2 at Hillsborough

		P	W	D	L	F	A	W	D	L	F	A	Pts
1	Sheffield United	42	15	3	3	60	27	10	7	4	37	28	60
2	Huddersfield Town	42	14	4	3	51	14	10	6	5	33	19	58
3	Luton Town	42	15	1	5	53	17	7	7	7	31	32	52
4	Plymouth Argyle	42	12	5	4	37	24	8	4	9	28	36	49
5	Leicester City	42	13	6	2	55	29	5	6	10	34	45	48
6	Birmingham City	42	11	3	7	44	38	8	7	6	27	28	48
7	Nottingham Forest	42	11	5	5	46	32	7	3	11	31	35	44
8	Fulham	42	14	1	6	52	28	3	9	9	29	43	44
9	Blackburn Rovers	42	12	4	5	40	20	6	4	11	28	45	44
10	Leeds United	42	13	4	4	42	24	1	11	9	29	39	43
11	Swansea Town	42	10	9	2	45	26	5	3	13	33	55	42
12	Rotherham United	42	9	7	5	41	30	7	2	12	34	44	41
13	Doncaster Rovers	42	9	9	3	26	17	3	7	11	32	47	40
14	West Ham United	42	9	5	7	38	28	4	8	9	20	32	39
15	Lincoln City	42	9	9	3	41	26	2	8	11	23	45	39
16	Everton	42	8	4	8	38	23	3	6	12	33	52	38
17	Brentford	42	8	8	5	38	29	5	3	13	21	47	37
18	Hull City	42	11	6	4	36	19	3	2	16	21	50	37
19	NOTTS COUNTY	42	11	5	5	41	31	3	3	15	19	57	36
20	Bury	42	10	6	5	33	30	3	3	15	20	51	35
21	Southampton	42	5	7	9	45	44	5	6	10	23	41	33
22	Barnsley	42	4	4	13	31	46	1	4	16	16	62	18

- 1952/53 Season -

Back: Allen, Simpson, Southwell, K.McPherson, Broome, Jackson, King
Standing: I.McPherson, Brunt, Johnston, Bradley, Wade, R.Smith, Cruickshank, Mann, Jarvis, McCormack, V.Smith
Sitting: Houghton (Man), Morley (Dir), Deans, Robinson, Evans, Leuty, Barnes (Pres), Baxter, Crookes, Wylie, Adamson
Front: Watts, Carver, Broadbent, Guyler, Groome

- 1953/54 Season -

Back: Wade, McCormack, T.Sewell, Smith, Linton, Bradley, Leuty, Adamson, Johnson
Standing: Potts (Asstt.Train.), Fisher (Sec.), Southwell, Brunt, Cruickshank, McGrath, Jarvis, Mann, Broadbent, Parry, Guyler,
Houghton (Man.), Moore (Train.).   Sitting: Watts, Laird, Carver, Morley (Dir.), Barnes(Pres), Wylie, Deans, Crookes
Front: Kirkham, Lovell, Hallam, Bulch, Rawson, Baxter

1953/54   14th in Division Two

#	Date	Opponent	Score	Scorers	Att	Bradley G	Southwell AA	Deans T	Adamson H	Leuty LH	Johnston TD	Laird A	Wylie RM	McCormack JC	Edwards J	Crookes RE	Brunt GR	Lovell FW	Broadbent AH	Allen HA	Jarvis H	Carver GF	Baxter WE	Wade A	Wills GF	Coole W	Leverton R	Chatham RH	Taylor JE	Cruickshank FJ
1	Aug 19	Leeds United	0-6		18432	1	2	3	4	5	6	7	8	9	10	11														
2	22	Bury	3-3	Johnston, McCormack, Lovell	12168	1	2	3	4	5	6		10	9		11	7	8												
3	27	OLDHAM ATHLETIC	2-0	McCormack 2	15091	1	2	3	4	5	6		10	9		11	7	8												
4	29	DONCASTER ROV.	1-5	Brunt	10117	1	2	3	4	5	6			9	10	11	7		8											
5	Sep 1	Oldham Athletic	3-1	Johnston 2, Carver	22083	1	2	3		5	10			9		11	7			4	6	8								
6	5	Blackburn Rovers	0-2		23244	1	2	3		5	10			9		11	7			4	6	8								
7	10	EVERTON	0-2		12515	1	2	3		5	10		7	9		11				4	6	8								
8	12	DERBY COUNTY	0-1		23899	1	2	3			7			9		11			10	4	6	8	5							
9	19	Brentford	0-0		12770	1	2	3			10		7	9		11				4	6	8	5							
10	23	Everton	2-3	Johnston, Wills	32005	1	2	3		9	10		7					8		4	6				5	11				
11	26	BRISTOL ROVERS	1-5	Lovell	16318	1		3		5	10		7	9		11		8		4	6			2						
12	Oct 3	Lincoln City	0-3		16448	1	2	3		5			8			11		10		4	6					7	9			
13	10	Nottm. Forest	0-5		30409	1	2	3		4			8		10	11					6		5			7	9			
14	17	LUTON TOWN	1-2	Leverton	12208	1	2	3		5	9		10			11				4	6					7	8			
15	24	Plymouth Argyle	3-3	Johnston, Wylie, Crookes	16656	1	2	3	4	5	9		10			11					6					7	8			
16	31	SWANSEA TOWN	3-0	Southwell, Johnston, Coole	12084	1	2	3	4	5	9		10			11					6					7	8			
17	Nov 7	Rotherham Utd.	1-0	Wylie	12189	1	2	3	4	5	9		10			11					6					7	8			
18	14	LEICESTER CITY	1-1	McCormack	27806	1	2	3	4	5	6		10	9		11										7	8			
19	21	Stoke City	1-0	Crookes	17887	1	2	3	4	5	9		10			11					6					7	8			
20	28	FULHAM	0-0		19336	1	2	3	4	5	9		10			11					6					7	8			
21	Dec 5	West Ham United	2-1	Johnston, Crookes	16236	1	2	3	4	5	9		10			11					6					7	8			
22	12	LEEDS UNITED	2-0	Johnston, Crookes	17552	1	2	3	4	5	9		10			11					6					7	8			
23	19	Bury	0-0		12494	1	2	3	4	5	9		10			11					6					7	8			
24	25	Birmingham City	0-3		30489	1	2	3	4	5	9		10			11					6					7	8			
25	26	BIRMINGHAM CITY	2-1	McCormack, Leverton	20986	1	2	3	6	5	11		8	9			4									7	10			
26	Jan 2	Doncaster Rov.	2-4	Johnston, McCormack	14233	1	2	3	6	5	11		8	9						4							7	10		
27	16	BLACKBURN ROVERS	0-5		15044	1	2	3	4	5	11		8	9							6						7	10		
28	23	Derby County	0-0		18302	1	2	3	4	5	9		8			11										7	10	6		
29	Feb 6	BRENTFORD	2-0	Crookes 2	10507	1	2	3	4	5	9		8			11										7	10	6		
30	13	Bristol Rovers	1-1	Chatham	20719	1	2	3	4	5	9		8			11										7	10	6		
31	20	LINCOLN CITY	1-1	Johnston	21009	1		3	4	5	9		8			11					2					7		6	8	
32	27	NOTTM. FOREST	1-1	Taylor	36929	1		3	4	5	9		8			11					2					7		6	8	
33	Mar 6	Luton Town	1-2	Taylor	14623	1	2	3	4	5	9		8			11										7		6	8	
34	13	PLYMOUTH ARGYLE	2-0	Johnston, Crookes	11157	1	2	3	4	5	9		8			11										7		6	8	
35	20	Swansea Town	2-2	Coole, Taylor	15794	1	2		4	5			10			11										7	9	6	8	3
36	27	STOKE CITY	2-1	Crookes, Taylor	11877	1	2		4	5			10			11					3					7	9	6	8	
37	Apr 3	Fulham	3-4	Johnston 2, Wylie	17796	1	2	3	4	5	9		10			11										7		6	8	
38	10	ROTHERHAM UTD.	1-2	Wylie	11894	1	2	3	4	5	9		10			11										7		6	8	
39	16	Hull City	2-0	Crookes, Taylor	24031	1	2	3	6	5	9		10			11								7				4	8	
40	17	Leicester City	2-2	Johnston 2	32142	1	2	3	6	5	9		10			11										7		4	8	
41	19	HULL CITY	1-1	Wylie	13022	1	2	3	6	5			10	9		11										7		4	8	
42	24	WEST HAM UNITED	3-1	McCormack 2, Johnston	9971	1	2	3	4	5	6		10	9		11										7			8	
		Apps				42	39	40	32	39	38	1	38	16	4	37	6	6	1	13	20	5	3	2	3	29	21	14	12	1
		Goals					1				16		5	8		9	1	2				1			1	2	2	1	5	

F.A. Cup

#	Date	Opponent	Score	Scorers	Att	Bradley G	Southwell AA	Deans T	Adamson H	Leuty LH	Johnston TD	Laird A	Wylie RM	McCormack JC	Edwards J	Crookes RE	Brunt GR	Lovell FW	Broadbent AH	Allen HA	Jarvis H	Carver GF	Baxter WE	Wade A	Wills GF	Coole W	Leverton R	Chatham RH	Taylor JE	Cruickshank FJ
R3	Jan 9	Everton	1-2	Wylie	49737	1	2	3	4	5	11		8	9							6					7	10			

		P	W	D	L	F	A	W	D	L	F	A	Pts
1	Leicester City	42	15	4	2	63	23	8	6	7	34	37	56
2	Everton	42	13	6	2	55	27	7	10	4	37	31	56
3	Blackburn Rovers	42	15	4	2	54	16	8	5	8	32	34	55
4	Nottingham Forest	42	15	5	1	61	27	5	7	9	25	32	52
5	Rotherham United	42	13	4	4	51	26	8	3	10	29	41	49
6	Luton Town	42	11	7	3	36	23	7	5	9	28	36	48
7	Birmingham City	42	12	6	3	49	18	6	5	10	29	40	47
8	Fulham	42	12	3	6	62	39	5	7	9	36	46	44
9	Bristol Rovers	42	10	7	4	32	19	4	9	8	32	39	44
10	Leeds United	42	12	5	4	56	30	3	8	10	33	51	43
11	Stoke City	42	8	8	5	43	28	4	9	8	28	32	41
12	Doncaster Rovers	42	9	5	7	32	28	7	4	10	27	35	41
13	West Ham United	42	11	6	4	44	20	4	3	14	23	49	39
14	NOTTS COUNTY	42	8	6	7	26	29	5	7	9	28	45	39
15	Hull City	42	14	1	6	47	22	2	5	14	17	44	38
16	Lincoln City	42	11	6	4	46	23	3	3	15	19	60	37
17	Bury	42	9	7	5	39	32	2	7	12	15	40	36
18	Derby County	42	9	5	7	38	35	3	6	12	26	47	35
19	Plymouth Argyle	42	6	12	3	38	31	3	4	14	27	51	34
20	Swansea Town	42	11	5	5	34	25	2	3	16	24	57	34
21	Brentford	42	9	5	7	25	26	1	6	14	15	52	31
22	Oldham Athletic	42	6	7	8	26	31	2	2	17	14	58	25

1954/55 7th in Division Two

Results

No	Date		Opponent	Score	Scorers	Att.
1	Aug	21	DERBY COUNTY	2-3	Coole, Wylie	29528
2		23	Port Vale	1-1	Taylor	26805
3		28	West Ham United	0-3		19638
4	Sep	2	PORT VALE	1-1	Chatham	17723
5		4	BLACKBURN ROVERS	3-1	Coole, Crookes, McCormack	14918
6		9	PLYMOUTH ARGYLE	2-0	Chatham, McCormack	14497
7		11	Fulham	1-3	Johnston	26619
8		15	Plymouth Argyle	3-1	Taylor, Wills, Broadbent	17173
9		18	SWANSEA TOWN	2-1	Taylor 2	17928
10		25	Nottm. Forest	1-0	McCormack	30198
11	Oct	2	Liverpool	1-3	Wills	37643
12		9	STOKE CITY	1-0	Leverton	22266
13		16	Middlesbrough	0-2		20585
14		23	LINCOLN CITY	2-1	Wylie, McCormack	19474
15		30	Hull City	2-5	Johnston, Broadbent	22995
16	Nov	6	LUTON TOWN	3-3	Johnston, Wylie, Broadbent	10395
17		13	Rotherham Utd.	0-2		11740
18		20	LEEDS UNITED	1-2	Broadbent	14519
19		27	Bury	2-1	Wylie, Broadbent	12495
20	Dec	4	BIRMINGHAM CITY	3-2	Johnston 2, Broadbent	13477
21		11	Ipswich Town	1-0	Wylie	12442
22		18	Derby County	1-1	Wylie	15842
23		25	BRISTOL ROVERS	2-0	Wylie, Broadbent	19647
24		27	Bristol Rovers	4-1	Broadbent, Leverton, Jackson 2	28885
25	Jan	1	WEST HAM UNITED	5-1	Jackson 4, Broadbent(p)	20290
26		15	Blackburn Rovers	5-4	Jackson 2, Wills 2, Wylie	18664
27	Feb	5	Swansea Town	0-3		21527
28		12	NOTTM. FOREST	4-1	Wills 2, Jackson, Broadbent	31018
29	Mar	3	LIVERPOOL	0-3		11026
30		5	MIDDLESBROUGH	1-3	Jackson	22354
31		16	Lincoln City	2-1	Wills, Leverton	8082
32		19	HULL CITY	3-1	Wylie, Jackson, Roby	15103
33		26	Luton Town	1-3	Wills	16917
34		28	Stoke City	0-3		8173
35	Apr	2	ROTHERHAM UTD.	3-2	Crookes, Wills, Broadbent	15812
36		8	Doncaster Rov.	2-4	Wylie, Graham(og)	12223
37		9	Leeds United	0-2		24564
38		11	DONCASTER ROV.	4-0	Jackson 3, Cruickshank	13144
39		16	BURY	2-1	Jackson, Redman(og)	12545
40		23	Birmingham City	1-1	Wills	28018
41		27	FULHAM	0-0		8236
42		30	IPSWICH TOWN	2-1	Jackson 2	10812

Appearances (shirt numbers)

No	Bradley G	Southwell AA	Deans T	Adamson H	Leuty LH	Chatham RH	Coole W	Taylor JE	Johnston TD	Wylie RM	Crookes RE	Carver GF	McCormack JC	Wills GF	Broadbent AH	Leverton R	Jarvis H	Wade A	Rawson K	Jackson J	Roby D	Cruickshank FJ	Lister E	Loxley H
1	1	2	3	4	5	6	7	8	9	10	11													
2	1	2	3	4	5	6	7	8	9	10	11													
3	1	2	3	4		5	7	9	6	10	11	8												
4	1	2	3	4	5	6	7	8		10	11		9											
5	1	2	3	4	5	6	7	8		10	11		9											
6	1	2	3	4	5	6	7	8		10	11		9											
7	1	2	3	4	5		7	8	6	10			9	11										
8	1	2	3	4	5			8	6	10			9	7	11									
9	1	2	3	4	5			8	6	10			9	7	11									
10	1	2	3	4	5			8		10			9	7	11									
11	1	2	3	4	5	6		8		10			9	7	11									
12	1	2	3	4	5	6		8		10				7	11	9								
13	1	2	3	4	5	6				10		8		7	11	9								
14	1	2	3	4	5	6			10	8			9	7	11									
15	1	2	3	4	5				10	8			9	7	11		6							
16	1	2	3	4					10	8			9	7	11		6	5						
17	1	2	3	4	5				10	8	11			7	9		6							
18	1	2	3	4	5				9	10		8		7	11		6							
19	1	2	3	4					6	8				9	7	11			5	10				
20	1	2	3	4					6	8				9	7	11			5	10				
21	1	2	3	4	5				6	8				9	7	11				10				
22	1	2	3	4	5				6	8				9	7	11				10				
23	1	2	3	4	5				6	8				7	11	10				9				
24	1	2	3	4	5				6	8				7	11	10				9				
25	1	2	3	4	5				6	8				7	11	10				9				
26	1	2	3	4	5				6	8				7	11	10				9				
27	1	2	3	4	5				6	8				7	11	10				9				
28	1	2	3	4	5				6	8				7	11	10				9				
29	1	2	3	4	5				6	8				7	11	10				9				
30	1	2	3	4	5				6	8				7	11	10				9				
31	1	2	3	4	5				6	8				11		10				9	7			
32	1	2	3	4	5				6	8				11		10				9	7			
33	1	2	3	4	5	6				8				11		10				9	7			
34	1	4	3		5	6				8					11	10				9	7	2		
35	1	2	3	4	5	6				8	11			7		10				9				
36	1	2	3	4	5	6				8	11			7		10				9				
37	1		3	4	5	6				8	11			7		10				9		2		
38	1		3	4	5	6			8	10				7	11					9		2		
39	1		3	4	5	6			8	10				7	11					9		2		
40	1		3	4	5	6			8	10				7	11					9		2		
41	1		3	4	5	6			8	10				7	11					9		2		
42	1	2	3	4	5				8	10				7	11					9				6
Apps	42	37	42	41	38	20	7	17	25	42	10	3	15	36	30	18	4	1	2	20	4	6	1	1
Goals						2	2	4	5	10	2		4	10	11	3				17	1	1		

Two own goals

F.A. Cup

Rd	Date		Opponent	Score	Scorers	Att.	Bradley G	Southwell AA	Deans T	Adamson H	Leuty LH	Johnston TD	Wylie RM	Wills GF	Broadbent AH	Leverton R	Jackson J
R3	Jan	8	Middlesbrough	4-1	Wylie 2, Broadbent, Wills	30503	1	2	3	4	5	6	8	7	11	10	9
R4	Jan	29	Sheffield Wednesday	1-1	Conwell (og)	53138	1	2	3	4	5	6	8	7	11	10	9
rep	Feb	3	SHEFFIELD WEDNESDAY	1-0	Jackson	36506	1	2	3	4	5	6	8	7	11	10	9
R5	Feb	19	CHELSEA	1-0	Broadbent	41457	1	2	3	4	5	6	8	7	11	10	9
R6	Mar	12	YORK CITY	0-1		47310	1	2	3	4	5	6	8	7	11	10	9

R4 replay after extra time

Final Table

		P	W	D	L	F	A	W	D	L	F	A	Pts
1	Birmingham City	42	14	4	3	56	22	8	6	7	36	25	54
2	Luton Town	42	18	2	1	55	18	5	6	10	33	35	54
3	Rotherham United	42	17	1	3	59	22	8	3	10	35	42	54
4	Leeds United	42	14	4	3	43	19	9	3	9	27	34	53
5	Stoke City	42	12	5	4	38	17	9	5	7	31	29	52
6	Blackburn Rovers	42	14	4	3	73	31	8	2	11	41	48	50
7	NOTTS COUNTY	42	14	3	4	46	27	7	3	11	28	44	48
8	West Ham United	42	12	4	5	46	28	6	6	9	28	42	46
9	Bristol Rovers	42	15	4	2	52	23	4	3	14	23	47	45
10	Swansea Town	42	15	3	3	58	28	2	6	13	28	55	43
11	Liverpool	42	11	7	3	55	37	5	3	13	37	59	42
12	Middlesbrough	42	13	1	7	48	31	5	5	11	25	51	42
13	Bury	42	10	5	6	44	35	5	6	10	33	37	41
14	Fulham	42	10	5	6	46	29	4	6	11	30	50	39
15	Nottingham Forest	42	8	4	9	29	29	8	3	10	29	33	39
16	Lincoln City	42	8	6	7	39	35	5	4	12	29	44	36
17	Port Vale	42	10	6	5	31	21	2	5	14	17	50	35
18	Doncaster Rovers	42	10	5	6	35	34	4	2	15	23	61	35
19	Hull City	42	7	5	9	30	35	5	5	11	14	34	34
20	Plymouth Argyle	42	10	4	7	29	26	2	3	16	28	56	31
21	Ipswich Town	42	10	3	8	37	28	1	3	17	20	64	28
22	Derby County	42	6	6	9	39	34	1	3	17	14	48	23

- 1954/55 Season -

Back: Adamson, Leuty, Johnston, Bradley, Southwell, Taylor, Cruickshank
Front: Wills, Wylie, Jackson, Deans, Leverton, Broadbent, McCormack

- 1955/56 Season -

Back: Sheridan, Cruickshank, Abthorpe, Leuty, Broome(Assistant Manager), Wade, Kirkham, Parry, Groome
Standing: Potts(Trainer), Southwell, Bulch, McGrath, Bradley, Adamson, Linton, Johnston, Lister, Poyser(Manager)
Sitting: Noon, Wills, Taylor, Jackson, Deans, Wylie, Crookes, Leverton
Front: Roby, Bircumshaw, Hill

1955/56   20th in Division Two

#	Date	Opponent	Score	Scorers	Att.	Bradley G	Southwell AA	Cruickshank FJ	Adamson H	Leuty LH	McGrath, John	Wills GF	Roby D	Jackson J	Wylie RM	Crookes RE	Chatham RH	Linton JA	Taylor JE	Abthorpe J	Coole W	Johnston TD	Lister E	Bulch RS	Leverton R	Deans T	Groome PB	Smith GH	Loxley H	McCormack JC	Russell PW
1	Aug 20	Middlesbrough	0-3		20291	1	2	3	4	5	6	7	8	9	10	11															
2	25	BARNSLEY	2-2	Jackson 2	15517	1	2	3	4	5	6	7	8	9	10	11															
3	27	BRISTOL CITY	3-2	Cruickshank(p), Wills, Roby	14596	1	2	3	4		6	7	8	9	10	11	5														
4	31	Barnsley	1-3	Wylie	16636	1	2	3	4		6	7	8	9	10	11	5														
5	Sep 3	West Ham United	1-6	Abthorpe	16710		2	3	4		6	7			10	11	5	1	8	9											
6	7	Fulham	1-1	Johnston	16455		2	3	4		6		8		10		5	1				7	9	11							
7	10	Port Vale	0-0		14733		2	3			6		8		10		5	1				7	9	11	4						
8	15	FULHAM	3-4	Johnston 2, McGrath	9563		2	3			6		8		10		5	1				7	9	11	4						
9	17	Rotherham Utd.	1-1	Johnston	10479		2	3			6		8		10		5	1				7	9	11	4						
10	24	SWANSEA TOWN	1-5	Cruickshank	16679		2	3			6	11	8		10		5	1		9		7			4						
11	Oct 1	Nottm. Forest	2-0	Crookes 2	26223		2		4			7	8		10	11	5	1				6				9	3				
12	8	SHEFFIELD WEDNESDAY	1-1	Roby	23356		2		4			7	8		10	11	5	1				6				9	3				
13	15	Doncaster Rov.	1-1	Abthorpe	10170		2		4			7	8		10	11	5	1		9		6					3				
14	22	BLACKBURN ROVERS	1-2	Wills	13926		2		4			7	8		10	11	5	1		9		6					3				
15	29	Stoke City	2-0	Crookes 2	15737		2		4			7	8		10	11	5	1		9		6					3				
16	Nov 5	PLYMOUTH ARGYLE	3-0	Wills, Crookes, Abthorpe	12466		2		4			7	8		10	11	5	1		9		6					3				
17	12	Liverpool	1-2	Jackson	32654		2		4			7		9	10	11	5	1				6					3				
18	19	LEICESTER CITY	1-1	McGrath	25622		2		4			7		9	10	11	5	1				6					3				
19	26	Lincoln City	0-2		12815		2		4			7	8	9	10	11	5	1				6					3				
20	Dec 3	BRISTOL ROVERS	5-2	Wylie 3, Roby, Taylor	15525		2		4			7	8	9	10		5	1	11			6					3				
21	10	Hull City	0-2		12842		2		4			7	8	9	10		5	1	11			6					3				
22	17	MIDDLESBROUGH	5-0	Roby 2, Jackson, Crookes, Taylor	9693		2		4			7	8	9	10	11	5	1				6					3				
23	24	Bristol City	3-1	Taylor 2, Roby	24075		2		4			7	8	9	10	11	5	1				6					3				
24	26	Leeds United	0-1		24869		2		4			7	8	9	10	11	5	1				6					3				
25	27	LEEDS UNITED	2-1	Cruickshank(p), Jackson	23910		2	3	4			7	8	9	10	11	5	1				6									
26	31	WEST HAM UNITED	0-1		18708		2	3	4			7	8	9	10	11	5	1				6									
27	Jan 14	Port Vale	1-3	Bulch	17370		2	3	4			7	8		10	11	5	1				6		9							
28	21	ROTHERHAM UTD.	1-2	Taylor(p)	12616		2	3	4			7	8		10	11	5	1				6			9						
29	Feb 4	Swansea Town	1-5	Coole	13114		2	3	4			11	8	9	10		5	1			7	6									
30	11	NOTTM. FOREST	1-3	Jackson	17509		2	3	4			11	8	9	10		5	1			7	6									
31	18	Leicester City	0-4		25977	1	2	3	4		6	11	8	9	10		5				7										
32	25	DONCASTER ROV.	3-2	Wills, Chatham, McCormack	13762	1	2		4			11	7	8	10		6										3			9	
33	Mar 3	Blackburn Rovers	0-2		18697	1	2		4			11	7	8	10		6										3			9	
34	10	HULL CITY	0-2		12707	1	2		4			10	7	8		11	6										3			9	
35	17	Plymouth Argyle	1-1	Wills	19946	1	2					7	8		10	11	6										3		4	9	5
36	24	LIVERPOOL	2-1	McCormack 2(1p)	13915	1	2					11	7	8	10		6										3		4	9	5
37	30	Bury	0-4		11708	1	2					11	7	8	10		6								9		3		4		5
38	31	Sheffield Wednesday	0-1		31330	1	2					11	7	8	9		6		10								3		4		5
39	Apr 2	BURY	2-1	Loxley, Wylie	13742	1	2					11	7	8	10		6										3		4	9	5
40	7	LINCOLN CITY	2-2	McCormack, Jackson	14234	1	2					11	7	8	10		6										3		4	9	5
41	14	Bristol Rovers	0-2		15455	1	2					11	7	8	10		6										3		4	9	5
42	21	STOKE CITY	1-3	Jackson	10918	1	2					11	7	8	10		4										3		6	9	5
				Apps		16	23	31	16	2	20	32	38	24	40	20	40	14	14	5	6	28	4	6	6	9	21	12	13	9	8
				Goals				3			2	5	6	8	5	6	1		5	3	1	4		1					1	4	

Played in games 17 and 18: GF Carver (8).
Played in games 32, 33 and 34: A Wade (5).

F.A. Cup

Round	Date	Opponent	Score	Att.	Southwell AA	Adamson H	Wills GF	Roby D	Jackson J	Wylie RM	Crookes RE	Chatham RH	Linton JA	Taylor JE	Johnston TD	Groome PB
R3	Jan 7	FULHAM	0-1	21500	2	4	7	9	8		11	5		10	6	3

		P	W	D	L	F	A	W	D	L	F	A	Pts
1	Sheffield Wed.	42	13	5	3	60	28	8	8	5	41	34	55
2	Leeds United	42	17	3	1	51	18	6	3	12	29	42	52
3	Liverpool	42	14	3	4	52	25	7	3	11	33	38	48
4	Blackburn Rovers	42	13	4	4	55	29	8	2	11	29	36	48
5	Leicester City	42	15	3	3	63	23	6	3	12	31	55	48
6	Bristol Rovers	42	13	3	5	53	33	8	3	10	31	37	48
7	Nottingham Forest	42	9	5	7	30	26	10	4	7	38	37	47
8	Lincoln City	42	14	5	2	49	17	4	5	12	30	48	46
9	Fulham	42	15	2	4	59	27	5	4	12	30	52	46
10	Swansea Town	42	14	4	3	49	23	6	2	13	34	58	46
11	Bristol City	42	14	4	3	49	20	5	3	13	31	44	45
12	Port Vale	42	12	4	5	38	21	4	9	8	22	37	45
13	Stoke City	42	13	2	6	47	27	7	2	12	24	35	44
14	Middlesbrough	42	11	4	6	46	31	5	4	12	30	47	40
15	Bury	42	9	5	7	44	39	7	3	11	42	51	40
16	West Ham United	42	12	4	5	52	27	2	7	12	22	42	39
17	Doncaster Rovers	42	11	5	5	45	30	1	6	14	24	66	35
18	Barnsley	42	10	5	6	33	35	1	7	13	14	49	34
19	Rotherham United	42	7	5	9	29	34	5	4	12	27	41	33
20	NOTTS COUNTY	42	8	5	8	39	37	3	4	14	16	45	31
21	Plymouth Argyle	42	7	6	8	33	25	3	2	16	21	62	28
22	Hull City	42	6	4	11	32	45	4	2	15	21	52	26

1956/57   20th in Division Two

Match results

No	Date		Opponent	Score	Scorers	Att
1	Aug	18	BURY	2-2	Taylor, Jackson	14857
2		23	LIVERPOOL	1-1	Wills	14691
3		25	Grimsby Town	1-2	Wills	18462
4		29	Liverpool	3-3	Wylie, Lane, Jackson	41095
5	Sep	1	DONCASTER ROV.	1-2	Lane	14412
6		8	Stoke City	0-6		18556
7		13	LEYTON ORIENT	1-3	Lane	10447
8		15	MIDDLESBROUGH	2-1	Russell, Jackson	10190
9		22	Leicester City	3-6	Bradley, Jackson, Wills	28806
10		29	BRISTOL ROVERS	0-2		12720
11	Oct	6	Bristol City	1-1	Lane	12005
12		13	Sheffield United	1-5	Wills	21737
13		20	NOTTM. FOREST	1-2	Lane	31585
14		27	Port Vale	2-1	Lane, Wills	13137
15	Nov	3	ROTHERHAM UTD.	1-5	Lane	12870
16		10	Lincoln City	0-1		11615
17		17	SWANSEA TOWN	1-4	Wills	10248
18		24	Fulham	1-5	McGrath	15360
19	Dec	1	BARNSLEY	3-2	Wills 3	11133
20		8	West Ham United	1-2	Wills	14875
21		15	Bury	1-2	Jackson	8364
22		22	GRIMSBY TOWN	0-1		4869
23		24	HUDDERSFIELD T	1-2	Wills	9165
24		26	Huddersfield T	0-3		7485
25		29	Doncaster Rov.	2-4	Loxley, Wills	11911
26	Jan	12	STOKE CITY	5-0	Jackson 2, Wylie 2, McGrath	13620
27		19	Middlesbrough	0-0		23085
28	Feb	2	LEICESTER CITY	0-0		42489
29		9	Bristol Rovers	0-3		17081
30		20	Bristol City	0-3		19288
31		23	SHEFFIELD UNITED	2-2	Russell 2	5712
32	Mar	9	PORT VALE	3-1	Jackson 2, Russell	17234
33		16	Rotherham Utd.	0-0		9482
34		23	LINCOLN CITY	3-0	Wylie, Wills, Tucker	17375
35		30	Swansea Town	1-2	Wills	13826
36	Apr	6	FULHAM	0-0		17121
37		13	Barnsley	1-1	Tucker	7652
38		19	Blackburn Rovers	1-1	Wills	24367
39		20	WEST HAM UNITED	4-1	Wills 2, Russell, Tucker	17803
40		23	BLACKBURN ROVERS	2-0	Taylor 2	27613
41		27	Leyton Orient	2-2	Wills 2	12424
42	May	1	Nottm. Forest	4-2	Taylor 2, Roby, Wylie	31896

Player appearances (shirt numbers)

No	Bradley G	Cruickshank FJ	Groome PB	Loxley H	Russell PW	Chatham RH	Wylie RM	Taylor JE	Lane JG	Jackson J	Wills GF	Roby D	Smith GH	Carver GF	Maddison F	Southwell AA	McGrath John	Lister E	Linton JA	Johnston TD	Kirkham R	Bulch RS	Bircumshaw PB	Tucker K
1	1	2	3	4	5	6	7	8	9	10	11													
2	1	2	3	4	5	6	7	8	9	10	11													
3	1	2	3	4	5	6	8		9	10	11	7												
4	1	2	3	4	5	6	8		9	10	11	7												
5		2	3	4	5	6	8		9	10	11	7	1											
6	1	2	3	4	5	6	8		9	10	11	7												
7	1	2	3		5	4	8		9	6	11	7		10										
8	1	2		4	5	6	8			9	11	7		10	3									
9	1	2	3	4	5	6	8			9	11	7		10										
10		2	3	4	5	6	8			9	11	7	1	10										
11				4	6	5	7		9		11	8	1	10		3	2							
12				4	6	5	7		9		11	8	1	10		3	2							
13				4	5	6	8		9		11	7	1	10		3	2							
14				4	5	6	8		9		11	7	1	10		3	2							
15				4	5	6	8		9		11	7	1	10		3	2							
16					6	5	8		9		11	7	1	10		3	2	4						
17					6	5	8		9		11	7		10		3	2	4	1					
18					5	6	8	10			11	7		9		3	2	4	1					
19		3			5		8			10	9	7		6		2		4	1	11				
20		3			5		8			10	9	7		6		2		4	1	11				
21		3		6	5		8			10	9	7				2		4	1	11				
22		3			5		8			10	9	7		6		2		4	1	11				
23		3	2	6	5		8			11	9	7		10				4	1					
24		3	2	6	5		8			11	9	7		10				4	1					
25		3		6	5	4	8			11	9	7		10					1	2				
26		3			5		7			10	9	11		8		6	2		1			4		
27		3			5		7			10	9			8		6	2		1			4	11	
28		3			5		7			10	9	11		8		6	2		1			4		
29		3			5		7			10	9	11		8		6	2		1			4		
30		3			5		7	8		10	9	11	1	6		2						4		
31		3			5		7			10	9			8		6	2		1			4	11	
32		3			5	2	7			10	9			6			8		1			4		11
33		3			5	2	7			10	9			6			8		1			4		11
34		3			5	2	7			10	9			6			8		1			4		11
35		3			5	2	7			10	9			6			8		1			4		11
36		3			5	2	7			10	9			6			8		1			4		11
37		3			5	2	7	8		10	9			6					1			4		11
38		3			5	2	7	8		10	9			6					1			4		11
39		3			5	2	7	8		10	9			6					1			4		11
40		3		6	5	2	7	8		10	9								1			4		11
41		3		6	5	2	7	8		10	9								1			4		11
42		3			5	2	7	8		10	9	6							1			4		11
Apps	8	34	11	22	42	28	39	10	21	25	41	33	9	33	8	18	17	3	25	4	1	17	2	11
Goals	1			1	5		5	5	7	9	19	1					2							3

F.A. Cup

Round	Date		Opponent	Score	Scorers	Att
R3	Jan	5	RHYL	1-3	Bircumshaw	16231

F.A. Cup appearances: Cruickshank 3, Loxley 6, Russell 5, Wylie 8, Wills 9, Roby 7, Carver 10, McGrath 2, Linton 1, Bulch 4, Bircumshaw 11.

League table — Division Two

		P	W	D	L	F	A	W	D	L	F	A	Pts
1	Leicester City	42	14	5	2	68	36	11	6	4	41	31	61
2	Nottingham Forest	42	13	4	4	50	29	9	6	6	44	26	54
3	Liverpool	42	16	1	4	53	26	5	10	6	29	28	53
4	Blackburn Rovers	42	12	6	3	49	32	9	4	8	34	43	52
5	Stoke City	42	16	2	3	64	18	4	6	11	19	40	48
6	Middlesbrough	42	12	5	4	51	29	7	5	9	33	31	48
7	Sheffield United	42	11	6	4	45	28	8	2	11	42	48	46
8	West Ham United	42	12	4	5	31	24	7	4	10	28	39	46
9	Bristol Rovers	42	12	5	4	47	19	6	4	11	34	48	45
10	Swansea Town	42	12	3	6	53	34	7	4	10	37	56	45
11	Fulham	42	13	1	7	53	32	6	3	12	31	44	42
12	Huddersfield Town	42	10	3	8	33	27	8	3	10	35	47	42
13	Bristol City	42	13	2	6	49	32	3	7	11	25	47	41
14	Doncaster Rovers	42	12	5	4	51	21	3	5	13	26	56	40
15	Leyton Orient	42	7	8	6	34	38	8	2	11	32	46	40
16	Grimsby Town	42	12	4	5	41	26	5	1	15	20	36	39
17	Rotherham United	42	9	7	5	37	26	4	4	13	37	49	37
18	Lincoln City	42	9	4	8	34	27	5	2	14	20	53	34
19	Barnsley	42	8	7	6	39	35	4	3	14	20	54	34
20	NOTTS COUNTY	42	7	6	8	34	32	2	6	13	24	54	30
21	Bury	42	5	3	13	37	47	3	6	12	23	49	25
22	Port Vale	42	7	4	10	31	42	1	2	18	26	59	22

- 1956/57 Season -

Back: McGrath, Wills, Bradley, Linton, Southwell, Bulch
Middle: Roby, Carver, Broome(Acting Manager), Cruickshank, Wylie
Front: Jackson, Loxley, Russell, Taylor

- 1957/58 Season -

Back: P.Russell, Carver, Noon, Parry, Lane, Hill, Bulch, McGrath
Standing: Dixon(Masseur), Dickinson(C/Scout), Groome, Wills, Loxley, Linton, Bradley, Cruickshank, Harvey, Kilford, Heath(Sec), Wheeler(Train).
Sitting: Broome(Ass Man), Jackson, Wylie, Sherwood(Dir), Machin(Chair), Edwards(Dir), Linnell(Dir), Sheridan, Roby, Lawton(Man).
Front: Asher, Gissing

1957/58 21st in Division Two (Relegated)

No		Date	Opponent	Score	Scorers	Att	Linton JA	Groome PB	Cruickshank FJ	Bulch RS	Russell PW	Loxley H	Roby D	Wills GF	Newsham S	Wylie RM	Tucker K	McGrath John	Jackson J	Carver GF	Lane JG	Asher T	Maddison F	Sheridan J	Robledo E	Bradley G	Gissing JW	Pritchard RT	Rawson K	Chatham RH	Noon H	Parry C
1	Aug	24	Sheffield United	0-1		20920	1	2	3	4	5	6	7	8	9	10	11															
2		29	FULHAM	1-5	Tucker	18238	1	2	3	4	5	6	7	8	9	10	11															
3		31	BLACKBURN ROVERS	1-1	Wills	17927	1	2	3	4	5			7	8	10	11	6	9													
4	Sep	4	Fulham	0-1		14607	1	2	3		5		7	11	8	10			4	9	6											
5		7	Ipswich Town	1-2	Jackson	17018	1	2	3	4	5		7	11	8			6	10	9												
6		12	SWANSEA TOWN	2-4	Wills 2	11397	1	2	3		5		7	8			11	6	4	9	10											
7		14	HUDDERSFIELD T	1-1	McGrath	15584	1		2		5		7	9			11	8		6		10	3	4								
8		19	Swansea Town	3-1	Asher, Carver, Tucker	19353	1		2		5		7	9			11	8		6		10	3	4								
9		21	LINCOLN CITY	1-0	Newsham	18059	1		2		5		7	9	8		11	6				10	3	4								
10		28	Bristol Rovers	2-5	Roby, Russell	20415	1	2	3		5		7	9	10		11	8		6					4							
11	Oct	5	DERBY COUNTY	1-0	Newsham	23966		2			5		7	9	10		11			6			3	4	8	1						
12		12	Grimsby Town	0-2		14328	1	2			5		7	9	10		11			6		8	3	4								
13		19	STOKE CITY	1-2	Newsham	13125	1	2			5		7	9	10		11	8		6			3	4								
14		26	Bristol City	1-3	Carver	18394	1	2			9	5		11	10					6	8		3	4				7				
15	Nov	2	CARDIFF CITY	5-2	Wills 2, Newsham 2, Lane	14911	1	2						11	8					6	9	10	4					7	3	5		
16		9	Liverpool	0-4		39735	1	2			5			11	8					6	9	10	4					7	3			
17		16	MIDDLESBROUGH	2-0	Lane, Asher	13292	1	2			5			11	8				4	6	9	10						7	3			
18		23	Leyton Orient	2-2	Wills, Asher	12361	1	2						11	8				4	6	9	10						7	3	5		
19		30	CHARLTON ATHLETIC	2-1	Lane, Asher	14961			3					11	8				4	6	9	10				1		7	5	2		
20	Dec	7	Doncaster Rov.	0-4		8674			3				7	9	8		11		4			10				1			5	2		6
21		14	ROTHERHAM UTD.	1-0	Newsham	10857			3			6		11	8				4	9	10					1			5	2		7
22		21	SHEFFIELD UNITED	1-0	Lane	12070			3			6		11	8				4	9	10					1			5	2		7
23		25	BARNSLEY	2-3	Loxley, Wills	11343			3			6		11	8				4	9	10					1			5	2		7
24		26	Barnsley	1-1	Sheridan	20307			3		5	6		11					4	9	10			8		1				2		7
25		28	Blackburn Rovers	0-3		24605			3		5	6	10	11					4	9				8		1				2		7
26	Jan	11	IPSWICH TOWN	0-3		13612			3		5	6	10	7			11	8	4	9						1				2		
27		18	Huddersfield T	0-3		9173			3			6		11	8				4	9	10					1			5	2		7
28	Feb	1	Lincoln City	2-2	Wills, Lane	8573	1				5	4	7	11	8			6		9	10								3	2		
29		15	Derby County	1-2	Lane	21304	1				5	4	7	11	8			6		9	10								3	2		
30		22	LEYTON ORIENT	0-1		11494	1				5		7	11	8			6		9	10		4						3	2		
31	Mar	1	Stoke City	1-0	Lane	16452	1				5	4	7	11	10			8	6	9									3	2		
32		8	BRISTOL CITY	0-1		9942	1					4	7	11	10			8	6	9								5	3	2		
33		15	Cardiff City	0-2		11116	1					4	7	11	10			8	6	9								5	3	2		
34		22	LIVERPOOL	0-2		13040	1				5	4	7	9	10	8	11	6											3	2		
35		29	Middlesbrough	1-3	Lane	14879	1					4	7	9	8		11	6			10							5	3	2		
36	Apr	4	West Ham United	1-3	Wills	29866	1		3			4	7	9	8		11	6			10								5	2		
37		5	GRIMSBY TOWN	2-0	Lane, Wylie	11555						4	7	9	8		11	6			10						1	3	5	2		
38		8	WEST HAM UNITED	1-0	Wills(p)	18317			3			4	7	9	8			6			10						1	11	5	2		
39		12	Charlton Athletic	1-4	Lane	21612			3			4	11	9	8			6			10						1	7	5	2		
40		19	DONCASTER ROV.	0-5		16102						4	7	9	8		11	6			10						1	3	5	2		
41		23	BRISTOL ROVERS	0-0		13467	1		3			4		9	10		11	6						8				7	5	2		
42		26	Rotherham Utd.	3-1	Newsham 2, Lane	7110	1		3			6		11	9				4		10			8				7	5	2		
Apps							27	7	28	4	24	24	25	42	31	13	17	17	11	28	26	20	7	17	2	15	10	18	19	23	1	6
Goals											1	1	1	10	8	1	2	1	1	2	11	4		1								

F.A. Cup

		Date	Opponent	Score	Scorers	Att	Linton JA	Groome PB	Cruickshank FJ	Bulch RS	Russell PW	Loxley H	Roby D	Wills GF	Newsham S	Wylie RM	Tucker K	McGrath John	Jackson J	Carver GF	Lane JG	Asher T	Maddison F	Sheridan J	Robledo E	Bradley G	Gissing JW	Pritchard RT	Rawson K	Chatham RH	Noon H	Parry C
R3	Jan	4	TRANMERE ROVERS	2-0	Tucker(p), Jackson	13394			3		5	6	10	7			11	4	8	9						1				2		
R4	Jan	25	BRISTOL CITY	1-2	Pritchard	18395					5	4	10	7	8		11		9	6						1		3		2		

Division Two — Final Table

		P	W	D	L	F	A	W	D	L	F	A	Pts
1	West Ham United	42	12	8	1	56	25	11	3	7	45	29	57
2	Blackburn Rovers	42	13	7	1	50	18	9	5	7	43	39	56
3	Charlton Athletic	42	15	3	3	65	33	9	4	8	42	36	55
4	Liverpool	42	17	3	1	50	13	5	7	9	29	41	54
5	Fulham	42	13	5	3	53	24	7	7	7	44	35	52
6	Sheffield United	42	12	5	4	38	22	9	5	7	37	28	52
7	Middlesbrough	42	13	3	5	52	29	6	4	11	31	45	45
8	Ipswich Town	42	13	4	4	45	29	3	8	10	23	40	44
9	Huddersfield Town	42	9	8	4	28	24	5	8	8	35	42	44
10	Bristol Rovers	42	12	5	4	52	31	5	3	13	33	49	42
11	Stoke City	42	9	4	8	49	36	9	2	10	26	37	42
12	Leyton Orient	42	14	2	5	53	27	4	3	14	24	52	41
13	Grimsby Town	42	13	4	4	54	30	4	2	15	32	53	40
14	Barnsley	42	10	6	5	40	25	4	6	11	30	49	40
15	Cardiff City	42	10	5	6	44	31	4	4	13	19	46	37
16	Derby County	42	11	3	7	37	36	3	5	13	23	45	36
17	Bristol City	42	9	5	7	35	31	4	4	13	28	57	35
18	Rotherham United	42	8	3	10	38	44	6	2	13	27	57	33
19	Swansea Town	42	8	3	10	48	45	3	6	12	24	54	31
20	Lincoln City	42	6	6	9	33	35	5	3	13	22	47	31
21	NOTTS COUNTY	42	9	3	9	24	31	3	3	15	20	49	30
22	Doncaster Rovers	42	7	5	9	34	40	1	6	14	22	48	27

1958/59   23rd in Division Three (Relegated)

#	Date	Opponent	Score	Scorers	Att	Linton JA	Chatham RH	Cruickshank FJ	Loxley H	Russell PW	Carver GF	Roby D	Wylie RM	Lane JG	Newsham S	Langford JW	Kilford JD	Parry C	Russell ET	Sheridan J	Asher T	Gissing JW	Bircumshaw PB	Noon H	Hateley A	Butler JH	Horobin R	Brown K	Withers A	Forrest JR	Stone M
1	Aug 23	ACCRINGTON STANLEY	1-1	Newsham	14872	1	2	3	4	5	6	7	8	9	10	11															
2	27	Wrexham	2-3	Wylie, Parry	15541	1		3	4	5	6	7	8		10	11	2	9													
3	30	Halifax Town	1-1	Newsham	9789	1		3	4	5		7	8		10	11	2	9	6												
4	Sep 4	WREXHAM	2-0	Roby, Newsham	11906	1		3		5		7	8		9	11	2		6	4	10										
5	6	NEWPORT COUNTY	1-1	Roby	12249	1		3		5		10	8		9	11	2		6	4		7									
6	11	HULL CITY	1-1	Parry	8584	1		3		5	6	10	8		9	11	2	7		4											
7	13	Chesterfield	0-1		12774	1		3		5	6	10			9	11	2		7	4	8										
8	15	Hull City	0-5		8521	1		3		5	6	7		9	10	11	2		4	8											
9	20	BURY	1-1	Roby	10077	1		3		5		7	8	9	10	11	2		6	4											
10	25	SOUTHAMPTON	1-2	Roby	6171	1		3		5		7	10	9	8	11	2		6	4											
11	27	MANSFIELD TOWN	3-4	Roby 2, Newsham(p)	16510	1		3		5		7	10	9	8	11	2		6	4											
12	Oct 1	Southampton	0-3		16548	1		3	4	5	6	7	8	9		11	2		10												
13	4	Swindon Town	1-3	Wylie	13478	1		3	4	5	6	7	10			11	2		9	8											
14	9	BRENTFORD	0-0		4359	1		3	4	5	6	7	10		9	11	2			8											
15	11	Rochdale	2-1	Newsham 2(1p)	5306	1		3	4	5	6	10			9		2			8						7	11				
16	18	DONCASTER ROV.	2-2	Newsham 2	9341	1		3	4	5	6	10	8		9		2									7	11				
17	25	Plymouth Argyle	0-3		25750	1		3		5	6	10	8		9	11	2			4							7				
18	Nov 1	TRANMERE ROVERS	1-1	Roby	9107	1		3		5		11	8	9	10		2			4		7	6								
19	8	Stockport County	1-1	Hateley	10181	1		3		5		10	11				2			4	8	7	6		9						
20	22	Norwich City	3-3	Carver, Newsham, Sheridan	13637	1		3			6	10	7		9		2			4			11		5	8					
21	29	BOURNEMOUTH	4-3	Horobin 2, Newsham, Loxley	7643	1		3		6		10	7		9		2			4			11		5		8				
22	Dec 13	SOUTHEND UNITED	1-4	Lane	7121	1	2	3			6	7		9	10	11				4					5	8					
23	20	Accrington Stanley	0-3		5299	1		3	9	5	6	7			10		2			4			11			8					
24	26	BRADFORD CITY	1-3	Loxley	8376	1		3	9	5	6	7					2		8	4	10						11				
25	27	Bradford City	1-4	Roby	16230	1		3	6	5		11					2		7	4	8					9	10				
26	Jan 3	HALIFAX TOWN	4-4	Horobin 2, Loxley, Brown	8909	1		3	4	5	6	7					2			10							8	9	11		
27	10	Reading	3-1	Cruickshank, Horobin, Withers	10156	1		3		5	6	7					2			4	10						8	9	11		
28	31	CHESTERFIELD	3-1	Brown 2, Newsham	14871	1		3		5	6	7			10		2			4							8	9	11		
29	Feb 7	Bury	1-0	Forrest	6555	1		3		5	6	7								4						2	8	9	11	10	
30	14	Mansfield Town	0-3		13374	1		3		5		7								4				6		2	8	9	11	10	
31	21	SWINDON TOWN	1-0	Forrest	10575	1		3		5		7								4				6		2	8	9	11	10	
32	23	Colchester Utd.	1-4	Horobin	4404	1		3		5		7		9						4				6		2	8		11	10	
33	28	ROCHDALE	1-1	Roby	6394	1		3		5	6	7		9						4						2	8		11	10	
34	Mar 7	Doncaster Rov.	1-2	Carver	4663	1		3	4	5	6	7		9												2	8		11	10	
35	14	PLYMOUTH ARGYLE	1-2	Withers	7369			3		5	6	7		9						4						2	8		11	10	
36	16	Newport County	1-3	Horobin	5869			3		5		7		9						4						2	8		11	10	
37	21	Tranmere Rovers	3-0	Roby 2, Brown	9493	1		3		5	6	7								4						2	8	9	11	10	
38	27	Queens Park Rangers	1-2	Roby	12044	1		3		5	6	10	8									7				9	2		11		
39	28	Stockport County	0-2		9761	1		3		5	6	7								4		11				9	2		8	10	
40	30	QUEENS PARK RANGERS	0-1		6956			3	4	5	6	7											11				2	8	9	10	1
41	Apr 4	Reading	1-3	Roby	8285			3	4	5	6	7							8	10							11		9		1
42	11	NORWICH CITY	1-3	Horobin	13289			3	4	5	6	7		9											2		8		11	10	1
43	18	Bournemouth	0-0		8130			3	4	5	6	7		9											2		8		11	10	1
44	21	Brentford	0-4		11720			3	4	5	6	7		9											2		7		11	10	1
45	25	COLCHESTER UTD.	0-1		4733			3	4	5	6														2		7		11	10	1
46	29	Southend United	2-5	Withers, Anderson(og)	5774			3		5	6				10				8	4					2		7		11	9	1
		Apps				37	2	46	33	32	33	43	16	10	28	16	26	6	9	34	11	8	6	11	4	15	27	8	17	17	7
		Gls						1	3		2	13	2	1	11			2		1					1		8	4	3	2	

Played in game 41: J Newton (2). In game 45: AN Bates (9).
Played in games 35 and 36: RL Twigg (1).

One own goal

F.A. Cup

#	Date	Opponent	Score	Scorers	Att	Linton JA	Cruickshank FJ	Russell PW	Carver GF	Roby D	Wylie RM	Lane JG	Kilford JD	Russell ET	Bircumshaw PB	Noon H
R1	Nov 15	BARROW	1-2	Bircumshaw	11030	1	3	5	6	10	7	9	2	8	11	4

		P	W	D	L	F	A	W	D	L	F	A	Pts
1	Plymouth Argyle	46	14	7	2	55	27	9	9	5	34	32	62
2	Hull City	46	19	3	1	65	21	7	6	10	25	34	61
3	Brentford	46	15	5	3	49	22	6	10	7	27	27	57
4	Norwich City	46	13	6	4	51	29	9	7	7	38	33	57
5	Colchester United	46	15	2	6	46	31	6	8	9	25	36	52
6	Reading	46	16	4	3	51	21	5	4	14	27	42	50
7	Tranmere Rovers	46	15	3	5	53	22	6	5	12	29	45	50
8	Southend United	46	14	6	3	52	26	7	2	14	33	54	50
9	Halifax Town	46	14	5	4	48	25	7	3	13	32	52	50
10	Bury	46	12	9	2	51	24	5	5	13	18	34	48
11	Bradford City	46	13	4	6	47	25	5	7	11	37	51	47
12	Bournemouth	46	12	9	2	40	18	5	3	15	29	51	46
13	Queen's Park Rgs.	46	14	6	3	49	28	5	2	16	25	49	46
14	Southampton	46	12	7	4	57	33	5	4	14	31	47	45
15	Swindon Town	46	13	4	6	39	25	3	9	11	20	32	45
16	Chesterfield	46	12	5	6	40	26	5	5	13	27	38	44
17	Newport County	46	15	2	6	43	24	2	7	14	26	44	43
18	Wrexham	46	12	6	5	40	30	2	8	13	23	47	42
19	Accrington Stanley	46	10	8	5	42	31	5	4	14	29	56	42
20	Mansfield Town	46	11	5	7	38	42	3	8	12	35	56	41
21	Stockport County	46	9	7	7	33	23	4	3	16	32	55	36
22	Doncaster Rovers	46	13	2	8	40	32	1	3	19	10	58	33
23	NOTTS COUNTY	46	5	9	9	33	39	5	3	16	22	57	29
24	Rochdale	46	8	7	8	21	26	0	5	18	16	53	28

- 1958/59 Season -

Back: Kilford, Blenkinsop, Butler, Twigg, Linton, Stone, Noon, Sheridan, Loxley
Standing: Dixon(Masseur), Harvey, Hateley, Rawson, Cruickshank, Chatham, P.Russell, E.T.Russell, Kirkham, Wheeler(Train)
Sitting: Ramirez, Wylie, Roby, Carver, Lane, Newsham, Asher, Hill
Front: Felice, Newton, Parry

- 1959/60 Season -

Back: Gibson, Butler, Forrest, Smith, Loxley, Hateley, Noon
Middle: Wheeler (Trainer), Roby, Joyce, Sheridan, Carver, Bircumshaw, Hill (Manager)
Front: Withers, Newsham, Horobin

1959/60 — 2nd in Division Four (Promoted)

#	Date		Opponent	Score	Scorers	Att.	Smith GH	Butler JH	Cruickshank FJ	Sheridan J	Rawson K	Carver GF	Roby D	Joyce C	Forrest JR	Horobin R	Withers A	Noon H	Newsham S	Bircumshaw PB	Gissing JW	Gibson APS	Loxley H	Beely O	Edwards RT	Hateley A	Newton J
1	Aug	22	CHESTER	2-1	Roby, Horobin	9652	1	2	3	4	5	6	7	8	9	10	11										
2		26	Crewe Alexandra	1-2	Roby	10283	1	2	3		5	6	7	8	9	10	11	4									
3		29	Crystal Palace	1-1	Newsham	16466	1	2	3		5	6	8	7			9	4	10	11							
4	Sep	3	CREWE ALEXANDRA	4-1	Newsham 2, Horobin 2	9861	1	2	3	4	5	6	7		10	8	11		9								
5		5	BRADFORD PARK AVE.	0-1		12139	1	2	3	4	5	6	8		10		11		9		7						
6		7	Gateshead	0-0		6618	1	2			5	6	7	8	10		11	3	9			4					
7		12	Stockport County	1-3	Forrest	7662	1	2		4	5	6	7		10	8	11	3	9								
8		17	GATESHEAD	4-0	Forrest 3, Withers	8793	1	2		4	5	6	7		10	8	11	3	9								
9		19	EXETER CITY	3-0	Roby, Horobin, Forrest	11982	1	2		4	5	6	7		10	8	11	3	9								
10		21	Hartlepool Utd.	4-2	Newsham 2, Roby, Forrest	3926	1	2		4	5	6	7		10	8	11	3	9								
11		26	Watford	2-4	Forrest, Carver	10131	1	2				6	7		10	8	11	3	9				4	5			
12	Oct	1	HARTLEPOOL UTD.	4-0	Newsham 2(1p), Horobin, Withers	10732	1	2				6	7		10	8	11	4	9				5	3			
13		3	OLDHAM ATHLETIC	3-1	Roby, Horobin, Carver	14015	1	2				6	7		10	8	11	4	9				5	3			
14		6	Carlisle Utd.	0-2		9004	1	2				6	7		10	8	11	4	9				5	3			
15		10	WORKINGTON	2-0	Newsham 2(1p)	13282	1	2				6	7		10	8	11	4	9				5	3			
16		15	CARLISLE UTD.	2-1	Newsham 2	12232	1	2				6	7		10	8	11	4	9				5	3			
17		17	Doncaster Rov.	4-0	Newsham 3, Forrest	4705	1	2				6	7		10	8	11	4	9				5	3			
18		24	NORTHAMPTON T	2-1	Newsham, Withers	14867	1	2				6	7		10	8	11	4	9				5	3			
19		31	Torquay United	1-3	Newsham	8196	1	2				6	7		10	8	11	4	9				5	3			
20	Nov	7	MILLWALL	2-1	Newsham, Withers	16018	1	2				6			10	8	11	4	9	11			5	3			
21		21	GILLINGHAM	3-1	Horobin, Forrest, Bircumshaw	13856	1	2				6			10	8	7	4	9	11			5	3			
22		28	Barrow	3-4	Newsham 2(1p), Forrest	5308	1	2	6			10			4	8	7		9	11			5	3			
23	Dec	12	Darlington	2-5	Newsham(p), Forrest	3977	1	2		4		6			10	8	7		9	11			5	3			
24		19	Chester	1-2	Forrest	4208	1	2	6				7	8	10			4	9	11			5	3			
25		26	ROCHDALE	2-1	Bircumshaw 2	14582	1	2	6				7	8	10			4	9	11			5		3		
26		28	Rochdale	4-1	Bircumshaw 2, Forrest, Roby	4044	1	2	6				7	8	10			3	9	11			4	5			
27	Jan	2	CRYSTAL PALACE	7-1	Joyce 3, Bircumshaw 2, Forrest, Roby	15804	1	2	6				7	8	10			3	9	11			4	5			
28		9	Southport	1-2	Burcumshaw, Joyce	4161	1	2	6				7	8	10			3	9	11			4	5			
29		16	Bradford Park Ave.	1-1	Newsham	8114	1	2	6				7	8	10			3	9	11			4	5			
30		23	STOCKPORT COUNTY	3-0	Joyce 2, Bircumshaw	13113	1	2	6				7	8	10			3	9	11			4	5			
31		30	ALDERSHOT	5-3	Bircumshaw 2, Newsham, Roby, Joyce	12879	1	2	6				7	8	10			3	9	11			4	5			
32	Feb	6	Exeter City	3-3	Bircumshaw 2, Joyce	9479	1	2	6				7	8	10			3	9	11			4	5			
33		13	WATFORD	2-1	Forrest, Bircumshaw	18423	1	2	6				7	8	10			3	9	11			4	5			
34		27	Workington	1-0	Newsham	4983	1	2	6				7	8	10			3	9	11			4	5			
35	Mar	5	DONCASTER ROV.	3-4	Bircumshaw 2, Joyce	16469	1	2	6				7	8	10			3	9	11			4	5			
36		12	Northampton T	2-4	Bircumshaw 2	8902	1	2	6				7	8	10			3	9	11			4	5			
37		19	TORQUAY UNITED	1-1	Hateley	15051	1	2		4		6	7		8	10		3		11			5			9	
38		26	Millwall	1-1	Withers	11996	1	2		4		6			10	8	11	3		7			5			9	
39	Apr	2	SOUTHPORT	4-1	Hateley 2, Forrest, Withers	12320	1	2		4		6	7		10	8	11	3					5			9	
40		9	Gillingham	1-0	Forrest	7636	1	2		4		6	7		10	8		3		11			5			9	
41		16	BARROW	1-2	Hateley	15634	1	2		4		6	7		10	8		3		11			5			9	
42		18	WALSALL	2-1	Roby, Hateley	22788	1	2		4		6	7	8	10		11	3					5			9	
43		19	Walsall	2-2	Withers, Forrest	14752	1	2		4			7	8	10		11	3				6	5			9	
44		23	Aldershot	1-1	Hateley	6669	1	2					7	8	10		11	3				6	5			9	4
45		30	DARLINGTON	5-4	Roby 2, Forrest, Joyce, Withers	13386	1	2					7	8	10		11	3				6	5			9	4
46	May	3	Oldham Athletic	3-0	Hateley 2, McGill(og)	3628	1	2					7	8	10		11	3				6	5			9	4
			Apps				46	46	5	26	10	31	42	22	44	25	31	41	34	22	1	17	36	13	1	10	3
			Goals									2	11	10	19	7	8		23	18						8	

One own goal

F.A. Cup

	Date		Opponent	Score	Scorers	Att.	Smith GH	Butler JH	Cruickshank FJ	Sheridan J	Rawson K	Carver GF	Roby D	Joyce C	Forrest JR	Horobin R	Withers A	Noon H	Newsham S	Bircumshaw PB	Gissing JW	Gibson APS	Loxley H	Beely O	Edwards RT	Hateley A	Newton J
R1	Nov	14	Hastings United	2-1	Bircumshaw 2	5757	1	2				6			10	8	7	4	9	11			5	3			
R2	Dec	5	BATH CITY	0-1		25889	1	2		4		6	7		10	8	11		9				5	3			

		P	W	D	L	F		A	W	D	L	F	A	Pts
1	Walsall	46	14	5	4	57		33	14	4	5	45	27	65
2	NOTTS COUNTY	46	19	1	3	66		27	7	7	9	41	42	60
3	Torquay United	46	17	3	3	56		27	9	5	9	28	31	60
4	Watford	46	17	2	4	62		28	7	7	9	30	39	57
5	Millwall	46	12	8	3	54		28	6	9	8	30	33	53
6	Northampton Town	46	13	6	4	50		22	9	3	11	35	41	53
7	Gillingham	46	14	2	4	47		21	4	6	13	27	48	52
8	Crystal Palace	46	12	6	5	61		27	7	6	10	23	37	50
9	Exeter City	46	13	7	3	50		30	6	4	13	30	40	49
10	Stockport County	46	15	6	2	35		10	4	5	14	23	44	49
11	Bradford Park Ave.	46	12	10	1	48		25	5	5	13	22	43	49
12	Rochdale	46	15	4	4	46		19	3	6	14	19	41	46
13	Aldershot	46	14	5	4	50		22	4	4	15	27	52	45
14	Crewe Alexandra	46	14	3	6	51		31	4	6	13	28	57	45
15	Darlington	46	11	6	6	40		30	6	3	14	23	43	43
16	Workington	46	10	8	5	41		20	4	6	13	27	40	42
17	Doncaster Rovers	46	13	3	7	40		23	3	7	13	29	53	42
18	Barrow	46	11	8	4	52		29	4	3	16	25	58	41
19	Carlisle United	46	9	6	8	28		28	6	5	12	23	38	41
20	Chester	46	10	8	5	37		26	4	4	15	27	51	40
21	Southport	46	9	7	7	30		32	1	7	15	18	60	34
22	Gateshead	46	12	3	8	37		27	0	6	17	21	59	33
23	Oldham Athletic	46	5	7	11	20		30	3	5	15	21	53	28
24	Hartlepools United	46	9	2	12	40		41	1	5	17	19	68	27

1960/61 5th in Division Three

#	Date		Opponent	Score	Scorers	Att	Smith GH	Butler JH	Noon H	Sheridan J	Loxley H	Carver GF	Roby D	Joyce C	Hateley A	Forrest JR	Withers A	Horobin R	Gibson APS	Simcoe KE	Bircumshaw PB	Rawson K	Edwards RT	Hampton IK	Gissing JW	Bircumshaw A	Newton J
1	Aug	20	Watford	2-2	Joyce, Forrest	16218	1	2	3	4	5	6	7	8	9	10	11										
2		25	QUEENS PARK RANGERS	2-1	Withers, Horobin	15174	1	2	3	4	5	6	7	8	9		11	10									
3		27	BOURNEMOUTH	3-2	Hateley 2, Joyce	12015	1	2	3	4	5	6	7	8	9		11	10									
4		29	Queens Park Rangers	0-2		8365	1	2	3	4		6	7	8	9				5	10	11						
5	Sep	3	Bradford City	2-2	PB Bircumshaw, Hateley	9689	1	2	3	4	5	6	7	8	9		10				11						
6		8	READING	4-2	PB Bircumshaw 2, Joyce, Hateley	13309	1	2	3	4	5	6	7	8	9		10				11						
7		10	BARNSLEY	5-1	Hateley 3, PB Bircumshaw, Sheridan	13934	1	2	3	4	5	6	7	8	9		10				11						
8		14	Reading	0-2		6327	1	2	3	4	5		7	8	9		10		6		11						
9		17	Newport County	2-2	Hateley, Joyce	7799	1	2	3	4			8	9	10	7			6		11	5					
10		20	Bristol City	1-2	Roby	14839	1	2	3	4	5		7	8	9	10	11		6								
11		24	COLCHESTER UTD.	4-2	Hateley 2, Roby, Joyce	14134	1	2	3	4	5	6	7	8	9	10	11										
12		29	BRISTOL CITY	3-0	Hateley, Roby, Forrest	14230	1	2	3	4	5	6	7	8	9	10	11										
13	Oct	1	Grimsby Town	1-1	Hateley	12448	1	2	3	4	5	6	7	8	9	10	11										
14		3	Hull City	1-3	PB Bircumshaw	12199	1	2	3	4	5	6	7	8	9	10					11						
15		8	SWINDON TOWN	1-0	PB Bircumshaw	11483	1	2	3	4	5	6	7	8	9	10					11						
16		15	Torquay United	2-2	Joyce, Hateley	8081	1	2	3	4	5	6	7	8	9	10	11										
17		22	PORT VALE	2-2	Hateley, PB Bircumshaw	10725	1	2	3	4	5	6		8	9	10		7			11						
18		29	Southend United	1-3	Forrest	5296	1	2	3	4	5	6		8	9	10		7			11						
19	Nov	12	Bury	0-7		8884	1	2	3	4		6	7		9	10	11	8				5					
20		19	WALSALL	3-1	Joyce, Hateley, PB Bircumshaw	12154	1	2	3	4		6	7	8	9	10					11	5					
21	Dec	10	Tranmere Rovers	3-2	Horobin, Forrest, Hateley	5668	1	2	3	4	5	6	7		9	10	11	8									
22		17	WATFORD	3-1	Forrest 2, Hateley	10262	1	2	3	4	5	6	7		9	10	11	8									
23		26	Coventry City	2-2	Horobin, Forrest	18793	1	2	3	4	5	6	7		9	10	11	8									
24		27	COVENTRY CITY	3-0	Carver, Roby(p), Austin(og)	26759	1	2	3	4		6	7		9	10	11	8	5								
25		31	Bournemouth	3-1	Horobin 3	7974	1	2	3	4		6	7		9	10	11	8	5								
26	Jan	14	BRADFORD CITY	2-1	Hateley, Horobin	12421	1	2	3	4		6	7		9	10	11	8	5								
27		21	Barnsley	2-5	Horobin, Forrest	5522	1	2	3	4		6	7		9	10	11	8	5								
28		28	CHESTERFIELD	1-0	Forrest	7555	1	2	3	4		6	7		9	10	11	8	5								
29	Feb	4	NEWPORT COUNTY	6-0	Withers 3, Horobin 2, Hateley	10673	1	2	3	4		6	7		9	10	11	8	5								
30		11	Colchester Utd.	2-1	Hateley, Withers	4634	1	2	3		4	6	7		9	10	11	8	5								
31		18	GRIMSBY TOWN	0-1		22292	1	2	3		4	6	7		9	10	11	8	5								
32		25	Halifax Town	1-0	Hateley	4242	1	2	3		5	6	7		9	10	11	8	4								
33	Mar	4	TORQUAY UNITED	0-1		14181	1	2	3		5	6	7	10	9		11	8	4								
34		8	Shrewsbury Town	0-4		8330	1	2	3		5	6	7		9		10	8	4		11						
35		11	Port Vale	3-1	PB Bircumshaw 3	10931	1	2	3		5	6	7		9		10	8	4		11						
36		18	SOUTHEND UNITED	1-2	Hateley	10530	1	2	3		5	6	7		9		10	8	4		11						
37		23	HALIFAX TOWN	1-1	Hateley	8346	1		3	4		6	7		9		10	8	5		11		2				
38		25	Chesterfield	1-3	Gissing	6154	1		3	4					9		10	8	5		11		2	6	7		
39	Apr	1	BURY	0-3		10489	1		3	4		6			9	10	11	8	5				2		7		
40		3	Brentford	0-3		5416	1			4		6				10		8	5	9	11		2		7	3	
41		4	BRENTFORD	0-0		3933	1				5	6	7		9	10		8			11		2			3	4
42		8	Walsall	1-2	Christie(og)	14508	1		3	4	5	6	7	11	9	10		8					2				
43		15	SHREWSBURY TOWN	2-1	Hateley, Forrest	7271	1		3	4	5	6	7	11	9	10		8					2				
44		22	Swindon Town	0-1		8904	1		3	4	5	6	7	11	9	10		8					2				
45		27	HULL CITY	2-1	Horobin, Hateley	4941	1		3	4	5	6	7	10	9			8			11		2				
46		29	TRANMERE ROVERS	4-1	Hateley 2, Withers, Joyce	7076	1		3	4	5	6	7	10	9		11	8					2				

	Smith GH	Butler JH	Noon H	Sheridan J	Loxley H	Carver GF	Roby D	Joyce C	Hateley A	Forrest JR	Withers A	Horobin R	Gibson APS	Simcoe KE	Bircumshaw PB	Rawson K	Edwards RT	Hampton IK	Gissing JW	Bircumshaw A	Newton J
Apps	46	36	44	38	32	42	40	25	45	31	34	31	21	2	19	3	10	1	3	2	1
Goals			1		1	4	8	27	10	6	11				11				1		

Two own goals

F.A. Cup

						Att																			
R1	Nov	5	Aldershot	0-2		7498	1	2	3	4	5	6	7	8	9	10		11								

F.L. Cup

						Att																			
R1	Oct	20	BRIGHTON & HOVE ALB.	1-3	Noon	10449	1	2	3	4	5	6	7	8	9	10	11									

		P	W	D	L	F	A	W	D	L	F	A	Pts
1	Bury	46	18	3	2	62	17	12	5	6	46	28	68
2	Walsall	46	19	4	0	62	20	9	2	12	36	40	62
3	Queen's Park Rgs.	46	18	4	1	58	23	7	6	10	35	37	60
4	Watford	46	12	7	4	52	27	8	5	10	33	45	52
5	NOTTS COUNTY	46	16	3	4	52	24	5	6	12	30	53	51
6	Grimsby Town	46	14	4	5	48	32	6	6	11	29	37	50
7	Port Vale	46	15	3	5	63	30	2	12	9	33	49	49
8	Barnsley	46	15	5	3	56	30	6	2	15	27	50	49
9	Halifax Town	46	14	7	2	42	22	2	10	11	29	56	49
10	Shrewsbury Town	46	13	7	3	54	26	2	9	12	29	49	46
11	Hull City	46	13	6	4	51	28	4	6	13	22	45	46
12	Torquay United	46	8	12	3	37	26	6	5	12	38	57	45
13	Newport County	46	12	7	4	51	30	5	4	14	30	60	45
14	Bristol City	46	15	4	4	50	19	2	6	15	20	49	44
15	Coventry City	46	14	6	3	54	25	2	6	15	26	58	44
16	Swindon Town	46	13	6	4	41	16	1	9	13	21	39	43
17	Brentford	46	10	9	4	41	28	3	8	12	15	42	43
18	Reading	46	13	5	5	48	29	1	7	15	24	54	40
19	Bournemouth	46	8	7	8	34	39	7	3	13	24	37	40
20	Southend United	46	10	8	5	38	26	4	3	16	22	50	39
21	Tranmere Rovers	46	11	5	7	53	50	4	3	16	26	65	38
22	Bradford City	46	8	8	7	37	36	3	6	14	28	51	36
23	Colchester United	46	8	5	10	40	44	3	6	14	28	57	33
24	Chesterfield	46	9	6	8	42	29	1	6	16	25	58	32

- 1960/61 Season -

Back: Noon, Simcoe, Horobin, Edwards, Dixon(Physio), Newsham, Gibson, Roby, Withers
Middle: Beeby, Joyce, Smith, Rawson, Forrest, McDowall, Hateley, Loxley
Front: Hill(Manager), Butler, Newton, Sheridan, Gissing, Carver, Bircumshaw, Wheeler(Trainer)

- 1961/62 Season -

Back: P.B.Bircumshaw, Astle, J.H.Butler, Edwards, A.Bircumshaw
Standing: Carver, Gibson, Smith, Loxley, P.L.Butler, Sheridan, Moore
Sitting: Wheeler (Trainer), Joyce, Horobin, Forrest, Hateley, Hill (Manager)
Front: Noon, Withers

1961/62 13th in Division Three

#	Date		Opponent	Score	Scorers	Att.	Smith GH	Edwards RT	Noon H	Sheridan J	Loxley H	Carver GF	Joyce C	Horobin R	Hateley A	Forrest JR	Withers A	Bircumshaw PB	Gibson APS	Butler JH	Newsham S	Astle J	Butler PL	Moore B	Bircumshaw A	Fry KF	Hampton IK	Flower AJ	Jones B	Woodford R
1	Aug	19	BRISTOL CITY	1-0	Horobin(p)	10203	1	2	3	4	5	6	7	8	9	10	11													
2		23	Crystal Palace	1-4	Withers	28567	1	2	3	4	5	6	7	8	9	10	11													
3		26	Bradford Park Ave.	2-3	Hateley, Forrest	11476	1	2	3	4	5	6	7	8	9	10	11													
4		31	CRYSTAL PALACE	0-0		11633	1	2	3	4	5	6	7	8	9	10	11													
5	Sep	2	GRIMSBY TOWN	2-0	Forrest, Welbourne(og)	9289	1	2	3	4	5	6	7	8	9	10	11													
6		7	PETERBOROUGH UTD.	2-2	Hateley, Loxley	19466	1	2	3		5	6		8	9	10	7	11	4											
7		9	Coventry City	2-2	Horobin, PB Bircumshaw	13329	1	2	3	4		6		8	9	10	7	11	5											
8		16	BRENTFORD	3-1	Edwards, Hateley, Newsham	7979	1	7	3	4	5	6		8	9			11		2	10									
9		21	Port Vale	2-3	Hateley 2	8676	1		3	4	5	6	7	8	9	10	11			2										
10		23	Reading	2-4	Horobin, Withers	11084	1	10	3	4	5	6		8			11			2	9	7								
11		25	Port Vale	0-1		11707		7	3	4	5	6	8			10	11			2	9	1								
12		30	NEWPORT COUNTY	8-1	*See below	6356			3	4	5		7	8			11	9	6	2	10	1								
13	Oct	4	Bournemouth	1-2	Forrest	15610			3	4	5		7	8			11	9	6	2	10									
14		7	PORTSMOUTH	2-1	PB Bircumshaw 2	9889	1	2	3	4	5	6	8	7				11	9											
15		12	BOURNEMOUTH	3-2	Hateley 3	11859	1	2	3	4	5	6	8	7	10			11	9											
16		14	Barnsley	0-2		6992	1	2	3	4	5	6	8	7	10			11	9											
17		28	Watford	1-3	PB Bircumshaw	10077	1	2	3	4	5	6	10	8	9			7	11											
18	Nov	11	Torquay United	3-3	Horobin 2, Hateley	3687	1	2	3	4	5	6		8	9	10	7	11												
19		18	LINCOLN CITY	1-0	Forrest	9215	1	2	3	4	5	6		8	9	10	7	11												
20	Dec	2	QUEENS PARK RANGERS	0-0		7980	1		3	4	5	6		8	9	10	11			2				7						
21		16	Bristol City	0-6		12552	1		3	4	5	6		8	9	10	11			2				7						
22		23	BRADFORD PARK AVE.	4-2	Hateley 3, Horobin	6868	1	2		4		6		10	9		11		5			8		7	3					
23		26	SHREWSBURY TOWN	3-2	Horobin(p), Moore, Walters(og)	10197	1	2		4		6		10	9		11		5			8		7	3					
24	Jan	13	Grimsby Town	1-2	Sheridan	5773		2		4		6		10	9		11		5			8	1	7	3					
25		20	COVENTRY CITY	2-0	Hateley 2	8827		2		4		6		10	9	8	11		5				1	7	3					
26		27	Northampton T	2-1	Withers, Hateley	11813		2		4		6		10	9		11		5				1	7	3					
27	Feb	2	Brentford	1-0	Hateley	9227		2		4		6		10	9	8	11		5				1	7	3					
28		10	READING	2-2	Horobin, Spiers(og)	9312		2		4		6		10	9		11		5			8	1	7	3					
29		17	Newport County	0-2		2597				4		6		10	9	8	11		5				1	7	3					
30		24	Portsmouth	0-0		14438					6			10	9		11	8	5	2			1		3	7				
31	Mar	3	BARNSLEY	0-2		7379				4		6		10	9		11	8	5	2			1		3	7				
32		10	Hull City	1-2	Moore	3911	1	2		4		6	8		9	10			5					7			3	11		
33		17	WATFORD	1-0	PB Bircumshaw	6987	1	2		4		6	10	8	9				5						3	7				
34		23	Swindon Town	0-1		7477	1	2		4		6	10					8	5	11					3	7				
35		28	Shrewsbury Town	0-3		3880	1	2		4		6		8	9	10			5						3	7		11		
36		31	TORQUAY UNITED	2-0	Jones, PB Bircumshaw	4975	1	2		4		6			10			8	5	11					3	7			9	
37	Apr	3	HULL CITY	3-0	Hateley 2, PB Bircumshaw (p)	3688	1	2		4		6		8	10				5	11					3	7			9	
38		6	Lincoln City	2-2	Jones, Hateley	5929	1	2		4		6		8	10				5	11					3	7			9	
39		9	Halifax Town	2-1	Sheridan, Fry	3037	1	2		4		6			10				5	11		8			3	7			9	
40		12	SWINDON TOWN	0-1		5369	1	2	6	4				8	10		11		5	9					3	7				
41		14	NORTHAMPTON T	1-4	PB Bircumshaw	5974	1	2	6	4				8	10		11		5	9					3	7				
42		20	Southend United	2-3	Horobin, Forrest	8310		2		4		6		8	9	10			11				1		3	7	2			
43		21	Queens Park Rangers	0-2		9911		5		4		6		8	9	10			11				1		3	7	2			
44		23	SOUTHEND UNITED	2-0	Horobin(p), Forrest	5158		2				6		8	9	10			5			1		11	3	7				4
45		28	HALIFAX TOWN	0-0		4822		2				6		8	9				5			8	1	11		7	3	10		4
46		30	Peterborough Utd.	0-2		7873	1		6		5		10	8				7	11	2					9	3				4

*Scorers in game 12: PB Bircumshaw 3, Withers 2, Newsham, Horobin, Herrity (og).

	Smith GH	Edwards RT	Noon H	Sheridan J	Loxley H	Carver GF	Joyce C	Horobin R	Hateley A	Forrest JR	Withers A	Bircumshaw PB	Gibson APS	Butler JH	Newsham S	Astle J	Butler PL	Moore B	Bircumshaw A	Fry KF	Hampton IK	Flower AJ	Jones B	Woodford R
Apps	31	37	25	42	21	40	15	40	40	25	35	23	27	12	6	7	15	14	23	15	3	2	5	3
Goals		1			2	1		11	19	6	5	11			2			2		1			2	

Four own goals

F.A. Cup

	Date		Opponent	Score	Scorers	Att.	Smith GH	Edwards RT	Noon H	Sheridan J	Loxley H	Carver GF	Horobin R	Hateley A	Forrest JR	Withers A	Bircumshaw PB	Gibson APS	Astle J	Bircumshaw A	Fry KF
R1	Nov	4	YEOVIL TOWN	4-2	Withers 2, Hateley, PB Bircumshaw	11375	1	2	3	4	5	6	8	9	10	7	11				
R2	Nov	15	Margate	1-1	Loxley	7864	1		3	4	5	6	8	9	10	7	11		2		
rep	Nov	30	MARGATE	3-1	PB Bircumshaw 2, Hateley	12302	1		3	4	5	6	8	9	10	7	11		2		
R3	Jan	6	MANCHESTER CITY	0-1		25015	1	2		4		6	10	9			11	5	8	7	3

F.L. Cup

	Date		Opponent	Score	Scorers	Att.	Smith GH	Edwards RT	Noon H	Sheridan J	Loxley H	Carver GF	Horobin R	Hateley A	Forrest JR	Withers A	Gibson APS	Butler JH
R1	Sep	14	DERBY COUNTY	2-2	Horobin 2	14654	1	7	3	4		6	8	9	10	11	5	2
rep	Sep	27	Derby County	2-3	PB Bircumshaw, Forrest	12494	1		3	4	5	6	7	9	8	11	10	2

R1 replay after extra time

		P	W	D	L	F	A	W	D	L	F	A	Pts
1	Portsmouth	46	15	6	2	48	23	12	5	6	39	24	65
2	Grimsby Town	46	18	3	2	49	18	10	3	10	31	38	62
3	Bournemouth	46	14	8	1	42	18	7	9	7	27	27	59
4	Queen's Park Rgs.	46	15	3	5	65	31	9	8	6	46	42	59
5	Peterborough Utd.	46	16	0	7	60	38	10	6	7	47	44	58
6	Bristol City	46	15	3	5	56	27	8	5	10	38	45	54
7	Reading	46	14	5	4	46	24	8	4	11	31	42	53
8	Northampton Town	46	12	6	5	52	24	8	5	10	33	33	51
9	Swindon Town	46	11	8	4	48	26	6	7	10	30	45	49
10	Hull City	46	15	2	6	43	20	5	6	12	24	34	48
11	Bradford Park Ave.	46	13	5	5	47	27	7	2	14	33	51	47
12	Port Vale	46	12	4	7	41	23	5	7	11	24	35	45
13	NOTTS COUNTY	46	14	5	4	44	23	3	4	16	23	51	43
14	Coventry City	46	11	6	6	38	26	5	5	13	26	45	43
15	Crystal Palace	46	8	8	7	50	41	6	6	11	33	39	42
16	Southend United	46	10	7	6	31	26	3	9	11	26	43	42
17	Watford	46	10	9	4	37	26	4	4	15	26	48	41
18	Halifax Town	46	9	5	9	34	35	6	5	12	28	49	40
19	Shrewsbury Town	46	8	7	8	46	37	5	5	13	27	47	38
20	Barnsley	46	9	6	8	45	41	4	6	13	26	54	38
21	Torquay United	46	9	4	10	48	44	6	2	15	28	56	36
22	Lincoln City	46	4	10	9	31	43	5	7	11	26	44	35
23	Brentford	46	11	3	9	34	29	2	5	16	19	64	34
24	Newport County	46	6	5	12	29	38	1	3	19	17	64	22

1962/63 — 7th in Division Three

#	Date	Opponent	Res	Scorers	Att	Butler PL	Edwards RT	Agnew DY	Sheridan J	Gibson APS	Carver GF	Fry KF	Brown R	Jones B	Hateley A	Tait RJ	Daykin B	Flower AJ	Withers A	Moore B	Astle J	Loxley H	Smith GH	Hampton IK	Bircumshaw A
1	Aug 18	Coventry City	0-2		22832	1	2	3	4	5	6	7	8	9	10	11									
2	23	WATFORD	1-3	Brown	6121	1	2	3	4	5		7	8		9		6	10	11						
3	25	BOURNEMOUTH	2-0	Hateley, Moore	6749	1	2	3	4	5			8		9	11	6			7	10				
4	28	Watford	0-4		11423	1	2	3		5		7	8		9	11	6				10	4			
5	Sep 1	BARNSLEY	2-0	Brown, Hateley(p)	6347				4	5			8	7	9	11					10	6	1	2	3
6	6	READING	1-0	Hateley	5791				4	5			8	7	9	11					10	6	1	2	3
7	8	Colchester Utd.	2-2	Jones, Astle	5399				4	5		7	8	9		11					10	6	1	2	3
8	12	Reading	1-1	Astle	5780				4	5		7	8	9		11					10	6	1	2	3
9	15	SOUTHEND UNITED	2-1	Brown, Astle	7128				4	5		7	8	9		11					10	6	1	2	3
10	20	BRISTOL CITY	3-2	Loxley, Fry, Jones	5993				4	5		7	8	9		11					10	6	1	2	3
11	22	Millwall	2-0	Jones 2	15953		6		4	5		7	8	9		11					10		1	2	3
12	29	SHREWSBURY TOWN	1-5	Jones	10363		3		4	5		7	8	9		11					10	6	1	2	
13	Oct 1	Port Vale	1-1	Jones	9245		3		4	5		7	8	9		11					10	6	1	2	
14	6	Queens Park Rangers	1-0	Jones	15594		3		4	5	8	7		9		11					10	6	1	2	
15	11	PORT VALE	1-0	Tait	14320	2			4	5	8	7		9		11					10	6	1	3	
16	13	HULL CITY	1-1	Fry	9595		3		4	5	8	7		9		11					10	6	1	2	
17	20	Crystal Palace	1-1	Carver	13700		3		4	5	8	7		9		11					10	6	1	2	
18	27	WREXHAM	3-2	Jones 2, Astle	8649		3		4	5	8	7		9		11					10	6	1	2	
19	Nov 10	BRISTOL ROVERS	1-3	Hateley(p)	5950		3		4	5			8	7	9				11		10	6	1	2	
20	17	Brighton & Hove Alb.	3-1	Edwards 2, Bircumshaw	6187	10	8		5	6				9						7	11	4	1	2	3
21	Dec 1	Swindon Town	1-3	Jones	11977	10	8		5	6				9						7	11	4	1	2	3
22	8	PETERBOROUGH UTD.	2-0	Hateley, Edwards	5640	10			4	5		7			9	11					8	6	1	2	3
23	15	COVENTRY CITY	1-1	Astle	6784	10			4	5		7			9	11					8	6	1	2	3
24	22	Bournemouth	1-3	Edwards	9629	10			4	5		7			9	11					8	6	1	2	3
25	26	NORTHAMPTON T	2-1	Astle, Hateley	6614	10			4	5		7			9				11		8	6	1	2	3
26	Jan 12	Barnsley	1-3	Hateley	7719	10				5	4	7			9				11		8	6	1	2	3
27	Feb 23	QUEENS PARK RANGERS	3-2	Hateley 3 (2p)	8268	10			4	5	6	7		11	9						8		1	2	3
28	Mar 9	CRYSTAL PALACE	0-2		5536	10			4	5	6	7		11	9						8		1	2	3
29	12	Carlisle Utd.	2-4	Hateley 2 (1p)	6732				4	5	6	10	7		9	11					8		1	2	3
30	16	Wrexham	1-5	Jones	8059				4	5	6	7	10	9		11					8		1	2	3
31	21	CARLISLE UTD.	1-0	Astle	3455	10			4	5				9					11	7	8	6	1	2	3
32	23	HALIFAX TOWN	5-0	Hateley 3, Astle, Edwards	5076	10			4	5				9					11	7	8	6	1	2	3
33	30	Bristol Rovers	1-1	Astle	5970	10			4	5				9					11	7	8	6	1		3
34	Apr 2	Northampton T	2-2	Astle, Hateley	14606	2			4	5					9	10			11	7	8	6	1		3
35	6	BRIGHTON & HOVE ALB.	0-1		7001	2			4	5					9	10			11	7	8	6	1		3
36	12	BRADFORD PARK AVE.	3-2	Astle, Loxley, Tait	6382	2			4	5			10		9	11		7			8	6	1		3
37	16	Bradford Park Ave.	0-5		8258	2			4	5			10		9	11		7			8	6	1		3
38	20	SWINDON TOWN	2-0	Hateley 2	5609	2			4	5					9	10			11	7	8	6	1		3
39	24	Shrewsbury Town	2-2	Astle, Hateley	4381	2			4	5					9	10			11	7	8	6	1		3
40	27	Peterborough Utd.	0-0		10287	2			4	5					9	10			11	7	8	6	1		3
41	30	Bristol City	1-1	(og)	12197	2			4	5					9	10			11	7	8	6	1		3
42	May 4	MILLWALL	3-3	Tait 2, Hateley	6459	2			4	5					9	10			11	7	8	6	1		3
43	7	Halifax Town	1-2	Tait	1781	2			4	5		7			9	10			11		8	6	1		3
44	13	Southend United	2-1	Astle, Flower	8210	2			4	5		7			9	10			11		8	6	1		3
45	17	COLCHESTER UTD.	6-0	Astle 2, Hateley 2(1p), Flower, Tait	4103	2			4	5		7			8	10			11		9	6	1		3
46	20	Hull City	1-1	Astle	4145	2			4	5		7			8	10			11		9	6	1		3
		Apps				4	38	4	44	46	13	26	18	22	32	34	3	18	4	13	44	38	42	29	34
		Goals					5				1	2	3	11	22	6		2		1	16	2			1

One own goal

F.A. Cup

| R1 | Nov 3 | PETERBOROUGH UTD. | 0-3 | | 24473 | | 3 | | 4 | 5 | 8 | 7 | | 9 | | 11 | | | | | 10 | 6 | 1 | 2 | |

F.L. Cup

R2	Sep 26	Southend United	3-2	Astle, Brown, Fry	5500		6		4	5		7	8	9		11					10		1	2	3
R3	Oct 17	SWINDON TOWN	5-0	Astle 2, Jones, Loxley, Sheridan	7012		3		4	5	8	7		9		11					10	6	1	2	
R4	Nov 14	Birmingham City	2-3	Moore, Sheridan	13187	10	8		5	6				9					11	7	4		1	2	3

		P	W	D	L	F	A	W	D	L	F	A	Pts
1	Northampton Town	46	16	6	1	64	19	10	4	9	45	41	62
2	Swindon Town	46	18	2	3	60	22	4	12	7	27	34	58
3	Port Vale	46	16	4	3	47	25	7	4	12	25	33	54
4	Coventry City	46	14	6	3	54	28	4	11	8	29	41	53
5	Bournemouth	46	11	12	0	39	16	7	4	12	24	30	52
6	Peterborough Utd.	46	11	5	7	48	33	9	6	8	45	42	51
7	NOTTS COUNTY	46	15	3	5	46	29	4	10	9	27	45	51
8	Southend United	46	11	7	5	38	24	8	5	10	37	53	50
9	Wrexham	46	14	6	3	54	27	6	3	14	30	56	49
10	Hull City	46	12	6	5	40	22	7	4	12	34	47	48
11	Crystal Palace	46	10	7	6	38	22	7	6	10	30	36	47
12	Colchester United	46	11	6	6	41	35	7	5	11	32	58	47
13	Queen's Park Rgs.	46	9	6	8	44	36	8	5	10	41	40	45
14	Bristol City	46	10	9	4	54	38	6	4	13	46	54	45
15	Shrewsbury Town	46	13	4	6	57	41	3	8	12	26	40	44
16	Millwall	46	11	6	6	50	32	4	7	12	32	55	43
17	Watford	46	12	3	8	55	40	5	5	13	27	45	42
18	Barnsley	46	12	6	5	39	28	3	5	15	24	46	41
19	Bristol Rovers	46	11	8	4	45	29	4	3	16	25	59	41
20	Reading	46	13	4	6	51	30	3	4	16	23	48	40
21	Bradford Park Ave.	46	10	9	4	43	36	4	3	16	36	61	40
22	Brighton & Hove A.	46	7	6	10	28	38	5	6	12	30	46	36
23	Carlisle United	46	12	4	7	41	37	1	5	17	20	52	35
24	Halifax Town	46	8	3	12	41	51	1	9	13	23	55	30

- 1962/63 Season -

Back: Wheeler (Trainer), Astle, Butler, Loxley, Sheridan, Smith, Daykin, Coleman (Manager)
Middle: Ford (Asst.Train), Agnew, Bircumshaw, Carver, Fry, Brown, Flower, Hateley
Front: Gibson, Edwards, Withers, Jones, Tait

- 1963/64 Season -

Back: Brown, Wheeler (Trainer), Jones, Butler, Loxley, Smith, Bircumshaw, Ford (Asst.Trainer), Woodfield
Middle: Barber, Holder, Carver, R.J.Tait, Flower, Fry, Agnew
Front: Astle, Edwards, Gibson, Sheridan

1963/64 24th in Division Three (Relegated)

#	Date	Opponent	Score	Scorers	Att	Smith GH	Edwards RT	Bircumshaw A	Sheridan J	Gibson APS	Loxley H	Povey VR	Astle J	Bly TG	Tait RJ	Barber MJ	Hampton IK	Carver GF	Jones B	Butler PL	Flower AJ	Fry KF	Holder DJ	Agnew DY	Lowe E	Woolley R	Robinson LJ	Woodfield T	Froggatt J	Bates B
1	Aug 24	Brentford	1-4	Bly	13320	1	2	3	4	5	6	7	8	9	10	11														
2	29	COVENTRY CITY	0-3		18669	1	2	3	4	5	6	7	8	9	10	11														
3	31	SHREWSBURY TOWN	0-1		7788	1	2	3	4	5	6	7	8	9	10	11														
4	Sep 7	Bristol City	0-2		9440	1	4	3		5		7	8	9	10		2	6	11											
5	10	Coventry City	0-2		27796		4	3		5		7	10	9			2	6	8	1	11									
6	14	PORT VALE	2-0	Bly, Tait	7309		4	3		5			8	9	10		2	6		1	11	7								
7	16	Mansfield Town	0-4		16560		4	3	6	5			8	9	10	11	2			1		7								
8	21	Peterborough Utd.	1-5	Astle	11791		4	3		5			8	9	10	11	2	6		1		7								
9	28	Crewe Alexandra	1-0	Barber	5284		4	3		5	6		10	9		11	2		8	1		7								
10	Oct 3	MANSFIELD TOWN	1-0	Jones	14014		4	3		5	6		10	9		11	2		8	1		7								
11	5	CRYSTAL PALACE	1-1	Bly	7207		4	3		5	6		10	9		11	2		8	1		7								
12	9	Reading	2-3	Edwards, Astle	8403		4	3		5	6	8	10	9		11	2			1		7								
13	12	WATFORD	1-2	Astle	6887		4	3		5	6	8	10	9		11	2			1		7								
14	17	READING	0-1		5271		4	3		5	6		8	9	10	11	2			1		7								
15	19	Queens Park Rangers	2-3	Edwards, Astle	7175		4	3		5	6		8		10	11	2		9	1		7								
16	24	WALSALL	0-1		6548		4	3			6		8			11	2		9	1	10	7	5							
17	26	WREXHAM	3-0	Edwards, Tait, Barber	4724		4	3			6		8		10	11	2		9	1		7	5							
18	29	Walsall	1-2	Astle	10598		4	3			6		8		10	11	2		9	1		7	5							
19	Nov 2	Bournemouth	1-1		9762		4	3			6		8		10	11	2		9	1		7	5							
20	23	MILLWALL	2-0	Tait, Snowden(og)	5205		4	3			6		8		10		2		9	1	11	7	5							
21	30	Colchester Utd.	0-4		4377		4	2			6		8		10	9				1	11	7	5	3						
22	Dec 14	BRENTFORD	2-0	Fry, Barber	3744	1	4	2	8	5	6		9		10	11						7		3						
23	21	Shrewsbury Town	2-5	Astle, Tait	3738	1	4	2		5	6		8	9	10	11						7		3						
24	26	Oldham Athletic	0-2		15869		4	2		5			8	9		11		10		1		7		3	6					
25	28	OLDHAM ATHLETIC	4-2	Astle 3, Fry	7976		4	2		5			8	9		11		10				7		3	6					
26	Jan 11	BRISTOL CITY	1-1	Edwards	5824	1	4	2		5			8	9		11		10				7		3	6					
27	18	Port Vale	1-0	Astle	7337	1	4	2		5			8	9		11		10						3	6					
28	25	HULL CITY	0-1		6742	1	4	2		5		7	8	9		11		10						3	6					
29	Feb 1	PETERBOROUGH UTD.	0-0		7206	1	4	2	8	5		7	9			11		10						3	6					
30	8	CREWE ALEXANDRA	0-0		5380	1	4	2	8	5		7	9		10	11		6						3						
31	15	Crystal Palace	0-2		15867	1	4	2	8	5		7	9		10	11		6						3						
32	22	Watford	0-2		11370	1	4		9	5	6	7	8		10	11	2							3						
33	29	SOUTHEND UNITED	1-1	Flower	3608	1	4		9	5		7	8				2	10			11			3	6					
34	Mar 3	Barnsley	1-2	Bly	3709	1	4		9	5	6	7		8			2	10			11			3						
35	7	Wrexham	0-4		4836	1	4		9	5	6	7	8			11	2	10						3						
36	14	BOURNEMOUTH	1-3	Fry(p)	2640	1	4		8	5	6			9			2	10			11	7		3						
37	20	Southend United	1-3	Edwards	7575	1	4		8	5					10		2		9		11	7		3	6					
38	26	LUTON TOWN	1-1	Jones	4406	1			4	5				9	10		2	6	8		11	7		3						
39	28	BARNSLEY	1-1	Flower	3607	1			4	5				9	10		2	6	8		11	7		3						
40	30	Luton Town	0-2		8387	1			4	5			8				2	6	9		11	7		3						
41	Apr 4	Millwall	1-6	Fry	5418	1	2		4	5			8	9				6			11	7				10				
42	9	BRISTOL ROVERS	3-4	Fry 2(1p), Woolley	3882	1		2		5			8		10			6			11	7				9	3	4		
43	11	COLCHESTER UTD.	3-1	Flower 2, Woolley	3912			2			6		8		10					1	11	7	5			9	3	4		
44	18	Bristol Rovers	0-4		7102			2			6		8							1		7	5			9	3	4	10	11
45	22	Hull City	1-4	Flower	5106			2		5	6		8	9						1	11	7		3				4	10	
46	25	QUEENS PARK RANGERS	2-2	Flower, Tait	2861					5			8	9	10		2	6		1	11	7		3				4		
		Apps				24	39	35	18	38	25	16	41	27	26	28	27	22	15	22	17	32	8	23	8	4	3	5	2	1
		Goals					5						11	4	5	3			2		6	6				2				

One own goal

F.A. Cup

#	Date	Opponent	Score	Scorers	Att	Smith GH	Edwards RT	Bircumshaw A	Sheridan J	Gibson APS	Loxley H	Povey VR	Astle J	Bly TG	Tait RJ	Barber MJ	Hampton IK	Carver GF	Jones B	Butler PL	Flower AJ	Fry KF	Holder DJ	Agnew DY
R1	Nov 16	FRICKLEY COLLIERY	2-1	Astle, Tait	5896		4	3			6		8		10		2		9	1	11	7	5	
R2	Dec 7	Doncaster Rovers	1-1	Bly	8810	1	4	2		5	6		8	9	10	11						7		3
rep	Dec 10	DONCASTER ROVERS	1-2	Tait	10607	1	4	2		5	6		8	9	10	11						7		3

F.L. Cup

#	Date	Opponent	Score	Scorers	Att	Smith GH	Edwards RT	Bircumshaw A	Gibson APS	Loxley H	Astle J	Bly TG	Tait RJ	Barber MJ	Hampton IK	Jones B	Butler PL	Flower AJ	Fry KF	Holder DJ	Agnew DY
R2	Sep 25	BLACKBURN ROVERS	2-1	Jones, Astle	7030		4	3	5	6	10	9		11	2	8	1		7		
R3	Nov 5	BRADFORD PARK AVE.	3-2	Astle, Fry(p), Edwards	4002		4	3		6	8		10	11	2	9	1		7	5	
R4	Nov 13	PORTSMOUTH	3-2	Tait 2, Fry(p)	6132		4	3		6	8		10		2	9	1	11	7	5	
R5	Dec 17	MANCHESTER CITY	0-1		7330	1	4	2	5	6	8	9	10	11					7		3

		P	W	D	L	F	A	W	D	L	F	A	Pts
1	Coventry City	46	14	7	2	62	32	8	9	6	36	29	60
2	Crystal Palace	46	17	4	2	38	14	6	10	7	35	37	60
3	Watford	46	16	6	1	57	28	7	6	10	22	31	58
4	Bournemouth	46	17	4	2	47	15	7	4	12	32	43	56
5	Bristol City	46	13	7	3	52	24	7	8	8	32	40	55
6	Reading	46	15	5	3	49	26	6	5	12	30	36	52
7	Mansfield Town	46	15	8	0	51	20	5	3	15	25	42	51
8	Hull City	46	11	9	3	45	27	5	8	10	28	41	49
9	Oldham Athletic	46	13	3	7	44	35	7	5	11	29	35	48
10	Peterborough Utd.	46	13	6	4	52	27	5	5	13	23	43	47
11	Shrewsbury Town	46	13	6	4	43	19	5	5	13	30	61	47
12	Bristol Rovers	46	9	6	8	52	34	10	2	11	39	45	46
13	Port Vale	46	13	6	4	35	13	3	8	12	18	36	46
14	Southend United	46	9	10	4	42	26	6	5	12	35	52	45
15	Queen's Park Rgs.	46	13	4	6	47	34	5	5	13	29	44	45
16	Brentford	46	11	4	8	54	36	4	10	9	33	44	44
17	Colchester United	46	10	8	5	45	26	2	11	10	25	42	43
18	Luton Town	46	12	2	9	42	41	4	8	11	22	39	42
19	Walsall	46	7	9	7	34	35	6	5	12	25	41	40
20	Barnsley	46	9	9	5	34	29	5	3	14	34	65	39
21	Millwall	46	9	4	10	33	29	5	6	12	20	38	38
22	Crewe Alexandra	46	10	5	8	29	26	1	7	15	21	51	34
23	Wrexham	46	9	4	10	50	42	4	2	17	25	65	32
24	NOTTS COUNTY	46	7	8	8	29	26	2	1	20	16	66	27

1964/65   13th in Division Four

No	Date	Opponent	Score	Scorers	Att	Smith GH	Edwards RT	Agnew DY	Sheridan J	Gibson APS	Carver GF	Kavanagh E	Astle J	Bly TG	Hannah G	Barber MJ	Hampton IK	Lowe E	Docherty B	Flower AJ	Bircumshaw A	Tait B	Froggatt J	Rayner J	Robinson LJ	Coates DP	Povey VR	Pace DJ	Fawell D	Woolley R	Bates B
1	Aug 22	Wrexham	0-4		7911	1	2	3	4	5	6	7	8	9	10	11															
2	27	TRANMERE ROVERS	2-4	Astle, Flower(p)	7694	1		3	4	5		7	9		8		2	6	10	11											
3	29	SOUTHPORT	0-0		4916	1	5	3	4	6		7	9		8		2		10	11											
4	31	Tranmere Rovers	0-4		11407	1	5		4	6		7	8				2		10	11	3	9									
5	Sep 5	Bradford Park Ave.	2-2	Kavanagh, Gibson(p)	7064	1	5		4	6		7	9			11	2		10		3		8								
6	10	DARLINGTON	4-2	Sheridan, Docherty, Rayner, Astle	8460	1	5		4	6		7	9			11	2		10		3			8							
7	12	ALDERSHOT	0-0		7659	1	5		4	6		7	9			11	2		10		3			8							
8	14	Darlington	1-5	Gibson	5125	1	5		4	6		7	9						10	11	3			8	2						
9	18	Doncaster Rov.	0-0		11362	1	5	3	4	6		7	9						10	11	2			8							
10	26	CHESTERFIELD	5-1	Raynor 3, Kavanagh, Astle	7482	1	5	3	4	6		7	9						10	11	2			8							
11	28	Newport County	1-3	Astle	5802	1	5	3	4			7	9	8					10	11	2			6							
12	Oct 3	YORK CITY	3-1	Sheridan, Rayner, Povey	6490	1	5	3	4			7			8				10		2			9		6	11				
13	8	NEWPORT COUNTY	1-0	Povey	6137	1	5	3	4			7			8				10		2			9		6	11				
14	10	Brighton & Hove Alb.	0-6		14195	1	5	3	4			7			8						2		10	9		6	11				
15	17	OXFORD UNITED	0-0		4971	1	5	3	4						8	11			10		2			9		6	7				
16	22	CREWE ALEXANDRA	2-0	Docherty, Rayner	3970	1	5	3	4						8				10	11	2			9		6	7				
17	24	Barrow	0-2		2149	1	5	3	4	6									10	11	2			9		8	7				
18	29	STOCKPORT COUNTY	2-0	Hannah, Rayner	4312	1	9		4	5		7					2		10	11	3			8		6					
19	31	HARTLEPOOL UTD.	1-0	Edwards	4924	1	9	3	4	5		7							10	11	2			8		6					
20	Nov 7	Rochdale	1-1	Sheridan	4804	1	9	3	4	5		7							10	11	2			8		6					
21	21	Bradford City	2-0	Edwards, Flower	3127	1	9	3	4	5		7							10	11	2			8		6					
22	28	CHESTER	1-1	Rayner	5898	1	9	3	4	5		7							10	11	2			8		6					
23	Dec 12	WREXHAM	1-3	Rayner	4706	1	10	3	4	5		7								11	2			8		6		9			
24	19	Southport	0-0		1800	1		3	4	5					10					11	2	8				6	7	9			
25	26	Lincoln City	0-1		4969	1		3	4	5					10					11	2			8		6	7	9			
26	28	LINCOLN CITY	2-1	Pace 2	4472	1		3	4	5					10					11	2			8		6	7	9			
27	Jan 2	BRADFORD PARK AVE.	3-3	Rayner 2, Pace	6205	1		3	4	5					10					11	2			8		6	7	9			
28	16	Aldershot	2-1	Flower, Pace	3901	1		3	4	5					10					11	2			8		6	7	9			
29	23	DONCASTER ROV.	5-2	Pace 3, Walton 2(2og)	8045	1		3	4	5					10					11	2			8		6	7	9			
30	Feb 6	Chesterfield	0-0		7014	1		3	4	5					10					11	2			8		6	7	9			
31	13	York City	1-2	Flower	6188	1		3	4	5					10					11	2			8		6	7	9			
32	20	BRIGHTON & HOVE ALB.	1-2	Coates	5002	1	2	3	4	5		7			10					11				8		6		9			
33	24	Torquay United	1-2	Pace	3905	1	2	3	4	5		7			10					11				8		6		9			
34	27	Oxford United	0-4		7837	1	2	3		5	4	7			10					11						6		9	8		
35	Mar 6	BARROW	4-1	Pace, Povey, Kavanagh, Gibson(p)	4295	1	2	3		5	4	7			10									8		6	11	9			
36	10	Crewe Alexandra	1-2	Kavanagh	4094	1	2	3		5	4	7			10									8		6	11	9			
37	13	Hartlepool Utd.	2-2	Gibson(p), Pace	5031	1	2	3	4	5	6				10					11						8		9		7	
38	20	ROCHDALE	0-0		3219	1	2	3	4	5	6				10					11						8		9		7	
39	27	Millwall	1-4	Pace	6324	1	5	3	4	6									10	11	2			8				9		7	
40	Apr 3	BRADFORD CITY	1-0	Pace	3707	1	5		4	6							2		10	11	3			8		7		9			
41	10	Chester	1-4	Flower	5684	1	5		4	6							2		10	11	3			8		7		9			
42	17	TORQUAY UNITED	0-0		5046	1	8		4	5							2		10		3					6		9		7	11
43	19	Halifax Town	1-1	Bates	1913	1	8		4	5							2		10		3					6		9		7	11
44	20	HALIFAX TOWN	4-0	Edwards 2, Rayner, Flower	4080	1	8		4	5							2			7	3			10		6		9			11
45	23	Stockport County	1-0	Rayner	5880	1	8		4	5							2			7	3			10		6		9			11
46	29	MILLWALL	1-2	Edwards	7322	1	8		4	5							2			7	3			10		6		9			11
		Apps				46	37	33	43	40	6	25	11	2	22	5	15	1	25	35	35	3	2	32	1	34	19	24	1	4	5
		Goals					5		3	4		4	4		1				2	6				13		1	3	12			1

Two own goals

F.A. Cup

Rd	Date	Opponent	Score	Scorers	Att	Smith	Edwards	Agnew	Sheridan	Gibson	Kavanagh	Docherty	Flower	Bircumshaw	Rayner	Coates
R1	Nov 14	CHELMSFORD CITY	2-0	Rayner, Kavanagh	9870	1	9	3	4	5	7	10	11	2	8	6
R2	Dec 5	Brentford	0-4		9400	1	9	3	4	5	7	10	11	2	8	6

F.L. Cup

Rd	Date	Opponent	Score	Scorers	Att	Smith	Edwards	Agnew	Sheridan	Gibson	Kavanagh	Astle	Barber	Hampton	Docherty	Flower	Bircumshaw	Froggatt	Rayner	Coates
R1	Sep 2	NEWPORT COUNTY	3-2	Astle 2, Froggatt	2881	1	5		4	6	7	9	11	2	10		3	8		
R2	Sep 23	Torquay United	2-1	Astle 2	4734	1	5	3	4	6	7	9		2	10	11			8	
R3	Oct 26	Chelsea	0-4		6596	1	5		4	6	7			2	10	11	3		9	8

Division Four — Final Table

	Team	P	W	D	L	F	A	W	D	L	F	A	Pts
1	Brighton & Hove A.	46	18	5	0	68	20	8	6	9	34	37	63
2	Millwall	46	13	10	0	45	15	10	6	7	33	30	62
3	York City	46	20	1	2	63	21	8	5	10	28	35	62
4	Oxford United	46	18	4	1	54	13	5	11	7	33	31	61
5	Tranmere Rovers	46	20	2	1	72	20	7	4	12	27	36	60
6	Rochdale	46	15	4	4	46	22	7	10	6	28	31	58
7	Bradford Park Ave.	46	14	8	1	52	22	6	9	8	34	40	57
8	Chester	46	19	1	3	75	26	6	5	12	44	55	56
9	Doncaster Rovers	46	13	6	4	46	25	7	5	11	38	47	51
10	Crewe Alexandra	46	11	8	4	55	34	7	5	11	35	47	49
11	Torquay United	46	11	5	7	41	33	10	2	11	29	37	49
12	Chesterfield	46	13	5	5	36	22	7	3	13	22	48	48
13	NOTTS COUNTY	46	12	7	4	43	23	3	7	13	18	50	44
14	Wrexham	46	12	5	6	59	37	5	4	14	25	55	43
15	Hartlepools United	46	11	10	2	44	28	4	3	16	17	57	43
16	Newport County	46	14	5	4	54	26	3	3	17	31	55	42
17	Darlington	46	14	2	7	52	30	4	4	15	32	57	42
18	Aldershot	46	14	3	6	46	25	1	4	18	18	59	37
19	Bradford City	46	9	2	12	37	36	3	6	14	33	52	32
20	Southport	46	5	9	9	35	45	3	7	13	23	44	32
21	Barrow	46	9	4	10	30	38	3	2	18	29	67	30
22	Lincoln City	46	8	4	11	35	33	3	3	18	23	66	28
23	Halifax Town	46	9	4	10	37	37	2	2	19	17	66	28
24	Stockport County	46	8	4	11	30	34	2	3	18	14	53	27

- 1964/65 Season -

Back: Gibson, Sheridan, Astle, Edwards, Coates, Woolley, Flower, Lee, Hampton, Shrewsbury
Middle: Coleman (Scout), Agnew, Hannah, Bircumshaw, Butler, Smith, Froggatt, Woodfield, L.Robinson, Bly, Wheeler(Train)
Front: B.Tait, Kavanagh, Docherty, Ward, J.Robinson, Lowe (Player/manager), Barber, Carver, Stead, Povey

- 1965/66 Season -

Back: Coates, Hampton, Bates, Moulden, Shiels, Woolley, Gibson, Hannah, Carver, Pace
Middle: Bircumshaw, Flower, Barber, Smith, Sheridan, Butler, Kirkup, Still, Edwards
Front: Wheeler(Trainer), Agnew, Stead, Northridge, Rogers, Beresford, Ward, Coleman

1965/66 8th in Division Four

#	Date	Opponent	Score	Scorers	Att	Smith GH	Hampton IK	Bircumshaw A	Coates DP	Gibson APS	Still RG	Moulden A	Edwards RT	Pace DJ	Beresford J	Kirkup F	Bates B	Hannah G	Shiels D	Sheridan J	Agnew DY	Woolley R	Flower AJ	Carver GF	Butler PL	McNamee P	Benskin D	Thompson T	Vincent R	Ward J	Needham DW
1	Aug 21	DARLINGTON	0-0		7388	1	2	3	4	5	6			9		11	7	8	10												
2	23	Stockport County	3-1	Bates 2, Shiels	11670	1	2	3	4	5	6			9		11	7	8	10												
3	28	Lincoln City	2-1	Pace 2	6613	1	2	3	4	5	6			9		11	7	8	10												
4	Sep 4	SOUTHPORT	1-2	Pace	5903	1	2	3	4	5	6			9		11	7	8	10												
5	11	CHESTER	3-3	Bates 2, Shiels	4916	1	2	3	6	5		8			10	11	7		9	4											
6	16	STOCKPORT COUNTY	1-1	Beresford	6623	1	2	3		5	6	8			10	11	7		9	4											
7	18	Halifax Town	1-0	Moulden	2523	1	2	3		5	6	8			10	11	7		9	4											
8	25	PORT VALE	3-1	Bates 2, Shiels	6086	1	2	3		5	6	8			10	11	7		9	4											
9	Oct 1	Crewe Alexandra	0-1		3760	1	2			5		8	10		6	11	7		9	4	3										
10	7	COLCHESTER UTD.	1-0	Hampton	5681	1	2			5		8			6	11	7		10	4	3	9									
11	9	Bradford Park Ave.	0-4		4501	1	2	7		5		8			6	11			10	4	3	9									
12	16	ALDERSHOT	2-0	Beresford 2	5407	1	2			5		8		3	10	11			9	4			7	6							
13	25	Newport County	2-1	Kirkup, Rowland(og)	3985	1	2			5				3	10	11			9	4			8	6							
14	30	TORQUAY UNITED	1-1	Bates	7174	1	2			5			3	9	10	11	7			4			8	6							
15	Nov 6	Chesterfield	0-0		8575	1	2			5			3		10	11	7			4			8	6							
16	20	Luton Town	1-5	Shiels	6486		2	3	4	5	10	8					7		9	6			11			1					
17	22	Colchester Utd.	1-4	Still	2768		2	3	4	5	10	8					7		9	6			11			1					
18	27	BARROW	0-2		3442	1	2	3	8	5	6					11	7		9	4			10								
19	Dec 11	DONCASTER ROV.	1-2	Still	5049	1	2	3		5	9	10	6			11	8						7	4							
20	27	Tranmere Rovers	3-0	Still 2, Shiels	10592	1	2	3		5	9	10	6			11	8						7	4							
21	Jan 1	BRADFORD PARK AVE.	2-0	Still, Bates	6277	1	2	3		5	9	10	6			11	8						7	4							
22	8	Rochdale	2-0	Sheridan, Flower	2677	1	2	3		5	9	10	6			11	8						7	4							
23	15	NEWPORT COUNTY	1-1	Bates	4605	1	2	3		5	9	10	6			11	8						7	4							
24	29	Darlington	0-1		7712	1	2	3		5	9	10	6			7							8	4				11			
25	Feb 5	LINCOLN CITY	2-1	Still, Beresford	5122	1	2	3		5	9		6		10	7			12	4			8					11			
26	12	Barnsley	1-1	Gibson(p)	2516	1	2			5	9	10	6			11	8			4	3		7								
27	19	Southport	0-1		5297	1	2	7		5	9	10	6				8			4	3		7								
28	26	Chester	1-1	Benskin	8704	1	2			5	9	10	6				8			4	3		7				11				
29	Mar 5	BARNSLEY	0-1		5894	1	2			5	9	10	6				8			4	3		7	12				11			
30	9	Aldershot	0-0		3593	1	2			5		10	6						9		3		7	8				11	4		
31	12	HALIFAX TOWN	1-1	Carver	3961	1	2			5		10	6			11			9		3		7	8					4		
32	19	Port Vale	1-0	Flower	5619	1	2			5			10		6						3		7	8				11	4	9	
33	26	CREWE ALEXANDRA	0-1		3256		2			5	9		8		6	11					3		7	10	1			4			
34	Apr 2	CHESTERFIELD	2-0	Still 2	1927	1	2			5	9		6		10	11	8				3		7	4							
35	8	Wrexham	3-1	Beresford, Kirkup, Thompson	7262	1	2			5	9		6		10	11					3		7	4				8			
36	9	Hartlepool Utd.	0-2		4001	1	2			5	9		6		10	11					3		7	4				8			
37	11	WREXHAM	3-1	Still, Beresford, Shiels	4667	1	2			5	9		6		10				7		3		11	4				8			
38	16	LUTON TOWN	1-1	Edwards	4740	1	2			5	9		6		10	11					3		7	4				8			
39	23	Barrow	1-2	Agnew	4151	1	2			5	9		6		10	11					3		7	4				8			
40	27	Bradford City	4-0	Beresford 2, Still, Flower	2370	1				5	9		6		10	11					3		7	4			2	8			
41	30	HARTLEPOOL UTD.	1-0	Kirkup	4448	1	12			6	9				10	11					3		7	4			2	8			5
42	May 6	Doncaster Rov.	3-0	Gibson, Beresford 2	16389	1				6	9				10	11					3		7	4			2	8			5
43	9	Torquay United	0-2		8298	1				6	9				10	11					3		7	4			2	8			5
44	13	TRANMERE ROVERS	1-2	King(og)	4816	1	3			6	9				10	11							7	4			2	8			5
45	18	BRADFORD CITY	2-1	Still, Beresford	3130	1	2			6	9				10	11					3		7	4				8			5
46	21	ROCHDALE	3-3	Still 2, Bates	3488	1				6	9	2			10	11					3		7	4				8			5
		Apps				43	42	19	8	46	34	23	29	5	29	29	26	3	29	25	23	1	35	22	3	4	4	16	1	5	6
		Goals					1			2	13	1	1	3	11	3	10		6	1	1		3	1			1	1		1	

Two own goals

F.A. Cup

Rd	Date	Opponent	Score	Scorers	Att	Smith GH	Hampton IK	Gibson APS	Edwards RT	Beresford J	Kirkup F	Bates B	Shiels D	Sheridan J	Flower AJ	Carver GF
R1	Nov 13	Southend United	1-3	Sheridan	5375	1	2	5	3	10	11	7	9	4	8	6

F.L. Cup

Rd	Date	Opponent	Score	Scorers	Att	Smith GH	Hampton IK	Bircumshaw A	Coates DP	Gibson APS	Still RG	Moulden A	Edwards RT	Pace DJ	Kirkup F	Bates B	Hannah G	Shiels D	Sheridan J	Agnew DY
R1	Sep 1	CHESTERFIELD	0-0		6076	1	2	3	4	5	6			9	11	7	8	10		
rep	Sep 8	Chesterfield	1-2	Bates	2188	1	2	3	6	5		10	8		11	7			4	9

	P	W	D	L	F	A	W	D	L	F	A	Pts
1 Doncaster Rovers	46	15	6	2	49	21	9	5	9	36	33	59
2 Darlington	46	16	3	4	41	17	9	6	8	31	36	59
3 Torquay United	46	17	2	4	43	20	7	8	8	29	29	58
4 Colchester United	46	13	7	3	45	21	10	3	10	25	26	56
5 Tranmere Rovers	46	15	1	7	56	32	9	7	7	37	34	56
6 Luton Town	46	19	2	2	65	27	5	6	12	25	43	56
7 Chester	46	15	5	3	52	27	5	7	11	27	43	52
8 NOTTS COUNTY	46	9	8	6	32	25	10	4	9	29	28	50
9 Newport County	46	14	6	3	46	24	4	6	13	29	51	48
10 Southport	46	15	6	2	47	20	3	6	14	21	49	48
11 Bradford Park Ave.	46	14	2	7	59	31	7	3	13	43	61	47
12 Barrow	46	12	8	3	48	31	4	7	12	24	45	47
13 Stockport County	46	12	4	7	42	29	6	2	15	29	41	42
14 Crewe Alexandra	46	12	4	7	42	23	4	5	14	19	40	41
15 Halifax Town	46	11	6	6	46	31	4	5	14	21	44	41
16 Barnsley	46	11	6	6	43	24	4	4	15	31	54	40
17 Aldershot	46	12	6	5	47	27	3	4	16	28	57	40
18 Hartlepools United	46	13	4	6	44	22	3	4	16	19	53	40
19 Port Vale	46	12	7	4	38	18	3	2	18	10	41	39
20 Chesterfield	46	8	9	6	37	35	4	4	14	25	43	39
21 Rochdale	46	12	1	10	46	27	4	4	15	25	60	37
22 Lincoln City	46	9	7	7	37	29	4	4	15	20	53	37
23 Bradford City	46	10	5	8	37	34	2	8	13	26	60	37
24 Wrexham	46	10	4	9	43	43	3	5	15	29	61	35

1966/67 20th in Division Four

#	Date	Opponent	Score	Scorers	Att	Smith GH	Chalmers L	Hampton IK	Thompson T	Gibson APS	Edwards RT	Bates B	Marshall S	Still RG	Beresford J	Bowers J	Flower AJ	Clarke D	Thorne T	Agnew DY	Needham DW	Garner W	Cargill J	Smith, Jack	Upton F	Harkin T	Coates DP	Shrewsbury P	Rose MJ	Wileman R	Watson DV	Crispin T
1	Aug 20	Bradford Park Ave.	1-4	Bates	6283	1	2	3	4	5	6	7	8	9	10	11																
2	27	PORT VALE	0-0		5648	1	2	3	4	5	6	7		9	10		8	11														
3	Sep 3	Crewe Alexandra	1-4	Edwards	3098	1	2	3	4	5	6	7		9	10		11	8														
4	7	WREXHAM	2-2	Thompson, Marshall	3878	1	2		8	6	4		10				7	11		3	5	9										
5	10	BARROW	2-2	Marshall 2	4029			2	8	6	4	7	10					11		3	5	9	1									
6	16	York City	1-4	Baker(og)	4909		2	3	4	5	6	7	8	9				11					1	10								
7	19	Southport	1-2	Marshall	6249		2	3	4	5	6	7	8	9				11					1	10								
8	24	LINCOLN CITY	2-1	Marshall 2	5167	1	2	3		5	4	7	8					11						10	6	9						
9	26	Wrexham	2-3	Marshall. Gibson(p)	6554	1	2	3		5	4	7	8					11						10	6	9						
10	Oct 1	Chesterfield	1-1	Harkin	5341	1	2	3		5	4		8				7	11						10	6	9						
11	8	ALDERSHOT	3-0	Beresford 2, Harkin	4911	1	2	3		5	4				10		7	11						8	6	9						
12	15	Luton Town	5-2	Upton 2, Harkin 2, Gibson(p)	5743	1	2	3		5	4				10		7	11						8	6	9						
13	19	SOUTHPORT	0-1		6491	1	2	3		5	4				10		7	11						8	6	9						
14	22	BARNSLEY	0-3		6373	1	2	3		5	4				10		7	11						8	6	9						
15	29	Newport County	0-1		3670	1	2		3	5	4	7	8	12										10	6	9						
16	Nov 1	CREWE ALEXANDRA	1-1	Harkin	2919	1		2	3	5	4		12		10		7	11						8	6	9						
17	5	BRENTFORD	3-2	Harkin 2, J Smith	3883	1		2	3	5	4				10		7	11						8	6	9						
18	12	Halifax Town	2-5	J Smith 2	2416	1		2	3	5	4				10		7	11						8	6	9						
19	19	HARTLEPOOL UTD.	0-0		3922	1	2		3	5	6	7		9				11	4					8		10						
20	Dec 3	BRADFORD CITY	1-3	J Smith	3913	1	2		3	5	4		8				7	11						10	6	9						
21	17	BRADFORD PARK AVE.	2-1	Bates 2	3051	1	2		3	5		8	7			12		11						10	6	9	4					
22	27	ROCHDALE	2-0	J Smith 2	4810	1	2		3	5		8	7			12		11						10	6	9	4					
23	31	Port Vale	0-0		5359	1	2		3	5		8	7					11						10	6	9	4		12			
24	Jan 14	Barrow	1-0	Edwards	7243	1	2		3	5		8	7					11						10	6	9	4					
25	21	YORK CITY	2-0	Edwards, Harkin	4718		2		3	5		8	7					11					1	10	6	9	4					
26	27	Rochdale	1-1	J Smith	2358		2		3	5		8	7					11					1	10	6	9	4					
27	Feb 4	Lincoln City	1-2	Harkin	5122		2		3	5		8	7					11					1	10	6	9	4					
28	11	CHESTERFIELD	0-2		5791		2		3	5		8			10			11					1	12	6	9	4	7				
29	18	Southend United	0-1		8476		2	12	3	5		8	10		7			11					1		6	9	4					
30	25	Aldershot	1-4	Chalmers	3855		2		3	5		8			7			11			12		1		9	10	4					
31	Mar 4	LUTON TOWN	1-2	Harkin	3909		2		3		6		7				11				5		1	8	9	10	4					
32	10	SOUTHEND UNITED	1-0	Bates	3858		2		3	5		7	8				11				6		1	10	9		4					
33	18	Barnsley	0-0		5278		2		3	6		7	8								5			11	9	10	4		1			
34	24	Chester	2-1	J Smith, Gibson(p)	4292		2		3	6		7	8				10				5				9		4			1	11	
35	25	EXETER CITY	0-1		4258		2		3	6		7	8				10				5				9		4		12	1	11	
36	28	CHESTER	3-0	Bates, Marshall 2	3398		2				4	7	8		11						5				9	10	6		1			3
37	Apr 1	Brentford	0-1		7764		2			3	4	7	8	10	11						5				9		6		1			
38	8	HALIFAX TOWN	2-1	Still 2	3024		2			3	4	7	8	10	11						5				9		6		1			
39	10	Stockport County	0-2		8556		2			3	4	7	8	10	11						5				9		6		1			
40	15	Hartlepool Utd.	1-2	Bates	4674		2				3	5	11	7	10						6				9		4		1		8	
41	22	NEWPORT COUNTY	2-1	Marshall 2	3455		2					6	7	8	10		11				5						4		1		9	3
42	26	STOCKPORT COUNTY	2-2	Marshall, Bates	4536	1	2	10	6			7	8				11				5				9		4					3
43	29	Bradford City	1-3	Upton	3856	1	2	10	6			7	8				11				5				9		4		12			3
44	May 6	TRANMERE ROVERS	0-0		4209		2	10	6			7					11				5		12	9	8		4		1			3
45	13	Exeter City	0-1		3417		2				6	5	7	8			11				4			10	9				1			3
46	17	Tranmere Rovers	0-3		6817		2				6	5	7				11				4			10	9				1		8	3
		Apps				24	35	24	37	46	30	35	25	12	21	5	22	24	2	2	17	2	10	32	34	28	24	2	12	2	4	6
		Goals					1		1	3	3	7	12	2	2									8	3	10						

One own goal

F.A. Cup

	Date	Opponent	Score	Scorers	Att	Smith GH	Chalmers L	Hampton IK	Thompson T	Gibson APS	Edwards RT	Bates B	Marshall S	Still RG	Beresford J	Bowers J	Flower AJ	Clarke D	Thorne T	Agnew DY	Needham DW	Garner W	Cargill J	Smith, Jack	Upton F	Harkin T	Coates DP	Shrewsbury P	Rose MJ	Wileman R	Watson DV	Crispin T
R1	Nov 26	Oldham Athletic	1-3	Marshall	12200	1	2		3	5	4		8				7	11						10	6	9						

F.L. Cup

	Date	Opponent	Score	Scorers	Att	Smith GH	Chalmers L	Hampton IK	Thompson T	Gibson APS	Edwards RT	Bates B	Marshall S	Still RG	Beresford J	Bowers J	Flower AJ	Clarke D	Thorne T	Agnew DY	Needham DW	Garner W	Cargill J	Smith, Jack	Upton F	Harkin T	Coates DP	Shrewsbury P	Rose MJ	Wileman R	Watson DV	Crispin T
R1	Aug 24	MANSFIELD TOWN	1-1	Beresford	7002	1	2	3	4	5	6	7		9	10		8	11														
rep	Aug 29	Mansfield Town	0-3		6081	1	2	3	4	5	6	7	12	9	10		8	11														

		P	W	D	L	F	A	W	D	L	F	A	Pts
1	Stockport County	46	16	5	2	41	18	10	7	6	28	24	64
2	Southport	46	19	2	2	47	15	4	11	8	22	27	59
3	Barrow	46	12	8	3	35	18	12	3	8	41	36	59
4	Tranmere Rovers	46	14	6	3	42	20	8	8	7	24	23	58
5	Crewe Alexandra	46	14	5	4	42	26	7	7	9	28	29	54
6	Southend United	46	15	5	3	44	12	7	4	12	26	37	53
7	Wrexham	46	11	12	0	46	20	5	8	10	30	42	52
8	Hartlepools United	46	15	3	5	44	29	7	4	12	22	35	51
9	Brentford	46	13	7	3	36	19	5	6	12	22	37	49
10	Aldershot	46	14	4	5	48	19	4	8	11	24	38	48
11	Bradford City	46	13	4	6	48	31	6	6	11	26	31	48
12	Halifax Town	46	10	11	2	37	27	5	3	15	22	41	44
13	Port Vale	46	9	7	7	33	27	5	8	10	22	31	43
14	Exeter City	46	11	6	6	30	24	3	9	11	20	36	43
15	Chesterfield	46	13	6	4	33	16	4	2	17	27	47	42
16	Barnsley	46	8	7	8	30	28	5	8	10	30	36	41
17	Luton Town	46	15	5	3	47	23	1	4	18	12	50	41
18	Newport County	46	9	9	5	35	23	3	7	13	21	40	40
19	Chester	46	8	5	10	24	32	7	5	11	30	46	40
20	NOTTS COUNTY	46	10	7	6	31	25	3	4	16	22	47	37
21	Rochdale	46	10	4	9	30	27	3	7	13	23	48	37
22	York City	46	11	5	7	45	31	1	6	16	20	48	35
23	Bradford Park Ave.	46	7	6	10	30	34	4	7	12	22	45	35
24	Lincoln City	46	7	8	8	39	39	2	5	16	19	43	31

- 1966/67 Season -

Back: Bates, Gibson, Edwards, Still, Coates, Thorne, Needham, Flower, Garner, J.Marshall
Standing: Millborne, Chalmers, S.Marshall, Cargill, Beresford, G.Smith, Clarke, Agnew, Hyde
Sitting: Burkitt (Man), Hampton, Thompson, Laurie (Dir), Levin (Dir), Hopcroft (Chair), Pounder (Dir), Bateman (Dir), Crispin,
Wileman, Wheeler (Train)   Front: Stewart, Battle, Gamble, Preston

- 1967/68 Season -

Back: Ball, K.W.Smith, Rose, J.Smith, Needham, Gibson
Front: Oakes, Pring, Bates, Bradd, J.B.Murphy, Elliott

1967/68   17th in Division Four

Player columns (left to right):
Rose MJ · Cartwright M · Gibson APS · Rushton B · Watson DV · Oakes DR · Weaver E · Marshall S · Smith Jack · Smith KW · Bates B · Chalmers L · Thompson T · Elliott JW · Needham DW · Yeomans K · Crispin T · Bradd LJ · Farmer RJ · Murphy F. John · Ball GH · Gadsby MD · Pring KD · McGovern P · Murphy James B

#	Date	Opponent	Score	Scorers	Att
1	Aug 19	CHESTER	1-2	Marshall	6599
2	26	Chesterfield	0-4		5932
3	Sep 2	EXETER CITY	1-0	J Smith	3741
4	6	PORT VALE	0-0		4338
5	9	Darlington	2-2	Marshall, KW Smith	4642
6	16	ALDERSHOT	0-1		4451
7	23	Workington	1-5	Marshall	2109
8	25	Port Vale	1-4	KW Smith	4021
9	30	LINCOLN CITY	0-0		6239
10	Oct 4	CREWE ALEXANDRA	1-0	DV Watson	5550
11	7	BRADFORD PARK AVE.	0-0		7355
12	14	Brentford	1-2	Elliott	7443
13	21	ROCHDALE	2-0	Bradd, Elliott	5832
14	25	Crewe Alexandra	0-4		6308
15	28	York City	2-4	Bates 2	4982
16	Nov 4	NEWPORT COUNTY	3-1	Weaver, Bradd, Collins(og)	4456
17	10	Hartlepool Utd.	1-3	Weaver	4141
18	15	Exeter City	3-3	Gibson, Weaver, Farmer	4009
19	18	SWANSEA TOWN	3-2	Weaver, J Smith, Thompson	5180
20	25	Barnsley	1-3	Marshall	8361
21	Dec 2	WREXHAM	1-1	Elliott	4878
22	16	Chester	3-1	Bradd 2, Farmer(p)	3567
23	23	CHESTERFIELD	1-0	FJ Murphy	9990
24	26	Bradford City	1-5	Farmer	11013
25	30	BRADFORD CITY	1-0	Bates	7404
26	Jan 13	DARLINGTON	0-0		4426
27	20	Aldershot	0-0		4345
28	Feb 3	WORKINGTON	2-1	Bradd 2	5259
29	10	Lincoln City	3-1	Farmer, KW Smith (p), Marshall	6554
30	17	HALIFAX TOWN	1-3	KW Smith (p)	5880
31	24	Swansea Town	0-2		12483
32	Mar 2	BRENTFORD	2-1	JB Murphy, Farmer	4486
33	8	Doncaster Rov.	1-3	Pring	9765
34	16	Rochdale	0-0		1895
35	23	YORK CITY	1-1	Bradd	4174
36	30	Newport County	0-1		2023
37	Apr 6	HARTLEPOOL UTD.	0-3		4976
38	12	Luton Town	0-2		16631
39	13	Bradford Park Ave.	4-1	JB Murphy, FJ Murphy, Bates, Burgin(og)	2165
40	15	LUTON TOWN	2-2	Bates, JB Murphy(p)	7920
41	20	BARNSLEY	1-4	Elliott	8674
42	22	Southend United	1-0	Bradd	9673
43	27	Wrexham	0-2		3933
44	May 1	DONCASTER ROV.	0-2		4070
45	4	SOUTHEND UNITED	4-3	Bradd 2, Elliott, J Smith	3848
46	10	Halifax Town	1-0	Pring	1802

Played in game 44: CR Watson (1).

Appearances and goals:

	Rose MJ	Cartwright M	Gibson APS	Rushton B	Watson DV	Oakes DR	Weaver E	Marshall S	Smith Jack	Smith KW	Bates B	Chalmers L	Thompson T	Elliott JW	Needham DW	Yeomans K	Crispin T	Bradd LJ	Farmer RJ	Murphy F.John	Ball GH	Gadsby MD	Pring KD	McGovern P	Murphy James B
Apps	34	15	39	3	21	25	17	24	33	45	19	16	13	40	31	1	2	28	30	18	28	11	17	3	16
Goals		1		1			4	5	3	4	5			1	5			10	5	2			2		3

Two own goals

F.A. Cup

	Date	Opponent	Score		Att
R1	Dec 9	Runcorn	0-1		6246

F.A. Cup line-up (shirt numbers): Rose 1, Gibson 3, Weaver 7, Smith Jack 9, Smith KW 6, Chalmers 4, Thompson 11, Elliott 5, Bradd 10, Farmer 8, Ball 2, Pring 12

F.L. Cup

	Date	Opponent	Score		Att
R1	Aug 23	ROTHERHAM UTD.	0-1		4492

F.L. Cup line-up (shirt numbers): Rose 1, Cartwright 2, Gibson 3, Rushton 11, Watson 5, Oakes 4, Marshall 8, Smith Jack 9, Smith KW 10, Bates 7, Thompson 6, Elliott 12

Division Four — Final Table

		P	W	D	L	F	A	W	D	L	F	A	Pts
1	Luton Town	46	19	3	1	55	16	8	9	6	32	28	66
2	Barnsley	46	17	6	0	43	14	7	7	9	25	32	61
3	Hartlepools United	46	15	7	1	34	12	10	3	10	26	34	60
4	Crewe Alexandra	46	13	10	0	44	18	7	8	8	30	31	58
5	Bradford City	46	14	5	4	41	22	9	6	8	31	29	57
6	Southend United	46	12	8	3	45	21	8	6	9	32	37	54
7	Chesterfield	46	15	4	4	47	20	6	7	10	24	30	53
8	Wrexham	46	17	3	3	47	12	3	10	10	25	41	53
9	Aldershot	46	10	11	2	36	19	8	6	9	34	36	53
10	Doncaster Rovers	46	12	8	3	36	16	6	7	10	30	40	51
11	Halifax Town	46	10	6	7	34	24	5	10	8	18	25	46
12	Newport County	46	11	7	5	32	22	5	6	12	26	41	45
13	Lincoln City	46	11	3	9	41	31	6	6	11	30	37	43
14	Brentford	46	13	4	6	41	24	5	3	15	20	40	43
15	Swansea Town	46	11	8	4	38	25	5	2	16	25	52	42
16	Darlington	46	6	11	6	31	27	6	6	11	16	26	41
17	NOTTS COUNTY	46	10	7	6	27	27	5	4	14	26	52	41
18	Port Vale	46	10	5	8	41	31	2	10	11	20	41	39
19	Rochdale	46	9	8	6	35	32	3	6	14	10	40	38
20	Exeter City	46	9	7	7	30	30	2	9	12	15	35	38
21	York City	46	9	6	8	44	30	2	8	13	21	38	36
22	Chester	46	6	6	11	35	38	3	8	12	22	40	32
23	Workington	46	8	8	7	35	29	2	3	18	19	58	31
24	Bradford Park Ave.	46	3	7	13	18	35	1	8	14	12	47	23

1968/69 — 19th in Division Four

#	Date		Opponent	Result	Scorers	Att.
1	Aug	10	Lincoln City	0-5		8177
2		17	SOUTHEND UNITED	2-2	Bradd 2	5227
3		24	Bradford Park Ave.	1-1	JB Murphy	2395
4		28	HALIFAX TOWN	1-2	Bradd	4980
5		31	ALDERSHOT	0-2		5300
6	Sep	7	NEWPORT COUNTY	3-1	KW Smith, Bradd, JB Murphy	3579
7		14	Darlington	2-3	JB Murphy, Masson	6291
8		17	Grimsby Town	0-2		2361
9		21	SWANSEA TOWN	0-3		4167
10		28	Wrexham	2-3	Bradd, Masson	4522
11	Oct	5	Chesterfield	2-0	Bradd, JB Murphy	5611
12		8	Halifax Town	1-3	Bradd	3030
13		12	PORT VALE	0-0		4127
14		19	Exeter City	0-0		4148
15		26	BRENTFORD	0-2		4173
16	Nov	4	Peterborough Utd.	0-1		4553
17		9	CHESTER	3-2	Bates, Bradd, Masson	3089
18		23	YORK CITY	0-0		3295
19		30	Rochdale	0-0		2673
20	Dec	7	Bradford City	1-1	Needham	4280
21		14	Port Vale	2-0	J Smith, Elliott	4169
22		21	EXETER CITY	3-1	Bradd 2, Masson	4605
23		26	CHESTERFIELD	2-1	Masson(p), Barker	9801
24	Jan	4	Scunthorpe Utd.	1-2	Barker	3311
25		11	BRADFORD CITY	0-2		4776
26		18	Chester	1-3	Masson	4846
27		25	PETERBOROUGH UTD.	2-1	Masson, Butlin	5740
28	Feb	1	DONCASTER ROV.	1-1	Needham	6587
29		22	Colchester Utd.	1-1	Butlin	6612
30	Mar	1	LINCOLN CITY	0-0		5870
31		5	SCUNTHORPE UTD.	1-0	Butlin	3311
32		7	Southend United	0-4		11052
33		11	Doncaster Rov.	0-0		10232
34		15	BRADFORD PARK AVE.	5-0	Butlin 2, Barker 2, Brown(og)	3629
35		22	Aldershot	0-0		5352
36		26	Brentford	0-0		3361
37		29	Newport County	0-0		1749
38	Apr	5	WREXHAM	5-0	Masson 2, Butlin, Elliott, Barker	5325
39		7	GRIMSBY TOWN	2-1	Butlin, Masson	6307
40		8	Workington	1-1	Masson	1749
41		12	Swansea Town	0-3		1984
42		16	WORKINGTON	0-0		4305
43		19	DARLINGTON	0-0		4444
44		23	York City	0-2		3095
45		28	ROCHDALE	1-1	Butlin	3678
46	May	2	COLCHESTER UTD.	2-0	Masson 2	3576

Player appearances (shirt numbers; 12 = substitute)

#	Rose MJ	Cartwright M	Ball GH	Smith, Jack	Needham DW	Gibson APS	Pring KD	Bates B	Bradd LJ	Murphy, James B.	Elliott JW	Smith KW	Wilson A	Smith GWC	Murphy, F.John	Oakes DR	Farmer RJ	Worthington PR	Masson DS	Stubbs BH	Barker RJ	Butlin BD
1	1	2	3	4	5	6	7	8	9	10	11					12						
2	1		2	4	5	6	7	8	9	10	11	3				12						
3	1		2	4	5	6	7	8	9	10	11	3				12						
4	1		2	4	5	6	11	8	9	10		3	7									
5			2	4	5	6	11	7	9	8		3		1	10	12						
6			2	4	5		7	11	9	10		3		1		6	8					
7			2	4	5			11	9	8		6		1		12	7	3	10			
8			2	4	5		11	8		9		6		1		7		3	10			
9			2		5	12	11	9	7			6		1		4		3	10	8		
10	1		2		5	7	11	9	8							4	6	3	10			
11	1		2		5	6	7	11	9	8						4		3	10			
12	1		2		5	6	7	11	9	8						12	4	3	10			
13	1		2		5	6	7	11	9	8						4		3	10			
14	1		2	8	5	6		11	9							7	4	3	10			
15	1		2	8	5	6		11	9							7	4	3	10			
16	1		2		5	6	7	8	9		11	3				10	4					
17	1		2		5	6	7	8	9		11	3				4			10			
18	1				5	6	7	9	8		11	3				4		2	10			
19	1			12	5	6	7	9	8		11	3				4		2	10			
20	1			9	5	6	7	8			11	3				4		2	10			
21	1			9	5	6	7	8			11	3				4		2	10			
22					5	6	7	9			11	3		1		4		2	10		8	
23					5	6	7	9			11	3				4		2	10		8	
24	1	12			5	6	7	9			11	3				4		2	10		8	
25	1		2		5	6	7	9			11					4		3	10		8	
26	1		2		5	6	7	9			11	12				4		3	10		8	
27					5	6	11	7				3				4		2	10		8	9
28	1				5	3	11	7			12					6	4	2	10		8	9
29					5		11	7						1		3	4	2	10	6	8	9
30					5		11	4	7					1		3	6	2	10		8	9
31					5		11	4	7					1		3	6	2	10		8	9
32					5	3	12	11	7					1		6	4	2	10		8	9
33	1		2		5			7			11					6	4	3	10		8	9
34	1		2		5			7			11					6	4	3	10		8	9
35	1		2		5			7			11					6	4	3	10		8	9
36	1		2		5			7			11					6	4	3	10		8	9
37	1		2		5			7		12	11					6	4	3	10		8	9
38	1		2		5			7								6	4	3	10		8	9
39	1		2		5			7			11					6	4	3	10		8	9
40	1		2		5	4	11	7								6		3	10		8	9
41	1		2		5		7				11					6	4	3	10		8	9
42	1		2		5		11		7		12					6	4	3	10		8	9
43	1		2		5		11	7	10							6	4	3			8	9
44	1		2		5		11	7								6	4	3	10		8	9
45	1		2		5		11	7								6	4	3	10		8	9
46	1		2		5		11	7				12				6	4	3	10		8	9
Apps	36	1	34	13	44	27	27	42	31	17	24	20	1	10	1	31	39	38	38	2	25	20
Goals				1	2			1	10	4	2	1							13		5	8

One own goal

F.A. Cup

	Date		Opponent	Result	Att.	Rose MJ	Ball GH	Needham DW	Gibson APS	Pring KD	Bates B	Bradd LJ	Elliott JW	Smith KW	Oakes DR	Worthington PR	Masson DS
R1	Nov	16	Doncaster Rov.	0-1	8318	1		5	6	7	8	9	11	3	4	2	10

F.L. Cup

	Date		Opponent	Result	Att.	Rose	Ball	SmJ	Need	Gib	Pring	Bates	Bradd	MurJ	Ell	SmKW	Oakes
R1	Aug	14	Grimsby Town	0-0	4627	1	2	4	5	6	7	8	9	10	11	3	12
rep	Aug	21	GRIMSBY TOWN	0-1	6082	1	2	4	5	6	7	8	9	10	11	3	

Division Four 1968/69 — Final Table

		P	W	D	L	F	A	W	D	L	F	A	Pts
1	Doncaster Rovers	46	13	8	2	42	16	8	9	6	23	22	59
2	Halifax Town	46	15	5	3	36	18	5	12	6	17	19	57
3	Rochdale	46	14	7	2	47	11	4	13	6	21	24	56
4	Bradford City	46	11	10	2	36	18	7	10	6	29	28	56
5	Darlington	46	11	6	6	40	26	6	12	5	22	19	52
6	Colchester United	46	12	8	3	31	17	8	4	11	26	36	52
7	Southend United	46	15	3	5	51	21	4	10	9	27	40	51
8	Lincoln City	46	13	6	4	38	19	4	11	8	16	33	51
9	Wrexham	46	13	7	3	41	22	5	7	11	20	30	50
10	Swansea Town	46	11	8	4	35	20	8	3	12	23	34	49
11	Brentford	46	12	7	4	40	24	6	5	12	24	41	48
12	Workington	46	8	11	4	24	17	7	6	10	16	26	47
13	Port Vale	46	12	8	3	33	15	4	6	13	13	31	46
14	Chester	46	12	4	7	43	24	4	9	10	33	42	45
15	Aldershot	46	13	3	7	42	23	6	4	13	24	43	45
16	Scunthorpe United	46	10	5	8	28	22	8	3	12	33	38	44
17	Exeter City	46	11	8	4	45	24	5	3	15	21	41	43
18	Peterborough Utd.	46	8	9	6	32	23	5	7	11	28	34	42
19	NOTTS COUNTY	46	10	8	5	33	22	2	10	11	15	35	42
20	Chesterfield	46	7	7	9	24	22	6	8	9	19	28	41
21	York City	46	12	8	3	36	25	2	3	18	17	50	39
22	Newport County	46	9	9	5	31	26	2	5	16	18	48	36
23	Grimsby Town	46	5	7	11	25	31	4	8	11	22	38	33
24	Bradford Park Ave.	46	5	8	10	19	34	0	2	21	13	72	20

- 1968/69 Season -

Back: Bradd, J.Smith, Rose, Needham, Gadsby, Stubbs, D.Smith
Standing: Wheeler (Trainer), Imlach (Coach), Ball, Farmer, Pring, Hallam, Cartwright, Jackson (Asst.Trainer), Gray (Manager)
Sitting: Elliott, F.J.Murphy, Saunders, J.B.Murphy, Gibson, Oakes, K.W.Smith, Bates
Front: Walsh, Rowe

- 1969/70 Season -

Back: Redmile, K.Smith, Worthington, Bradd, Ryan, Gould
Standing: Butlin, Needham, Stubbs, Rose, Watling, Jones, Jones, McMorran, Oakes
Sitting: Wheeler(Trainer), Terry, Hubson, Barker, Masson, Ball, McDerment, Jackson(Asst Train)
Front: McGlinchey, Holder, Limb

1969/70   7th in Division Four

#		Date	Opponent	Score	Scorers	Att	Rose MJ	Worthington PR	McDerment WS	Jones M	Needham DW	Smith KW	Ryan J	Barker RJ	Butlin BD	Masson DS	Gould G	Ball GH	Oakes DR	McMorran J	Bradd LJ	Hobson J	Stubbs BH	Buxton IR	Billington B	Watling BJ	Nixon JC	Crickmore C	Holder S
1	Aug	9	OLDHAM ATHLETIC	0-0		6584	1	2	3	4	5	6	7	8	9	10	11												
2		16	Brentford	0-1		6364	1	3		4	5		7			10		2	6	8	9	11							
3		23	COLCHESTER UTD.	1-1	Hobson	4901	1	3		4	5		7		12	10		2	6	8	9	11							
4		27	Crewe Alexandra	1-1	Masson	2963	1	3			5		7	8		10		2	6	4	9	11							
5		30	Peterborough Utd.	0-1		5986	1	3			5		7	8		10		2	6	4	9	11							
6	Sep	6	GRIMSBY TOWN	2-1	Masson, Butlin	4991	1				5	3	7	8	9	10		2	6	4			11	12					
7		13	Chester	1-0	Barker	3645	1				5	3		8	9	10		2	6	7			11	4					
8		17	LINCOLN CITY	2-0	Butlin 2	6479	1				5	3	7	8	9	10		2	6				11	4					
9		20	EXETER CITY	4-0	Masson, Butlin, Barker, Hobson	6358	1				5	3	7	8	9	10		2	6				11	4	12				
10		27	Aldershot	0-2		5139	1		12		5	3	7	8	9	10		2	6				11	4					
11		30	Northampton T	1-3	Needham	6609	1				5	3	7	8	9	10		2	6				11	4					
12	Oct	4	YORK CITY	0-2		5883	1			4	5	3	7	8	9	10		2	6				11						
13		8	BRENTFORD	1-0	Hobson	4664	1	3			5	12	7			10	4	2	6		9	11			8				
14		11	Chesterfield	0-5		10170	1	3			5	2	7			10	4		6		9	11			8				
15		16	NEWPORT COUNTY	4-1	Buxton, Barker 2, Butlin	4394	1	3			5				9	10	4	2		12		7	11	6	8				
16		25	Bradford Park Ave.	3-1	Smith, Bradd, Masson(p)	3219	1	3			5	8	7			10	4	2	6		9	11							
17	Nov	1	SWANSEA TOWN	0-1		5604	1	3			5	12	7			10	4	2	6		9	11			8				
18		8	Wrexham	0-2		8805	1	3			10				8		4	2	6		9	7	5		11				
19		22	Workington	2-0	Barker, Masson	1916	1	3			5		7	8		10		2	4		9	11	6						
20		29	SCUNTHORPE UTD.	3-1	Masson 2, Smith	3497	1				5	3	7	8		10		2	4		9	11	6						
21	Dec	13	CHESTER	3-0	Masson 2, Barker	4231	1				5	3	7	9		8		2	4		10	11	6		12				
22		26	Colchester Utd.	1-2	Ryan	4759	1	12			5	3	7	8		10		2	4		9	11	6						
23		27	PETERBOROUGH UTD.	2-2	Barker, Masson(p)	6924	1	12			5	3	7		10	8		2			9	11	4		6				
24	Jan	3	Grimsby Town	1-2	Barker	3791	1				5	3	7	8		10		2	4		9	11	6						
25		10	Exeter City	1-1	Barker	3872	1			4	5	3				9		2				11	6		10	1	7		
26		17	ALDERSHOT	3-0	Bradd, Masson 2	4854		3			5					10		2	4		8	11	6			1	7		
27		24	Southend United	5-2	Needham, Stubbs, Barker 2, Bradd	5263		3			5			9		10		2	4		8	11	6			1	7		
28		31	York City	2-1	Nixon 2	3482		3		12	5					10		2	4		9	11	6			1	7		
29	Feb	7	CHESTERFIELD	1-1	Hobson	15346		3			5			9		10		2	4		8	11	6			1	7		
30		14	Oldham Athletic	0-5		3943		3			5		12			9		2	4		8	11	6		10	1	7		
31		21	WREXHAM	3-2	Barker, Masson, Nixon	6742	1	3			5			9	8	10		2	4			11	6				7		
32		28	Newport County	0-1		1339	1	3			5			9	8	10		2	4			11	6			12	7		
33	Mar	2	Hartlepool Utd.	0-4		1797		3			5			9		10		2	4		8	11	6			12	7		
34		11	DARLINGTON	4-1	Masson 2, Hobson, Bradd	3742		3			5		7	9		10		2	4		8	11	6			12			
35		14	Scunthorpe Utd.	3-2	Masson 2, Barker	3960		3			5			9		10		2	4		8	7	6			1		11	
36		18	SOUTHEND UNITED	2-0	Masson, Barker	5828		3			5			9		10		2	4		8	7	6			1		11	
37		21	HARTLEPOOL UTD.	1-0	Bradd	5313		3			5			9		10		2	4		8	7	6			1		11	
38		28	Darlington	2-1	Hobson, Masson(p)	1768		3			5			9		10		2	4		8	7	6			1		11	
39		30	BRADFORD PARK AVE.	5-2	Masson 2(1p), Crickmore, Bradd 2	8897		3			5			9		10		2	4		8	7	6			1		11	
40		31	Swansea Town	1-1	Barker	13983		3			5			9		10		2	4		8	7	6			1		11	
41	Apr	4	CREWE ALEXANDRA	0-1		7014		3			5		12	9		10		2	4		8	7	6			1		11	
42		8	PORT VALE	1-2	Barker	5070		3			5			9		10		2	4		8	7	6			1		11	
43		15	Lincoln City	4-2	Barker 2, Bradd, Masson	5518		3			5			9		10		2	4		8	7	6			1		11	
44		16	Port Vale	1-1	Masson	8042		3			5				8	10		2	4		9	7	6			1		11	
45		21	WORKINGTON	0-3		3155		3			5			9		10		2	4		8	7	6			1		11	
46		24	NORTHAMPTON T	2-0	Barker, Stubbs	2456				4	5	3		9		10		2			8	7	6			1		11	12
			Apps				27	34	3	6	45	24	24	44	10	43	1	43	43	6	35	45	36	5	7	20	9	12	1
			Goals								2	2	1	19	5	23					8	6	2	1			3	1	

F.A. Cup

| R1 | Nov | 15 | ROTHERHAM UTD. | 0-3 | | 8769 | 1 | 3 | | | 4 | | 7 | 8 | | 10 | | 2 | 6 | | | 9 | 11 | 5 | 12 | | | | |

F.L. Cup

| R1 | Aug | 13 | Mansfield Town | 1-3 | Barker | 6727 | 1 | 2 | 3 | 4 | 5 | 6 | 7 | 8 | 9 | 10 | | | | | | 11 | | | | | | | |

		P	W	D	L	F	A	W	D	L	F	A	Pts
1	Chesterfield	46	19	1	3	55	12	8	9	6	22	20	64
2	Wrexham	46	17	6	0	56	16	9	3	11	28	33	61
3	Swansea Town	46	14	8	1	43	14	7	10	6	23	31	60
4	Port Vale	46	13	9	1	39	10	7	10	6	22	23	59
5	Brentford	46	14	8	1	36	11	6	8	9	22	28	56
6	Aldershot	46	16	5	2	52	22	4	8	11	26	43	53
7	NOTTS COUNTY	46	14	4	5	44	21	8	4	11	29	41	52
8	Lincoln City	46	11	8	4	38	20	6	8	9	28	32	50
9	Peterborough Utd.	46	13	8	2	51	21	4	6	13	26	48	48
10	Colchester United	46	14	5	4	38	22	3	9	11	26	41	48
11	Chester	46	14	3	6	39	23	7	3	13	19	43	48
12	Scunthorpe United	46	11	6	6	34	23	7	4	12	33	42	46
13	York City	46	14	7	2	38	16	2	7	14	17	46	46
14	Northampton Town	46	11	7	5	41	19	5	5	13	23	36	44
15	Crewe Alexandra	46	12	6	5	37	18	4	6	13	14	33	44
16	Grimsby Town	46	9	9	5	33	24	5	6	12	21	34	43
17	Southend United	46	12	8	3	40	28	3	2	18	19	57	40
18	Exeter City	46	13	5	5	48	20	1	6	16	9	39	39
19	Oldham Athletic	46	11	4	8	45	28	2	9	12	15	37	39
20	Workington	46	9	9	5	31	21	3	5	15	15	43	38
21	Newport County	46	12	3	8	39	24	1	8	14	14	50	37
22	Darlington	46	8	7	8	31	27	5	3	15	22	46	36
23	Hartlepool	46	8	7	7	31	30	3	3	17	11	52	30
24	Bradford Park Ave.	46	6	5	12	23	32	0	6	17	18	64	23

1970/71 Champions of Division Four - Promoted

#		Date	Opponent	Score	Scorers	Att.	Watling BJ	Brindley JC	Worthington PR	Oakes DR	Needham DW	Stubbs BH	Nixon JC	Bradd LJ	Barker RJ	Masson DS	Crickmore C	Jones M	Brown RE	Hateley A	Ball GH	Cozens JW	Hobson J
1	Aug	15	York City	0-0		4476	1	2	3	4	5	6			9	8	10	11					7
2		22	BARROW	3-1	Crickmore, Barker 2	5826	1	2	3	4	5		7	8	9	10	11	6					
3		29	Aldershot	1-0	Nixon	8689	1	2	3	4	5	6	7	8	9	10	11						12
4	Sep	2	CREWE ALEXANDRA	5-1	Barker 2, Crickmore, Needham, Nixon	6463	1	2	3	4	5		7	8	9	10	11	6					12
5		5	SOUTHEND UNITED	2-1	Bradd, Masson	9025	1	2	3	4	5		7	8		10	11	6				9	12
6		12	Colchester Utd.	3-2	Stubbs, Barker, Bradd	4285	1	2	3	4	5	6	7	8	9	10	11						
7		19	BRENTFORD	0-0		10281	1	2	3	4	5	6	7	8	9	10	11						
8		23	NEWPORT COUNTY	2-0	Barker, Nixon	8445	1	2	3	4	5	6	7	8	9	10	11						
9		26	Exeter City	1-0	Barker	6093	1	2	3	4	5	6	7	8	9	10	11						
10		30	Hartlepool Utd.	1-2	Bradd	2772	1	2	3	4	5	6	7	8	9	10	11	12					
11	Oct	3	WORKINGTON	2-2	Bradd, Masson	7474	1	2	3	4	5	6	7	8	9	10	11	12					
12		10	Grimsby Town	1-2	Nixon	5482	1	2	3	4	5	6	7	8	9	10	11						
13		17	YORK CITY	2-1	Barker 2	7690		2	3	4	5	6	7	8	9	10	11		1				
14		21	DARLINGTON	3-0	Crickmore(p), Nixon, Masson	6285		2	3		5	6	7	8	9	10	11	4	1				
15		24	OLDHAM ATHLETIC	2-0	Needham, Crickmore	10028		2	3		5	6	7	8	9	10	11	4	1				
16		31	Scunthorpe Utd.	1-0	Masson	5801	1	2	3	12	5	6	7	8	9	10	11	4					
17	Nov	7	NORTHAMPTON T	1-0	Nixon	21012	1	2	3		5	6	7		9	10	11	4		8			
18		11	LINCOLN CITY	0-0		10276	1	2	3		5	6	7	12		10	11	4		8			
19		14	Southport	2-0	Hateley 2	3392	1	2	3		5	6	7		8	10	11	4		9			
20		28	Peterborough Utd.	1-1	Hateley	7116	1	2	3	12	5	6	7	10	8		11	4		9			
21	Dec	5	BOURNEMOUTH	2-1	Crickmore(p), Hateley	11711	1		3		5	6	7	10	8		11	4		9	2		
22		19	Barrow	2-1	Hateley, Bradd	2672	1		3		5	6	7	10	8		11	4		9	2		
23		26	CAMBRIDGE UNITED	4-1	Jones, Needham 2, Bradd	15722	1		3	12	5	6	7	8	9		11	4			2	10	
24	Jan	9	HARTLEPOOL UTD.	3-0	Barker 2, Hateley	11540	1		3		5	6	7		8	10	11	4		9	2		
25		16	Darlington	3-2	Hateley, Albeson (2 og)	5096	1		3	12	5	6	7		8	10	11	4		9	2		
26		23	Chester	1-2	Edwards (og)	5835	1		3	12	5	6	7		8	10	11	4		9			
27		30	PETERBOROUGH UTD.	6-0	Masson, Bradd, Hateley 3, Needham	9440	1	2	3		5	6	7	8	12	10	11	4		9			
28	Feb	6	Bournemouth	1-1	Hateley	15431	1	2	3		5	6	7	8		10	11	4		9			
29		13	CHESTER	2-1	Bradd, Nixon	10545	1	2	3		5	6	7	8		10	11	4		9			
30		20	Lincoln City	1-0	Masson	10849	1	2	3		5	6	7	8	12	10	11	4		9			
31		22	Stockport County	0-1		2926	1	2	3		5	6	7	8		10	11	4		9			
32		27	SCUNTHORPE UTD.	3-0	Masson, Bradd, Crickmore	10750	1	2	3		5	6	7	8	12	10	11	4		9			
33	Mar	6	Oldham Athletic	3-1	Bradd, Hateley 2	17953	1	2	3		5	6	7	8	12	10	11	4		9			
34		9	Newport County	1-2	Masson	2129	1	2	3		5	6	7	8		10	11	4		9			
35		13	SOUTHPORT	3-1	Masson, Barker, Hateley	11182	1	2	3		5	6	7	8	12	10	11	4		9			
36		17	STOCKPORT COUNTY	5-1	Masson, Nixon, Crickmore 2, Stubbs	10704	1	2	3		5	6	7	8		10	11	4		9			
37		20	Northampton T	1-1	Hateley	11923	1	2	3	6		5	7	8		10	11	4		9			
38		26	Southend United	0-1		7010	1	2	3		5	6	7	8		10	11	4		9			
39	Apr	3	ALDERSHOT	3-0	Crickmore, Masson, Hateley	8747	1	2	3		5	6	7	8	12	10	11	4		9			
40		8	Workington	1-0	Barker	2986	1	2	3		5	6	7		8	10	11	4		9			
41		10	Cambridge United	1-2	Hateley	6935	1	2	3		5	6	7		8	10	11	4		9			
42		12	COLCHESTER UTD.	4-0	Hateley 3, Masson	14084	1	2	3	6	5		7		8	10	11	4		9			
43		17	GRIMSBY TOWN	1-0	Masson	12182	1	2	3		5	6	7		8	10	11	4		9			
44		24	Brentford	2-2	Crickmore, Hateley	9299	1	2	3		5	6	7	12	8	10	11	4		9			
45		28	Crewe Alexandra	2-1	Bradd, Masson	4222	1	2	3		5	6	7	8		10	11	4		9			
46	May	1	EXETER CITY	1-1	Hateley	18002	1	2	3	4	5	6	7	8	12	10	11			9			
			Apps				43	41	46	21	45	42	45	37	37	42	46	37	3	29	5	2	4
			Goals								5	2	8	11	13	14	10	1		22			

Three own goals

F.A. Cup

	Date	Opponent	Score	Scorers	Att.	Watling BJ	Brindley JC	Worthington PR	Oakes DR	Needham DW	Stubbs BH	Nixon JC	Bradd LJ	Barker RJ	Masson DS	Crickmore C	Jones M	Brown RE	Hateley A	Ball GH	Cozens JW	Hobson J
R1	Nov 21	PORT VALE	1-0	Crickmore(p)	15965	1	2	3		5	6	7	10	8		11	4		9			
R2	Dec 12	Bury	1-1	Nixon	6968	1		3	12	5	6	7	10	8		11	4		9	2		
rep	Dec 21	BURY	3-0	Hateley, Crickmore, Needham	15508	1		3	12	5	6	7	10	8		11	4		9	2		
R3	Jan 2	Leicester City	0-2		33770	1		3		5	6	7	10	8		11	4		9	2		

F.L. Cup

	Date	Opponent	Score		Att.	Watling BJ	Brindley JC	Worthington PR	Oakes DR	Needham DW	Stubbs BH	Nixon JC	Bradd LJ	Barker RJ	Masson DS	Crickmore C	Jones M	Brown RE	Hateley A	Ball GH	Cozens JW	Hobson J
R1	Aug 17	Aston Villa	0-4		17843	1	2	3	4	5	6		8	9	10	11				12		7

		P	W	D	L	F	A	W	D	L	F	A	Pts
1	NOTTS COUNTY	46	19	4	0	59	12	11	5	7	30	24	69
2	Bournemouth	46	16	5	2	51	15	8	7	8	30	31	60
3	Oldham Athletic	46	14	6	3	57	29	10	5	8	31	34	59
4	York City	46	16	6	1	45	14	7	4	12	33	40	56
5	Chester	46	17	2	4	42	18	7	5	11	27	37	55
6	Colchester United	46	14	6	3	44	19	7	6	10	26	35	54
7	Northampton Town	46	15	4	4	39	24	4	9	10	24	35	51
8	Southport	46	15	2	6	42	24	6	4	13	21	33	48
9	Exeter City	46	12	7	4	40	23	5	7	11	27	45	48
10	Workington	46	13	7	3	28	13	5	5	13	20	36	48
11	Stockport County	46	12	8	3	28	17	4	6	13	21	48	46
12	Darlington	46	15	3	5	42	22	2	8	13	16	35	45
13	Aldershot	46	8	10	5	32	23	6	7	10	34	48	45
14	Brentford	46	13	3	7	45	27	5	5	13	21	35	44
15	Crewe Alexandra	46	13	1	9	49	35	5	7	11	26	41	44
16	Peterborough Utd.	46	14	3	6	46	23	4	4	15	24	48	43
17	Scunthorpe United	46	9	7	7	36	23	6	6	11	20	38	43
18	Southend United	46	8	11	4	32	24	6	4	13	21	42	43
19	Grimsby Town	46	13	4	6	37	26	5	3	15	20	45	43
20	Cambridge United	46	9	9	5	31	27	6	4	13	20	39	43
21	Lincoln City	46	11	4	8	45	33	2	9	12	25	38	39
22	Newport County	46	8	3	12	32	36	2	5	16	23	49	28
23	Hartlepool	46	6	10	7	28	27	2	2	19	6	47	28
24	Barrow	46	5	5	13	25	38	2	3	18	26	52	22

- 1970/71 Season -

Back: Jones, Needham, Bradd, Watling, Stubbs, Worthington, Wheeler(Trainer)
Front: Nixon, Barker, Masson, Sirrel(Manager), Hateley, Brindley, Crickmore

- 1971/72 Season -

Back: Fenton, Cooper, Cozens, Brown, Watling, Stubbs, Needham, Worthington
Middle: Wheeler(Trainer), Crickmore, Dyer, Richardson, Brindley, Barker, Bradd, Jones, Vinter, Bolton
Front: Nixon, Ball, Hateley, Dunnett(Chairman), Sirrell(Manager), Hopcroft(Director), Masson, Mansley, Newell

League Tables 1971/72 to 1978/79

	1971/72 Division 3	*P*	*W*	*D*	*L*	*F*	*A*	*W*	*D*	*L*	*F*	*A*	*Pts*
1	Aston Villa	46	20	1	2	45	10	12	5	6	40	22	70
2	Brighton & Hove A.	46	15	5	3	39	18	12	6	5	43	29	65
3	Bournemouth	46	16	6	1	43	13	7	10	6	30	24	62
4	NOTTS COUNTY	46	16	3	4	42	19	9	9	5	32	25	62
5	Rotherham United	46	12	8	3	46	25	8	7	8	23	27	55
6	Bristol Rovers	46	17	2	4	54	26	4	10	9	21	30	54
7	Bolton Wanderers	46	11	8	4	25	13	6	8	9	26	28	50
8	Plymouth Argyle	46	13	6	4	43	26	7	4	12	31	38	50
9	Walsall	46	12	8	3	38	16	3	10	10	24	41	48
10	Blackburn Rovers	46	14	4	5	39	22	5	5	13	15	35	47
11	Oldham Athletic	46	11	4	8	37	35	6	7	10	22	28	45
12	Shrewsbury Town	46	13	5	5	50	29	4	5	14	23	36	44
13	Chesterfield	46	10	5	8	25	23	8	3	12	32	34	44
14	Swansea City	46	10	6	7	27	21	7	4	12	19	38	44
15	Port Vale	46	10	10	3	27	21	3	5	15	16	38	41
16	Wrexham	46	10	5	8	33	26	6	3	14	26	37	40
17	Halifax Town	46	11	6	6	31	22	2	6	15	17	39	38
18	Rochdale	46	11	7	5	35	26	1	6	16	22	57	37
19	York City	46	8	8	7	32	22	4	4	15	25	44	36
20	Tranmere Rovers	46	9	7	7	34	30	1	9	13	16	41	36
21	Mansfield Town	46	5	12	6	19	26	3	8	12	22	37	36
22	Barnsley	46	6	10	7	23	30	3	8	12	9	34	36
23	Torquay United	46	8	6	9	31	31	2	6	15	10	38	32
24	Bradford City	46	6	8	9	27	32	5	2	16	18	45	32

	1972/73 Division 3												
1	Bolton Wanderers	46	18	4	1	44	9	7	7	9	29	30	61
2	NOTTS COUNTY	46	17	4	2	40	12	6	7	10	27	35	57
3	Blackburn Rovers	46	12	8	3	34	16	8	7	8	23	31	55
4	Oldham Athletic	46	12	7	4	40	18	7	9	7	32	36	54
5	Bristol Rovers	46	17	4	2	55	20	3	9	11	22	36	53
6	Port Vale	46	15	6	2	41	21	6	5	12	15	48	53
7	Bournemouth	46	14	6	3	44	16	3	10	10	22	28	50
8	Plymouth Argyle	46	14	3	6	43	26	6	7	10	31	40	50
9	Grimsby Town	46	16	2	5	45	18	4	6	13	22	43	48
10	Tranmere Rovers	46	12	8	3	38	17	3	8	12	18	35	46
11	Charlton Athletic	46	12	7	4	46	24	5	4	14	23	43	45
12	Wrexham	46	11	9	3	39	23	3	8	12	16	31	45
13	Rochdale	46	8	8	7	22	26	6	9	8	26	28	45
14	Southend United	46	13	6	4	40	14	4	4	15	21	40	44
15	Shrewsbury Town	46	10	10	3	31	21	5	4	14	15	33	44
16	Chesterfield	46	13	4	6	37	22	4	5	14	20	39	43
17	Walsall	46	14	3	6	37	26	4	4	15	19	40	43
18	York City	46	8	10	5	24	14	5	5	13	18	32	41
19	Watford	46	11	8	4	32	23	1	9	13	11	25	41
20	Halifax Town	46	9	8	6	29	23	4	7	12	14	30	41
21	Rotherham United	46	12	4	7	34	27	5	3	15	17	38	41
22	Brentford	46	12	5	6	33	18	3	2	18	18	51	37
23	Swansea City	46	11	5	7	37	29	3	4	16	14	44	37
24	Scunthorpe United	46	8	7	8	18	25	2	3	18	15	47	30

	1973/74 Division 2												
1	Middlesbrough	42	16	4	1	40	8	11	7	3	37	22	65
2	Luton Town	42	12	5	4	42	25	7	7	7	22	26	50
3	Carlisle United	42	13	5	3	40	17	7	4	10	21	31	49
4	Orient	42	9	8	4	28	17	6	10	5	27	25	48
5	Blackpool	42	11	5	5	35	17	6	8	7	22	23	47
6	Sunderland	42	11	6	4	32	15	8	3	10	26	29	47
7	Nottingham Forest	42	12	6	3	40	19	3	9	9	17	24	45
8	West Bromwich Alb.	42	8	9	4	28	24	6	7	8	20	21	44
9	Hull City	42	9	9	3	25	15	4	8	9	21	32	43
10	NOTTS COUNTY	42	8	6	7	30	35	7	7	7	25	25	43
11	Bolton Wanderers	42	12	5	4	30	17	3	7	11	14	23	42
12	Millwall	42	10	6	5	28	16	4	8	9	23	35	42
13	Fulham	42	11	4	6	26	20	5	6	10	13	23	42
14	Aston Villa	42	8	9	4	33	21	5	6	10	15	24	41
15	Portsmouth	42	9	8	4	26	16	5	4	12	19	46	40
16	Bristol City	42	9	5	7	25	20	5	5	11	22	34	38
17	Cardiff City	42	8	7	6	27	20	2	9	10	22	42	36
18	Oxford United	42	8	8	5	27	21	2	8	11	8	25	36
19	Sheffield Wed.	42	9	6	6	33	24	3	5	13	18	39	35
20	Crystal Palace	42	6	7	8	24	24	5	5	11	19	32	34
21	Preston North End	42	7	8	6	24	23	2	6	13	16	39	31
22	Swindon Town	42	6	7	8	22	27	1	4	16	14	45	25

	1974/75 Division 2												
1	Manchester United	42	17	3	1	45	12	9	6	6	21	18	61
2	Aston Villa	42	16	4	1	47	6	9	4	8	32	26	58
3	Norwich City	42	14	3	4	34	17	6	10	5	24	20	53
4	Sunderland	42	14	6	1	41	8	5	7	9	24	27	51
5	Bristol City	42	14	5	2	31	10	7	3	11	16	23	50
6	West Bromwich Alb.	42	13	4	4	33	15	5	5	11	21	27	45
7	Blackpool	42	12	6	3	31	17	2	11	8	7	16	45
8	Hull City	42	12	8	1	25	10	3	6	12	15	43	44
9	Fulham	42	9	8	4	29	17	4	8	9	15	22	42
10	Bolton Wanderers	42	9	7	5	27	16	6	5	10	18	25	42
11	Oxford United	42	14	3	4	30	19	1	9	11	11	32	42
12	Orient	42	8	9	4	17	16	3	11	7	11	23	42
13	Southampton	42	10	6	5	29	20	5	5	11	24	34	41
14	NOTTS COUNTY	42	7	11	3	34	26	5	5	11	15	33	40
15	York City	42	9	7	5	28	18	5	3	13	23	37	38
16	Nottingham Forest	42	7	7	7	24	23	5	7	9	19	32	38
17	Portsmouth	42	9	7	5	28	20	3	6	12	16	34	37
18	Oldham Athletic	42	10	7	4	28	16	0	8	13	12	32	35
19	Bristol Rovers	42	10	4	7	25	23	2	7	12	17	41	35
20	Millwall	42	8	9	4	31	19	2	3	16	13	37	32
21	Cardiff City	42	7	8	6	24	21	2	6	13	12	41	32
22	Sheffield Wed.	42	3	7	11	17	29	2	4	15	12	35	21

	1975/76 Division 2	*P*	*W*	*D*	*L*	*F*	*A*	*W*	*D*	*L*	*F*	*A*	*Pts*
1	Sunderland	42	19	2	0	48	10	5	6	10	19	26	56
2	Bristol City	42	11	7	3	34	14	8	8	5	25	21	53
3	West Bromwich Alb.	42	10	9	2	29	12	10	4	7	21	21	53
4	Bolton Wanderers	42	12	5	4	36	14	8	7	6	28	24	52
5	NOTTS COUNTY	42	11	6	4	33	13	8	5	8	27	28	49
6	Southampton	42	18	2	1	49	16	3	5	13	17	34	49
7	Luton Town	42	13	6	2	38	15	6	4	11	23	36	48
8	Nottingham Forest	42	13	1	7	34	18	4	11	6	21	22	46
9	Charlton Athletic	42	11	5	5	40	34	4	7	10	21	38	42
10	Blackpool	42	9	9	3	26	22	5	5	11	14	27	42
11	Chelsea	42	7	9	5	25	20	5	7	9	28	34	40
12	Fulham	42	9	8	4	27	14	4	6	11	18	33	40
13	Orient	42	10	6	5	21	12	3	8	10	16	27	40
14	Hull City	42	9	5	7	29	23	5	6	10	16	26	39
15	Blackburn Rovers	42	8	6	7	27	22	4	8	9	18	28	38
16	Plymouth Argyle	42	13	4	4	36	20	0	8	13	12	34	38
17	Oldham Athletic	42	11	8	2	37	24	2	4	15	20	44	38
18	Bristol Rovers	42	7	9	5	20	15	4	7	10	18	35	38
19	Carlisle United	42	9	8	4	29	22	3	5	13	16	37	37
20	Oxford United	42	7	7	7	23	25	4	4	13	16	34	33
21	York City	42	8	3	10	28	34	2	5	14	11	37	28
22	Portsmouth	42	4	6	11	15	23	5	1	15	17	38	25

	1976/77 Division 2												
1	Wolverhampton Wan.	42	15	3	3	48	21	7	10	4	36	24	57
2	Chelsea	42	15	6	0	51	22	6	7	8	22	31	55
3	Nottingham Forest	42	14	3	4	53	22	7	7	7	24	21	52
4	Bolton Wanderers	42	15	2	4	46	21	5	9	7	29	33	51
5	Blackpool	42	11	7	3	29	17	6	10	5	29	25	51
6	Luton Town	42	13	5	3	39	17	8	1	12	28	31	48
7	Charlton Athletic	42	14	5	2	52	27	2	11	8	19	31	48
8	NOTTS COUNTY	42	11	5	5	29	20	8	5	8	36	40	48
9	Southampton	42	12	6	3	40	24	5	4	12	32	43	44
10	Millwall	42	9	6	6	31	22	6	7	8	26	31	43
11	Sheffield United	42	9	8	4	32	25	5	4	12	22	38	40
12	Blackburn Rovers	42	12	4	5	31	18	3	5	13	11	36	39
13	Oldham Athletic	42	11	6	4	37	23	3	4	14	15	41	38
14	Hull City	42	9	8	4	31	17	1	9	11	14	36	37
15	Bristol Rovers	42	8	9	4	32	27	4	4	13	21	41	37
16	Burnley	42	8	9	4	27	20	3	5	13	19	44	36
17	Fulham	42	9	7	5	39	25	2	6	13	15	36	35
18	Cardiff City	42	7	6	8	30	30	5	4	12	26	37	34
19	Orient	42	4	8	9	18	23	5	8	8	19	32	34
20	Carlisle United	42	7	7	7	31	33	4	5	12	18	42	34
21	Plymouth Argyle	42	5	9	7	27	25	3	7	11	19	40	32
22	Hereford United	42	6	9	6	28	30	2	6	13	29	48	31

	1977/78 Division 2												
1	Bolton Wanderers	42	16	4	1	39	14	8	6	7	24	19	58
2	Southampton	42	15	4	2	44	16	7	9	5	26	23	57
3	Tottenham Hotspur	42	13	7	1	50	19	7	9	5	33	30	56
4	Brighton & Hove A.	42	15	5	1	43	21	7	7	7	20	17	56
5	Blackburn Rovers	42	12	4	5	33	16	4	9	8	23	44	45
6	Sunderland	42	11	6	4	36	17	3	10	8	31	42	44
7	Stoke City	42	13	5	3	38	16	3	5	13	15	33	42
8	Oldham Athletic	42	9	10	2	32	20	4	6	11	22	38	42
9	Crystal Palace	42	9	7	5	31	20	4	8	9	19	27	41
10	Fulham	42	9	8	4	32	19	5	5	11	17	30	41
11	Burnley	42	11	6	4	35	20	4	4	13	21	44	40
12	Sheffield United	42	13	4	4	38	22	3	4	14	24	51	40
13	Luton Town	42	11	4	6	35	20	3	6	12	19	32	38
14	Orient	42	8	11	2	30	20	2	7	12	13	29	38
15	NOTTS COUNTY	42	10	9	2	36	22	1	7	13	18	40	38
16	Millwall	42	8	8	5	23	20	4	6	11	26	37	38
17	Charlton Athletic	42	11	6	4	38	27	2	6	13	17	41	38
18	Bristol Rovers	42	10	7	4	40	26	3	5	13	21	51	38
19	Cardiff City	42	12	6	3	32	23	1	6	14	19	48	38
20	Blackpool	42	7	8	6	35	25	5	5	11	24	35	37
21	Mansfield Town	42	6	6	9	30	34	4	5	12	19	35	31
22	Hull City	42	6	6	9	23	25	2	6	13	11	27	28

	1978/79 Division 2												
1	Crystal Palace	42	12	7	2	30	11	7	12	2	21	13	57
2	Brighton & Hove A.	42	16	3	2	44	11	7	7	7	28	28	56
3	Stoke City	42	11	7	3	35	15	9	9	3	23	16	56
4	Sunderland	42	13	3	5	39	19	9	8	4	31	25	55
5	West Ham United	42	12	7	2	46	15	6	7	8	24	24	50
6	NOTTS COUNTY	42	8	10	3	23	15	6	6	9	25	45	44
7	Preston North End	42	7	11	3	36	23	5	7	9	23	34	42
8	Newcastle United	42	13	3	5	35	24	4	5	12	16	31	42
9	Cardiff City	42	12	5	4	34	23	4	5	12	22	47	42
10	Fulham	42	10	7	4	35	19	3	8	10	15	28	41
11	Orient	42	11	5	5	32	18	4	5	12	19	33	40
12	Cambridge United	42	7	10	4	22	15	5	6	10	22	37	40
13	Burnley	42	11	6	4	31	22	3	6	12	20	40	40
14	Oldham Athletic	42	10	7	4	36	23	3	6	12	16	38	39
15	Wrexham	42	10	6	5	31	16	2	8	11	14	26	38
16	Bristol Rovers	42	10	6	5	34	23	4	4	13	14	37	38
17	Leicester City	42	7	8	6	28	23	3	9	9	15	29	37
18	Luton Town	42	11	5	5	46	24	2	5	14	14	33	36
19	Charlton Athletic	42	6	8	7	28	28	5	5	11	32	41	35
20	Sheffield United	42	9	6	6	34	24	2	6	13	18	45	34
21	Millwall	42	7	4	10	22	29	4	6	11	20	32	32
22	Blackburn Rovers	42	5	8	8	24	29	5	2	14	17	43	30

1971/72   4th in Division Three

#	Date	Opponent	Score	Scorers	Att	Brown RE	Brindley JC	Worthington PR	Jones M	Needham DW	Barker RJ	Stubbs BH	Nixon JC	Bradd LJ	Hateley A	Masson DS	Mansley A	Cooper T	Ball GH	Carlin W	Cozens JW	Carter SC	Crickmore C	Watling BJ	Hulme J	Bolton IR	Richardson J
1	Aug 14	ROCHDALE	4-0	Mansley, Masson, Stubbs, Hateley	10879	1	2	3	4	5	12	6	7	8	9	10	11										
2	21	Chesterfield	2-1	Bradd, Hateley	12276	1	2	3	4		12	6	7	8	9	10	11	5									
3	28	BOLTON WANDERERS	1-2	Hateley	15658	1		3	4	5	12	6	7	8	9	10	11	2									
4	30	Port Vale	3-0	Masson, Bradd, Hateley	5298		2	3	4	5		6	7	8	9	10	11										
5	Sep 4	Walsall	2-1	Hateley 2	6780	1	2	3	4	5	12	6	7	8	9	10	11										
6	11	SHREWSBURY TOWN	1-0	Mansley	13328	1	2	3	6	5	12		7	8	9	10	11			4							
7	18	Brighton & Hove Alb.	1-1	Needham	13443	1	2	3	6	5	12		7	8	9	10	11			4							
8	25	BRISTOL ROVERS	2-3	Masson(p), Roberts(og)	13101	1	2	3	12	5		6	7	8	9	10	11			4							
9	29	BOURNEMOUTH	1-1	Masson(p)	13342	1	2	3	12	5		6	7	8	9	10	11			4							
10	Oct 2	Swansea City	1-1	Masson	9703	1	2	3	4	5		6	7	8	9	10	12				11						
11	9	PLYMOUTH ARGYLE	1-0	Bradd	11828	1	2	3	12	5		6	7	8		10	11			4	9						
12	16	Rochdale	1-1	Bradd	4848	1	2	3	12	5		6	7	8		10	11			4	9						
13	20	Blackburn Rovers	2-0	Bradd 2	6935	1	2	3	12	5		6	7	8	9	10				4	11						
14	23	OLDHAM ATHLETIC	2-0	Needham 2	14419	1	2	3	12	5		6	7	8	9	10				4	11						
15	30	York City	2-0	Nixon, Hateley	8302	1	2	3	12	5		6	7	8	9	10				4	11						
16	Nov 6	MANSFIELD TOWN	2-0	Bradd, Needham	16905	1	2	3		5		6	7	8	9	10				4	11						
17	13	Aston Villa	0-1		37462	1	2	3	12	5		6	7	8	9	10				4	11						
18	27	Bradford City	3-2	Bradd, Cooper(og), Cozens	6826	1	2	3	12	5		6	7	8	9	10				4	11						
19	Dec 4	BARNSLEY	3-0	Cozens 2, Bradd	12639	1	2	3	12	5		6	7	8	9	10				4	11						
20	18	WALSALL	3-0	Bradd 2, Hateley	11775	1	2	3		5		6	7	8	9	10				4	11						
21	27	Wrexham	1-1	Cozens	12680	1	2	3	12	5		6	7	8	9	10				4	11						
22	Jan 1	BRIGHTON & HOVE ALB.	1-0	Bradd	16401	1	2	3	12	5		6	7	8	9	10				4	11						
23	8	Bolton Wanderers	2-1	Cozens, Carlin	8380	1	2	3		5		6	7	8	9	10				4	11						
24	22	Bournemouth	0-2		21154	1	2	3		5		6	7	8	9	10	12			4	11						
25	29	BLACKBURN ROVERS	1-0	Bradd	12375	1	2	3	6			5	7	8	9	10				4	11						
26	Feb 12	Oldham Athletic	1-0	Hateley	8621	1	2	3	6			5	12	8	9	10				4	11	7					
27	19	YORK CITY	2-2	Hateley, Bradd	12351	1	2	3	6			5	12	8	9	10				4	11	7					
28	26	Mansfield Town	1-1	Bradd	16784	1	2	3	6			5	12	8	9	10				4	11	7					
29	Mar 4	ASTON VILLA	0-3		34208	1	2	3	5			6	7	8	9	10				4			11				
30	11	Plymouth Argyle	1-1	Bradd	12157		2	3	4			6	7	9		10				8	11				1	5	
31	14	Rotherham Utd.	2-2	Masson, Cozens	10359		2	3	4			5	7	9		10				8	11			6	1		
32	18	CHESTERFIELD	1-4	Stubbs	14701		2	3	4			5	7	10	9					8	11			6	1		12
33	22	ROTHERHAM UTD.	1-1	Worthington	11522	1	2	3	4			5	7	9		10				8	12	11		6			
34	25	Shrewsbury Town	1-1	Bradd	5211	1	2	3	4			5	7	9		10				8	11			6			
35	Apr 1	WREXHAM	1-0	May(og)	12060	1		3	4			5	7	9		10			2	8	12	11		6			
36	3	SWANSEA CITY	5-0	Bradd, Masson, Cozens 2, Nixon	14019	1		3	4	5		2	7	9		10		6		8	11						
37	4	Bristol Rovers	2-0	Carter, Cozens	11998	1		3	4	5		2	7	9		10		6			8	11					12
38	8	Torquay United	1-1	Masson(p)	6478	1		3	4	5		2	7	9		10		6		8	11						12
39	12	HALIFAX TOWN	3-1	Cozens 2, Carter	14979	1	2	3	4	5		6	7	9		10					8	11					
40	15	BRADFORD CITY	2-0	Bradd, Cozens	16315	1	2	3	4	5		6	7	9		10					8	11					
41	18	Halifax Town	1-3	Bradd	3943	1	2	3	4	5		6	7	9		10		12			8	11					
42	22	Barnsley	1-2	Masson	6264	1	2	3	4	5		6	7	9		10					8	11					
43	26	PORT VALE	2-1	Masson(p), Carter	9033	1	2	3	4	5		6	7	9		10		12			8	11					
44	29	TRANMERE ROVERS	1-0	Cozens	9885	1	2	3	4	5		6	7	9		10		12			8	11					
45	May 3	TORQUAY UNITED	2-1	Bradd, Masson	8921	1	2	3	4	5		6	7	9		10					8	11					
46	8	Tranmere Rovers	1-2	Needham	4212	1	2	3	6	5			7	9		10		12		4	8	11					
				Apps		43	41	46	44	32	6	43	46	46	28	45	11	8	2	31	33	18	1	3	8	1	2
				Goals					1	5		2	2	21	10	11	2			1	13	3					

Three own goals

F.A. Cup

#	Date	Opponent	Score	Scorers	Att	Brown RE	Brindley JC	Worthington PR	Jones M	Needham DW	Barker RJ	Stubbs BH	Nixon JC	Bradd LJ	Hateley A	Masson DS	Mansley A	Cooper T	Ball GH	Carlin W	Cozens JW	Carter SC	Crickmore C	Watling BJ	Hulme J	Bolton IR	Richardson J
R1	Nov 20	NEWPORT COUNTY	6-0	Hateley, Cozens, Bradd, Nixon, Stubbs, Carlin	11976	1	2	3		5		6	7	8	9	10				4	11						
R2	Dec 11	South Shields	3-1	Masson, Cozens, Bradd	8144	1	2	3		5		6	7	8	9	10				4	11						
R3	Jan 15	Watford	4-1	Cozens 2, Nixon, Masson	13488	1	2	3	5			6	7	8	9	10				4	11						
R4	Feb 5	Derby County	0-6		39450	1	2	3	6			5	7	8	9	10				4	11						

F.L. Cup

#	Date	Opponent	Score	Scorers	Att	Brown RE	Brindley JC	Worthington PR	Jones M	Needham DW	Barker RJ	Stubbs BH	Nixon JC	Bradd LJ	Hateley A	Masson DS	Mansley A	Cooper T	Ball GH	Carlin W	Cozens JW	Carter SC	Crickmore C	Watling BJ	Hulme J	Bolton IR	Richardson J
R1	Aug 17	Leyton Orient	1-1	Nixon	8263	1	2	3	6		4		7	8	9	10	11	5									
rep	Aug 25	LEYTON ORIENT	3-1	Hateley, Nixon, Bradd	3607	1		3	4	5	12	6	7	8	9	10	11										2
R2	Sep 8	GILLINGHAM	1-2	Bradd	12650	1	2	3	4	5	12	6	7	8	9	10	11										

1972/73 2nd in Division Three · Promoted

#		Match	Score	Scorers	Att	Brown RE	Brindley JC	Worthington PR	Jones M	Needham DW	Stubbs BH	Nixon JC	Cooper T	Cozens JW	Mann AF	Scanlon I	Vinter M	Masson DS	Randall K	Bradd LJ	Carter SC	Carlin W	McManus CE	Dyer P
1	Aug 12	Shrewsbury Town	0-0		3775	1	2	3	4	5	6	7	8	9	10	11	12							
2	19	BOLTON WANDERERS	1-0	Masson	11129	1	2	3	4	5	6	7			11			8	9	10				
3	26	York City	1-1	Masson(p)	4318	1	2	3	4	5	6	7			11			10	9	8				
4	28	Tranmere Rovers	2-0	Randall 2	3651	1	2	3	4	5	6	7		12	11			8	9	10				
5	Sep 2	WALSALL	1-1	Nixon	9554	1	2	3	4	5	6	7			11	12		10	9	8				
6	9	Southend United	1-2	Bradd	6035	1	2		4	5	6	7		11	3			8	9	10	12			
7	16	ROCHDALE	2-2	Needham, Nixon	7991	1	2		4	5	6	7			3			8	9	10	11			
8	19	Charlton Athletic	1-6	Bradd	6156	1	2		6	5		7		4	3			10	8	9	11			
9	23	Watford	0-1		8363	1		3	6	5	2	7		4	12			10	8	9	11			
10	27	SWANSEA CITY	2-0	Nixon, Masson	6118	1	2	3		5	6	7			10			4	8	9	11			
11	30	BRENTFORD	1-0	Randall	8152	1	2	3	12	5	6	7			10			4	8	9	11			
12	Oct 7	Halifax Town	1-0	Masson(p)	3233	1	2	3		5	6			7	8			4	9	10	11			
13	14	BOURNEMOUTH	0-2		11914	1	2	3		5	6	12		7	10			4	8	9	11			
14	21	Wrexham	0-2		5404	1	2	3		5	6			8	10				7	9	11	4		
15	25	ROTHERHAM UTD.	2-0	Needham, Bradd	6199	1	2	3		5	6	7			11			10	8	9		4		
16	28	PORT VALE	1-1	Randall	8544	1	2	3		5	6	7			11			10	9	8	12	4		
17	Nov 4	Swansea City	0-3		3508	1	2	3		5	6	7			11			10	8	9		4		
18	7	Bristol Rovers	0-1		6695		2	3	4	5	6	12		11				10	7	9		8	1	
19	11	CHARLTON ATHLETIC	3-1	Randall 2 (1p), Needham	7069	1	2	3		5	6	7			11			10	8	9		4		
20	25	OLDHAM ATHLETIC	2-4	Randall(p), Bradd	7329	1	2	3		5	6	7					12	10	8	9	11	4		
21	Dec 2	Grimsby Town	1-3	Randall(p)	9149	1	2	3	12	5	6	7						10	9	8	11	4		
22	16	CHESTERFIELD	2-0	Nixon, Randall(p)	6891	1	2	3		5	6	7			12			10	8	9	11	4		
23	23	Scunthorpe Utd.	0-1		3983	1	2	3	12	5	6	7			10			4	8	9	11			
24	26	WATFORD	1-0	Franks(og)	9282	1	2	3		5	6	7			10			4	8	9	11			
25	30	Bolton Wanderers	2-2	Stubbs, Bradd	17800	1	2	3		5	6	7			10			4	9	8	11			
26	Jan 6	YORK CITY	1-0	Masson	6202	1	2	3		5	6	7			10			4	8	9	11			
27	23	Walsall	3-1	Randall, Stubbs, Carlin	4395	1	2	3			5	7			10			4	8	9	11	6		
28	27	SOUTHEND UNITED	2-0	Bradd, Nixon	7903	1	2	3		5	6	7			10			4	8	9	11	12		
29	30	Rotherham Utd.	4-1	Nixon 2, Randall, Masson	6572	1	2	3		5	6	7			10			4	8	9	11	12		
30	Feb 3	BRISTOL ROVERS	2-0	Randall, Nixon	11938	1	2	3		5	6	7			10			4	8	9	11			
31	10	Rochdale	1-4	Nixon	3092	1	2	3		5	6	7			10			4	8	9	11	12		
32	17	SHREWSBURY TOWN	1-0	Nixon	8903	1	2	3		5	6	7			11			4	8	9			10	12
33	24	Chesterfield	2-0	Masson 2	8755	1	2	3		5	6	7						4	8	9	11	10		
34	Mar 3	HALIFAX TOWN	3-0	Stubbs, Nixon, Bradd	9820	1		3		5	2	7			6			4	8	9	11	10		12
35	7	Blackburn Rovers	0-2		13626	1		3		5	2	7			6	11		4	8	9		10		12
36	10	Bournemouth	1-1	Nixon	14830	1	2	3		5	6	7			11			4	8	9		10		
37	17	WREXHAM	1-0	Bradd	10068	1	2	3		5		7			6		8	4	10	9		11		12
38	21	PLYMOUTH ARGYLE	2-0	Vinter, Randall	12889	1	2	3		5		7			6		8	4	11	9		10		12
39	24	Port Vale	1-1	Randall(p)	8920	1	2	3		5		7			6		10	4	9	8		11		12
40	31	Oldham Athletic	1-1	Needham	12570	1	2	3		5	6	7			11			4	8	9		10		
41	Apr 7	GRIMSBY TOWN	4-0	Randall 2, Nixon, Mann	16208	1	2	3		5	6	7			10			4	8	9	12	11		
42	14	Plymouth Argyle	4-1	Nixon 2, Carter, Randall	11997	1	2	3		5	6	7			10			4	9		8	11		
43	20	Brentford	1-1	Needham	11658	1	2	3		5	6	9			11			4	8		7	10		
44	21	BLACKBURN ROVERS	0-0		22712		2	3		5	6	7			11			4	8	9		10	1	
45	23	SCUNTHORPE UTD.	2-0	Bradd, Nixon	15697		2	3		5	6	7			11			4	8	9		10	1	
46	28	TRANMERE ROVERS	4-1	Nixon, Randall(2p), Needham	23613		2	3		5	6	7			11			4	9	8		10	1	
		Apps				42	43	43	13	45	42	44	1	9	42	4	4	44	45	43	27	28	4	6
		Goals								6	3	17			1		1	8	19	9	1	1		

One own goal

F.A. Cup

		Match	Score	Scorers	Att	Brown RE	Brindley JC	Worthington PR	Jones M	Needham DW	Stubbs BH	Nixon JC	Cooper T	Cozens JW	Mann AF	Scanlon I	Vinter M	Masson DS	Randall K	Bradd LJ	Carter SC	Carlin W	McManus CE	Dyer P
R1	Nov 18	Altrincham	1-0	Randall(p)	4211	1	2	3		5	6	7			11			10	8	9		4		
R2	Dec 9	LANCASTER CITY	2-1	Randall(p), Bradd	6613	1	2	3	6	5		7			11			10	8	9		4		
R3	Jan 13	SUNDERLAND	1-1	Bradd	15142	1	2	3		5	6	7			10			4	9	8	11			
rep	Jan 15	Sunderland	0-2		30033	1	2	3		5	6	7			10			4	8	9	11			

F.L. Cup

		Match	Score	Scorers	Att	Brown RE	Brindley JC	Worthington PR	Jones M	Needham DW	Stubbs BH	Nixon JC	Cooper T	Cozens JW	Mann AF	Scanlon I	Vinter M	Masson DS	Randall K	Bradd LJ	Carter SC	Carlin W	McManus CE	Dyer P
R1	Aug 16	YORK CITY	3-1	Randall, Nixon, Mann	8078	1	2	3	4	5	6	7		8	11			9	10					
R2	Sep 6	SOUTHPORT	3-2	Needham, Mann, Cozens	7004	1	2		4	5	6	7		11	3			8	9	10				
R3	Oct 3	Southampton	3-1	Cozens 2, Bradd	11095	1	2	3		5	6			7	10			4	8	9	11			
R4	Oct 31	STOKE CITY	3-1	Randall(p), Bradd, Stubbs	20297	1	2	3		5	6	7			11			10	8	9		4		
R5	Nov 22	Chelsea	1-3	Osgood(og)	22580	1	2	3		5	6	7			11			10	8	9		4		

Watney Cup

		Match	Score	Scorers	Att	Brown RE	Brindley JC	Worthington PR	Jones M	Needham DW	Stubbs BH	Nixon JC	Cooper T	Cozens JW	Mann AF	Scanlon I	Vinter M	Masson DS	Randall K	Bradd LJ	Carter SC	Carlin W	McManus CE	Dyer P
R1	Jul 29	SHEFFIELD UNITED	0-3		14405	1	2		4	5	6	7	8		3	11		10		9				

-1972/73 Season -

Back: Stubbs, Brown, Bradd, Vinter, McManus, Dyer
Standing: Fenton(Yth Coach), Scanlon, Jones, Bolton, Cozens, Worthington, Needham, Cooper, Potrac, not known, Wheeler(Train)
Sitting: Nixon, Brindley, Masson, Sirrell(Manager), Hopcroft(Director), Dunnett(Chairman), Levin(Director), Carlin, Mann, Carter
Front: Newell, Richards

- 1973/74 Season -

Back: Cliff, Randall, Needham, McManus, Brown, Worthington, Stubbs, Bradd
Front: Nixon, Brindley, Mann, Carter, Masson, Carlin, Probert

1973/74   10th in Division Two

#	Date	Opponent	Score	Scorers	Att	Brown RE	Brindley JC	Worthington PR	Masson DS	Stubbs BH	McVay DR	Carter SC	Nixon JC	Randall K	Probert EW	Mann AF	Vinter M	Needham DW	Carlin W	Bradd LJ	McManus CE	Collier G	Cliff E	Bolton IR	Dyer P	O'Brien R	Scanlon I
1	Aug 25	Crystal Palace	4-1	Stubbs, Vinter, Randall 2	20841	1	2	3	4	5	6	7	8	9	10	11	12										
2	Sep 1	SUNDERLAND	1-4	Carter	15322	1	2	3	4	6		11	7	10			12	5	8	9							
3	8	Carlisle Utd.	0-3		6109		2	3	4	6		11	7	9	10			5		8	1						
4	11	LUTON TOWN	1-1	Bradd	8509		2	3	4	6			7	8	10	11		5		9	1						
5	15	SWINDON TOWN	2-0	Randall, Bradd	9264		2	3	4	6			7	8	10	11		5		9	1						
6	19	Oxford United	1-2	Bradd	6995		2	3	4	6			7	8	10	11		5		9	1						
7	22	Portsmouth	2-1	Mann, Bradd	14443		2	3	4	6			7	8	10	11	12	5		9	1						
8	29	ASTON VILLA	2-0	Probert, Bradd	15872		2	3	4	6			7	8	10	11	12	5		9	1						
9	Oct 2	OXFORD UNITED	0-0		9927		2	3	4	6			7	8	10	11		5		9	1						
10	6	Blackpool	1-0	Mann	11072		2	3	4	6			7	8	10	11	12	5		9	1						
11	13	FULHAM	2-1	Masson(2p)	11981		2	3	4	6			7	8	10	11		5		9	1	12					
12	20	PRESTON NORTH END	2-1	Stubbs, Mann	12479		2	3	4	6			7	8	10	11		5		9	1						
13	27	Sheffield Wednesday	0-0		14252		2	3	4	6			7	8	10	11		5		9	1						
14	Nov 3	MILLWALL	3-3	Nixon, Dorney(og), Needham	12243		2	3	4	6			7	9	10	11		5		8	1						
15	10	West Bromwich Alb.	1-2	Randall	15564		2	3	4	6			7	8	10	11		5		9	1						
16	17	Bolton Wanderers	3-1	Stubbs, Randall 2	12139		2	3	4	6			7	8	10	11		5		9	1						
17	24	MIDDLESBROUGH	2-2	Bradd, Masson	16314		2	3	4	6			7	8	10	11	12	5		9	1						
18	Dec 1	Bristol City	2-2	Masson(p), Mann	10436		2	3	4		6		7	9	10	11	12	5		8	1						
19	8	LEYTON ORIENT	2-4	Bradd, Masson(p)	11264		2	3	4				7	8	10	11		5		9	1						
20	15	HULL CITY	3-2	Stubbs, Nixon(p), Masson	8574	1	2	3	4	6	12		7	8	10	11		5		9							
21	22	Aston Villa	1-1	Randall(p)	20825	1	2	3	4		6		7	8	10	11		5		9							
22	26	NOTTM. FOREST	0-1		32310	1	2	3	4		6		7	8	10	11		5		9		12					
23	29	CARLISLE UTD.	0-3		10209	1	2	3	4		6		7	8	10	11		5		9		12					
24	Jan 1	Sunderland	2-1	Masson 2	22581	1	2		4		6	7	9	8	10	11		5					3				
25	20	CRYSTAL PALACE	1-3	Randall	14748	1	2	3			6	11	7	8	4	10		5		9							
26	26	Cardiff City	0-1		8432		2	3			6	11		8		10		5		9	1			4	7		
27	Feb 2	Hull City	0-1		6384		2		4		6	7		8	10	11		5		9	1		3	12			
28	5	Luton Town	1-1	Probert	4908		2		8		4	11	12	7	10	6				9	1		3	5			
29	9	PORTSMOUTH	4-0	Randall 2, Masson(p), Roberts(og)	8665		2	8	3	4	11		7	10	6			5		9	1		3				
30	16	Fulham	0-2		7515		2	10	6	4	7		9	11	3			5		8	1			12			
31	19	Swindon Town	4-1	Masson, Randall 2, Bradd	3482		2	8	6	4	11		7	10	3			5		9	1						
32	23	BLACKPOOL	0-3		11092		2	8	6	4	11	12	7	10	3			5		9	1						
33	Mar 3	Nottm. Forest	0-0		29962		2	8	6	4			7	10	11			5		9	1		3				
34	9	SHEFFIELD WEDNESDAY	1-5	Mann	9378		2	8	6	4			7	10	11			5		9	1		3				
35	16	Preston North End	2-0	Stubbs, Bradd	8907		2	8	6	5	12		7	10	11					9	1			4	3		
36	23	WEST BROMWICH ALB.	1-0	Stubbs	9672		2	10	6	8			12	7	11			5		9	1			4	3		
37	30	Millwall	0-0		5906		2	10	6	8			12	7	11			5		9	1			4	3		
38	Apr 6	Middlesbrough	0-4		27823		2	8	6	4			12	9		10		5		7	1				3	11	
39	13	BOLTON WANDERERS	0-0		8349		2	8	4	10			12	7		11		5		9	1			6	3		
40	15	CARDIFF CITY	1-1	Randall	6975		2	8	6			12		9	7	10		5			1			4	3		11
41	20	Leyton Orient	1-1	Masson	11711		2	4	5	8			7		11			9		10	1		6		3		12
42	27	BRISTOL CITY	2-1	Rodgers(og), Bradd	6991		2	4	5	8			7		10			9		11	1		6		3		
		Apps				8	42	25	40	32	25	14	31	42	35	40	6	39	1	39	34	3	5	12	1	8	2
		Goals							11	6	1	2		13	2	5	1	1		10							

Three own goals

F.A. Cup

	Date	Opponent	Score		Att	Brown RE	Brindley JC	Worthington PR	Masson DS	Stubbs BH	McVay DR	Carter SC	Nixon JC	Randall K	Probert EW	Mann AF	Vinter M	Needham DW
R3	Jan 5	West Bromwich Albion	0-4		13022	1	2	3	4		6	7	9	8	10	11	12	5

F.L. Cup

	Date	Opponent	Score	Scorers	Att	Brown RE	Brindley JC	Worthington PR	Masson DS	Stubbs BH	McVay DR	Carter SC	Nixon JC	Randall K	Probert EW	Mann AF	Vinter M
R1	Aug 28	DONCASTER ROV.	3-4	Randall 2, Stubbs	7735	1	2	3	4	5	6	7	8	9	10	11	12

1974/75   14th in Division Two

#	Date	Opponent	Score	Scorers	Att	McManus CE	Brindley JC	O'Brien R	Masson DS	Needham DW	Stubbs BH	Nixon JC	Probert EW	Randall K	Bradd LJ	Mann AF	Carter SC	Scanlon I	Brown RE	Bolton IR	Vinter M	McVay DR	Richards P	Benjamin T
1	Aug 17	Bristol Rovers	0-0		14319	1	2	3	4	5	6	7	8	9	10	11	12							
2	20	FULHAM	1-1	Bradd	9468	1	2	3	4	5	6	7	8	9	10	11								
3	24	OLDHAM ATHLETIC	1-0	Needham	9353	1	2	3	4	5	6	8	7	9	10	11		12						
4	28	Fulham	0-3		9373	1	2	3	4	5	6	12	7	9	10			11						
5	31	York City	2-2	Bradd 2	6558	1	2	3	4	5	6		8	7	9	10		11						
6	Sep 7	SOUTHAMPTON	3-2	Randall, Stubbs, Masson(p)	8923	1	2	3	4	5	6		8	7	9	10		11						
7	14	Norwich City	0-3		17362		2	3	4	5	6		8	7	9	10		11	1		12			
8	21	WEST BROMWICH ALB.	0-0		10004		2	3	4	5	6		8	7	9	10		11	1					
9	24	LEYTON ORIENT	1-1	Scanlon	7883		2	3	4	5	6		8	7	9	10		11	1					
10	28	Bolton Wanderers	1-1	Scanlon	10347		2	3	4	5	6		8	7	9	10		11	1					
11	Oct 5	PORTSMOUTH	1-1	Stubbs	8573		2	3	4	5	6		8	7	9	10	12	11	1					
12	12	Manchester Utd.	0-1		46565		2	3	4	5	6		8		9	10	7	11	1					
13	15	Oldham Athletic	0-1		9240		2	3	4	5	6		8		9	10	7	11	1					
14	19	OXFORD UNITED	4-1	Scanlon 2, Bradd, Carter	8116		2	3	4	5	6		8		9	10	7	11	1		12			
15	26	Bristol City	0-3		10343		2	3	4	5	6		8		9	10	7	11	1					
16	Nov 2	HULL CITY	5-0	O'Brien, Randall(p), Scanlon, Probert, Vinter	9032		2	3	8	5	6		10	9			7	11	1		12	4		
17	9	Aston Villa	1-0	Needham	22182		2	3	4	5	6		9		10		7	11	1	8	12			
18	16	SHEFFIELD WEDNESDAY	3-3	Scanlon 3(1p)	14170		2	3	4	5	6		9			10	7	11	1	8	12			
19	23	Sunderland	0-3		25677		2		4	5	6		9			10	7	11	1	8	12		3	
20	30	MILLWALL	2-1	Bolton, Randall	9248		2		4	5	6		10	9			7	11	1	8	12		3	
21	Dec 7	Blackpool	1-3	Vinter	4922		2	3	4	5	6		10	9			7	11	1	8	12			
22	14	BRISTOL ROVERS	3-2	Aitkin(og), Randall, Stubbs	7628		2			5	6		8	9		10	7	11	1		4		3	
23	21	Cardiff City	0-0		6646	1	2			5	6		8	9	12	10	7	11			4		3	
24	26	NORWICH CITY	1-1	Mann	13977	1	2			5	6		8	9		10	7	11			4		3	
25	28	Nottm. Forest	2-0	Bradd, Carter	25013	1	2			5	6		8	9	10	12	7	11			4		3	
26	Jan 11	BLACKPOOL	0-0		10601	1	2			5	4		8		10	12	7	11		6				
27	18	Millwall	0-3		4963		2	3		5	6		8	9	10	11	7			4	12			
28	Feb 1	ASTON VILLA	1-3	Scanlon	16651	1	2	3		5	6		8	9	10		7	11		4				
29	8	Hull City	0-1		6700	1	2	3		5	6		8	7	9			11		4		10		
30	15	SUNDERLAND	0-0		15855	1	2	3		5	6		8	9				11		4	7	10		
31	22	Sheffield Wednesday	1-0	Vinter	14900	1	2	3		5	4		8	7			12	11		6	9	10		
32	Mar 1	YORK CITY	2-1	Bradd, Needham	8835	1	2	3		5	6		8		12		7	11		4	9	10		
33	8	Leyton Orient	1-0	Scanlon	4352	1	2	3		5	6		8		12		7	11		4	9	10		
34	15	BOLTON WANDERERS	1-1	Vinter	8196	1	2	3		5	6		8		12		7	11		4	9	10		
35	22	Southampton	2-3	Scanlon 2	12973	1	2	3		5	6		8		12		7	11		4	9	10		
36	25	NOTTM. FOREST	2-2	Scanlon, Richardson(og)	20303	1	2	3		5	6		8		12		7	11		4	9	10		
37	29	CARDIFF CITY	0-2		8105	1	2	3		5	6		8		12		7	11		4	9	10		
38	Apr 2	West Bromwich Alb.	1-4	McVay	7812	1	2	3		5			8								9	4		6
39	5	Bristol City	1-2	Probert	7227		2	3		5			4	9	10		7	11	1		8			6
40	12	Portsmouth	1-1	Scanlon	10966	1	2	3		5	6		10	9			7	11		4	8			
41	19	MANCHESTER UTD.	2-2	Probert, Randall	17320	1	2	3		5	6		10	9			7	11		4	8			
42	26	Oxford United	2-1	Randall 2	6316	1	2	3		5	6		8	9			7			4	11	10		

| | | | | | Apps | 25 | 42 | 35 | 21 | 42 | 40 | 4 | 39 | 30 | 30 | 28 | 31 | 32 | 17 | 25 | 20 | 15 | 7 | 2 |
| | | | | | Goals | | | 1 | 1 | 3 | 3 | | 3 | 7 | 6 | 1 | 2 | 14 | | 1 | 4 | 1 | | |

Two own goals

F.A. Cup

Rd	Date	Opponent	Score	Scorers	Att	McManus CE	Brindley JC	O'Brien R	Masson DS	Needham DW	Stubbs BH	Nixon JC	Probert EW	Randall K	Bradd LJ	Mann AF	Carter SC	Scanlon I	Brown RE	Bolton IR	Vinter M	McVay DR	Richards P	Benjamin T
R3	Jan 3	PORTSMOUTH	3-1	Randall 2, Needham	14723	1	2			5	6		8	9	10	11	7			4			3	
R4	Jan 24	Queens Park Rangers	0-3		23428	1	2	3		5	6		8	9	10	11	7			4				

F.L. Cup

Rd	Date	Opponent	Score	Scorers	Att	McManus CE	Brindley JC	O'Brien R	Masson DS	Needham DW	Stubbs BH	Nixon JC	Probert EW	Randall K	Bradd LJ	Mann AF	Carter SC	Scanlon I	Brown RE	Bolton IR	Vinter M	McVay DR	Richards P	Benjamin T
R2	Sep 10	Southampton	0-1		10649		2	3	4	5	6		8	7	9	10		11	1		12			

- 1974/75 Season -

Back: McVay, Brindley, Randall, McManus, Brown, Needham, Stubbs, Wheeler(Trainer)
Front: O'Brien, Nixon, Probert, Scanlon, Sirrell(Manager), Masson, Bradd, Bolton, Mann

- 1975/76 Season -

Back: Probert, P.Richards, Bradd, Randall, Benjamin, Mann
Standing: Wheeler(Trainer), McVay, Needham, McManus, Regan, Lane, Stubbs, Bolton, O'Brien, Fenton(Coach)
Sitting: Brindley, Carter, Scanlon, Sirrell(Manager), Dunnett(Chairman), McCool, Kane, Smith
Front: Weightman, L.Richards, Towle

1975/76 5th in Division Two

No.	Date	Opponent	Score	Scorers	Att.	McManus CE	Brindley JC	Richards P	Bolton IR	Needham DW	Stubbs BH	Carter SC	McVay DR	Bradd LJ	Probert EW	Scanlon I	Randall K	Mann AF	O'Brien R	Vinter M	Sims J	King J	Lane F	Birchenall AJ	Smith DF	Richards LG	Benjamin T
1	Aug 16	Charlton Athletic	2-1	Bradd, Probert	9618	1	2	3	4	5	6	7	8	9	10	11	12										
2	19	Leyton Orient	1-1	Probert	5223	1		2	4	5	6	7	10	9	8	11			3								
3	23	SOUTHAMPTON	0-0		9439	1		2	4	5	6	7	10	9	8	11	12		3								
4	30	Nottm. Forest	1-0	Bradd	19757	1		2	4	5	6	7	10	9	8	11			3								
5	Sep 6	CARLISLE UTD.	1-0	Probert	8005	1		2	4	5	6	7	10	9	8	11			3								
6	13	York City	2-1	Scanlon(p), McVay	6129	1		2	4	5	6	7	10	9	8	11			3	12							
7	20	LUTON TOWN	1-0	Scanlon	11173	1		2	4	5	6	7	10	9	8	11			3								
8	23	Hull City	2-0	Bradd 2	8068	1		2	4	5	6	7	10	9	8	11			3								
9	27	Sunderland	0-4		27565	1		2	4	5	6	7	10	9	8	11			3	12							
10	Oct 4	BRISTOL CITY	1-1	Needham	10802	1		2	4	5	6	7	10	9	8	11			3	12							
11	11	OXFORD UNITED	0-1		11742	1	2	3	4	5	6	7	8	9		11			10	12							
12	18	Bolton Wanderers	1-2	Bolton	16659	1		2	4	5	6		8	9		11	7	10	3								
13	25	PORTSMOUTH	2-0	Scanlon(p), Probert	9594	1		2	4	5	6		8	9	10	11	7		3	12							
14	Nov 1	West Bromwich Alb.	0-0		12610	1	12	2	4	5	6	7		9	8	11			10	3							
15	4	PLYMOUTH ARGYLE	1-0	Scanlon	9239	1		2	12	5	6	7	8	9		11		4	10	3							
16	8	BRISTOL ROVERS	1-1	Bradd	10930	1		2		5	6	7	8	9		11		4	10	3							
17	15	Chelsea	0-2		18229	1	12	2		5	6	7	8	9		11		4	10	3							
18	22	BOLTON WANDERERS	1-1	Bradd	12964	1		2	4	5	6	7	8	9		11			10	3							
19	29	Blackpool	0-1		5747	1		2	4	5	6	7		9		11			10	3	12						
20	Dec 6	BLACKBURN ROVERS	3-0	Bolton, Bradd, Scanlon	10252	1		2	4	5	6			9	8	11			10	3	7						
21	13	Southampton	1-2	Vinter	12571	1		2	4	5	6		12	9	8	11			10	3	7						
22	20	CHARLTON ATHLETIC	2-0	O'Brien, Sims	10017	1		2	4	5	6			9	8	11			10	3	7						
23	26	Fulham	2-3	Vinter, Scanlon	11887	1		2		5	6	7		9		11		4	10	3	12	8					
24	27	OLDHAM ATHLETIC	5-1	Bradd 2, Scanlon 2, Sims	14706	1		2	7	5	6			9		11		4	10	3		8					
25	Jan 10	YORK CITY	4-0	Sims 2, Bradd, Vinter	10136	1		2		5	6			9				4	10	3	11	7	8				
26	17	Carlisle Utd.	2-1	Bradd, Vinter	7654	1		2	12	5	6			9				4	10	3	7	8					
27	Feb 7	Plymouth Argyle	3-1	Probert, Scanlon, Vinter	11576	1		2		5	6			9		11		4	10	3	12	8	7				
28	14	Bristol Rovers	0-0		7946	1		2	4	5	6			9	8	11			10	3	12	7					
29	21	CHELSEA	3-2	Scanlon, Sims, Bradd	14528	1		2		5	6		12	9		11		4	10	3	7	8					
30	24	HULL CITY	1-2	Bolton	15293	1		2	12	5	6	7		9		11		4	10	3		8					
31	28	Portsmouth	3-1	Bradd 2, Scanlon	9126	1	2		7	5	6			9		11		4	10	3	12	8					
32	Mar 6	WEST BROMWICH ALB.	0-2		20032	1	2		4	5	6			9	8	11			10	3	12	7					
33	13	Oxford United	1-2	Sims	5737	1	2			5	6			9		11		4	10	3	12	7		1	8		
34	20	BLACKPOOL	1-2	Mann	10427	1	2			5	6				12	11		4	10	3	9	7		1	8		
35	27	Blackburn Rovers	1-2	Mann	8472	1	2			5	6	12		9				4	10	3	11	7			8		
36	Apr 3	SUNDERLAND	0-0		14811	1	2			5	6	11		9					10	3	7			8	4		
37	10	Luton Town	1-1	Sims	8277	1	2			5	6	11		9			12		10	3	7			8	4		
38	13	NOTTM. FOREST	0-0		29279	1	2			5	6	7		9		11			10	3				8	4		12
39	17	FULHAM	4-0	Bradd, O'Brien, Scanlon, Benjamin	8819	1	2			5	6		8	9		11			10	3	7				4		12
40	19	Oldham Athletic	2-2	Bradd, Mann	7346	1	2			5	6	7		9		11			10	3				8	4		12
41	24	Bristol City	2-1	O'Brien, Benjamin	24614	1	2			5	6	8		9		11			10	3	7				4		12
42	27	LEYTON ORIENT	2-0	Needham, Sims	8515	1	2			5	6	7		9					10	3		8			4	12	11
		Apps				40	14	32	27	42	40	24	27	42	30	38	4	31	40	20	19	3	2	5	7	1	5
		Goals							3	2			1	16	5	12		3	3	5	8						2

F.A. Cup

Rd	Date	Opponent	Score	Scorers	Att.	McManus CE	Brindley JC	Richards P	Bolton IR	Needham DW	Stubbs BH	Carter SC	McVay DR	Bradd LJ	Probert EW	Scanlon I	Randall K	Mann AF	O'Brien R	Vinter M	Sims J	King J	Lane F	Birchenall AJ	Smith DF	Richards LG	Benjamin T
R3	Jan 3	LEEDS UNITED	0-1		31192	1		2	4	5	6	12		9		11			10	3	7	8					

F.L. Cup

Rd	Date	Opponent	Score	Scorers	Att.	McManus CE	Brindley JC	Richards P	Bolton IR	Needham DW	Stubbs BH	Carter SC	McVay DR	Bradd LJ	Probert EW	Scanlon I	Randall K	Mann AF	O'Brien R	Vinter M	Sims J	King J	Lane F	Birchenall AJ	Smith DF	Richards LG	Benjamin T
R2	Sep 9	SUNDERLAND	2-1	Stubbs, Bradd	10384	1		2	4	5	6	7	10	9	8	11			3	12							
R3	Oct 8	Leeds United	1-0	Scanlon	19122	1	2	3	4	5	6	7	8	9		11			10								
R4	Nov 11	Everton	2-2	Scanlon(p), Stubbs	19169	1	12	2		5	6	7	8	9		11		4	10	3							
rep	Nov 25	EVERTON	2-0	Bradd 2	23404	1		2		5	6	7	8	9		11		4	10	3							
R5	Dec 3	Newcastle United	0-1		31223	1		2	8	5	6	7		9		11		4	10	3						12	

1976/77   8th in Division Two

#	Date	Opponent	Score	Scorers	Att.	McManus CE	Richards P	O'Brien R	Probert EW	Needham DW	Stubbs BH	McVay DR	Vinter M	Bradd LJ	Smith DF	Scanlon I	Mann AF	Benjamin T	Sims J	Carter SC	Bolton IR	Ross I	Busby MG	Mair G	Richards LG	Hooks P
1	Aug 21	MILLWALL	1-2	Bradd	8469	1	2	3	4	5	6	7	8	9	10	11	12									
2	25	Chelsea	1-1	Probert	17426	1	2	3	4	5		10	7	9	8	11	6	12								
3	28	Plymouth Argyle	2-1	Sims, Vinter	14539	1	2	3	4	5	6	10	7		8		11	12	9							
4	Sep 4	BOLTON WANDERERS	0-1		9347	1	2	3	4	5	6	10	7		8	9		12		11						
5	11	Cardiff City	3-2	Needham, Vinter 2	11960	1	2	3	4	5	6		7		8	11	10		9	12						
6	18	BLACKPOOL	2-0	Scanlon, Mann	9598	1	2	3	4	5	6		7		8	11	10		9	12						
7	25	Bristol Rovers	1-5	Needham	6251	1	2		4	5	6		9		8	11	3		10	7	12					
8	Oct 2	OLDHAM ATHLETIC	1-0	Scanlon(p)	9123	1	2	3	4	5	6	12	7		8	11	10		9							
9	9	Blackburn Rovers	1-6	Probert	7993	1	2		4	5	6	10	7		8	11	3		9		12					
10	16	LEYTON ORIENT	0-1		8192	1	2		10	5			8	9		11	6			12	7	3	4			
11	23	Hereford United	4-1	Sims 2, Needham, Busby	7462	1	2		10	5	6		8			11	3		7				4	9		
12	30	CARLISLE UTD.	2-1	Ross, Probert	8327	1	2		10	5	6		8			11	3		7	12			4	9		
13	Nov 6	Sheffield United	0-1		18355	1	2		10	5	6		8			11	3		7	12			4	9		
14	13	WOLVERHAMPTON W.	1-1	Bradd	14234	1	2	3	4	5	6		7	9		11	10			12			8			
15	20	Fulham	5-1	Vinter 2, Carter, Busby, Howe(og)	12191	1	2		4	5			8	9		11	6						10	12		
16	27	LUTON TOWN	0-4		10009	1	2		4	5	6		8	9		11	3		12	7			10			
17	Dec 4	Southampton	1-2	Vinter	14153	1	2		4		5	3	8	9		11	6			7			10			
18	27	HULL CITY	1-1	Needham	10634	1	2	3	4	5	12		8	9		11	6			7			10			
19	Jan 3	Carlisle Utd.	2-0	Vinter, Mann	8295	1	2	3		5	6		8	9	11		10			7			4			
20	22	Millwall	5-2	Bradd 2, Vinter 3	10240	1	2	3		5	6		8	9	11		10			7			4			
21	29	Charlton Athletic	1-1	Needham	8863	1	2	3		5	6		8	9	11		10			7			4			
22	Feb 5	PLYMOUTH ARGYLE	2-0	Needham, Mann	9079	1	2	3		5	6		8	9	11		10			7			4			
23	12	Bolton Wanderers	0-4		22355	1	2	3		5	6		8	9	11		10			12	7		4			
24	15	CHELSEA	2-1	Stubbs, Carter(p)	11902	1	2	3		5	6		8	9	11		10			7			4			
25	19	CARDIFF CITY	1-0	Bradd	9401	1	2	3		5	6		8	9	11	12	10			7			4			
26	26	Blackpool	1-1	Vinter	10275	1	2	3		5			8	9	10	11	6			7			4			
27	Mar 2	BURNLEY	5-1	Carter 2(2p), Thompson(og), Vinter, Bradd	8492	1	2	3		5			8	9	10	11	6			7			4	12		
28	5	BRISTOL ROVERS	2-1	Busby, Carter	10058	1	2	3		5	6		8	9	10	12	11			7			4			
29	8	Nottm. Forest	2-1	Anderson(og), Carter(p)	31004	1	2	3		5			8	9	11	12	4	6		7			10			
30	12	Oldham Athletic	1-1	Bradd	9771	1	2	3		5				9	10	11	6			12	7		4	8		
31	19	BLACKBURN ROVERS	0-0		9343	1	2	3		5	6			9		11	10			7			4	8		
32	26	Leyton Orient	0-1		4635	1	2	3		5	6	8		9		11	10	12		7			4			
33	28	SHEFFIELD UNITED	2-1	Carter 2(1p)	9275	1	2	3		5	6			9		11	10			7	8		4			
34	Apr 1	HEREFORD UNITED	3-2	Bradd 2, Scanlon	8080	1	2	3		5	6			9	12	11	10			7	8		4			
35	8	Hull City	1-0	Daniel(og)	7225	1	2	3		5	6			9		11	10			7	8		4			
36	9	NOTTM. FOREST	1-1	Bradd	32518	1		3		5	6	12	9	8		11		2		7	10		4			
37	11	Wolverhampton Wand.	2-2	Bradd, Mann	25549	1	2	3		5	6		8	9	11	12	10			7			4			
38	16	FULHAM	0-0		14847	1	2	3		5	6		8	9	10	12	11			7			4			
39	23	Luton Town	2-4	Bradd, Mann	9585	1	2	3		5	6		8	9	11	12	10			7			4			
40	30	SOUTHAMPTON	3-1	Carter(p), Richards P, Scanlon	11021	1	2			5	6		12	9		11	10			8	7	3	4			
41	May 7	Burnley	1-3	Scanlon	11699	1	2	3		5			12	9		11	10			8	7	6	4			
42	14	CHARLTON ATHLETIC	0-1		7845	1	2	3		5							12		6	8	7		4	9	10	11
		Apps				42	41	33	18	41	33	8	36	30	29	31	41	7	20	36	5	4	32	5	1	1
		Goals					1		3	6	1		12	12		5	5		3	9			1	3		

Four own goals

F.A. Cup

	Date	Opponent	Score	Att.	McManus CE	Richards P	O'Brien R	Probert EW	Needham DW	Stubbs BH	McVay DR	Vinter M	Bradd LJ	Smith DF	Scanlon I	Mann AF	Benjamin T	Sims J	Carter SC	Bolton IR	Ross I	Busby MG
R3	Jan 8	ARSENAL	0-1	17328	1	2	3		5	6		8	9	11		10			7			4

F.L. Cup

	Date	Opponent	Score	Scorers	Att.	McManus CE	Richards P	O'Brien R	Probert EW	Needham DW	Stubbs BH	McVay DR	Vinter M	Bradd LJ	Smith DF	Scanlon I	Mann AF	Sims J	Carter SC
R2	Sep 1	Scunthorpe Utd.	2-0	McVay, Vinter	6208	1	2	3	4	5	6	7	8		10	11		9	12
R3	Sep 22	Derby County	1-1	O'Brien	24881	1	2	3	4	5	6		8		7	11	10	9	12
rep	Oct 4	DERBY COUNTY	1-2	Scanlon(p)	16276	1	2	3	4	5		10	8		7	11	6	9	12

Anglo-Scottish Cup

	Date	Opponent	Score	Scorers	Att.	McManus CE	Richards P	O'Brien R	Probert EW	Needham DW	Stubbs BH	McVay DR	Vinter M	Bradd LJ	Smith DF	Scanlon I	Mann AF	Benjamin T	Sims J
QR	Aug 7	NOTTM. FOREST	0-0		4258	1	2	3	4	5	6	8		9		11	10	12	7
QR	Aug 10	Bristol City	0-2		3372	1	2	3	4	5	6	8		9		11	10	12	7
QR	Aug 14	West Bromwich Alb.	1-3	Sims	6396	1	2	3	4	5	6	10	9		8	11		12	7

- 1976/77 Season -

Back: P.Richards, Scanlon, McManus, Bradd, Benjamin
Standing: Wheeler (Trainer), L.Richards, Vinter, McVay, Sprigg, Lane, Probert, Bolton, O'Brien, Addison(Coach)
Sitting: Smith, Towle, Needham, Fenton (Manager), Carter, Stubbs, Mann
Front: Mair, Mitchell, Hooks

- 1977/78 Season -

Back: Scanlon, P.Richards, Chapman, McManus, Sims, Benjamin
Middle: Wheeler (Trainer), Bradd, Mair, Hooks, L.Richards, Stubbs, Jones (Coach)
Front: Busby, Carter, Vinter, Fenton (Manager), Mann, O'Brien, Smith

1977/78 15th in Division Two

No	Date	Opponent	Res	Scorers	Att	McManus CE	Richards P	O'Brien R	Busby MG	Chapman RD	Benjamin T	Carter SC	Vinter M	Bradd LJ	Smith DF	Scanlon I	Hooks P	Richards LG	Sims J	Stubbs BH	Birchenall AJ	Mann AF	Ladd I	McVay DR	Hunt D	Wood GT
1	Aug 20	BLACKBURN ROVERS	1-1	Bradd	8237	1	2	3	4	5	6	7	8	9	10	11	12									
2	Aug 23	Bristol Rovers	2-2	Carter, Busby	5167	1	2	3	4	5	6	7	8	9	10	11			12							
3	Aug 27	Tottenham Hotspur	1-2	Vinter	25839	1	2	3	4	5	6	7	8		10				11	9	12					
4	Sep 3	SOUTHAMPTON	2-3	Sims, Bradd	9088	1	2	3		4	6	7	8	12	10				11	9	5					
5	Sep 10	CARDIFF CITY	1-1	O'Brien	7330	1	2	3	4	5		7		9	10					8	6	11	12			
6	Sep 17	Fulham	1-5	Bradd	6064	1	2	3	4	5		7	8	9	10		11			6	12					
7	Sep 24	BLACKPOOL	1-1	Stubbs	7200	1		3		5	2	4	11	12		7		8		6	9	10				
8	Oct 1	Luton Town	0-2		7593	1	4	3		8	2			9			10		12	6	7	11	5			
9	Oct 4	Sheffield United	1-4	Hooks	12495	1		3		4	2	7					8	11	9	5	10	6				
10	Oct 8	LEYTON ORIENT	1-1	Bradd	7482	1	2	3		5		7	8	9	4		12			6	10	11				
11	Oct 15	Oldham Athletic	1-2	Vinter	8717	1	2	3		5		10	7	9	4	12				6	8	11				
12	Oct 22	CHARLTON ATHLETIC	2-0	Carter, Vinter	8273	1	2	3		5	6	7	11		8				9	4		10				
13	Oct 29	Mansfield Town	3-1	O'Brien, Mann, Vinter	12237	1	2	3		5	6	7	11	12					9	4	8	10				
14	Nov 5	BRIGHTON & HOVE ALB.	1-0	Vinter	9549	1	2	3		4		7	11				12		9	5	6	10		8		
15	Nov 12	Burnley	1-3	Carter(p)	9734	1	2	3		6		7	9				12		8	5	10	11		4		
16	Nov 19	SUNDERLAND	2-2	Bradd, Mann	12247	1	2	3		4		7	8	9			12			5	6	11		10		
17	Nov 26	Millwall	0-0		5654	1	2	3		4			11	9	12		7			5	6	10		8		
18	Dec 3	STOKE CITY	2-0	Vinter, Hooks	9309	1	2	3		4		7	9				8			5	10	11		6		
19	Dec 10	Crystal Palace	0-2		14691	1	2	3		4		7	9			12	11			5	6	10		8		
20	Dec 17	BURNLEY	3-0	Hooks, Thompson(og), Vinter	7639	1	2	3		4		7	9				10			5	6	11		8		
21	Dec 26	Bolton Wanderers	0-2		24559	1		3		4			9	8		12	11	7		5	6	10		2		
22	Dec 27	HULL CITY	2-1	O'Brien 2	9486	1		3		4			9	8			11	7	12	5	6	10		2		
23	Dec 31	BRISTOL ROVERS	3-2	Bradd 2, Hooks	8471	1		3		4			9	8			11	7	12	5	6	10		2		
24	Jan 2	Blackburn Rovers	0-1		14394	1		3		4			9	8			11	7		5	6	10		2		
25	Jan 14	TOTTENHAM HOTSPUR	3-3	Bradd 2, Vinter	15709	1	2	3		4		7	11	9					8	5		10		6		
26	Jan 21	Southampton	1-3	Vinter	20174	1	2	3		4		7	11	9			12		8	5		10		6		
27	Feb 25	LUTON TOWN	2-0	Bradd, Mann	8558	1	2	3		4		7	11	9			12			5	8	10		6		
28	Mar 4	Leyton Orient	0-0		5828	1	2	3		4		7	11	9						5	6	10		8		
29	Mar 7	Blackpool	2-2	O'Brien, Carter	6783	1	2	3		4		7	8	9					12	5	6	11		10		
30	Mar 11	OLDHAM ATHLETIC	3-2	Vinter 2, Carter(p)	8916	1	2	3		4		7	8	9					12	5	6	11		10		
31	Mar 17	Charlton Athletic	0-0		5856	1	2	3		4	5	7	11	9					12		10			8	6	
32	Mar 21	MANSFIELD TOWN	1-0	Vinter	10587	1	2	3		4		7	11	9						5	6			10	8	
33	Mar 25	Hull City	1-1	Vinter	5392	1	2	3		4		7	11	9			12			5	6			8	10	
34	Mar 27	BOLTON WANDERERS	1-1	Vinter	15718	1	2	3		4		7	11	9			12			5	6			10	8	
35	Apr 1	Brighton & Hove Alb.	1-2	Vinter	20315	1	2	3		4	5	7	11	9			12				6			8	10	
36	Apr 4	FULHAM	1-1	Vinter	7378	1	2	3		4	5	7	11	9					8					10	6	
37	Apr 8	MILLWALL	1-1	Vinter	7509	1	2	3		4	5	7	11	9			12				6	10		8		
38	Apr 15	Sunderland	1-3	Sims	14673	1	2			4	5	7	11	9					8		6				10	3
39	Apr 22	CRYSTAL PALACE	2-0	Vinter, Bradd	7710	1	2	3		4		7	11	9						5		10		8	6	
40	Apr 25	SHEFFIELD UNITED	1-2	Vinter	8234	1	2	3		4		7	11	9			12			5		10		8	6	
41	Apr 29	Stoke City	1-1	Bradd	13890	1	2	3		4	12	7	11	9						5		10		8	6	
42	May 3	Cardiff City	1-2	O'Brien	9506	1	2	3		4	10	7	11	9						5		10		8	6	
		Apps				42	36	41	5	42	16	36	39	34	14	4	19	7	22	35	28	31	1	27	12	1
		Goals						6	1			5	19	12			4			2	1	3				

One own goal

F.A. Cup

	Date	Opponent	Res	Scorers	Att	McManus CE	Richards P	O'Brien R	Busby MG	Chapman RD	Benjamin T	Carter SC	Vinter M	Bradd LJ	Smith DF	Scanlon I	Hooks P	Richards LG	Sims J	Stubbs BH	Birchenall AJ	Mann AF	Ladd I	McVay DR	Hunt D	Wood GT
R3	Jan 6	Charlton Athletic	2-0	Vinter 2	9228	1		3		4			11	9	8	7	12			5	6	10		2		
R4	Jan 31	Brighton & Hove Alb.	2-1	Vinter 2	23590	1	2	3		4		7	11	9			12			5	6	10		8		
R5	Feb 18	Millwall	1-2	Chapman	12176	1	2	3		4		7	11	9			12			5	6	10		8		

F.L. Cup

	Date	Opponent	Res	Scorers	Att	McManus CE	Richards P	O'Brien R	Busby MG	Chapman RD	Benjamin T	Carter SC	Vinter M	Bradd LJ	Smith DF	Scanlon I	Hooks P	Richards LG	Sims J	Stubbs BH	Birchenall AJ	Mann AF	Ladd I	McVay DR	Hunt D	Wood GT
R2	Aug 30	Birmingham City	2-0	Carter(p), Sims	14993	1	2	3	4	5	6	7	8		10			11	9							
R3	Oct 25	Nottm. Forest	0-4		26931	1	2	3		4	6	7	11		8	12			9	5		10				

Anglo-Scottish Cup

	Date	Opponent	Res	Scorers	Att	McManus CE	Richards P	O'Brien R	Busby MG	Chapman RD	Benjamin T	Carter SC	Vinter M	Bradd LJ	Smith DF	Scanlon I	Hooks P	Richards LG	Sims J	Stubbs BH	Birchenall AJ	Mann AF	Ladd I	McVay DR	Hunt D	Wood GT
PR	Aug 6	HULL CITY	1-0	Vinter	4020	1	2	3	4	5	6	7	9		8	11			10							
PR	Aug 9	Oldham Athletic	0-0		3243	1	2	3	4	5	6	7	9		8	11		12	10							
PR	Aug 12	Sheffield United	5-4	Chapman, Sims 2, Scanlon, Hooks	8000	1	2	3	4	5		7	9		10	11	12			8	6					
PO	Sep 6	SHEFFIELD UNITED	3-0	Smith, Stubbs, O'Brien	5279	1	2	3	4	5		7		9	10	11	12			8	6					
QF1	Sep 13	Motherwell	1-1	Bradd	4734	1	2	3	4		6	12	9			7			10	5		11				
QF2	Sep 27	MOTHERWELL	1-0	Vinter	5396	1		3		5	2		12	9			11		4	8	6		7	10		
SF1	Oct 18	ST. MIRREN	1-0	Mann	5384	1	2	3		4		7	11	9	8					5	6	10				
SF2	Nov 1	St. Mirren	0-2		4345	1	2	3		4		7	11	9	8	12			9	5		10		6		

A play off with Sheffield United was required.
SF2 game after extra time.

EW Probert played in third PR game (at 8) and in QF1 (8)

1978/79   6th in DIvision Two

#		Date	Opponent	Score	Scorers	Att	McManus CE	Richards P	O'Brien R	Benjamin T	Blockley JP	Stubbs BH	Carter SC	McCulloch I	Hooks P	Mann AF	Vinter M	McVay DR	Green R	Wood GT	Hunt D	Masson DS	Mair G
1	Aug	19	West Ham United	2-5	McCulloch 2	25387	1	2	3	4	5	6	7	8	9	10	11	12					
2		22	MILLWALL	1-1	Vinter	7060	1	2	3	4	5	6	7	8	9	10	11	12					
3		26	BLACKBURN ROVERS	2-1	Blockley, Vinter	7774	1	2	3	4	5	6		7	9	8	11		10				
4	Sep	2	Burnley	1-2	McCulloch	9787	1	2	3	4	5	6		7	12	10	11		9		8		
5		9	Leicester City	1-0	Vinter	14485	1	2	3	4	5	6		7			11		9		10	8	
6		16	LEYTON ORIENT	1-0	Masson	8190	1	2	3	4	5	6		7					9		10	8	
7		22	Charlton Athletic	1-1	Vinter	8643	1	2	3	4	5	6		7		12	11		9		10	8	
8		30	NEWCASTLE UNITED	1-2	Hooks	11813	1	2	3	4		5		7	12	6	11		9		10	8	
9	Oct	7	Cardiff City	3-2	Hooks 2, McCulloch	7952	1	2	3	4	5	6		7	9	10	11				12	8	
10		14	BRISTOL ROVERS	2-1	Vinter, O'Brien(p)	8646	1	2	3	4		5		7	9	6	11				10	8	
11		21	Luton Town	0-6		8561	1	2	3	4		5		7	9	6	11	12			10	8	
12		28	CAMBRIDGE UNITED	1-1	McCulloch	8437	1		3	4		5		7	9	6	11	2	12		10	8	
13	Nov	4	Wrexham	1-3	O'Brien	10891	1		3	4		5		7	9		11	2		10	6	8	
14		11	WEST HAM UNITED	1-0	O'Brien(p)	11002	1	2	3	4		5		7	9	6	11				10	8	
15		18	Blackburn Rovers	4-3	Hooks, Vinter, Masson, Hunt	7833	1	2	3	4		5		7	9	6	11	12			10	8	
16		21	BURNLEY	1-1	Masson	8520	1	2	3	4		5		7	9	6	11				10	8	
17		25	BRIGHTON & HOVE ALB.	1-0	Hooks	8851	1	2	3	4		5		7	9	6	11				10	8	
18	Dec	2	Fulham	1-1	Hooks	7591	1	2	3	4		5		7	9	6	11				10	8	
19		9	CRYSTAL PALACE	0-0		11011	1	2	3	4		5		7	9	6	11				10	8	
20		16	Preston North End	1-1	Vinter	10730	1	2	3	4		5		7	9	6	11				10	8	
21		23	SUNDERLAND	1-1	O'Brien(p)	11281	1	2	3	4	6	5		7	9	10	11					8	
22		26	Oldham Athletic	3-3	Hooks, Vinter, Blockley	8262	1	2	3	4	12	5		7	9	6	11				10	8	
23		30	Stoke City	0-2		21393	1	2	3	4	12	5		7	9	6	11				10	8	
24	Jan	20	Leyton Orient	0-3		4803	1	2	3	4		5		7	9	6	11	12			10	8	
25	Feb	3	CHARLTON ATHLETIC	1-1	Mann	7958	1	2	3		4	5		7	9	6	11				10	8	
26		24	Bristol Rovers	2-2	Hooks, Vinter	6887	1	2	3		4	5		7	9	6	11				10	8	
27	Mar	3	LUTON TOWN	3-1	Mann, Hunt, Hooks	7624	1	2	3		4	5		7	9	6	11				10	8	
28		10	Cambridge United	1-0	Mann	5157	1	2	3		4	5		7	9	6	11	12			10	8	
29		13	SHEFFIELD UNITED	4-1	Vinter 3, McCulloch	10372	1	2	3		4	5		7	9	6	11				10	8	
30		24	Millwall	1-0	O'Brien	5679	1	2	3		4	5		7	9	6	11	12			10	8	
31		27	CARDIFF CITY	1-0	McCulloch	8211	1	2	3	12	4	5		7	9	6	11				10	8	
32		31	Brighton & Hove Alb.	0-0		21382	1	2	3		4	5		7	9	6	11				10	8	
33	Apr	7	FULHAM	1-1	Blockley	9465	1	2	3	12	4	5		7	9	6	11				10	8	
34		10	Sheffield United	1-5	McCulloch	15186	1	2	3		4	5		7	9	6	11				10	8	
35		13	Sunderland	0-3		34027	1	2	3		4	5		7	9	6	11		12		10	8	
36		14	OLDHAM ATHLETIC	0-0		7023	1	2	3	12	4	5		7	9	6	11				10	8	
37		18	Newcastle United	2-1	Hooks, O'Brien(p)	12017	1	2	3		4	5		7	9	6	11	12			10	8	
38		21	PRESTON NORTH END	0-0		7009	1	2	3		4	5		7	9	6	11				10		8
39		24	LEICESTER CITY	0-1		8702	1	2	3		4	5		7	9	12	11				10	8	6
40		28	Crystal Palace	0-2		23454	1	2	3		4	5		7	9	6	11		12		10	8	
41	May	1	WREXHAM	1-1	Mair	4374	1	2			4	5		7	9	12	11			3	10	8	6
42		5	STOKE CITY	0-1		21571	1	2	3		4	5		7	9	10	11					8	6
			Apps				42	40	41	27	29	42	2	42	38	40	41	11	9	2	37	37	4
			Goals					6		3				8	10	3	12				2	3	1

F.A. Cup

Rnd		Date	Opponent	Score	Scorers	Att	McManus CE	Richards P	O'Brien R	Benjamin T	Blockley JP	Stubbs BH	Carter SC	McCulloch I	Hooks P	Mann AF	Vinter M	McVay DR	Green R	Wood GT	Hunt D	Masson DS	Mair G
R3	Jan	9	READING	4-2	Vinter, Hooks, Mann, Masson	8265	1	2	3		4	5		7	9	6	11				10	8	
R4	Jan	27	Arsenal	0-2		39173	1	2	3		4	5		7	9	6	11				10	8	

F.L. Cup

Rnd		Date	Opponent	Score	Scorers	Att	McManus CE	Richards P	O'Brien R	Benjamin T	Blockley JP	Stubbs BH	Carter SC	McCulloch I	Hooks P	Mann AF	Vinter M	McVay DR	Green R	Wood GT	Hunt D	Masson DS	Mair G
R1/1	Aug	12	Scunthorpe Utd.	1-0	Hooks	2389	1	2	3	4	5	6	7		8	10	9		11				
R1/2	Aug	15	SCUNTHORPE UTD.	3-0	Carter 2, Hooks	5064	1	2	3	4	5	6	7	8	9	10	11		12				
R2	Aug	30	Crewe Alexandra	0-2		3178	1	2	3	4	5	6		7	9	10	11				12	8	

Anglo-Scottish Cup

Rnd		Date	Opponent	Score	Scorers	Att	McManus CE	Richards P	O'Brien R	Benjamin T	Blockley JP	Stubbs BH	Carter SC	McCulloch I	Hooks P	Mann AF	Vinter M	McVay DR	Green R	Wood GT	Hunt D	Masson DS	Mair G
PR	Jul	31	Mansfield Town	0-1		5354	1	2	3		5	6	12	7		10	11	8	9		4		
PR	Aug	5	NORWICH CITY	2-1	Blockley, Carter	4209	1	2	3	4	5	6	12	7	9	10	11				8		
PR	Aug	8	Leyton Orient	3-2	Vinter, Benjamin, Carter(p)	2511	1	2	3	4	5	6	7	8	9		11				12	10	

- 1978/79 Season -

Back: Chapman, Hunt, McVay, Mann, Richards, Benjamin
Middle: Wheeler(Trainer), Stubbs, Green, King, McManus, Blockley, Sims, Murphy(Coach)
Front: Carter, Hooks, McCulloch, Sirrell(Manager), Vinter, O'Brien, Smith

- 1979/80 Season -

Back: Wheeler(Train), Hunt, Christie, Blockley, Leonard, Avramovic, McCulloch, Benjamin, Stubbs, Kilcline, Sirrell(Man)
Front: Mair, Manns, Hooks, Richards, Wood, Doherty, Masson, O'Brien

1979/80   17th in Division Two

#	Date	Opponent	Res	Scorers	Att	Avramovic R	Richards P	O'Brien R	Blockley JP	Stubbs BH	Mair G	McCulloch I	Masson DS	Hooks P	Hunt D	Christie T	Benjamin T	Leonard MC	Kilcline B	Manns P	Beavon MS	Doherty J	Wood GT	Shelton G
1	Aug 18	CARDIFF CITY	4-1	McCulloch, Mair, Richards, Masson	7157	1	2	3	4	5	6	7	8	9	10	11								
2	21	Shrewsbury Town	1-1	Christie	7369	1	2	3	6	5	11	7	8	10	4	9								
3	25	Burnley	1-0	Mair	7005	1	2	3	6	5	11	7	8	10	4	9	12							
4	Sep 1	QUEENS PARK RANGERS	1-0	Masson	8745	1	2	3	6	5	11	7	8	10	4	9								
5	8	Leicester City	0-1		16595	1	2	3	6	5	11	7	8	10	4	9								
6	15	LUTON TOWN	0-0		9582		2	3	6	5	11	7	8	10	4	9	12	1						
7	22	SWANSEA CITY	0-0		8319		2	3	6	5	11	7	8	10	4	9		1						
8	29	Wrexham	0-1		9173		2	3	6	5	11	7	8	10	4	9	12	1						
9	Oct 6	Bristol Rovers	3-2	Blockley, McCulloch, Christie	5422		2	3	4		11	7	8	6	9	10		1	5	12				
10	9	SHREWSBURY TOWN	5-2	Mair, O'Brien 2(2p), McCulloch, Benjamin	7361		2	3	6	5	11	7	8	12	4	9	10	1						
11	13	OLDHAM ATHLETIC	1-1	Masson	8540		2	3	4	5	11	7	8	12	6	9	10	1						
12	20	Fulham	3-1	Hooks, McCulloch 2	6280	1	2	3	6	5	11	7	8	9	4		10							
13	27	WEST HAM UNITED	0-1		12256	1	2	3	6	5	11	7	8	9	4	12	10							
14	Nov 1	PRESTON NORTH END	2-1	Blockley, Hunt	8316		2	3	6	5	11	7	8	9	4	12	10	1						
15	3	Cardiff City	2-3	Mair, Christie	8602	1	2	3	6	5	11	7	8	9	4	12	10							
16	17	Sunderland	1-3	Masson	21896	1	2	3	6	5	11	7	8	9	4	12	10							
17	24	CHELSEA	2-3	Hooks, O'Brien	12646	1	2	3		5	11	7	8	9	4	12	10				6			
18	Dec 1	Watford	1-2	O'Brien	12170	1	2	3	6	5	11	7	8	9	10	12	4							
19	8	BIRMINGHAM CITY	1-1	O'Brien(p)	11383	1	2	3	6	5	11	7	8	9	4	12					10			
20	15	Leyton Orient	0-1		4115	1	2	3	6		11	7	8	9	4	12			5		10			
21	22	NEWCASTLE UNITED	2-2	O'Brien 2(2p)	11224	1	2	3	6	5	11	7	8	9	4	12					10			
22	26	Charlton Athletic	0-0		6894	1		3	6	5	11	7	8	9	4	12	2				10			
23	29	BURNLEY	2-3	Hunt, Christie	7596	1		3	6	5	11	7	8	9	4	12	2				10			
24	Jan 1	CAMBRIDGE UNITED	0-0		7722	1		3	6	5	11	7	8		4	9	2				10			
25	12	Queens Park Rangers	3-1	Christie, Hooks, Hunt	9613			3	6		11		8	10	4	9	2	1	5			7	12	
26	19	Leicester City	0-1		14849			3	6		11		8	10	4	9	2	1	12			7		
27	Feb 2	Luton Town	1-2	Donaghy(og)	9007	1		3	6	5	11	7	8	10	4	9	2					12		
28	9	Swansea City	1-0	Hooks	13213	1		3	6	5	11		8	9	4	7	2					10		
29	23	Oldham Athletic	0-1		7241	1		3	6	5	10		8	9	4	11	2		12			7		
30	26	WREXHAM	1-1	O'Brien(p)	6684	1		3	6	5	11	7	8		4	9	2					10		
31	Mar 1	FULHAM	1-1	Hunt	6968	1		3	6	5	11	7	8		4	9	2					10		
32	11	West Ham United	2-1	Christie, Stubbs	24894	1	2	3		5	11	7	8		10	9	4				6			
33	15	BRISTOL ROVERS	0-0		5693	1	2			5	10	11	8	12	4	9			6		3			7
34	22	Preston North End	0-2		7407	1	2	3		5	11	7	8	12		9			6					4
35	29	SUNDERLAND	0-1		10817	1	2	3		5	11	7	8	12	10	9			6					4
36	Apr 2	Newcastle United	2-2	Christie, Benjamin	22005	1	2	3		5	11	7	8	12	10	9			6					4
37	5	CHARLTON ATHLETIC	0-0		6254	1	2	3		5	11	7	8	12	10	9			6					4
38	8	Cambridge United	3-2	McCulloch, Christie, O'Brien	5546	1	2	3		5	11	7	8		10	9			6					4
39	12	WATFORD	1-2	Hooks	7279	1	2	3		5	11	7		8	12	10	9		6					4
40	19	Chelsea	0-1		24002	1	2	3		5	11	7		8	9	10			6					4
41	26	LEYTON ORIENT	1-1	O'Brien(p)	5505	1	2	3		5	11	7	8		4	9	10		6					
42	May 3	Birmingham City	3-3	Mair, Christie, Kilcline	33863	1	2	3		5	11	7	8	12	10	9	4		6					
		Apps				33	32	41	30	39	42	38	40	34	38	41	34	9	16	3	6	5	1	8
		Goals					1	10	2	1	5	6	4	5	4	9	2		1					

One own goal

F.A. Cup

	Date	Opponent	Res	Scorers	Att	Avramovic R	Richards P	O'Brien R	Blockley JP	Stubbs BH	Mair G	McCulloch I	Masson DS	Hooks P	Hunt D	Christie T	Benjamin T	Leonard MC	Kilcline B
R3	Jan 5	WOLVERHAMPTON W.	1-3	Hunt	15668			3	6		11	7	8	10	4	9	2	1	5

F.L. Cup

	Date	Opponent	Res	Scorers	Att	Avramovic R	Richards P	O'Brien R	Blockley JP	Stubbs BH	Mair G	McCulloch I	Masson DS	Hooks P	Hunt D	Christie T	Benjamin T	Kilcline B	Manns P
R2/1	Aug 28	TORQUAY UNITED	0-0		5865	1	2	3	6	5	11	7	8	10	4		12		9
R2/2	Sep 5	Torquay United	1-0	Hooks	4531	1	2	3	6		11	7	8	10	4	9		5	
R3	Sep 25	Grimsby Town	1-3	O'Brien(p)	11881		2	3	6	5	11	7	8	10	4	9			

Played in game 3: C King (at no. 1)

Anglo-Scottish Cup

	Date	Opponent	Res	Scorers	Att	Avramovic R	Richards P	O'Brien R	Blockley JP	Stubbs BH	Mair G	McCulloch I	Masson DS	Hooks P	Hunt D	Christie T	Benjamin T	Manns P	Doherty J
PR	Aug 4	Mansfield Town	1-0	Christie	3587	1	2	3	6	5		7	10	11	4	9	8		12
PR	Aug 7	SHEFFIELD UNITED	0-1		4340	1	2	3	6	5	12	7	10		4	9	8	11	
PR	Aug 11	CAMBRIDGE UNITED	1-3	Hooks	2553	1	2	3	6	5		7	10	11	4	9	8	12	

League Tables 1979/80 to 1986/87

	1979/80 Division 2	*P*	*W*	*D*	*L*	*F*	*A*	*W*	*D*	*L*	*F*	*A*	*Pts*
1	Leicester City	42	12	5	4	32	19	9	8	4	26	19	55
2	Sunderland	42	16	5	0	47	13	5	7	9	22	29	54
3	Birmingham City	42	14	5	2	37	16	7	6	8	21	22	53
4	Chelsea	42	14	3	4	34	16	9	4	8	32	36	53
5	Queen's Park Rgs.	42	10	9	2	46	25	8	4	9	29	28	49
6	Luton Town	42	9	10	2	36	17	7	7	7	30	28	49
7	West Ham United	42	13	2	6	37	21	7	5	9	17	22	47
8	Cambridge United	42	11	6	4	40	23	3	10	8	21	30	44
9	Newcastle United	42	13	6	2	35	19	2	8	11	18	30	44
10	Preston North End	42	8	10	3	30	23	4	9	8	26	29	43
11	Oldham Athletic	42	12	5	4	30	21	4	6	11	19	32	43
12	Swansea City	42	13	1	7	31	20	4	8	9	17	33	43
13	Shrewsbury Town	42	12	3	6	41	23	6	2	13	19	30	41
14	Orient	42	7	9	5	29	31	5	8	8	19	23	41
15	Cardiff City	42	11	4	6	21	16	5	4	12	20	32	40
16	Wrexham	42	13	2	6	26	15	3	4	14	14	34	38
17	NOTTS COUNTY	42	4	11	6	24	22	7	4	10	27	30	37
18	Watford	42	9	6	6	27	18	3	7	11	12	28	37
19	Bristol Rovers	42	9	8	4	33	23	2	5	14	17	41	35
20	Fulham	42	6	4	11	19	28	5	3	13	23	46	29
21	Burnley	42	5	9	7	19	23	1	6	14	20	50	27
22	Charlton Athletic	42	6	6	9	25	31	0	4	17	14	47	22

	1980/81 Division 2	*P*	*W*	*D*	*L*	*F*	*A*	*W*	*D*	*L*	*F*	*A*	*Pts*
1	West Ham United	42	19	1	1	53	12	9	9	3	26	17	66
2	NOTTS COUNTY	42	10	8	3	26	15	8	9	4	23	23	53
3	Swansea City	42	12	5	4	39	19	6	9	6	25	25	50
4	Blackburn Rovers	42	12	8	1	28	7	4	10	7	14	22	50
5	Luton Town	42	10	6	5	35	23	8	6	7	26	23	48
6	Derby County	42	9	8	4	34	26	6	7	8	23	26	45
7	Grimsby Town	42	10	8	3	21	10	5	7	9	23	32	45
8	Queen's Park Rgs.	42	11	7	3	36	12	4	6	11	20	34	43
9	Watford	42	13	5	3	34	18	3	6	12	16	27	43
10	Sheffield Wed.	42	14	4	3	38	14	3	4	14	15	37	42
11	Newcastle United	42	11	7	3	22	13	3	7	11	8	32	42
12	Chelsea	42	8	6	7	27	15	6	6	9	19	26	40
13	Cambridge United	42	13	1	7	36	23	4	5	12	17	42	40
14	Shrewsbury Town	42	9	7	5	33	22	2	10	9	13	25	39
15	Oldham Athletic	42	7	9	5	19	16	5	6	10	20	32	39
16	Wrexham	42	5	8	8	22	24	7	6	8	21	21	38
17	Orient	42	9	8	4	34	20	4	4	13	18	36	38
18	Bolton Wanderers	42	10	5	6	40	27	4	5	12	21	39	38
19	Cardiff City	42	7	7	7	23	24	5	5	11	21	36	36
20	Preston North End	42	8	7	6	28	26	3	7	11	13	36	36
21	Bristol City	42	6	10	5	19	15	1	6	14	10	36	30
22	Bristol Rovers	42	4	9	8	21	24	1	4	16	13	41	23

	1981/82 Division 1	*P*	*W*	*D*	*L*	*F*	*A*	*W*	*D*	*L*	*F*	*A*	*Pts*
1	Liverpool	42	14	3	4	39	14	12	6	3	41	18	87
2	Ipswich Town	42	17	1	3	47	25	9	4	8	28	28	83
3	Manchester United	42	12	6	3	27	9	10	6	5	32	20	78
4	Tottenham Hotspur	42	12	4	5	41	26	8	7	6	26	22	71
5	Arsenal	42	13	5	3	27	15	7	6	8	21	22	71
6	Swansea City	42	13	3	5	34	16	8	3	10	24	35	69
7	Southampton	42	15	2	4	49	30	4	7	10	23	37	66
8	Everton	42	11	7	3	33	21	6	6	9	23	29	64
9	West Ham United	42	9	10	2	42	29	5	6	10	24	28	58
10	Manchester City	42	9	7	5	32	23	6	6	9	17	27	58
11	Aston Villa	42	9	6	6	28	24	6	6	9	27	29	57
12	Nottingham Forest	42	7	7	7	19	20	8	5	8	23	28	57
13	Brighton & Hove A.	42	8	7	6	30	24	5	6	10	13	28	52
14	Coventry City	42	9	4	8	31	24	4	7	10	25	38	50
15	NOTTS COUNTY	42	8	5	8	32	33	5	3	13	29	36	47
16	Birmingham City	42	8	6	7	29	25	2	8	11	24	36	44
17	West Bromwich Alb.	42	6	6	9	24	25	5	5	11	22	32	44
18	Stoke City	42	9	2	10	27	28	3	6	12	17	35	44
19	Sunderland	42	6	5	10	19	26	5	6	10	19	32	44
20	Leeds United	42	6	11	4	23	20	4	1	16	16	41	42
21	Wolverhampton Wan.	42	8	5	8	19	20	2	5	14	13	43	40
22	Middlesbrough	42	5	9	7	20	24	3	6	12	14	28	39

	1982/83 Division 1	*P*	*W*	*D*	*L*	*F*	*A*	*W*	*D*	*L*	*F*	*A*	*Pts*
1	Liverpool	42	16	4	1	55	16	8	6	7	32	21	82
2	Watford	42	16	2	3	49	20	6	3	12	25	37	71
3	Manchester United	42	14	7	0	39	10	5	6	10	17	28	70
4	Tottenham Hotspur	42	15	4	2	50	15	5	5	11	15	35	69
5	Nottingham Forest	42	12	5	4	34	18	8	4	9	28	32	69
6	Aston Villa	42	17	2	2	47	15	4	3	14	15	35	68
7	Everton	42	13	6	2	43	19	5	4	12	23	29	64
8	West Ham United	42	13	3	5	41	23	7	1	13	27	39	64
9	Ipswich Town	42	11	3	7	39	23	4	10	7	25	27	58
10	Arsenal	42	11	6	4	36	19	5	4	12	22	37	58
11	West Bromwich Alb.	42	11	5	5	35	20	4	7	10	16	29	57
12	Southampton	42	11	5	5	36	22	4	7	10	18	36	57
13	Stoke City	42	13	4	4	34	21	3	5	13	19	43	57
14	Norwich City	42	10	6	5	30	18	4	6	11	22	40	54
15	NOTTS COUNTY	42	12	4	5	37	25	3	3	15	18	46	52
16	Sunderland	42	7	10	4	30	22	5	4	12	18	39	50
17	Birmingham City	42	9	7	5	29	24	3	7	11	11	31	50
18	Luton Town	42	7	7	7	34	33	5	6	10	31	51	49
19	Coventry City	42	10	5	6	29	17	3	4	14	19	42	48
20	Manchester City	42	9	5	7	26	23	4	3	14	21	47	47
21	Swansea City	42	10	4	7	32	29	0	7	14	19	40	41
22	Brighton & Hove A.	42	8	7	6	25	22	1	6	14	13	46	40

	1983/84 Division 1	*P*	*W*	*D*	*L*	*F*	*A*	*W*	*D*	*L*	*F*	*A*	*Pts*
1	Liverpool	42	14	5	2	50	12	8	9	4	23	20	80
2	Southampton	42	15	4	2	44	17	7	7	7	22	21	77
3	Nottingham Forest	42	14	4	3	47	17	8	4	9	29	28	74
4	Manchester United	42	14	3	4	43	18	6	11	4	28	23	74
5	Queen's Park Rgs.	42	14	4	3	37	12	8	3	10	30	25	73
6	Arsenal	42	10	5	6	41	29	8	4	9	33	31	63
7	Everton	42	9	9	3	21	12	7	5	9	23	30	62
8	Tottenham Hotspur	42	11	4	6	31	24	6	6	9	33	41	61
9	West Ham United	42	10	4	7	39	24	7	5	9	21	31	60
10	Aston Villa	42	14	3	4	34	22	3	6	12	25	39	60
11	Watford	42	9	7	5	36	31	7	2	12	32	46	57
12	Ipswich Town	42	11	4	6	34	23	4	4	13	21	34	53
13	Sunderland	42	8	9	4	26	18	5	4	12	16	35	52
14	Norwich City	42	9	8	4	34	20	3	7	11	14	29	51
15	Leicester City	42	11	5	5	40	30	2	7	12	25	38	51
16	Luton Town	42	7	5	9	30	33	7	4	10	23	33	51
17	West Bromwich Alb.	42	10	4	7	30	25	4	5	12	18	37	51
18	Stoke City	42	11	4	6	30	23	2	7	12	14	40	50
19	Coventry City	42	8	5	8	33	33	5	6	10	24	44	50
20	Birmingham City	42	7	7	7	19	18	5	5	11	20	32	48
21	NOTTS COUNTY	42	6	7	8	31	36	4	4	13	19	36	41
22	Wolverhampton Wan.	42	4	8	9	15	28	2	3	16	12	52	29

	1984/85 Division 2	*P*	*W*	*D*	*L*	*F*	*A*	*W*	*D*	*L*	*F*	*A*	*Pts*
1	Oxford United	42	18	2	1	62	15	7	7	7	22	21	84
2	Birmingham City	42	12	6	3	30	15	13	1	7	29	18	82
3	Manchester City	42	14	4	3	42	16	7	7	7	24	24	74
4	Portsmouth	42	11	6	4	39	25	9	8	4	30	25	74
5	Blackburn Rovers	42	14	3	4	38	15	7	7	7	28	26	73
6	Brighton & Hove A.	42	13	6	2	31	11	7	6	8	23	23	72
7	Leeds United	42	12	7	2	37	11	7	5	9	29	32	69
8	Shrewsbury Town	42	12	6	3	45	22	6	5	10	21	31	65
9	Fulham	42	13	3	5	35	26	6	5	10	33	38	65
10	Grimsby Town	42	13	1	7	47	32	5	7	9	25	32	62
11	Barnsley	42	11	7	3	27	12	3	9	9	15	30	58
12	Wimbledon	42	9	8	4	40	29	7	2	12	31	46	58
13	Huddersfield Town	42	9	5	7	28	29	6	5	10	24	35	55
14	Oldham Athletic	42	10	4	7	27	23	5	4	12	22	44	53
15	Crystal Palace	42	8	7	6	25	27	4	5	12	21	38	48
16	Carlisle United	42	8	5	8	27	23	5	3	13	23	44	47
17	Charlton Athletic	42	8	7	6	34	30	3	5	13	17	33	45
18	Sheffield United	42	7	6	8	31	28	3	8	10	23	38	44
19	Middlesbrough	42	6	8	7	22	26	4	2	15	19	31	40
20	NOTTS COUNTY	42	6	5	10	25	32	4	2	15	20	41	37
21	Cardiff City	42	5	3	13	24	42	4	5	12	23	37	35
22	Wolverhampton Wan.	42	5	4	12	18	32	3	5	13	19	47	33

	1985/86 Division 3	*P*	*W*	*D*	*L*	*F*	*A*	*W*	*D*	*L*	*F*	*A*	*Pts*
1	Reading	46	16	3	4	39	22	13	4	6	28	29	94
2	Plymouth Argyle	46	17	3	3	56	20	9	6	8	32	33	87
3	Derby County	46	13	7	3	45	20	10	8	5	35	21	84
4	Wigan Athletic	46	17	4	2	54	17	6	10	7	28	31	83
5	Gillingham	46	14	5	4	48	17	8	8	7	33	37	79
6	Walsall	46	15	7	1	59	23	7	2	14	31	41	75
7	York City	46	16	4	3	49	17	4	7	12	28	41	71
8	NOTTS COUNTY	46	12	6	5	42	26	7	8	8	29	34	71
9	Bristol City	46	14	5	4	43	19	4	9	10	26	41	68
10	Brentford	46	8	8	7	29	29	10	4	9	29	32	66
11	Doncaster Rovers	46	7	10	6	20	21	9	6	8	25	31	64
12	Blackpool	46	11	6	6	38	19	6	6	11	28	36	63
13	Darlington	46	10	7	6	39	33	5	6	12	22	45	58
14	Rotherham United	46	13	5	5	44	18	2	7	14	17	41	57
15	Bournemouth	46	9	6	8	41	31	6	3	14	24	41	54
16	Bristol Rovers	46	9	8	6	27	21	5	4	14	24	54	54
17	Chesterfield	46	10	6	7	41	30	3	8	12	20	34	53
18	Bolton Wanderers	46	10	4	9	35	30	5	4	14	19	38	53
19	Newport County	46	7	8	8	35	33	4	10	9	17	32	51
20	Bury	46	11	7	5	46	26	1	6	16	17	41	49
21	Lincoln City	46	7	9	7	33	34	3	7	13	22	43	46
22	Cardiff City	46	7	5	11	22	29	5	4	14	31	54	45
23	Wolverhampton Wan.	46	6	6	11	29	47	5	4	14	28	51	43
24	Swansea City	46	9	6	8	27	27	2	4	17	16	60	43

	1986/87 Division 3	*P*	*W*	*D*	*L*	*F*	*A*	*W*	*D*	*L*	*F*	*A*	*Pts*
1	Bournemouth	46	19	3	1	44	14	10	7	6	32	26	97
2	Middlesbrough	46	16	5	2	38	11	12	5	6	29	19	94
3	Swindon Town	46	14	5	4	37	19	11	7	5	40	28	87
4	Wigan Athletic	46	15	5	3	47	26	10	5	8	36	34	85
5	Gillingham	46	16	5	2	42	14	7	4	12	23	34	78
6	Bristol City	46	14	6	3	42	15	7	8	8	21	21	77
7	NOTTS COUNTY	46	14	6	3	52	24	7	7	9	25	32	76
8	Walsall	46	16	4	3	50	27	6	5	12	30	40	75
9	Blackpool	46	11	7	5	35	20	5	9	9	39	39	64
10	Mansfield Town	46	9	9	5	30	23	6	7	10	22	32	61
11	Brentford	46	9	7	7	39	32	6	8	9	25	34	60
12	Port Vale	46	8	6	9	43	36	7	6	10	33	34	57
13	Doncaster Rovers	46	11	8	4	32	19	3	7	13	24	43	57
14	Rotherham United	46	10	6	7	29	23	5	6	12	19	34	57
15	Chester City	46	7	9	7	32	28	6	8	9	29	31	56
16	Bury	46	9	7	7	30	26	5	6	12	24	34	55
17	Chesterfield	46	11	5	7	36	33	2	10	11	20	36	54
18	Fulham	46	8	8	7	35	41	4	9	10	24	36	53
19	Bristol Rovers	46	7	8	8	26	29	6	4	13	23	46	51
20	York City	46	11	8	4	34	29	1	5	17	21	50	49
21	Bolton Wanderers	46	8	5	10	29	26	2	10	11	17	32	45
22	Carlisle United	46	7	5	11	26	35	3	3	17	13	43	38
23	Darlington	46	6	10	7	25	28	1	6	16	20	49	37
24	Newport County	46	4	9	10	26	34	4	4	15	23	52	37

1980/81   2nd in Division Two - Promoted

#	Date		Opponent		Scorers	Att	Avramovic R	Benjamin T	O'Brien R	Kelly EP	Kilcline B	Richards P	McCulloch I	Masson DS	Christie T	Hunt D	Hooks P	Wood GT	Mair G	Harkouk R	Doherty J	Manns P	Leonard MC	McParland LJ	Beavon DG	Goodwin M
1	Aug	16	BOLTON WANDERERS	2-1	Christie, Hooks	7459	1	2	3	4	5	6	7	8	9	10	11									
2		20	Newcastle United	1-1	Masson	17272	1	2	3	4	5	6	7	8	9	10	11	12								
3		23	SHEFFIELD WEDNESDAY	2-0	Christie, McCulloch	10246	1	2	3	4	5	6	7	8	9	10	11		12							
4		30	West Ham United	0-4		21769	1	2	3	4	5	6	7	8	9	10	11		12							
5	Sep	6	QUEENS PARK RANGERS	2-1	Christie, Hunt	7097	1	2	3	4	5	6	7	8	9	10			12	11						
6		13	Swansea City	1-1	Kilcline	10921	1	2	3	4	5	6	7	8	9	10			12	11						
7		20	Bristol City	1-0	Masson	8253	1	2	3	4	5	6	7	8		10	11	12		9						
8		27	CARDIFF CITY	4-2	Kelly, McCulloch, O'Brien(p), Hooks	7229	1	2	3	4	5	6	7		9	10	11			8						
9	Oct	4	Luton Town	1-0	Hunt	8786	1	2	3	4	5	6	7	8	9	10	11									
10		7	GRIMSBY TOWN	0-0		7800	1	2	3	4	5	6	7	8	9	10	11									
11		11	BRISTOL ROVERS	3-1	Harkouk, Hooks, Christie	7292	1	2	3	4	5	6	7	8	9	10	11			12						
12		18	Leyton Orient	2-0	Gray(og), McCulloch	5829	1	2	3	4	5	6	7	8	9	10	11			12						
13		21	Oldham Athletic	1-0	McCulloch	5876	1	2	3		5	6	7	8	9	10	11			4						
14		25	BLACKBURN ROVERS	2-0	McCulloch 2	13500	1	2	3		5	6	7	8	9	10	11			4						
15	Nov	1	Wrexham	1-1	Hooks	6221	1	2	3	12	5	6	7	8	9	10	11			4						
16		8	Derby County	0-0		16560	1	2	3		5	6	7		9	10	11			8						
17		11	NEWCASTLE UNITED	0-0		8093	1	2	3	4	5	6	7		9	10	11	12		8						
18		22	Shrewsbury Town	1-1	Christie	5352	1	2	3	4	5	6	7		9	10	11			8	12					
19		25	Bolton Wanderers	0-3		7344	1	2	3	4	5	6	7	8	9	10	11			12						
20		29	CHELSEA	1-1	Harkouk	14419	1	2	3	4	5	6	7	8	9	10	11			12						
21	Dec	6	Watford	0-2		11180	1	2	3	4	5	6	7	8	9	10		12		11						
22		13	OLDHAM ATHLETIC	0-2		6565	1	2	3		5	6		8		10			11	9	4	7				
23		19	Bristol Rovers	1-1	McCulloch	3552		2	3	4	5	6	9	8		10			11	7	12		1			
24		27	Preston North End	2-2	Harkouk, Manns	6551		2			5			8	9	6		3		10	4	7	1	12	11	
25	Jan	10	SHREWSBURY TOWN	0-0		7139		2			5			8	9	4	11	3		10		7	1	12	6	
26		17	WEST HAM UNITED	1-1	Hooks	13745	1	2	3	4	5	6	7	8	9	10	11									
27		31	Sheffield Wednesday	2-1	Christie, McCulloch	22685	1	2	3	4	5	6	7	8	9	10	11			12						
28	Feb	7	SWANSEA CITY	2-1	Masson, McCulloch	8628		2	3	4	5	6	7	8	9	10	11						1			
29		14	Queens Park Rangers	1-1	McCulloch	11457	1	2	3	4	5	6	7	8	9	10	11									
30		20	Cardiff City	1-0	Christie	4958	1	2	3	4	5	6	7	8	9	10	11			12						
31		28	BRISTOL CITY	2-1	O'Brien(p), Christie	7609	1	2	3	4	5	6	7	8	9	10	11			12						
32	Mar	7	LUTON TOWN	0-1		8075	1	2	3	4	5	6	7	8	9	10	11			12						
33		14	Grimsby Town	1-2	Christie	12184	1	2	3		5	6	7	8	9	10									11	4
34		21	LEYTON ORIENT	1-0	O'Brien	6846	1	2	3		5	6	7	8	9	10	11									4
35		28	Blackburn Rovers	0-0		14391	1	2	3		5	6	7	8	9	10	11									4
36	Apr	5	WREXHAM	1-1	Hunt	10959	1	2	3		5	6	7	8	9	10	11									4
37		11	Derby County	2-2	Goodwin, Christie	17922	1	2	3		5	6	7	8	9	10									11	4
38		18	PRESTON NORTH END	0-0		8485	1	2	3		5	6	7	8	9	10				12					11	4
39		20	Cambridge United	2-1	Christie 2	5507	1	2	3		5	6	7	8	9	10	11									4
40		25	WATFORD	1-2	Goodwin	10345	1	2	3		5	6	7	8	9	10	11			12						4
41	May	2	Chelsea	2-0	Christie, Harkouk	13324	1	2	3		5	6	7		9	10	11			8						4
42		5	CAMBRIDGE UNITED	2-0	Christie, McCulloch	12489	1	2	3		5	6	7		9	10	11			8						4
			Apps				38	42	40	27	42	40	39	36	39	42	36	7	4	25	3	4	4	2	5	10
			Goals						3	1	1		11	3	14	3	5			4		1				2

One own goal

F.A. Cup

Rd	Date		Opponent		Scorers	Att	Av	Be	OB	Ke	Ki	Ri	McC	Ma	Ch	Hu	Ho	Wo	Mai	Ha	Do	Mn	Le	McP	Bv	Go
R3	Jan	3	BLACKBURN ROVERS	2-1	Manns, Christie	7885		2			5			8	9	4	11	3		10		7	1		6	
R4	Jan	24	PETERBOROUGH UTD	0-1		11714	1	2	3	4	5	6	7	8	9	10	11			12						

F.L. Cup

Rd	Date		Opponent		Scorers	Att	Av	Be	OB	Ke	Ki	Ri	McC	Ma	Ch	Hu	Ho	Wo	Mai	Ha	Do	Mn	Le	McP	Bv	Go
R1/1	Aug	8	Grimsby Town	0-1		7402	1	2	3	4	5	6	7	8	9	10	11		12							
R1/2	Aug	12	GRIMSBY TOWN	3-0	Christie, Kelly, Mair	4718	1	2	3	4	5	6	7	8	9	10	11		12							
R2/1	Aug	26	Newport County	1-1	Hunt	6708	1	2	3	4	5	6	7	8	9	10	11		12							
R2/2	Sep	2	NEWPORT COUNTY	2-0	O'Brien(p), Christie	4714	1	2	3	4	5	6	7	8	9	10			11							
R3	Sep	23	QUEENS PARK RANGERS	4-1	O'Brien(p), Christie, Kelly, Hooks	6644	1	2	3	4	5	6	7	8	9	10	11									
R4	Oct	29	Manchester City	1-5	Christie	26363	1	2	3		5	6	7	8	9	10	11	12		4						

Anglo-Scottish Cup

Rd	Date		Opponent		Scorers	Att	Av	Be	OB	Ke	Ki	Ri	McC	Ma	Ch	Hu	Ho	Wo	Mai	Ha	Do	Mn	Le	McP	Bv	Go
Q	Aug	2	LEYTON ORIENT	2-2	Hunt, Harkouk	2450	1		3	4		6	2	7	10	9		8	12	11						
Q	Aug	4	Fulham	1-0	O'Brien(p)	1500	1	2	3	4	5	6	7	8	10	9					11					
Q	Aug	6	Bristol City	1-1	Hooks	1678	1	2		4	5	6	9	8		10				11	7	3				
QF1	Sep	16	MORTON	2-0	Christie, Hunt	3558	1	2	3	4		6	7	8	9	10	11									
QF2	Sep	30	Morton	1-1	O'Brien	3500	1	2	3		5	6	7	8	9	10	11	12		4						
SF1	Nov	4	Kilmarnock	2-1	Robertson(og), Harkouk	2900	1	2		4	5	6	7	8		10	11	3		9	12					
SF2	Nov	18	KILMARNOCK	5-2	*See below	4314	1	2	3	4	5	6		8	9	10	11			7	12					
F1	Mar	24	Chesterfield	0-1		10190	1	2	3	10	5	6	7	8	9		11									4
F2	Mar	31	CHESTERFIELD	1-1	Masson	12951	1	2	3		5	6	7	8	9	10	11			12						4

Scorers in SF2: O'Brien(p), Harkouk, Kilcline, Christie, Hooks   Played in first game: BH Stubbs (5)

Second leg of final after extra time. Chesterfield won on aggregate scores.

- 1980/81 Season -

Back: Christie, Kelly, Leonard, Avramovic, Richards, Harkouk
Middle: Wheeler(Trainer), Hunt, Wood, Kilcline, Stubbs, O'Brien, Benjamin, Walker(Youth Coach)
Front: Masson, Hooks, Mair, Sirrel(Manager), Wilkinson(Coach), Manns, McCulloch, Doherty

- 1981/82 Season -

Back: Dykes, Hunt, Christie, Kilcline, O'Brien, Benjamin, Lahtinen
Middle: Wilkinson (Chief Coach), McParland, Hooks, Goodwin, Leonard, Harkouk, Avramovic, Wood, Worthington, Richards,
Walker (Res/Youth Coach).   Front: McCulloch, Chiedozie, Masson, Sirrell (Manager), Wheeler (Trainer/Physio), Manns, Doherty, Mair

1981/82 15th in Division One

#	Date	Opponent	Score	Scorers	Att	Avramovic R	Benjamin T	O'Brien R	Harkouk R	Kilcline B	Richards P	Chiedozie J	McCulloch I	Christie T	Hunt D	Hooks P	Goodwin M	Lahtinen A	Masson DS	Mair G	Worthington N	McParland IJ
1	Aug 29	Aston Villa	1-0	McCulloch	31978	1	2	3	4	5	6	7	8	9	10	11	12					
2	Sep 1	MANCHESTER CITY	1-1	Christie	14493	1	2	3	4	5	6	7	8	9	10	11	12					
3	5	COVENTRY CITY	2-1	Christie, Hunt	10891	1	2	3		5	6	7	8	9	10	11	4					
4	12	Swansea City	2-3	O'Brien(p), McCulloch	14738	1	2	3		5	6	7	8	9	10	11	4		12			
5	19	IPSWICH TOWN	1-4	Osman(og)	12540	1	2	3		5	6	7	10	9	4	11			12	8		
6	22	Everton	1-3	McCulloch	22186	1	2	3		5	6	7	9		10	11	4			8		12
7	26	Wolverhampton Wand.	2-3	Berry(og), Goodwin	11594	1	2			5	6	7	9		10	11	4			8	3	
8	Oct 3	ARSENAL	2-1	Hunt, Kilcline	10785	1	2			5	6	7	9		10	11	4		12	8	3	
9	10	SUNDERLAND	2-0	Christie 2	10668	1	2	3		5	6	7		9	10	11	4			8		
10	17	Southampton	1-3	Mair	18900	1	2	3		5	6	7	9		10	11	4			8		
11	24	WEST HAM UNITED	1-1	Masson	12456	1	2	3		5	6	7	9		10	11	4		8			
12	31	Manchester Utd.	1-2	McCulloch	45928	1	2	3		5	6	7	9		10	11	4		12	8		
13	Nov 7	Leeds United	0-1		19552	1	2	3		5	6	7	9		10	11	4		12	8		
14	21	Brighton & Hove Alb.	2-2	McCulloch, Mair	13851	1	2	3		5	6	7	9		10	11	4			8		
15	24	EVERTON	2-2	Hooks, McCulloch	7749	1	2	3		5	6	7	9		10	11	4			8		
16	28	TOTTENHAM HOTSPUR	2-2	O'Brien, Kilcline	15550	1	2	3		5	6	7	9		10	11	4			8		
17	Dec 5	Birmingham City	1-2	McCulloch	11914	1	2	3		5	6	7	9		10	11	4			8		
18	Jan 16	ASTON VILLA	1-0	Christie	9590	1	2	3		5	6		9	12	10		4	8		11		7
19	23	Nottm. Forest	2-0	Hooks, Christie	26158	1	2	3		5	6		9	10		11	4	8				7
20	26	LIVERPOOL	0-4		14399	1	2	3		5	6	12	9	10		11	4	8				7
21	30	Ipswich Town	3-1	Mair, Kilcline, Hooks	21614	1	2	3		5	6	7	9	12	10	11	4			8		
22	Feb 6	SWANSEA CITY	0-1		10062	1	2	3		5	6	7	9	12	10	11	4			8		
23	13	Arsenal	0-1		18229	1	2	3		5	6	7	9	12	10	11	4			8		
24	16	Coventry City	5-1	Goodwin, Harkouk, Mair, Christie, Chiedozie	10237	1	2	3	8	5	6	7	9	10			4			11		
25	20	WOLVERHAMPTON W.	4-0	McCulloch 2, Mair 2	10168	1	2	3	8	5	6	7	9	10			4			11		
26	27	Sunderland	1-1	McCulloch	12910	1	2	3	8	5	6	7	9	12	10		4			11		
27	Mar 6	SOUTHAMPTON	1-1	Mair	12465	1	2	3	8	5	6	7	9	10			4			11		
28	13	West Ham United	0-1		23654	1	2	3	8	5	6	7	9	12	10		4			11		
29	20	MANCHESTER UTD.	1-3	Harkouk	17048	1	2	3	8	5	6		9	10			4			11		7
30	24	West Bromwich Alb.	4-2	McCulloch 3, Mair	12637	1	2	3	8	5	6		9	10	12		4			11		7
31	27	LEEDS UNITED	2-1	Harkouk, Hunt	13307	1	2	3	8	5	6		9	10	12		4			11		7
32	Apr 2	Liverpool	0-1		30126	1	2	3	8	5	6		10	9	12		4			11		7
33	10	Middlesbrough	0-3		10402	1	2	3	8	5	6	7	9	12	10		4			11		
34	12	NOTTM. FOREST	1-2	Christie	19304	1	2	3	8	5	6	7	9	10			4			11		12
35	17	BRIGHTON & HOVE ALB.	4-1	Christie 3, Goodwin	7916	1	2	3	8	5	6	7	9	10			4			11		12
36	24	Tottenham Hotspur	1-3	McCulloch	38017	1	2	3		5	6	7	9	10			4	8		11		12
37	26	STOKE CITY	3-1	McCulloch, Harkouk(p), Mair	8650	1	2	3	8	5	6	7	9	10	12		4			11		
38	May 1	BIRMINGHAM CITY	1-4	McCulloch	10704	1	2	3	8	5	6	7	9	10			4			11		
39	5	Manchester City	0-1		24443	1	2	3		5	6	7	9	10			4	8		11		12
40	8	Stoke City	2-2	Christie(p), Richards	11011	1	2	3		5	6	7	9	10			4	8		11		
41	11	MIDDLESBROUGH	0-1		6707	1	2	3	12	5	6	7	9	10			4	8		11		
42	15	WEST BROMWICH ALB.	1-2	Chiedozie	8726	1	2			5	6	7	9	10			4	8		11		12
	Apps					42	41	39	18	36	40	32	40	35	30	28	38	8	16	34	2	12
	Goals							2	4	3	1	2	16	12	3	3	3		1	9		

Two own goals

F.A. Cup

Rd	Date	Opponent	Score	Scorers	Att	Avramovic R	Benjamin T	O'Brien R	Harkouk R	Kilcline B	Richards P	Chiedozie J	McCulloch I	Christie T	Hunt D	Hooks P	Goodwin M	Lahtinen A	Masson DS	Mair G	Worthington N	McParland IJ
R3	Jan 5	ASTON VILLA	0-6		12321		2	3			6	7	12		4	9	10		5	8	11	

Played at no. 1: MC Leonard

F.L. Cup

Rd	Date	Opponent	Score	Scorers	Att	Avramovic R	Benjamin T	O'Brien R	Harkouk R	Kilcline B	Richards P	Chiedozie J	McCulloch I	Christie T	Hunt D	Hooks P	Goodwin M	Lahtinen A	Masson DS	Mair G	Worthington N	McParland IJ
R2/1	Oct 7	Lincoln City	1-1	Hooks	4943	1	2	3		5	6	7	9		10	11	4			8		
R2/2	Oct 27	LINCOLN CITY	2-3	Mair, Masson	6292	1	2	3		5	6	7	9		10	11	4		12	8		

F.L. Group Cup

Rd	Date	Opponent	Score	Scorers	Att	Avramovic R	Benjamin T	O'Brien R	Harkouk R	Kilcline B	Richards P	Chiedozie J	McCulloch I	Christie T	Hunt D	Hooks P	Goodwin M	Lahtinen A	Masson DS	Mair G	Worthington N	McParland IJ
PR	Aug 15	Lincoln City	1-1	Mair	2959	1	2	3			6	7	9		10	8	4				11	5
PR	Aug 19	Peterborough Utd.	1-3	Manns	2463	1	2	3			6	7			10	8	4				11	5
PR	Aug 22	Norwich City	0-3		4038	1	2	3			6		8		10	9	4				11	5

P Manns played in each game, in position 12, 9 and 12 respectively

1982/83   15th in Division One

No	Mon	Date	Opponent	Res	Scorers	Att	Avramovic R	Benjamin T	Worthington N	Hunt D	Kilcline B	Richards P	McParland LJ	Harkouk R	Christie T	Chiedozie J	Mair G	Lahtinen A	Goodwin M	McCulloch I	Hooks P	Clarke DA	Fashanu J	Leonard MC	O'Brien R
1	Aug	28	SWANSEA CITY	0-0		8048	1	2	3	4	5	6	7	8	9	10	11	12							
2	Sep	1	Sunderland	1-1	Christie	18997	1	2	3	4	5	6	12	8	9	7	11	10							
3		4	Luton Town	3-5	Kilcline, Chiedozie, Goodwin	9071	1	2	3	4	5	6	12	8	9	7	11		10						
4		7	MANCHESTER CITY	1-0	Goodwin	9369	1	2	3	4	5	6		8	9	7	11		10						
5		11	EVERTON	1-0	Harkouk(p)	9188	1	2	3	4	5	6		8	9	7	11		10						
6		18	Arsenal	0-2		20556	1	2	3	4	5	6		8	9	7		11	12	10					
7		25	IPSWICH TOWN	0-6		8475	1	2	3	4	5	6		8	9	7			10	11					
8	Oct	2	Southampton	0-1		16230	1	2	3	4	5	6	11	8		7			10	9	12				
9		9	ASTON VILLA	4-1	Mortimer(og), Christie, Mair, McCulloch	8977	1	2	3	4	5	6			8	7	11		12	9	10				
10		16	Coventry City	0-1		8314	1	2	3	4	5	6			8	7	11		12	9	10				
11		23	Tottenham Hotspur	2-4	Christie, Chiedozie	26183	1		3	4	5	6			8	7	11	2	12	9	10				
12		30	WATFORD	3-2	Kilcline, McCulloch, Hooks	9158	1		3	4	5	6			8	7	11		2	9	12	10			
13	Nov	6	Norwich City	2-1	Mair, Christie	12591	1		3		5	6			8	7	11		2	9	4	10			
14		13	BIRMINGHAM CITY	0-0		9118	1		3		5	6			8	7	11	12	2	9	4	10			
15		20	LIVERPOOL	1-2	Christie	16897	1	2	3		5	6			8	7	11	12	10	9	4				
16		27	Brighton & Hove Alb.	2-0	McCulloch 2	9971	1	2	3	4	5	6			8	7	11			9	10				
17	Dec	4	NOTTM. FOREST	3-2	McCulloch, Hooks, Christie	23552	1	2	3	4	5	6			8	7	11			9	10				
18		11	Manchester Utd.	0-4		33618	1	2	3	4	5	6			8	7	11		12	9	10				
19		18	WEST HAM UNITED	1-2	Worthington	8441	1	2	3	4	5	6			9	7	11				10	12	8		
20		27	West Bromwich Alb.	2-2	Fashanu, Goodwin	17756	1	2	3	4	5	6			12	7	11		10	9			8		
21		28	STOKE CITY	4-0	Mair, McCulloch 2, Goodwin	22591	1	2	3	4	5	6				7	11		10	9	12		8		
22	Jan	1	Liverpool	1-5	Fashanu	33663	1	2	3	4	5	6				7	11		10	9	12		8		
23		3	SUNDERLAND	0-1		9317	1	2	3	4	5	6				7	11		10	9	12		8		
24		15	Swansea City	0-2		8999	1	2	3	4	5	6	7		12		11		10	9			8		
25		22	ARSENAL	1-0	Fashanu	9718	1	2	3	4	5	6			12	7	11		10	9		12	8		
26	Feb	5	Everton	0-3		14546	1	2	3	4	5	6				7	11		10	9			8		
27		15	SOUTHAMPTON	1-2	McCulloch	5846	1	2		4	5	6				7	11		10	9	12	3	8		
28		19	Manchester City	1-0	Fashanu	21199			3	4		6	12			7			5	2	9	11	8	1	10
29		26	COVENTRY CITY	5-1	Fashanu 2, Lahtinen, McCulloch, Hooks	8676			3	4		6	12			7			5	2	9	11	8	1	10
30	Mar	5	TOTTENHAM HOTSPUR	3-0	Hunt, Chiedozie 2	11841			3	4	5	6	12			7			2	9	11		8	1	10
31		8	Aston Villa	0-2		17452			3	4	5	6				7			2	9	11		8	1	10
32		12	Watford	3-5	Christie, Worthington, Fashanu	16273		4	3		5	6	12		10	7			2	9			11	8	1
33		19	NORWICH CITY	2-2	Worthington, Christie(p)	8059		2	3	4	5	6	12		10	7				9			11	8	1
34		26	Birmingham City	0-3		11744	1	2	3	4	5	6			7		10		8	9			12		11
35	Apr	2	Stoke City	0-1		16316	1	2	11	4	5	6			7			8	12	9	10	3			
36		4	WEST BROMWICH ALB.	2-1	McCulloch, Christie(p)	8696	1	2	11		5	6			8	7		10	4	9		3			
37		9	Ipswich Town	0-0		15945	1	2	11	3	5	6	12		8	7		10	4	9					
38		16	LUTON TOWN	1-1	Chiedozie	8897	1	2	11	3	5	6	12		8	7		10	4	9					
39		23	Nottm. Forest	1-2	Lahtinen	25554	1	2	11	3	5	6	12		8	7		10	4	9					
40		30	BRIGHTON & HOVE ALB.	1-0	Kilcline	7326	1	2	11	3	5	6			8	7		10	4	9			12		
41	May	7	West Ham United	0-2		17534	1	2	11	3	5	6			8	7		10	4	9			12		
42		14	MANCHESTER UTD.	3-2	Harkouk 2, McParland	14395	1	6	5	2	3	4	11	7	10	9			8						
			Apps				36	34	41	37	40	42	11	14	33	39	25	17	34	34	17	16	15	6	5
			Goals					3	1	3			1	3	9	5	3	2	4	10	3		7		

One own goal

F.A. Cup

No	Mon	Date	Opponent	Res	Scorers	Att	Avramovic R	Benjamin T	Worthington N	Hunt D	Kilcline B	Richards P	McParland LJ	Harkouk R	Christie T	Chiedozie J	Mair G	Lahtinen A	Goodwin M	McCulloch I	Hooks P	Clarke DA	Fashanu J	Leonard MC	O'Brien R
R3	Jan	8	Leicester City	3-2	Fashanu 2, McCulloch	18384	1	2	3	4	5	6				7	11		10	9			8		
R4	Jan	29	Middlesbrough	0-2		17114	1	2	3	4	5	6			12	7	11		10	9			8		

The Milk Cup

No	Mon	Date	Opponent	Res	Scorers	Att	Avramovic R	Benjamin T	Worthington N	Hunt D	Kilcline B	Richards P	McParland LJ	Harkouk R	Christie T	Chiedozie J	Mair G	Lahtinen A	Goodwin M	McCulloch I	Hooks P	Clarke DA	Fashanu J	Leonard MC	O'Brien R
12/1	Oct	6	Aston Villa	2-1	Chiedozie, Clarke	16312	1	2	3	4	5	6		8	9	7	11				10	12			
12/2	Oct	26	ASTON VILLA	1-0	Hunt	6921	1		3	4	5	6			8	7	11		2	9	12	10			
R3	Nov	9	CHELSEA	2-0	Christie(p), Hooks	8852	1		3		5	6			8	7	11	12	2	9	4	10			
R4	Dec	7	WEST HAM UNITED	3-3	McCulloch, Christie, Hunt	7525	1	2	3	4	5	6			8	7	11			9	10				
R5	Dec	21	West Ham United	0-3		12906	1	2	3	4	5	6			8	7	12			10			11	9	

- 1982/83 Season -

Back: Richards, Christie, Leonard, Avramovic, Hunt, Benjamin, O'Brien
Middle: Wheeler (Physio), Hooks, Worthington, Lahtinen, Kilcline, Harkouk, Wood, Walker (Youth Coach), Wilkinson (Team Man.)
Front: McCulloch, Manns, Mair, Sirrell (Club Man.), McParland, Chiedozie, Goodwin

- 1983/84 Season -

Back: McDonagh, Christie, Kilcline, Harkouk, Lahtinen, Leonard
Middle: Lloyd(Team Manager), Worthington, Richards, Hunt, Fashanu, Benjamin, O'Brien, Short(Trainer)
Front: McCulloch, Mair, Chiedozie, Sirrel(Club Manager), Clarke, Goodwin, McParland

1983/84 21st in Division One - Relegated

#	Date		Opponent	Score	Scorers	Att	McDonagh JM	Lahtinen A	Worthington N	Goodwin M	Kilcline B	Hunt D	Chiedozie J	Fashanu J	Christie T	Harkouk R	O'Neill M	McParland IJ	McCulloch I	Benjamin T	Mair G	Richards P	Roeder G	Clarke DA	Leonard MC	Hodson S	Armstrong KC	Davis DJ	Jones MR
1	Aug	27	Leicester City	4-0	O'Neill, Christie 3	15583	1	2	3	4	5	6	7	8	9	10	11	12											
2		30	BIRMINGHAM CITY	2-1	Harkouk 2	11031	1	2	3	4	5	6	7	8	9	10	11		12										
3	Sep	3	IPSWICH TOWN	0-2		9023	1	2	3	4	5	6	7	8	12	10	11		9										
4		6	Coventry City	1-2	Fashanu	11016	1	2	3	4	5	6	7	8		10	11		9										
5		10	Watford	1-3	Harkouk	12896	1	2	3	4	5	6	7	8	12	10	11		9										
6		17	ARSENAL	0-4		10217	1		3	4	5	6	7	8	12	10	11		9		2								
7		24	West Ham United	0-3		20613	1		3		5	6	12	8		10	4	7	9	2	11								
8	Oct	1	EVERTON	0-1		7949	1		3	4	5	6	7	8		10	11		9		2	12							
9		16	Nottm. Forest	1-3	Christie(p)	26657	1		3	4	5	6	7	8	9	10	11					2			12				
10		22	STOKE CITY	1-1	Kilcline	7684	1		3	4	5	6		8	9	10	12				2	11	7						
11		29	Tottenham Hotspur	0-1		29198	1		3	4	5	6		8	9	10	12				2	11	7						
12	Nov	5	West Bromwich Alb.	0-2		10760	1		3	4	5			8	9	10	12				2	11	7	6					
13		12	NORWICH CITY	1-1	Fashanu	7882	1		3	2		5	11	8	9	10	7					4	6						
14		19	Southampton	2-0	Christie, Fashanu	15009	1		3	2		5	11	8	9	10	7					4	6						
15		26	ASTON VILLA	5-2	Christie 2(1p), Chiedozie 2, Harkouk	8960	1		3	2		5	11	8	9	10	7					4	6						
16	Dec	3	Queens Park Rangers	0-1		10217	1		3	2		5	11	8	9	10	7					4		6					
17		10	SUNDERLAND	6-1	*See below	7123	1		3	2		5	11	8	9			7	10			4		6					
18		17	Liverpool	0-5		22436	1		3	2		5	11	8	9			7	10	12		4		6					
19		26	LUTON TOWN	0-3		9789	1		3	2	6	5	11	8	9	12		7	10			4							
20		27	Manchester Utd.	3-3	Christie(p), Fashanu 2	41544	1		3	2	6	5	11	8	9	10		7				4			12				
21		31	Ipswich Town	0-1		14170	1		3	2	6	5	11	8	9	10		7				4			12				
22	Jan	2	WEST HAM UNITED	2-2	Christie, O'Neill	8667	1		3	2	6	5	11		9	10		7				4		8					
23		14	LEICESTER CITY	2-5	Chiedozie, Harkouk	10707	1		3	2	6	5	11		9	10		7	12	8		4							
24		21	Arsenal	1-1	Chiedozie	20110	1		10		6	5	11		9	12		7		8	2	4		3					
25	Feb	4	Everton	1-4	McParland(p)	13191				7	6	5	11			10			9	8	2	4		3	1				12
26		11	WATFORD	3-5	Harkouk, Christie 2(1p)	8070					6	5	11		9	10		7		8	2	4		3	1				
27		21	TOTTENHAM HOTSPUR	0-0		7943			12		6	5	11		9	10		7		8	2	4		3	1				
28		25	Stoke City	0-1		11725			12		5	6	11		9	10		7		8	2	4		3	1				
29	Mar	3	WEST BROMWICH ALB.	1-1	Christie(p)	7373		2			5	6	11		9	10		7	12	8		4		3	1				
30		13	Norwich City	1-0	O'Neill	12116						6	11		9		7		10	8		4		3	1	5	2		
31		17	COVENTRY CITY	2-1	O'Neill, Christie(p)	6564						6	11		9		7		10	8		4		3	1	5	2		
32		24	Birmingham City	0-0		9040						6	11		9		7		10	8		4		3	1	5	2		
33		31	NOTTM. FOREST	0-0		18357						6	11		9		7		10	8		4		3	1	5	2		
34	Apr	7	Wolverhampton Wand.	1-0	Hunt	7481						6	11		9		7	12	10	8		4		3	1	5	2		
35		14	MANCHESTER UTD.	1-0	Christie	13911						6	11		9		7	12	10	8		4		3	1	5	2		
36		21	Luton Town	2-3	Christie, Chiedozie	8181						6	11		9		7	12	10	8		4		3	1	5	2		
37		28	Aston Villa	1-3	Chiedozie	13052						6	11		9		7		10	8		4		3	1	5	2		
38	May	1	WOLVERHAMPTON W.	4-0	Chiedozie, Christie 2, Hunt	5378						6	11		9		7	12	10	8		4		3	1	5	2		
39		5	QUEENS PARK RANGERS	0-3		7309						6	11		9		7		10	8		4		3	1	5	2		
40		7	Sunderland	0-0		14517					6		11		9		7	12	10	8		4			1	5	2	3	
41		12	LIVERPOOL	0-0		18745					6	5	11		9		7		10	8		4		3	1		2		
42		17	SOUTHAMPTON	1-3	Christie	6035					6	5	11		9		7		10	8		4		3	1		2		12

*Scorers in game 17: Christie, Worthington, McParland, Chiedozie 2, Richards

	McDonagh JM	Lahtinen A	Worthington N	Goodwin M	Kilcline B	Hunt D	Chiedozie J	Fashanu J	Christie T	Harkouk R	O'Neill M	McParland IJ	McCulloch I	Benjamin T	Mair G	Richards P	Roeder G	Clarke DA	Leonard MC	Hodson S	Armstrong KC	Davis DJ	Jones MR
Apps	24	6	24	29	24	39	40	17	39	32	38	21	22	15	17	34	4	20	18	13	10	1	2
Goals			1		1	2	9	5	19	6	4	2				1							

F.A. Cup

Rd	Date		Opponent	Score	Scorers	Att	McDonagh JM	Worthington N	Goodwin M	Kilcline B	Hunt D	Chiedozie J	Christie T	Harkouk R	McParland IJ	McCulloch I	Benjamin T	Mair G	Richards P	Clarke DA	Leonard MC
R3	Jan	8	BRISTOL CITY	2-2	Cristie 2(1p)	11042	1	3	2	6	5	11	9	10	7	12			4	8	
rep	Jan	10	Bristol City	2-0	Kilcline, McCulloch	16107	1	3	2	6	5	11	9	10	7	12			4	8	
R4	Feb	1	Huddersfield Town	2-1	Kilcline, Harkouk	13634	1		6	5	11		9	10	7	12	8	2	4	3	1
R5	Feb	18	MIDDLESBROUGH	1-0	Chiedozie	17487	1			5	6	11	9	10	7		8	2	4	3	1
R6	Mar	10	EVERTON	1-2	Chiedozie	19534		2	12	5	6	11		8	7	10	9		4	3	1

The Milk Cup

Rd	Date		Opponent	Score	Scorers	Att	McDonagh JM	Worthington N	Goodwin M	Kilcline B	Hunt D	Chiedozie J	Fashanu J	Christie T	Harkouk R	O'Neill M	McParland IJ	McCulloch I	Mair G	Richards P	Roeder G	Clarke DA
R2/1	Oct	3	Aldershot	4-2	Kilcline, Christie 2, Fashanu	4458	1	3	4	5	6	7	9	8	10	11			2			
R2/2	Oct	25	ALDERSHOT	4-1	Hunt 2, Christie 2	3439	1	3	4	5	6	8		9	10	12			2	11	7	
R3	Nov	8	Birmingham City	2-2	Harkouk, Chiedozie	10484	1	3	2	5		8		9	4	10	11			7	6	12
rep	Nov	22	BIRMINGHAM CITY	0-0		8268	1	3	2	5		11	8	9	10	7				4	6	
r2	Nov	29	Birmingham City	0-0		9678	1	3	2	5		11	8	9	10	7				4	6	
r3	Dec	5	BIRMINGHAM CITY	1-3	O'Neill	7361	1	3	2	5		11	8	9	10	7	12			6		4

R3 replay and replay 2 after extra time

1984/85 20th in Division Two · Relegated

#	Date	Opponent	Res	Scorers	Att	Leonard MC	Hodson S	Clarke DA	Jones MR	Lahtinen A	Hunt D	O'Neill M	Fashanu J	Downing K	Harkouk R	McParland IJ	Goodwin M	Sims SF	Young AF	Richards P	Benjamin T	Beaver D	Burke SJ	McDonagh JM	Waitt M	Robinson MJ	Burns K	Watson DV	Daws A	Davis DJ	Yates D
1	Aug 25	LEEDS UNITED	1-2	Harkouk	12497	1	2	3	4	5	6	7	8	9	10	11															
2	28	Brighton & Hove Alb.	1-2	Fashanu	13773	1	2	3	4	5	6	7	8	9	10	11	12														
3	Sep 1	Charlton Athletic	0-3		4656	1	2	3	4	5	6	7	8	9	10	11	12														
4	4	BARNSLEY	0-2		4703	1	2	3	4	5	6	7	8	9	10	11															
5	8	MIDDLESBROUGH	3-2	Goodwin, Harkouk, Hunt	4911	1	2	3			6	4	8	11	10	7	12	5	9												
6	15	Sheffield United	0-3		12628	1	2	3			6	7	8		10	11	9	5		4											
7	22	BLACKBURN ROVERS	0-3		5246	1	2	11			6	7	8		10		9	5		4	3										
8	29	Shrewsbury Town	2-4	Harkouk 2	3504	1	2				6	7	8		10		9	5		4	3	11						12			
9	Oct 6	Wolverhampton Wand.	3-2	Harkouk, O'Neill, Pender(og)	7676	1		3	2		6	7	8		10		11	5	9	4								12			
10	14	CARDIFF CITY	0-2		5893	1	2		3		6	7	8		10		11	5	9	4											
11	20	BIRMINGHAM CITY	1-3	Goodwin	5788	1	2		3		6	7	8	10			11	4	5	9											
12	27	Oldham Athletic	2-3	Harkouk, Sims	3273	1	2				4	9	8		10		7	5	12	6	3					11					
13	Nov 3	GRIMSBY TOWN	1-1	Fashanu	5750	1	2				5	9	8		10		7	6		4	3					11					
14	10	Portsmouth	1-3	Goodwin	12287	1	2				5	9	8		10		7	6		4	3					11					
15	17	HUDDERSFIELD T	0-2		6051		2					9	12		10		7	6	5	8	4	3		1		11					
16	24	Carlisle Utd.	0-1		3165						3	11	7	8	10		6		9	4	2			1	12			5			
17	Dec 1	OXFORD UNITED	2-0	Hunt, Young	6282			3			10	7	9			12	8	6	11	4	2			1				5			
18	8	Manchester City	0-2		20109			3			11	7			10	12	4	6	9	8	2			1				5			
19	16	FULHAM	2-1	Harkouk(p), Young	4917			3			11	7		9		12	8	6	10	4	2			1				5			
20	26	Wimbledon	2-3	Harkouk 2	2992			3			11	7		9			8	6	12	4	2			1	10			5			
21	29	Barnsley	0-0		7447			3			11	7		9			8	6		4	2			1	10			5			
22	Jan 1	CRYSTAL PALACE	0-0		5725			3			11	7	10		9		8	6		4	2			1				5			
23	12	SHEFFIELD UNITED	0-0		8119			3				7			4	11	8	6	9	2				1	10			5			
24	19	Leeds United	0-5		11364	1		3				7			4	11		6	9	2					10			5			
25	26	CHARLTON ATHLETIC	0-0		3409			3		2	11	7			10		8	6	9	4				1	12			5			
26	Feb 2	SHREWSBURY TOWN	1-3	Hunt	4421			3		2	11	7	8				10	6	12	4	5				1			9			
27	9	Middlesbrough	1-0	Waitt	3364	1		3		2	11		8				7	6	10	4	5				12			9			
28	23	Grimsby Town	0-2		4967	1		3		2	11				10		7	6					8		12	9	4	5			
29	Mar 2	OLDHAM ATHLETIC	0-0		4202	1		3				8			10	11	7	6			2				12	9	4	5			
30	9	Birmingham City	1-2	Sims	9071	1		3				8			10	11	7	6			2				12	9	5	4			
31	17	Cardiff City	4-1	Daws, Harkouk, Young 2	3631	1									10		7	6	9	4	2					11		5	8	3	
32	23	WOLVERHAMPTON W.	4-1	Fashanu, Harkouk 2, Young	5561	1							8		10		7	6	9	4	2					11		5		3	
33	30	Blackburn Rovers	0-1		7132	1							8		10		7	6	9	4	2					11		5	9	3	
34	Apr 2	PORTSMOUTH	1-3	Harkouk	5631	1							8		10		7	6		4	2				12	11		5	9	3	
35	6	WIMBLEDON	2-3	Fashanu, Harkouk	4800	1						11	8		4		7	6			3				10	9		5	12		2
36	9	Crystal Palace	0-1		4744	1						10	8	3	7		4	6			2				12	9			11		5
37	14	Brighton & Hove Alb.	1-2	Richards	4671	1						10		3	7		4	6	9		2				12			5	11		8
38	20	Huddersfield T	2-1	Fashanu, Young(p)	4117	1						10	8		11		7	6	9	3	2				12			5			4
39	27	CARLISLE UTD.	3-0	Fashanu, Goodwin(p), Watson	4051	1						10	8	3	11		7	6	9						2			5			4
40	May 4	Oxford United	1-1	Fashanu	9944	1				6	10	8	3				7		9		2							5			4
41	6	MANCHESTER CITY	3-2	Fashanu, Harkouk, Young	17812	1						10	8	3	11	12	7	6	9		2							5			4
42	11	Fulham	0-1		4891	1				5	10	8		3	11		7	6	9		2							12			4
		Apps				31	14	22	4	14	37	26	32	12	35	20	38	34	24	35	21	1	5	11	13	14	2	25	7	4	8
		Goals									3	1	8		15		4	2	7	1					1			1	1		

One own goal

F.A. Cup

Rd	Date	Opponent	Res	Scorers	Att	Leonard MC	Hodson S	Clarke DA	Jones MR	Lahtinen A	Hunt D	O'Neill M	Fashanu J	Downing K	Harkouk R	McParland IJ	Goodwin M	Sims SF	Young AF	Richards P	Benjamin T	Beaver D	Burke SJ	McDonagh JM	Waitt M	Robinson MJ	Burns K	Watson DV	Daws A	Davis DJ	Yates D
R3	Jan 5	GRIMSBY TOWN	2-2	McParland 2	6202			3			11	7			4	12	8	6	9	2				1	10			5			
rep	Jan 8	Grimsby Town	2-4	Harkouk, Wilkinson(og)	6743			3		2		7			6	11	8	5	9	4				1	10						

The Milk Cup

Rd	Date	Opponent	Res	Scorers	Att	Leonard MC	Hodson S	Clarke DA	Jones MR	Lahtinen A	Hunt D	O'Neill M	Fashanu J	Downing K	Harkouk R	McParland IJ	Goodwin M	Sims SF	Young AF	Richards P	Benjamin T	Beaver D	Burke SJ	McDonagh JM	Waitt M	Robinson MJ	Burns K	Watson DV	Daws A	Davis DJ	Yates D
R2/1	Sep 25	Charlton Athletic	1-0	Goodwin	4012	1	2				6	7	8		10		9	5		4	3	11									
R2/2	Oct 9	CHARLTON ATHLETIC	2-0	O'Neill, Harkouk(p)	3453	1	2		3		6	7	8		10		11	5	9	4											
R3	Oct 30	BOLTON WANDERERS	6-1	Harkouk 3, Sims, Richards, Young	4547	1	2				6	7			10	8	12	5	9	4	3		11								
R4	Nov 21	Norwich City	0-3		14540				3			7	8		10		6		9	4	2			1	11			5			

- 1984/85 Season -

Back: Beaver, Clarke, Dalton, McDonagh, Hunt, Richards
Middle: Walker(Coach), Jones, Lahtinen, Leonard, O'Neill, Harkouk, Short(Physio)
Front: Benjamin, Downing, Fashanu, Lloyd(Manager), Hodson, McParland, Goodwin

- 1985/86 Season -

Back: Richards, Clarke, Hunt, Dalton, Benjamin, Davis, Goodwin
Middle: Walker(Coach), Downing, Smalley, Young, Waitt, Robinson, Yates, Short(Physio)
Front: McDonagh, Daws, Harkouk, Sirrell(Manager), Sims, McParland, Leonard

1985/86   8th in Division Three

						Leonard MC	Richards P	Clarke DA	Benjamin T	Sims SF	Yates D	McParland IJ	Goodwin M	Young AF	Harkouk R	Downing K	Smalley P	Hunt D	Waitt M	Harbottle M	Fairclough W	Robinson MJ	Davs A	Hesford I	Davis DJ	Edge D	Kevan DJ	Barnes PL	Mimms R	Davies JG
1	Aug 17	CARDIFF CITY	1-4	Young	3856	1	2	3	4	5	6	7	8	9	10	11														
2	24	Blackpool	3-1	Clarke, Young, Harkouk	4011	1	2	3	4	5	6	7	8	9	10		12	11												
3	26	DONCASTER ROV.	1-1	McParland	3922	1	2	3	4	5	6	7		9	10	11	12	8												
4	31	Plymouth Argyle	1-0	Harkouk	5105	1	2	3	4	5	6	7	8	9	10			11												
5	Sep 7	GILLINGHAM	1-1	Young	3624	1	2	3	4	5	6	7	8	9				11	10											
6	14	Bournemouth	0-0		4235	1	2	3	4	5	6	7	8	9				11	10											
7	17	YORK CITY	3-1	Goodwin, Young, McParland	3708	1	2	3	4	5	6	7	8	9				11	10	12										
8	22	Darlington	3-2	Harbottle, McParland, Waitt	3786	1		3	4	5	6	7	8					11	9	10	2	12								
9	28	BURY	2-2	Young, Waitt	4528	1	2	3	4	5	6	7	8	9				11	10			12								
10	Oct 1	Bristol Rovers	1-1	McParland	3549	1	2	3	4	5	6	7	8	9				11	10											
11	5	Derby County	0-2		14406	1	2	3	4	5	6	7	8	9				11	10			12								
12	12	BRISTOL CITY	4-0	Hunt 3, McParland	4332	1	2	3	4	5	6	7	8	9				11	10		12									
13	19	CHESTERFIELD	2-1	Waitt, Goodwin(p)	5776	1	2	3	4	5	6	7	8	9				11	10			12								
14	22	Wigan Athletic	1-3	Robinson	3374	1	2	3	4	5	6	7	8	9				11		12		10								
15	27	LINCOLN CITY	3-2	Harkouk 2, McParland	6120	1	2	3	4	5	6	7	8	9	10			11				12								
16	Nov 2	Walsall	0-0		4967	1	2	3	4	5	6	7	8	9	10			11												
17	6	Reading	1-3	Harkouk(p)	6986	1	2	3	4	5	6	7	8	9	10			11				12								
18	9	BOLTON WANDERERS	1-0	Yates	4497	1	2	3	4	5	6	7	8	9				11				10								
19	23	Newport County	2-1	McParland, Goodwin	1946	1		3	4	5	6	7	8		10		2	11	9			12								
20	30	SWANSEA CITY	3-0	Hunt, Goodwin(p), McParland	3912			3	4	5	6	7	8				2	11	9			10	1							
21	Dec 14	Rotherham Utd.	0-1		3820			3	4	5	6	7	8	9			2	11	10			12	1							
22	22	BLACKPOOL	1-2	Hunt	5926			3	4		6	7	8	9	12		2	11	10				1	5						
23	26	WOLVERHAMPTON W.	4-0	Harkouk, McParland, Waitt, Goodwin	5264			3	4	5	6	7	8		10		2	11	9				1			12				
24	28	Doncaster Rov.	1-2	Edge	3673			3	4	5		7	8				2	11	9	12			1		6	10				
25	Jan 11	PLYMOUTH ARGYLE	2-0	Hunt, McParland	4953	1		3	4	5		7	8					11	9		2	12			6	10				
26	18	Cardiff City	3-1	Waitt, Mullen(og), McParland	2410				4	5	6	7	8				2	11	9				1	3	10					
27	21	Brentford	1-1	Hunt	4002				4		6	7	8			3	2	11	9				1	5	10					
28	Feb 1	Gillingham	0-4		4368			3	4		6	7			10		8	11	9		2		1	5		12				
29	4	WIGAN ATHLETIC	1-1	Yates	3369			3	4		6	7			7		8	11	9		2		1	5	10		12			
30	8	Chesterfield	2-2	Edge, Waitt	3623			3		5	6		8		7		4	11	9		2		1		10					
31	Mar 1	Bury	4-2	Waitt, Hunt, Harkouk, Barnes	2379	1		3		5	2	7	8		10		4	11	9						6			12		
32	4	BRISTOL ROVERS	0-0		3183	1		3		5	2	7	8				4	11	9						6	10		12		
33	8	DERBY COUNTY	0-3		13086			3	4	5	2	7	8		10			11	9						6	12				
34	15	Bristol City	0-3		5701		3		4	5	6	12	8		10		2	11	9									7	1	
35	22	Lincoln City	2-0	Waitt 2	3468				4	5	6	7	8		10		2	11	12						3			9	1	
36	29	BRENTFORD	0-4		3857			12	4	5	6	7	8		10		2		9						3			11		1
37	31	Wolverhampton Wand.	2-2	Waitt, Goodwin	3774			11	4	5	6	7	8		10		2		9						3	12				1
38	Apr 5	READING	0-0		3711			11	4	5	6	7	8		10		2		9						3					1
39	8	WALSALL	3-1	Waitt 2, Barnes	2490			11	4	5	6	7	8				2		9						3			10		1
40	12	Bolton Wanderers	0-1		4688	5		11	4		6	7	8				2		9						3			10		1
41	15	BOURNEMOUTH	3-1	Davis, McParland, Waitt	2423			11	4	5	6	7	8				2		9						3			10		1
42	19	NEWPORT COUNTY	1-2	Waitt	3279			11	4	5	6	7	8				2		9						3			10		1
43	22	York City	2-2	Barnes, McParland (p)	3211			11	4	5	6	7	8				2		9						3			10		
44	26	Swansea City	0-0		3869	12		11	4	5	6	7	8				2		9						3			10		1
45	May 3	ROTHERHAM UTD.	1-0	McParland	3123			11	2	5	6	7	8						9						3		4	10		1
46	6	DARLINGTON	5-0	Yates 2, McParland, Clarke, Barnes	2345			11	2	5	6	7	8						9						3		4	10		

Played in game 43: R Dalton (1). In game 46: C Jackson (12).

	Leonard MC	Richards P	Clarke DA	Benjamin T	Sims SF	Yates D	McParland IJ	Goodwin M	Young AF	Harkouk R	Downing K	Smalley P	Hunt D	Waitt M	Harbottle M	Fairclough W	Robinson MJ	Davs A	Hesford I	Davis DJ	Edge D	Kevan DJ	Barnes PL	Mimms R	Davies JG
Apps	23	20	42	43	41	44	44	43	19	20	3	26	34	37	4	5	12	1	10	22	10	3	14	2	10
Goals		2				4	15	6	5	7			8	14	1		1			1	2		4		

One own goal

F.A. Cup

						Leonard MC	Richards P	Clarke DA	Benjamin T	Sims SF	Yates D	McParland IJ	Goodwin M	Young AF	Harkouk R	Downing K	Smalley P	Hunt D	Waitt M	Harbottle M	Fairclough W	Robinson MJ	Davs A	Hesford I	Davis DJ	Edge D
R1	Nov 17	SCARBOROUGH	6-1	Hunt, Harkouk 3, Young, McParland	5621	1	2	3	4	5	6	7	8	9	10			11								
R2	Dec 7	WREXHAM	2-2	Waitt 2	4569	1		3	4	5	6	7	8	9			2	11	10							
R3	Dec 10	Wrexham	3-0	Clarke, Waitt, McParland	2645	1		3	4	5	6	7	8	9			2	11	10							
R4	Jan 13	Stoke City	2-0	Waitt, McParland	12219	1		3	4	5	2	7	8					11	9			12			6	10
R5	Jan 25	TOTTENHAM HOTSPUR	1-1	McParland	17546	1			4		6	7	8		12		5	11	9		2				3	10
rep	Jan 29	Tottenham Hotspur	0-5		17393	1			4	5	6	7					8	2	11	9					3	10

The Milk Cup

						Leonard MC	Richards P	Clarke DA	Benjamin T	Sims SF	Yates D	McParland IJ	Goodwin M	Young AF	Harkouk R	Downing K	Smalley P	Hunt D	Waitt M	Harbottle M	Fairclough W	Robinson MJ	Davs A	Hesford I	Davis DJ
R1/1	Aug 20	DONCASTER ROVERS	1-0	Clarke	2425	1	2	11	4	5	6	7	8	9	10		12								3
R1/2	Sep 3	Doncaster Rovers	1-2	Goodwin	2679	1	2	3	4	5	6	7	8	9	10			11	12						
R2/1	Sep 24	Fulham	1-1	Goodwin	2324	1	2	3	4	5	6	7	8					11	9	12		10			
R2/2	Oct 8	FULHAM	2-4	Young, McParland	3054	1	2	11	4	5	6	7		9				8	10		12				3

R1 won an away goals. R2/2 after extra time

Freight Rover Trophy

						Leonard MC	Richards P	Clarke DA	Benjamin T	Sims SF	Yates D	McParland IJ	Goodwin M	Young AF	Harkouk R	Downing K	Smalley P	Hunt D	Waitt M	Harbottle M	Fairclough W	Robinson MJ	Davs A	Hesford I	Davis DJ	Edge D	Kevan DJ
R1	Jan 16	DONCASTER ROVERS	1-0	McParland	1642			3	4	5	2	7	8				12	11	9			14		1	6	10	
R1	Mar 11	Mansfield Town	0-1		3447	1			4	5	2	7	8		10		6	11	9						3		
rep	Mar 20	MANSFIELD TOWN	0-1		2409				4	5	6	7	8		10		2	11	9						3	12	1

1986/87 — 7th in Division Three

#	Date	Opponent	Score	Scorers	Att	Leonard MC	Smalley P	Davis DJ	Benjamin T	Sims SF	Yates D	Thompson DS	Goodwin M	Waitt M	Hunt D	McParland IJ	Young RA	Clarke DA	Fairclough W	Kevan DJ	Crichton P	Downing K	Campbell DA	Jackson C
1	Aug 23	WIGAN ATHLETIC	2-0	Waitt, McParland(p)	3533	1	2	3	4	5	6	7	8	9	10	11	12							
2	31	Swindon Town	2-1	McParland, Goodwin	7350	1	2	3	4	5	6	7	8	9	10	11								
3	Sep 6	BOURNEMOUTH	1-1	Waitt	3619	1	2	3	4	5	6	7	8	9	10	11			12					
4	13	Darlington	1-2	Yates	1814	1	2		4	5	6	7	8	9	10	11			3	12				
5	16	Port Vale	1-1	Waitt	3725	1	2	3	4	5	6	7	8	9	10				12	11				
6	20	FULHAM	2-3	McParland, Thompson	4452	1	2	3	4	5	6	12	8	9	10	7			11					
7	27	Chesterfield	2-1	McParland, Clarke	3249	1	12	3	2	5	6	4	8		10	7	9	11						
8	30	BRISTOL ROVERS	3-0	Clarke, Yates, Sims(p)	3409	1	12	3	2	5	6	4	8		10	7	9	11						
9	Oct 4	Bolton Wanderers	1-1	Hartford(og)	4248	1	12	3	2	5	6	4	8			7	9	11		10				
10	11	ROTHERHAM UTD.	5-0	Sims 2(2p), McParland 2, Thompson	4132	1	2	3		5	6	4	8			7	9	11	12	10				
11	18	Blackpool	1-3	Young	5325	1	2	3	6		5	4	8			7	9	11	12	10				
12	21	MIDDLESBROUGH	1-0	McParland	4405		2	3	6		5	4	8			7	9	11		10	1			
13	25	DONCASTER ROV.	3-1	Young, McParland 2	4179		2	3	6		5	4	8			7	9	11		10	1			
14	Nov 1	Newport County	1-1	Young	1980		2	3	6		5	4	8	12		7	9	11		10	1			
15	4	Brentford	0-1		3057		2	3	6		5	4	8	12		7	9	11		10	1			
16	8	WALSALL	2-1	McParland, Clarke	5267		2	3	6		5	4	8	12		7	9	11		10	1			
17	22	Gillingham	1-3	Waitt	5514	1	2	3			5	4	8	12		7	9	11		10				
18	29	BRISTOL CITY	2-0	Goodwin, McParland	3987	1	2	3	6		5	4	8	9		7		11		10				
19	Dec 13	YORK CITY	5-1	Yates 2, Thompson 2, Clarke	3614	1	2	3	6		5	4	8	9		7	12	11		10				
20	21	Carlisle Utd.	2-0	Yates, Waitt	2811	1	2	3	6		5	4	8	9	11	7				10				
21	26	MANSFIELD TOWN	0-0		8820	1	2	3	6		5	4	8	9	11	7	12			10				
22	27	Bury	2-0	Clarke, McParland	3232	1	2	3	6		5	4	8	9		7	12	11		10				
23	Jan 3	GILLINGHAM	3-1	Waitt 3	5832	1	2	3			5	4	8	9	6	7	12	11		10				
24	24	Bournemouth	0-3		6022	1	2	3	6		5	4	8	9		7		11		10				
25	31	DARLINGTON	2-2	Yates 2	4196	1	6	3	2		5	4	8	9		7	12			10			11	
26	Feb 7	PORT VALE	4-1	McParland 3(1p), Waitt	5277	1					5	4	8	9	6	7	12			10			11	
27	14	Fulham	1-3	McParland	3054	1	2	3			5	4	8	9	6	7				10			11	
28	17	Chester City	2-1	Thompson, Goodwin	2792	1	2	3			5	4	8	9	6	7				10			11	
29	21	CHESTERFIELD	2-1	McParland 2(1p)	5020	1	2	3			5	4	8	9	6	7	12			10			11	
30	28	Bristol Rovers	0-0		2978	1	2	3			5	4	8	9		7	12			10			11	6
31	Mar 3	NEWPORT COUNTY	5-2	Goodwin, Waitt, McParland 2, Kevan	3814	1	2	3			5	4	8	9		7	12			10			11	6
32	7	Doncaster Rov.	2-1	Waitt 2	2564	1	2	3			5	4	8	9		7			6	10			11	
33	14	BLACKPOOL	3-2	Campbell, Yates, Young	5920	1	2	3			5	4	8	9	6	7	12			10			11	
34	17	Middlesbrough	0-2		9845	1	2	3			5	4	8	9	6	7				10			11	
35	21	Rotherham Utd.	1-1	McParland	3787	1	2	3			5	4	8	9	6	7				10			11	
36	24	Wigan Athletic	0-1		3171	1	2	3			5	4	8	9	6	7	12			10			11	
37	28	BOLTON WANDERERS	0-0		4776	1	2	3			5	4	8	9	6	7	12			10			11	
38	Apr 4	Walsall	1-1	Downing	5206	1	2	3			5	4	8	9	6	7				10		12	11	
39	11	BRENTFORD	1-1	Yates	4358	1	2	3			5	4	8	9	6	7				10			11	
40	18	CHESTER CITY	1-1	Thompson	4528	1	2	3			5	4	8	9	6	7				10		12	11	
41	21	Mansfield Town	2-1	Hunt, Thompson	6094	1	2	3			5	4	8	9	6	7				10		12	11	
42	26	CARLISLE UTD.	2-1	Hunt, Campbell	4808	1	2	3			5	4	8	9	6	7				10		12	11	
43	28	SWINDON TOWN	2-3	Hunt, McParland	6354	1	2	3				4	8	9	6	7				10		12	11	5
44	May 2	Bristol City	1-3	McParland	9189	1	2	3	6	11	5	4	8	9		7	12			10				
45	4	BURY	1-2	Clarke	4457	1	2	3			5	4	8	9	6	7	12	11		10				
46	9	York City	1-1	Young	3760	1	2	3			5	4	8	9	6	7	12	11		10				
	Apps					41	46	45	24	10	42	46	45	32	30	45	35	23	9	33	5	8	18	4
	Goals									3	9	7	4	12	2	24	5	6		1		1	2	

One own goal

F.A. Cup

	Date	Opponent	Score	Scorers	Att	Leonard MC	Smalley P	Davis DJ	Benjamin T	Sims SF	Yates D	Thompson DS	Goodwin M	Waitt M	Hunt D	McParland IJ	Young RA	Clarke DA	Fairclough W	Kevan DJ	Crichton P	Downing K	Campbell DA	Jackson C
R1	Nov 15	CARLISLE UNITED	1-1	Davis	4626	1	2	3	6		5	4	8	12		7	9	11		10				
rep	Nov 18	Carlisle United	3-0	Young, McParland 2	3742	1	2	3	6		5	4	12	8		7	9	11		10				
R2	Dec 7	MIDDLESBROUGH	0-1		7415	1	2	3	6		5	4	8	9	14	7	12	11		10				

Littlewoods Challenge Cup

	Date	Opponent	Score	Scorers	Att	Leonard MC	Smalley P	Davis DJ	Benjamin T	Sims SF	Yates D	Thompson DS	Goodwin M	Waitt M	Hunt D	McParland IJ	Young RA	Clarke DA	Fairclough W	Kevan DJ	Crichton P	Downing K	Campbell DA	Jackson C
R1/1	Aug 26	PORT VALE	1-3	McParland	2127	1	2	3	4	5	6	7	8	9	10	11	12							
R1/2	Sep 3	Port Vale	1-4	Waitt	3436	1		3	2	5	4	7	8	9	6	11	12			10				

Freight Rover Trophy

	Date	Opponent	Score	Scorers	Att	Leonard MC	Smalley P	Davis DJ	Benjamin T	Sims SF	Yates D	Thompson DS	Goodwin M	Waitt M	Hunt D	McParland IJ	Young RA	Clarke DA	Fairclough W	Kevan DJ	Crichton P	Downing K	Campbell DA	Jackson C
PR	Nov 24	GILLINGHAM	0-5		1668	1	2	3	12		5	4	8	9	6	7	14	11		10				
PR	Jan 5	Northampton Town	0-3		3578	1	2	3			5	4	8	9	6	7		11		10				

Played in game 2: Barnes (at no. 12)

- 1986/87 Season -

Back: Davis, Benjamin, Leonard, Hunt, Barnes
Middle: Jones(Physio), Sims, Waitt, Yates, Bate(Chief Coach)
Front: Smalley, Clarke, Edge, Sirrell(Manager), Kevan, Harbottle, McParland

- 1987/88 Season -

Back: Thompson, Smalley, Davis, Yates, Mills, McParland
Middle: Lund, Belford, Birtles, Hart, Gray, Leonard, Jackson
Front: Snook, Kevan, Kimberley, Barnwell(Manager), Pike, Barnes, Harbottle

League Tables 1987/88 to 1994/95

	1987/88 Division 3	*P*	*W*	*D*	*L*	*F*	*A*	*W*	*D*	*L*	*F*	*A*	*Pts*
1	Sunderland	46	14	7	2	51	22	13	5	5	41	26	93
2	Brighton & Hove A.	46	15	7	1	37	16	8	8	7	32	31	84
3	Walsall	46	15	6	2	39	22	8	7	8	29	28	82
4	NOTTS COUNTY	46	14	4	5	53	24	9	8	6	29	25	81
5	Bristol City	46	14	6	3	51	30	7	6	10	26	32	75
6	Northampton Town	46	12	8	3	36	18	6	11	6	34	33	73
7	Wigan Athletic	46	11	8	4	36	23	9	4	10	34	38	72
8	Bristol Rovers	46	14	5	4	43	19	4	7	12	25	37	66
9	Fulham	46	10	5	8	36	24	9	4	10	33	36	66
10	Blackpool	46	13	4	6	45	27	4	10	9	26	35	65
11	Port Vale	46	12	8	3	36	19	6	3	14	22	37	65
12	Brentford	46	9	8	6	27	23	7	6	10	26	36	62
13	Gillingham	46	8	9	6	45	21	6	8	9	32	40	59
14	Bury	46	9	7	7	33	26	6	7	10	25	31	59
15	Chester City	46	9	8	6	29	30	5	8	10	22	32	58
16	Preston North End	46	10	6	7	30	23	5	7	11	18	36	58
17	Southend United	46	10	6	7	42	33	4	7	12	23	50	55
18	Chesterfield	46	10	5	8	25	28	5	5	13	16	42	55
19	Mansfield Town	46	10	6	7	25	21	4	6	13	23	38	54
20	Aldershot	46	12	3	8	45	32	3	5	15	19	42	53
21	Rotherham United	46	8	8	7	28	25	4	8	11	22	41	52
22	Grimsby Town	46	6	7	10	25	29	6	7	10	23	29	50
23	York City	46	4	7	12	27	45	4	2	17	21	46	33
24	Doncaster Rovers	46	6	5	12	25	36	2	4	17	15	48	33

	1988/89 Division 3												
1	Wolverhampton Wan.	46	18	4	1	61	19	8	10	5	35	30	92
2	Sheffield United	46	16	3	4	57	21	9	6	8	36	33	84
3	Port Vale	46	15	3	5	46	21	9	9	5	32	27	84
4	Fulham	46	12	7	4	42	28	10	2	11	27	39	75
5	Bristol Rovers	46	9	11	3	34	21	10	6	7	33	30	74
6	Preston North End	46	14	7	2	56	31	5	8	10	23	29	72
7	Brentford	46	14	5	4	36	21	4	9	10	30	40	68
8	Chester City	46	12	6	5	38	18	7	5	11	26	43	68
9	NOTTS COUNTY	46	11	7	5	37	22	7	6	10	27	32	67
10	Bolton Wanderers	46	12	8	3	42	23	4	8	11	16	31	64
11	Bristol City	46	10	3	10	32	25	8	6	9	21	30	63
12	Swansea City	46	11	8	4	33	22	4	8	11	18	31	61
13	Bury	46	11	7	5	27	22	5	6	12	28	45	61
14	Huddersfield Town	46	10	8	5	35	25	7	1	15	28	48	60
15	Mansfield Town	46	10	8	5	32	22	4	9	10	16	30	59
16	Cardiff City	46	10	9	4	30	16	4	6	13	14	40	57
17	Wigan Athletic	46	9	5	9	28	22	5	9	9	27	31	56
18	Reading	46	10	6	7	37	29	5	5	13	31	43	56
19	Blackpool	46	10	6	7	36	29	4	7	12	20	30	55
20	Northampton Town	46	11	2	10	41	34	5	4	14	25	42	54
21	Southend United	46	10	9	4	33	26	3	6	14	23	49	54
22	Chesterfield	46	9	5	9	35	35	5	2	16	16	51	49
23	Gillingham	46	7	3	13	25	32	5	1	17	22	49	40
24	Aldershot	46	7	6	10	29	29	1	7	15	19	49	37

	1989/90 Division 3												
1	Bristol Rovers	46	15	8	0	43	14	11	7	5	28	21	93
2	Bristol City	46	15	5	3	40	16	12	5	6	36	24	91
3	NOTTS COUNTY	46	17	4	2	40	18	8	8	7	33	35	87
4	Tranmere Rovers	46	15	5	3	54	22	8	6	9	32	27	80
5	Bury	46	11	7	5	35	19	10	4	9	35	30	74
6	Bolton Wanderers	46	12	7	4	32	19	6	8	9	27	29	69
7	Birmingham City	46	10	7	6	33	19	8	5	10	27	40	66
8	Huddersfield Town	46	11	5	7	30	23	6	9	8	31	39	65
9	Rotherham United	46	12	6	5	48	28	5	7	11	23	34	64
10	Reading	46	10	9	4	33	21	5	10	8	24	32	64
11	Shrewsbury Town	46	10	9	4	38	24	6	6	11	21	30	63
12	Crewe Alexandra	46	10	8	5	32	24	5	9	9	24	29	62
13	Brentford	46	11	4	8	41	31	7	3	13	25	35	61
14	Leyton Orient	46	9	6	8	28	24	7	4	12	24	32	58
15	Mansfield Town	46	13	2	8	34	25	3	5	15	16	40	55
16	Chester City	46	11	7	5	30	23	2	8	13	13	32	54
17	Swansea City	46	10	6	7	25	27	4	6	13	20	36	54
18	Wigan Athletic	46	10	6	7	29	22	3	8	12	19	42	53
19	Preston North End	46	10	7	6	42	30	4	3	16	23	49	52
20	Fulham	46	8	8	7	33	27	4	7	12	22	39	51
21	Cardiff City	46	6	9	8	30	35	6	5	12	21	35	50
22	Northampton Town	46	7	7	9	27	31	4	7	12	24	37	47
23	Blackpool	46	8	6	9	29	33	2	10	11	20	40	46
24	Walsall	46	6	8	9	23	30	3	6	14	17	42	41

	1990/91 Division 2												
1	Oldham Athletic	46	17	5	1	55	21	8	8	7	28	32	88
2	West Ham United	46	15	6	2	41	18	9	9	5	19	16	87
3	Sheffield Wed.	46	12	10	1	43	23	10	6	7	37	28	82
4	NOTTS COUNTY	46	14	4	5	45	28	9	7	7	31	27	80
5	Millwall	46	11	6	6	43	28	9	7	7	27	23	73
6	Brighton & Hove A.	46	12	4	7	37	31	9	3	11	26	38	70
7	Middlesbrough	46	12	4	7	36	17	8	5	10	30	30	69
8	Barnsley	46	13	7	3	39	16	6	5	12	24	32	69
9	Bristol City	46	14	5	4	44	28	6	2	15	24	43	67
10	Oxford United	46	10	9	4	41	29	4	10	9	28	37	61
11	Newcastle United	46	8	10	5	24	22	6	7	10	25	34	59
12	Wolverhampton Wan.	46	11	6	6	45	35	2	13	8	18	28	58
13	Bristol Rovers	46	11	7	5	29	20	4	6	13	27	39	58
14	Ipswich Town	46	9	8	6	32	28	4	10	9	28	40	57
15	Port Vale	46	10	4	9	32	24	5	8	10	24	40	57
16	Charlton Athletic	46	8	7	8	27	25	5	10	8	30	36	56
17	Portsmouth	46	10	6	7	34	27	4	5	14	24	43	53
18	Plymouth Argyle	46	10	10	3	36	20	2	7	14	18	48	53
19	Blackburn Rovers	46	8	6	9	26	27	6	4	13	25	39	52
20	Watford	46	5	8	10	24	32	7	7	9	21	27	51
21	Swindon Town	46	8	6	9	31	30	4	8	11	34	43	50
22	Leicester City	46	12	4	7	41	33	2	4	17	19	50	50
23	West Bromwich Alb.	46	7	11	5	26	21	3	7	13	26	40	48
24	Hull City	46	6	10	7	35	32	4	5	14	22	53	45

	1991/92 Division 1	*P*	*W*	*D*	*L*	*F*	*A*	*W*	*D*	*L*	*F*	*A*	*Pts*
1	Leeds United	42	13	8	0	38	13	9	8	4	36	24	82
2	Manchester United	42	12	7	2	34	13	9	8	4	29	20	78
3	Sheffield Wed.	42	13	5	3	39	24	8	7	6	23	25	75
4	Arsenal	42	12	7	2	51	22	7	8	6	30	24	72
5	Manchester City	42	13	4	4	32	14	7	6	8	29	34	70
6	Liverpool	42	13	5	3	34	17	3	11	7	13	23	64
7	Aston Villa	42	13	3	5	31	16	4	6	11	17	28	60
8	Nottingham Forest	42	10	7	4	36	27	6	4	11	24	31	59
9	Sheffield United	42	9	6	6	29	23	7	3	11	36	40	57
10	Crystal Palace	42	7	8	6	24	25	7	7	7	29	36	57
11	Queen's Park Rgs.	42	6	10	5	25	21	6	8	7	23	26	54
12	Everton	42	8	8	5	28	19	5	6	10	24	32	53
13	Wimbledon	42	10	5	6	32	20	3	9	9	21	33	53
14	Chelsea	42	7	8	6	31	30	6	6	9	19	30	53
15	Tottenham Hotspur	42	7	3	11	33	35	8	4	9	25	28	52
16	Southampton	42	7	5	9	17	28	7	5	9	22	27	52
17	Oldham Athletic	42	11	5	5	46	36	3	4	14	17	31	51
18	Norwich City	42	8	6	7	29	28	3	6	12	18	35	45
19	Coventry City	42	6	7	8	18	15	5	4	12	17	29	44
20	Luton Town	42	10	7	4	25	17	0	5	16	13	54	42
21	NOTTS COUNTY	42	7	5	9	24	29	3	5	13	16	33	40
22	West Ham United	42	6	6	9	22	24	3	5	13	15	35	38

	1992/93 Football League Division 1												
1	Newcastle United	46	16	6	1	58	15	13	3	7	34	23	96
2	West Ham United	46	16	5	2	50	17	10	5	8	31	24	88
3	Portsmouth	46	19	2	2	48	9	7	8	8	32	37	88
4	Tranmere Rovers	46	15	4	4	48	24	8	6	9	24	32	79
5	Swindon Town	46	15	5	3	41	23	6	8	9	33	36	76
6	Leicester City	46	14	5	4	43	24	8	5	10	28	40	76
7	Millwall	46	14	6	3	46	21	4	10	9	19	32	70
8	Derby County	46	11	2	10	40	33	8	7	8	28	24	66
9	Grimsby Town	46	12	6	5	33	25	7	1	15	25	32	64
10	Peterborough Utd.	46	7	11	5	30	26	9	3	11	25	37	62
11	Wolverhampton Wan.	46	11	6	6	37	26	5	7	11	20	30	61
12	Charlton Athletic	46	10	8	5	28	19	6	5	12	21	27	61
13	Barnsley	46	12	4	7	29	19	5	5	13	27	41	60
14	Oxford United	46	8	7	8	29	21	6	7	10	24	35	56
15	Bristol City	46	10	7	6	29	25	4	7	12	20	42	56
16	Watford	46	8	7	8	27	30	6	6	11	30	41	55
17	NOTTS COUNTY	46	10	7	6	33	21	2	9	12	22	49	52
18	Southend United	46	9	8	6	33	22	4	5	14	21	42	52
19	Birmingham City	46	10	4	9	30	32	3	8	12	20	40	51
20	Luton Town	46	6	13	4	26	26	4	8	11	22	36	51
21	Sunderland	46	9	6	8	34	28	4	5	14	16	36	50
22	Brentford	46	7	6	10	28	30	6	4	13	24	41	49
23	Cambridge United	46	8	6	9	29	32	3	10	10	19	37	49
24	Bristol Rovers	46	6	6	11	30	42	4	5	14	25	45	41

	1993/94 Division 1												
1	Crystal Palace	46	16	4	3	39	18	11	5	7	34	28	90
2	Nottingham Forest	46	12	9	2	38	22	11	5	7	36	27	83
3	Millwall	46	14	8	1	36	17	5	9	9	22	32	74
4	Leicester City	46	11	9	3	45	30	8	7	8	27	29	73
5	Tranmere Rovers	46	15	3	5	48	23	6	6	11	21	30	72
6	Derby County	46	15	3	5	44	25	5	8	10	29	43	71
7	NOTTS COUNTY	46	16	3	4	43	26	4	5	14	22	43	68
8	Wolverhampton Wan.	46	10	10	3	34	19	7	7	9	26	28	68
9	Middlesbrough	46	12	6	5	40	19	6	7	10	26	35	67
10	Stoke City	46	14	4	5	35	19	4	9	10	22	40	67
11	Charlton Athletic	46	14	3	6	39	22	5	5	13	22	36	65
12	Sunderland	46	14	2	7	35	22	5	6	12	19	35	65
13	Bristol City	46	11	7	5	27	18	5	9	9	20	32	64
14	Bolton Wanderers	46	10	8	5	40	31	5	6	12	23	33	59
15	Southend United	46	10	5	8	34	28	7	3	13	29	39	59
16	Grimsby Town	46	7	14	2	26	16	6	6	11	26	31	59
17	Portsmouth	46	10	6	7	29	22	5	7	11	23	36	58
18	Barnsley	46	9	3	11	25	26	7	4	12	30	41	55
19	Watford	46	10	5	8	39	35	5	4	14	27	45	54
20	Luton Town	46	12	4	7	38	25	2	7	14	18	35	53
21	West Bromwich Alb.	46	9	7	7	38	31	4	5	14	22	38	51
22	Birmingham City	46	9	7	7	28	29	4	5	14	24	40	51
23	Oxford United	46	10	5	8	33	33	3	5	15	21	42	49
24	Peterborough Utd.	46	6	9	8	31	30	2	4	17	17	46	37

	1994/95 Division 1												
1	Middlesbrough	46	15	4	4	41	19	8	9	6	26	21	82
2	Reading	46	12	7	4	34	21	11	3	9	24	23	79
3	Bolton Wanderers	46	16	6	1	43	13	5	8	10	24	32	77
4	Wolverhampton Wan.	46	15	5	3	39	18	6	8	9	38	43	76
5	Tranmere Rovers	46	17	4	2	51	23	5	6	12	16	35	76
6	Barnsley	46	15	6	2	42	19	5	6	12	21	33	72
7	Watford	46	14	6	3	33	17	5	7	11	19	29	70
8	Sheffield United	46	12	9	2	41	21	5	8	10	33	34	68
9	Derby County	46	12	6	5	44	23	6	6	11	22	28	66
10	Grimsby Town	46	12	7	4	36	19	5	7	11	26	37	65
11	Stoke City	46	10	7	6	31	21	6	8	9	19	32	63
12	Millwall	46	11	8	4	36	22	5	6	12	24	38	62
13	Southend United	46	13	2	8	33	25	5	6	12	21	48	62
14	Oldham Athletic	46	12	7	4	34	21	4	6	13	26	39	61
15	Charlton Athletic	46	11	6	6	33	25	5	5	13	25	41	59
16	Luton Town	46	8	6	9	35	30	7	7	9	26	34	58
17	Port Vale	46	11	5	7	30	24	4	8	11	28	40	58
18	Portsmouth	46	9	8	6	31	28	6	5	12	22	35	58
19	West Bromwich Alb.	46	13	3	7	33	24	3	7	13	18	33	58
20	Sunderland	46	5	12	6	22	22	7	6	10	19	23	54
21	Swindon Town	46	9	6	8	28	27	3	6	14	26	46	48
22	Burnley	46	8	7	8	36	33	3	6	14	13	41	46
23	Bristol City	46	8	8	7	26	28	3	4	16	16	35	45
24	NOTTS COUNTY	46	7	8	8	26	28	2	5	16	19	38	40

1987/88 4th in Division Three

No	Date	Opponent	Score	Scorers	Att	Leonard MC	Smalley P	Davis DJ	Kevan DJ	Yates D	Gray AM	McParland IJ	Lund G	Birtles G	Pike G	Mills G	Thompson DS	Belford D	Hart P	Fairclough W	Barnes PL	Withe C	Thorpe A	McStay W
1	Aug 15	WIGAN ATHLETIC	4-4	Pike 2(1p), Birtles 2	6344	1	2	3	4	5	6	7	8	9	10	11	12							
2	22	York City	5-3	McParland 2, Thompson, McKenzie(og), Pike	2939		2	3	4	5	6	8	12	9	10	7	11	1						
3	29	GRIMSBY TOWN	0-0		5322	1	2	3	4	5	12	8	9	6	10	7	11							
4	Sep 1	Fulham	0-0		4767	1	2	3	4	5	11	8	12	9	10	7			6					
5	5	SOUTHEND UNITED	6-2	McParland 2, Lund, Pike 3(2p)	4166	1	2	3	4	5		8	12	9	10	7	11		6		14			
6	12	Northampton T	1-0	Lund	6023	1	2	3	4	5		8	11	9	10	7			6		14	12		
7	15	ALDERSHOT	2-1	Lund, Pike	4835	1	2	3	4	5		8	11	9	10	7			6		12			
8	19	BRISTOL CITY	0-1		5705	1	2		4	5		8	11	9	10	7	12		6		3			
9	26	Chesterfield	0-2		3466	1	2		4	5		8	12	9	10	7	11		6		3			
10	29	BRISTOL ROVERS	1-1	Birtles	4334	1	2		4	5		8		9	10	7	11		6		3			
11	Oct 3	Chester City	2-1	Mills, Pike	3375	1	2		4	5		8	12	9	10	7	11		6		14	3		
12	11	MANSFIELD TOWN	1-1	Mills	8573	1	2		4	5			8	9	10	7			6		11	3		
13	17	Doncaster Rov.	1-0	Lund	2645	1	2		4	5			8	9	10	7			6		11	3		
14	20	BURY	3-0	Lund 2, Birtles	4044	1	2		4	5		12	8	9	10	7			6		11	3		
15	24	Gillingham	1-3	Withe	5551	1	2		4	5		8		9	10	7			6		11	3		
16	31	SUNDERLAND	2-1	Birtles 2	8854	1	2		4	5		8	12	9	10	7	11		6		14	3		
17	Nov 3	Rotherham Utd.	1-1	Green(og)	4175	1	2		4	5		8		9	10	7			6		11	3		
18	7	BRENTFORD	3-0	Withe, McParland 2	5634	1	2		4	5		8		9	10	7			6		11	3	12	
19	21	WALSALL	3-1	McParland 2, Lund	7211	1	2	12	4	5		8	9	6	10	7						3	11	
20	28	Brighton & Hove Alb.	1-1	Yates	8733	1	2	12		5		8	14	9	10	7			6		4	3	11	
21	Dec 12	Port Vale	3-1	Pike, McParland 2	3358	1	2		4	5		8		9	10	7			6			3	11	
22	19	PRESTON NORTH END	4-2	McParland 2, Pike 2	5734	1	2		4	5		8	9	6	10	7				12		3	11	
23	26	CHESTERFIELD	2-0	Lund, Mills	8677	1	2		4	5		8	9	6	10	7						3	11	
24	28	Blackpool	1-1	Lund	4627	1	2		4	5		8	9	6	10	7						3	11	
25	Jan 1	Grimsby Town	0-0		5297	1	2		4	5		8	9		10	7			6	12		3	11	
26	2	NORTHAMPTON T	3-1	Lund, Thorpe 2	8153	1	2		4	5		8	9	6	10	7				12	14	3	11	
27	9	YORK CITY	3-0	Mills, Thorpe, Lund	5924	1	2		4	5		8	9	6	10	7						3	11	
28	16	Bristol City	1-2	Lund	9558	1	2		4	5		8	9	6	10	7				12	14	3	11	
29	30	FULHAM	5-1	McParland 3(1p), Yates, Lund	6110	1	2	3	4	5		8	9	6	10	7				12			11	
30	Feb 5	Southend United	2-1	Pike, McParland(p)	3905	1	2		4	5		8	9	6	10	7						3	11	
31	13	BLACKPOOL	2-3	McParland(p), Thorpe	5803	1	2		4	5		8	9	6	10	7						3	11	
32	20	Wigan Athletic	1-2	McParland	5182	1	2	3		5		8	9		10	7			6			4	11	
33	23	Aldershot	2-0	McParland 2	2880	1	2			5		8	9		10	7			6			3	11	4
34	27	CHESTER CITY	1-0	Lund	5869	1	2			5		8	12	9	10	7			6		14	3	11	4
35	Mar 2	Bristol Rovers	1-1	Twentyman(og)	4075	1	2			5		8	9	6	10	7						3	11	4
36	5	DONCASTER ROV.	2-0	Lund 2	5816	1	2		4	5		8	9	6	10	7						3	11	
37	12	Mansfield Town	1-1	Pike(p)	8002	1	2	3	4	5		8	9	6	10	7				14	12	11		
38	19	Sunderland	1-1	Barnes	24071	1	2		4	5		8	9	6	10	7					12	3	11	
39	26	GILLINGHAM	0-1		6478	1	2	3	4	5		8	9	6	10	7				12	14	11		
40	Apr 2	Brentford	0-1		4388	1	2		4	5		8	11	9	10	7			6		12	3		
41	4	BRIGHTON & HOVE ALB.	1-2	Barnes	7422	1	2		4	5		8	9	6	10	7				12	11	3		14
42	9	Bury	1-0	Birtles	2527	1	2			5		8	9		10	7			6	12		11	3	4
43	23	ROTHERHAM UTD.	4-0	Lund 3, Mills	7021	1	2		4	5			9	6	10	7					8	3	11	12
44	30	Walsall	1-2	Lund	11913	1	2		4	5		14	9	6	10	7				12	8	3	11	
45	May 2	PORT VALE	1-2	Thorpe	7702	1	2		4	5		8	9	6	10	7				12		3	11	14
46	7	Preston North End	2-1	McParland, Pike	5822	1	12			5		8	9	6	10	7				4		3	11	2
				Apps		45	46	20	32	46	4	43	40	43	46	46	9	1	23	29	11	35	23	9
				Goals						2		21	20	7	14	5	1				2	2	5	

Three own goals

Play Offs

	Date	Opponent	Score	Scorers	Att	Leonard MC				Yates D		McParland IJ	Lund G	Birtles G	Pike G	Mills G			Hart P	Fairclough W	Barnes PL	Withe C	Thorpe A	McStay W
SF1	May 15	WALSALL	1-3	Yates	11522	1				5		8	9	6	10	7				4	12	3	11	2
SF2	May 18	Walsall	1-1	Yates	8901	1				5		14	12	9	10	7			6	4	8	3	11	2

F.A. Cup

	Date	Opponent	Score	Scorers	Att	Leonard MC	Smalley P		Kevan DJ	Yates D		McParland IJ	Lund G	Birtles G	Pike G	Mills G			Hart P	Fairclough W	Barnes PL	Withe C	Thorpe A	
R1	Nov 15	CHESTERFIELD	3-3	Kevan, McParland, Birtles	4850	1	2		4	5		8		9	10	7			6			3	11	
rep	Nov 17	Chesterfield	1-0	Pike(p)	4482	1	2		4	5		8	9	6	10	7						3	11	
R2	Dec 5	Port Vale	0-2		5039	1	2			5		8	9		10	7			6	4	12	3	11	

Littlewoods Challenge Cup

	Date	Opponent	Score	Scorers	Att	Leonard MC	Smalley P	Davis DJ	Kevan DJ	Yates D	Gray AM	McParland IJ	Lund G	Birtles G	Pike G	Mills G	Thompson DS							
R1/1	Aug 18	Wolverhampton Wand.	0-3		5980	1	2	3	4	5	6	7	8	9	10	11	12							
R1/2	Aug 25	WOLVERHAMPTON W.	1-2	Gray	2730	1	2	3	4	5	9	8		6	10	7	11							

Played in R1/1: C Jackson (14)

Sherpa Van Trophy

	Date	Opponent	Score	Scorers	Att	Leonard MC	Smalley P	Davis DJ	Kevan DJ	Yates D		McParland IJ	Lund G	Birtles G	Pike G	Mills G			Hart P	Fairclough W	Barnes PL	Withe C	Thorpe A	McStay W
PR	Oct 13	NORTHAMPTON T	1-0	Withe	2351	1	2		4	5		8	9		10	7			6		11	3		
PR	Nov 24	Brentford	2-3	Birtles, McParland	2005	1	2			5		8	9	6	10	7				4		3	11	
R1	Jan 20	CARDIFF CITY	2-0	Barnes, McParland	2704	1	2	3	4	5		12	9	6		7				14	8	10	11	
QF	Feb 9	Colchester Utd.	3-2	McParland, Thorpe, Lund	1564	1	2		4	5		8	9	6	10	7						3	11	
SFS	Mar 9	Brighton & Hove Alb.	5-1	Thorpe, McParland 2, Barnes 2	8499	1	2		4	5		8	9	6	10	7					12	3	11	
FS1	Apr 12	WOLVERHAMPTON W.	1-1	McParland	10041	1	2		4	5		8	12	9	10	7			6			3	11	14
FS2	Apr 19	Wolverhampton Wand.	0-3		18413	1	2			5		8	12	9	10	7			6			3	11	4

1988/89   9th in Division Three

#		Date	Opponent	Result	Scorers	Att	Leonard MC	Norton D	Withe C	O'Riordan D	Yates D	Law N	Mills G	McParland IJ	Birtles G	Pike G	Thorpe A	Lund G	McStay W	Draper M	Johnson T	Kevan DJ	Fairclough W	Barnes PL	Rimmer S	Cherry S	Palmer C	Turner P	Davison AJ
1	Aug	27	BRISTOL CITY	0-0		6285	1	2	3	4	5	6	7	8	9	10	11	12											
2	Sep	3	Blackpool	1-0	Mills	4669	1	2	3	4	5	6	7	8	9	10	11	12											
3		10	NORTHAMPTON T	0-1		6340	1	2	3	4	5	6	7	8	9	10	11		12										
4		17	Wolverhampton Wand.	0-0		10870	1	2	3	4	5	6	7	8	9	10			12	11									
5		20	Huddersfield T	1-3	Yates	5655	1	2	3	4	5	6	7	8	9	10	11	12											
6		24	PRESTON NORTH END	0-0		5045	1	2	3	4	5	6	7	8			11	9	10		14	12							
7	Oct	1	Mansfield Town	1-1	McParland	5908	1		3		5	6	7	8	9	10	11		2				4	12					
8		4	CHESTERFIELD	4-0	Thorpe, McStay, Yates, Pike(p)	4520	1		3		5	6	7		9	10	11	8	2				4						
9		9	CHESTER CITY	2-2	Birtles 2	5771	1		3		5	6	7	8	9	10	11		2				4						
10		15	Bristol Rovers	0-2		4183	1		3	14	5	6	7		9	10	11	12	2				4	8					
11		22	READING	3-3	Thorpe, Law, Mills(p)	5170	1		3	14	5	6	7	8	9	10	11	12					4	2					
12		29	FULHAM	0-1		5214	1	2	3	4	5	6	7		9	10	11	8						12					
13	Nov	5	Bury	1-1	Lund	2692	1	2	3	4	5	6	7		9	10	11	8	12					14					
14		8	Brentford	1-2	O'Riordan	4013	1		3	4	5	6	7		9	10	11	8	2										
15		12	SOUTHEND UNITED	1-1	Mills	5037	1		3	4	5		7		6		11	9	2				10		8				
16		26	GILLINGHAM	1-2	Rimmer	4611	1		3	2	5	12	7		6	10	11	9					4		8				
17	Dec	3	Aldershot	3-2	Kevan, Lund, Rimmer	2191	1		3	6	2	5		12	11	9	7	8	4			10							
18		18	Wigan Athletic	1-0	McParland	3016	1		3	4	2	5	7	8	6	10		9	12					11					
19		26	SHEFFIELD UNITED	1-4	Pike	11590	1		3	4	6	5	7	8		10	14	9	2					11	12				
20		31	BOLTON WANDERERS	2-0	Lund, Law	5097	1		3	4		5	7	8	6	10		9	2					11					
21	Jan	2	Port Vale	0-1		7084	1		3	4		5	7	8	6	10	12	9	2					11					
22		7	Swansea City	0-2		5808	1		3	4	5	12	7	8	6	10		9	2					11					
23		14	BLACKPOOL	1-1	Lund	4748	1		3	4	5	6	7	8		10	12	9	2					11					
24		21	Northampton T	3-1	McParland 2(1p), Draper	3704	1		3	4	5		7	8		10	11	9		12			6	2					
25		29	WOLVERHAMPTON W.	1-1	O'Riordan	9058	1		3	4	5	2	7	8		12	11	9		10			6						
26	Feb	4	MANSFIELD TOWN	2-1	Pike, Coleman(og)	5924	1		3	4	5	2	7	8	6		11	9		10	14			12					
27		11	Chesterfield	0-3		4943	1		3	4	5	2	7	8	6		11	9		10			14	12					
28		18	Chester City	0-1		3165			3	4	5	6	7			10		9			11			8		1	2		
29		25	BRISTOL ROVERS	1-0	Barnes	5176			3		5	6	7	12		10		9	2		11			8		1	4		
30		28	CARDIFF CITY	2-0	Kevan, Withe	4266			3		5	6	7			10		9	2			11		8		1	2		
31	Mar	4	Reading	3-1	Barnes 3	4153			3	4	5	6				10	14	9		12		11		8		1	2	7	
32		11	BURY	3-0	Lund, Barnes, McParland	5727			3	4	5	6		12		10		9	2			11		8		1		7	
33		14	Fulham	1-2	McParland(p)	3402			3	4	5	6		12		10		9	2		14	11		8		1		7	
34		18	Bristol City	4-0	Barnes 2, O'Riordan, Draper	6407			3	4	5	6				10	12	9	2	11			14	8		1		7	
35		25	PORT VALE	1-4	Yates	7328			3	4	5	6		12		10		9	2	11				8		1		7	
36		27	Sheffield United	1-1	Yates	13039			3	4	5	6					11	9	2	12			10	8		1		7	
37	Apr	1	WIGAN ATHLETIC	1-0	Thorpe	4929			3	4	5	6				12	11	9	2	10			14	8		1		7	
38		4	SWANSEA CITY	1-0	Lund	3940			3	4	5	6					11	9	2	12				8		1		7	
39		8	Bolton Wanderers	3-3	Turner, Thorpe, Crombie(og)	4521			3	4	5	6				10	11	9	2	12				8		1		7	
40		15	Preston North End	0-3		6735					5	6				10	11	9	2	8	12		3				4	7	1
41		18	Cardiff City	1-0	Yates	3073			3	12	5	6					11	9			10	4	8			1	2	7	
42		22	HUDDERSFIELD T	3-0	Draper, Johnson 2	5499			3	4	5	6						9		8	11		10			1	2	7	
43		28	Southend United	1-1	Johnson	3931			3	4	5	6						9	12	8	11		10			1	2	7	
44	May	1	BRENTFORD	3-0	Lund, Bates(og), Yates	4989			3	4	5	6					12	9		10	8	11	14			1	2	7	
45		6	ALDERSHOT	4-1	Lund, Turner, Johnson, Law(p)	4261			3	4	5	6						9		10	8	11		12		1	2	7	
46		13	Gillingham	1-2	Law(p)	2871			3	4	5	6					12	9		10	8	11		14		1	2	7	
			Apps				27	8	45	43	41	44	29	23	20	36	36	42	33	20	10	18	20	15	4	18	11	16	1
			Goals						1	3	6	4	3	6	2	3	4	8	1	3	4	2		7	2			2	

Three own goals

F.A. Cup

		Date	Opponent	Result	Scorers	Att	Leonard MC	Norton D	Withe C	O'Riordan D	Yates D	Law N	Mills G	McParland IJ	Birtles G	Pike G	Thorpe A	Lund G	McStay W	Draper M	Johnson T	Kevan DJ	Fairclough W	Barnes PL	Rimmer S	Cherry S	Palmer C	Turner P	Davison AJ
R1	Nov	19	Darlington	2-1	Thorpe, Pike	2110	1		3	2	5		7		6	10	11	9					4		8				
R2	Dec	10	Hartlepool Utd.	0-1		3182	1		3	4	2	5	7	12	6	10		9						11	8				

Littlewoods Challenge Cup

		Date	Opponent	Result	Scorers	Att	Leonard MC	Norton D	Withe C	O'Riordan D	Yates D	Law N	Mills G	McParland IJ	Birtles G	Pike G	Thorpe A	Lund G	McStay W	Draper M	Johnson T	Kevan DJ	Fairclough W	Barnes PL	Rimmer S	Cherry S	Palmer C	Turner P	Davison AJ
R1/1	Aug	30	MANSFIELD TOWN	5-0	McParland 3, Pike, Mills	4428	1	2	3	4	5	6	7	8	9	10	11	12											
R1/2	Sep	6	Mansfield Town	0-1		2695	1	2	3	4	5	6	7	8	9	10			12	14	11								
R2/1	Sep	27	TOTTENHAM HOTSPUR	1-1	Birtles	9279	1		3		5	6	7	8	9	10	11		2		12	4							
R2/1	Oct	11	Tottenham Hotspur	1-2	Thorpe	14953	1		3		5	6	7	8	9	10	11		2			4							

Sherpa Van Trophy

		Date	Opponent	Result	Scorers	Att	Leonard MC	Norton D	Withe C	O'Riordan D	Yates D	Law N	Mills G	McParland IJ	Birtles G	Pike G	Thorpe A	Lund G	McStay W	Draper M	Johnson T	Kevan DJ	Fairclough W	Barnes PL	Rimmer S	Cherry S	Palmer C	Turner P	Davison AJ
PR	Nov	29	Mansfield Town	1-1	Yates	2477	1		3	10	5	6					11	9	2	7			4	12	14	8			
PR	Dec	6	CHESTERFIELD	1-1	Yates	2005	1		3	6	2	5					9	12	8	11		4	7	14	10				
R1	Jan	17	Brentford	0-2		3194	1		3	4	5	6	7				14	9	2	12		10	11	8					

- 1988/89 Season -

Back: Machin, Fairclough, Atkin, Leonard, Davison, Norton, Draper, Johnson
Middle: Barnwell(Man), Walker(Yth Coach), Law, Yates, Smalley, Lund, Jackson, Kevan, Hart(Player Coach), Newman(Ass Man)
Front: Withe, McParland, McStay, Birtles, Pike, O'Riordan, Mills, Thorpe

- 1989/90 Season -

Back: Pike, Norton, McStay, Fairclough, Machin, Cox, Kevan
Middle: Robinson, Palmer, Law, Yates, Cherry, Davison, Short (Craig), O'Riordan, Stant, Newman (Asst.Man.)
Front: Lund, Barnes, Johnson, Warnock(Manager), Turner, Draper, Platnauer

1989/90 3rd in Division Three - Promoted after Play Off

Player columns (left to right): Cherry S, Palmer C, Platnauer N, Fairclough W, Yates D, Robinson PJ, Draper M, O'Riordan D, Lund G, Stant P, Turner P, Short Craig, Johnson T, Barnes PL, McStay W, Kevan DJ, Chapman G, Norris S, Norton D, Law N, Chiedozie J, Fleming G, Bartlett K, Thomas D

#	Date	Opponent	Score	Scorers	Att	Che	Pal	Pla	Fai	Yat	Rob	Dra	O'R	Lun	Sta	Tur	Sho	Joh	Bar	McS	Kev	Cha	Nor S	Nor D	Law	Chi	Fle	Bar K	Tho
1	Aug 19	Leyton Orient	1-0	Stant	5364	1	2	3		5	6	7	8	9	10	11													
2	26	BLACKPOOL	0-1		4852	1	2	3		5	6	7	8	9	10	11	4	12	14										
3	Sep 2	Bristol Rovers	2-3	Yates, Johnson	4753	1	2	3	7	5	6			9	10		4	11		14									
4	9	READING	0-0		4697	1	2	3		5	6	7			10		8	4	11		9								
5	15	Chester City	3-3	Chapman, Short, Draper	2394	1	2	3		5	6	7		9	10		8	4	12		14	11							
6	23	ROTHERHAM UTD.	2-0	Chapman 2	5891	1	2	3		5	6	7		9			8	4	10			11							
7	26	BOLTON WANDERERS	2-1	Johnson, Lund	5392	1	2	3		5	6	7		9			8	4	10			11							
8	30	Swansea City	0-0		3075	1	2	3		5	6	7		9	12		8	4	10			11							
9	Oct 7	Walsall	2-2	Johnson, Draper	4592	1	2	3		5	6	7		9			8	4	10			11							
10	14	TRANMERE ROVERS	1-0	Chapman	6332	1	2	3		5	6	7		9			8	4	10	12		11							
11	17	Bristol City	0-2		8331	1	2	3		5	6	7		9	12		8	4	10	14		11							
12	21	PRESTON NORTH END	2-1	Palmer, Johnson	5276	1	2	3		5	6	7		9			8	4	10			11							
13	28	Northampton T	0-0		3734	1	2	3	5		6	7	10	9	12		8	4				11							
14	31	BRENTFORD	3-1	Turner, Lund 2	4586	1	2	3		5	6	7	14	9	12		8	4	10			11							
15	Nov 4	Mansfield Town	3-1	Robinson, Johnson 2	6016	1	2	3		5	6	7		9	12		8	4	10			11							
16	11	WIGAN ATHLETIC	1-1	Lund	5443	1	2	3		5	6	7		9	12		8	4	10			11							
17	25	Huddersfield T	2-1	Turner, Yates	5416	1	2	3		5	6	7	11	9	10		8	4											
18	Dec 2	FULHAM	2-0	Johnson, Robinson	5133	1	2	3		5	6	12	11	9	10		8	4	7			14							
19	16	Cardiff City	3-1	Stant 2, Turner	3610	1	2	3		5	6	7	11	9	10		8	4				12							
20	26	SHREWSBURY TOWN	4-0	Stant 2, Yates, Turner	7819	1	2	3	12	5	6	7		9	10		8	4	11										
21	30	BIRMINGHAM CITY	3-2	Palmer, Johnson, Lund	7786	1	2	3	12	5	6	7		9	10		8	4	11										
22	Jan 1	Crewe Alexandra	0-1		4786	1	2	3	8	5	6	7	11	9	10			4	12			14							
23	6	BURY	0-4		6059	1	2	3	12	5	6	7		9	10		8	4	11	14									
24	13	Blackpool	0-0		3146	1	2	3		5	6	7		9			8	4	11	10									
25	20	LEYTON ORIENT	1-0	Palmer	5344	1	2	3		5	6	7		9			8	4	11	10									
26	Feb 3	Rotherham Utd.	2-1	Barnes, Yates	7218	1	2	3		5	6	7	11	9			8	4	10										
27	10	CHESTER CITY	0-0		5184	1		3	2	5	6	12	11	9			8	4	7	10				14					
28	17	Fulham	2-5	Yates, Johnson	4625	1		3		5	6	7	11	9			8	4	12	10				2	14				
29	24	HUDDERSFIELD T	1-0	Lund	7632	1	2	3		5	6	7		9			8	4	11	10				12					
30	Mar 3	Bury	2-3	Johnson, Draper(p)	3007	1	2	3		5	6	12	11	9			8	4	7	10				14					
31	6	SWANSEA CITY	2-1	Lund, Palmer	4859	1	2			5	6	7		9			8	4	11					10	14	3	12		
32	10	Bolton Wanderers	0-3		8420	1		3		5	6	7	14	9				12						10	11	4	2		
33	17	WALSALL	2-0	Bartlett, Johnson	5207	1		3		5	6	7		9			8	4	11					12	14			2	10
34	19	Tranmere Rovers	0-2		9718	1	2			5	6		11	9			8	4	12					7				3	10
35	24	BRISTOL CITY	0-0		9598	1		3		5	6		11				8	4	7					2				9	10
36	31	Preston North End	4-2	Norton, Yates, Bartlett 2	5810	1		3		5	6	7	14				8	4	11					12			2	9	10
37	Apr 7	Brentford	1-0	Bartlett	5105	1		3		5	6		12				8	4	11					7			2	9	10
38	10	NORTHAMPTON T	3-2	Johnson(p), Thomas, Stant	5396	1		3		5	6	7					8	4	11					2				9	10
39	14	CREWE ALEXANDRA	2-0	Johnson, Bartlett	6403	1		3		5	6	7					8	4	11					2				9	10
40	17	Shrewsbury Town	2-2	Johnson, Bartlett	3536	1	12	3		5	6	7					8	4	11					2				9	10
41	21	CARDIFF CITY	2-1	Short, Bartlett	5532	1	2	3		5	6				10		8	4	11					12				9	7
42	24	Birmingham City	2-1	Lund, Palmer	10533	1	2	3		5	6	12			10		8	4	11					7				9	
43	26	BRISTOL ROVERS	3-1	Turner, Johnson 2(1p)	10151	1	2	3		5	6				10		8	4	11									9	7
44	28	Wigan Athletic	1-1	A Johnson (og)	2433	1	2	3		5	6				10		8	4	11					12	14			9	7
45	May 3	Reading	1-1	Bartlett	3132	1	2	3		5	6				10		8	4	11									9	7
46	5	MANSFIELD TOWN	4-2	Lund, Turner, Johnson 2(1p)	6906	1	2	3		5	6				10		8	4	11									9	7

	Che	Pal	Pla	Fai	Yat	Rob	Dra	O'R	Lun	Sta	Tur	Sho	Joh	Bar	McS	Kev	Cha	Nor S	Nor D	Law	Chi	Fle	Bar K	Tho
Apps	46	37	44	8	45	46	34	17	40	22	44	44	40	13	3	3	19	1	15	3	1	3	14	10
Goals		5			6	2	3		9	6	6	2	18	1			4		1				8	1

One own goal

Play offs

	Date	Opponent	Score	Scorers	Att	Che	Pal	Pla	Yat	Rob	Sta	Tur	Sho	Joh	Bar	Nor D	Bar K	Tho
SF1	May 13	Bolton Wanderers	1-1	Lund	15108	1	2	3	5	6	10		8	4	11	12	9	7
SF2	May 16	BOLTON WANDERERS	2-0	Johnson, Bartlett	15197	1	4	3	5	6		9	11	10		2	8	7
F	May 27	Tranmere Rovers	2-0	Johnson, Short	29252	1	2	3	5	6	10		8	4	11		9	7

Final at Wembley Stadium

F.A. Cup

	Date	Opponent	Score	Att	Che	Pal	Pla	Yat	Rob	Dra	Lun	Sta	Sho	Joh	Bar	Nor S
R1	Nov 18	Doncaster Rovers	0-1	3817	1	2	3	5	6	7	9	12	8	4	10	11

Littlewoods Challenge Cup

	Date	Opponent	Score	Scorers	Att	Che	Pal	Pla	Fai	Yat	Rob	Dra	O'R	Lun	Sta	Tur	Sho	Joh	Bar	McS
R1/1	Aug 22	Shrewsbury Town	0-3		2848	1	2	3	4	5	6	7	8	9	10	11			14	12
R1/2	Aug 29	SHREWSBURY TOWN	3-1	Robinson, Short, Stant	2559	1	2	3	12	5	6	7		9	10	11	4	8		

Leyland-DAF Cup

	Date	Opponent	Score	Scorers	Att	Che	Pal	Pla	Fai	Yat	Rob	Dra	O'R	Lun	Sta	Sho	Joh	Bar	McS	Kev	Nor D	Law	Chi	Fle
PR	Nov 28	Fulham	1-0	Palmer	1317	1	2	3	14	5	6	7	11	9	10	8	4	12						
PR	Dec 12	PETERBOROUGH UTD.	2-2	Draper, Lund	1616	1	2	3	6	5		7	12	9	10	8	4	11	14					
R1	Jan 23	Bristol City	1-0	Barnes	4902	1	2	3		5	6	7	11	9		8	4	10						
QF	Feb 21	Hereford United	1-1	Barnes	3409	1	2	3	7	5	6	12	14	9		8	4	11	10					
SFS	Mar 14	Maidstone United	1-0	Turner	2114	1		3		5	6		11	9		8	4	10				7	4	2
FS1	Mar 28	Bristol Rovers	0-1		6480	1		3		5	6	7	12			8	4	11	9		10			2
FS2	Apr 2	BRISTOL ROVERS	0-0		10057	1		3		5	6	7	12	14		8	4	11	9		10			2

QF won 4-3 on penalties after extra time. SFS after extra time.

1990/91   4th in Division Two - Promoted after Play Off

#	Date		Opponent	Score	Scorers	Att	Cherry S	Palmer C	Platnauer N	Short Craig	Yates D	Robinson PJ	Thomas D	Draper M	Bartlett K	Lund G	Johnson T	Norton D	Brook G	Chapman G	Turner P	Regis D	Harding P	Short Chris	O'Riordan D	Nelson G	Paris A	Davis SM
1	Aug	25	Hull City	2-1	Palmer, Lund	7385	1	2	3	4	5	6	7	8	9	10	11	12										
2	Sep	1	OXFORD UNITED	3-1	Johnson, Lund, Melville(og)	6398	1	4	3		5	6	7	8	9	10	11	2										
3		8	Middlesbrough	0-1		17301	1	4	3		5	6	7	8	9	10	11	2	12									
4		15	PORTSMOUTH	2-1	Draper, Thomas	6433	1	2	3	4	5	6	7	8	9	10	11				12							
5		18	BARNSLEY	2-3	Robinson, Lund	7187	1	2	3	4	5	6	7	8	9	10	11											
6		22	Watford	3-1	Platnauer, Dublin(og), Bartlett	7973	1	2	3	4	5	6	7	8	9	10	11				12							
7		29	BRISTOL ROVERS	3-2	Yates, Thomas, Robinson	6562	1	2	3	4	5	6	7	8	9	10	11				12	14						
8	Oct	1	Port Vale	1-0	Johnson(p)	7723	1	2	3	4	5	6	7	8	9	10	11				12							
9		6	Leicester City	1-2	Johnson	13597	1	2	3	4	5	6	7	12	9	10	11				8	14						
10		13	WOLVERHAMPTON W.	1-1	Thomas	12835	1	2	3	4	5	6	7	12	9	10	11				8	14						
11		20	MILLWALL	0-1		7605	1	2	3	4	5	6	7	12	9	10	11				8	14						
12		23	Plymouth Argyle	0-0		6651	1	2		4	5	6	7	11	9	10					8		3					
13		27	Oldham Athletic	1-2	Regis	12940	1	2	3	4	5	6	7	8	9	10	11					14	12					
14		30	CHARLTON ATHLETIC	2-2	Balmer(og), Bartlett	5086	1	2	3	4	5	6	7	8	9	10	11					14		12				
15	Nov	3	WEST HAM UNITED	0-1		10950	1	2		4	5		7	11	9							8	10	3	6			
16		10	WEST BROMWICH ALB.	4-3	Bartlett 2, Regis, Draper(p)	8162	1	2		4	5	12	7	11	9							8	10	3	6	14		
17		17	Ipswich Town	0-0		10573	1	2		4	5		7	11	9							8	10	3	6			
18		24	SWINDON TOWN	0-0		6091	1	2		4	5		7	11	9							8	10	3	6	12		
19	Dec	1	Sheffield Wednesday	2-2	Draper(p), Bartlett	23474	1	2		4	5		7	11	9							8	10	3	6			
20		15	HULL CITY	2-1	Regis, Bartlett	5537	1	2		4	5		7	11	9							8	10	3	6			
21		22	BRISTOL CITY	3-2	Regis 2, Draper	6586	1	2		4	5		7	11	9					12		8	10	3	6			
22		26	Blackburn Rovers	1-0	Bartlett	8648	1	2		4	5		7	11	9							8	10	3	6			
23		29	Newcastle United	2-0	Bartlett, Draper(p)	17536	1				5	4	7	11	9		8	2				10	3	12	6			
24	Jan	1	BRIGHTON & HOVE ALB.	2-1	Bartlett, Chivers (og)	8238	1			4	5		7	11	9							8	10	3	2		6	
25		12	Oxford United	3-3	Robinson, Turner, Yates	5358	1	2		4	5	3	7	11			9				8	10		12	6			
26		19	MIDDLESBROUGH	3-2	Draper, Regis, Johnson	9323	1	2		4	5	3	7	11			9				8	10		12	6			
27		22	Charlton Athletic	1-3	Regis	4516	1	2		4	5	6	7	11			9			12	8	10	3					
28	Feb	2	Portsmouth	1-2	Johnson	12680	1	2		4	5		7	11			9			12	8	10	3		6		14	
29		23	West Bromwich Alb.	2-2	Bartlett 2	11068	1	2		4	5			11	9	10		12			8	14	3		6		7	
30	Mar	2	SHEFFIELD WEDNESDAY	0-2		15546	1	2		4	5		7	11	9						8	10	3		6			
31		12	PORT VALE	1-1	Johnson	6305	1	2		4	5		7	11	9	10					8	14	3		6			
32		16	Bristol Rovers	1-1	Johnson	4878	1			4	5		7	11		10					8	14	3	2	6		12	
33		19	Wolverhampton Wand.	2-0	Johnson, Bartlett	12375	1			4	5		7		9		11				8	10		2	6		3	
34		23	LEICESTER CITY	0-2		11532	1	12		4	5		7	14	9		11				8	10		2	6		3	
35		30	BLACKBURN ROVERS	4-1	Bartlett, Johnson 3	6831	1			4	5		7	10	9		11				8	14	12	2	6		3	
36	Apr	1	Bristol City	2-3	Johnson, O'Riordan	13466	1			4	5		7	10	9		11				8			2	6		3	
37		6	NEWCASTLE UNITED	3-0	Regis 2, Chris Short	7806	1	5		4			7	10	9						12	8	11	3	6		2	
38		9	Barnsley	0-1		9801	1	5		4			7	10	9						12	8	11	3	6		2	14
39		13	Brighton & Hove Alb.	0-0		9864	1	5		4			7	10	9						8	11	12	2	6		3	
40		16	WATFORD	1-0	Paris	6168	1	2		4	5		7	10			11				12	8	9		6		3	
41		20	Millwall	2-1	Yates, Regis	10162	1	2		4	5		7	10			11				12	8	9		6		3	
42		23	Swindon Town	2-1	Yates, Johnson	8287	1	2		4	5		7	10	14		11				12	8	9		6		3	
43		27	PLYMOUTH ARGYLE	4-0	Draper, Regis 3(1p)	7370	1	2		4	5		7	10	14		11				12	8	9		6		3	
44	May	4	OLDHAM ATHLETIC	2-0	Regis, Johnson	12311	1	2		4	5		7	10	14		11				8	9	12		6		3	
45		7	IPSWICH TOWN	3-1	Johnson 2(1p), Regis	6902	1	2		4			7	10			11				8	9	12	5	6		3	
46		11	West Ham United	2-1	Draper 2	26551	1	2		4				10			11				8	9	7	5	6		3	12

	Cherry S	Palmer C	Platnauer N	Short Craig	Yates D	Robinson PJ	Thomas D	Draper M	Bartlett K	Lund G	Johnson T	Norton D	Brook G	Chapman G	Turner P	Regis D	Harding P	Short Chris	O'Riordan D	Nelson G	Paris A	Davis SM
Apps	46	40	13	43	41	19	44	45	40	16	37	4	1	6	38	37	24	15	31	2	15	2
Goals		1	1	4		3	3	9	13	3	16				1	15		1	1		1	

Four own goals

Play offs

	Date		Opponent	Score	Scorers	Att	Cherry S	Palmer C	Short Craig	Draper M	Bartlett K	Johnson T	Turner P	Regis D	Harding P	Short Chris	O'Riordan D	Paris A
SF1	May	19	Middlesbrough	1-1	Turner	22343	1	2	4	12	10	11	8	9	7	5	6	3
SF2	May	22	MIDDLESBROUGH	1-0	Harding	18249	1	2	4	12	10	11	8	9	7	5	6	3
F	Jun	2	Brighton & Hove Alb.	3-1	Johnson 2, Regis	59940	1	2	4	12	10	11	8	9	14		6	3

Final at Wembley Stadium

F.A. Cup

	Date		Opponent	Score	Scorers	Att	Cherry S	Palmer C	Short Craig	Yates D	Robinson PJ	Thomas D	Draper M	Bartlett K	Lund G	Johnson T	Turner P	Regis D	Harding P	Short Chris	O'Riordan D	Paris A
R3	Jan	5	Hull City	5-2	*See below	6655	1		4	5	12	7	11	9	10		8		3	2	6	
R4	Jan	26	OLDHAM ATHLETIC	2-0	Turner, Craig Short	14002	1	2	4	5		7	11	9	10		8		3		6	
R5	Feb	16	MANCHESTER CITY	1-0	Lund	18979	1	2	4	5			11	9	10		8		3	12	6	7
R6	Mar	10	Tottenham Hotspur	1-2	O'Riordan	29686	1	2	4	5		7	11	9	10	12	8		3		6	

*Scorers in R3: Buckley(og), Turner, O'Riordan, Bartlett, Lund

Rumbelows League Cup

	Date		Opponent	Score	Scorers	Att	Cherry S	Palmer C	Platnauer N	Short Craig	Yates D	Robinson PJ	Thomas D	Draper M	Bartlett K	Lund G	Johnson T	Norton D	Turner P	Regis D	O'Riordan D
R1/1	Aug	29	Exeter City	1-1	Bartlett	3858	1	2	3	4	5	6	7	8	9	10	11	12			
R1/2	Sep	4	EXETER CITY	1-0	Johnson	4204	1	4	3		5	6	7	8	9	10	11	2			12
R2/1	Sep	25	OLDHAM ATHLETIC	1-0	Johnson	7089	1	2	3	4	5	6	7	8	9	10	11		12		
R2/2	Oct	10	Oldham Athletic	2-5	Johnson(p), Robinson	10757	1	2	3	4	5	6	7	14	9	10	11		8	12	

R2 second leg after extra time

Zenith Data Systems Cup

	Date		Opponent	Score	Scorers	Att	Cherry S	Palmer C	Short Craig	Yates D	Robinson PJ	Thomas D	Draper M	Bartlett K	Johnson T	Chapman G	Turner P	Regis D	Harding P	Short Chris	O'Riordan D
R1	Nov	20	PORT VALE	1-0	Regis	2320	1	2	4	5		7	11	9	12		14	8	10	3	6
R2	Dec	11	SUNDERLAND	2-2	Bartlett, Draper (p)	3003	1	2	4	5	12	7	11	9	14			8	10	3	6

R2 lost 1-3 on penalties after extra time

- 1990/91 Season -

Back: Finch, Browne, Cox, O'Riordan, Walker, Telford, Thompson, Aldridge, Wells
Middle: Jones (Asst.Man.), Stant, Palmer, Yates, Cherry, Blackwell, Short (Craig), Lund, Platnauer, Wilson (Physio)
Front: Robinson, Norton, Johnson, Turner, Pavis (Chairman), Warnock (Manager), Draper, Bartlett, Thomas, Chapman

- 1991/92 Season -

Back: Jones (Asst.Man), Harding, Dryden, Palmer, Yates, Cherry, Blackwell, Short (Short), Paris, Regis, O'Riordan, Wilson (Physio)
Front: Robinson, Short (Chris), Johnson, Turner, Pavis (Chairman), Warnock (Manager), Draper, Bartlett, Thomas, Chapman

1991/92 21st in Division One - Relegated

League (Division One)

#	Date	Opponent	Res	Scorers	Att
1	Aug 17	Manchester Utd.	0-2		46278
2	20	SOUTHAMPTON	1-0	Yates	9613
3	24	NOTTM. FOREST	0-4		21044
4	28	Chelsea	2-2	T Johnson, Bartlett	15847
5	31	West Ham United	2-0	Bartlett 2	20093
6	Sep 3	SHEFFIELD WEDNESDAY	2-1	T Johnson 2(1p)	12297
7	7	LIVERPOOL	1-2	T Johnson	16051
8	14	Coventry City	0-1		10685
9	17	Sheffield United	3-1	Bartlett 2, Rideout	19375
10	21	NORWICH CITY	2-2	Rideout, Bowen(og)	9488
11	28	Luton Town	1-1	T Johnson(p)	7629
12	Oct 6	MANCHESTER CITY	1-3	Thomas	11878
13	19	LEEDS UNITED	2-4	Lund, T Johnson	12964
14	26	Arsenal	0-2		30011
15	Nov 2	OLDHAM ATHLETIC	2-0	Rideout, T Johnson	7634
16	16	Aston Villa	0-1		23020
17	23	Everton	0-1		24230
18	30	QUEENS PARK RANGERS	0-1		7901
19	Dec 7	Tottenham Hotspur	1-2	Craig Short	23364
20	20	Southampton	1-1	Slawson	11054
21	26	CHELSEA	2-0	Yates, T Johnson	11933
22	28	WEST HAM UNITED	3-0	Turner, Harding, Agana	11163
23	Jan 1	Crystal Palace	0-1		14202
24	11	Nottm. Forest	1-1	Dryden	30168
25	18	MANCHESTER UTD.	1-1	T Johnson(p)	21055
26	Feb 1	Leeds United	0-3		27224
27	8	ARSENAL	0-1		11221
28	22	Queens Park Rangers	1-1	Bartlett	8300
29	25	WIMBLEDON	1-1	Craig Short	6198
30	Mar 7	Wimbledon	0-2		4196
31	10	ASTON VILLA	0-0		8389
32	14	Oldham Athletic	3-4	Draper, Williams, Lund	12125
33	17	EVERTON	0-0		7480
34	21	Sheffield Wednesday	0-1		23910
35	28	CRYSTAL PALACE	2-3	Craig Short, Wilson	7674
36	31	Liverpool	0-4		25457
37	Apr 7	TOTTENHAM HOTSPUR	0-2		9205
38	11	COVENTRY CITY	1-0	Sansom(og)	6655
39	18	Norwich City	1-0	Matthews	12100
40	20	SHEFFIELD UNITED	1-3	Bartlett	12605
41	25	Manchester City	0-2		23426
42	May 2	LUTON TOWN	2-1	Matthews 2	11380

Played in game 36: PJ Robinson (11). In game 41: PR Cox (14).

Appearances / line-ups

#	Cherry S	Palmer C	Paris A	Short, Craig	Yates D	O'Riordan D	Thomas D	Turner P	Regis D	Draper M	Johnson T	Bartlett K	Short, Chris	Harding P	Dryden R	Rideout P	Lund G	Johnson M	Agana T	Slawson S	Wells M	Williams A	McClelland J	Wilson K	Farina F	Devlin P	Matthews R
1	1	2	3	4	5	6	7	8	9	10	11	12	14														
2	1	2	3	4	5		7	8	9	10	11			6													
3	1	2	3	4	5		7	8	9	10	11	12	14	6													
4	1	2	3	4	5		7		9	12	11	10	14	6	8												
5	1	2	3	4	5		7	12	9	6	11	10			8												
6	1	2	3	4	5		7	8		6	11	10			12	9											
7	1	2	3	4	5		7	8	12	6	11	10				9											
8	1	2	3	4	5		7	8	12	6	11	10	14			9											
9	1		3	4	5		7			6	11	10	2		8	9											
10	1	12	3	4	5		7	14		6	11	10	2		8	9											
11	1	8	3	4	5		7	14		12	11	10	2	6		9											
12	1	2	3	4	5		7	14	12	8	11	10		6		9											
13	1	2	3	4	5		7	8	12	6	11	10					14		9								
14	1	2	3		5		7	8		6	11	12		14	10		9	4									
15	1	2	3	4			7	14		6	11	10			8	5	9	12									
16	1	2	3	4	5		7			6	11					8	9		10								
17	1	2	3	4	5		7	12		6	11		14			8	9		10								
18	1	2	14	4			7	12		6	11		5	8	3		9		10								
19	1	2	3	4			7	8	12		11		5	6			9		10								
20	1	2	3	4	5		7	8			11			6		9			10	12							
21	1	2	3	4	5		7	8			11			6		9			10								
22	1	2	3	4	5		7	8			11			6		9			10	12	14						
23	1	2	3	4	5		7	8			11			6		9			10	12	14						
24	1	2	3	4			7	8			11	12		6	9	5			10		14						
25	1	2	3	4			7	8		6	11	10	5	9													
26	1	2	3	4			7	8		6	11	10		5					9			12	14				
27	1	2	3	4			7	8		6	11	10	5	9								12		14			
28	1	2		4			7				11	10	5	6	3				9			8					
29	1	2		4			7				11	10	5	6	3				9	12		8					
30	1	2					10			6	11	12	5	8	3				9	14				7	4		
31	1	2						8		6	11	10	5	9	3					14		12		7	4		
32	1	2		4	11					8		6		10			14	3	9			12	5	7			
33	1	2		4	12					8		6		10	5			3	9				7	11			
34	1	2		4	5		7			6			10	8	14	3			9			12		11			
35	1	2		4	5					8		6			3				9			12		7	11	10	14
36	1	2		4	5					8		6			12				3			9		7		10	14
37	1	2		4				12		6				5	8	3			9			14		7		10	11
38	1	2		4				12		6		10			8	3				5				7		11	9 · 14
39	1	2		4			9			6		10	12	8	3					5				7		11	14
40	1	2		4			9			6		10			8	3				5				7		11	12
41	1	2								6		10			8	3			4 · 5 · 9					7		11	12
42	1	2		4			3			6					5	8				9				7		11	12 · 10
Apps	42	41	27	38	25	1	36	29	9	35	31	29	27	29	29	11	13	5	13	13	1	15	6	8	3	2	5
Goals				3	2		1	1		1	9	7		1	1	3	2		1	1		1		1			3

Two own goals

F.A. Cup

	Date	Opponent	Res	Scorers	Att
R3	Jan 5	WIGAN ATHLETIC	2-0	T Johnson, Turner	5913
R4	Feb 4	BLACKBURN ROVERS	2-1	Lund, Draper	12173
R5	Feb 15	Norwich City	0-3		14511

Rumbelows League Cup

	Date	Opponent	Res	Scorers	Att
R2/1	Sep 24	Port Vale	1-2	T Johnson	4722
R2/2	Oct 9	PORT VALE	3-2	Bartlett 2, T Johnson(p)	4419

Lost on away goals rule a.e.t.

Zenith Data Systems Cup

	Date	Opponent	Res	Scorers	Att
R2	Oct 22	Sheffield United	3-3	Draper, Bartlett, Slawson	3291
QF	Nov 26	SHEFFIELD WENESDAY	1-0	Harding	4118
SF	Jan 8	LEICESTER CITY	1-2	Chris Short	11559

SF after extra time

1992/93 — 17th in Division One of the Football League

(Divisions renumbered
Division Two became Division One)

Player columns (left to right): Cherry S, Palmer C, Thomas D, Short Craig, Johnson M, O'Riordan D, Draper M, Williams A, Agana T, Matthews R, Smith D, Wilson K, Dijkstra M, Slawson S, Turner P, Catlin R, Short Chris, Murphy S, Lund G, Robinson D, Devlin P, Smith M, Bartlett K, Turner R, Dryden R, Cox PR, Walker R, Reeves D

#	Date	Opponent	Score	Scorers	Att.	Cherry S	Palmer C	Thomas D	Short C	Johnson M	O'Riordan D	Draper M	Williams A	Agana T	Matthews R	Smith D	Wilson K	Dijkstra M	Slawson S	Turner P	Catlin R	Short Chris	Murphy S	Lund G	Robinson D	Devlin P	Smith M	Bartlett K	Turner R	Dryden R	Cox PR	Walker R	Reeves D
1	Aug 16	Birmingham City	0-1		10614	1	2	3	4	5	6	7	8	9	10	11	12																
2	22	LEICESTER CITY	1-1	D Smith(p)	10502	1	2		4	5	6	7	8	9		11	12	3	10	14													
3	25	WATFORD	1-2	Slawson	6276	1	2			5	6	7	8	9		11	12	3	10	4													
4	29	Peterborough Utd.	3-1	D Smith, Wilson, Williams	6720		2			4	6	7	8			11	9	3	10	12	1	5											
5	Sep 5	BARNSLEY	1-3	Craig Short	6205		2	14	4		6	7				11	9	5	10	8	1	3	12										
6	12	Watford	3-1	Draper, Lund, Slawson	7077	1	2				6	7				11	10	5	12	8		3	4	9									
7	19	Millwall	0-6		6689	1		3			6	7				11	10	2	12	8		4	9	5									
8	26	LUTON TOWN	0-0		5992	1	5	3		4	6	7				11			10	8		2		9		12							
9	29	Tranmere Rovers	1-3	Murphy	5410	1		3		4	6	7				11			8		2	5	9	10									
10	Oct 3	Bristol Rovers	3-3	Bartlett, D Smith, O'Riordan	5015	1		3		5	6	7				11			8		2	12	9	14		4		10					
11	10	GRIMSBY TOWN	1-0	Lund	6442	1	2	3		5	6	7							8				9	11		4		10					
12	17	Swindon Town	1-5	Thomas	7912	1	2	3		5	6	7							12	8		14	9	11		4		10					
13	24	OXFORD UNITED	1-1	Turner P	5228	1	4	3		5	6	7	8	10					12	2			9	11									
14	31	Sunderland	2-2	Chris Short, Slawson	15501	1	4	3		5		7	6	10			11		12	8		2		9									
15	Nov 3	DERBY COUNTY	0-2		14268	1	4	3		5		7	6	10					11	8		2		9		12							
16	7	West Ham United	0-2		12345	1	4	3		5		10	6						11	8		2		9		7		12					
17	14	WOLVERHAMPTON W.	2-2	Bartlett 2	8494	1	4	3		5	6		10				14		11	8		2		9		7		12					
18	21	Southend United	1-3	Bartlett	2651	1	4	3			6	7	8						12			2	14	9		11		10	5				
19	28	Bristol City	0-1		9086	1	2	4		6	14	8		9		11	7	3	12									10	5				
20	Dec 5	NEWCASTLE UNITED	0-2		14841	1	2	4			14	7		9		11	8	3	12		6							10	5				
21	12	CAMBRIDGE UNITED	1-0	R Turner	5037	1	6	4				7	14	9		11	8	3				2		12				10	5				
22	19	Portsmouth	0-0		8943	1	2	4				7	6	9		11	8	3										12	10	5			
23	28	BRENTFORD	1-1	Agana	6892	1	6	4				7		9		11	8	3				2						10	5				
24	Jan 9	MILLWALL	1-2	Thomas	6148	1	6	4				7		9	12	11	8					2	14					3	10	5			
25	16	Luton Town	0-0		6729	1	5	4		6		7	2	9	12	11	10							8					3				
26	23	Leicester City	1-1	Draper	15716	1		4		6	8		9	12	11	10					2	7						3	5				
27	26	TRANMERE ROVERS	5-1	*See below	5642	1	6	4		3		8		9	10	11	12					2	7							5				
28	30	Charlton Athletic	1-2	Draper	8337	1	6	4		3		8	14	9	10	11	12					2	7							5				
29	Feb 6	BIRMINGHAM CITY	3-1	D Smith(p), Matthews, Bartlett	8550	1	6			3		8	4	9	10	11						2	7					12		5				
30	21	PETERBOROUGH UTD.	1-0	D Smith(p)	7468	1	6			3		8	4	9	7	11						2	10					12		5				
31	27	Grimsby Town	3-3	Devlin, Draper, Lund	5871	1	6	4		3		8	12	9		11						2	7	10						5				
32	Mar 6	BRISTOL ROVERS	3-0	Draper 2, Devlin	6455	1	6	4		3		8		9		11						2	7	10				12		5				
33	9	Wolverhampton Wand.	0-3		11482	1	6	4		3		8	14			11	12					2	7	10				9		5				
34	13	WEST HAM UNITED	1-0	Walker	10272	1		4		3		8	10			11	9					2	7	12						5		6		
35	16	Barnsley	0-0		6372	1		4		3		8	2				9		11				7	10						5		6		
36	20	Newcastle United	0-4		29871	1		4		3		8	14			11	9		12			2	7	10						5		6		
37	23	SOUTHEND UNITED	4-0	Lund, Cox, Draper 2	6109	1		4		3		8				11	9		12			2	7	10					14	5		6		
38	Apr 3	BRISTOL CITY	0-0		6634	1		4		3		8			12	11	9					2	7	10						5		6		14
39	6	Cambridge United	0-3		4583	1	14	4		3		8			12	11						2	7	10						5		6		9
40	10	CHARLTON ATHLETIC	2-0	Thomas, Draper	6202	1	2	4		3		8			7	11	14		12					10						5		6		9
41	12	Brentford	2-2	Devlin, Walker	8045	1		4		3		8			7	11	2		14					10						5		6		9
42	17	PORTSMOUTH	0-1		11014	1		4		3		8			7	11	14					2		12						5		6		9
43	24	SWINDON TOWN	1-1	Reeves	8382	1				3		8			12	11	4			2			7	10						5		6		9
44	May 1	Oxford United	1-1	Walker	6171	1				3		8			12	11	4			2			7	10						5		6		9
45	5	Derby County	0-2		13326	1				3		8			12	11	4			2		14	7	10						5		6		9
46	8	SUNDERLAND	3-1	Reeves, D Smith, Draper	14417	1	6			3		8			12	11	4			2			7	10						5				9
		Apps				44	31	37	3	37	17	44	22	29	8	37	32	11	20	20	2	31	8	28	1	32	5	16	8	2	21	12	9
		Goals					3	1			1	11	1	2	2	8	1		3	1		1	1	4		3		5	1		1	3	2

*Scorers in game 27: Matthews, D Smith 2(1p), Agana, Draper
Played in game 1: P Harding (14). In game 41, M Wells (12)

F.A. Cup

Rd	Date	Opponent	Score	Att.	Cherry S	Palmer C	Thomas D				Draper M	Agana T	Matthews R	Smith D	Wilson K		Slawson S			Short Chris	Murphy S	Lund G				Bartlett K	Turner R				
R3	Jan 12	SUNDERLAND	0-2	8522	1	6	4				7	9	10	11	8		14			2		12				5	3				

Coca Cola Cup

Rd	Date	Opponent	Score	Scorers	Att.																													
R2/1	Sep 22	WOLVERHAMPTON W.	3-2	Lund 2, Robinson	4197	1		3		4	6	7				11			10	8		2		9	5								
R2/2	Oct 7	Wolverhampton Wand.	1-0	O'Riordan	11146	1	2	3		5	6	7				4			8			12	9			11		10					
R3	Oct 27	CAMBRIDGE UNITED	2-3	Draper, Agana	3742	1	4	3				7	8	10			12		6			2		9		11						5	

Anglo-Italian Cup

Rd	Date	Opponent	Score	Scorers	Att.																													
PR	Sep 2	Derby County	2-4	Craig Short, O'Riordan	6767			3	4	5	6	7				11	9		10	8	1	2											14
PR	Sep 15	BARNSLEY	1-1	Palmer	2115	1	2	12		4	6	7				11	10	3	14	8		5	9										

Played in first PR game: T Gallagher (no. 12)

- 1992/93 Season -

Back: Worboys, R.Walker, Williams, Dijkstra, Wilson, Johnson, Matthews, Short (Chris), Harding, Cox, Slawson, Wells
Middle: Lawson (Physio), Devlin, Dryden, Palmer, Yates, J.Walker, Catlin, Cherry, Short(Craig), Paris, O'Riordan, Gallagher, Jones (Asst.Man).   Front: Smith, Agana, Turner, Pavis (Chairman), Warnock(Manager), Draper, Bartlett, Thomas

- 1993/94 Season -

Back: Agana, D.Smith, Cox, Slawson, Yates, Williams, R.Turner, Robinson, Reeves
Middle: Walker, Short(Chris), Dijkstra, M.Smith, Murphy, Catlin, Cherry, Lund, Harding, Palmer, Worboys, Paris
Front: Slade(Ass Man), Draper, Legg, McSwegan, Thomas, Pavis(Chair), Walker(Man), Turner, Wilson, Devlin, Johnson, Lawson(Phy)

1993/94 7th in Division One

League — Division One

#		Date	Opponent	Score	Scorers	Att	Cherry S	Wilson K	Johnson M	Turner P	Cox PR	Walker R	Devlin P	Draper M	McSwegan G	Reeves D	Legg A	Lund G	Williams A	Short, Chris	Simpson M	Slawson S	Dijkstra M	Thomas D	Agana T	Gallagher T	Palmer C	King P	Matthews R	Sherlock P	Foster CJ	Reid P	Murphy S
1	Aug 14	MIDDLESBROUGH	2-3	Draper(p), Lund	9392	1	2	3	4	5	6	7	8	9	10	11	12	14														
2	21	Peterborough Utd.	1-1	Draper	6890		2	3	4	5		7	8		12	11	9	10														
3	28	SUNDERLAND	1-0	Draper	9166	1	2	3			6	7	8			11	9		4	5	10											
4	Sep 4	Tranmere Rovers	1-3	Simpson	6317	1	2	3			6	7	8	12		11	9		4	5	10											
5	11	WEST BROMWICH ALB.	1-0	Draper	9870	1	2	3	5		6	7	8	12		11	9		4		10											
6	18	Watford	1-3	Draper	6959	1	2	3	5		6	7	8	9	12		10		14		11	4										
7	25	DERBY COUNTY	4-1	McSwegan 3, P Turner	11000	1			4		5	7	8	9		11	10		2			6		3	12							
8	Oct 2	Leicester City	2-3	Draper(p), McSwegan	16319	1			4	5	6	7	8	9		11	10		2					3								
9	9	BRISTOL CITY	2-0	McSwegan(p), Draper	6418	1			4		5	7	8	9		11	10							3		2	6					
10	16	Luton Town	0-1		6366	1		14	3		12	5	7	8	9	11	10		4							2	6					
11	20	Millwall	0-2		5887	1	8	3	4	5	6	7		12		11	10							9	2							
12	23	PORTSMOUTH	1-1	Walker	6683	1			4	5	6	7		9		11	10							8	12	2	3					
13	30	Nottingham Forest	0-1		26721	1		11	4			5	7	8	12		10							6	9	2	3					
14	Nov 2	Wolverhampton Wan.	0-3		15989	1			4	6	12	5	7	8	9		10							14	11	2	3					
15	6	CRYSTAL PALACE	3-2	McSwegan 2(1p), Lund	6904	1			4	5	6		7	8	9		10			12				14	11	2	3					
16	13	Charlton Athletic	1-5	Agana	7226	1		5	6		4	7	8				10							11	2		3	12				
17	20	STOKE CITY	2-0	Robinson, P Turner	9815	1	10	5	6			7	8				9							11	2		3					
18	28	OXFORD UNITED	2-1	Devlin, Agana	5302	1	10	3	6		5	7	8				9							11	2							
19	Dec 5	Crystal Palace	2-1	Devlin 2	13704	1	10	3	6		5	7	8				9							11	2	4						
20	11	MILLWALL	1-3	Lund	6516	1	10	3	6		5	7	8	12			9							11	2	4						
21	18	Middlesbrough	0-3		7869	1	10	3	6	2	5	7	8	12			9							11		4						
22	27	Grimsby Town	2-2	Lund, Devlin	7781	1		3	4	2	6	7	8	10			9					5		11								
23	Jan 1	Bolton Wanderers	2-4	P Turner, Lund	11041	1	2	5	6	3		7	8	10			9			11		4						12				
24	3	SOUTHEND UNITED	2-1	Draper, Dijkstra	6503	1	2	5	6	4		7	8	10			9					3						11				
25	11	BIRMINGHAM CITY	2-1	Devlin, McSwegan	7212	1		4				7	8	12		10	9			6		3						11	2	5		
26	15	LUTON TOWN	1-2	Agana	6589	1		4	6			7	8	12		10	9					3		11						5		
27	22	Bristol City	2-0	Legg, Agana	7458	1			6			7	8			10	9							11		4			3	5		
28	Feb 5	Portsmouth	0-0		9359	1			4			7	8				9					6		11		2			3	5	10	
29	12	NOTTM. FOREST	2-1	McSwegan, Palmer	17911	1		6	4			7	8	11		12	9					14			2				3	5	10	
30	19	Birmingham City	3-2	McSwegan, Wilson, Legg	12913	1	14	6	4			8	10			11	9					3			2				5	7		
31	22	PETERBOROUGH	2-1	McSwegan 2	6106	1	11		4	12		8	10			7	9					3			2				6	5		
32	Mar 1	BARNSLEY	3-1	Draper 2, Lund	6297	1			4	2		7	8			11	9					3			6				12	5		
33	5	Sunderland	0-2		16269	1	4			2		7	8	10		11	9					3							12	6	5	
34	12	WATFORD	1-0	Lund	6379	1			4	6	5	7	8	10		3	9								2						11	
35	16	West Bromwich Alb.	0-3		14594	1	2	5	4	6		7	8	10		3	9											12			11	
36	26	LEICESTER CITY	4-1	McSwegan, Matthews, Lund 2	11907	1	2	5	4			8	10			11	9								6			7				3
37	30	Southend United	0-1		3758	1	2	5	4			8	10			11	9					12			6			7				3
38	Apr 2	GRIMSBY TOWN	2-1	Matthews, Draper	7205	1	2	5	4			12	8	10		11	9								6			7				3
39	4	Barnsley	3-0	Devlin, Lund, McSwegan	6827	1	2	5	4			7	8	10		11	9								6							3
40	9	BOLTON WANDERERS	2-1	Murphy, Devlin	7270	1	2	5	4			7	8	10		11	9								6							3
41	12	TRANMERE ROVERS	0-0		6318	1	2	5	4			7	8	10		11	9								6			12				3
42	16	Wolverhampton W.	0-2		13438	1	2		4			7	8	12		11	9					5			6			10				3
43	20	Derby County	1-1	Draper	18602	1			4	6		7	8	12		11	9					5			10	2						3
44	23	Stoke City	0-0		16453	1	2	12	4			7	8	11			9					5			10	6						3
45	30	CHARLTON ATHLETIC	3-3	Draper(p), Lund, McSwegan	7019	1	2	5	4			7	8	10			9								11	6						3
46	May 8	Oxford United	1-2	Draper	8487	1	2	5					8	10		11	9					4			7	6		12				3
				Apps		45	29	34	40	19	21	41	44	37	4	30	46	2	6	6	4	18	7	20	13	22	6	12	7	9	5	11
				Goals			1		3		1	7	14	15		2	11			1		1		4		1		2				1

R Catlin played in game 2, at 1
S Goater played in game 16 at 9
D Robinson played in games 17 and 18 at 4, scoring once
JP Gannon played in games 26 and 27, at 2. D Yates played in 46, at 14

F.A. Cup

		Date	Opponent	Score	Scorers	Att	Cherry S	Wilson K	Johnson M	Turner P	Cox PR	Walker R	Devlin P	Draper M	McSwegan G	Reeves D	Legg A	Lund G	Dijkstra M	Agana T	Palmer C	Matthews R	Sherlock P	Murphy S
R3	Jan	8	SUTTON UNITED	3-2	Draper, Agana, Devlin	6805	1	2	5	6	4		7	8	10		12	9	3	11		14		
R4		29	WEST HAM UNITED	1-1	Lund	14952	1			4	14		7	8	12		10	9	6	11	2		3	5
rep	Feb	9	West Ham United	0-1		23273	1		5	4			7	8	11		10	9	6		2	12	3	

R4 replay after extra time

Coca Cola Cup

		Date	Opponent	Score	Scorers	Att																					
1/1	Aug	17	HULL CITY	2-0	Lund, Cox	3003	2	3	12	5	6	7	8	9	14	11	10	4									
1/2		24	Hull City	1-3	Draper	2222	1	2	3	10	5	6	7	8		9	11		4		12	14					
2/1	Sep	22	Newcastle United	1-4	Smicek(og)	25887	1	11	3	5			6	14	8	9		10		2	7		12	4			
2/2	Oct	5	NEWCASTLE UTD.	1-7	McSwegan	6068	1			3	5	4	7	8	9		11	14	2			6	12	10			

Round 1 won on away goals   Played in R1/1: R Catlin (1)

Anglo-Italian Cup

		Date	Opponent	Score	Scorers	Att																							
PR	Aug	31	DERBY CO.	3-2	Legg 2, Lund	3276	1	2	3			6	7				11	9	4	5	10	8							
PR	Sep	15	Nottingham Forest	1-1	Lund	7347	1	4	3	5		6	7	8	9		11	14		12	10	2							
IR	Oct	12	ASCOLI	4-2	Legg, Lund 2, Draper	3756	1			4	12	5	7	8	9		11	10				3		2	6				
IR	Nov	9	PISA	3-2	Agana, Devlin, Lund	3253	1		5	6			7	8				10		12	9	4	11	2		3	14		
IR		16	Brescia	1-3	Draper	2000	1						7	8				10			11		2		3	9			
IR	Dec	22	Ascona	1-0	McSwegan	1000	1	12	5	6	2	3	7	8	10			9		4	11								
SF1	Jan	26	Southend United	0-1		3708	1		2	6			7	8			11	9		6	10	4				3	5		
SF2	Feb	16	SOUTHEND UNITED	1-0	Devlin	5485	1		6	4			7	8	11		10	9		3		2			12	5		
F	Mar	20	Brescia	0-1		17185	1	2	5	4			7	8	10		11	9		3	12	6						

SF2 won 4-3 on penalties a.e.t.   Final at Wembley Stadium

1994/95 24th in Division One (Relegated)

#	Date	Opponent	Score	Scorers	Att	Cherry S	Johnson M	Turner P	Murphy S	Yates D	Agana T	Legg A	Lund G	McSwegan G	Simpson M	Sherlock P	Emenalo M	Matthews R	Devlin P	Gallagher T	Jemson NB	Walker R	Mills G	Williams JN	Butler PJF	Reece PJ	Daniel R	Marsden C	White DW	Nicol S	Hogg GJ	Russell KJ	Short, Chris	Galloway M
1	Aug 13	Portsmouth	1-2	Sherlock	10487	1	3	4	5	6	7	8	9	10	11	12																		
2	21	WOLVERHAMPTON W.	1-1	Simpson	8569	1		4	5	6	7	8	9	10	11		3	12																
3	27	Sheffield United	3-1	Lund, McSwegan 2	15301	1		4	5	6	7	8	9	10	12		3	11																
4	30	OLDHAM ATHLETIC	1-3	McSwegan	6604	1		4	5		7	8	9	10		2	3	12	11															
5	Sep 3	SWINDON TOWN	0-1		6537	1		4	5	6	12	8	9	10			3	11	7															
6	10	Bristol City	1-2	Jemson	6670	1	5	3		6		8	12	10			4	9			2	7												
7	13	Barnsley	1-1	Lund	3928	1	5	4		6		8	12	10				9	2	7	3													
8	17	STOKE CITY	0-2		8282	1	5	4		6		8	12	10	11		3		9	2	7													
9	24	CHARLTON ATHLETIC	3-3	Agana,Lund,Sturgess(og)	5726	1	5	4	3	6	11	8	9	12		2			7		10													
10	Oct 1	Reading	0-2		7465	1	3	4	6	5	11	8	9					12	7		10		2											
11	8	PORT VALE	2-2	Williams, Agana	6903	1	3	4	6	5	11		9					12	7				8	2	10									
12	15	Watford	1-3	Williams	7008	1	3		6	5	11		9		4				7			12	14	2	10	8								
13	23	DERBY COUNTY	0-0		6390		6	4		5	11		9						7			12	3	2	10	8	1							
14	29	Burnley	1-2	Davis (og)	12876			4		5	11	9		10					7	2			3		12	8	1	6						
15	Nov 1	Southend United	0-1		4302			4		5	11			10		14		9	7	2		6			12	8	1	3						
16	5	SUNDERLAND	3-2	Devlin 2, Legg	8890		6	4		5	11	10				12		9	7	2					8	1	3							
17	19	Bolton Wanderers	0-2		11698		6	4	5		11		12					9	7			2			8	1	3	10						
18	26	WEST BROMWICH ALB.	2-0	Turner, Lund	10088	1	6	4		5	11		9					7	10			2			8		3							
19	Dec 3	Derby County	0-0		14278	1	6	4	12	5	11	3	9	10				7				2			8									
20	6	TRANMERE ROVERS	1-0	Devlin	4703	1	6		12	5	11	3	9	10				7				2			8			4						
21	10	Wolverhampton Wan.	0-1		25786	1	6	4	12	5	11	3	9					7		14		2			8			10						
22	17	PORTSMOUTH	0-1		6383	1	6	4	14	5	11	3	9					7		12		2			8			10						
23	26	MILLWALL	0-1		6758	1	6	4		5	11	3		10				7				2			8				9					
24	28	Middlesbrough	1-2	McSwegan	21558	1	6	4	5		11	3		10				14			12	2			8			7	9					
25	31	LUTON TOWN	0-1		6249	1	6	4	5			3		11				12	7		14	2			8			10	9					
26	Jan 14	BURNLEY	3-0	Devlin, White, McSwegan	8698	1	6	4	5		12	3		10				11	7			2			8				9					
27	21	Sunderland	2-1	Lund, Matthews	14334		6	4	5			3	9					11	7			2			8			12	10					
28	28	Grimsby Town	1-2	White	5161		6	4	5			3	9					11	7			2			8			12	10					
29	Feb 4	Tranmere Rovers	2-3	Legg, Devlin (p)	6105		11	4	5		9	3				12			7			2						8	14	10	6			
30	7	BOLTON WANDERERS	1-1	Matthews	7374		11	4	5		9	3			8			12	7			2								10	6			
31	11	SOUTHEND UNITED	2-2	Legg, Matthews	6768		11	4	5		9	3	14		12			8	7			2								10	6			
32	18	West Bromwich Alb.	2-3	Devlin 2	13748		11	4	5		3	12	9	14				8	7			2								10	6			
33	25	READING	1-0	Agana	7184		14	4	5		12	11		10				8	7			2								6	9			
34	Mar 4	Charlton Athletic	0-1		13863		14	4	5		11								7			2							12	10	6	9	8	
35	11	SHEFFIELD UNITED	2-1	Simpson, White	11102				5		12	11		4					7			2							8	10	6	9	14	
36	14	Oldham Athletic	1-1	Devlin	5465				5		12	11		4					7			2							8	10	6	9	14	
37	21	BRISTOL CITY	1-1	White	5692	1	14	12			9	11							7			2							8	10	6	4	3	
38	25	Stoke City	1-2	White	10170	1		4	5			11					9		7			14							8	10	6	12	2	
39	Apr 1	BARNSLEY	1-3	Devlin	6834	1	14	4				11	9						7			3							8	10	6		2	
40	8	Luton Town	0-2		6428	1	11	4							7			12				3							8	10		9	2	14
41	15	MIDDLESBROUGH	1-1	White	9377			4	5		12				7							3			1				8	10	6	9	2	11
42	19	Millwall	0-0		5471			4	5			12			7			14				3			1				8	10	6	9	2	11
43	22	GRIMSBY TOWN	0-2		5286				5			14			7			12				3			4	1			8	10	6	9	2	11
44	29	WATFORD	1-0	White	5083				5						14			9				3			4	1			8	10	6	12	2	11
45	May 3	Swindon Town	0-3		8262				5						12			9				3			4	1			8	10	6		2	11
46	7	Port Vale	1-1	McSwegan	9452				5					9	7							4	3		1				8	10	6		2	11

CR Hoyle played in games 1,2 and 40 at 2,2 and 6
PR Cox played in games 4-6 at 2, 6, 2
M Kuhl played in games 6 and 7 at 11, 11
JB Kearton played in games 27 -36 at 1 (10 games). M Forsyth played at 3 in games 33 to 36, 38 and at 5 in games 37 and 39 (7 appearances).
S Slawson played in game 39 (at 12). I Ridgway in game 45 (14).

| | Apps | 25 | 31 | 38 | 35 | 21 | 31 | 34 | 23 | 22 | 19 | 5 | 7 | 18 | 40 | 7 | 11 | 7 | 34 | 5 | 20 | 11 | 5 | 7 | 20 | 19 | 17 | 11 | 13 | 7 |
| | Goals | | 1 | | | 3 | 3 | 5 | 6 | 2 | 1 | | | 3 | 9 | | 1 | | | 2 | | | | | | | | | | |

Two own goals

F.A. Cup

	Date	Opponent	Score	Scorers	Att	Cherry S	Johnson M	Turner P	Murphy S	Agana T	McSwegan G	Devlin P	Jemson NB	Walker R	Butler PJF	White DW
R3	Jan 8	MANCHESTER CITY	2-2	White, Matthews	12376	1	6	4	5	3	10	11	7	2	8	9
rep	18	Manchester City	2-5	McSwegan, Matthews	14261	1	6	4	5	3	12 10	11	7	2	8	9

Coca Cola Cup

	Date	Opponent	Score	Scorers	Att	Cherry S	Johnson M	Turner P	Murphy S	Yates D	Agana T	Legg A	Lund G	McSwegan G	Simpson M	Emenalo M	Devlin P	Jemson NB	Walker R	Daniel R	Marsden C	White DW
2/1	Sep 20	Bristol City	1-0	Devlin	2546	1	5	4	3	6	14	8	9	10	11	2	7	12				
2/2	27	BRISTOL CITY	3-0	Lund 2, Jemson	2721	1	3	4	6	5	11	8	9				12 7	10	2			
R3	Oct 26	TOTTENHAM HOTSPUR	3-0	McSwegan 2, Agana	16952		6	4	12	5	11	9		10			14 7		3 2	8	1	
R4	Nov 30	Norwich C	0-1		14030	1	6	4		5	11	3	9	10			7		2	8		

Anglo-Italian Cup

	Date	Opponent	Score	Scorers	Att	Cherry S	Johnson M	Turner P	Murphy S	Yates D	Agana T	Legg A	Lund G	McSwegan G	Simpson M	Sherlock P	Emenalo M	Matthews R	Devlin P	Gallagher T	Jemson NB	Walker R	Butler PJF	Marsden C	White DW	Nicol S	Hogg GJ	Russell KJ	Short, Chris
PR	Aug 24	Ascoli	1-1	Devlin	1300	1		4	6	5	10		9			11	8	3	12	7									
PR	Sep 6	LECCE	1-0	Turner	2495		5	4	6	9	8		10	12		3	11	7	2				1						
PR	Oct 5	Atalanta	1-1	Agana	2300	1		4	6	5	11	12	9			3	7			10	8	2							
PR	Nov 15	VENEZIA	3-3	Devlin, Marsden, Murphy	2861		6	4	12	5	11						9	7	2			8	1	3	10				
SF1	Jan 24	STOKE CITY	0-0		5135		6	4	5		3	9					12	7			2	8			11	10			
SF2	Dec 31	Stoke City	0-0		10741	12	4	5	9	3		7						14			2	8			11	10	6		
F	Mar 19	Ascoli	2-1	Agana, White	11704	1	6	4	5	9	11			10			12	7	14		3		13		8			2	

SF2 after extra time. County won 3-2 on penalties
Final played at Wembley Stadium
Played in first PR game; CR Hoyle (2), PR Cox (14). Played in SF1 amd SF2; JB Kearton (1). Played in SF1; S Slawson (14)

Friendly games since 1888

Games listed as "CC" were for the Notts FA
County Cup (1936/37 onwards)

1888/89

Sep	8	Grantham Rovers	a	3-0
	13	Wirksworth	a	2-0
	27	Boston	a	3-0
Oct	4	Canadians	h	2-0
Dec	1	Nottm. Forest	a	0-3
	26	Nottm. Forest	h	4-1
Jan	3	Casuals	h	1-0
Feb	9	Queen's Park	h	0-6
Mar	2	Notts Rangers	h	3-1
	23	Long Eaton Rangers	h	1-1
	30	Nottm. Forest	a	5-2

Benefit for H Emmitt & S. Norman (Forest)

1889/90

Sep	2	Nottm Jardines	h	3-1
Oct	3	Sheffield Wednesday	h	6-1
	21	Sheffield United	a	3-2
	31	South of England	h	6-3
Nov	30	Nottm. Forest	a	4-2
Dec	26	Nottm. Forest	h	1-1
	28	Dumfries	h	13-3
Feb	8	Halliwell	h	3-2
Mar	22	Sunderland Albion	h	2-0
	29	Derby County	a	2-3
Apr	4	Lincoln City	a	2-2
	6	Bootle	h	2-0
	7	Aston Villa	a	1-3
	8	Rotherham Town	a	0-4
	12	Celtic	a	1-1
	14	Third Lanark	a	0-4
	15	St. Bernards	a	0-7
	19	Sunderland	a	1-2
	21	Sunderland Albion	a	3-6
	22	Newcastle East End	a	1-1
	23	Middlesbro' Ironopolis	a	0-0
	24	Grimsby Town	a	1-1
	26	Bootle	a	2-4
	27	Burslem Port Vale	a	0-2
May	1	Everton	a	1-0

1890/91

Sep	1	Nottm. Jardines	h	7-0
	3	Burton Wanderers	a	4-0
	11	Newark	a	6-0
Oct	4	Sheffield Wednesday	h	3-1
Dec	26	Nottm. Forest	h	0-0
Feb	7	Stoke	h	3-1
	21	Corinthians	h	1-2
Mar	23	Derby County	a	0-2
	27	Lincoln City	a	1-0
	28	Stoke	a	1-1
	30	Sheffield Wednesday	a	2-3
	31	Preston North End	h	0-4
Apr	4	Everton	a	0-1
	8	Burton Swifts	a	3-4

Bass Charity Vase

	11	Sunderland	a	0-6
	13	Aston Villa	a	0-2
	18	Nottm. Forest	a	4-2
	23	Everton	h	0-1
	25	Wolves	a	1-2
	27	Leicester Fosse	a	2-2
	30	Newark	a	4-0

1891/92

Sep	2	Lincoln City	a	4-0
	7	Sheffield United	a	1-4
	10	Newark Town	h	6-1
	14	Leicester Fosse	a	4-3
	23	Mansfield Town	a	2-1
Oct	3	Nottm. Forest	h	1-3
	22	Newark Town	a	5-0
Nov	5	Royal Arsenal	h	4-3
	11	Cambridge University	a	3-0
	19	Oxford University	h	8-0
Dec	26	Nottm. Forest	h	0-1
Jan	25	Preston North End	a	2-6

Ordered by Football League

	30	Derby County	h	5-1
Feb	8	Oxford University	a	4-2
	13	Sheffield United	a	0-0
Mar	5	Cambridge University	h	5-2
	12	Burton Swifts	a	5-0

Bass Charity Vase

	14	Sheffield Wednesday	a	5-2
	17	Sheffield United	h	2-0
	31	Royal Arsenal	a	4-2
Apr	2	Sheffield Wednesday	h	2-5
	6	Wolves	a	2-1

Bass Charity Vase

	18	Ardwick	a	1-2
	19	Distillery	a	5-2
	24	Wolves	h	2-0
	27	Derby County	a	0-5

Bass Charity Vase

	30	Newton Heath	a	0-0

1892/93

Sep	1	Gainsborough Trinity	h	3-1
	12	Middlesbro' Ironopolis	a	0-4
Oct	13	Newark	a	4-0
	24	Kimberley	a	7-0
	27	Cambridge University	h	10-1
Nov	2	Greenhalgh's	a	4-2
	7	Bulwell United	a	1-2
	24	Grantham Rovers	a	2-0
Dec	3	Ardwick	a	3-3
	26	Nottm. Forest	h	0-1
	27	Preston North End	h	1-1
Jan	2	Aberdeen	a	4-0
	3	Celtic	a	1-1
	4	Wishaw Thistle	a	2-5
Feb	18	Newcastle United	a	2-3
	20	Aston Villa	a	2-6
Mar	4	Bootle	a	3-4
	23	Stoke	a	0-2

Bass Charity Vase

Apr	1	Middlesbro' Ironopolis	h	3-0
	10	Kettering Town	a	4-0
	12	Mansfield Town	a	4-1
	15	Bury	a	2-5
	25	Hucknall	a	3-1
	26	Sutton	a	3-2
	29	Grimsby Town	a	1-3

1893/94

Sep	4	Bulwell United	h	9-0
	18	Greenhalgh's	a	3-2
	23	Chester	h	5-1
	25	Leicester Fosse	a	2-1
	28	Burton Wanderers	h	1-2
Oct	2	West Bromwich Alb.	a	0-2
	7	Chatham	a	7-0
	9	Sheffield Wednesday	a	2-1
Nov	10	Loughborough	a	1-4
	11	Nottm. Forest	a	2-1
	13	Wolves	a	1-4
	7	Aston Villa	h	0-2
	21	Everton	h	0-0
	23	Corinthians	h	4-1
	26	Nottm. Forest	h	1-1
Jan	1	Kettering T	a	5-0
	4	WBA	h	3-1
Apr	5	Wolves	h	2-0

Bass Charity Vase

	12	Stoke	a	0-2

Bass Charity Vase

	14	Crouch End	a	6-1
	16	Burton Wanderers	a	1-2
	21	Newark Town	a	2-1
	23	Everton	a	0-3
	30	Rangers	a	1-3

1894/95

Oct	20	Nottm. Forest	a	0-2
Nov	1	Vampires	h	5-2
	8	Derby County	h	0-6

HB Daft's benefit

	12	Bulwell United	a	3-0
	17	Corinthians	a	4-3
Dec	26	Nottm. Forest	h	1-1
Feb	16	Small Heath	h	3-3
	27	Midlands XI	h	4-4

E May's benefit

Mar	2	Grimsby Town	a	0-4
	28	Norfolk County	a	3-0
Apr	3	Mansfield Town	a	0-2
	13	Leicester Fosse	a	1-2
	15	Rangers	h	1-0
	29	Nottm. Forest	a	0-1

1895/96

Sep	2	Loughborough	h	3-1
	9	Hucknall St. John's	a	2-1
Oct	21	Kimberley	a	8-0
Nov	11	Bulwell United	a	5-2
Dec	5	Sheffield Wednesday	h	1-3

Calderhead's benefit

	19	Notts Olympic	h	7-1
	26	Nottm. Forest	h	1-1
Jan	4	Millwall Athletic	a	1-5
	23	Barking Woodville	a	5-0
	25	Tottenham Hotspur	a	5-1
Feb	15	Nottm. Forest	a	1-3
Mar	28	Small Heath	a	4-3
Apr	16	Derby County	h	6-1
	18	Gravesend United	a	1-1
	22	Mansfield Town	a	3-2
	23	Hucknall Torkard	a	2-3
	25	Liverpool South End	a	0-4
	27	Worksop	a	2-1

1896/97

Sep	1	Millwall Athletic	a	1-2
	2	Luton Town	a	1-2
	7	Hucknall St. John's	a	1-1
	14	Mansfield Town	a	2-0
	22	Sheffield United	a	1-0
		At Huddersfield		
Oct	19	Kimberley	a	7-1
Nov	5	Vampires	h	7-3
	9	Bulwell United	a	3-1
	12	Wolves	h	3-1
		G. Toone's benefit		
Dec	26	Nottm. Forest	h	1-2
	29	Corinthians	h	4-1
Feb	17	Burton Swifts	a	1-0
		Burford Cup		
	20	Stockport County	a	4-1
Mar	11	Lincoln City	h	3-1
		Burford Cup		
	18	Casuals	a	2-1
Apr	5	Fairfield	a	1-1
		Burford Cup		
	28	Leicester Fosse	h	0-2
	29	Aston Villa	h	1-2
		C Bramley's benefit		

1897/98

Sep	13	Lincoln City	a	2-0
	27	Wolves	a	1-1
Oct	18	Kimberley	a	4-2
Nov	8	Bulwell United	a	1-2
	10	Mansfield Town	a	6-2
	13	Manchester City	a	2-3
	20	Small Heath	a	3-2
Dec	27	Nottm. Forest	h	0-1
	28	Sheffield Wednesday	a	1-1
Jan	8	Grimsby Town	a	1-2
	19	Loughborough	a	1-1
Feb	12	Bristol City	a	2-2
Mar	23	Ilkeston	a	3-1
	26	Corinthians	a	0-1
Apr	16	Walsall	a	2-3
	25	Leicester Fosse	a	1-2
		Burford Cup tie		

1898/99

Sep	1	Grimsby Town	a	2-1
Oct	20	Grimsby Town	h	3-1
Dec	26	Bristol City	h	2-4
Jan	30	Sheffield Wednesday	a	3-1
Feb	25	Brighton United	a	2-1
Mar	2	Derby County	h	2-0
		TG Prescott's benefit		
	4	Corinthians	a	2-1
	31	Nottm. Forest	a	5-1
Apr	24	Woolwich Arsenal	a	1-2

1899-1900

Sep	4	Tottenham Hotspur	a	1-4
	27	Brighton United	a	1-3
Nov	27	Burslem Port Vale	a	2-3
Dec	26	Nottm. Forest	h	2-4
Feb	24	Corinthians	a	1-1
Mar	27	Lincoln City	a	1-3

1900/01

Sep	27	Tottenham Hotspur	h	4-1
		Calderhead's second benefit		
Oct	8	Tottenham Hotspur	a	1-1
Nov	12	Bulwell United	a	4-1
Dec	8	Corinthians	a	1-4
	24	Leicester Fosse	a	4-3
Mar	14	Sheffield Wednesday	h	1-2
	30	Aberdare	a	7-1
Apr	1	South Wales League	a	2-0
	20	Woolwich Arsenal	a	0-3
	27	Celtic	a	2-1

1901/02

Sep	2	Chesterfield	a	4-1
Dec	25	Rangers	h	2-3
	30	Wolves	a	2-5
Jan	2	Rangers	a	3-2
	16	Wolves	h	2-3
		J. Goode's benefit		
Feb	22	Clapton	a	2-2
Mar	1	Walsall	a	1-1
	15	Corinthians	a	4-2

1902/03

Sep	1	Northampton Town	a	4-1
Nov	10	Bulwell United	a	2-0
	25	Oxford University	a	2-2
Dec	11	Oxford University	h	4-4
	13	Clapton	a	3-3
Mar	14	Corinthians	a	2-1
	21	Coventry City	a	2-0
Apr	25	Sheffield Wednesday	a	0-2
		At Plymouth		
	27	Aberaman	a	1-2

1903/04

Sep	8	Grimsby Town	a	3-4
	14	Leicester Fosse	a	2-0
Nov	18	Oxford University	a	2-0
Dec	10	Oxford University	h	5-1
		J Montgomery's benefit		
	28	Corinthians	h	3-5
Mar	5	Northampton Town	a	2-2
	12	Corinthians	a	1-2
Apr	9	Clapton	a	2-0
	16	Plymouth Argyle	a	1-0
	30	Grimsby Town	a	2-2

1904/05

Sep	1	Hull City	a	2-2
Dec	10	Clapton	a	3-1
Mar	4	Corinthians	a	5-2
Apr	12	Stafford Rangers	a	1-0

1905/06

Mar	10	Corinthians	a	3-3
Apr	17	Leicester Fosse	a	1-1

1906/07

Sep	26	Lincoln City	a	3-3
Feb	16	Corinthians	a	1-4
Apr	30	Grimsby Town	a	2-0

1907/08

Sep	16	Norwich City	a	2-2
	23	Leicester Fosse	a	3-6
Feb	22	Brighton & Hove Alb.	a	1-3

1908/09

Nov	11	Lincoln City	a	1-1
Feb	6	Hull City	a	1-1

1909/10

Apr	27	Chesterfield	a	3-0
Jun	1	Danish XI	a	2-2
	3	Danish XI	a	4-2
	5	Danish XI	a	2-1

1910/11

Sep	13	Grimsby T	a	1-2

1911/12, 1912/13 no games

1913/14

Jan	31	Nottm. Forest	h	0-5
		Notts FA Senior Cup		
Apr	25	Swansea Town	a	2-2
	27	Merthyr Town	a	0-1
May	31	Barcelona	a	3-1
Jun	4	Barcelona	a	4-2
	7	Barcelona	a	10-3

1914/15

Apr	17	Rangers	a	1-1

1916/17

Apr	28	Dr. Coutts-Wood's XI	a	4-1

1917/18

Apr	20	Nottm. Forest	a	0-1
		Notts FA Senior Cup		

1918/19

Apr	26	West Ham United	a	1-1
May	17	Coventry City	a	2-3

1919/20

May	8	Nottm. Forest	h	0-2
		Nottm Hospital Fund		
Jul	19	Derby County	a	4-5

1921/22

Apr	24	Norwich City	a	2-0
		Norwich Hospital Cup		
May	25	St. Mirren	a	1-2(e)
		In Barcelona		
	27	Barcelona	a	4-2
	28	Barcelona	a	1-1

1922/23

Dec	13	Nottm. Forest	a	0-2
		Notts Senior Cup (for Children's Xmas Fund)		
May	7	Boston	a	2-0
		Boston Hospital Cup		
	?	Copenhagen XI	a	3-0
	27	Copenhagen XI	a	1-0
	?	Danish XI	a	3-2

1923/24

Apr	3	RAF	a	0-0
	30	Lincoln City	a	0-3
		Wilson Hospital Cup		

1924/25

Apr	20	Lincoln City	a	0-0
		Wilson Hospital Cup		
	??	Burton Town	a	0-1
		Bass Charity Vase		
May	7	Vienna Sports Club	a	1-0
	11	Prague	a	0-1
	?	Prague	a	1-1
	?	Ostrau	a	1-3

1925/26

Apr	26	RAF	a	1-2
		For RAF Memorial Fund, at Cranwell		

1928/29

May	4	Carlisle United	a	2-5

1930/31

Apr	20	Grimsby Town	a	4-2
		Grimsby Hospital Cup		
	29	Wealdstone	a	8-3
May	4	Chesterfield	a	2-2
		Chesterfield Hospital Cup		

1932/33

Jan	28	Airdrie	h	4-1
May	1	Coventry City	a	0-2
		Coventry Hospital Cup		

1933/34

Apr	23	Dolphin	a	5-2
	30	Exeter City	a	5-5

1934/35

May	6	Nottm. Forest	h	3-2(e)
		Notts FA Senior Cup		

1935/36

Sep	30	Hearts	h	2-4
		Testimonial for Alf Feebery		
Apr	20	Heanor Town	a	3-1

1936/37

Oct	14	Mansfield Town	a	5-1	CC
	28	Nottm. Forest	h	1-0(e)	CC

1937/38

Oct	13	Nottm. Forest	a	0-1	CC
May	9	Chesterfield	a	1-2	
		Chesterfield Hospital Cup			

1938/39

Aug	20	Nottm. Forest	a	1-4	
		Football League Jubilee Fund			
Sep	19	Boston	a	2-1	
Oct	19	Mansfield Town	h	2-3	CC

1939/40

See main section

1945/46

Aug	15	Nottm. Forest	a	2-3
		Celebration of VJ Day		
Oct	10	British Army XI	a	5-2
		In Cologne		
Apr	27	Cardiff City	a	1-5
May	11	Leicester City	h	5-0
		Bolton Disaster Relief Fund		

1946/47

Sep	30	Coventry City	a	1-4
		Testimonial for George T. Taylor		

1947/48

Dec	6	Port Vale	h	2-2
Apr	26	Brighton & Hove Alb.	a	7-1
May	8	Chesterfield	a	1-2
		Chesterfield Hospital Cup		
	22	Shelbourne	a	4-1

1948/49

Apr	11	Airdrie	h	1-1
	27	Celtic	h	2-1

1949/50

May	2	Clyde	h	2-0
	3	Leicester City	a	0-3

1950/51

Oct	11	Chesterfield	h	4-1
		Creswell Col. Disaster Fund		
Jan	27	Everton	a	2-3
Feb	10	Everton	h	0-3
Apr	16	Third Lanark	h	2-4
	18	Buxton	a	2-1
May	10	FC Austria	h	1-1
		Festival of Britain match		

1951/52

Feb	23	Middlesbrough	a	1-2
Apr	28	Dudley Town	a	6-1

1952/53

Feb	28	Middlesbrough	h	4-1
Mar	16	Derby County	a	0-3
	23	Derby County	h	1-1
Apr	9	East Fife	h	2-5
	16	Hartlepools United	a	1-2
	27	Dudley Town	a	0-1
		Andy Langford benefit		

1953/54

Dec	1	Admira Wien	h	3-5
Apr	28	Mansfield Town XI	a	6-3
		E Barks/S Watson benefit		
	29	All Stars XI	h	6-1
May	5	Apeldoorn	a	2-3
	8	Wageningen	a	2-2
	12	North Holland Select	a	1-1

1954/55

Oct	11	Clyde	h	0-2
		T. Dean's benefit (floodlit)		
Nov	3	Maccabi, Tel Aviv	h	4-2
May	4	All Stars XI	a	3-3
		Oscar Hold's benefit, at March Town		

1955/56

Jan	28	Brentford	a	4-0
May	3	Wolves	h	4-2
		L. Leuty fund		

1956/57

Feb	16	Manchester City	h	1-2
Mar	2	Queen of the South	h	3-0
Apr	29	King's Lynn	a	
		Peter Robinson benefit		

1957/58

Oct	30	Budowlani (Poland)	h	3-0
Apr	29	Select XI (at March)	a	6-1
		S Garratt/M Reagan benefit		
May	1	Kettering Town	h	4-0

1958/59

Dec	6	Exeter City	a	0-2
Jan	24	Man. Utd. Reserves	a	0-4
		13,770 spectators		

1959/60

Oct	26	Nottm. Forest	h	3-1
Nov	4	Headington United	a	2-2

1960/61

May	8	Nottm. Forest	a	3-4(e)	CC

1961/62

May	2	England XI	h	1-3	
		Centenary match			
	8	Nottm. Forest	h	1-2	CC

1962/63

Aug	11	Ilkeston Town	a	5-3	
Nov	24	Oldham Athletic	a	0-2	
May	23	Mansfield Town	h	4-3	CC
	27	Nottm. Forest	a	2-1(e)	CC

1963/64

Aug	17	Ilkeston Town	a	1-2	
Apr	14	Nottm. Forest	h	1-5	CC

1964/65

Aug	10	Grantham	a	0-6	
	17	Burton Albion	a	4-3	
	18	Sutton Town	a	0-0	
Jan	30	Bury	h	1-2	
May	3	Mansfield Town	a	0-1	CC

1966/67

Aug	10	Birmingham City	h	2-2	
	13	Cambridge United	a	1-2	
Oct	3	All Stars	h	6-3	
		Testimonial for Mike Barber			
	25	Mansfield Town	h	4-0	CC
Apr	18	Partick Thistle	h	1-4	
May	9	Nottm. Forest	a	0-2	CC

1967/68

Aug	14	Eastwood Town	a	1-1	
Mar	25	Mansfield Town	a	1-0	CC
May	14	Nottm. Forest	a	0-3	CC

1968/69

Aug	3	Ilkeston Town	a	1-2	
	5	Nuneaton Borough	a	0-1	
May	3	Mansfield Town	a	3-1	CC
	7	Nottm. Forest	a	1-2	CC

1969/70

Oct	22	Mansfield Town	h	2-0	CC
Dec	6	Chesterfield	a	1-2	
Apr	28	Nottm. Forest	a	0-2(e)	CC

1970/71

Aug	1	Sheffield Wednesday	h	1-2	
	4	Leicester City	h	1-2	
	7	South Shields	a	0-0	
	10	Sutton Town	a	3-0	
Mar	30	Mansfield Town	h	0-1	CC
May	10	Nottm. Forest	a	1-4	
		Alan Hill testimonial			
Jun	1	Rimini	a	4-2	
	2	Cesena	a	2-1	

1971/72

July	31	Bohemian CKD Prague	h	3-1	
Aug	7	Watford	a	3-3	
	12	Nuneaton Borough	a		
Nov	8	Nottm. Forest	h	0-2	
		Jack Wheeler's testimonial			
May	10	Nottm. Forest	h	3-0	CC
	15	Mansfield Town	a	1-3	CC
	17	Boston United	a		
		Howell's testimonial			

1972/73

Aug	2	Lincoln City	a	0-1	
	5	Wolves	h	0-3	
	7	Nuneaton Borough	a	1-2	
Mar	27	Gibraltar	a	7-0	
May	2	Nottm. Forest	h	0-1	CC

1973/74

Jul	30	Arbroath	a	0-3	
Aug	1	Elgin City	a	2-0	
	3	Inverness Thistle	a	4-2	
	11	Leicester City	h	1-2	
	15	Hereford United	a	1-2	
	18	Coventry City	h	0-2	
May	1	Mansfield Town	h	4-2	CC
	7	Nottm. Forest	a	2-3	CC

1974/75

Aug	3	Torquay United	a	1-1	
	6	Exeter City	a	2-0	
	9	Swindon Town	a	1-1	
May	1	Mansfield Town	a	0-0	CC
		Won 5-4 on pens.			
	8	Nottm. Forest	a	1-0	CC
	9	Minsk Dynamo	h	4-4	
		30th anniversary of VE day; lost on pens 4-3			
	13	Fulham	a	2-2	
		In Gibraltar			
	15	Fulham	a	3-2	
		In Gibraltar			

1975/76

Aug	2	Peterborough United	h	3-2
	5	Cambridge United	a	0-1
	9	Kettering Town	a	4-3
		Above three games for Shipp Cup		
	11	Colchester United	a	2-0
Jan	24	Sheffield United	h	3-0
May	29	Abaluhya (Nairobi)	a	2-0
	30	Gor Mahia (Nairobi)	a	3-1
Jun	5	Kenya Breweries(M'basa)	a	0-2
	6	Mwenge (Mombasa)	a	1-2

1976/77

Oct	26	Nottm. Forest	h	1-0	CC
		Held over from 1975/76			
Apr	18	Midlands International XI	h	2-1	
		Testimonial for Dave Needham.			
		Played by "Nottingham XI"			
May	25	St. Mirren	a	2-2	
		In Gibraltar			
	26	St. Mirren	a	2-1	
		Jubilee Cup won 4-3 on aggregate			

1977/78

Aug	15	Nottm. Forest	a	1-1	CC
		Held over from 1976/77. Lost 2-3 on pens.			
Apr	12	Nottm. Forest	h	0-1	
		Testimonial for Les Bradd			
May	8	Mansfield Town	a	0-2	CC

1978/79

Mar	5	Mansfield Town	a	0-3	CC

1979/80

Aug	1	Oxford United	a	3-1	
Nov	12	Mansfield Town	a	2-2	CC
		won on penalties 7-6			
Feb	16	Crystal Palace	a	2-2	
Mar	7	Manchester City	h	0-2	
May	6	Nottm. Forest	a	1-2	CC

1980/81

Sep	8	Nottm. Forest	h	2-3	
		Testimonial for Brian Stubbs			
Apr	13	Mansfield Town	h	1-2	CC
May	7	Nottm. Forest	a	'0-3	
		Testimonial for Jimmy Gordon			

1981/82

Nov	3	Forest "All Star XI"	h	3-5	
		Testimonial for Jimmy Sirrel			
Dec	19	Queens Park Rangers	a	0-3	
Mar	8	Gibraltar	a	1-0	
Apr	6	International XI	h	5-5	
		Don Masson's testimonial			
	19	Mansfield Town	a	1-1	CC
		won on penalties 4-3			
May	18	Nottm. Forest	a	1-7	CC

1982/83

Aug	14	Sheffield Wednesday	a	0-5	
	17	Barnsley	a	1-0	
	23	Leicester City	a	1-2	
Mar	23	Boston U	a	5-5	
		John Moyes testimonial			
Apr	26	Mansfield Town	h	2-1	CC
May	9	Nottm. Forest	a	3-4	CC

1983/84

Aug	5	Jerez	a	1-1	
		Won on penalties			
	6	Americo di Mexico	a	1-3	
		4 team tournament in Jerez			
	13	Grimsby Town	a	1-1	
	17	Doncaster Rovers	a	3-1	
	20	Derby County	h	2-1	
Feb	?	Magaluf (Spain)	a	0-1	
	28	Mansfield Town	a	0-4	CC
May		Cargo (Kenya)	a	5-4	
		Leopards	a	2-4	
		Gor Mahia	a	2-1	
		Kenya tour			

1984/85

Aug	4	Burton Albion	a	1-3	
	11	Lincoln City	a	0-4	
	13	Exeter City	a	1-0	
	15	Bristol City	a	2-2	
	18	Sheffield Wednesday	h	1-1	
		Ray O'Brien testimonial			
Dec	11	Lincoln C	a	3-1	
Feb	19	Lincoln City	a	2-0	
	26	Nottm. Forest	h	1-2	
		Pedro Richards testimonial			

1985/86

Aug	3	Ipswich Town	h	1-1	
	10	Mansfield Town	h	2-2	CC
		won on penalties 3-2			
	12	Leicester City	h	2-1	
Sep	11	Nottm. Forest	a	2-1	CC
		(CC games held over from 84/85)			
Oct	24	Manchester United	h	1-2	
		Ian McCulloch testimonial			
Feb	15	Queens Park Rangers	a	2-2	
	18	Luton Town	a	2-4	
	24	Nottm. Forest	a	1-4	
		Loughborough Univ. artificial surface			
May	8	Nottm. Forest	a	0-2	CC

1986/87

Jul	26	Grantham	a	0-3	
	30	Boston United	a	1-1	
Aug	9	Sheffield Wednesday	h	0-3	
	12	Mansfield Town	a	0-3	CC
	16	Coventry City	h	0-2	
Oct	14	Nottm. Forest	h	2-5	
		For Lifeline trophy			

1987/88

Jul	25	Buxton	a	0-2	
	28	Kettering Town	a	4-3	
Aug	1	Hednesford Town	a	0-1	
	4	Derby County	a	3-3	
	9	Nottm. Forest	h	4-4	CC
		won on penalties 4-3			
	11	Mansfield Town	a	2-2	CC
		lost on penalties 4-5			
Oct	14	Hinckley Town	a	4-1	
Mar	6	Shepshed Charterhouse	a	2-1	
		Mark Robinson testimonial			

1988/89

Aug	6	Sheffield Wed.		0-0	
	8	Shepshed	a	1-1	
	9	Derby County		1-2	
	13	Aston Villa	h	3-2	
	16	Gainsborough Trin.	a	7-1	
	21	Nottm. Forest	h	1-1	CC
		won on penalties 4-2			
	23	Mansfield T	a	2-3	CC

1989/90

Jul	22	Warminster	a	5-0	
	25	Stapenhill	a	3-1	
	29	Boston U	a	2-1	
Aug	1	Sheffield Utd.	h	0-1	
	5	Luton T	h	2-0	
	8	Whitby T	a	2-0	
Aug	13	Nottm. Forest	a	1-3	CC

1990/91

Jul	31	Stapenhill	a	3-0	
Aug	4	Boston U	a	4-0	
	7	Barnet	a	1-1	
	9	Sheffield Utd.	h	2-0	
	13	Darlington	a	3-0	
	15	Pickering T	a	6-0	
Aug	22	Mansfield T	a	3-3	CC
		Lost 1-4 on penalties			
Dec	4	Karpaty (Ukraine)	h	2-0	
May	13	Nottm. Forest	h	2-1	
		Mick Walker testimonial			

1991/92

Jul	27	Burton Albion	a	4-1	
	29	Boston U	a	4-0	
	31	Tranmere Rovers	h	1-0	
Aug	2	Armitage	a	4-1	
	3	Pickering T	a	2-1	
	7	Mansfield T	h	4-0	CC
	11	Nottm. Forest	a	1-2	CC
Jan	2	Hucknall T	a	5-0	

1992/93

Jul	23	Romsey	a	9-0	
	25	Waterlooville	a	4-1	
	28	Lincoln C	a	1-0	
Aug	1	Boston U	a	2-0	
	4	Hartlepool U	a	1-2	
	6	Pickering T	a	4-0	
	8	Scarborough	a	0-0	
Mar	26	Gibraltar	a	4-0	
Apr	20	Mansfield T	h	3-0	CC
May	11	Nottm. Forest	a	0-3	CC
		Att. 12,493; Brian Clough's farewell			

1993/94

Jul	16	Armitage	a	6-1	
	20	Shepshed Albion	a	6-0	
	29	Stafford Rangers	a	1-3	
Aug	2	Gedling T	a	8-0	
	4	Chester City	a	0-1	
	8	Mansfield T	h	2-1	CC

1994/95

Jul	16	Armitage	a	6-0	
	19	Slovan Bratislava	a	0-1	
	19	Cozika	a	1-0	
		Mini-tournament; 50 min. games			
	28	Northampton T	a	1-1	
		At Wellingborough			
Aug	3	Rotherham U	a	1-0	
	6	Birmingham C	a	2-0	
		At Bescot Stadium, Walsall			
	9	Ipswich T	a	0-1	
		At Grantham			
Nov	11	Nottm Forest	a	1-3	CC
		Final held over from 1993/94			

ADVANCED SUBSCRIBERS

Derek Pavis, Chairman
John Mounteney, Vice Chairman
Bill Barrowcliffe, Director
Vivien Pavis, Director
Douglas Ward, Director
Maurice Youdell, MBE. Director
Frank Sherwood, President
Neal Hook, Nottingham
Mr. Les Scrimshaw, Bingham
Carl R. Skinner, Giltbrook
Bryce John Clare, Meadows
Michael, Craig, Lisa Fiddes
Richard Blaney, Beeston
Nick King, Rise Park
Mr. & Mrs. W.A. Towers, Nuthall
John Beniston, East Leake
Roy Thorne, Wollaton, Nottingham
Richard Hucknall, Groby, Leicester
Jeff Grain
Steve Adcock, Woodthorpe, Nottingham
E.E. Weeks, Nottingham
Stephen Leahy, Nottingham
Trevor & Robert North, Arnold
Ian Brewster, Awsworth, Notts.
Stuart Jackson, Keyworth
Bruv Singleton of Bingham
Vic King, Bray, Berks.
Benjamin John Bramwell, Kimberley
David Nigel Smith
Kevin Goldsbury, Chilwell, Nottingham
Brian Greensmith, Bilborough, Nottingham
Alec Smalley, Chilwell, Notts.
Bill Jalland, Daventry, Northants.
Julian Drinkwater, Wollaston, Stourbridge
Trevor & Joanne Knight, Bradford
Peter Kisby, Huthwaite
David Greenwood, Thrumpton
Brian Easom, Carlton
William Sims
Andy Lambley, Chilwell, Magpie
Robert Ogg, Laurencekirk, Scotland
Robert C. Copley
Mark Hoskings, London
Michael & Marion Knapton
Robert Nattrass, Sneinton
Justin Cast, Sneinton, Nottingham
Trevor Smith, Rothwell, Northamptonshire
Ian Langham, Clifton Estate
Matthew Kerry, Sneinton
Steve Jeffery, Daybrook, Nottingham
Helen, Love Always, Adrian
Desmond Handley, Hayes, Kent
Phil Jones, West Bromwich
Mr. Ken Hallam, Bilborough
Mr. David Hallam, Daybrook
Michael Raymond Wright, Nottingham
Allan Michael Wright, Nottingham
Melving & Craig Eatherington, Nottingham
Gwilym Goronwy, Stapleford
Steven Smith, Ruddington
Fred Loakes, Radcliffe-on-Trent
Harry Gillett, Clifton Estate
Mark Kenny, Morden, Surrey
Richard Ward, Horsley, Derby
A Wisher, Keyworth, Nottingham
Geoff Gibbs, Long Eaton
Thomas Clay, Nottingham
Paul & Mark Fulwood, Preston
Dennis Spurr, Carlton, Nottingham
J.B. Cracknell, Stanton-By-Dale

John Jarman, Hucknall
Pete Storey, Loughborough, Leicestershire
Tom Brumfield, Gwen Brumfield
Mike Overton, Kempsford, Gloucester
Robert Turner, Cinderhill
Katherine Taylor, Papplewick, Nottingham
Leslie Breffit, Southend, Essex
Mark Smith, Ruddington
Luke Woolhouse, Carlton, Nottingham
Mr. Glyn Light, Gloucester
A. Hallam, Nottingham
Neil Tomlinson
D. Montgomery, Basford, Nottingham
Michael Harrison, Bulwell, Nottingham
Scott Harrison, Thorneywood, Nottingham
Paul Harrison, Thorneywood, Nottingham
Clive Thorneloe, Beeston
Donna Thorneloe, Beeston
Gerald & Anita Indcox, Nottingham
David Richmond, Sutton-in-Ashfield
A.C. Tatlow, Arnold
The Watts Family, Nottingham
Leslie & Lee Potter, Radcliffe-on-Trent
Alan Camplin, Beeston, Notts.
Charles and Malc. Smith
David Steele, Basford, Lincs
Edward Barkham, Boston, Lincs.
Jared Wilson, Sherwood, Notts.
Malcolm Dean, Nottingham
Patrick Murray
Steven Booth, Ravenshead, Nottingham
David Tye, Oxton, Notts.
Thomas Lydon Woolley, Clifton
Alan Underwood, Nottingham
Trevor/Sean Welsh, Shrewsbury
Fred Bales, Nottingham
Paul Bradley, Ramsgate Branch
Clive Newman, Melton Mowbray
Bill Brown, Melton Mowbray
Darren Smart, Beeston, Nottingham
Mark Berehowskyj, Beeston, Notts.
Dave Harvey, Petrograd
Richard Taylor, Bramcote, Nottingham
Tim Taylor, Bramcote, Nottingham
Sarah Taylor, Bramcote, Nottingham
Andrew Taylor, Bramcote, Nottingham
J.H. Rawle, Newark, Notts.
Chris Granger, Alvechurch, Worcestershire
Martin J. Dabell, Birmingham
Paul Gregory, Bradder White
Andrew Ward, Long Eaton
A Swift, Meadows, Nottingham
Colin Sisson, Aspley, Nottingham
Mike Jackson of Arnold
John E. Lamb, Arnold, Nottingham
Alan Dell, Dunbar, Scotland
Frank Key, Broxtowe, Nottingham
Alan Standeven, Tadcaster
J. Colton, Keyworth, Nottingham
Mick Worthington, Bulwell
Michael D. Briscoe, London
Ian J. Mills, Nottingham
Adrian Alan Jukes, Nottingham
Stuart Hardy, Arnold, Nottingham
George Claye, Allestree, Derby
Ken Allsop, Gamston, Nottingham
Robert L. Jackson, Chilwell
Nicholas C. Jackson, Exeter
Lisa Hardwick, Gamston Village
Kelvin Stevens, Burton Joyce

Michael Hessey, Beeston, Nottingham
B. Austin, Nottingham
Michael Galpin, Nottingham
James McCabe, County Antrim
Andy Whibberley, Derby
Ivan Jones, Sutton-in-Ashfield
Darren Jones, Sutton-in-Ashfield
Fred Spooner, Tintagel, Cornwall
Arthur Pidgeon, Colwick, Nottingham
Brian Clay, Stapleford
Karen Knight, Sherwood
Richard Williams, Clifton, Nottingham
J. Robinson, Whitemoor, Nottingham
Malcolm Shearstone, Aspley, Nottingham
Mr. Victor Kingswood, West Bridgford
The Bakers of Stapleford
Gordon Hugh Halliday
Neil John Parker, New Westwood
J. Perry, West Bridgford
Jeremy Donovan, Bingham, Notts.
George Smalley, Chaddesden, Derby
Mick/Hayley Morris, Attenborough
John Parker, West Bridgford
Marcus Darwent, Gotham
I. Devonport, Chilwell
J. Devonport, Wilford
John W. Mills, Hucknall
Peter Copley, Little Dalby
S.A. Smedley, Boston
Alicia Jaworek, Nottingham
Daniel Murdock
Andrew Murden, Sandiacre, Nottingham
Kevin Thomas, Newcastle, Australia
The Pettifor Family
Robert Green, Stapleford, Nottingham
Percy & Grenville White, Carlton
Gareth John Hughes
Dave Simkiss, Sandiacre, Nottingham
Neil Smith, Bingham, Notts.
Bill Beardmore, Gedling, Notts.
Adrian and Mark Fairhurst
Kevin & Neil Greally, Tollerton
Neal Putnam, Biddulph, Staffs
R. Walters, Bulwell, Nottingham
B. & J. Ellis, Radcliffe-on-Trent
Alan Swift, Awsworth, Nottingham
David Brown, Carlton, Nottingham
David Coote, Winthorpe, Notts.
Andrew Birch, Clifton, Nottingham
Dean Gollin of Carlton
Brian Rose, North Hykeham
Colin Guy, Newton, Derbyshire
Mike Leahy, Ripley, Derbyshire
Sally Brealey, Chilwell, Nottingham
P. Whiteley, Newark, Notts.
Dr. Michael Bramley, Northamptonshire
Gary & Julie Fewkes, Bracknell
Darren Ferris, Nottingham
Jonathan Harby, Sutton-in-Ashfield
Simon Brodbeck, London NW11
N.W.F. Davy, Newark
R.S. Davy, Radcliffe-on-Trent
Frederick Hickton, Teversal
John Crocker, London
Barrie Cousins, Plungar, Nottingham
Cliff and Jimmy Smith
Paul Swanwick, Clifton, Nottingham
Brian Bent, Sherwood, Nottingham
Martin Cumberworth, Notts.
Harry Beighton, Chilwell, Notts.

ADVANCED SUBSCRIBERS

Malcolm Mills, Thetford, Norfolk
Sandra Lakin, Bulwell
Matthew Edward Cowlishaw, Nottingham
Mark Durkin, Burton Joyce
Philip David Whittaker, Mansfield
Mike Disney, Oswaldtwistle, Lancs.
Graham Andrews, Colwick, Notts.
John Richard Hindson, Stapleford
Ashley Daws, Aspley, Nottingham
Paul Belshaw, Clifton Grove, Nottingham
David Gore, Wistow, Cambs.
Phillip Holland, Bulwell, Nottingham
Graham Kerry, Kimberley, Notts.
Andrew Marshall, Singapore
Dave Oakley, Chilwell
Dave Evans, Chilwell
Richard Tomlinson, Hucknall, Nottingham
Alan, Janet Henshaw, Derby
Ian Couper, Carlton, Notts.
Desmond Barsby, Bulwell
Dr. Mick Chappell, Nottingham
Steve Shepherd, Darley Abbey
Harold Mace, Bakersfield
Mick West, Keyworth
Lisa & Stuart Lister, Calverton
David/Francesca Thorpe, Lincoln
S.J. Hutton, Plymouth
Simon Roche, Toton
Ian Warbrick, Hazlemere, Bucks
Jody Hughes, Basford, Nottingham
Brian Burman, Arnold, Notts.
John Douglas Allwood, Calverton
J.A. Dale, Carlton
Stuart Cromme, Bulwell, Nottingham
John B. Pritchard, Kimberley
Douglas Knight, Calverton
Ian & Chris McLaughlin
Keith A. Worthington, Gedling
David & Abbi Brumfield
Kilborn Family, Wollaton Park
Michael Derek Prudham
Allan Reynolds, Derby
Alan Cooke, Oakwood, Derby
Malcolm Mortimer, Woodthorpe
Lou Mortimer, Woodthorpe
Ailsa Gyles, Newton, Derbyshire
Mike Gyles, Newton, Derbyshire
Ken, Chris, Helen Atherton
Graham Kershaw, Meadows
Ashley Waterfall, Bingham, Nottingham
Trevor West, Nottingham
Graham Hopcroft, Beeston, Nottingham
Keith Waterfall, West Bridgford
Darren Paul Flint, Hucknall
The Moores, Woodthorpe, Nottingham
Neil Glenn, Gotham
Julian Morris, Nottingham
Glyn Lewis, Melton Mowbray
Peter Joseph Whitt, Wollaton
Russell Jonathan Whitt, Nottingham
Martin Bostock, Hucknall, Notts.
Deryck Flowers, Nottingham
John Walker, Long Bennington
Mr. K. Murden BA - Beeston
Mr. D.L. Murden BA - Beeston
Ken & Blanche Bonsall, Bulwell
Ken Pryer, Chilwell, Nottingham
Sokal Family, Wollaton Park
Richard Wright, Sneinton Magpies
Peter Crannage, Long Eaton
Jim Haywood, Chilwell, Nottingham

George Oliver, Wilford, Nottingham
Paul Anthony Jukes
Bernard West, Wollaton, Nottingham
Richard Bartles, Long Eaton
Philip Smith, Alton, Hampshire
Barrie Smith, Nottingham
Geoff Askew, Sutton-in-Ashfield
Chris Wildsmith, Sutton-in-Ashfield
Gordon Smith, Hucknall, Blackpool
Allan Start, Kent
Frederick Start, Kent
Dale Huskinson, Warsop
Joe Simpson, Trowell Park, Notts.
Percy Chilton, Kirkby-in-Ashfield
Alan Molyneaux, Huthwaite
Mr. W.L. Bainbridge, Radcliffe-on-Trent
D. Selby
Ken Swift, Chilwell, Notts.
Peter Orme, Long Eaton
Kevin Charlton Ward, Arnold
Jon Templeman, Portsmouth, Hants.
David Clark, Arnold, Notts.
P.E. Norton, Clifton
Robin Burton, Toton
Ian Burton, Toton
John Burton, Chilwell
K.D. Wilson, Chilwell, Notts.
N.J. Wilson, Chilwell, Notts.
R.F. Wilson, Chilwell, Notts.
Rev. Fr. P. Scott, Los Angeles, U.S.A.
Anthony Cooper, Austrey, Warwickshire
Mark Scothon, Woodthorpe, Nottingham
Steve Williams, Edinburgh
Paul Johnson, Grantham, Lincs.
John T. Palmer, Nottingham
Ian McCondach, Halifax, Yorks.
Stephen Silver, Bestwood, Nottingham
Michelle Wakelin, Chilwell, Nottingham
Simon Neal, Arnold
Mark Andrew Pardoe
John Wallis, Sandiacre, Notts.
Ron Gent, Woodthorpe
Steve & Patricia Broxham
Cliff & Steve Wakelin, Beeston
Christopher Tantum from Grandad
Michael R. Patterson, Farndon, Newark
Sarah Hamilton, Mascot Wembley 1995
Lee Sigona, Clifton Grove
Catherine Ryland, Mapperley, Nottingham
Kevin Sharpe of Carlton
Anthony Lucas, Long Eaton
'Electric Steve' Westby, Radcliffe
Stephen Pilcher, Gedling
Peter Dennis, Arnold, Nottingham
David K. Parker
Anne & Graham Palmer
Anthony Bullin, Scarborough
Stephen Bullin, Shrewsbury
Peter Smith, Boyfield, Arnold
Paul Wilkinson, Skegness
Jack & Alex. Retford
Helen Pollard, Nottingham
Howard Brown, East Bridgford
Duncan Brown, East Bridgford
Keith Warsop
Michael Day
John Day
Paul Wain
Arran Matthews, Tylers Green
Nicholas Matthews, Tylers Green
C. Phillips, Bucks.

John Treleven
Raymond Shaw
Steve Emms
Graham Spackman
Dave McPherson, Colchester
Richard Wells
Derek Hyde
David Keats, Thornton Heath
M.J. Cripps, Burgess Hill
Peter Cogle, Aberdeen
Chris Harte, Bickley
David Robert Earnshaw, Belper
Phil Hollow
Donald Noble
Mark Tyler, Billericay Town F.C.
".....still hate Forest!"
John Motson
George Painter, Castle Cary
Geoff Allman
Harry Kay, West Yorkshire
Jeremy Taylor, Matlock
David Downs and Marion
John Ringrose
Alan Davies
John Byrne
Philip Whitehead
L.A. Zammit
Fred Lee, Plymouth Argyle
Jonny Stokkeland, Kvinesdal, Norway
K.P. Wood, Holbrook
Jonathan Hall
A.N. Other
John Rawnsley, Pudsey
Gordon Macey
A.H. Atkins, Ontario, Canada
Martin Simons
Arthur A. Hackett
Joseph A. Hackett
Ray Bickel
W.D. Phillips
B.H. Standish
Geoffrey Wright
Stephen Kieran Byrne
Willy Østby, Norway
Terry Frost
Bob Lilliman
Robert M. Smith
Moira & Frederick Furness
Stephen Carr, Wednesbury, Staffs.
Duncan Watt
Dave Smith
Christer Svensson
Jim Rogers Loyal Supporter
Andrew Anderson, Dorchester
Peter Baxter
Svein Borge Pettersen, (Sandefjord)
David Lumb
Keith Coburn and Alison
Chrissie Sheila Mary Hooker
Andrew & Janet Waterman
Trond Isaksen, Norway
Roland Hansson
Peter Kirby, Maidstone
David Jowett
B.R. Phillips
Peter M. Freeman
Noreen (Chalmers) Crofts
Richard W. Lane, Newark
R.V. Calmels
Gordon Small
David Wood, A Bristol Babe